International Review of
Industrial
and Organizational
Psychology
1997   Volume 12

International Review of Industrial and Organizational Psychology
1997   Volume 12

Edited by

Cary L. Cooper
and
Ivan T. Robertson

University of Manchester
Institute of Science & Technology, UK

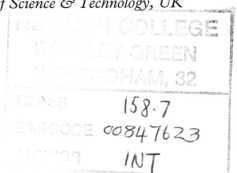
JOHN WILEY & SONS
Chichester · New York · Weinheim · Brisbane · Singapore · Toronto

The Library of Congress has cataloged this serial publication as follows:

International review of industrial and organizational psychology.
    —1986—Chichester; New York; Wiley, c1986—
    v.: ill.; 24 cm.
    Annual.
    ISSN 0886–1528 = International review of industrial and organizational psychology

    1. Psychology, Industrial—Periodicals.   2. Personnel management—Periodicals.
    [DNLM: 1. Organization and Administration—periodicals. 2. Psychology,
Industrial—periodicals. W1IN832U]
    HF5548.7.157   I58.7'05—dc19 86-643874
                              AACR 2 MARC-S
Library of Congress [8709]

ISBN 0-471-97004-2

Typeset in 10/12pt Plantin by Dorwyn Ltd, Rowlands Castle, Hants.
Printed and bound in Great Britain by Biddles Ltd, Guildford and King's Lynn.
This book is printed on acid-free paper responsibly manufactured from sustainable forestation,
for which at least two trees are planted for each one used for paper production.

CONTENTS

ABOUT THE EDITORS

Cary L. Cooper
Ivan T. Robertson

Manchester School of Management, University of Manchester Institute of Science and Technology, PO Box 88, Manchester, M60 1QD, UK.

Cary L. Cooper is currently Professor of Organizational Psychology at the Manchester School of Management (UMIST) and Pro Vice Chancellor of the University of Manchester Institute of Science and Technology. Professor Cooper is the author of over 80 books (on stress, women at work, and industrial and organizational psychology), has written over 250 articles for academic journals, and is a frequent contributor to national newspapers, TV, and radio. Founding President of the British Academy of Management, he is currently Editor-in-Chief of the *Journal of Organizational Behaviour,* and a Fellow of the British Psychological Society, Royal Society of Arts and The Royal Society of Medicine.

Ivan Robertson is Professor of Occupational Psychology in the Manchester School of Management, UMIST. He is a Fellow of the British Psychological Society and a Chartered Psychologist. Professor Robertson received his BSc degree from the University of Exeter. His career includes several years experience working as an applied psychologist on a wide range of projects for a variety of different organizations. His PhD was awarded by the Open University in 1976. Professor Robertson's research and teaching interests focus on individual differences and organizational factors related to human performance. His other publications include 15 books and over 100 scientific articles and conference papers.

CONTRIBUTORS

John Arnold — *Loughborough University Business School, Ashby Road, Loughborough, LE11 3TU, UK.*

Thomas J. Bouchard, Jr — *Department of Psychology, Institute of Human Genetics, University of Minnesota, Elliot Hall, Minneapolis, Minnesota 55455-0344, USA.*

Russell Cropanzano — *Department of Psychology, Colorado State University, Fort Collins, Colorado 80523-1876, USA.*

Gordon Foxall — *Department of Commerce, University of Birmingham, Edgbaston, Birmingham, B15 2TT, UK.*

Jerald Greenberg — *Faculty of Management and Human Resources, Ohio State University, Columbus, Ohio 43210-1399, USA.*

Michael M. Harris — *School of Business Administration, University of Missouri, St Louis, MO 63121-4499, USA.*

Gary Johns — *Department of Management, Concordia University, Montreal, Quebec, H3G 1M8, CANADA.*

Elchanan I. Meir — *Department of Psychology, Tel-Aviv University, ISRAEL.*

John P. Meyer — *Department of Psychology, The University of Western Ontario, London, Ontario, N6A 5C2, CANADA.*

Phyllis Tharenou — *Department of Business Management, Monash University, Caulfield East 3145, Melbourne, AUSTRALIA.*

Michael L. Trusty — *Anheuser–Busch Companies, 1 Busch Place, St Louis, MO 63118, USA.*

Aharon Tziner — *School of Business Administration, Bar-Ilan University, Box 45, Ramat Gan 52900, ISRAEL.*

EDITORIAL FOREWORD

The *International Review of Industrial and Organizational Psychology* is now into its twelfth year, with contributions in this volume from the US, Australia, Israel, Canada and the UK. As with previous volumes, the chapters are 'stand alone' reviews of important existing or new topic areas within the field of industrial and organizational psychology. The *Review* is not meant to represent a coherent, integrated volume with a single topic or theme, but to provide self-contained state-of-the-art reviews of empirical and/or conceptual topics of current concern or new seminal areas of possible future significance.

As usual, in this particular volume, we provide up-to-date reviews of topics of more recent interest to I/O psychologists such as organizational justice, drugs and alcohol in the workplace and genetic influences on occupationally relevant individual difference variables. These reviews are presented alongside reviews of established topics in the I/O psychology field, such as absenteeism, organizational commitment—both of which have been reviewed in earlier volumes of the *International Review*. The subtheme of occupational development and adjustment is explored in three chapters dealing with work adjustment, careers and managerial career advancement. Chapters addressing learning strategies, occupational training and consumer behaviour complete this volume.

The international aspects of the series remains a key feature. In the last five years we have published 46 reviews from ten different countries. The dominant North American influence on the literature and thinking in I/O psychology is reflected in the fact that most of the chapters in each volume have been written by authors from North America. Together with our authors we have worked hard to enable contributions from non-English-speaking countries to appear in the series; although there is no such contribution in this particular volume, such contributions will continue to appear in future volumes.

CLC
ITR
March 1996

Chapter 1

THE PSYCHOLOGY OF CAREERS IN ORGANIZATIONS

John Arnold
Loughborough University Business School

In one sense an exhaustive review of the literature on the psychology of careers is overdue—the last one in this series was provided by Michael Driver in 1988. But on the other hand there is no shortage of more recent reviews of career-related topics. In 1991, the *Journal of Vocational Behavior* commissioned a veritable blitz of reviews to mark its 20th anniversary (Borgen, 1991; Chartrand & Camp, 1991; Hackett, Lent and Greenhaus, 1991; London & Greller, 1991; Meier, 1991). Since then, its traditional annual reviews of the whole field of vocational behavior have been replaced by annual reviews of subareas of the field, each subarea appearing once every three years, usually right at the end of the year (Swanson, 1992; Blau, Linnehan, Brooks and Hoover, 1993; Fouad, 1994; Watkins and Subich, 1995). The *Career Development Quarterly* also publishes annual reviews, these mostly concerning the theory and practice of counseling (e.g. Salomone, 1993; Subich, 1994). Meanwhile, in the *Journal of Management*, Ornstein and Isabella (1993) produced a review of aspects of careers more exclusively orientated towards organizational issues. Feldman (1989) did a similar job four years earlier. Also, as we shall see shortly, some topics I would consider to be specific aspects of careers have been reviewed elsewhere, including in this present volume.

I want to use the existence of the generous supply of thorough reviews (albeit from a North American perspective) as an opportunity to take a different approach. Rather than seeking to mention briefly all research and theory produced in recent years in a kind of prose catalogue, I will present some observations and arguments about certain aspects of the psychology of careers in organizations. My primary purposes are to examine what careers are about in a changing world, to identify some topics which reflect current and future concerns, and to report and critically examine literature in those areas.

Ornstein and Isabella (1993, p. 244) commented that a review of the whole field of careers would be 'impossible and somewhat unnecessary' due to the

International Review of Industrial and Organizational Psychology, 1997 Volume 12
Edited by C.L. Cooper and I.T. Robertson. © 1997 John Wiley & Sons Ltd.

large number of disciplinary approaches brought to bear upon it, and the variety of target audiences for different segments of it. Driver (1988) noted that other writers have characterized the study of careers as fragmented and unsatisfactory in important respects (see also Hall, 1991). Part of the reason for this may be that even amongst behaviorally-orientated writers there seems little consensus about what careers are, or rather what they are construed as being. An examination of some definitional differences will help us to clarify the many strands of career and begin to identify a framework for a structured examination.

WHAT IS A CAREER?

Some authors perhaps wisely do not attempt to define what a career is. Others have grasped the nettle. Below are some not very systematically chosen definitions of career, including some older ones because they have influenced or reflect subsequent work:

1. A sequence of positions occupied by a person during the course of a lifetime (Super & Hall, 1978).
2. A series of related job experiences that fit into some meaningful pattern. If you have a series of odd jobs all your working life, that is hardly a career (DuBrin, 1983).
3. A succession or an accumulation of role-related experiences over time (London & Mone, 1988).
4. A sequence of jobs occupied and performed throughout a person's working lifetime (Gray, Gault, Meyers and Walther, 1990).
5. Occupations that are characterized by interrelated training and work experiences, in which a person moves upward through a series of positions that require greater mastery and responsibility, and that provide increasing financial return (Perlmutter & Hall, 1992).
6. The sequence of negotiations and renegotiations of the psychological contract which the individual conducts with organizations during his or her work life (adapted from Herriot, 1992, referring to organizational careers).
7. The pattern of work-related experiences that span the course of a person's life (Greenhaus & Callanan, 1994).
8. Accumulations of information and knowledge embodied in skills, expertise, and relationship networks acquired through an evolving sequence of work experiences over time. In this context, work experiences constitute the primary mechanism by which careers occur though they are not in themselves a career (Bird, 1994).

Most academics familiar with careers literature agree that a career is NOT confined to upward and/or predictable movement within one kind of work.

Yet this is the image conveyed in definition 2 (in a self-help 'how to be successful' guide), and definition 5 (a lifespan development text). Worse, it is not uncommon to see advertisements along the lines of 'Enrol at Salaryhike College if you want a career, not just a job'. The local newspaper in my current home town entitles its situations vacant section 'Jobs and Careers'. Readers can no doubt think of similar examples of this apparent dual labor market. Therefore, a continuing and pressing concern is that career *is* often thought of as something like definitions 2 and 5 by many people, including some who write about careers. Wider use of less restrictive implicit or explicit definitions of career would surely help social scientists to apply theories and concepts more effectively, enable popular writers to purvey more effective advice, and assist mere mortals to manage their careers better.

One fairly evident common feature of all these definitions is that they refer to *more than one* role, experience, or event. Words like series, sequence, succession, pattern and accumulation are used. This is a key point. The study of career involves study over time rather than taking snapshots of supposedly stable situations. Note also that although the above definitions agree on the 'more than one' aspect, what there is more than one of is in doubt. We are offered positions, related job experiences, role-related experiences, jobs occupied and performed, upward sequence of positions, negotiations, work-related experiences and skills, expertise and relationship networks. In other words, the studies of careers have variously focused on sequences of roles, experiences in those roles, behaviors in the roles, and personal attributes derived from the roles. No wonder it is a diverse field.

For present purposes, we can be said to be considering career if we are thinking about (i) potential or actual sequences of employment-related positions, roles, activities or experiences encountered by, or available to, one or more persons; (ii) their plans, decisions and attitudes concerning such sequences; (iii) their adjustment and development in new or changed employment-related positions, etc.; (iv) their preparation for future ones; and (v) their sense-making about past employment-related positions etc in relation to their present ones. We are also in the realm of careers when we consider (vi) attempts made by focal individuals themselves or others to influence (normally facilitate or shape) any of the first five phenomena; and finally (vii) the interplay between personal and macro- or micro-situational variables and any of the preceding six phenomena.

THE CONTEXT OF CAREERS

It is now well known that the context of employment in the Western world has changed and is still changing. Pressures brought about by globalization of economies and technological advance have led to some quite dramatic transformations in work organizations.

More than one *guru* has skilfully and eloquently described the new landscape. Bridges (1995) has argued that jobs and traditional employment are gone forever. Handy (1989, 1994) described various organizational forms that are emerging. They have in common a core of full-time employees who consider themselves members of the organization, and a periphery of casualized workers, some highly skilled carrying out specialized and limited-term projects and others semi- or unskilled working in contracted-out functions such as cleaning and catering. Some interesting questions revolve around managing the performance and commitment of these latter two groups (Pearce, 1993; Beard and Edwards, 1995). Along similar but more pessimistic lines, UK journalist Will Hutton (Hutton, 1995) has predicted the advent of a 30/30/40 society: 30% either unemployed or economically inactive, 30% in insecure and intermittent employment with few benefits, and 40% relatively privileged usually with marketable skills in relatively stable employment or self-employment. Particularly in countries which embraced the concept (and cost) of a welfare state after World War II, such scenarios have profound implications for social fabric and order, and for personal financial planning which in many countries has long been based on a norm of stable employment.

Perhaps mainly with Hutton's 40% in mind, some writers have referred to new kinds of career. This too has a rather longer history than might be first thought. Hall (1976) referred to the Protean career, where the individual is his or her own agent. More recently, people are urged to regard themselves as self-employed even if they have an employer (Bridges, 1995); to carry a portfolio of skills and experiences and make strategic moves which equip them for future employability (Kanter, 1989; Handy, 1989). Arthur (1994) has coined the term 'boundaryless career' to sum up the trend towards employment experiences which take individuals across employer boundaries. These boundaries are in any case blurred due to the proliferation of mergers and acquisitions (Cartwright & Cooper, 1992), wholly-owned subsidiaries, and autonomous business units. The boundaryless career may well also take a person across different types of work, and it is validated and supported by networks such as professional groups.

Some further trends in employment, and in demography, add detail to this picture. The average age of the population in most Western countries is increasing due to increased longevity and historical patterns of birth rates. In the UK, out of a total labor force of about 30 million, an increase of 2.4 million in the number of 35 to 54 year olds and a drop of 1.6 million under 35s is expected between 1993 and 2006 (*Social Trends*, 1993). Increased participation by women in the labor market is occurring in many countries (Offermann and Gowing, 1990; Wheeler, 1990; Davidson, 1996), and an increasing proportion of the total jobs available are part-time (the two trends are not unconnected, since at present a greater proportion of women than men work part-time). Although somewhat vulnerable to the economic cycle, the proportion of people in self-employment has increased significantly in the UK and to a lesser extent in other European Union countries (Meager, Kaiser & Dietrich, 1992). The number and proportion of people working in small and medium enterprises (SMEs) has increased in many countries—a salutary reminder that analyses of organizational careers must not assume a large organization (in any case, as many have wryly observed, the sure-fire way to run a small business these days is to start with a large one).

So, with the earlier analysis of the nature of careers in mind, what issues arise from the trends described above that should interest psychologists? In no particular order, they seem to me to be those listed below. Having identified the issues, in each case I will then briefly examine recent literature in that area.

1. Job changes happen with increasing frequency (Inkson, 1995), and perhaps involve more radical change for individuals and less predictability than was once the case. Individuals and organizations are under pressure to perform quickly and creatively. Louis (1982) argued that career transitions had been neglected hitherto—has this been rectified in recent years? Psychological investigations of work-role transitions (Nicholson, 1989), relocation, newcomer information-seeking and socialization are all relevant here. So is the literature on commitment, but that is reviewed in Meyer's chapter in this volume. Hence it is not covered here. Also, teleworking, and the transition to it, have been covered recently in this series by Chapman, Sheehy, Heywood, Dooley and Collins (1995). Transitions involving unemployment received some attention from Winefield (1995), also in this series.

2. In some organizations individuals are explicitly told that it is up to them to manage their own careers—the organization as a corporate body will take no part and provide no support. In others, some responsibility is being taken for equipping individuals to manage their own career within a general framework that offers some signposts but fewer than was once the case. There is a strong case to be made that demographic changes and increasing competition mean that organizations need to utilize *all* their people better (Herriot & Pemberton, 1995b). What is the current contribution of the psychologically oriented literature concerning career interventions and their impact upon individuals and organizations?

3. Individuals are having to make and remake career decisions more frequently. They may experience periods of education and training scattered through their life, not just in their childhood and adolescence. The proportion of older people in the population of many countries is increasing. What can the psychological literatures on career, decision-making, aging and lifespan development contribute to an understanding of career?

These three issues seem to me to fall naturally out of the current context. That is not to say there are no others. In particular, I am aware of the need to include in each of the above three areas relevant literature on gender, ethnicity and internationalization in careers. Two other important issues arising from the current context but omitted here due to space constraints and coverage elsewhere are:

4. For many people working in organizations, the old understanding of their employment relationship has been disconfirmed by experiences over the last few years. What implications does this have for their interpretation of present experience relative to past and future? Recent literature on the psychological contract (e.g. Shore & Tetrick, 1994; Herriot, Pemberton, 1995a) and related issues has addressed this.
5. Delayering and downsizing have made promotions harder to obtain, and some organizations have shifted to project- or competency-bases (Lawler, 1994) where relatively constant job descriptions do not exist. For both reasons, externally verifiable career success is more difficult to obtain and to define. Indeed any sort of career map is hard to find. Within a managerial context, issues concerning career success are reviewed by Tharenou (this volume).

CHANGE AND TRANSITION

Incidence and Types of Change

One symptom of what Stephens (1994) has appropriately described as 'increasingly discontinuous and unstable work lives' is increased frequency of voluntary and involuntary work-role transitions. These include changes between jobs, substantial shifts in the requirements or opportunities inherent in an existing job or other employment situation, transitions into and out of employment, relocation of employment, and also changes in attitude to features of one's objective career. Regarding managers, Nicholson and West (1988) reported increasing frequency of job change in the UK. More recent work by Inkson (1995) and Cawsey and Inkson (1992) has reaffirmed this trend in the UK and New Zealand respectively, and noted that it has been relatively impervious to the economic cycle. Also, much of the increase in job changes for managers is accounted for by involuntary and/or sideways or downward status moves. Around half of managers' job changes involve a change of employer. Thus it is appropriate that no less than 12 of Hall's (1991) 'Twenty Questions: research needed to advance the field of careers' specifically refer to work-role transitions.

Potentially useful general typologies and models of work-role transitions were developed some time ago (e.g. Louis, 1980a, b; Nicholson, 1984, 1989) but have been used relatively little in subsequent research, though there are signs that this may be changing. Ashforth and Saks (1995) tested some predictions derived from Nicholson (1984) concerning whether business school graduates in the early months of employment would seek to change their roles (innovate) or be changed by them (personal change). Contrary to prediction, the amount of personal change was unrelated to the discretion and novelty of the new work role. However, as predicted, discretion was positively related to self-reported role innovation. Commenting upon the moderate level of support for their predictions, the authors noted that Nicholson's theory may be limited in that adjustment to new work roles is portrayed as a relatively asocial process. In line with this proposition, Major, Kozlowski, Chao and Gardner (1995) have recently reported that interactions with colleagues and supervisors in the early weeks of a new job can reduce the negative impact of unmet expectations.

In a review of some of the literature in this area, Stephens (1994) has integrated some concepts from the Nicholson (1984) model with others from lifelong approaches to career development. Stephens argued that the Nicholson model is more comprehensive than the perhaps better known Theory of Work Adjustment (Dawis & Lofquist, 1984). Certainly, to me, the Theory of Work Adjustment has a strangely dated appearance. Its prediction that satisfactoriness (of an employee's performance) and satisfaction (the extent to which the job meets the employees' needs) jointly determine job tenure seems to portray stability as the norm, disrupted only by unsatisfactory circumstances. This seems rather implausible these days. Returning to Stephens (1994), he also noted a dearth of research on the effects of work-role transitions on non-transitioners. This is a theme that has been mentioned in socialization literature and recently in job rotation literature but as yet rarely pursued.

Bruce and Scott (1994) adapted Louis' (1980a) typology of transitions to fit the context of the US Navy, where the structured career development system enabled them to test propositions in relatively controlled fashion. The five types of transition were entry events, promotion events, lateral moves, resignation, and retirement. The authors commented as follows upon their results (p. 26): 'In general, the career events studied were moderately high in magnitude and desirability, low in strain and role ambiguity, and seen as causing moderate adjustment difficulty. These events were seen as resulting in gains in both individuals' personal lives and their careers, and there was moderate eagerness toward all events.' Nicholson and West (1988) also noted that many work-role transitions are experienced quite positively, and questioned whether stress-based models were appropriate. Longitudinal work with degree-qualified samples by Newton and Keenan (1990) and Arnold (1994) supports the notion that job-changing produces either neutral or positive outcomes for psychological well-being, though this does not rule out the possibility that stress models may be useful in investigating the *process* of adjustment. The amount of stress experienced by a transitioner may depend partly upon the resources they bring to the transition. Heppner, Multon and Johnston (1994) reported the development and validation of the 40-item Career Transitions Inventory. Five subscales emerged. They did not precisely coincide with the theoretical constructs originally identified by the authors. The subscales are readiness, confidence, perceived support, control, and decision-independence. The Career Transitions Inventory may well prove to be a useful instrument in research and practice.

Relocation

Relocation occurs when one or more employees of an organization move geographically whilst retaining the same employer. They may or may not be performing the same job in their new location as their old, and the move may or may not be of their own instigation. J. M. Brett, Stroh and Reilly (1992) reviewed the then-existing literature in volume 7 of this series. Their own work (Brett, Stroh & Reilly, 1993) with mobile managers in leading US corporations contradicted much earlier research by finding that sex, race and number of children at home were *not* related to willingness to relocate. Neither were work attitudes such as job satisfaction and company loyalty—as the authors point out, this is not surprising since the object of those attitudes is the job or company, not the relocation. The main factor predicting willingness to relocate was age. Older employees were less willing. These findings may be partly due to the sample, which consisted of managers who had relocated in the previous two years. Although not about relocation, a recent article by J.F. Brett, Cron and Slocum (1995) suggests a variable that has been neglected in relocation research. This is economic dependency on work. For some people, relocation is the only way of keeping a job, particularly in group moves.

Munton, Forster, Altman and Greenbury (1993) reported data from over 200 relocating employees and their families at relocation, and then three months and six months later. Respondents' worries focused mostly on extra-employment concerns such as property transactions and guilt at forcing children to move. Fisher and Shaw (1994) reported a study of 150 relocating military employees who provided data before and then three months after their move. Adjustment and attitudes toward the move were more strongly related to anticipated, and then actual, features of the new location than were demographic and pre-move location attributes. Past experience of moves was strongly negatively correlated with adjustment difficulty. However, this last point has not been the case in all research. Martin (1995) found some evidence, albeit in a small sample, that adjustment to relocation was most difficult for those with little experience of it and those with a great deal of experience. In the former case lack of know-how and disruption of community ties may have been the cause. In the latter group it may have been more a case of being worn down by yet another round of tedious and taxing tasks. Lawson and Angle (1994) found a more straightforward effect of prior experience of moving helping adjustment in their survey of 200 families involved in a company move. Overall, family and other extra-employment factors were better predictors of adjustment than were employment-related ones.

The concept of adjustment has come under rather closer scrutiny in the literature on international relocation. Brewster (1994) argues that it is most often construed by researchers as psychological comfort, but in the discussion of data researchers 'find themselves discussing the steps that the expatriate takes to bring his or her behavior into line with that of the host country' (p. 50). Brewster found that Swedish managers in the UK tended to adopt styles more characteristic of the UK than Sweden, and suggested that expatriates' behaviors may change more completely and quickly than is often realized. Janssens (1995) has pointed out that integration into a new environment should not necessarily be seen as a desirable outcome of work-role transitions. Sometimes (and particularly in international assignments) the employing organization's top managers may want the relocatee to retain a 'head office' perspective rather than 'go native'. She found that contact of international relocatees with members and the culture of the host country increased steadily as they spent longer there. This increase was still evident after 5 years and longer. Contrary to Brewster, then, some aspects of adjustment may be long drawn out.

There are of course individual differences in how international relocation is handled. Black and Gregersen (1992) distinguished two dimensions: maintenance of own cultural identity and contact with the host culture. This enabled a 2 × 2 classification: free agent (low, low); go native (low, high); heart at home (high, low); and dual citizen (high, high). Recent empirical work has reinforced earlier assertions that adjustment of family members is crucial to the work and general adjustment of the international relocatee him or herself. Nicholson and Imaizumi (1993, p. 130) have described this as '. . . a significant flow of adjustment from the domestic to the employment sphere.' W. Arthur and Bennett (1995) found that family situation was perceived as more important in determining success of international location than were job knowledge and motivation, relational skills, flexibility/adaptability and even extra-cultural openness. Furthermore, this finding from a sample of 338 international assignees in 45 multinational companies applied across different types of work and types of company. In an interesting analysis from a psychoanalytical perspective Schneider and Asakawa (1995) examined the role in international adjustment of dependency, separation and individualization, autonomy and control, and intimacy. They contrasted aspects of child-rearing in an attempt to identify differential adult adjustment patterns.

Experiencing Work-role Transitions

Much research on work-role transitions has used samples of young people entering full-time employment for the first time. This is sometimes for good theoretical reasons, but often for convenience. Earlier work (see Arnold, 1990, for a review) tended to find that navigating the transition was not as difficult as previous theorizing had suggested it might be. That work tended to concentrate on adjustment to unfulfilling work for school-leavers, but utilization of skills and commitment in graduate samples. More recent work by

Arnold and Nicholson (1991) and Fournier and Payne (1994) with graduates has examined the nature and extent of self-concept change in the early months and years of employment. There is significant qualitative change, though not necessarily towards potential role models in the organization.

There is perhaps good reason why the education to employment transition of young people has been going out of fashion. Trends towards higher unemployment, education interspersed throughout life, and work experience during education have made this transition less clearcut and uniform than it once was. Nevertheless, a special issue of the *Journal of Vocational Behavior* was recently devoted to the transition for non-college-educated youth. In the lead article, Feij, Whitely, Peiró and Taris (1995) reported a large-scale longitudinal study with cross-validation of young people in eight countries over the first 18 months of school to work transition. The sample was chosen on the basis of being employed in certain occupations. They formulated, tested and modified a model of the development of job content innovation and career enhancing strategies on the part of the young people. They proposed that supervisor relations, work centrality, work values and correspondence between individual and work were implicated in this. Findings supported the importance of relations with the supervisor in influencing the outcome variables.

A series of invited articles critiqued the Feij et al. paper. Hesketh (1995) examined the potential contribution of the Theory of Work Adjustment (Dawis & Lofquist, 1984) to the framing of the study and interpreting its findings. Blustein (1995) argued that it would have been strengthened by inclusion of theoretical constructs from career development and lifespan development theory, as well as more attention to the cultural contexts of the countries concerned. The most critical commentary was by Eldredge (1995), who highlighted Feij et al.'s inappropriate use of some existing literature and their failure to use concepts and measures of socialization and innovation.

One area Eldredge (1995) concentrated upon was the impact of socialization on the role orientation of newcomers. A recent reanalysis by Baker (1995) of data reported by Allen and Meyer (1990) has suggested that socialization tactics adopted by organizations with newcomers have their effect partly through the degree of role certainty as proposed by Allen and Meyer, but also partly through the degree of interaction with incumbents. Baker reiterated Jones' (1986) earlier conclusion that it is difficult to socialize newcomers in such a way that both commitment and innovation are fostered.

At the other end of employed life, there has been a little recent attention to retirement. This too is an increasingly ambiguous transition with respect to its timing, voluntariness, and suddenness. A model of psychological aspects of retirement has recently been presented in this series (McGoldrick, 1996), so coverage here is very brief. Feldman (1994) has called for more research linking decision to retire with subsequent adjustment. He drew on image theory (Beach & Mitchell, 1978) to identify sustaining a stable self-image, resolving approach-avoidance conflicts, and maintaining or regaining control over one's future as three themes that should be central to retirement re-search. No less than 14 hypotheses for future research were specified. Hanisch (1994) has reported research which made some links between reasons for retiring (work, personal, or health reasons) and subsequent attitudes and behaviors. Talaga and Beehr (1995) uncovered several factors (e.g. presence of dependents in the household) which had differential impacts on the retirement decisions of men relative to women.

Socialization and Information-seeking

The notion that individuals have inflated expectations of their new environment when starting work or making subsequent job changes has a long history (e.g. Vroom, 1966). It has subsequently been developed into unmet expectations—i.e. failure of the reality to live up to anticipation. Although recent research in this area is scant compared with the 1970s and 1980s, Wanous, Poland, Premack and Davis (1992) reported a meta-analysis of 31 studies which showed quite strong relationships between met expectations and job satisfaction, organizational commitment, and intention to leave, and a smaller but still significant one with actual job survival. Study design (experimental vs non-experimental) did not moderate these relationships. Wanous et al. acknowledged some conceptual and methodological limitations of met expectations.

One practical application of the met expectations literature has been realistic job previews—that is, attempts to portray the job to applicants 'warts and all' rather than in an entirely positive light. Again, published research in this area seems to have passed its peak, at least for the time being. However, Meglino, Denisi and Ravlin (1993) reported an investigation of a large sample of correctional officers. Surprisingly, a realistic job preview had significant effects on applicants who already had experience of the role, often in the opposite direction from those who did not have such experience. Findings were also different during the probationary period than subsequently. However, most of the effects were relatively small.

Researchers have devoted quite a lot of attention to learning and socialization in new jobs. Many studies in this area demonstrate a particularly painstaking and thorough approach on the part of their authors. For example, R.F. Morrison and Brantner (1992) investigated correlates of self-reported learning of departmental head jobs in a military setting. Reassuringly, in-creasing time in the job was positively correlated with learning, though a significant effect in regression analysis for time squared indicated a leveling off of learning towards the end of the 18-month assignments. Learning the job was also associated with low job challenge (presumably the benefits of simplicity more than offset any motivational problems caused by low challenge), and by high perceived importance to the real work of the organization. Self-efficacy (see also Saks, 1995) and role clarity were also positively correlated with learning. One interesting inhibitor of learning was prior experience of the role but in a different context and a subordinate position. The cross-sectional nature of this research inevitably leaves open the question of causality. Some of the correlates listed above could quite plausibly be outcomes of learning.

Chao, O'Leary-Kelly, Wolf, Klein and Gardner (1994) reported a large, impressive and informative study of organizational socialization. Construing organizational socialization as learning on the part of an individual who is adjusting to a new or changed role within an organization, they set out to examine content rather than process. They identified six areas of socialization: performance proficiency, people, politics, language, organizational goals and values, and history. A measure was developed, the factor structure of which reflected the theoretical concepts very well. The questions for four of the factors reflect learning 'about' or 'how to'. Those concerning people reflect social acceptance by others, whilst goals and values predominantly concerns personal acceptance or internalization of those goals and values. Longitudinal data showed that self-reported socialization had a positive impact on the career-related outcomes of career involvement, identity resolution and adaptability. People socialization however showed no relationships with outcomes, and history socialization showed negative ones!

Several studies have built upon earlier work (e.g. Ashford, 1986) concerning the information and feedback-seeking strategies of newcomers. This work is very much in the social-cognitive tradition. The newcomer is viewed as seeking to make sense of their new environment by acquiring and processing various forms of information in a social context. Miller and Jablin (1991) produced an exhaustive conceptual overview of types, sources and tactics of information-seeking as well as its potential costs and outcomes and individual differences. They specified a number of propositions for subsequent research. Some of these have subsequently been addressed (Ostroff & Koslowski, 1992; E.W. Morrison, 1993). Among Ostroff and Koslowski's findings were that newcomers focus primarily on acquiring information about task and role (as opposed to group and organization) and that acquisition of knowledge from supervisors and task knowledge was associated with positive changes in satisfaction, commitment and adjustment. Using somewhat different classifications of types and sources of information, E.W. Morrison (1993) also found cross-time relationships between certain aspects of information and adjustment outcomes.

Overall, the research on work-role transitions could benefit from a more consistent approach to what adjustment is. The term is used a lot, sometimes to mean integration or well-being, and sometimes to signal the individual's approach to their role. The same, only more so, applies to socialization. In spite of quite a rich and long-running literature in this area (see for example Brim, 1968), it is still conceptualized in many different ways. In keeping with the current dominance of social cognition in psychology, current work tends to construe it as learning various aspects of how to be an organizational member. Even so, distinctions are not always made between learning what to do, learning how to do it, and learning when to do it, let alone wanting to do it, believing it is the right thing to do, and viewing oneself as the kind of person who does it. In other words, socialization may cover cognitive learning, behavioral compliance, identification and internalization even though the first has had the vast majority of attention in recent research. The last of these in particular involves change in the self-concept, or at least the constellation of social selves (Schein, 1971). The methods used in most psychological research in this area also miss some of the richness of socialization and adjustment. Many writers have argued, for example, that socialization of women in male-dominated work environments presents women with a number of difficulties and dilemmas that may be qualitatively different from those experienced by men (Alvesson & Billing, 1992) and more acute the more the preponderance of males (Ely, 1994). These include how to respond to uncongenial value systems, whether or not to participate in organizational politics and adopt assertive behavior, with implications for self-concept and integrity. Marshall (1995) has reviewed much of this and other work, and has examined the dilemmas of advocating change whilst also speaking within academic conventions.

Commitment

There is an extraordinarily large literature on organizational commitment, much of it quite recent, and relatively little challenging (as opposed to refining) the concept (for an exception, see Coopey & Hartley, 1991). The organizational commitment literature is reviewed in this volume by one of its leading contributors (Meyer, Chapter 5).

Commitment is not confined to organizations, however. For many years it has been recognized that for some people at work, commitments may be to other referents. Meyer, Allen and Smith (1993) have provided some tentative evidence that the three aspects of organizational commitment (normative, continuance and affective) are also observable in commitment to occupations. The related construct of career commitment has also been developed and measured in recent years. Building on the earlier work of Blau (e.g. 1985), Carson and Bedeian (1994) have recently developed the 12-item Career Commitment Measure (CCM), which incorporates the three dimensions of career identity, career planning and career resilience. The authors argued on the basis of their data that their measure exhibits good construct and content validity, whilst also avoiding some of the problems of Blau's (1985) measure. Carson and Bedeian went to some lengths to explain to people completing the CCM that career includes concepts like line of work, profession, occupation and vocation, but even so the measure clearly refers to quite a narrow concept of career. Another line of research in this area has concerned the compatibility or otherwise of commitment to organization and to occupation. Wallace (1993) reported a meta-analysis of 15 published studies which showed a positive correlation between the two types of commitment. This suggests that the two can go hand in hand. Whilst this is no doubt true in some workplaces, Herriot (1992) amongst others has presented an analysis which shows very clearly that it cannot be taken for granted.

CAREER INTERVENTIONS IN ORGANIZATIONS

Overview

As already noted, the state of flux in most organizations, and contraction in many, is widely held to have led to the abandonment of attempts to manage careers in organizations. This has been replaced by an emphasis on the need for employees to engage in self-development. This concept may be helpful. It has a history in the applied psychology and management literature, and at least some people seem to engage purposefully in it (McEnrue, 1989). However, it now seems to be accompanied by the message that the organization will not even give any clues about what skills and experiences it wants its people to have. So people are expected not only to look after their own development, but also to do so in the absence of any information (Hirsh, Jackson & Jackson, 1995).

Nevertheless, there is a strong case to be made that now more than ever it is advantageous for an organization to play a part in the management of careers. If career paths are necessarily ambiguous (Callanan & Greenhaus, 1992; Arnold & Mackenzie Davey, 1994) and if an organization's competitive advantage lies in its use of human resources (Lawler, 1994), then the organization's task is to provide a context where employees can learn to manage their own careers in conditions of change and uncertainty. This means providing a supportive context without actually doing the managing. It probably also means a shift from using the narrower definitions of career emphasizing advancement within one line of work to much broader definitions (Adams, 1991). Tensions often exist between employee and organizational interests, and it is often argued that successful interventions must reflect both (Gutteridge, Leibowitz & Shore, 1993). In workplaces with many outsourced contract workers, issues arise as to who should be eligible to participate in interventions (Pearce, 1993). Clarity is required about the purpose of any given intervention. Is it for assessment, identifying career options, action planning, skill development, vacancy filling, or some prioritized combination of these? (Hirsh, Jackson & Jackson, 1995). It is doubtful whether the Human Resource Management strategy of making line managers responsible for facilitating the career development of subordinates (Storey, 1992) will be effective. This doubt stems from many observations, not least gaps in perception, understanding and interest between line manager and subordinate (Arnold & Mackenzie Davey, 1992; Herriot, Pemberton & Pinder, 1994).

Career interventions in organizations can take a variety of forms (Russell, 1991). These include internal vacancy notification, career workbooks, career workshops, individual counseling (including outplacement), skills inventories, personal development plans, career pathing, educational opportunities, mentoring, development centers, succession planning, and developmental work experiences. In recognition of the less organizationally-based nature of careers, there are some initiatives to set up career centers for use by individuals but to some extent sponsored by employing organizations (Waterman, Waterman & Collard, 1994).

In spite of quite thorough analyses of how organizational career interventions might be evaluated (e.g. London & Stumpf, 1982, ch. 5), there is little good-quality research assessing the impact of these interventions, nor the necessary conditions for them to work well. As Herr and Cramer (1992, pp. 482–483) put it: 'In some ways the current state of the literature pertaining to career planning in organizations is reminiscent of the writing and research related to the condition of school counseling in the late 1950s and early 1960s—role studies, suggestions, reports of tentative programs, recommendations for practice, rudimentary attempts to link theory with practice, and very little empirical or evaluative research.' Of course it is understandable that evaluation is thin on the ground. It takes time to conduct, especially in a field like careers where any benefits will be medium rather than short term. Some organizations will not wish to go public about what they do and whether it works. The legitimate demands of journal editors for rigor are hard to meet in field settings, particularly over substantial time periods with (almost by definition) a potentially mobile population. Nevertheless, the correlation between use of certain HRM practices and organizational performance at least in some industries (Terpstra & Rozell, 1993; J.B. Arthur, 1994) does give some prospect of career interventions having a demonstrable impact on the bottom line.

Mentoring

Mentoring is the intervention most often investigated in applied psychological research. To some extent this is justified by its apparent increasing popularity, although thorough information about the uptake of interventions is thin on the ground (Iles and Mabey, 1993). In turn, this popularity may be a function of the relatively small visible demands made by mentoring on a training budget and its resonance with preoccupations of baby-boomers reaching middle age. Mentoring can take a number of forms, but probably the most common one fits with the general definition provided by Kram (1985, p. 2): '. . . a relationship between a younger adult and an older, more experienced adult that helps the individual learn to navigate in the world of work.' The person in receipt of mentoring is often referred to as the protégé. A distinction is often made between informal mentoring (Levinson, Darrow, Klein, Levinson & McKee, 1978), where a relationship between mentor and protégé springs up spontaneously, and formal mentoring, where relationships are arranged and overseen by an employing or professional organization.

There is evidence that having had a mentoring relationship as opposed to not having had one is associated with indices of career success and/or socialization (e.g. Whitely, Dougherty & Dreher, 1991; Scandura, 1992; Ostroff & Kozlowski, 1993; Aryee & Chay, 1994), though see Chao, Walz and Gardner (1992) for more equivocal results. An interesting recent study (Pollock, 1995) has found that protégé benefits from mentoring seem to increase after the initial stages of the relationship, though this finding may be jeopardized by the method of asking respondents for retrospective accounts of their mentoring relationships, and leaving unspecified the time period associated with early, middle and late stages of the relationship. There are also data consistent with the idea that protégé individual differences such as socio-economic status (Whitely, Dougherty & Dreher, 1991) and personality (Turban & Dougherty, 1994) mediate and/or moderate the beneficial effects of mentoring for the protégé. Particular concern has been voiced about gender issues in mentoring. There is some feeling that women protégés may be at a disadvantage relative to male ones in obtaining a mentoring relationship and then profiting from it, especially if the mentor is male (e.g. Ragins & Cotton, 1991).

A number of writers seem willing on the basis of the above studies or their own experience and intuition to accept that mentoring normally produces benefits for mentor, protégé and employing organization, particularly the protégé (Clutterbuck, 1993). Attention therefore turns to how mentoring can be implemented effectively and pitfalls avoided. To be sure, those are vital issues, and the practicalities and politics of such interventions are often neglected by I/O psychologists (Johns, 1993). However, it really is necessary to point out a few important truths about the research cited above. Most of it did not distinguish between formal and informal mentoring. In the latter case, it may be that people who were clearly going to be successful were attractive to potential mentors, and that's why they received mentoring. Some experimental evidence in support of this conjecture has been provided by Olian, Carroll and Giannantonio (1993). With the exception of Chao, Walz and Gardner (1992) there were no comparable control groups of people who did not receive mentoring. The range of potentially confounding variables controlled for is rarely comprehensive, and certainly less comprehensive than in some of the related career success literature cited in Tharenou (this volume). Sometimes mentoring is defined as having someone the respondent calls their mentor, and sometimes as being in receipt of functions or benefits associated with mentoring, whatever the source. The research is very predominantly cross-sectional and/ or retrospective. Interestingly, where an assessment is made of what immediate benefits of mentoring are experienced by the protégé, they have been fairly modest (Noe, 1988; Chao, Waltz and Gardner, 1992).

Succession

There has been quite an extensive literature over the years on succession, particularly succession of Chief Executive Officers (CEOs). Unlike most other research on work-role transitions (see above) CEO succession literature focuses very little upon the experiences and adjustments of the incoming CEO. Instead, it concentrates on characteristics of the CEO and impact of his or her arrival upon organizational performance and employees. This is understandable given the supposed influence of CEOs, but it might be informative if more studies addressed how new CEOs are (for example) socialized. Even more to the point, research on other, 'ordinary' work-role transitions could place more emphasis upon the impact of the new arrival on those around them.

The literature on executive succession has recently been reviewed very thoroughly by Kesner and Sebora (1994), who noted that CEO succession happens relatively infrequently, with average CEO tenure of 14 years. They traced succession literature through from the 1950s and 1960s to the 1990s, identifying themes, ambiguities and progress along the way. Kesner and Sebora noted that one recurring theme was successor origin—particularly whether the incoming executive was an organizational insider or outsider. Research in this area has not drawn a clear conclusion about when each type of succession occurs, or whether one produces consistently better results than the other. The search is now on for moderator variables which may account for the variable findings. Cannella and Lubatkin (1993) for example found that in poor performing organizations, appointment of an outside CEO was likely only if there was no heir apparent and if the old CEO had little influence on the selection decision. Mabey and Iles (1993) have also made the point that succession is often a highly political process. Kesner and Dalton (1994) found that outsider CEOs induced more turnover in other upper management positions than outsider CEOs, but contrary to hypothesis, this latter turnover was unrelated to organizational performance. It should be noted, finally, that the outsider vs insider distinction is very broad. There is scope for greater use of more refined typologies of executive career path, such as that recently proposed by White, Smith and Barnett (1994).

Development Centers

There is increasing interest in using assessment center technology to identify developmental needs of existing employees, with a view to possible future job placement, training or promotion rather than immediate selection for a specific post. There is some evidence that candidates see assessment centers as relatively fair means of selecting people for jobs (Robertson, Iles, Gratton & Sharpley, 1991), so on the face of it one might expect those who experience a development center to act upon the feedback they obtain.

Jones and Whitmore (1995) conducted a 10-year follow-up of employees in an insurance company and found that acceptance of the feedback on the part of the assessees was quite high, and that (on the basis of self-report) 48% of developmental recommendations were implemented. This percentage was positively correlated with subsequent promotion, but close analysis showed that this was due to just two of the seven areas of developmental activity investigated. Engelbrecht and Fischer (1995) have also reported a study of insurance company employees. They compared experimental and control groups in an investigation of whether attendance at a development center was positively associated with work performance (supervisor ratings) relative to non-attendees three months later. It was, on nine of the eleven scales measured. However, there was no pre-test, and supervisors were aware of who had attended development centers so conclusions must be tentative.

Development Through the Job

Various factors have provoked a recent career-oriented focus on how people can be developed for future work via present work. The most significant are probably the well-documented problems of transfer of learning in training courses to everyday work (see for example Baldwin & Padgett, 1993) and the increased pressure in organizations for development to interfere with immediate performance as little as possible.

Campion, Cheraskin and Stevens (1994) have reported an investigation of managerial job rotation amongst 255 employees in a large pharmaceutical company. They construed rotation as non-promotional job moves where the employee usually does not remain permanently in the new job but nor does he or she return to the old one. In their study, rotations occurred every one to five years. They found that self-reported knowledge and skill outcomes factored out into three areas: technical, administrative and business. What they termed career management outcomes of rotation included career affect, organizational integration, stimulating work and personal development, though only the last of these could be said directly to reflect on individuals' felt ability to manage their career. Potential costs of job rotation included workload and productivity and learning curve. On the whole, respondents gave numerically higher ratings to the benefits of rotation than to the costs, though they suggested an additional cost of lost motivation or commitment amongst those not rotating. Rate of job rotation was positively correlated with promotion and salary increases, being in early career, being highly educated, and perceived increase in skills. These findings are interesting, though there may well have been an element of self-fulfilling prophecy about some of them. Also, in some contexts job rotation is used to try to maintain the performance and motivation of plateaued staff (see for example Tremblay, Roger & Toulouse, 1995) so it may be of some concern that early career (presumably pre-plateau) employees were more interested in rotation than later career ones. The association between rotation and promotion may also not be replicated elsewhere. Campion and colleagues pointed out that further research could address generalizability issues and a finer analysis of which skills are most effectively developed through rotation as opposed to other means.

In another important line of work, McCauley and colleagues (e.g. McCauley, Ruderman, Ohlott & Morrow, 1994) have developed and validated the Development Challenge Profile, which is a self-report instrument for assessing the developmental opportunities inherent in managerially oriented jobs. They identified 15 developmental features of jobs, two of which concerned job transitions, nine task-related characteristics and four obstacles. Particularly in the last category, there were some features such as difficult boss that one presumably would not normally seek to build into a job. This leads to the question of what can truly be called developmental as opposed to just plain difficult, and the authors conceded that they underestimated the degree of stress associated with some of the developmental challenges. Ohlott, Ruderman and McCauley (1994) found that although there were no widespread differences between male and female managers in terms of the developmental challenges they experienced, women tended to experience more of the obstacles.

The contribution of on-the-job experiences to career is a fruitful area for further development, and one suspects that much more in this line will be done in the next few years.

Career Counseling

Most counseling occurs outside the person's work organization, but it is sometimes offered to employees as a stand-alone service or as part of a package such as outplacement or a career development workshop. A review of theory and research on career counseling theory, techniques and practice is outside the scope of this chapter, and is in any case provided elsewhere (e.g. Egan, 1990; Nathan & Hill, 1992; Sharf, 1992; see also Hermansson, 1993, for an interesting example of the application of some of Egan's ideas to counseling in organizations). Here I will confine comment to a few points about the evaluation of career counseling.

Most counselors do not seek to give advice. To use an old distinction, they help people to make decisions wisely, not wise (as judged by the counselor) decisions (Katz, 1969). This becomes ever more true as the pace of change increases and it is difficult to discern with confidence what a wise decision is. The need for ready access to counseling by adults throughout their career is increasingly evident (Watts, 1994) as non-normative events buffet us frequently (Vondracek & Schulenberg, 1992). Some of the earlier research evaluating careers counseling and guidance used stability in a job or occupation as a dependent variable, but this seems inappropriate as a goal of counseling now, and perhaps then too (Killeen, White & Watts, 1992). Given the number of other things happening in a person's life, it is difficult if not impossible to isolate the impact of a counseling intervention, which may in any case be additional to earlier interventions with the same person. The interconnections and continuities between different parts of a person's life at any one time also mean that any career counseling intervention must encompass, and may have an impact upon, leisure, personal relationships and so on (Krumboltz, 1993).

However, to the extent that it can be done, evaluation of career counseling work needs to be in terms of the client's cognitive processes (Kidd & Killeen, 1992) as well as outcomes such as job satisfaction. The latter are becoming more ephemeral and in any case are unlikely to be achieved without cognitive processes. These include reflecting on the past and present, monitoring and evaluating self, and exploration, as well as meta-cognitive skills such as knowing when to use these processes. This is touched on again in the next section.

CAREER MANAGEMENT AND LIFESPAN DEVELOPMENT OF INDIVIDUALS

The Nature of Vocational Personality

John Holland's theory (e.g. Holland, 1985) remains the dominant one in the field of vocational personality measurement. Holland has proposed the existence of six 'pure types' of vocational personality, each of which any given individual or work environment can resemble to greater or lesser degrees. The types can be thought of as arranged at the vertices of a hexagon, with their positioning defining the relative similarity of the types. Holland's fundamental proposition concerning effective vocational choices is that a person whose personality is congruent with (i.e. similar to) their environment will, other things being equal, experience more satisfaction in it and perform better than a person not in congruent environment. Surprisingly perhaps, a recent meta-analytic review revealed little support for this prediction (Tranberg, Slane & Ekeberg, 1993).

If we assume that *some* kind of match between person and environment facilitates satisfaction and/or performance, the negative results reported by Tranberg, Slane and Ekeberg may indicate that Holland has not hit upon the optimal way of describing people and environments. One conclusion might be that something like Schein's (1993) career anchors might do a better job. There is no direct evidence for that, but Nordvik (1991) has shown that scores on career anchor measures are relatively independent of scores on Holland vocational personality measures. This leaves open the possibility that career anchors may tap aspects of personality more meaningful to congruence than Holland's. Tokar and Swanson (1995) have found that scores on Holland types correlate in interpretable ways with parts of the five-factor model of personality (McCrae & Costa, 1987), particularly Openness and

Extroversion. This is encouraging for Holland's typology in that it should indeed link with other conceptualizations of personality, but discouraging in that large areas of the 'Big Five' do not seem well reflected in the Holland typology.

There have been recent debates concerning the structure of vocational personality. Gati (1991) argued for a hierarchical structure of vocational interests rather than a hexagonal or circular one. A stimulating series of articles in the *Journal of Vocational Behavior* (1992) debated Holland's hexagonal structure. Prediger and Vansickle (1992) advocated a two-dimensional model in which the axes (data-ideas and things-people) could be superimposed onto the hexagon, but with more utility and sensitivity than could be achieved by Holland type scores. Holland and Gottfredson (1992) presented a counter-argument which focused on how some patterns of scores would not be adequately reflected by the Prediger and Vansickle reformulation. Dawis (1992) offered some perceptive further comments, including the observation that the choice of six clusters is arbitrary, and other formulations specify different numbers. Rounds and Tracey (1993) analyzed data from a large number of US studies in an attempt to identify which non-hierarchical structure, if any, best fitted the data. They concluded (p. 886) that '. . . a very simple circular-ordering structure can be validly used in thinking about RIASEC interests.' This means that the Prediger and Vansickle axes are not obviously any better or worse than any other pair of orthogonal axes, and that choosing different numbers and positions on the circle could lead to description of 'pure types' different from those of Holland, but equally valid. Rounds and Tracey also noted the presence of a general factor in response to vocational interest inventories: that is, a tendency to express (or not) interest in activities of all kinds. The interpretation of this factor was identified as an important issue for future research.

Decision Processes and Individual Differences

Holland's theory concerns the content of decisions more than the process of making decisions. Quite a lot of developmentally oriented theorizing some years ago attempted to map out how individuals clarify their sense of self and integrate this with vocational and other life choices (Super & Hall, 1990). Using concepts derived from this line of thinking, Blustein, Pauling, DeMania and Faye (1994) found that the extent to which students reported engaging in exploratory behavior was correlated with progress in vocational decision-making, whereas indices of congruence (see above) were not.

Recently a little attention has been paid to the detail of how individuals go about making and implementing decisions. The literature here concerns either on the one hand 'career' or 'vocation' (normally defined as an area of work) or on the other hand, job. Integration with work on decision-making from other areas of psychology is not particularly high, though for an exception see Gati,

Fassa, and Houminer (1995). Use of concepts from social cognitive psychology is however more prevalent. Moss and Frieze (1993) found that students' preferences amongst job offers could be explained both by the extent to which offers matched students' desired job attributes and by the extent to which students' stereotypes of people working in the jobs offered matched their self-concept. The first of these explained more of the variance in preferences than the second. Gianakos (1995) extended an existing line of research applying sex-role self-concept to career variables. She found that androgynous individuals (i.e. those who described themselves in both stereotypically masculine and feminine terms) felt more able to tackle career decision-making tasks than others, and significantly more so than undifferentiated individuals (i.e. those who scored low on both traditionally feminine and masculine aspects of self-concept). However, in studies of this kind it is important to establish that a person's sex *per se* does not account for the variance in the dependent variable.

A recent monograph by Lent, Brown and Hackett (1994) has applied social cognitive theory to interests, choices and performance in employment and academic settings. The authors argued that existing work tended to view persons in overly static terms, with behavior being seen as a product of a person–situation interaction rather than an aspect of it. They continued: 'By contrast, social cognitive theory emphasizes the situation and domain-specific nature of behavior, relatively dynamic aspects of the self-system, and the means by which individuals exercise personal agency' (p. 82). With an emphasis on self-efficacy, outcome expectancies and personal goals, Lent, Brown and Hackett then built models of interests, choices and performance and specified many hypotheses, some of which they were able to test. This work may well succeed in doing what the authors hoped—to advance on the static trait-oriented views of decision-making and add specificity to the more learning-oriented but rather general development approaches.

The Lent, Brown and Hackett approach may be particularly well suited to a world where people need to make choices with a weather eye toward their future marketability in terms of skills and experiences as well as the congruence between present self and work requirements. Furthermore, individuals have fewer external markers of their progress (see above) and less opportunity to pursue a pre-defined sequence of jobs. All this places a greater emphasis on self-awareness and assessment, learning from experience and coping with uncertainty and setbacks. Some other recent work is also relevant here. Waterman, Waterman and Collard (1994) have referred to career-resilient workers, where career resilience is defined in terms of self-knowledge, long-term goals independent of an employing organization, knowledge of the market, flexibility, and willingness to move on when they no longer fit the organization. Although it was developed in the specific context of Silicon Valley in California, USA, and reflects economic rather than psychological imperatives, the concept of career resilience probably has wider applicability.

London (1993) has explored the concept of career motivation. He suggested that it has three components: career insight, career identity and career resilience. The last of these was defined (rather differently from Waterman, Waterman & Collard) as the ability to adapt to changing circumstances. Career insight is the realism and clarity of the person's career goals, and career identity is the extent to which a person defines him or herself in terms of work. The three constructs and their measurement are clearly important to the study of careers, but combining them and assigning the label motivation to the composite seems less than helpful despite London's attempt to equate them to the energizing, direction and persistence components of motivation. Carson, Carson and Bedeian (1995) have developed a self-report measure of career entrenchment, which is in some respects the opposite of career resilience. It has three components: career investments, emotional costs of changing careers, and limitedness of career alternatives.

Regarding self-assessment of attributes and/or performance, the earlier literature (e.g. Mabe & West, 1982) tended to concentrate on the degree of accuracy of self-assessment (or at least agreement with others' assessments), often with the assumption that accuracy would facilitate effective decision-making. More recent work has taken two rather different directions. First, it seems that agreement of self-ratings with those made by colleagues at work may reflect the possession of some social or self-insight skills which also contribute to a person's objective career success (Bass & Yammarino, 1991; Furnham & Stringfield, 1994). Second, self-efficacy theory suggests, with a little evidence to back the claim, that moderately over-optimistic self-estimates should enhance subsequent performance (Lent, Brown & Hackett, 1994).

Life-span Development and Aging

The influence of development approaches was hinted at in the previous section. Led by the late Donald Super and others, developmental analyses of careers have emphasized the unfolding nature of cognition, emotion and behavior concerning careers. At first, these approaches tended to be confined purely to employment, and quite closely tied to normative age-related phenomena. But the developmental approaches themselves developed. They have increasingly considered roles other than employment and in some cases close links with age have been loosened (Super, 1990; see also Chi-Ching, 1995, for an empirical example).

As Super (1990, p. 194) put it: '. . . what I have contributed is not an integrated, comprehensive and testable theory, but rather . . . a loosely unified set of theories dealing with specific aspects of career development taken from developmental, differential, social and phenomenological psychology and held together by self-concept or personal-construct psychology.' Developmental ideas, even more than most, require longitudinal examination. Thus it is perhaps not surprising that the use of developmental ideas in careers research and practice is common, but tests of theoretical propositions are rare. In the former category, Dix and Savickas (1995) have recently reported an interesting piece of work attempting to elicit from 50 successful male workers how they had tackled the six developmental tasks of the establishment stage of career. The authors pointed out that this helps to make explicit some of the tacit knowledge associated with successful career development. Through use of interviews, critical incident techniques, and content categorizing by expert judges, Dix and Savickas identified between three and eight coping behaviors for each of the six tasks. A similar exercise with female workers is planned, which is important given that this study focused on males, and that developmental approaches are often heavily criticized for working from male, middle-class perspectives.

One contribution often seen as particularly vulnerable on this last point is that of Levinson et al. (1978), (see also Levinson, 1986). On the basis of interviews with 40 men, they proposed a closely age-related developmental pattern which alternated between stable and transitional periods. The former is where a person pursues stable goals within a life structure, and the latter is where they question and perhaps change their goals and/or life structure. Smart and Peterson (1994) have tested these ideas in a cross-sectional analysis of 498 Australian professional women. There were 12 dependent variables, including for example professional commitment, intent to remain and need for achievement. They concluded that the pattern postulated by Levinson et al. was evident for only one of the dependent variables (pay satisfaction). However, it is not obvious to me why one would expect trends in the dependent variables consistent with Levinson et al. As Levinson et al. pointed out, stable periods are not necessarily experienced as stable or calm. A person may have stable goals, and these may include (for example) leaving their employer. During a transitional period they may be considering a different lifestyle, but still intend to build this around (for example) their current profession. Levinson's ideas can only really be tested using detailed case material, with all the practical and analytical problems that involves.

Recently Helms and Piper (1994) have lamented the small amount and simplistic nature of research on racial aspects of vocational behavior and development. Typically racial groups have been defined in nominal terms—that is, people are assigned to a category regardless of how they view themselves. But, '. . . unless one believes that vocational behavior is biogenetically determined and racial classification is a valid indicator of persons' biogenetic endowments, then there is no valid reason for explaining or anticipating consistent between-group differences on the basis of race *per se* on any of the commonly investigated vocational behavior.' In the same issue of the *Journal of Vocational Behavior*, Evans and Herr (1994) reported results which supported that assertion. Helms and Piper argued that use of racial identity theory (e.g. Helms, 1990) could further our understanding of the vocational development blacks and whites alike. The theory traces stages in the development of racial identity, and may have some parallels with other developmental approaches in careers and in adult cognitive development more generally (see e.g. Commons, Sinnott, Richards & Armon, 1989). Helms and Piper further suggested that racial identity should be seen as a dependent variable (i.e. an outcome of events and experiences) as well as an independent variable.

There is increasing recognition that the demographic trends described earlier require more attention to the psychology of aging and its integration with employment-related contexts (see Davies, Matthews & Wong, 1991 for a review). Sterns and Miklos (1995) have provided a helpful recent review of some key areas here. They disaggregated the concept of aging into five different and not necessarily consistent aspects (chronological/legal, functional, psychosocial, organizational and lifespan) and reviewed research related to each. Consistent with Neugarten's (1977) notion of 'fanning out' of members of a cohort as they progress through adulthood, Sterns and Miklos noted that 'Late careers are often more difficult to study than early careers because there is less consistency in the development tasks' (p. 259). In an article in the same edition of the *Journal of Vocational Behavior*, Hall and Mirvis (1995) have put forward some interesting propositions about the nature of career at midlife and beyond. They argued that the changing nature of the workplace holds both threats and opportunities for older workers. For example, older workers may be better able than younger ones to engage in 'relational' work such as helping and supporting others. This work is especially important when an organization is under pressure, but often goes unnoticed (or worse, it is seen as non-productive) and unrewarded. Hall and Mirvis also drew upon systems theory to suggest that an organization needs to contain at least as much complexity as is present in its environment. One form of complexity is diversity, and one form of diversity is age. 'Careers too are becoming more complex: We would argue that what we are seeing now, instead of one set of career stages spanning a lifespan (as the Super model posits), is a series of many shorter learning cycles over the span of a person's work life. . . . As a result, people's careers will become increasingly a succession of 'mini-stages' (or short-cycle learning stages) of exploration – trial – mastery – exit, as they move in and out of various product areas, technologies, functions, organizations, and other work environments. . . . Thus, the half-life of a career stage would be driven by the half-life of the competency field of that career work' (p. 277). Hall and Mirvis added that if older workers can be removed from various job and health insecurities, they are likely to be able to engage in the continuous learning (as opposed to isolated retraining) demanded by the labour market.

A number of studies have shown that stereotypes of older workers, whilst not wholly negative, are not particularly flattering. A comprehensive recent study in this area has been reported by Warr and Pennington (1994). In a study with 1140 personnel managers, they found that non-managerial jobs perceived as mainly for older workers were also perceived to make fewer cognitive demands, be slower paced and less demanding of energy than those for younger workers. Sterns and Miklos (1995) cited a study by Russell and Curtis (1992) which found that 63% of companies offered pre-retirement programs, but only 23% had programs to reduce obsolescence or plateauing. This is consistent with barriers to the effective development of older workers identified by Hall and Mirvis (1995), which included the perceptions that investment in the development of older workers is too costly, and that older workers are too inflexible and difficult to train.

These perceptions exist alongside research showing that there is little relationship between age and job performance (McEvoy & Cascio, 1989), except within early adulthood. Other work shows that, despite age-related decrements in some aspects of information-processing, the task performance of older people is often at least as good as that by younger people especially where tasks are of a relatively familiar kind and the use of learning strategies is encouraged (e.g. Salthouse, 1990). On the other hand the pace of change in the workplace more often requires learning *un*familiar tasks. Alwin (1994) has noted the existence of different patterns of stability in psychological constructs during adulthood. He suggested that the evidence on intelligence and personality traits indicated a pattern of persistently high stability from early adulthood to old age. Data on self-concepts and attitudes suggested a rather different pattern of low stability in early adulthood followed by stability in midlife and either further stability or more change thereafter. These findings might suggest another problem for older people—they really are less open to change than younger people. On the other hand, as Alwin and others have pointed out, it is wellnigh impossible to disentangle different influences on lifespan development. The pattern of findings may principally reflect typically low pressure in the past for people to change after early adulthood. Nowadays and in the future we may find that necessity is the mother of instability.

Future theory and practice in careers would do well to pay more attention to work on lifespan development, of which Alwin (1994) is just one example, though an impressively far-sighted one. Warr and Conner (1992) presented another impressive contribution in their attempt to link research on intelligence, cognitive style and expertise with job competence, whilst Warr (1993) analyzed key differences between cognitive tasks and linked them to expected patterns of performance of people of different ages. Extension of this kind of work to the cognitive demands made by the self-management of careers offers an exciting and profitable way forward in helping all people, especially older ones, tackle the demands of contemporary life (Kegan, 1994). Another avenue here is the recent work on wisdom by Baltes and colleagues (e.g. Staudinger, Smith & Baltes, 1992). Although this might be criticized for taking a rather narrow and culture-specific view of what wisdom is (Assmann, 1994) it offers a measure of ways of thinking which may be very well suited to career management as we approach the millennium.

CONCLUSIONS

The psychological literature on careers is appropriately diverse in content, though less so in method. Recent years have seen important advances in research in some areas, particularly (in my opinion) the psychological contract and work-role transitions and socialization. In some areas empirical research is relatively plentiful but over-arching theory rather thin. In others, especially developmental approaches to careers, the reverse is true.

A number of impressive contributions exhibiting at least two of methodological excellence, theory development, and practical application have been published in recent years. Most of these are either substantial longitudinal empirical studies or ground-breaking theoretical contributions which more often than not draw heavily upon work in other areas of psychology, particularly social cognition. Indeed, this last point is a real source of optimism— there are signs of increasing integration of career psychology with the rest of the discipline.

Of course, not all in the garden is rosy. A number of papers, including some mentioned in this review, have made at best a modest contribution to our understanding of careers (though in most cases I would have been proud enough to have produced them!). For the purposes of this review (including areas I have excluded from this chapter because of space limitations), I was most consistently impressed by the content of *Academy of Management Journal* and *Personnel Psychology*. Contributions in these journals seemed to me most often to combine rigor with a sensitive attempt to tackle issues of real importance in organizational life. *Journal of Applied Psychology* and *Journal of Vocational Behavior* carried many excellent articles but at times seemed in danger of over-emphasizing 'technical correctness' at the expense of contribution to understanding of issues of practical importance. The *Journal of Organizational Behavior* and *Human Relations* were also very valuable sources of good material, and the latter in particular published papers with diverse methods and varied theoretical orientations. But these two more than the other four journals mentioned also seemed to carry some of the modest contributions alluded to earlier. Often, but not always, cross-sectional and entirely self-report data were the limiting factor.

With large datasets and/or a longitudinal study design it is of course often appropriate for multiple papers to be published. Nevertheless, I felt there were some instances where researchers produced multiple articles from the same data even though a single bigger and more integrative contribution might have developed the field better. There is also a tendency (evident also in this article I suspect) for authors to over-emphasize research conducted in their own country or continent even though they are writing on issues of international importance for international audiences.

The career literature is beginning to reorientate to take account of the changing world of employment. There is much still to be done in developing analyses of how individuals can and should manage their careers, achieve success against their own standards, and make appropriate decisions, but in many of the areas reviewed a start has been made. The Hall and Mirvis (1995) paper is a particularly good example of this.

One of several profitable lines of enquiry will be how people explain to themselves and others their past, present and future in a world with relatively few fixed points or signposts. This endeavor requires attention to discourse and narrative (e.g. Gergen, 1988) which would represent a useful addition to, and change from, the vast majority of existing careers research. It may depart from the positivist assumption that there is one 'truth' (albeit a complex one) waiting to be found. Interestingly, this assumption reflects quite a low level of development in models of cognitive development! But even if it is not really so novel, there is likely to be much value in placing somewhat more emphasis on people's accounts of their behavior and thinking (e.g. Dix & Savickas, 1995), and also more emphasis on direct observation of behavior and assessment of thinking strategies.

REFERENCES

Adams, J. (1991) Issues in the management of careers. In R. F. Morrison and J. Adams (eds), *Contemporary Career Development Issues*. Hillsdale, NJ: Erlbaum.

Allen, N. J. & Meyer, J. P. (1990) Organizational socialization tactics: A longitudinal analysis of links to newcomers' commitment and role orientation. *Academy of Management Journal*, **33**, 847–858.

Alvesson, M. & Billing, Y. D. (1992) Gender and organization: Towards a differentiated understanding. *Organization Studies*, **13**, 73–102.

Alwin, D. F. (1994) Aging, personality and social change: The stability of individual differences over the adult life span. In D. L. Featherman, R. M. Lerner & M. Perlmutter (eds), *Life-Span Development and Behavior*, Vol. 12. Hillsdale, NJ: Erlbaum.

Arnold, J. (1990) From education to labor markets. In S. Fisher and C.L. Cooper (eds), *On The Move: The Psychological Effects of Change and Transition*. Chichester: Wiley.

Arnold, J. (1994) Opportunity for skill use, job changing, and unemployment as predictors of psychological well-being amongst graduates in early career. *Journal of Occupational and Organizational Psychology*, **67**, 355–370.

Arnold, J. & Mackenzie Davey, K. (1992) Self-ratings and supervisor ratings of graduate employees' competences during early career. *Journal of Occupational and Organizational Psychology*, **65**, 235–250.

Arnold, J. & Mackenzie Davey, K. (1994) Graduate experiences of organizational career management. *International Journal of Career Management*, **6**, 14–18.

Arnold, J. & Nicholson, N. (1991) Construing of self and others at work in the early years of corporate careers. *Journal of Organizational Behavior*, **12**, 621–639.

Arthur, J. B. (1994) Effects of human resource systems on manufacturing performance and turnover. *Academy of Management Journal*, **37**, 670–687.

Arthur, M.B. (1994) The boundaryless career: A new perspective for organizational enquiry. *Journal of Organizational Behavior*, **15**, 295–306.

Arthur, W. & Bennett, W. (1995) The international assignee: The relative importance of factors perceived to contribute to success. *Personnel Psychology*, **48**, 99–114.

Aryee, S. & Chay, Y. W. (1994) An examination of the impact of career-oriented mentoring on work commitment attitudes and career satisfaction among professional and managerial employees. *British Journal of Management*, 5, 241–249.

Ashford, S. J. (1986) Feedback-seeking in individual adaptation: A resource perspective. *Academy of Management Journal*, 29, 465–487.

Ashforth, B. E. & Saks, A. M. (1995) Work-role transitions: A longitudinal examination of the Nicholson model. *Journal of Occupational and Organizational Psychology*, 68, 157–175.

Assmann, A. (1994) Wholesome knowledge: Concepts of wisdom in a historical and cross-cultural perspective. In D. L. Feathermen, R. M. Lerner & M. Perlmutter (eds), *Life-Span Development and Behavior*, Vol. 12. Hillsdale, NJ: Erlbaum.

Baker, W. K. (1995) Allen and Meyer's (1990) longitudinal study: A reanalysis and reinterpretation using structural equation modeling. *Human Relations*, 48, 169–186.

Baldwin, T.T. and Padgett, M. (1993) Management development. In C. L. Cooper and I. T. Robertson (eds), *International Review of Industrial and Organizational Psychology*, Vol. 8. Chichester: Wiley.

Bass, B. M. & Yammarino, F. J. (1991) Congruence of self and others' leadership ratings of naval officers for understanding successful performance. *Applied Psychology: An International Review*, 40, 437–454.

Beach, L.R. & Mitchell, T.R. (1978) A contingency theory for the selection of decision strategies. *Academy of Management Review*, 3, 439–449.

Beard, K. M. & Edwards, J. R. (1995) Employees at risk: Contingent work and the psychological experience of contingent workers. In C. L. Cooper and D. M. Rousseau (eds), *Trends in Organizational Behavior*, Vol. 2. Chichester: Wiley.

Bird, A. (1994) Careers as repositories of knowledge: A new perspective on boundaryless careers. *Journal of Organizational Behavior*, 15, 325–344.

Black, J. S. & Gregersen, H. B. (1992) Serving two masters: Managing the dual allegiance of expatriate employees. *Sloan Management Review*, Summer, 61–71.

Blau, G. (1985) The measurement and prediction of career commitment. *Journal of Occupational Psychology*, 58, 277–288.

Blau, G., Linnehan, F., Brooks, A. & Hoover, D. K. (1993) Vocational behavior 1990–1992: Personnel practices, organizational behavior, workplace justice, and industrial/organizational measurement issues. *Journal of Vocational Behavior*, 43, 133–197.

Blustein, D. L. (1995) Toward a contextual perspective of the school-to-work transition: A reaction to Feij et al. *Journal of Vocational Behavior*, 47, 257–265.

Blustein, D. L., Pauling, M. L., DeMania, M. E. & Faye, M. (1994) Relation between exploratory and choice factors and decisional progress. *Journal of Vocational Behavior*, 44, 75–90.

Borgen, F. H. (1991). Megatrends and milestones in vocational behavior: A 20-year counseling psychology retrospective. *Journal of Vocational Behavior*, 39, 263–290.

Brett, J. F., Cron, W. L. & Slocum, J. W. (1995) Economic dependency on work: A moderator of the relationship between organizational commitment and performance. *Academy of Management Journal*, 38, 261–271.

Brett, J. M. (1992) Job transfer. In C. L. Cooper and I. T. Robertson (eds), *International Review of Industrial and Organizational Psychology*. Vol. 7. Chichester: Wiley.

Brett, J. M., Stroh, L. K. & Reilly, A. H. (1992) Job transfer. In C. L. Cooper and I. T. Robertson (eds), *International Review of Industrial and Organizational Psychology*, Vol. 7. Chichester: Wiley.

Brett, J. M., Stroh, L. K. & Reilly, A. H. (1993) Pulling up roots in the 1990s: Who's willing to relocate? *Journal of Organizational Behavior*, 14, 49–60.

Brewster, C. (1994) The paradox of adjustment: UK and Swedish expatriates in Sweden and the UK. *Human Resource Management Journal*, 4, 49–62.

Bridges, W. (1995) *Jobshift: How to Prosper in a Workplace Without Jobs.* London: Nicholas Brealey.

Brim, O. G. (1968) Adult socialization. In J. A. Clausen (ed.), *Socialization and Society.* Boston: Little, Brown.

Bruce, R. A. & Scott, S. G. (1994) Varieties and commonalities of career transitions: Louis' typology revisited. *Journal of Vocational Behavior*, **45**, 17–40.

Callanan, G. A. & Greenhaus, J. H. (1992) The career indecision of managers and professionals: An examination of multiple subtypes. *Journal of Vocational Behavior*, **41**, 212–231.

Campion, M. A., Cheraskin, L. & Stevens, M. J. (1994) Career-related antecedents and outcomes of job rotation. *Academy of Management Journal*, **37**, 1518–1542.

Cannella, A. A. & Lubatkin, M. (1993) Succession as a sociopolitical process: Internal impediments to outsider selection. *Academy of Management Journal*, **36**, 763–793.

Carson, K. D. & Bedeian, A. G. (1994) Career commitment: Construction of a measure and examination of its psychometric properties. *Journal of Vocational Behavior*, **44**, 237–262.

Carson, K. D., Carson, P. P. & Bedeian, A. G. (1995) Development and construct validation of a career entrenchment measure. *Journal of Occupational and Organizational Psychology*, **68**, 301–320.

Cartwright, S. & Cooper, C. L. (1992) *Mergers and Acquisitions: The Human Factor.* Oxford: Butterworth & Heinemann.

Cawsey, T. & Inkson, K. (1992) Patterns of managerial job change: A New Zealand study. *New Zealand Journal of Business*, **14**, 14–25.

Chao, G. T., O'Leary-Kelly, A. M., Wolf, S., Klein, H. J. & Gardner, P. D. (1994) Organizational socialization: Its content and consequences. *Journal of Applied Psychology*, **79**, 730–743.

Chao, G. T., Walz, P. M. & Gardner, P. D. (1992) Formal and informal mentorships: A comparison on mentoring functions and contrast with nonmentored counterparts. *Personnel Psychology*, **45**, 619–636.

Chapman, A. J., Sheehy, N. P., Heywood, S., Dooley, B. & Collins, S. C. (1995) The organizational implications of teleworking. In C. L. Cooper and I. T. Robertson (eds), *International Review of Industrial and Organizational Psychology*, Vol. 10. Chichester: Wiley.

Chartrand, J. M. & Camp, C. C. (1991) Advances in the measurement of career development constructs: A twenty-year review. *Journal of Vocational Behavior*, **39**, 1–39.

Chi-Ching, Y. (1995) The effects of career salience and life-cycle variables on perceptions of work–family interfaces. *Human Relations*, **48**, 265–284.

Clutterbuck, D. (1993) *Everyone Needs a Mentor*, 2nd edn. London: Institute of Personnel Management.

Collin, A. & Watts, A. G. (1996) The death and transfiguration of career—and careers guidance? *British Journal of Guidance and Counselling*, in press.

Commons, M. L., Sinnott, J. D., Richards, F. F. & Armon, C. (eds) (1989) *Adult Development: Comparisons and Applications of Developmental Models.* New York: Praeger.

Coopey, J. & Hartley, J. (1991) Reconsidering the case for organizational commitment. *Human Resource Management Journal*, **1**, 18–32.

Davidson, M. J. (1996) Women and Employment. In P. B. Warr (ed.), *Psychology at Work.* Harmondsworth: Penguin.

Davies, D. R., Matthews, G. & Wong, C. S. K. (1991) Ageing and work. In C. L. Cooper and I. T. Robertson (eds), *International Review of Industrial and Organizational Psychology*, Vol. 6. Chichester: Wiley.

Dawis, R. V. (1992) The structure(s) of occupations: Beyond RIASEC. *Journal of Vocational Behavior*, **40**, 171–178.

Dawis, R. V. & Lofquist, L. H. (1984) *A Psychological Theory of Work Adjustment.* Minneapolis, MN: University of Minnesota Press.

Dix, J. E. & Savickas, M. L. (1995) Establishing a career: Developmental tasks and coping responses. *Journal of Vocational Behavior,* **46**, 93–107.

Driver, M. J. (1988) Careers: A review of personal and organizational research. In C. L. Cooper and I. T. Robertson (eds), *International Review of Industrial and Organizational Psychology,* Vol. 3. Chichester: Wiley.

DuBrin, A. J. (1983) *Human Relations for Career and Personal Success.* Reston, VA: Reston Publishing Co.

Egan, G. (1990) *The Skilled Helper* 4th edn. Pacific Grove: Brooks/Cole.

Eldredge, B. D. (1995) Some things not considered: Evaluation of a model of career enhancing strategic and content innovation with respect to organizational socialization. *Journal of Vocational Behavior,* **47**, 266–273.

Ely, R. J. (1994) The effects of organizational demographics and social identity on relationships among professional women. *Administrative Science Quarterly,* **39**, 203–238.

Engelbrecht, A. S. & Fischer, A. H. (1995) The managerial performance implications of a developmental assessment center process. *Human Relations,* **48**, 387–404.

Evans, K. M. & Herr, E. L. (1994) The influence of racial identity and the perception of discrimination on the career aspirations of African American men and women. *Journal of Vocational Behavior,* **44**, 173–184.

Feij, J. A., Whitely, W. T., Peiró, J. M. & Taris, T. W. (1995) The development of career-enhancing strategies and content innovation: A longitudinal study of new workers. *Journal of Vocational Behavior,* **47**, 231–256.

Feldman, D. C. (1989) Careers in organizations: Recent trends and future directions. *Journal of Management,* **15**, 135–156.

Feldman, D. C. (1994) The decision to retire early: A review and reconceptualization. *Academy of Management Review,* **19**, 285–311.

Fisher, C. D. & Shaw, J. B. (1994) Relocation attitudes and adjustment: A longitudinal study. *Journal of Organizational Behavior,* **15**, 209–224.

Fouad, N. A. (1994) Annual review 1991–1993: Vocational choice, decision-making, assessment, and intervention. *Journal of Vocational Behavior,* **45**, 125–176.

Fournier, V. & Payne, R. (1994) Change in self-construction during the transition from university to employment: A personal construct psychology approach. *Journal of Occupational and Organizational Psychology,* **67**, 297–314.

Furnham, A. & Stringfield, P. (1994) Congruence of self and subordinate ratings of managerial practices as a correlate of supervisor evaluation. *Journal of Occupational and Organizational Psychology,* **67**, 57–67.

Gati, I. (1991) The structure of vocational interests. *Psychological Bulletin,* **109**, 309–324.

Gati, I., Fassa, N. & Houminer, D. (1995) Applying decision theory to career counseling practice: The sequential elimination approach. *Career Development Quarterly,* **43**, 211–220.

Gergen, M. (1988) Narrative structures in social explanation. In C. Antaki (ed.), *Analyzing Everyday Explanation: A Casebook of Methods.* London: Sage.

Gianakos, I. (1995) The relation of sex-role identity to career decision-making self-efficacy. *Journal of Vocational Behavior,* **46**, 131–143.

Gray, D. A., Gault, F. M., Meyers, H. H. & Walther, J. E. (1990) Career planning. In J. C. Quick et al. (eds) *Career Stress in Changing Times.* New York: Haworth Press.

Greenhaus, J. H. & Callanan, G.A. (1994) *Career Management,* 2nd edn. London: Dryden Press.

Gutteridge, T. G., Leibowitz, Z. B. & Shore, J. E. (1993) *Organizational Career Development.* Reading, MA: Addison-Wesley.

Hackett, G., Lent, R.W. & Greenhaus, J. H. (1991) Advances in vocational theory and research: A twenty-year retrospective. *Journal of Vocational Behavior*, **38**, 3–38.

Hall, D. T. (1976) *Careers in Organizations*. Glenview, IL: Scott Foresman.

Hall, D. T. (1991) Twenty questions: Research needed to advance the field of careers. In R. F. Morrison and J. Adams (eds) *Contemporary Career Development Issues*. Hillsdale, NJ: Erlbaum.

Hall, D. T. & Mirvis, P. H. (1995) The new career contract: Developing the whole person at midlife and beyond. *Journal of Vocational Behavior*, **45**, 328–346.

Handy, C. (1989) *The Age of Unreason*. London: Business Books.

Handy. C. (1994) *The Empty Raincoat*. London: Hutchinson.

Hanisch, K. A. (1994) Reasons people retire and their relations to attitudinal and behavioral correlates in retirement. *Journal of Vocational Behavior*, **45**, 1–16.

Helms, J. E. (1990) *Black and White Racial Identity*. New York: Greenwood Press.

Helms, J. E. & Piper, R. E. (1994) Implications of racial identity theory for vocational psychology. *Journal of Vocational Behavior*, **44**, 124–138.

Heppner, M. J., Multon, K. D. & Johnston, J. A. (1994) Assessing psychological resources during career change: Development of the Career Transitions Inventory. *Journal of Vocational Behavior*, **44**, 55–74.

Hermansson, G. L. (1993) Counsellors and organizational change: Egan's systems model as a tool in organizational consulting. *British Journal of Guidance and Counselling*, **21**, 133–144.

Herr, E. L. & Cramer, S. H. (1992) *Career Guidance and Counseling through the Life Span*, 4th edn. New York: Harper Collins.

Herriot, P. (1992) *The Career Management Challenge*. London: Sage.

Herriot, P. & Pemberton, C. (1995a) *New Deals*. Chichester: Wiley.

Herriot, P. & Pemberton, C. (1995b) *Competitive Advantage Through Diversity*. London: Sage.

Herriot, P., Pemberton, C. & Pinder, R. (1994) Misperceptions by managers and their bosses of each other's preferences regarding the managers' careers: A case of the blind leading the blind? *Human Resource Management Journal*, **4**, 39–51.

Hesketh, B. (1995) Personality and adjustment styles: A Theory of Work Adjustment approach to career enhancing strategies. *Journal of Vocational Behavior*, **47**, 274–282.

Hirsh, W., Jackson, C. & Jackson, C. (1995) *Careers in Organizations: Issues for the Future*. Brighton: Institute for Employment Studies.

Holland, J. L. (1985) *Making Vocational Choices*, 2nd edn. Englewood Cliffs, NJ: Prentice-Hall.

Holland, J. L. & Gottfredson, G. D. (1992) Studies of the hexagonal model: An evaluation (or, the perils of stalking the perfect hexagon). *Journal of Vocational Behavior*, **40**, 158–170.

Hutton, W. (1995) *The State We're In*. London: Cape.

Iles, P. & Mabey, C. (1993) Managerial career development programmes: Effectiveness, availability and acceptability. *British Journal of Management*, **4**, 103–118.

Inkson, K. (1995) Effects of changing economic conditions on managerial job changes and careers. *British Journal of Management*, **6**, 183–194.

Janssens, M. (1995) Intercultural interaction: A burden on international managers? *Journal of Organizational Behavior*, **16**, 155–167.

Johns, G. (1993) Constraints on the adoption of psychology-based personnel practices: Lessons from organizational innovation. *Personnel Psychology*, **46**, 569–592.

Jones, G. R. (1986) Socialization tactics, self-efficacy, and newcomers' adjustments to organizations. *Academy of Management Journal*, **29**, 262–279.

Jones, R. G. & Whitmore, M. D. (1995) Evaluating developmental assessment centers as interventions. *Personnel Psychology*, **48**, 377–388.

Kanter, R. M. (1989) *When Giants Learn to Dance*. New York: Simon & Schuster.

Katz, M. R. (1969) Can computers make guidance decisions for students? *College Board Review*, No. 72, Summer.

Kegan, R. (1994) *In Over our Heads: The Mental Demands of Modern Life.* Cambridge, MA: Harvard University Press.

Kesner, I. F. & Dalton, D. R. (1994) Top management turnover and CEO succession: An investigation of the effects of turnover on performance. *Journal of Management Studies*, 31, 701–713.

Kesner, I. F. & Sebora, T. C. (1994) Executive succession: Past, present and future. *Journal of Management*, 20, 327–372.

Kidd, J. & Killeen, J. (1992) Are the effects of careers guidance worth having? *Journal of Occupational and Organizational Psychology*, 65, 219–234.

Killeen, J., White, M. & Watts, A. G. (1992) *The Economic Value of Careers Guidance.* London: Policy Studies Institute.

Kram, K. E. (1985) *Mentoring at Work.* Lanham, MD: University Press of America.

Krumboltz, J. D. (1993) Integrating career and personal counseling. *Career Development Quarterly*, 42, 143–148.

Kuhl, J. (1992) A theory of self-regulation: Action versus state orientation, self-discrimination, and some applications. *Applied Psychology: An International Review*, 41, 97–129.

Lawler, E. (1994) From job-based to competency-based organizations. *Journal of Organizational Behavior*, 15, 3–16.

Lawson, M. B. & Angle, H. (1994) When organizational relocation means family relocation: An emerging issue for strategic human resource management. *Human Resource Management*, 33, 33–54.

Lent, R. W., Brown, S. D. & Hackett, G. (1994) Toward a unifying social cognitive theory of career and academic interest, choice and performance. *Journal of Vocational Behavior*, 45, 79–122.

Levinson, D. J. (1986) A conception of adult development. *American Psychologist*, 41, 3–13.

Levinson, D. J., Darrow, C. N., Klein, E. B., Levinson, M. H. & McKee, B. (1978) *Seasons of a Man's Life.* New York: Knopf.

London, M. (1993) Relationships between career motivation, empowerment and support for career development. *Journal of Occupational and Organizational Psychology*, 66, 55–69.

London, M. & Greller, M. M. (1991) Demographic trends and vocational behavior: A twenty year retrospective and agenda for the 1990s. *Journal of Vocational Behavior*, 38, 125–164.

London, M. & Mone, E. (1988) *Career Growth and Human Resources Strategies.* New York: Quorum Books.

London, M. & Stumpf, S. A. (1982) *Managing Careers.* Reading, MA: Addison-Wesley.

Louis, M. R. (1980a) Surprise and sense-making: What newcomers experience in entering unfamiliar organizational settings. *Administrative Science Quarterly*, 25, 226–251.

Louis, M. R. (1980b) Career transitions: Varieties and commonalities. *Academy of Management Review*, 5, 329–340.

Louis, M. R. (1982) Career transitions: A missing link in career development. *Organizational Dynamics*, 10, 68–77.

Mabe, P. A. & West, S. G. (1982) Validity of self-evaluation of ability: A review and meta-analysis. *Journal of Applied Psychology*, 67, 280–296.

Mabey, C. & Iles, P. (1993) The strategic integration of assessment and development practices: Succession planning and new manager development. *Human Resource Management Journal*, 3, 16–34.

Major, D. A., Kozlowski, S. W. J., Chao, G. T. & Gardner, P. D. (1995) A longitudinal investigation of newcomer expectations, early socialization outcomes, and the moderating effects of role development factors. *Journal of Applied Psychology*, **80**, 418–431.

Marshall, J. (1995) Gender and management: A critical review of research. *British Journal of Management*, **6** (Special Issue), S53–S62.

Martin, R. (1995) The effects of prior job moves on job relocation stress. *Journal of Occupational and Organizational Psychology*, **68**, 49–56.

McCauley, C.D., Ruderman, M. N., Ohlott, P. J. & Morrow, J. E. (1994) Assessing the developmental components of managerial jobs. *Journal of Applied Psychology*, **79**, 544–560.

McCrae, R. R. & Costa, P. T. (1987) Validation of the five-factor model of personality across instruments and observers. *Journal of Personality and Social Psychology*, **56**, 586–595.

McEnrue, M. P. (1989) Self-development as a career management strategy. *Journal of Vocational Behavior*, **34**, 57–68.

McEvoy, G. M. & Cascio, W. F. (1989) Cumulative evidence of the relationship between employee age and job performance. *Journal of Applied Psychology*, **74**, 11–17.

McGoldrick, A. E. (1996) A psychological model of retirement decision and impact. In C. L. Cooper and I. T. Robertson (eds), *International Review of Industrial and Organizational Psychology*, Vol. 11. Chichester: Wiley.

Meager, N., Kaiser, M. & Dietrich, H. (1992) *Self-Employment in the UK and Germany*. London: Anglo-German Foundation for the Study of Industrial Society.

Meglino, B. M., Denisi, A. S. & Ravlin, E. C. (1993) Effects of previous job exposure and subsequent job status on the functioning of a realistic job preview. *Personnel Psychology*, **46** 803–822.

Meier, S. T. (1991) Vocational behavior, 1988–1990: Vocational choice, decision-making, career development interventions, and assessment. *Journal of Vocational Behavior*, **39**, 131–181.

Meyer, J. P., Allen, N. J. & Smith, C. A. (1993) Commitment to organizations and occupations: Extension and test of a three-component conceptualization. *Journal of Applied Psychology*, **78**, 538–551.

Miller, V. D. & Jablin, F. M. (1991) Information seeking during organizational entry: Influences, tactics, and a model of the process. *Academy of Management Review*, **16**, 92–120.

Morrison, E. W. (1993) Newcomer information-seeking: Exploring types, modes, sources and outcomes. *Academy of Management Journal*, **36**, 557–589.

Morrison, R. F. & Brantner, T. M. (1992) What enhances or inhibits learning in a new job? A basic career issue. *Journal of Applied Psychology*, **77**, 926–940.

Moss, M. K. & Frieze, H. (1993) Job preferences in the anticipatory socialization phase: A comparison of two matching models. *Journal of Vocational Behavior*, **42**, 282–297.

Munton, A. G., Forster, N., Altman, Y. & Greenbury, L. (1993) *Job Relocation: Managing People on the Move*. Chichester: Wiley.

Nathan, R. & Hill, L. (1992) *Career Counselling*. London: Sage.

Neugarten, B. L. (1977) Personality and aging. In J. E. Birren and K. W. Schaie (eds), *Handbook of the Psychology of Aging*. New York: Van Nostrand Reinhold.

Newton, T. J. & Keenan, A. (1990) Consequences of changing employers amongst young engineers. *Journal of Occupational Psychology*, **63**, 113–127.

Nicholson, N. (1984) A theory of work-role transitions. *Administrative Science Quarterly*, **29**, 172–191.

Nicholson, N. & West, M. A. (1989) Transitions, work histories and careers. In M. B. Arthur, D. T. Hall and B. S. Lawrence (eds) *Handbook of Career Theory*. Cambridge: Cambridge University Press.

Nicholson, N. (1990) The transition cycle: Causes, outcomes, processes and forms. In S. Fisher and C. L. Cooper (eds), *On The Move: The Psychological Effects of Change and Transition.* Chichester: Wiley.

Nicholson, N. & Imaizumi, A. (1993) The adjustment of Japanese expatriates to living and working in Britain. *British Journal of Management,* 4, 119–134.

Nicholson, N. & West, M. A. (1988) *Managerial Job Change: Men and Women in Transition.* Cambridge: Cambridge University Press.

Noe, R. A. (1988) An investigation of the determinants of successful assigned mentoring relationships. *Personnel Psychology,* 41, 457–479.

Nordvik, H. (1991) Work activity and career goals in Holland's and Schein's theories of vocational personalities and career anchors. *Journal of Vocational Behavior,* 38, 165–178.

Offermann, L. R. & Gowing, M. K. (1990) Organizations of the future. *American Psychologist,* 45, 95–108.

Ohlott, P. J., Ruderman, M. N. & McCauley, C. D. (1994) Gender differences in managers' developmental job experiences. *Academy of Management Journal,* 37, 46–67.

Olian, J. D., Carroll, S. J. & Giannantonio, C. M. (1993) Mentor reactions to protégés: An experiment with managers. *Journal of Vocational Behavior,* 43, 266–278.

Ornstein, S. & Isabella, L. A. (1993) Making sense of careers: A review 1989–1992. *Journal of Management,* 19, 243–267.

Ostroff, C. & Kozlowski, S. W. J. (1992) Organizational socialization as a learning process: The role of information acquisition. *Personnel Psychology,* 45, 849–874.

Ostroff, C. & Kozlowski, S. W. J. (1993) The role of mentoring in the information gathering processes of newcomers during early organizational socialization. *Journal of Vocational Behavior,* 43, 170–183.

Pearce, J. L. (1993) Toward an organizational behavior of contract laborers: Their psychological involvement and effects on employee coworkers. *Academy of Management Journal,* 36, 1082–1096.

Perlmutter, M. & Hall, E. (1992) *Adult Development and Aging.* 2nd edn. Chichester: Wiley.

Pollock, R. (1995) A test of conceptual models depicting the developmental course of informal mentor-protégé relationships in the workplace. *Journal of Vocational Behavior,* 46, 144–162.

Prediger, D. J. & Vansickle, T. R. (1992) Locating occupations on Holland's hexagon: Beyond RIASEC. *Journal of Vocational Behavior,* 40, 111–128.

Quick, J. C., Hess, R. E., Hermalin, J. & Quick, J. D. (eds) (1990) *Career Stress in Changing Times.* New York: Haworth Press.

Ragins, B. R. & Cotton, J. L. (1991) Easier said than done: Gender differences in perceived barriers to gaining a mentor. *Academy of Management Journal,* 34, 939–951.

Robertson, I. T., Iles, P. A., Gratton, L. & Sharpley, D. (1991) The impact of personnel selection and assessment methods on candidates. *Human Relations,* 44, 963–982.

Rounds, J. & Tracey, T. J. (1993) Prediger's dimensional representation of Holland's RIASEC circumplex. *Journal of Applied Psychology,* 78, 875–890.

Russell, J. E. A. (1991) Career development interventions in organizations. *Journal of Vocational Behavior,* 38, 237–287.

Russell, J. E. A. & Curtis, L. B. (1992) *Career development programs in the Fortune 500.* Paper presented at meeting of the Society for Industrial Organizational Psychology.

Saks, A. M. (1995) Longitudinal field investigation of the moderating and mediating effects of self-efficacy on the relationship between training and newcomer adjustment. *Journal of Applied Psychology,* 80, 211–225.

Salomone, P. R. (1993) Annual review: Practice and research in career counseling and development, 1993. *Career Development Quarterly,* 42, 99–128.

Salthouse, T. A. (1990) Cognitive competence and expertise in aging. In J. E. Birren and K. W. Schaie (eds), *Handbook of the Psychology of Aging*, 3rd edn. London: Academic Press.

Scandura, T. A. (1992) Mentorship and career mobility: An empirical investigation. *Journal of Organizational Behavior*, **13**, 169–174.

Scandura, T. A. & Ragins, B. R. (1993) The effects of sex and gender role orientation on mentorship in male-dominated occupations. *Journal of Vocational Behavior*, **43**, 251–265.

Schein, E. H. (1971) The individual, the organization, and the career: A conceptual scheme. *Journal of Applied Behavioral Science*, **7**, 401–426.

Schein, E. H. (1993) *Career Anchors: Discovering your Real Values*. Revised edn. London: Pfeiffer and Co.

Schneider, S. C. & Asakawa, K. (1995) American and Japanese expatriate adjustment: A psychoanalytic perspective. *Human Relations*, **48**, 1109–1127.

Sharf, R. F. (1992) *Applying Career Development Theory to Counseling*. Pacific Grove: Brooks/Cole.

Shore, L. & Tetrick, L. E. (1994) The psychological contract as an explanatory framework in the employment relationship. In C. L. Cooper and D. M. Rousseau (eds), *Trends in Organizational Behavior*, Vol. 1. Chichester: Wiley.

Smart, R. & Peterson, C. (1994) Stability versus transition in women's career development: A test of Levinson's theory. *Journal of Vocational Behavior*, **45**, 241–260.

Social Trends, (1993) No. 23. London: Central Statistical Office.

Staudinger, U. M., Smith, J. & Baltes, P. B. (1992) Wisdom-related knowledge in a life review task: Age differences and the role of professional specialization. *Psychology and Aging*, **7**, 271–281.

Stephens, G. K. (1994) Crossing internal career boundaries: The state of research on subjective career transitions. *Journal of Management*, **20**, 479–501.

Sterns, H. L. & Miklos, S. M. (1995) The aging worker in a changing environment: Organizational and individual issues. *Journal of Vocational Behavior*, **47**, 248–268.

Storey, J. (1992) *Developments in the Management of Human Resources*. Oxford: Blackwell.

Subich, L. M. (1994) Annual review: Practice and research in career counseling and development: 1993. *Career Development Quarterly*, **43**, 114–151.

Super, D. E. (1990) Career and life development. In D. Brown and L. Brooks (eds), *Career Choice and Development*, 2nd edn. San Francisco: Jossey-Bass.

Super, D. E. & Hall, D. T. (1978) Career development: exploration and planning. *Annual Review of Psychology*, **29**, 257–293.

Super, D. E. & Hall, D. T. (1990) Career development: Exploration and planning. *Annual Review of Psychology*, **29**, 333–372.

Swanson, J. L. (1992) Vocational behavior 1989–1991: Life-span career development and reciprocal interaction of work and nonwork. *Journal of Vocational Behavior*, **41**, 101–161.

Talaga, J. A. & Beehr, T. A. (1995) Are there gender differences in predicting retirement decisions? *Journal of Applied Psychology*, **80**, 16–28.

Terpstra, D. E. & Rozell, E. J. (1993) The relationship of staffing practices to organizational level measures of performance. *Personnel Psychology*, **46**, 27–48.

Tokar, D. M. & Swanson, J. L. (1995) Evaluation of the correspondence between Holland's vocational personality typology and the five-factor model of personality. *Journal of Vocational Behavior*, **46**, 89–108.

Tranberg, M., Slane, S. & Ekeberg, S. E. (1993) The relation between interest congruence and satisfaction: A meta-analysis. *Journal of Vocational Behavior*, **42**, 253–264.

Tremblay, M., Roger, A. & Toulouse, J-M. (1995) Career plateau and work attitudes: An empirical study of managers. *Human Relations*, **48**, 221–237.

Turban, D. B. & Dougherty, T. W. (1994) Role of protégé personality in receipt of mentoring and career success. *Academy of Management Journal*, **37**, 688–702.

Vondracek, F. & Schulenberg, J. (1992) Counseling for normative and nonnormative influences on career development. *Career Development Quarterly*, **40**, 291–301.

Vroom, V. H. (1966) A study of pre- and post-decision processes. *Organizational Behavior and Human Performance*, **1**, 212–225.

Wallace, J. E. (1993) Professional and organizational commitment: Compatible or incompatible? *Journal of Vocational Behavior*, **42**, 333–349.

Wanous, J. P., Poland, T. D., Premack, S. L. & Davis, K. S. (1992) The effects of met expectations on newcomer attitudes and behaviors: A review and meta-analysis. *Journal of Applied Psychology*, **77**, 288–297.

Warr, P. B. (1993) Age and employment. In M. Dunnette, L. Hough and H. Triandis (eds), *Handbook of Industrial and Organizational Psychology*, Vol. 4. Palo Alto: Consulting Psychologists Press.

Warr, P. B. & Conner, M. (1992) Job competence and cognition. *Research in Organizational Behavior*, **14**, 91–127.

Warr, P. B. & Pennington, J. (1994) Occupational age-grading: Jobs for older and younger non-managerial employees. *Journal of Vocational Behavior*, **45**, 328–346.

Waterman, R., Waterman, J. & Collard, B. (1994) Toward a career resilient workforce. *Harvard Business Review*, July/August.

Watkins, C. E. & Subich, L. M. (1995) Annual review, 1992–1994: Career development, reciprocal work/non-work interaction, and women's workforce participation. *Journal of Vocational Behavior*, **47**, 109–163.

Watts, A. G. (1994) *Lifelong Career Development: Towards a National Strategy for Careers Education and Guidance*. Cambridge, UK: Careers Research and Advisory Centre.

Wheeler, K. G. (1990) Career experiences: Current and future themes. In J C. Quick et al. (eds), *Career Stress in Changing Times*. London: Haworth Press.

White, M. C., Smith, M. & Barnett, T. (1994) A typology of executive career specialization. *Human Relations*, **47**, 473–486.

Whitely, W., Dougherty, T. W. & Dreher, G. F. (1991) Relationship of career mentoring and socioeconomic origin to managers' and professionals' early career progress. *Academy of Management Journal*, **34**, 331–351.

Whitely, W., Dougherty, T.W. & Dreher, G. F. (1992) Correlates of career-oriented mentoring for early career managers and professionals. *Journal of Organizational Behavior*, **13**, 141–154.

.

Chapter 2

MANAGERIAL CAREER ADVANCEMENT

Phyllis Tharenou
Monash University

It has become increasingly important to understand how advancement into managerial positions occurs. There is the need to advance as managers those who are most effective. The performance of organization leaders has been shown to contribute to organization failure (Levinson, 1994) and profitability (Day & Lord, 1988), with the proportion of effective managers thought to be less than 50% and executives about 33% (Forbes & Piercy, 1991; Hogan, 1994; Hogan, Curphy, & Hogan, 1994). There is the critical need to understand why women and minorities continue to be underrepresented in management (Northcraft & Gutek, 1993). There are different but not understood ways to advance to high positions in contemporary organizations than two decades ago (Kotter, 1995), when there was reliance on career paths based on job ladders, seniority, and tenure. Managerial positions are fewer in flatter, decentralized, downsized organizations, of necessity changing how advancement occurs (Offerman & Gowing, 1993). There are also changed human resources management practices for selection and promotion of managers. Selection practices for management positions are more structured and less subjective than a decade earlier (Shackleton & Newell, 1991), equal employment opportunity/affirmative action has been introduced, and applicant pools for managerial positions are increasingly diverse—more feminized, older, and of more ethnic groups and races (Khojasteh, 1994).

How people advance in the contemporary management hierarchy is not understood (Kotter, 1995). Are qualities of the individual (ambition, intelligence) more important than organizational factors (promotion ladders, line jobs, functional areas), or do they interact? Are merit, performance-based factors—human capital, managerial skills, job performance, job-relevant traits—more important than non-merit, non-performance-based factors—informal networks, discrimination, politics, job-irrelevant traits? Are 'informal' social factors—networks, mentors, politics, group similarity—more explanatory than 'formal' opportunity structures—internal labor markets, seniority, tenure? Knowledge of managerial advancement is from diverse, distinct, highly specific approaches, as yet resulting in questions remaining unanswered. Reviews of the literature have been confined to understanding causes of promotion (Forbes & Wertheim, 1995; Markham, Harlan, & Hackett, 1987; Stumpf & London, 1981) or women's advancement into management (Powell & Mainiero, 1992; Ragins & Sundstrom, 1989). This review examines the causes of career advancement of supervisors, managers, executives, and chief executive officers (CEOs) broadly in terms of managerial promotions, level and pay, as well as of subordinate entry to management positions. It is based on the contemporary empirical research published since 1990.

Managerial career advancement has usually been defined in terms of promotions within managerial ranks and the level of management position ultimately reached (e.g. Miner, Chen, & Yu, 1991), and as level of pay (Rosenbaum, 1984). Managerial promotions signify upward movement in the managerial hierarchy, and managers' levels and pay signify managerial achievement and success (Gattiker & Larwood, 1990; Miner, Chen, & Yu, 1991). Managerial promotions (number or rate) appear to precede increases in level and pay (Brett, Stroh, & Reilly, 1992a; Bretz & Judge, 1994; Gibbs, 1995), and managerial level is used to predict pay (e.g. Boxman, De Graaf, & Flap, 1991; Bretz & Judge, 1994; Lobel & St. Clair, 1992; Reskin & Ross, 1992; Schneer & Reitman, 1995), suggesting promotion increases level which increases pay. The term pay will be used to refer to salary, salary progression or total compensation because results do not differ by pay type and types are highly related (e.g. Judge, Cable, Boudreau, & Bretz, 1995).

The studies to be reviewed have examined organizational and individual causes of managerial career advancement, consistent with past reviews (e.g. Markham, Harlan, & Hackett, 1987; Ragins & Sundstrom, 1989; Stumpf & London, 1981). The studies published since 1990 cover several major categories of variables, as shown in Figure 2.1. In the organizational context, opportunity structures, social structures, the interpersonal context, and promotion processes have been examined, and in regard to individual factors, traits, human capital, managerial skills, and family.

THE ORGANIZATIONAL ENVIRONMENT

Opportunity Structures

Large organizations with long promotion ladders and high growth should provide opportunities for individuals to advance into management. On organization entry, individuals are faced with opportunity structures (Markham, Harlan, & Hackett, 1987). They enter jobs that vary in the extent to which promotion ladders are attached, entering on the bottom rung of the ladder in a

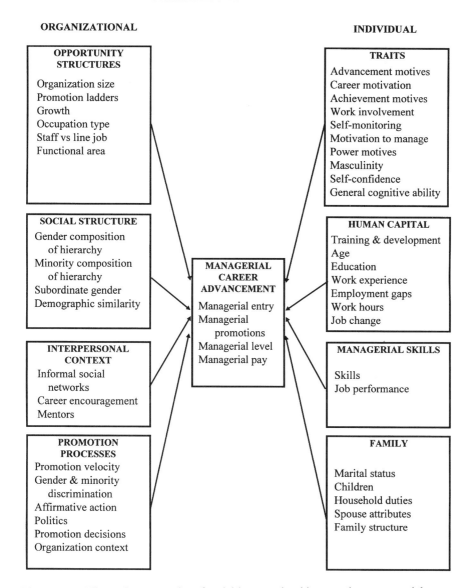

Figure 2.1 The major categories of variables examined in regard to managerial career advancement from the studies to be reviewed

closed internal labor market, or at higher rungs in a more open internal labor market. Promotion is achieved by moves between levels in the ladder, and so ladders need to be long with many levels and to lead to higher level jobs for promotion to occur, and vacancies need to arise. Occupations and job types and functions are also components of internal labor markets that vary in their capacity to allow individuals to move into, or advance in management. Primary jobs and 'organization' jobs (the firm labor market) provide more promotion opportunities than secondary jobs and 'occupation' jobs (Markham, Harlan, & Hackett, 1987). The studies to be reviewed are multivariate, primarily cross-sectional designs, assessing opportunity structures measured either by self-report, little validated measures at individual level, or by more objective means using company and industry records at organization level. Most studies of opportunity structures do not assess their indirect effects on advancement through intervening structures or other factors, and insufficient studies have compared the importance of opportunity structures to individual factors or to other organizational factors.

Organization size

Organization size has been found not related (Cox & Harquail, 1991; Dreher & Ash, 1990; Judge et al., 1995) or weakly related (Nkomo & Cox, 1990; Whiteley & Coetsier, 1993) to managers' promotion. Indirect effects may occur through internal labor markets. Larger organizations than smaller had internal promotion systems for executives (Friedman, 1991), and were more likely to have a fast track and use informal nominations for promotion to middle manager levels (Ferris, Buckley, & Allen, 1992). The influence on actual advancement was not assessed. Organization size was negatively related to managers' managerial levels (Cox & Harquail, 1991; Herriot, Gibson, Pemberton, & Pinder, 1993; Schneer & Reitman, 1994a, 1995), perhaps because larger organizations are more competitive or have fewer managerial positions. Organization size may have greatest effect in late career. Organization size did not increase managerial levels until mid-career when employees were 28 to 44 years old, reaching full impact for those greater than 44 years (Melamed, 1996a), and managers in larger organizations increased their level and pay when older than 44 than in middle years (Herriot et al., 1993). Organization size had inconsistent links to managers' and executives' pay: nonsignificant (Dreher & Ash, 1990; Reskin & Ross, 1992; Whitely & Coetsier, 1993), negative (Herriot et al., 1993; Ingham & Thompson, 1995; Judge et al., 1995), and positive (Meyerson, 1994; Pfeffer & Ross, 1990; Schneer & Reitman, 1995). Organization size was not related to managers' advancement comprising promotion, level and pay (Judge & Bretz, 1994). Organization size was related positively to selection of older business unit managers with more corporation tenure (Guthrie & Olian, 1991) and of insider CEOs than outsiders (Datta & Guthrie, 1994), suggesting larger organizations than smaller may advance insiders to executive positions, perhaps because of larger candidate pools. Organization size has been inconsistently related to women's or minorities' managerial advancement. Using large numbers of companies, organization size was not related to the proportion of women or minorities in management (Konrad & Linnehan, 1995; Konrad & Pfeffer, 1991; Leck &

Saunders, 1992a, b; Leck, Saunders, & St. Onge, 1991; Pfeffer, Davis-Blake, & Julius, 1995), although it has been related, particularly representatively, to hiring for management positions of male and female visible minorities (non-Caucasian, nonwhite) and the disabled (Konrad & Linnehan, 1995; Leck & Saunders, 1992a, b; Leck, Saunders, & St. Onge, 1991). For university executives and managers, organization size was negatively related to hiring of women (Konrad & Pfeffer, 1991) and to pay for positions continuously held by women and positions held by men but formerly held by women, compared to continuing male positions (Pfeffer & Ross, 1990). In summary, not consistent with internal labor markets for advancement, organization size is inconsistently related, either unrelated or weakly related, to managerial career advancement including of women and minorities.

Promotion ladders

Long promotion ladders were related to male and female managers' promotion (Tharenou & Conroy, 1994), but the number of management levels was not related to black managers' managerial promotions (Nkomo & Cox, 1990). Frequency of management vacancies was positively related (Blum, Fields, & Goodman, 1994; Nkomo & Cox, 1990) and unrelated to managers' promotions or managerial levels (Cox & Harquail, 1991). Promotion ladders were negatively related to managers' and executives' managerial levels (Herriot, Gibbons, Pemberton, & Jackson, 1994; Tharenou & Conroy, 1994), perhaps because shorter ladders are reported closer to the top. In a sample ranging in level (43% subordinates), an open versus closed internal labor market was not related to managerial level, but low cohort competition increased women's and not men's managerial levels (Melamed, 1995a). Management vacancies and low management salaries, reflecting institutional pressures, and promotion and development from within and the high proportions of professional and skilled organization positions, reflecting internal labor markets, were related to the percentage of women in management in 279 medium to large private firms (Blum, Fields, & Goodman, 1994). Industrial relations managers' perceptions of organization career reward systems and the fit of their preferences with the system were related, albeit weakly, to pay and job level (Bretz & Judge, 1994), suggesting advancement arises partly from person–environment fit. In summary, not supporting internal labor markets for advancement, promotion ladders are inconsistently related to managerial advancement.

Growth

Organizational growth in two 3-year periods did not assist promotion of two entry cohorts of managers in a US international company, having either small positive effects or negative effects (Hurley & Sonnenfeld, 1994). Periods of high growth had inconsistent links with promotion rates at all managerial levels, and did not assist women and minorities. The promotion rates of men and whites remained much higher (Hurley & Sonnenfeld, 1994). The growth era enhanced the promotions of whichever functional area (operations versus staff) had initially lower promotion rates, suggesting growth equalizes. Women were more likely than men to manage academic and nonacademic departments in two universities when they had smaller budgets and the department was nongrowing, whereas men got the job when the department had a larger budget or was growing (Stover, 1994). In summary, growth may not help managerial career advancement.

Occupation type

Occupations are classified by skill level based on their range and complexity of job duties and formal education, on-the-job training, and experience to do the job. Managerial and administrative occupations are classified highest in skill level and unskilled occupations lowest, with nonmanagerial/administrative occupations (e.g. clerical) having managerial positions. High skill level occupations (primary jobs) offer job security, skill development, and career paths as distinct from low level occupations (secondary jobs; Markham, Harlan, & Hackett, 1987). Using standard government occupational classifications, occupational level was related positively to women's and men's managerial levels for employees ranging in level (Melamed, 1995a), and holding a managerial versus nonmanagerial occupation to managers' higher pay (Reskin & Ross, 1992). The greater percentage of women in an occupation, the less likelihood employees held a supervisory position in a US national sample (Huffman, 1995) and the lower the pay of Australian managers (Martin, 1994). Job titles that qualified public servants to apply to take examinations for managerial positions were disproportionately held by males, with eligibility requirements reducing managerial promotions of women and minorities (Steinberg, Haignere, & Chertos, 1990). In summary, supporting the importance of primary versus secondary job labor markets, occupation level and male gender-linkage are positively related to managerial advancement.

Line versus staff job

Line rather than staff positions should provide more knowledge about the firm and opportunities for visible performance and credibility in critical functions, increasing opportunities for managerial advancement. Line rather than staff positions were related (Nkomo & Cox, 1990; Whitely & Coetsier, 1993) and not related (Cox & Harquail, 1991; Scandura, 1992) to managers' promotions, and not related to managers' levels (Bretz & Judge, 1994; Cox & Harquail, 1991). Women who reached vice-president level reported moving out of staff to line positions in mid-career (Mainiero, 1994a). Entering by line versus staff jobs was related inconsistently to managers' career advancement, and became less important with tenure in the firm (Hurley & Sonnenfeld, 1994). Line rather than staff jobs were positively related to managers' pay (Scandura, 1994) or had no links (Cox & Harquail, 1991; Whitely & Coetsier, 1993), and not related to industrial relations managers' advancement (promotions, level, pay; Judge & Bretz, 1994). In summary, line versus staff jobs are related inconsistently, often unrelated, to managerial career advancement.

Functional area

The type or breadth of functional areas managers occupy may influence opportunities for advancement through increased knowledge, visible performance, credibility, and familiarity (Forbes & Piercy, 1991). For managers, central areas of finance, marketing, and operations were not related to advancement (Cannings, 1991; Cannings & Montmarquette, 1991b; Dreher & Ash, 1990; Schneer & Reitman, 1990; Stroh, Brett, & Reilly, 1992; Whitely, Dougherty, & Dreher, 1991), although they are rarely compared to less central functions of human resources and community relations. Managers in finance had higher pay (Schneer & Reitman, 1994b, 1995). The number of functional areas, and thus breadth of experience, was not related to managers' promotion, level or pay (Cox & Harquail, 1991; Ellis & Heneman, 1990), except for younger compared to middle and older managers' managerial levels (Herriot et al., 1993). International experience was related to executives' promotion but not pay (Judge et al., 1995), and international jobs, living outside the US, and adding one year of international experience gave male managers extra salary payoffs per year but female managers pay reductions (Egan & Bendick, 1994). In studies using archival data and interviews, and without comparison groups, men and women who rose to executive levels had (i) successful performance in critical functional areas and experience on high visibility projects and task forces, especially in the first five years; (ii) experience in corporate headquarters, and breadth of experience through several functional areas, cross-functional areas, assistant to executive positions, and international assignments, especially in late early career, the second five years; (iii) broadening general management experience, especially in mid-career (10 to 20 years); and (iv) major organizational assignments and projects on specific organizational needs in late career (Forbes & Piercy, 1991; Mainiero, 1994a; Piercy & Forbes, 1991). In summary, apart from executive advancement, type and number of functional areas are usually not related to managerial career advancement.

Social Structure

Organizational social structures may influence opportunities for managerial career advancement. Processes of similarity and categorization operate for decision-makers, including when selecting for management jobs. Decision-makers compare themselves to others as similar or different and are attracted to those similar, and perceive and relate to others by social categories when detailed information and contact is lacking (Baron & Pfeffer, 1994). Kanter coined the term 'homosocial reproduction' when insiders replicate themselves when filling jobs (Kanter, 1977), and homophily operates when selectors prefer to choose similar others and job seekers prefer to work with similar individuals (Ibarra, 1993). Homophily is the degree of demographic and identity similarity of interacting individuals (Ibarra, 1993). Male managerial hierarchies are therefore more likely to result in selection and promotion of white men for managerial jobs. In the studies to be reviewed, there are insufficient direct tests of explanations (e.g. effects of similarity) posed for the effects, and few tests of interactions between social structures and individual attributes for managerial career advancement.

Gender composition of hierarchy

Most studies of the impact of gender composition of managerial hierarchies are cross-sectional, self-report survey designs with multivariate analyses and controls. For managers and executives, the extent to which the managerial hierarchy was male was related to women not being promoted but not men, but to neither's managerial levels (Tharenou & Conroy, 1994). Female CEOs were discriminated from matched samples of male CEOs and female top managers from amongst organizational (training, selection), interpersonal (male hierarchy, career encouragement), and individual (personality, non-work, early background) factors by two factors, one of which was the extent the managerial hierarchy was male (Tharenou, 1995). This suggests male hierarchies stop women breaking the glass ceiling, and more female hierarchies help them. In a structural equation analysis, male hierarchies did not affect male or female managers' and executives' career encouragement, and reduced men's and not women's training and development and thus in turn managerial advancement (Tharenou, Latimer, & Conroy, 1994). For middle managers of a finance company, the number of women already in top positions was related to women's motivation to be promoted, but not men's (Cannings & Montmarquette, 1991a).

Studies of university managers are consistent with processes of homosocial reproduction and homophily in selection and promotion practices based on the gender composition of managerial hierarchies. From analysis of objective longitudinal data of a national US sample of 821 colleges and universities, the proportion of female administrators predicted the proportion of female administrators five years later (Pfeffer, Davis-Blake, & Julius, 1995). If the president of the college was a woman or a minority, the greater were the proportion of female administrators and increase in their proportion over five years (Pfeffer, Davis-Blake, & Julius, 1995). A new hire for managerial and executive positions was more likely to be a woman if there was a greater percentage of women in the particular position across institutions and/or in all administrative positions in a university, and if the previous occupant was a woman (Konrad & Pfeffer, 1991). It was hard to get women into positions from which they were formerly excluded, but once first hired for those positions, they were more likely to be hired (Konrad & Pfeffer, 1991). For two university departments, women were more likely than men to manage departments previously managed by a woman (Stover, 1994). In summary, consistent with homophily and homosocial reproduction processes, male managerial hierarchies reduce women's managerial advancement, and increases in women in managerial jobs subsequently increase women's representation in management.

Minority composition of hierarchy

For university executives and managers, the percentage of minorities in management five years earlier and the CEO being a minority were related to the percentage of minorities in management (Pfeffer, Davis-Blake, & Julius, 1995). The greater percentage of minorities in that particular position, or all administrative positions in universities and the previous occupant being a minority were related to minorities being new hires (Konrad & Pfeffer, 1991). The organizations' percentage of black employees was not related to managerial promotions of black managers from self-reports of MBA graduates in several organizations (Nkomo & Cox, 1990). The overall trends are consistent with homophily and homosocial reproduction explanations. In summary, minorities in the managerial hierarchy increase minority representation in management.

Subordinate gender

Higher proportions of female than male subordinates were positively related to the number of women managers (Reskin & Ross, 1992) and university administrators (Stover, 1994), and the percentage of women in nonmanagement positions was related to the percentage of women in management in medium to large private firms (Blum, Fields, & Goodman, 1994). Men were more likely to manage men than women (Reskin & Ross, 1992). In summary, women are more likely to be managers when the subordinates are women rather than men.

Demographic similarity

Social similarity, by providing a familiar frame of reference, is thought to influence choice of job applicants when the decision is more uncertain (Salancik & Pfeffer, 1978), as would be found for high level management jobs. Hence, demographically similar candidates may be promoted to management jobs (Mittman, 1992). For male but not female business school graduates in the first 3 months of their jobs, when the work group had high proportions of women, men were more likely to be promoted at 14 months, but women were not when the workgroup was male (Kirchmeyer, 1995). Cultural (ethnicity, religion) and generational (age, education, lifestyle) similarity were not related to promotion. From analyses of objective public data, individuals' demographic dissimilarity to the team in age, tenure, education, military service and career experiences was not related to promotion from nonelite to elite status in 93 top management teams over a four-year period (Jackson, Brett, Sessa, Cooper, Julin, & Peyronnin, 1991). From archival data, future CEOs were found similar to the organization's executives in middle- or upper-class socioeconomic origins, education level from elite universities, being sons of business executives or professionals, and being from industrialized or metropolitan areas, all indicating familiarity and trust (Forbes & Piercy, 1991). In summary, not supporting a broad social similarity view, demographic similarity is inconsistently related to managerial promotion.

Interpersonal Context

Individuals may be provided in their work environment with emotional/expressive and career/instrumental support for advancement from multiple others or specific individuals. Instrumental behavior provides job-related resources including information and career support, whereas expressive behavior provides emotional support (Ibarra, 1993). Studies have examined multiple contacts using informal social networks. Informal network relationships influencing advancement are formed based on group similarity (i.e. homophily), with same-group ties thought to pull people into and up managerial hierarchies (Ibarra, 1993). Studies have examined individual support using mentors. Mentors provide intensive career and expressive support for advancement (Kram, 1983), using direct interventions, for example, through sponsoring protégés and providing legitimacy (Burt, 1992). Studies of social structure have rarely directly tested the inferred explanations for their effects.

Informal social networks

Employees are said to have a location in the social structure of an organization, giving each employee a network of contacts who are themselves connected to others (Burt, 1992). Social capital is the network of the player's relationships with other players who may be friends, colleagues or other contacts (Burt, 1992). They provide opportunities, because they have information, and enable the player to have more control in negotiations because there are multiple options or choices between them (Burt, 1993). Returns arise because employees are positioned to identify and develop more rewarding opportunities from the information and control benefits of these ties. Structural hole theory (Burt,

1992) proposes that, among similar managers, those who advance most have personal contacts in diverse groups within and beyond the firm. Structural holes are gaps between nonredundant relationships that allow network benefits partly because they are additive rather than overlapping. Networks should be large and have weak ties to provide information and control. The studies of informal networks have analyzed primarily objective data.

Social capital in terms of number of external ties was positively related to pay for executive team members in Swedish public firms through networks based on strong not weak ties (Meyerson, 1994). Social capital added to human capital (education, experience) to explain executives' pay (Meyerson, 1994). Dutch male and female senior managers primarily found their current jobs through informal channels with larger than smaller ranges, with weak ties the most frequent way, especially for those highest educated (Boxman, De Graaf, & Flap, 1991). Using structural equation analysis, social capital in terms of external work contacts and memberships increased managers' pay, net of human capital as education and experience and of position level as number of subordinates (Boxman, De Graaf, & Flap, 1991). Human capital increased social capital. The effects of human capital on pay were greatest for managers with little social capital, and smallest for those with a lot. For male managers in a high technology firm, early and greatest promotions went to managers with more social capital, through having unconstrained, nonredundant networks (Burt, 1992). Except when entry-rank, promotions came more slowly to managers with networks constrained by being too small, too strongly connected, and connected to a single central contact, especially promotions to highest ranks. In summary, supporting social network theorists, informal social networks within or outside the organization increase managerial advancement (pay), with larger networks better than smaller, although not necessarily those with weaker than stronger ties.

For female senior managers in a high technology firm, networks dominated by strong ties to strategic sponsors and few interconnected, redundant contacts led to greatest promotion, especially to highest ranks, opposite to the weak network ties that assisted men (Burt, 1992). Women managers are thought to be not fully trusted and to need greater sponsorship to achieve legitimacy, through an objective source of information, and need to borrow the social capital to get the information and control benefits of structural holes (Burt, 1992). Male managers are thought to have more favorable social networks and personal contacts than female, providing more information, support, and access to jobs, resulting in men gaining higher status jobs than women (Ragins & Sundstrom, 1989). Using confirmatory analysis, male middle managers in a finance company used informal networks for career advice, especially with organizational superiors, more than females did, resulting in more promotion offers (Canning & Montmarquette, 1991b). Women used formal meritocratic procedures in terms of performance, formal promotion bids and education more than men, and gained fewer promotions (Canning &

Montmarquette, 1991b). For managers in internationally related occupations, men gained an additional $5200 per year from using personal networks for job search, whereas women gained $3000 per year (Egan & Bendick, 1994). In summary, informal social networks may provide men with greater managerial career advancement than women.

Career encouragement

Career encouragement by superiors and colleagues in the organization was related to male and female managers' and executives' organizational promotion, but not to their managerial levels (Tharenou & Conroy, 1994). Using structural equation analysis, managers' and executives' career encouragement increased women's training and development more than men's, and training and development in turn led to managerial advancement (Tharenou, Latimer, & Conroy, 1994). Women who reached vice-president level reported widespread top level support in early career (Mainiero, 1994a). One of the two factors distinguishing matched female CEOs, male CEOs, and female top managers was career encouragement (Tharenou, 1995). The women CEOs reported the support was from female colleagues and superiors more than male, who would have been the majority available (Tharenou, 1995). Career encouragement from similar others may thus help women break the glass ceiling. Women are likely to need more interpersonal support than men to reach top jobs because they have substantial barriers, and interpersonal support facilitates persistence in the face of barriers. In summary, career encouragement increases managerial career advancement, perhaps more for women than men.

Mentors

Career mentoring, embracing sponsorship, challenging work, protection, coaching and visibility for the protégé (Kram, 1983), should be more directly related to career advancement than psychosocial mentoring, comprising role modeling, friendship, acceptance, and counseling. For example, sponsoring involves mentors using their influence to gain protéges desirable positions and advancement. Mentor processes are different to those used by nonmentors (supervisors) of managers, who provided fewer mentor functions and for whom a mentoring relationship with stages could not be detected (Pollock, 1995). Sponsored promotion in early career is thought to assist career progress in tournaments in which winning and losing occurs at each career round (Rosenbaum, 1984). Mentoring is thought to assist winning in early rounds, although there are no comparisons with later career stages to assess its early importance.

   In cross-sectional, chiefly self-report questionnaire studies controlling for human capital and job and organization variables, mentor presence and mentor career support were related positively to managers' pay and promotions in early career (Whitely & Coetsier, 1993; Whitely, Dougherty, & Dreher, 1991;

Yuen, 1995), as was overall mentor support (Dreher & Ash, 1990). Business graduates who had a mentor in the first 3 months of the job were more likely to be promoted at 14 months, with no effects for general supervisor support and work group fit (Kirchmeyer, 1995). General supervisor support was not related to black or white managers' promotability or plateauing by being in the same position seven or more years (Greenhaus, Parasuraman, & Wormley, 1990). For 183 managerial dyads in a manufacturing firm, supervisor- and subordinate-rated career mentoring were related to middle managers' pay and promotion rate from company records (Scandura & Schriesheim, 1994). Using structural equation analysis, initiation of mentoring resulted in mentoring, which then led to managers' and professionals' self-reported advancement, comprising pay and promotions (Turban & Dougherty, 1994). In early career, career mentoring has been more important to managers' promotions, though not to pay, than individual and other organization variables (Kirchmeyer, 1995; Whitely & Coetsier, 1993; Whitely, Dougherty, & Dreher, 1991), although there are no comparisons with later career stages.

The effects of psychosocial mentoring alone have not been assessed, and moderator effects of the mentoring-managerial advancement relationship appear likely, as found for protégé socio-economic status and promotion (Whitely, Dougherty, & Dreher, 1991). There are insufficient studies to say if mentoring similarly influences managerial advancement by gender or race. Mentor support was related similarly to the pay and promotion of male and female business graduates (Dreher & Ash, 1990), but a mentor was related to men's managerial level and not women's for accountants of whom over half supervised more than five employees (Johnson & Scandura, 1994). Presence of a mentor was related to black managers' managerial promotions (Nkomo & Cox, 1990) and promotability ratings and lack of plateauing (Greenhaus, Parasuraman, & Wormley, 1990). In summary, supporting the process of career mentoring, mentor presence and career support, rather than general supervisor support, increase managers' promotion, especially in early career, and pay.

Promotion Processes

Selection for managerial positions requires matching the candidate's competencies with the nature and demands of the job and organization. At lower management levels, the focus is on the performance demands of the job and the expectations of the organization, whereas at executive levels it is on the match with the organization's business strategy, culture and history and the fit with other senior executives (Forbes & Piercy, 1991).

Promotion velocity

Studies have assessed the effects of favorable starting circumstances and continuity of promotion on managerial career advancement. Career tournament theory proposes that, on organization entry, individuals join a tournament in which players must win rounds at each career round to advance to the next (Rosenbaum, 1990). Employees face a series of progressively more selective competitions. Those who do not win early are eliminated or restricted in play to consolation rounds, whereas winners proceed to the next round but need to keep winning to be still in the tournament (Rosenbaum, 1984, 1990). Those who advance early, by being younger than their peers on their status level, are offered more opportunities for advancement. Winners receive ability signals (job status, career velocity) that affect their prospects for the next higher competition. Promotion leads to more promotion as new jobs create more opportunities for development and networking and signal ability, creating 'career velocity' (Rosenbaum, 1990). Tournaments discourage late-emerging ability and impose low ceilings.

Starting at higher hierarchical levels was related to more managerial promotions and higher levels for managers (Cox & Harquail, 1991). For male and female managers, fast starters, trainees who spent less than average time in their first management job, compared to slow starters, attained higher management levels, and starting in a high power versus lower power department predicted greater promotion and pay over 10 years (Sheridan, Slocum, Buda, & Thompson, 1990). In early career, assignment to career-maker departments and high visibility projects was reported for women reaching vice-president level (Mainiero, 1994a), and promotion to the first management position by the first five years occurred for managers promoted to general manager or functional vice-president by age 39 for those who later became CEOs (Forbes & Piercy, 1991). Analysing longitudinal company data, managers who had been promoted upward still had high chances of being promoted to higher levels (Hurley & Sonnenfeld, 1994) and high advancement desires (Howard, 1991), whereas those who had not been promoted as much reported less chance of still being promoted and had low advancement desires, supporting career tournament theory. Starting opportunities may be less favorable to women's managerial advancement than men's. Female middle managers entered banking at initially lower job levels than male managers (Martin & Morgan, 1995; Morgan, Schor, & Martin, 1993). For university nonacademic staff ranging from subordinates to senior managers who had been promoted, structural equation analysis of objective data showed that the managerial level and status of the prior position influenced the hierarchical level of the new position and, independently, being a woman reduced the level and status of the prior position as well as the new position (Johnsrud & Heck, 1994). Unlike men's, female middle managers' promotion offers led to a decline in promotion bids, perhaps because of an invisible ceiling for women (Cannings & Montmarquette, 1991b). In summary, supporting career tournaments in early career, favorable starting opportunities lead to managerial advancement, but women's initially lower level placements than men's reduces their managerial advancement.

Gender discrimination

Female managers' promotions did not translate to as high managerial levels as males' (Cox & Harquail, 1991; Lewis, 1992). Compared to men, women gained more promotions to reach middle management (Martin & Morgan, 1995; Morgan, Schor, & Martin, 1993), and were promoted less into the professional grades through which public servants needed to pass to apply for supervisory jobs (Naff, 1994). In summary, promotion results in female managers gaining lower managerial levels than male managers.

Statistical discrimination studies assess if there are incremental effects of gender on advancement by first controlling for individuals' productivity and job and organizational variables, using hierarchical regression analysis (see Ragin & Bradshaw, 1991, for a critique). When the incremental variance is significant, statistical discrimination is said to operate. This is said to be based on employers expecting women, on average, to be less productive or to leave the firm sooner than men, and thus assigning individual women to lower level positions than men (Blau & Ferber, 1987; Strober, 1990). The generalizations from statistical reasoning processes about the attributes of average group members constitute gender stereotypes (see Schaller, Boyd, Yohannes, & O'Brien, 1995). Stereotypes save energy by simplifying information processing and response generation in evaluative processes, and are invoked more when evaluative processes are difficult and perceivers' resources depleted (Macrae, Milne, & Bodenhausen, 1994). This is consistent with the sizeable, complex information requirements and uncertain decision-making confronted in selection processes for higher level jobs with large applicant pools. Studies do not directly test the inferred explanations for statistical discrimination, nor test if stereotypes are involved.

The statistical discrimination studies are primarily cross-sectional self-report designs, and cover all career stages. For executives and managers comparable in age, productivity (i.e. work experience, education, performance), career paths and mobility (i.e. starting level, relocation, company changes, employment gaps), job type, organization, and industry, men compared to women were rated higher on promotion potential (Landau, 1995) and gained more managerial promotions (Cox & Harquail, 1991), and more pay (Cannings, 1991; Hanson Frieze, Olson, & Cain Good, 1990; Schneer & Reitman, 1994b, p <0.10; Stroh, Brett, & Reilly, 1992; Truman & Baroudi, 1994). Similarly, for employees ranging from subordinates to executives, men gained higher managerial levels than comparable women (Haberfeld, 1992; Melamed, 1995b; Wright, Baxter, & Birkelund, 1995). In an analysis of objective longitudinal data for university managers and executives, statistical discrimination was shown. Pay dropped when the incumbent changed from male to female and increased when the incumbent changed from female to male, worse in private than public universities (Pfeffer & Ross, 1990). Overall, the explanation by gender is weak, but can translate into substantial reductions in pay (e.g. Haberfeld, 1992). Some studies show no statistical discrimination: on managers' promotion (Dreher & Ash, 1990; Stroh, Brett, & Reilly, 1992) or managers' levels (Schneer & Reitman, 1994a; Truman & Baroudi, 1994). In an analysis of objective data, gender was first controlled, and effects assessed of five-year-earlier individual variables (human capital, family), change in individual variables in the five years, and organization (functional area) variables (Shenhav, 1992). Female white scientists and engineers in the private but not public sectors were more likely to be promoted into entry-level management positions than comparable white men, with no differences by race (Shenhav, 1992). In summary, overall, supporting statistical discrimination by gender, higher standards are used for women's managerial career advancement than men's.

Perceived discrimination predicted male and female MBAs' starting pay but not current pay in early to mid-career, although being female still also lowered starting and current pay (Hanson Frieze, Olson, & Cain Good, 1990). Each year since MBA graduation increased the probability that early career women perceived discrimination. In a longitudinal study tracking male and female cohorts of MBA graduates, mid-career was less helpful to women's managerial career advancement than early career, compared to men's (Schneer & Reitman, 1994b, 1995). The full-time women managers earned less and reached top management levels less often than the comparable males (Schneer & Reitman, 1995). The income gender difference first appeared 7–12 years post-MBA and grew larger in the last six years. Women continued to feel more subject to sex discrimination in relation to promotion or position in mid-career as early career than men, although men reported discrimination unlike in early career. Female Singaporean business graduates in mid- but not early career perceived that prejudice against women was negatively related to managerial level in relation to age and pay (Chi-Ching, 1992).

Minority discrimination

Statistical discrimination against minorities has been tested by the incremental variance added by minority status/race after controlling effects of productivity and other relevant variables. Stastical discrimination was shown on rated promotion potential for black compared to white and Asian compared to nonAsian managers and professionals although not Hispanics (Landau, 1995), on supervisor-rated promotability and career advancement opportunities and on career plateauing for black compared to white managers (some professionals; Igbaria & Wormley, 1995), on managers' and executives' pay for minority compared to nonminority status (Pfeffer & Ross, 1990), and on being supervisors or not for Asian American compared to white public servants varying in grade level (Kim & Lewis, 1994). Blacks and other nonwhite managers, especially when male, reported more discrimination for promotion and/or hiring than white managers in early to mid-career (Hanson Frieze,

Olson, & Cain Good, 1990). In a study in which gender was entered first in regression analyses, followed by five-year earlier individual variables, their change in five years, and organizational variables, black male or female scientists and engineers were more likely to be promoted to entry-level managerial positions over comparable whites and more in the public than private sectors (Shenhav, 1992). In summary, overall, supporting statistical discrimination by race, there are higher standards for blacks' managerial career advancement than whites', especially for promotion potential.

Affirmative action

Affirmative action/equal employment opportunity (AA/EEO) implementation was not related to black managers' promotion in a self-report study (Nkomo & Cox, 1990). From analyzing objective survey data for 231 universities, presence of a female or minority AA officer predicted the proportion of female or minority administrators five years later, respectively, with the higher the relative salary of the officer within the university, and thus presumably their status and ability to mobilize resources to get things done, the greater the effect (Pfeffer, Davis-Blake, & Julius, 1995). Studies have surveyed human resource managers to gather data on AA practices and proportions of women and minorities in management. Using structural equation analysis of 116 companies, equity-based (i.e. merit) and equality-based (i.e. target groups) human resource practices were related to the percentage of managers who were women or minorities, as was management support for EEO to minority proportion (Konrad & Linnehan, 1992). For 138 companies, formalized human resource management strategies to promote EEO and AA were in the main not related to women's and people of color's percentage in management and highest ranks (Konrad & Linnehan, 1995). This included identity-blind merit-based structures in which human resource practices do not identify protected groups, and management attitude, or being subject to lawsuits. Identity-conscious human resource management structures explicitly identifying their purpose for protected groups were weakly related to women's highest ranks and people of color in greatest percentages in management, and not being subject to compliance reviews to greater percentages of women in management (Konrad & Linnehan, 1995). The extent of formalization, comprehensiveness and management support of 294 Canadian employment equity programs (EEP) was correlated, weakly, with representative hiring from the external labor pool for management positions of female nonminorities and visible minorities (Leck, Saunders, & St. Onge, 1991), and of women and of male and female visible minorities but not of disabled persons and aboriginal peoples (Leck & Saunders, 1992a). EEP effectiveness explained additional variance in representative hiring for management positions of nonminority but not visible minority women (Leck & Saunders, 1992b; Leck, Saunders, & St. Onge, 1991) and of male and female visible minorities and women, but not disabled persons (Leck & Saunders, 1992a). In summary, affirmative action increases, although weakly, the advancement in management of women and perhaps minorities but not the disabled.

Politics

A political model of promotion is said to characterize the process as a negotiated reality, where the outcome is explained more by connections and interpersonal influence strategies, and less by objective qualifications, performance, and competence (Ferris, Buckley, & Allen, 1992), especially if situations are ambiguous and accountable such as managerial advancement decisions (Ferris & Judge, 1991). Political influence by candidates is defined as behavior designed to maximise short- or long-term interests, comprising primarily self-promotion and ingratiation (Ferris & Judge, 1991).

For middle manager positions, in chiefly interview studies of how promotion occurs in their organizations, politics were reported by candidates and decision-makers as influencing promotion through superiors' choice of managers for developmental opportunities such as training and task forces (Cianni & Romberger, 1995), by organizational connections (Deshpande, Schoderbek, & Joseph, 1994), and by identification of possible candidates, similarity of values and interests, bosses' level of personal comfort with candidates, candidate impression management and ingratiation, and promotion being a negotiated process (Ferris, Buckley, & Allen, 1992; Ruderman & Ohlott, 1994; Ruderman, Ohlott, & Kram, 1995). In a multivariate survey study, managers' use of supervisor-focused tactics based on ingratiation was related to higher overall career advancement, whereas job-focused tactics based on self-promotion were negatively related (Judge & Bretz, 1994). Women's progression from political naïviety to development may help reaching vice-president levels (Mainiero, 1994b). In surveys and interviews in 82 manufacturing and service organizations, organizational strategy was the major influence on promotion to middle manager, influencing who were the selectors, how the choice was made, the criteria utilized, and who was chosen (Ferris, Buckley, & Allen, 1992), resulting in a political process. Outsider CEOs were more likely to be chosen than insiders when organizational performance was poor but, suggesting political influence, especially when there were fewer insiders on the board of directors and less employee ownership, combined with the previous CEO being dismissed or younger than retirement age, or there being no heir apparent (Boeker & Goodstein, 1993; Cannella & Lubatkin, 1993; Cannella, Lubatkin, & Kapouch, 1991; Puffer & Weintrop, 1995). Political influence by candidates and selectors appears as important to managerial promotions as candidate performance, ability and human capital, and organization strategy, structure and needs (Deshpande, Schoderbeh, & Joseph, 1994; Ferris, Buckley, & Allen, 1992; Judge & Bretz, 1994; Ruderman & Ohlott, 1994; Ruderman, Ohlott, & Kram, 1995). In summary, partly supporting a political model of advancement, use of politics by candidates and decision-makers influences managerial career advancement, at least for middle manager to executive positions.

Promotion decisions

Interviews of successful candidates and their decision-makers have examined individual and organization factors perceived to influence managerial promotions. Promotion to middle and senior manager appears to be based on a combination of individual and organizational factors, meritorious and non-meritorious. The individual factors reported linked to promotion included ability, performance, work ethic, preparation, and results (Ferris, Buckley, & Allen, 1992; Ruderman & Ohlott, 1994). The organization factors were strategy, opportunity structure, messages sent by promotions, and long-range staffing goals. The social networks and political influence factors were to do with bosses' identification of, comfort with, and similarity to candidates, candidate impression management and ingratiation, and negotiation through mutual accommodation and adapting jobs for candidates (Ferris, Buckley, & Allen, 1992; Ruderman & Ohlott, 1994). Gender differences in 36 promotions were examined in one of the three companies of Ruderman and Ohlott (1994). Similar reasons were given for men's and women's promotion based on merit (Ruderman, Ohlott, & Kram, 1995). The key differences were bosses' reporting high personal comfort as important when they promoted men, but personal strength and familiarity with job responsibilities when they promoted women. Women, unlike men, reported having to push for the job after a trial. Bosses cited diversity when women were chosen on merit, whereas availability was cited for talented men. Women appeared to have to demonstrate personal strength and prove themselves extensively before they were promoted, in order to reduce perceived risk (Ruderman, Ohlott, & Kram, 1995).

Organization context

Resource dependency theory proposes that top staffing appointments (and removals) are affected by the organization's context (Pfeffer & Salancik, 1978). Top managers and executives are proposed to be selected who can cope with problems and critical internal and external contingencies of their environments. Managers and executives with more years of relevant organization experience who were older, and thus more likely to be insiders, were chosen as general managers of business units when low cost strategic goals were sought (Guthrie & Olian, 1991), and those with fewer years of organization experience, higher education, and in marketing and professional functions rather than engineering and operations, and thus more likely outsiders, when change was occurring through industry instability (Olian & Guthrie, 1991) or deregulation (Guthrie, Grimm, & Smith, 1991). Future CEOs were generalists who had had responsibility for an entire division or business within the same firm or industry when company or industry knowledge was needed and not change (Forbes & Piercy, 1991). Outsider CEOs were chosen, with specialties in one functional area, usually finance or law, gained from company changes, when change and specialized expertise were needed. From analyses of objective, often longitudinal data, insiders advanced to be CEO when insider knowledge was needed, whereas outsiders were more likely than insiders when times were unstable, change and diverse experience were needed, or organization performance was poor (Boeker & Goodstein, 1993; Cannella & Lubatkin, 1993; Cannella, Lubatkin, & Kapouch, 1991; Datta & Guthrie, 1994; Puffer & Weintrop, 1995). In summary, supporting resource dependency theory, organization context influences the attributes of those selected for top management.

INDIVIDUAL FACTORS

Traits

Traits are stable predispositions to certain kinds of actions that, when combined with other factors, are proposed to predict organizationally relevant behaviors, including managerial success (House, Howard, & Walker, 1991; Locke, 1991). Traits may predict advancement because individuals' motives, such as ambition, drive them to gratify their goals through managerial advancement, and because the tasks of the managerial role allow individuals to implement their self-concepts in occupational choice (Super, 1957) through fit. Traits such as cognitive ability, masculinity, and leadership motivation fit the tasks of the managerial role; intelligence, dominance, and masculinity were the traits perceived of leaders (Lord, De Vader, & Alliger, 1986). Traits may also indirectly influence advancement by interacting with the work situation (Fagenson, 1990a). Most studies have used standardized reliable, validated measures of personality and work-related motivation, and company records of managerial advancement, often being longitudinal predictions over many years, rendering confidence in the results. Studies are generally not conducted in which traits interact with the work situation, in which the relative importance of traits is compared to organizational or other individual factors, in which reverse effects are tested, in which comparisons occur of group differences (e.g. gender) in predicting advancement by traits, or in which traits chosen are based on job-relevance or vocational choice theory. Some traits can be classified within the 'Big Five' (Barrick & Mount, 1991). Conscientiousness, as will to achieve, measured as advancement motives, ambition and achievement motives, and openness to experience, measured as general cognitive ability, have clear support, with little evidence for extroversion, agreeableness, and emotional stability.

Advancement motives/ambition

Advancement motivation and need on entry to American Telephone & Telegraph company (AT&T) most predicted, of seven assessment centre dimensions, male managers' promotion into higher levels of management (Howard & Bray, 1990). Advancement motivation increased from entry up to 8 years, and at entry and at 8 years (strongly) predicted, and at 20 years less strongly predicted, 20-year managerial level. Ambition at entry at AT&T most predicted, of six composite measures from 37 personality and motivation tests, managerial level 20 years later (Howard & Bray, 1990). A single-item ambition measure was positively related to promotion and pay of executives and was as important as most human capital and organizational factors (Judge et al., 1995). In summary, advancement motives and ambition predict managerial career advancement.

Career motivation

Ratings of managers' overall career potential by trainers and by peers (trainees) in international management development programs predicted position levels 6 and 3.5 years later, respectively (Hofstede, 1994). Assessment center-rated career motivation in terms of desire for career advancement and development, but not ratings of knowledge or skill dimensions as communication and planning, predicted advancement to division level management 10 years later in an insurance company (Jones & Whitmore, 1995). Supervisor-rated and personality measures of managerial potential were related to managers' position level and pay in a single firm, similarly by gender and race when examined for pay (Thompson, 1994). In summary, career motivation is related to managerial career advancement.

Achievement motives

Achievement motivation as inner work standards, achievement motivation, and need for achievement, from personality tests and assessment center exercises, at 8 and 20 years rather than on entry predicted promotion to higher managerial levels after 20 years at AT&T (Howard & Bray, 1990). It was late-appearing in prediction becoming important by late, early career. Using the same sample, achievement motivation at entry predicted female but not male managers' level for those who stayed in AT&T to become middle managers 12 years later (Jacobs & McClelland, 1994). In summary, from one data set, achievement motivation may predict managerial level.

Work involvement

Managers' work involvement has been measured as either a personality trait, or as preferences. Work involvement, as work orientation, primacy of work, and occupational life theme from personality tests and assessment center exercises, predicted managers' promotion into higher levels of management at AT&T (Howard & Bray, 1990). Work involvement at 8 and especially 20 years, not entry, most strongly predicted 20-year managerial level, thus being late-appearing in prediction at late early career. Being family-involved on entry, measured from interviews, negatively predicted 20-year managerial level, with financial-acquisitive, service and occupational involvements positively predictive (Howard & Bray, 1990). Work centrality is chiefly measured as a single item according points to work out of several areas of life. It was not related to managers' promotions (Nkomo & Cox, 1990; Judge et al., 1995), with a positive exception (Whitely, Dougherty, & Dreher, 1991), nor to managers' and executives' levels (Judge et al., 1995; Schneer & Reitman, 1995; Yuen, 1995). Work centrality and significance were related to executives' and managers' pay (Judge et al., 1995; Lobel & St. Clair, 1992; Schneer & Reitman, 1995), although there were nonsignificant links (Whitely, Dougherty, & Dreher, 1991; Yuen, 1995). Preference for high income, but not for meaningful work, was positively related to male and female managers' pay (Jacobs, 1992). For mostly managers (some professionals), family-oriented women with preschoolers received higher merit increases than family-oriented men with preschoolers, and career-oriented women with preschoolers received lower merit increases than career-oriented women with preschoolers (Lobel & St. Clair, 1992), suggesting allocation based on conformity to gender role stereotypes. In summary, work involvement as personality may be related to managerial level, and work centrality in life is positively related to managers' pay but not promotion or level.

Self-monitoring

High self-monitors are said to regulate or control themselves according to situational and interpersonal cues, adjusting their self-presentations, whereas low self-monitors behave according to how they feel, being less attuned to role expectations and about making a positive impression on others (Snyder & Gangestad, 1982). Male and female managers in early career who were high self-monitors achieved more cross-company promotions five years later and obtained more internal promotions when they stayed in the same company than low self-monitors (Kilduff & Day, 1994). In a structural equation test, management graduates who were high self-monitors initiated more mentoring, which led to gaining more mentoring which, in turn, led to higher career advancement of promotion and pay (Turban & Dougherty, 1994). In summary, the few studies suggest that self-monitoring is related positively to managerial promotions and perhaps pay.

Motivation to manage

According to role motivation theory, motivation to change, the extent to which certain individuals enjoy and perform well in managerial positions in hierarchical organizations, should result in managerial success (Miner, 1993). Motivation to manage was assessed in 36 studies, 25 of managers of which seven were predictive over three to five years. Motivation to manage was moderately related to managers' success as advancement potential, hierarchic level and pay, and to business school students' managerial career choice, similarly for the 1960s to the 1990s (Miner, 1993; Miner, Ebrahimi, & Wachtel, 1995). The effects were found for hierarchic systems but not professional, task and group domains (Miner, 1993). Desire to compete and to exercise power were the most highly predictive subscales. A meta-analysis of 26 studies found that motivation to manage was related, albeit weakly, to managers' position level and pay, and to students' intention to pursue a career in management (Carson & Gilliard, 1993). In summary, supporting hierarchic role motivation theory, motivation to manage predicts career intentions to enter management and managerial career advancement.

Power motives

Three studies used the data of the AT&T sample (Howard & Bray, 1990). The leadership motive pattern on entry distinguished upper management men and women at higher levels (combining those in AT&T and those who left) from those at lower levels 12 years later (Jacobs & McClelland, 1994). The leadership motive pattern is a high need for power with low affiliation needs, tempered with high self-control. Need for power was positively related to men's and women's attained management level. Helpless power at entry was higher for those who remained in lower management levels than for those who attained upper levels 12 years later (Jacobs & McClelland, 1994). High responsible power, combining power motivation and responsibility, predicted managerial level after 16 years in AT&T for men in nontechnical jobs (Winter, 1991). Need for power of university women in senior year did not predict holding a supervisor job or not at age 35, 14 years later. It predicted career advancement comprising improved salary, status, or control positively and more for women in power-relevant jobs than women in nonpower-relevant jobs (self-employed, small business owners, technical managers; Jenkins, 1994). The positive relationship was for relational power jobs (psychologists, noncollege teachers) and not for directive power jobs (college faculty, journalists, nontechnical business executives) such as management. In summary, need for power is related to managerial career advancement depending on job type.

Masculinity/instrumentality

According to gender schema theory (Bem, 1981), gender role traits influence the way individuals organize and process information. The 'masculine' gender role is an instrumental, task orientation focusing on getting the job done or problem solved (Bem, 1981). Individuals high in masculinity process information in masculine terms, and should perceive themselves as suited to the managerial role. The managerial role is perceived as requiring masculine traits of leadership, dominance, forcefulness, tough-mindedness, lack of emotion, independence, and aggressiveness, as observed primarily in business students (e.g. Schein & Mueller, 1992; Schein, Mueller, Lituchy, & Liu, 1996). Masculine individuals emerged as leaders compared to feminine, in groups of undergraduate business students working throughout the semester on class presentations and assignments (Kent & Moss, 1994). In cross-sectional studies, higher level managers reported greater masculinity than lower level managers, male or female (Chusmir & Koberg, 1991; Chusmir, Koberg, & Stecher, 1992; Fagenson, 1990b), although reverse effects could occur. The lack of gender different effects does not support the gender role model (see Gutek, 1993) suggesting women have difficulty in using the sex-role behaviors needed for managing others, especially masculinity. In summary, masculinity is positively related to men's and women's managerial levels.

Self-confidence

Managers' self-confidence was related positively to hierarchical level for men or women (Chusmir, Koberg, & Stecher, 1992) but was not related to hierarchical level when masculinity was included for the same sample (Chusmir & Koberg, 1991). Self-confidence in relation to one's job was not related to managers' and executives' promotion and managerial level, whether male or female (Tharenou & Conroy, 1994). Self-confidence did not lead directly to managerial career advancement comprising level and pay in a structural equation test, but did so indirectly through increasing career encouragement and training and development, similarly for men and women (Tharenou, Latimer, & Conroy, 1994). Reverse effects did not occur on self-confidence. In analyses of the one data set, self-confidence had inconsistent gender differences in the prediction of managerial level, weakly related to male but not female managers' level (Koberg, Chusmir, & Carlin, 1992) or giving no gender differences (Chusmir, Kobert, & Stecher, 1992). Self-confidence was negatively related to female but positively to male public service managers' levels (Melamed, 1996b). On entry to AT&T and at 8 and 20 years, self-esteem, high feelings of self-worth, very weakly predicted 20-year managerial level (Howard & Bray, 1990). In summary, self-confidence is inconsistently related to managers' levels.

General cognitive ability

General cognitive ability, how much and how quickly a person learns, has been measured by validated, reliable verbal and numerical reasoning tests and at times other ability tests. Cognitive ability in early career predicted male and female oil company managers' job grades 5 to 10 years later controlling for skills (Shore, 1992), at entry predicted managerial level 20 years later for AT&T managers (Howard & Bray, 1990), and in the first two years of service predicted job level attained from the third to the twelfth year for oil company managers, as did management judgment (Sparks, 1990). Using the sample of oil company managers, early cognitive ability more strongly predicted job level 14–15 years later for those less successful in early career than more successful, measured as age-graded job level attained in the first four or five years (Dreher & Bretz, 1991), the authors speculating that acquiring knowledge, skills and information depends on cognitive ability when individuals are competing without the advantages of early career signals of high potential, and thus sponsorship. By contrast, general cognitive ability did not predict male middle managers' monetary bonuses one, two, three or four years later, nor did pre-employment cognitive ability (Tziner, Meir, Dahan, & Birati, 1994), or predict the promotions and pay of MBAs 3.5 to 4.5 years after graduation except in interaction with conscientiousness (O'Reilly & Chatman, 1994). A standard deviation increase in conscientiousness at higher cognitive ability levels was worth U.S. $18 780 more in salary and 0.56 more in promotions than at lower levels, similarly by race and ethnicity (O'Reilly & Chatman, 1994). Verbal and nonverbal reasoning were related to supervisors' and managers' level and pay (Thompson, 1994). In summary, general cognitive ability alone or combined with circumstances or other traits predicts long-term managerial career advancement from entry.

Other traits of the 'Big Five'

Extroversion was related to male but not female managers' managerial level (Melamed, in press). Conscientiousness comprising achievement, endurance and order did not directly predict promotion and pay of MBAs 3.5 to 4.5 years after graduation, but did when they were higher not lower in cognitive ability (O'Reilly & Chatman, 1994). Positiveness (i.e. optimism), measured at entry, predicted managerial level 20 years later at AT&T (Howard & Bray, 1990). Using structural equation analysis of the AT&T data, optimism, measured by optimism and general adjustment, and leadership role attractiveness, measured by attraction to the leader role and aversion to the follower role, predicted managerial level taking into account measurement error, stability of variables, and verbal and quantitative ability and education (House, Howard, & Walker, 1991). Entry optimism predicted 8-year managerial level, and 8-year leadership attraction predicted 20-year managerial level. In the only reverse effect, 8-year managerial level increased leadership role attraction at 20 years (House, Howard, & Walker, 1991). Personality traits, including extroversion and cognitive ability, did not start increasing managerial level until employees were 28 to 44 years, and had greatest effects when greater than 44 years (Melamed, 1996a).

Human Capital

Human capital theory proposes that investments in education, on-the-job training and work experience result in increased productivity, which leads to increased pay and job status, causing upward mobility in free market contests (Becker, 1975). Individuals choose to improve their human capital, which results in payoffs later in their careers (Becker, 1993). Gender differences in individuals' chosen investments and types of jobs then explain differences in pay and status. In signaling theory (Spence, 1973, 1974), employers make selection decisions guessing the applicant's productive capabilities from imperfect information. They therefore use signals, the applicants' investments in education, job experience and training, to estimate the probability the applicant will be productive based on conditional probabilities established through past experience. These signals of productivity have rates of return in pay and advancement. Studies providing empirical links for human capital inputs are multivariate, chiefly cross-sectional, self-report survey designs often assessing the importance of another factor (e.g. mentoring) for managerial advancement, and initially controlling human capital. Apart from training and development—usually of interest in its own right—the links found for human capital are for relative importance often when used as controls, prior to other predictor sets, in regression analyses.

Training and development

In human capital theory, on-the-job training increases employee pay and other rewards as work experience increases, because productivity increases, and employers are said to make specific investments such as executive training of their employees (Becker, 1993). Training and development are also proposed to lead to promotion to top management by developing knowledge, skills, credibility, and credentials and thus expertise and power (Ragins & Sundstrom, 1989). Development, learning activities for personal and professional growth and the long term as opposed to training for immediate job performance, is used to prepare managers for future jobs and to lead to promotion (e.g. Campion, Cheraskin, & Stevens, 1994). Using a case study approach, when an organization was faced with many middle managers and supervisors retiring, the strategy to replace them was to prepare individuals for advancement by training (Sandwith, 1993).

Participation in training and development courses over one's career was positively related to manufacturing managers' promotion and pay (Scandura, 1992) and to manager's and executives' managerial levels but not promotion (Tharenou & Conroy, 1994). For research and development professionals, whereas technical training was either not or negatively related, participation in managerial development increased the likelihood of gaining lower level supervisory positions four years later, all objective company measures (Roberts &

Biddle, 1994), and of assessment as promotable to technical management by supervisors, especially when higher on self-reported managerial interests and abilities (Cordero, DiTomaso, & Farris, 1994). Managerial interests also increased promotability indirectly through managerial development opportunities (Cordero, DiTomaso, & Farris, 1994). From company records, job rotation was positively related to managers' and professionals' pay growth and promotion rate (Campion, Cheraskin, & Stevens, 1994), job rotation opportunities in the first year were related to managers' salary progression four years later (Orpen, 1994), and entering by the company's 14-month on-the-job trainee program compared to direct hiring or internal promotion predicted greater managerial promotion and salary progression over 10 years for male and female public utility company managers, but nontrainees reached higher management levels (Sheridan et al., 1990). In a later analysis of the same sample, the training program increased promotion only on the first job and not subsequent jobs (Sheridan, Slocum, & Buda, in press). Implemented assessment center developmental recommendations were not related to attaining division level management 10 years later in an insurance company, nor was participation versus nonparticipation for nominated nonparticipants (Jones & Whitmore, 1995). In summary, consistent with human capital theory, participation in training and development increases managerial advancement, especially if management development.

Ragins and Sundstrom (1989) argued that access to training is used as part of a pattern of tracking that grooms men for promotion into management more than women. Studies have been of comparable men and women. For female but not male managers and executives, being prevented from attending training was related to lack of organizational promotion (Tharenou & Conroy, 1994). Using structural equation analysis, participation in training and development substantially increased managerial advancement for managers and executives, and not the reverse, more for men than women (Tharenou, Latimer, & Conroy, 1994). For managers in internationally related occupations, being designated in a fast-track development program earned men $10 900 per year but women $200 per year (Egan & Bendick, 1994). In summary, participation in training and development increases men's managerial career advancement more than comparable women's.

Age

In career tournament theory, age timetables are proposed in promotion (Rosenbaum, 1984, 1990). Advancement is said to decline with age because employees who do not win early in the tournament are eliminated or restricted later in play to consolation rounds, with sharp declines after a critical age. Some studies are consistent with age—advancement timetables. Age was negatively related to managers' promotion rate (Scandura, 1992) and supervisor-rated promotability (Igbaria & Wormley, 1995). Older managers plateaued more than younger, by having more years in their current position (Igbaria & Wormley, 1995; Tremblay & Roger, 1993). For younger but not older managers, position tenure and education were related positively to promotability (Cox & Nkomo, 1992), and number of jobs, functions and organizations to managerial level and pay (Herriot et al., 1993). High fliers (i.e. younger than their job grade norm) had the highest advancement expectations, and plateaued managers (i.e. older than their grade norm) the lowest for managers in an multinational corporation (Nicholson, 1993). Managerial level increases with age to a certain point and then the rate slows, the curvilinear link supporting career tournaments. Managers' age was related to supervisor-rated promotability when below but not over 45 years (Cox & Nkomo, 1992), and to job grade up to middle manager level with higher levels decreasingly related (Nicholson, 1993). Age positively and age squared negatively were related to the managerial level of employees ranging in level (Haberfeld, 1992). Pay may increase continuously with age. Age and age squared were related to CEOs' pay (Ingham & Thompson, 1995). In summary, there is some support for career tournament age timetables for promotion and managerial level.

Other studies do not test curvilinear links. Age has been used as a proxy for work experience to test human capital theory (Strober, 1990). Age was not related to male and female managers' and executives' promotion (Cox & Harquail, 1991; O'Reilly & Chatman, 1994; Tharenou & Conroy, 1994), with one positive exception (Judge et al., 1995). Age was not related to managers' and executives' managerial levels (Cox & Harquail, 1991; Tharenou & Conroy, 1994), with one positive exception (Herriot et al., 1993). Age may indirectly increase managerial career advancement. Using structural equation analysis, age increased male managers' and executives' years work experience more than females' which, in turn, increased participation in training and development, subsequently increasing managerial career advancement (Tharenou, Latimer, & Conroy, 1994). The impact of men's age was totally captured through work experience, unlike women's, for whom age directly increased managerial advancement. Age was positively related to male and female managers' and executives' pay (Cannings, 1991; Herriot et al., 1993, 1994; Ingham & Thompson, 1995; Judge et al., 1995; Scandura, 1992), although there are nonsignificant links (O'Reilly & Chatman, 1994; Schneer & Reitman, 1993) and negative links with merit increases (Lobel & St. Clair, 1992). In summary, overall, not supporting human capital theory, age is comparatively unimportant to managerial promotions and managerial levels but, in support of human capital theory, has a distinct positive link with managers' pay.

Education

Human capital and signaling theories predict that education increases managerial level and pay, the former theory through increasing knowledge and skills and thus productivity (Becker, 1993) and the latter through providing information when knowledge about potential productivity is imperfect (Spence, 1974; Strober, 1990). Education is likely not to be used as a signal for managerial promotion, because promotion is usually internal to the organization, where more certain information exists on candidates' performance than by external entry.

Education level was not related to male or female managers' and executives' promotion (Cannings & Montmarquette, 1991b; Judge et al., 1995; Powell & Butterfield, 1994; Scandura, 1992; Stroh, Brett, & Reilly, 1992; Tharenou & Conroy, 1994), nor to supervisor-rated promotability of black or white managers (Igbaria & Wormley, 1995), with one positive exception for promotability ratings of black and white managers (Greenhaus & Parasuraman, 1993). Education level was positively related to female and male managers' levels (Gattiker & Larwood, 1990; Melamed, 1996b; Tharenou & Conroy, 1994) and entry to management, although education change was not (Shenhav, 1992). Two studies applying structural equation analysis showed indirect as well as direct effects of education level. Education level directly increased the hierarchical level of jobs to which university administrative employees ranging in level had been promoted, but also indirectly, by increasing the status and level of the prior position held (Johnsrud & Heck, 1994). Education level increased managers' and executives' managerial advancement, similarly for men and women, but indirectly did so by increasing men's participation in training but not women's (Tharenou, Latimer, & Conroy, 1994). Education level was positively related to managers' pay (Gattiker & Larwood, 1990; Jacobs, 1992; Martin, 1994; Reskin & Ross, 1992; Scandura, 1992; Stroh, Brett, & Reilly, 1992; Whitely & Coetsier, 1993), although there were also no links (Cannings, 1991; Dreher & Ash, 1990; Lobel & St. Clair, 1992). In summary, supporting human capital and signaling theories, education level is not related to managers' promotion but is related to managerial level and pay.

Type of degree and educational institution are also relevant. Bachelors' degrees as opposed to noncollege education were positively related to managers' levels (Herriot et al., 1994) and pay (Egan & Bendick, 1994; Herriot et al., 1994; Judge et al., 1995; Martin, 1994), although not promotion (Judge et al., 1995) nor Singaporean business graduates' level or pay (Yuen, 1995). Bachelor degrees and professional majors in business or engineering predicted the first and subsequent promotions over a 10-year period of entry level public utility managers, with lack of them having negative effects for low performers, and resulted in faster promotion than for those with comparable performance who had different educational backgrounds (Sheridan, Slocum, & Buda, in press). Law degrees were more highly related to executives' pay than other degrees, but not to promotion (Judge et al., 1995). Masters' degrees, usually MBAs, were positively related to managers' pay (Bretz & Judge, 1994; Dreher & Ash, 1990; Egan & Bendick, 1994; Judge et al., 1995; Whitely & Coetsier,

1993; Whitely, Dougherty, & Dreher, 1991) but not managers' promotions (Dreher & Ash, 1990; Whitely & Coetsier, 1993; Whitely, Dougherty, & Dreher, 1991) nor pay, level and overall advancement (Bretz & Judge, 1994; Judge & Bretz, 1994; Judge et al., 1995). Masters' degrees had negative links with private sector scientists' and engineers' entry to management (Shenhav, 1992). PhDs had negative links to entry to and level in management (Bretz & Judge, 1994; Judge & Bretz, 1994; Shenhav, 1992) with a positive exception for managers' pay (Bretz & Judge, 1994). Ivy League schools and quality degrees versus others were positively related to managers' and executives' pay but not promotion (Judge et al., 1995). Grade point average was not related to managers' and executives' advancement (Bretz & Judge, 1994; Judge & Bretz, 1994; Judge et al., 1995). Men in internationally related occupations received greater additional pay per year than women from bachelor and graduate degrees, law or business degrees, and degrees from prestigious schools (Egan & Bendick, 1994). This is consistent with signaling theory. Employers offer returns on education using probability distributions that interact with unalterable observable indices such as gender, resulting in the rate of return to men's external signaling of education applying only to other men and not to women, for whom payoffs are different (Spence, 1973). In summary, gaining a bachelors' degree is positively related to managers' level and pay but not promotion, masters' degrees are related positively only to managers' pay, and PhDs decrease managerial advancement. Women may gain less managerial advancement indirectly or directly from educational attainment than men.

Work experience/tenure

Years of company tenure were positively related to managers' and executives' promotions (Cox & Harquail, 1991; Naff, 1994; Nkomo & Cox, 1990; Stroh, Brett, & Reilly, 1992), with one nonsignificant exception (Scandura, 1992). Although company tenure was positively related, average job tenure (i.e. job change) was negatively related to managers' promotion and level (Cox & Harquail, 1991), suggesting loyalty is rewarded. Similarly, stable company tenure from the second five years of employment, combined with less inter-firm and more intra-firm job change was found for men who rose to CEO status (Forbes & Piercy, 1991; Piercy & Forbes, 1991). Company tenure and company tenure squared were positively related to managers' promotions (Stroh, Brett, & Reilly, 1992), suggesting promotion continues to increase with tenure. Years of company tenure were positively related to managerial entry (Shenhav, 1992) and managers' levels (Herriot et al., 1993; Yuen, 1995) for men's and women's levels (Melamed, 1996b) with one exception (Gattiker & Larwood, 1990). It took fewer years of company experience for male middle managers in a bank to reach that level than female (Martin & Morgan, 1995; Morgan, Schor, & Martin, 1993). Company tenure was positively related to managers' pay (Cannings, 1991; Gattiker & Larwood,

1990; Herriot et al., 1993; Lobel & St. Clair, 1992; Reskin & Ross, 1992; Scandura, 1992; Stroh, Brett, & Reilly, 1992; Whitely, Dougherty, & Dreher, 1991; Yuen, 1995), with one negative exception (Judge et al., 1995). Company tenure but not company tenure squared were related to managers' pay (Stroh, Brett, & Reilly, 1992), suggesting a linear link. Using structural equation analysis, work experience of occupational and organizational years indirectly increased male managers' and executives' managerial advancement comprising level and pay more than females' through increasing men's participation in training and development more (Tharenou, Latimer, & Conroy, 1994). In summary, supporting human capital theory and also notions of rewards for loyalty, company tenure is positively related to managers' promotion, levels and pay.

Years of position tenure were negatively related to black and white managers' promotability ratings (Greenhaus & Parasuraman, 1993), and positively related to university executives' and managers' pay (Pfeffer & Ross, 1990). Suggesting a curvilinear link, position tenure in the current level was related to middle managers' promotion, being lowest in the first year, peaking in the second, and declining thereafter (Gibbs, 1995), and position tenure positively and position tenure squared negatively were related to managers' overall advancement (Judge & Bretz, 1994). Candidate employment in the hiring department, being at the highest grade and years at that grade, was positively related to panel evaluations and referrals for the senior executive service (Powell & Butterfield, 1994). Only employment in the hiring department was positively related to the selecting official's actual selection decision of those referred; years at the highest grade were negatively related. Position tenure squared was not related to building society CEOs' pay (Ingham & Thompson, 1994), implying a linear link. In summary, promotion may rise, peak and fall with position tenure, and position tenure may be positively related to managers' pay.

Total years of work experience were positively related to managers' promotion (Cox & Harquail, 1991; Dreher & Ash, 1990; Stroh, Brett, & Reilly, 1992; Whitely & Coetsier, 1993; Whitely, Dougherty, & Dreher, 1991), and negatively related to panel evaluations and referral decisions for the senior executive service, but not to the selecting official's actual selection decision of those referred (Powell & Butterfield, 1994). Total years of work experience had a curvilinear relationship with panel evaluations; highest evaluations were received by applicants with 10 years experience and lower evaluations as experience increased beyond 10 years. Total years of work experience were not related to managers' levels (Schneer & Reitman, 1994a, 1995) but combined with organizational and occupational years were related to managers' and executives' promotion and managerial level (Tharenou & Conroy, 1994). Total years of work experience were positively related to managers' pay (Dreher & Ash, 1990; Martin, 1994; Stroh, Brett, & Reilly, 1992; Whitely & Coetsier, 1993; Whitely, Dougherty, & Dreher, 1991) with no links in some early career studies (Cox & Harquail, 1991; Schneer & Reitman, 1995) and a negative link in mid-career (Schneer & Reitman, 1994a, 1995). Pay appears to rise, peak and then decrease in rate of rise with years of employment. Total years of work experience were positively related and total years squared negatively related to male or female managers' pay (Cannings, 1991; Jacobs, 1992; Martin, 1994), with one exception suggesting a linear link (Stroh, Brett, & Reilly, 1992). In summary, supporting human capital theory, total years of work experience are positively related to managerial promotions but, supporting a career tournament view, may have a curvilinear link with managers' pay.

Employment gaps

Employment gaps have often been measured as gaps/no gaps (continuous employment), reducing variance. Employment gaps were negatively related to managers' promotions (Dreher & Ash, 1990) when low not high in socioeconomic status (Whitely, Dougherty, & Dreher, 1991), but not related to managers' levels (Bretz & Judge, 1994; Schneer & Reitman, 1995; Yuen, 1995) or overall advancement (Judge & Bretz, 1994). Employment gaps were not related (Bretz & Judge, 1994; Schneer & Reitman, 1994a; Stroh, Brett, & Reilly, 1992; Whitely & Coetsier, 1993), positively related (Whitely, Dougherty, & Dreher, 1991), and negatively related (Yuen, 1995) to managers' pay. Employment gaps were related to lower pay for male but not female MBA graduates in early career (Schneer & Reitman, 1990), suggesting adverse effects for men who do not follow a traditional career path. For the same sample six years later, the impact of the early career employment gap on mid-career pay was not sustained when controlling for earlier pay, and mid-career gaps reduced mid-career pay, similarly for men and women (Schneer & Reitman, 1994b). In another MBA sample, early career employment gaps decreased early career pay and accumulated gaps at mid-career decreased mid-career pay, controlling for earlier pay (Schneer & Reitman, 1995). In summary, employment gaps may be negatively related to promotion, are not related to managerial level, and are either not or negatively related to managers' pay.

Work hours

Hours worked per week were not (Judge et al., 1995; Whitely, Dougherty, & Dreher, 1991) or positively (Whitely & Coetsier, 1993) related to managers' promotions. Hours worked per week were related to managers' job levels (Bretz & Judge, 1994) and pay (Bretz & Judge, 1994; Jacobs, 1992; Judge et al., 1995; Schneer & Reitman, 1993, 1995; Whitely & Coetsier, 1993; Whitely, Dougherty, & Dreher, 1991). Hours worked per week were not related to managers' pay (Reskin & Ross, 1992) including in mid-career for either early career or mid-career hours, when controlling for earlier pay

(Schneer & Reitman, 1994a). Hours worked per week were related to managers' overall advancement (Judge & Bretz, 1994). Evenings worked per month and desired work hours were related to executives' pay and promotion (Judge et al., 1995). Reverse effects were not tested for work hours. An additional eight hours work per week gained male middle managers in internationally related occupations an estimated extra $7300 per year but female managers an extra $4300, controlling relevant variables (Egan & Bendick, 1994). In summary, weekly hours are positively related to managers' pay.

Job change

Managers appear to change jobs frequently, every two years in a British study (Nicholson, 1990), and increased changing jobs and company relocations from 1978 to 1989 (Stroh, Brett, & Reilly, 1994). Managers on an executive search firm's files gave advancement as the reason for job search (Krausz & Reshef, 1992). Number of company/employer changes was not related to managers' promotion (Whitely & Coetsier, 1993), and organization and geographic moves were negatively related to managers' and executives' promotion (Tharenou & Conroy, 1994). Changing companies more frequently was associated, weakly, with managers' lower levels (Brett, Stroh, & Reilly, 1992a; Ellis & Heneman, 1990) or not related to managers' levels (Melamed, in press). Number of employing organizations was related positively to managers' levels and pay for those young but not middle-aged and older (Herriot et al., 1993). Number of company changes was not related to managers' pay (Cox & Harquail, 1991; Ellis & Heneman, 1990; Stroh, Brett, & Reilly, 1992; Whitely & Coetsier, 1993), and was negatively related for men and women (Brett, Stroh, & Reilly, 1992a). For managers from middle managers to CEOs, not changing companies increased advancement (Brett, Stroh, & Reilly, 1992a; Ellis & Heneman, 1994; Forbes & Piercy, 1991; Piercy & Forbes, 1991). In early and not mid-career, female Singaporean business graduates reported limited organization change was related to lower pay and age-adjusted managerial levels (Chi-Ching, 1992). Number of position changes was positively related to managers' levels (Melamed, 1996b) and to younger but not middle and older managers' levels and pay (Herriot et al., 1993). In summary, changing employers and positions is inconsistently related to managers' levels, and changing employers is not related to managers' pay.

Relocation moves for current and previous employers predicted high managerial level and pay for Fortune 500 transferees, most middle managers (Brett, Stroh, & Reilly, 1992a; Stroh, Brett, & Reilly, 1992). Relocation for the company was the most important predictor of several factors of female managers' managerial level, more than males' (Brett, Stroh, & Reilly, 1992a), and managers at high levels, mostly men, had not moved for their spouse's career (Stroh, Brett, & Reilly, 1992). The most highly paid managers relocated rather than not, and were promoted in their companies rather than changing companies. Relocation increased managerial levels for public sector middle managers (Lewis, 1992) and senior executive service officers (Naff, 1994). By contrast, relocations were not related to the pay or level of the male 45–50-year-old managers on an executive search firm's files (Ellis & Heneman, 1990). Moving for advancement was related to men's but not women's managerial levels (Tharenou & Conroy, 1994). In summary, job change by relocation may be positively related to managers' levels and pay.

Investment in human capital in early career is important to early and later managerial career advancement. Workforce experience, education, and employment gaps were more important than other individual variables for managers' advancement in early career (Cox & Harquail, 1991; Schneer & Reitman, 1990, 1995; Whitely & Coetsier, 1993; Whitely, Dougherty, & Dreher, 1991) although there is little comparison with organizational variables. Human capital (education, position tenure, job and organization changes) gained managers more advancement in early than in late career (Cox & Nkomo, 1992; Herriot et al., 1993). At an early career stage, career choices of short organization tenure and more job changes combined with choosing occupations with high levels and prestige explained managerial level, but other individual variables and organization opportunity structures did not for British employees ranging in level, 43% subordinates (Melamed, 1996a). Managerial level was more explained by human capital inputs, organizational structure, and career choices in late (>44 years) career than early (18 to 28 years old), conflicting with greater links of human capital with the advancement of younger than older managers (Cox & Nkomo, 1992; Herriot et al., 1993). Education level, but also traits, parenthood (negatively), and industry type and company size did not increase managerial level until mid-career when employees were 28 to 44 years old, reaching their full impact when greater than 44 years in late career (Melamed, 1996a).

Managerial Skills

Skills are important for leaders' effectiveness because they provide specific capacities for action from traits (Locke, 1991), and should increase performance and subsequently advancement. Managerial skills have been classified as people and administrative/task skills (Locke, 1991). Management performance has been classified into interpersonal dealings and communication, leadership and supervision (both people domains), technical activities and the mechanics of management (the task domain), and personal behavior and skills (Borman & Brush, 1993). Studies have not been based on theories of managerial skills or performance, and do not consider indirect links of skills to advancement through performance, nor the relative importance of managerial skills and performance compared to other factors.

Skills

Cross-sectional usually self-report studies have assessed managers' work-related skills, often with validated, reliable measures, as background experiences, skills demonstrated in assessment centers, and on-the-job leadership skills. Background experiences (self-rated leadership, general responsibility, personal financial management) were related positively to supervisors' and managers' levels and pay in a single firm (Thompson, 1994). Interpersonal skills and administrative skills assessed by an assessment center at entry predicted managerial level 20 years later at AT&T (Howard & Bray, 1990). For those who ultimately remained at lower management, managerial skills assessed in assessment centers decreased by the eighth year and further by the twentieth year compared to the increase for those who rose to higher levels in AT&T (Howard, 1991). Interpersonal skills and performance skills from an assessment center in early career each predicted oil company managers' job grade 5 to 10 years later, similarly for men and women, controlling for cognitive ability, the 'other' skill, and the overall assessment center rating (Shore, 1992). Female managers' higher performance skills than males' did not translate into higher advancement. Male middle managers' managerial performance, communication and interpersonal interaction abilities assessed in an assessment center did not predict monetary bonuses over the next four years (Tziner et al., 1994).

Subordinate- and self-reported problem-solving, planning/organizing, networking, clarifying, and motivating behaviors were correlated with mid- and upper-level managers' age-graded managerial level, similarly for self- and subordinate-reports (Kim & Yukl, 1995), although several behaviors were not consistently related or related at all. Bosses' assessments of 20 of 25 skills predicted managers' organization promotion (demoted/termination, no/lateral movement, promoted) 2 to 2.5 years later (McCauley & Lombardo, 1990). Most predictive were: perseveres, hires talented staff, builds team, learns quickly, easy with job transition, is flexible, resourceful, and is decisive. In early career, supervisory skills, technical skills, skills in critical functional areas and, additionally in mid- and late career, broadening and general management skills, appeared to facilitate men reaching CEO using archival data (Forbes & Piercy, 1991) and women reaching vice-president levels using self-report interviews (Mainiero, 1994a). In studies without comparison groups, retrospective interviews of senior executives or ratings by supervisors and peers, perhaps subject to self-serving distortions, indicated that poor managerial skills, including adaptability, strategic, interpersonal and participative skills derailed executives and managers in late career (McCauley & Ruderman, 1991; Van Velsor & Leslie, 1995). Derailed managers resign, are fired, retire early, do not rise further with high potential, or rise and fail.

The managerial skills found related to managerial advancement can be classified into people skills, both interpersonal and communication (interpersonal, clarifying, conflict management, team-building, networking) and leadership and supervision (leadership, motivating, supervisory, supporting), administrative skills/mechanics of management and technical skills (planning, decision-making, problem-solving, meeting objectives, administration, delegating, hiring, technical skills, performance), and personal behavior and skills (adaptability, responsibility, learning, flexibility, perseverance, resourceful). In summary, consistent with Borman and Brush's (1993) managerial performance dimensions, interpersonal, leadership, task, and personal skills are related to entry into and managerial advancement at all career stages, including later advancement.

Job performance

Studies of job performance have used chiefly company records of supervisor performance appraisal ratings, which are subject to errors and validity problems, reducing confidence in what the construct is being measured. Managers' job performance has been said to comprise task and contextual performance, the latter being the 'extras' employers look for in outstanding performance, such as citizenship and prosocial behavior (Landy, Shankster, & Kohler, 1994). Managers' job performance is usually judged by superiors, for whom high contextual performance is thought to lead to early promotion recommendations (Landy, Shankster, & Kohler, 1994). Studies are multivariate with substantial statistical controls.

Using across-organization samples, job performance was not related to managerial promotions, levels, or pay (Cannings, 1991; Cox & Harquail, 1991; Nkomo & Cox, 1990), or to panel evaluations and referral decisions for the senior executive service, but was positively related to the selecting official's actual selection of those referred (Powell & Butterfield, 1994). Successful early performance in critical functional areas was found for men reaching CEO status from archival data (Forbes & Piercy, 1991; Piercy & Forbes, 1991) and reported by women reaching vice-president level (Mainiero, 1994a). Using samples from single firms, job performance was related to promotability ratings of municipality supervisors by their managers, more for those below 45 years than above (Cox & Nkomo, 1992), to middle managers' promotion for performance measured currently and last year but not two years earlier (Gibbs, 1995), to male managers' promotions (Korenman & Neumark, 1991), and to entry to first level supervisor positions four years later for technical professionals (Roberts & Biddle, 1994). For US private sector white male scientists and engineers, managers came from higher paid technical workers, a proxy for performance, and successful managers were also more successful technicians in terms of pay (Biddle & Roberts, 1994). In summary, particularly within single firms, managers' job performance is positively related to managerial entry and advancement, especially for technical jobs.

Five studies analysed the same data set in multivariate analyses with substantial controls. For pairs of lower- to middle-level managers and their supervisors in three companies in communications, banks and electronics, job performance was related to supervisor-rated promotability for younger (23–49 or 23–54 years) but not older (50–63 or 55–63 years) managers (Siegel, 1993), consistent with the direction in Cox and Nkomo (1992). Younger managers appear preferred for promotion despite similar performance by older managers, with performance gaining managers more advancement in early than in late career. Using the communications company managers, job performance was positively related to promotability and to not being non-plateaued (Igbaria & Greenhaus, 1992). For black and white, chiefly managerial (rest professional) information systems employees of one of the companies, job performance was related to supervisor-rated promotability and future career advancement opportunities and to career plateauing (Igbaria & Wormley, 1995). Supervisor-rated internal performance attributions of ability and effort were not related to the advancement measures. Using the full sample from the three companies, black lower and middle level managers were rated lower on job performance by their supervisors than comparable whites, resulting in lower promotability assessments (Greenhaus, Parasuraman, & Wormley, 1990). Being black thus resulted in lower performance ratings which resulted in lower promotability ratings. In another analysis, blacks were rated as less promotable than whites primarily because they were rated as performing less effectively, but also because their job performance was less likely to be attributed to their ability than comparable performance of whites (Greenhaus & Parasuraman, 1993). Supervisors' ability attributions for the performance of their subordinate managers were associated with their promotability ratings; the strongest impact was when performance was moderately rather than highly successful, perhaps because performance is open to different explanations. In summary, supervisor performance attributions are not consistently related to managers' promotability ratings, but being black results in lower performance ratings and lower internal attributions for job performance than being white, resulting in lower promotability ratings.

Family

Psychological and labor market theories propose that a family has a negative impact on women's managerial career advancement, and a positive one on men's. Male managers are usually married fathers, whereas female managers are likely to be single or married and, if married, childless (Brett, Stroh, & Reilly, 1992a; Gutek, Searle, & Klepa, 1991; Lobel & St. Clair, 1992; Schneer & Reitman, 1995; Parasuraman & Greenhaus, 1993). From a psychological view, women's multiple roles of family and work impose time limitations and cause role overload and work–family role conflict, limiting factors leading to managerial advancement such as years of work experience, work hours, training, and relocation (Ragins & Sundstrom, 1989; Tharenou, 1990). By contrast, men's role in the workplace is consistent with the family 'provider' role (Bielby & Bielby, 1989), separating them from the home role and possible time constraints and role overload or conflict, resulting in a positive career impact. From a labor market view, men need to perform better in the labor market to support a family, and employers need to advance men to cater for family needs, unlike women. According to human capital theory, household duties reduce married women's time in the labor force, discourage their investment in human capital, and cause them to seek low-energy-intensive jobs (Becker, 1985), resulting in lower pay and status. According to distributive justice theory (Pfeffer & Ross, 1982), employers allocate rewards based on individual employee needs. Fathers need to provide for the family's financial needs, but women should be supported by spouses. According to wife-as-resource view (Kanter, 1977; Pfeffer & Ross, 1982), wives provide men with additional resources to invest in their careers through the extra roles they take on, especially if not employed outside the home, advantaging married over single men.

Studies assessing the impact of family are usually cross-sectional, self-report multivariate designs with extensive controls. Most do not consider the effects of family on intervening processes such as managers' tenure, work hours, or training that then affect managerial advancement, or directly test the theoretical explanations proposed for effects of family.

Marital status

Marital status was not related to male or female managers' and executives' promotion (Dreher & Ash, 1990; Judge et al., 1995; Korenman & Neumark, 1991; Tharenou & Conroy, 1994; Whitely, Dougherty, & Dreher, 1991). Marital status or marrying or changing to single did not predict the entry of scientists and engineers into managerial positions five years later (Shenhav, 1992), nor was marital status related to managers' levels (Melamed, 1996b). By contrast, single managers had lower managerial levels than married (Bretz & Judge, 1994), and marital status increased managers' levels which then increased pay, although there was a small wage premium on pay caused by marital status alone (Korenman & Neumark, 1991). Single managers had less overall managerial advancement than married (Judge & Bretz, 1994) and earned less (Bretz & Judge, 1994; Judge et al., 1995; Korenman & Neumark, 1991; Landau & Arthur, 1992), although there are also no links between marital status and pay (Dreher & Ash, 1990; Whitely, Dougherty, & Dreher, 1991). Being married was negatively related to female managers' pay and positively to males' (Jacobs, 1992). Single or never-married female managers and professionals earned less than married women, especially dual-career (Brett, Stroh, & Reilly, 1992b; Landau & Arthur, 1992; Schneer & Reitman, 1993). Single men earned less than divorced male managers and professionals who earned less than married men (Korenman & Neumark, 1991; Landau & Arthur, 1992). The lesser pay of single managers than married is consistent with distributive justice theory (less financial need), human capital theory (lack of stability), or social expectations theory (Pfeffer & Ross, 1982), not conforming to social stereotypes, although the explanations are not assessed. In summary, not consistent with a multiple role view, both female and male single managers may be lower in managerial level and are paid less than married managers.

Children

Number of children was not related to female or male managers' and executives' organization promotion (Tharenou & Conroy, 1994). For male and female scientists and engineers, number of children was not related to entry into management, and having children was negatively related to entry for the private not public sector (Shenhav, 1992). Children were related very weakly to managers' levels (Bretz & Judge, 1994), but not to female or male managers' levels (Melamed, 1996b). Number of children was not related to female or male managers' pay (Bretz & Judge, 1994; Cannings, 1991; Jacobs, 1992; Korabik & Rosin, 1995; Lobel & St. Clair, 1992), nor were pregnancy leave (Landau & Arthur, 1992) or preschool children (Lobel & St. Clair, 1992). Children under age six were negatively related to female but not male manager's pay (Jacobs, 1992). For a chiefly managerial sample (rest were professionals), men with children at home earned more than men with no children at home, whereas there was no relationship between having children and pay for women (Landau & Arthur, 1992). For a sample of Australian managers without post-secondary education and not necessarily full-time, women earned less than men increasingly more from having no children to one or two children to three or more children (Martin, 1994). Time devoted to dependant care was not related to executives' (93% men) pay or promotion (Judge et al., 1995), child-minding was not related to male or female managers' and executives' promotion or managerial level (Tharenou & Conroy, 1994), and dependant responsibilities were not related to managers overall advancement (two-third's men; Judge & Bretz, 1994). In summary, not consistent with a multiple role view, number or care of children is not related to managerial promotions, level, or pay for women (or men).

Marital status and children

Female CEOs could be discriminated from matched male CEOs but not from matched female top managers by being childless and not having a spouse (Tharenou, 1995), suggesting that lack of a family is not the reason women break the glass ceiling. A family, combining martial status and children, was not related to managers' and executives' managerial level or organization promotion (Tharenou & Conroy, 1994). For five of six countries (except Canada), the self-selection hypothesis whereby women voluntarily make themselves less available for promotion into management because of family responsibilities, was not supported for employees ranging from subordinates to top managers (Wright, Baxter, & Birkelund, 1995). There were no differences in workplace authority in terms of managerial level or authority between unmarried women, childless women with husbands providing household help, and mothers with little husband help (Wright, Baxter, & Birkelund, 1995). Parasuraman and Greenhaus (1993) proposed that families interrupt women's work experience, which reduces training amongst other things, and, in turn, affects career advancement. In support, structural equation analysis revealed that a family (spouse and children) reduced women's work experience but increased men's (Tharenou, Latimer, & Conroy, 1994). In turn, work experience led to training and development and subsequently managerial career advancement. In summary, marriage and children do not decrease women's managerial advancement but, consistent with a multiple role view, may reduce processes leading to it.

Household duties

Household responsibilities were not related to managers' (most men) overall advancement (Judge & Bretz, 1994). For married middle-level managers, household labor was more negatively related to men's levels and pay than women's, especially for those with graduate degrees (Konrad & Cannings, 1994). The career-family men (above the median on participation in household labor) of the sample had lower hierarchical levels than career-primary men (below the median), with career-family women in between (Konrad & Cannings, 1994). Employers may have sanctioned men for participating in household labor because it violates gender roles. Career-family women managers were paid less than career-primary men managers, who were similar in pay to career-family men (Konrad & Cannings, 1994). Extent of full responsibility for household duties were negatively related to women's but not men's pay (Cannings, 1991). In summary, inconsistent with multiple role effects for women alone, household duties may disadvantage men's or women's managerial advancement.

Spouse attributes

Male and female managers reported that spouse assistance had enhanced their careers (Grossbard-Shechtman, Izraeli, & Neuman, 1994). Spouse support was related to male and female managers' and executives' managerial level but not promotion (Tharenou & Conroy, 1994). Managers (87% male) with spouses working full-time rather than part-time had not plateaued more (Tremblay & Roger, 1993), and employed spouses were not related to male (chiefly) executives' promotion, but were to their lower pay (Judge et al., 1995). Managers' assessment that they had not constrained their careers for spouses gained male managers an extra $21 900 per year and women $1700 (Egan & Bendick, 1994). Work–family conflict was related to male and to female managers' and executives' managerial level but not promotion (Tharenou & Conroy, 1994). Because the study is cross-sectional, high managerial level could have caused role conflict. In summary, the few studies suggest that spouse support may help managers' levels, and spouse employment may affect male managers' pay.

Family structure

Family structures are derived from the interaction between marital status, parental status, and spousal employment status, providing family types: single childless, single-career families including traditional families with married fathers whose spouses are not employed outside the home, and dual-career families including post-traditional families of employed fathers or mothers whose spouses are also employed outside the home. Most studies assess only links with pay.

For managers, traditional men, fathers with not-employed spouses, earned more than other men, including childless counterparts and dual-career married fathers and childless men, and single childless men (Landau & Arthur, 1992; Schneer & Reitman, 1993), with greater salary progression and promotion in a longitudinal study than dual-career fathers (Brett, Stroh, & Reilly, 1992b). Effects were weak (Landau & Arthur, 1992). Post-traditional fathers do not necessarily earn less than other men, apart from traditional fathers. Dual-career fathers had similar pay compared to men combined from all other family structures for MBA graduates in mid-career (Schneer & Reitman, 1995) and to dual-earner childless men in early career (Schneer & Reitman, 1993). Dual-career fathers were promoted less than dual-career childless men and traditional single-earner fathers for managers who were all transferees (Brett, Stroh, & Reilly, 1992b), but had similar managerial levels to men combined into all other family structures (Schneer & Reitman, 1995). Post-traditional women, mothers with employed spouses, earned as much as other married women and mothers but more than single or never married women (Brett, Stroh, & Reilly, 1992b; Landau & Arthur, 1992; Schneer & Reitman, 1993, 1995), had similar promotion to dual-career childless women (Brett, Stroh, & Reilly, 1992b), and had similar managerial levels to women combined from all other family structures (Schneer & Reitman, 1995). Female managers whose spouses did not have a career earned more than dual-career counterparts (Landau & Arthur, 1992). In summary, for managers, traditional fathers earn more than other men, chiefly supporting distributive justice and wife as resource views; with that proviso, post-traditional fathers do not necessarily earn less; and post-traditional mothers earn as much as other women but more than single women, not supporting multiple role views.

INTEGRATORY STUDIES

Multivariate Studies

Organization or individual?

A few comprehensive, chiefly self-report studies were able to estimate the relative importance of organizational and individual factors simultaneously, most using hierarchical regression analysis. Most studies measured more individual than organizational variables, and only one (Bretz & Judge, 1994) considered interactions between the two in their effects on managerial career advancement. For 1270 Australian managers and executives (Tharenou & Conroy, 1994), managerial level and promotion were related to self-reported organization opportunity (organization size, promotion ladders, public sector) and social structures (male hierarchies, career encouragement) and training and development opportunities, but not to individuals' personalities (self-confidence, attributions, willingness to move), early socialization, and family responsibilities. Human capital (work experience, education) added to the explanation by the organization variables. In a stepwise regression analysis of 16 predictors for 136 British public service managers, human capital inputs (education, tenure), organizational opportunity structures (line position, promotion opportunities for the grade above), and personality (low self-control) explained managerial level, with other personality measures, mental ability, family (marital status, children), job changes, and objectively measured industry opportunities unimportant (Melamed, 1996b). Four studies measured more individual than organization variables, and so found they were more important. Using multivariate multiple regression, pay and promotion of 1388 US executives on a search firm's database were more related to human capital (education, tenure), demographic (male, marital status), and motivational (ambition, work hours) variables than to objectively measured organizational and industry opportunity variables (Judge et al., 1995). For 873 US industrial relations managers, human capital (education, work hours) most explained pay and job level, with explanation added by the perceived organization reward environment and the fit of the person's preferences to this reward environment, but little by demographic variables (gender, race, family), industry, or personal reward preferences alone (Bretz & Judge, 1994). For the same sample, political skills of the supervisor- and job-focused tactics and human capital inputs explained overall career advancement more than demographic, motivational and industry variables (Judge & Bretz, 1994). For 200 US managers from several firms, work experience was more important to managerial level than were career choice, success criteria and family influence on work (Gattiker & Larwood, 1990).

The multivariate studies show family variables have no or little relative importance, and human capital inputs have the most consistent relative importance. Organizations' internal labor markets as organization size, promotion ladders, line jobs and the reward environment have inconsistent links, but appear more related than family roles, early socialization, and personality. Personality is inconsistently related to managerial career advancement when compared to organizational and individual factors, but may be relatively important when conceptually linked (e.g. ambition). In summary, individual factors, especially human capital of education and work experience, and organization factors, mainly promotion opportunities, are related to managerial advancement.

Integratory models

Most studies testing integratory models have applied structural equation modeling to cross-sectional chiefly self-report questionnaire data. For 1359 senior Dutch private sector managers and executives, human capital increased position level and social networks, and all in turn increased pay (Boxman, De Graaf, & Flap, 1991). The internal locus of control, emotional stability and self-monitoring of 147 US managers and professionals led to initiating mentoring, resulting in mentoring gained that, in turn, increased overall career advancement (Turban & Dougherty, 1994). For 513 women and 501 men Australian public and private sector managers and executives, self-confidence increased the career encouragement and training and development received, and career encouragement increased women's participation in training and development more than men's (Tharenou, Latimer, & Conroy, 1994). Education increased men's, not women's participation in training and development and, for both, increased managerial advancement. A family increased men's work experience and reduced women's, and work experience led to greater participation in training and development by men than women. Training and development had the major impact on managerial advancement (Tharenou, Latimer, & Conroy, 1994). For 646 middle managers of a Canadian finance company, informal social networks increased men's offers of promotions more than women's, and human capital of performance and company tenure increased women's promotion more than men's, with men being offered more promotions (Cannings & Montmarquette, 1991b). In a study testing mediator effects by regression analysis for 457 British employees from subordinates to general manager level (Melamed, 1996a), human capital, but not organization structure, was related to career choices that influenced managerial level. Human capital of education and work experience, but also mental ability and being single were related to career choices of more prestigious and professional jobs and short tenure and frequent change of jobs, that in turn increased managerial levels.

In summary, tests of integratory models suggest that, apart from direct effects, individuals' human capital (work experience, education) and personality (e.g. self-confidence, self-monitoring) influence the use of organization social networks, career support, and training and development opportunities, and individuals' career choices that, in turn, lead to managerial career advancement. Marriage may affect career choices and reduce work experience, thus decreasing managerial career advancement.

CONCLUSION

Organization opportunity structures of internal labor markets, as provided by large organization size, long promotion ladders and growth, appear not important to advancing in management. The traditional path to advancement of employees stepping onto career ladders on entry and then subsequent promotion up the ladder may therefore not hold. The type of position and functional area is also not related to managerial advancement, although broadening experiences in critical functional areas, including general management at mid-career and late career, may assist advancement to executive levels. High level occupations with high percentages of males increase managerial level, providing opportunities for development of skills and the career paths needed to advance. Overall, being in the 'right' place at the 'right' time appears relatively unimportant to advancement, except being in the right occupation counts.

Social structures are important to managerial career advancement. Women are more likely to gain initial management jobs and advance in the hierarchy including to executive positions when the managerial hierarchy is less proportionately male and subordinates are women rather than men. Minorities are likely to advance under corresponding circumstances. Decision-makers appear attracted to those similar to them in identity and group affiliation, and comfortable with those with whom they are familiar, resulting in their reproducing themselves socially in selection and promotion. This causes white men to gain more managerial advancement than other groups. Who individuals are like counts.

Informal social networks and career support facilitate entering and advancing in management, at least in mid- and late career, and including to the top. Informal networks of personal contacts inside or external to the organization provide career information, control of options and support. Bigger networks are better. Networks assist men's managerial advancement more than women's, even though social networks with large range and strong sponsors are needed for women's managerial career advancement. Career encouragement from peers and supervisors increases managerial advancement, perhaps more for women than men, and interpersonal support appears especially important for women to overcome barriers including breaking the glass ceiling. Having a mentor who provides career support, as distinct from general supervisor support, results in increased managerial promotions, especially in early career, and managerial pay for men and women managers. Who individuals know and who knows them counts.

Promotion processes have important effects on entry into and advancement in the managerial hierarchy. Starting in favorable circumstances including higher levels and on faster tracks predicts later managerial advancement. Career tournaments operate from entry with winners and losers at each career stage, and winners may keep winning. They may do so because promotion provides developmental and network opportunities, opening up further promotion. Favorable starting processes are found more for men than women. Female managers also gain lower managerial levels and pay from promotion and incur higher promotion and advancement standards than comparable, similarly situated men, including in early and mid-career. This is discrimination, presumably based on stereotypes held about women as a group, perhaps in regard to productivity or labor force attachment or just lack of comfort of the male managerial majority through dissimilarity. Blacks appear discriminated against for managerial career advancement based on race. To counteract discrimination, affirmative action programs clearly delineating target groups increase entry into managerial jobs, increasing women's and minorities' representation in management. Politics influences who advances in management, especially from mid-career, including to the top. Use of political skills by candidates including managing impressions and ingratiation increases their managerial advancement, as does supervisor political influence through recommendations, candidate identification, comfort levels, and negotiations. How political individuals are counts. Promotion to middle and upper management and executive levels is determined by individuals' abilities and accomplishments and organization needs, including context, but also by social networks and politics. The organization's context and needs are important to characteristics of those chosen to be executives.

Individuals' traits predict managerial career advancement in the short and long term, and are important to initial managerial advancement and to reaching the top. Certain traits may allow taking advantage of organization opportunities, by seeking or accepting training and development and career support and making career choices that increase managerial advancement. There appear to be four major facets of individuals who advance in management. First, they are ambitious, advancement- and career-motivated, and self-monitoring, especially in early career, and have high achievement needs and work involvement, important as careers progress to mid- and late career to sustain advancement. These ambition and achievement motives drive individuals to seek and accept managerial advancement. Second, those likely to advance into management are motivated to manage, including prior to employment. Third, they are intelligent, especially relevant to early career progress in learning complex jobs. Fourth, they are instrumental, suited to the task demands of managerial jobs. The latter three traits allow individuals to implement their self-concepts in occupational choice; the traits fit with and are relevant to the managerial role. Drive and person fit count.

Human capital investments increase managerial career advancement. Managers who invest in their education level and quality, company tenure, full-time years of work experience, weekly work hours, geographical job transfers, and management training and development are likely to gain initial managerial positions and advance, including to the top. This is the traditional way of getting ahead, working hard and increasing skills and knowledge and thus productivity, for which rewards are given, and establishing credentials, credibility and visibility in the organization to provide signals on which advancement decisions are made. Human capital investments are as, or more important to, managerial career advancement as other significant factors. Human capital directly influences advancement into management and also indirectly through increasing factors that lead to advancement: social networks, training and development, and career choices. Investing in human capital, especially company tenure and education, pays back at the time in managerial advancement, and in mid- and late career. What individuals know and can do counts throughout their careers.

Managerial skills at each career stage increase managerial career advancement at that stage and later. Important are interpersonal, leadership, administrative, and personal skills. Ineffective people and strategic skills may derail managers in late career. Managers rated as high performers by their supervisors are more likely to gain entry into management and to advance as managers within organizations, reflecting task performance but perhaps also citizenship. High performance in critical functional areas is important to gain top level advancement. Age and racial bias may reduce promotability ratings, affected by attributions for performance. Overall, what individuals can do and how well counts.

Family roles appear relatively unimportant to advancement in management compared to other factors. Being a single male or female disadvantages, and being a traditional father advantages, managers' pay, perhaps because employers allocate pay based on individual need and/or perceived stability and conformity. Multiple roles of home and work do not appear to cause women's lesser managerial advancement than men's, and dual-career mothers advance as much as other women except singles, although women's multiple roles may impede processes that lead to advancement such as work experience and training.

In summary, the empirical literature since 1990 suggests that individual qualities and work environment factors combine to facilitate individuals entering and advancing in management in hierarchical organizations. Individuals choose certain occupations and, when they are high level occupations with high proportions of white men, they provide opportunities for advancement. Employees who are ambitious, want to manage, are instrumental, and intelligent seek advancement continuously. They invest in education, work experience, and training and development to do so, increasing their productivity and developing credentials, credibility and visibility. Because of these attributes, they are viewed as suitable for entry to, and advancement in management and seek and are provided with developmental experiences, social networks, career encouragement and mentor support, providing the information, resources, control, and support needed to advance. Interpersonal support comes from the male managerial hierarchies of organizations, more to men than women. Individuals who gain early promotion increase in the hierarchical level of their jobs, resulting in continued challenging work and development experiences, gaining credibility, visibility and familiarity, and thus more opportunities for promotion. The managerial momentum and career velocity need to be maintained. To be promoted, managers need to have high managerial skills especially in critical areas and general management, perceived so by their bosses, have favorable political circumstances and use political skills, and be similar in attributes to the majority of the managerial hierarchy. Decision-makers select and advance those who are similar to them and in the same social categories, and use stereotypes to help them process information about possible candidates. The selection and promotion process is thus imperfect, resulting in higher promotion standards for groups dissimilar to the majority. Advancement at highest levels in the hierarchy is influenced by similarity and fitting in, by politics, and with fulfilling organization needs, requiring a fit with organization context.

REFERENCES

Baron, J. N. & Pfeffer, J. (1994) The social psychology of organizations and inequality. *Social Psychology Quarterly*, **57**, 190–209.

Barrick, M. R. & Mount, M. K. (1991) The big five personality dimensions and job performance: A meta-analysis. *Personnel Psychology*, **44**, 1–26.

Becker, G. S. (1975) *Human Capital*. Chicago: University of Chicago Press.

Becker, G. S. (1985) Human capital, effort, and the sexual division of labor. *Journal of Labor Economics*, **3**, 533–558.

Becker, G. S. (1993) *Human Capital*. Chicago: University of Chicago Press.

Bem, S. L. (1981) Gender schema theory. *Psychological Review*, **88**, 354–364.

Biddle, J. & Roberts, K. (1994) Private sector scientists and engineers and the transition to management. *Journal of Human Resources*, **29**, 82–107.

Bielby, J. M. & Bielby, D. D. (1989) Family ties. *American Sociological Review*, **54**, 776–789.

Blau, F. D. & Ferber, M. A. (1987) Occupations and earnings of women workers. In K. S. Koziara, M. H. Moskow, & L. D. Tanner (eds), *Working Women: Past, Present, Future*. Washington, DC: Bureau of National Affairs.

Blum, T. C., Fields, D. L., & Goodman, J. S. (1994) Organization-level determinants of women in management, *Academy of Management Journal*, **37**, 241–268.

Boeker, W. & Goodstein, J. (1993) Performance and successor choice. *Academy of Management Journal*, **36**, 172–186.

Borman, W. C. & Brush, D. H. (1993) More progress toward a taxonomy of managerial performance requirements. *Human Performance*, **6**, 1–21.

Boxman, E. A. W., De Graaf, P. M., & Flap, H. D. (1991) The impact of social and human capital on the income attainment of Dutch managers. *Social Networks*, **13**, 51–73.

Brett, J. M., Stroh, L. K., & Reilly, A. H. (1992a) Job transfer. In C. L. Cooper and I. T. Robertson (eds), *International Review of Industrial and Organizational Psychology* (pp. 323–362). New York: Wiley.

Brett, J. M., Stroh, L. K., & Reilly, A. H. (1992b) What is it like being a dual career manager in the 1990s? In S. Zedeck (ed.), *Work, Families and Organizations* (pp. 138–167). San Francisco: Jossey-Bass.

Bretz, R. D. & Judge, T. A. (1994) Person–organization fit and the theory of work adjustment. *Journal of Vocational Behavior*, **44**, 32–54.

Burt, R. S. (1992) *Structural Holes: The Social Structure of Competition*. Cambridge, MA: Harvard University Press.

Burt, R. S. (1993) The social structure of competition. In R. Swedgerb (ed.), *Explanations in Economic Sociology* (pp. 65–103). New York: Russell Sage Foundation.

Campion, M. A., Cheraskin, L., & Stevens, M. J. (1994) Career-related antecedents and outcomes of job rotation. *Academy of Management Journal*, **37**, 1518–1542.

Cannella, A. & Lubatkin, M. (1993) Succession as a socio-political process. *Academy of Management Journal*, **36**, 763–793.

Cannella, A., Lubatkin, M., & Kapouch, M. (1991) Antecedents of executive selection. *Academy of Management Proceedings*, **51**, 11–15.

Cannings, K. (1991) An interdisciplinary approach to analyzing the managerial gender gap. *Human Relations*, **44**, 679–695.

Cannings, K. & Montmarquette, C. (1991a) The attitudes of subordinates to the gender of superiors in a managerial hierarchy. *Journal of Economic Psychology*, **12**, 707–724.

Cannings, K. & Montmarquette, C. (1991b) Managerial momentum. *Industrial and Labor Relations Review*, **44**, 212–228.

Carson, K. P. & Gilliard, D. J. (1993) Construct validity of the Miner Sentence Completion Scale. *Journal of Occupational and Organizational Psychology*, **66**, 171–175.

Chi-Ching, E. Y. (1992) Perceptions of external barriers and the career success of female managers in Singapore. *Journal of Social Psychology*, **132**, 661–674.

Chusmir, L. H. & Koberg, C. S. (1991) Relationship between self-confidence and sex-role identity among managerial women and men. *Journal of Social Psychology*, **131**, 781–790.

Chusmir, L. H., Koberg, C. S., & Stecher, H. D. (1992) Self-confidence of managers in work and social situations. *Sex Roles*, **26**, 495–512.

Chusmir, L. H. & Parker, B. (1991) Gender and situational differences in managers' values. *Journal of Business Research*, **23**, 325–335.

Cianni, M. & Romberger, B. (1995) Perceived racial, ethnic, and gender differences in access to developmental experiences. *Group & Organization Management*, **20**, 440–459.

Cordero, R., Di Tomaso, N., & Farris, G. F. (1994) Identifying and developing promotability in R&D laboratories. *Journal of Engineering and Technology Management*, **11**, 55–72.

Cox, T. H. & Harquail, C. V. (1991) Career paths and career success in the early career stages of male and female MBAs. *Journal of Vocational Behavior*, **39**, 54–75.

Cox, T. H. & Nkomo, S. M. (1991) A race and gender-group analysis of the early career experience of MBAs. *Work and Occupations*, **18**, 431–446.

Cox, T. H. & Nkomo, S. M. (1992) Candidate age as a factor in promotability ratings. *Public Personnel Management*, **21**, 197–210.

Datta, D. K. & Guthrie, J. P. (1994) Executive succession. *Strategic Management Journal*, **15**, 569–577.

Day, D. V. & Lord, R. G. (1988) Executive leadership and organizational performance. *Journal of Management*, **14**, 453–464.

Deshpande, S. P., Schoderbek, P. P., & Joseph, J. (1994) Promotion decisions by managers. *Human Relations*, **47**, 223–232.

Dreher, G. F. & Ash, R. A. (1990) A comparative study of mentoring among men and women in managerial positions. *Journal of Applied Psychology*, **75**, 539–546.

Dreher, G. F. & Bretz, R. D. (1991) Cognitive ability and career attainment. *Journal of Applied Psychology*, **76**, 392–397.

Egan, M. L. & Bendick, M. (1994) International business careers in the United States. *International Journal of Human Resource Management*, **5**, 33–50.

Ellis, R. & Heneman, H. G. (1990) Career pattern determinants of career success for mature managers. *Journal of Business and Psychology*, **5**, 3–20.

Fagenson, E. A. (1990a) At the heart of women in management research. *Journal of Business Ethics*, **9**, 1–8.

Fagenson, E. A. (1990b) Perceived masculine and feminine attributes as a function of sex and level in the organizational hierarchy. *Journal of Applied Psychology*, **75**, 204–211.

Ferris, G. R., Buckley, M. R., & Allen, G. M. (1992) Promotion systems in organizations. *Human Resource Planning*, **15**, 47–68.

Ferris, G. R. & Judge, T. A. (1991) Personnel/human resources management: A political perspective. *Journal of Management*, **17**, 447–488.

Forbes, J. B. & Piercy, J. E. (1991) *Corporate Mobility and Paths to the Top*. New York: Quorum Books.

Forbes, J. B. & Wertheim, S. E. (1995) Promotion, succession, and career systems. In R. Ferris, S. D. Rosen, & D. T. Barnum (eds), *Handbook of Human Resource Management* (pp. 494–510). Cambridge, MA: Blackwell Business.

Friedman, S. D. (1991) Why hire from within? *Academy of Management Best Paper Proceedings*, **51**, 272–276.

Gattiker, U. E. & Larwood, L. (1990) Predictors for career achievement in the corporate hierarchy. *Human Relations*, **43**, 703–726.

Gibbs, M. (1995) Incentive compensation in a corporate hierarchy. *Journal of Accounting and Economics*, **19**, 247–277.

Greenhaus, J. H. & Parasuraman, S. (1993) Job performance attributions and career advancement prospects. *Organizational Behavior and Human Decision Processes*, **55**, 273–297.

Greenhaus, J. H., Parasuraman, S., & Wormley, W. M. (1990) Effects of race on organizational experiences, job performance evaluations, and career outcomes. *Academy of Management Journal*, **33**, 64–86.

Grossbard-Shechtman, S. A., Izraeli, D. N., & Neuman, S. (1994) When do spouses support a career? *Journal of Socio-Economics*, **23**, 149–167.

Gutek, B. A. (1993) Changing the status of women in management. *Applied Psychology: An International Review*, **42**, 301–311.

Gutek, B. A., Searle, S., & Klepa, L. (1991) Rational versus gender-role expectations for work–family conflict. *Journal of Applied Psychology*, **76**, 560–568.

Guthrie, J. P., Grimm, C., & Smith, K. G. (1991) Environmental change and management staffing. *Journal of Management*, **17**, 735–748.

Guthrie, J. P. & Olian, J. D. (1991) Does context affect staffing decisions? *Personnel Psychology*, **44**, 261–291.

Haberfeld, Y. (1992) Employment discrimination: An organizational model. *Academy of Management Journal*, **35**, 161–180.

Hanson, Frieze, I., Olson, J. E., & Cain Good, D. (1990) Perceived and actual discrimination in the salaries of male and female managers. *Journal of Applied Social Psychology*, **20**, 46–67.

Herriot, P., Gibbons, P., Pemberton, C., & Jackson, P. R. (1994) An empirical model of managerial careers in organizations. *British Journal of Management*, 5, 113–121.

Herriot, P., Gibson, G., Pemberton, C., & Pinder, R. (1993) Dashed hopes. *Journal of Occupational and Organizational Psychology*, 66, 115–123.

Hofstede, G. (1994) Predicting managers' career success in an international setting. *Management International Review*, 34, 63–70.

Hogan, R. (1994) Trouble at the top: Causes and consequence of managerial incompetence. *Consulting Psychology Journal*, 46(1), 9–15.

Hogan, R., Curphy, G. J., & Hogan, J. (1994) What do we know about leadership? *American Psychologist*, 49, 493–504.

House, R. J., Howard, A., & Walker, G. (1991) The prediction of managerial success. *Academy of Management Best Paper Proceedings*, 51, 215–219.

Howard, A. (1991) Managerial roles that span careers. In J. W. Jones, B. D. Steffy, & D. W. Bray (eds), *Applying Psychology in Business* (pp. 452–462). Lexington, MA: Lexington Books.

Howard, A. & Bray, D. W. (1990) Predictions of managerial success over long periods of time. In K. E. Clark & M.B. Clark (eds), *Measures of Leadership* (pp. 113–130). West Orange, NJ: Leadership Library of America.

Huffman, M. L. (1995) Organizations, internal labor market policies, and gender inequality in workplace supervisory authority. *Sociological Perspectives*, 38, 381–397.

Hurley, A. E. & Sonnenfeld, J. A. (1994) Organizational growth and employee advancement. In M. London (ed.), *Employees, Careers and Job Creation* (pp. 31–48). San Francisco, CA: Jossey-Bass.

Ibarra, H. (1993) Personal networks of women and minorities in management: A conceptual framework. *Academy of Management Review*, 18, 57–87.

Ibarra, H. (1995) Race, opportunity, and diversity of social circles in managerial ranks. *Academy of Management Journal*, 38, 673–703.

Igbaria, M. & Greenhaus, J. H. (1992) The career advancement prospects of managers and professionals. *Decision Sciences*, 23, 478–499.

Igbaria, M. & Wormley, W. M. (1995) Race differences in job performance and career success. *Communication of the ACM*, 38 (3), 83–92.

Ingham, H. & Thompson, S. (1995) Mutuality, performance and executive compensation. *Oxford Bulletin of Economics and Statistics*, 57, 295–308.

Jackson, S. E., Brett, J. F., Sessa, V. I., Cooper, D. M., Julin, J. A., & Peyronnin, K. (1991) Some differences make a difference. *Journal of Applied Psychology*, 76, 675–689.

Jacobs, J. A. (1992) Women's entry into management. *Administrative Science Quarterly*, 37, 282–301.

Jacobs, R. L. & McClelland, D. C. (1994) Moving up the corporate ladder. *Consulting Psychology Journal*, 46, 32–41.

Jenkins, S. R. (1994) Need for power and women's careers over 14 years. *Journal of Personality and Social Psychology*, 66, 155–165.

Johnson, N. B. & Scandura, T. A (1994) The effects of mentoring and sex-role style on male–female earnings. *Industrial Relations*, 33, 263–274.

Johnsrud, L. K. & Heck, R. H. (1994) Administrative promotion within a university. *Journal of Higher Education*, 65, 23–43.

Jones, R. G. & Whitmore, M. D. (1995) Evaluating developmental assessment centers as interventions. *Personnel Psychology*, 48, 377-388.

Judge, T. A. & Bretz, R. D. (1994) Political influence processes and career success. *Journal of Management*, 20, 43–65.

Judge, T. A., Cable, D. M., Boudreau, J. W., & Bretz, R. D. (1995) An empirical investigation of the predictors of executive career success. *Personnel Psychology*, 48, 485–519.

Kanter, R. M. (1977) *Men and Women of the Corporation.* New York: Basic Books.

Kent, R. L. & Moss, S. E. (1994) Effects of sex and gender role on leader emergence. *Academy of Management Journal,* 37, 1335–1346.

Khojasteh, M. (1994) Workforce 2000 demographic characteristics and their impacts. *International Journal of Public Administration,* 17, 465–505.

Kilduff, M. D. & Day, D. V. (1994) Do chameleons get ahead? *Academy of Management Journal,* 37, 1047–1060.

Kim, H. & Yukl, G. (1995) Relationships of managerial effectiveness and advancement to self-reported and subordinate-reported leadership behaviors from the multiple-linkage model. *Leadership Quarterly,* 6, 361–377.

Kim, P. S. & Lewis, G. B. (1994) Asian Americans in the public service: Success, diversity and discrimination. *Public Administration Review,* 54, 285-290.

Kirchmeyer, C. (1995) Demographic similarity to the work group. *Journal of Organizational Behavior,* 16, 67–83.

Koberg, C. S., Chusmir, L. H., & Carlin, W. B. (1992) Gender and hierarchical level coalignment with managers' self-confidence. *Psychology, A Journal of Human Behavior,* 29, 14–17.

Konrad, A. M. & Cannings, K. (1994) Of mummy tracks and glass ceilings. *Relations Industrielles,* 49, 303–333.

Konrad, A. M. & Linnehan, F. (1992) The implementation and effectiveness of equal opportunity employment. *Academy of Management Best Paper Proceedings,* 52, 380–384.

Konrad, A. M. & Linnehan, F. (1995) Formalized HRM structures. *Academy of Management Journal,* 38, 787–820.

Konrad, A. M. & Pfeffer, J. (1991) Understanding the hiring of women and minorities in educational institutions. *Sociology of Education,* 64, 141–157.

Korabik, K. & Rosin, H. M. (1995) The impact of children on women managers' career behavior and organizational commitment. *Human Resource Management,* 34, 513–528.

Korenman, S. & Neumark, D. (1991) Does marriage really make men more productive? *Journal of Human Resources,* 26, 283–307.

Kotter, J. P. (1995) *The New Rules: How to Succeed in Today's Corporate World.* New York: Free Press.

Kram, K. E. (1983) Phases of the mentor relationship. *Academy of Management Journal,* 26, 608–625.

Krausz, M. & Reshef, M. (1992) Managerial job change. *Journal of Business and Psychology,* 6, 349–359.

Landau, J. (1995) The relationship of race and gender to managers' ratings of promotion potential. *Journal of Organizational Behavior,* 16, 391–400.

Landau, J. & Arthur, M. B. (1992) The relationship of marital status, spouse's career status, and gender to salary level. *Sex Roles,* 27, 665–681.

Landy, F. J., Shankster, L. J., & Kohler, S. S. (1994) Personnel selection and placement. *Annual Review of Psychology,* 45, 261–296.

Leck, J. D. & Saunders, D. M. (1992a) Canada's employment equity act. *Population Research and Policy Review,* 11, 21–49.

Leck, J. D. & Saunders, D. M. (1992b) Hiring women. *Canadian Public Policy – Analyse de Politiques,* 18, 203–220.

Leck, J. D., Saunders, D. M., & St. Onge, S. (1991) Achieving a diversified workforce with employment equity programs: Effects on hiring women. *Academy of Management Best Paper Proceedings,* 51, 385–389.

Levinson, H. (1994) Why the behemoths fall. *American Psychologist,* 49, 428–436.

Lewis, G. B. (1992) Men and women towards the top. *Public Personnel Management,* 21, 473–491.

Lobel, S. A. & St. Clair, L. (1992) Effects of family responsibilities, gender, and career identity salience on performance outcomes. *Academy of Management Journal*, **35**, 1057–1069.

Locke, E. A. (1991) *The Essence of Leadership*. New York: Lexington Books.

Lord, R. G., De Vader, C. L., & Alliger, G. M. (1986) A meta-analysis of the relationship between personality traits and leadership perceptions. *Journal of Applied Psychology*, **71**, 402–410.

Macrae, C. N., Milne, A. B., & Bodenhausen, G. V. (1994) Stereotypes as energy-saving devices: A peek inside the cognitive toolbox. *Journal of Personality and Social Psychology*, **64**, 37–47.

Mainiero, L. A. (1994a) Getting anointed for advancement: The case of executive women. *Academy of Management Executive*, **8**, 53–67.

Mainiero, L. A. (1994b) The political seasoning of powerful women executives. *Organizational Dynamics*, **22** (4), 5–20.

Markham, W. T., Harlan, S. L., & Hackett, E. J. (1987) Promotion opportunity in organization. *Research in Personnel and Human Resources Management* (pp. 223–287). New York: JAI Press.

Martin, L. R. & Morgan, S. (1995) Middle managers in banking. *Quarterly Journal of Business and Economics*, **34**, 55–68.

Martin, W. (1994) Understanding class segmentation in the labour market. *Work, Employment & Society*, **8**, 355–385.

McCauley, C. D. & Lombardo, M. M. (1990) Benchmarks. In K. E. Clark & M. B. Clark (eds), *Measures of Leadership* (pp. 535–545). West Orange, NJ: Leadership Library of America.

McCauley, C. D. & Ruderman, M. N. (1991) Understanding executive derailment. In J. W. Jones, B. D. Steffy, & D. W. Bray (eds), *Applying Psychology in Business* (pp. 483–488). Lexington, MA: Lexington Books.

Melamed, T. (1995a) Career success: The moderating effect of gender. *Journal of Vocational Behavior*, **47**, 35–60.

Melamed, T. (1995b) Barriers to women's career success. *Applied Psychology: An International Review*, **44**, 295–314.

Melamed, T. (1996a) Validation of a stage model of career success. *Applied Psychology: An International Review*, **45**, 35–66.

Melamed, T. (1996b) Career success: An assessment of a gender-specific model. *Journal of Occupational and Organizational Psychology*, **69**, 217–242.

Meyerson, E. M. (1994) Human capital, social capital and compensation. *Acta Sociologica*, **37**, 383–399.

Miner, J. B. (1993) *Role Motivation Theories*. Routledge: London.

Miner, J. B., Chen, C. C., & Yu, K. C. (1991) Theory testing under adverse conditions. *Journal of Applied Psychology*, **76**, 343–349.

Miner, J. B., Ebrahimi, B., & Wachtel, J. M. (1995) How deficiencies in motivation to manage contribute to the United States' competitiveness problem (and what can be done about it). *Human Resource Management*, **34**, 1–25.

Mittman, B. S. (1992) Theoretical and methodological issues in the study of organizational demography and demographic change. *Research in the Sociology of Occupations*, **10**, 3–53.

Morgan, S., Schor, S. M., & Martin, L. R. (1993) Gender differences in career paths in banking. *Career Development Quarterly*, **41**, 375–382.

Murrell, A. J., Olson, J. E., & Frieze, I. H. (1995) Sexual harassment and gender discrimination. *Journal of Social Issues*, **51**, 139–149.

Naff, K. C. (1994) Through the glass ceiling. *Public Administration Review*, **54**, 507–514.

Nicholson, N. (1990) The transition cycle. In S. Fisher & C. L. Cooper (eds), *The Psychology of Change and Transition* (pp. 83–108). New York: Wiley.

Nicholson, N. (1993) Purgatory or place of safety? *Human Relations*, **46**, 1369–1389.
Nkomo, S. M. & Cox, T. (1990) Factors affecting the upward mobility of black managers in private sector organizations. *Review of Black Political Economy*, **19**, 39–58.
Northcraft, G. & Gutek, B. (1993) Discrimination against women in management. In E. A. Fagenson (ed.), *Women in Management: Trends, Issues and Challenges in Managerial Diversity* (pp. 131–161). Newbury Park, CA: Sage Publications.
Offerman, L. R. & Gowing, M. K. (1993) Personnel selection in the future. N. Schmitt & W. C. Borman (eds), *Personnel Selection in Organizations* (pp. 385–417). San Francisco: Jossey-Bass.
O'Reilly, C. A. & Chatman, J. A. (1994) Working smarter and harder. *Administrative Science Quarterly*, **39**, 603–627.
Orpen, C. (1994) The effect of initial job challenge on subsequent performance among middle managers: A longitudinal study. *Psychology, A Journal of Human Behavior*, **31**, 51–52.
Parasuraman, S. & Greenhaus, J. H. (1993) Personal portrait. In E. A. Fagenson (ed.), *Women in Management* (pp. 186–211). Newbury Park, CA: Sage.
Pfeffer, J., Davis-Blake, A., & Julius, D. J. (1995) The effect of affirmative action officer salary changes on managerial diversity. *Industrial Relations*, **34**, 73–94.
Pfeffer, J. & Ross, J. (1982) The effects of marriage and a working wife on occupational and wage attainment. *Administrative Science Quarterly*, **27**, 66–80.
Pfeffer, J. & Ross, J. (1990) Gender-based wage differences: The effects of organization context. *Work and Occupations*, **17**, 55–78.
Pfeffer, J. & Salancik, G. R. (1978) *The External Control of Organizations: A Resource Dependence Perspective*. New York: Harper & Row.
Piercy, J. E. & Forbes, J. B. (1991) The phases of the chief executive's career. *Business Horizons*, **34**, 20–22.
Pollock, R. (1995) A test of conceptual models depicting the developmental course of informal mentor–protégé relationships in the workplace. *Journal of Vocational Behavior*, **46**, 144–162.
Powell, G. N. & Butterfield, D. A. (1994) Investigating the 'glass ceiling' phenomenon. *Academy of Management Journal*, **37**, 68–86.
Powell, G. N. & Mainiero, L. A. (1992) Cross-currents in the river of time. *Journal of Management*, **18**, 215–237.
Puffer, S. M. & Weintrop, J. B. (1995) CEO and board leadership. *Leadership Quarterly*, **6**, 49–68.
Ragin, C. C. & Bradshaw, Y. W. (1991) Statistical analysis of employment discrimination. *Research in Social Stratification and Mobility*, **10**, 199–228.
Ragins, B. R. & Sundstrom, E. (1989) Gender and power in organizations. *Psychological Bulletin*, **105**, 51–88.
Reskin, B. F. & Ross, C. E. (1992) Jobs, authority, and earnings among managers. *Work and Occupations*, **19**, 342–365.
Roberts, K. & Biddle, J. (1994) The transition into management by scientists and engineers. *Human Resource Management*, **33**, 561–579.
Rosenbaum, J. E. (1984) *Career Mobility in a Corporate Hierarchy*. New York: Academic Press.
Rosenbaum, J. E. (1990) Structural models of organizational careers. In R. L. Breiger (ed.), *Social Mobility and Social Structure* (pp. 272–397). Cambridge: Cambridge University Press.
Ruderman, M. N. & Ohlott, P. J. (1994) *The Realities of Management Promotion*. Greensboro, NC: Center for Creative Leadership.
Ruderman, M. N., Ohlott, P. J., & Kram, K. E. (1995) Promotion decisions as a diversity practice. *Journal of Management Development*, **14** (2), 6–23.

Salancik, G. R. & Pfeffer, J. (1978) Uncertainty, secrecy, and the choice of similar others. *Social Psychology*, **41**, 246–255.

Sandwith, P. (1993) A hierarchy of management training requirements: The competency domain model. *Public Personnel Management*, 22, 43–62.

Scandura, T. A (1992) Mentorship and career mobility: An empirical investigation. *Journal of Organizational Behavior*, **13**, 169–174.

Scandura, T. A. & Schriesheim, C. A. (1994) Leader–member exchange and supervisor career mentoring as complementary constructs in leadership research. *Academy of Management Journal*, 37, 1588–1602.

Schaller, M., Boyd, C., Yohannes, J., & O'Brien, M. (1995) The prejudiced personality revisited. *Journal of Personality and Social Psychology*, **68**, 544–555.

Schein, V. E. & Mueller, R. (1992) Sex role stereotyping and requisite management characteristics. *Journal of Organizational Behavior*, **13**, 439–447.

Schein, V. E., Mueller, R., Lituchy, T., & Liu, J. (1996) Think manager–think male. *Journal of Organizational Behavior*, **17**, 33–41.

Schneer, J. A. & Reitman, F. (1990) Effects of unemployment gaps on the careers of MBAs. *Academy of Management Journal*, **33**, 391–406.

Schneer, J. A. & Reitman, F. (1993) Effects of alternate family structures on managerial career paths. *Academy of Management Journal*, **36**, 830–843.

Schneer, J. A. & Reitman, F. (1994a) Effects of early and mid-career employment gaps on career outcomes. *Academy of Management Best Paper Proceedings*, **54**, 63–67.

Schneer, J. A. & Reitman, F. (1994b) The importance of gender in mid-career. *Journal of Organizational Behavior*, **15**, 199–207.

Schneer, J. A. & Reitman, F. (1995) The impact of gender as managerial careers unfold. *Journal of Vocational Behavior*, **47**, 290–315.

Shackleton, V. & Newell, S. (1991) Managerial selection. *Journal of Occupational Psychology*, **64**, 23–36.

Shenhav, Y. (1992) Entrance of blacks and women into managerial positions in scientific and engineering occupations. *Academy of Management Journal*, **35**, 889–901.

Sheridan, J. E., Slocum, J. W., Buda, R., & Thompson, R. C. (1990) Effects of corporate sponsorship and departmental power on career tournaments. *Academy of Management Journal*, **33**, 578–602.

Sheridan, J. E., Slocum, J. W., & Buda, R. (in press) Factors influencing the probability of employee promotions. *Journal of Business and Psychology*, **11**.

Shore, T. H. (1992) Subtle gender bias in the assessment of managerial potential. *Sex Roles*, **29**, 499–515.

Siegel, S. R. (1993) Relationship between current performance and likelihood of promotion for old versus young workers. *Human Resource Development Quarterly*, **4**, 39–50.

Snyder, M. & Gangestad, S. (1982) Choosing social situations. *Journal of Personality and Social Psychology*, **43**, 123–135.

Sparks, C. P. (1990) Testing for management potential. In K. E. Clark & M. B. Clark (eds), *Measures of Leadership* (pp. 103–111). West Orange, NJ: Leadership Library of America.

Spence, A. M. (1973) Job market signaling. *Quarterly Journal of Economics*, **87**, 355–375.

Spence, A. M. (1974) *Market Signaling: The Information Transfer of Hiring and Related Processes.* Cambridge, MA: Harvard University Press.

Steinberg, R. J., Haignere, L., & Chertos, C. H. (1990) Managerial promotion in the public sector. *Work and Occupations*, **17**, 284–301.

Stover, D. (1994) The horizontal distribution of female managers within organizations. *Work and Occupations*, **21**, 385–402.

Strober, M. H. (1990) Human capital theory: Implications for HR managers. *Industrial Relations*, **29**, 214–359.

Stroh, L. K., Brett, J. M., & Reilly, A. H. (1992) All the right stuff. *Journal of Applied Psychology*, 77, 251–260.

Stroh, L. K., Brett, J. M., & Reilly, A. H. (1994) A decade of change. *Human Resource Management*, 33, 531–548.

Stumpf, S. A. & London, M. (1981) Management promotions. *Academy of Management Review*, 6, 539–549.

Super, D. E. (1957) *The Psychology of Careers*. New York: Harper.

Tharenou, P. (1990) Psychological approaches for investigating women's career advancement. *Australian Journal of Management*, 15, 363–378.

Tharenou, P. (1995) Correlates of women's chief executive status. *Journal of Career Development*, 21, 201–212.

Tharenou, P. & Conroy, D. K. (1994) Men and women managers' advancement. *Applied Psychology: An International Review*, 43, 5–31.

Tharenou, P., Latimer, S., & Conroy, D. K. (1994) How do you make it to the top? *Academy of Management Journal*, 37, 899–931.

Thompson, J. W. (1994) An international validation of London House's STEP battery. *Journal of Business and Psychology*, 9, 81–99.

Tremblay, M. & Roger, A. (1993) Individual, familial, and organizational determinants of career plateau. *Group and Organization Management*, 18, 411–435.

Truman, G. E. & Baroudi, J. J. (1994) Gender differences in the information systems managerial ranks. *MIS Quarterly*, 18, 129–142.

Turban, D. B. & Dougherty, T. W. (1994) Role of protégé personality in receipt of mentoring and career success. *Academy of Management Journal*, 37, 688–702.

Tziner, A., Meir, E., Dahan, M., & Birati, A. (1994) An investigation into the predictive validity and economic utility of the Assessment center for the high management level. *Canadian Journal of Behavioral Science*, 26, 228–245.

Van Velsor, E. & Leslie, J. B. (1995) Why executives derail. *Academy of Management Executive*, 9 (4), 62–73.

Whitely, W. T. & Coetsier, P. (1993) The relationship of career mentoring to early career outcomes. *Organization Studies*, 14, 419–441.

Whitely, W. T., Dougherty, T. W., & Dreher, G. F. (1991) Relationship of career mentoring and socioeconomic origin to managers' and professionals' early career progress. *Academy of Management Journal*, 34, 331–351.

Winter, D. G. (1991) A motivational model of leadership. *Leadership Quarterly*, 2 (2), 67–80.

Wright, E. O., Baxter, J., & Birkelund, G. E. (1995) The gender of workplace authority. *American Sociological Review*, 60, 407–435.

Yuen, E. C. (1995) Does having a mentor make a difference? *International Journal of Employment Studies*, 3, 1–15.

Chapter 3

WORK ADJUSTMENT; EXTENSION OF THE THEORETICAL FRAMEWORK

Aharon Tziner
Université de Montréal
and
Elchanan I. Meir
Tel-Aviv University

The concept of person–environment (P–E) fit has received ample attention in the literature in the context of work attitudes and work behavior (Edwards, 1991; Edwards & van Harrison, 1993; Tziner, 1990). This fit is based on the interaction between an individual's work-related characteristics and the attributes of the work environment in which the person functions. The central proposition is that fit enhances manifestations of well adjustment or well-being at work (e.g. high performance, organizational commitment), whereas misfit serves as a major cause of negative outcomes (e.g. absenteeism, dissatisfaction).

A close perusal of the P–E fit literature in the work context reveals that although both subscribing to the same proposition noted above, two major theories have emerged in an attempt to explain how and why various attitudinal and behavioral outcomes result from fit/misfit. These are: (i) The Theory of Work Adjustment (Dawis & Lofquist, 1984), where fit/misfit is referred to as correspondence/discorrespondence; and (ii) Holland's (1973, 1985) Congruence Theory, where fit/misfit is termed congruence/lack of congruence or incongruence.

We shall first offer a review of each of these theories, with suggested amendment judged necessary. Subsequently, we shall attempt to incorporate both into a single theoretical framework.

International Review of Industrial and Organizational Psychology, 1997 Volume 12
Edited by C.L. Cooper and I.T. Robertson. © 1997 John Wiley & Sons Ltd.

THE THEORY OF WORK ADJUSTMENT (Dawis & Lofquist, 1984)

Correspondence and Work Adjustment

An individual's adjustment to the work milieu has long attracted interest because it is construed as an essential component of effective organization functioning (Cascio, 1991). The theoretical frame that has offered the most compelling explanation of the process leading to this state is the Theory of Work Adjustment (Dawis & Lofquist, 1984).

Central to this theory is the notion of correspondence between the individual and his or her work environment. In the earlier formulation of this theory, correspondence was defined as a 'harmonious relationship between the individual and his environment: suitability of the individual to the environment and of the environment to the individual, and a reciprocal and complementary relationship between the individual and his environment' (Lofquist & Dawis, 1969, p. 45). A basic tenet of this theory is that the individual seeks to achieve, and acts to maintain, such mutual correspondence. Thus, attaining and sustaining work adjustment is a continuous and dynamic process.

Moreover, within the context of work organizations, two types of correspondence must prevail in order for work adjustment to emerge. These are:

Correspondence I: The individual's skills, knowledge, abilities and personality traits must match the requirements of the job, as well as the expectations deriving from the organization's culture and particular structural features (e.g. managerial procedures, communication systems, etc.).

Correspondence II: The job and organizational environment must satisfy the employee's work-related needs. For instance, Bretz, Ash, and Dreher (1989) reported that employees with a high need for achievement tend to be attracted to environments that encourage and reward competitive effort and accomplishments.

Correspondence I has been postulated to lead to satisfactoriness, denoting the degree to which the individual employee meets job requirements and organizational expectations. Correspondence II has been assumed to result in work satisfaction, the extent to which the individual employee experiences fulfillment of his or her work-related needs. Both work satisfaction and satisfactoriness are necessary for the employee to develop work adjustment. Following Dawis & Lofquist (1984), this state is indicated by an employee deliberately choosing to be associated with a particular work organization over alternative employment opportunities (voluntary tenure). However, it should be noted that the decision to maintain a contractual relationship is not the sole prerogative of the employee: the organization also retains those employees whom it considers to possess work qualities appropriate to the task.

This notion has been neatly incorporated into Schneider's (1983, 1987) attraction–selection–attrition conceptual scheme, which clearly demonstrates that forces within the organization operate over time to attract, select and retain those individuals who are the most congruent with the organization's characteristics and expectations. This results in the creation of increasingly homogeneous groups of employees, with respect to background, work abilities and orientation, and work personality.

Several typologies have been presented in the literature to describe the relationship between workers' personality traits and the work conditions conducive to their adjustment to work environment (Correspondence I). For example, Holland (1985) describes individual employees with a realistic type of personality who share certain personality and functional attributes (interests, skills, abilities, traits) and who seek to create a congruent environment (i.e. one that allows them to satisfy their needs and interests).

In the same vein, Friedman & Rosenman (1974) have described the high Type A personality as typically a highly competitive achiever, constantly struggling against time and people, and expressing excessive hostility in response to frustration. Following this paradigm, Burke & Dezca (1982) have posited that a less structured work environment may be perceived by such a person as potentially less coercive, restrictive and frustrating, thus offering better opportunities for personal objectives to be realized. Likewise, Bretz, Ash, & Dreher (1989) have shown that high achievers prefer organizations in which workers are rewarded according to accomplishments, rather than seniority.

While confirming the previous observation, Turban & Keon (1993) have also demonstrated that employees with a high need to achieve are attracted to smaller organizations. They suggest that the relatively small size is perceived as providing more opportunities to be personally responsible for outcomes and to receive personalized feedback and rewards, conditions that are highly compatible to the needs of high achievers.

With respect to the degree of centralization in an organization, Turban & Keon (1993) found that such employees with low self-esteem were more attracted to decentralized structures. In such environments, opportunities for exercising responsibility are likely to be diffused or shared, and the participatory nature of the decision-making process tends to offer increased opportunities for recognition and satisfaction.

Likewise, Tziner & Falbe (1990) have demonstrated that individuals acting in an organizational milieu which they perceived as corresponding to their achievement orientation, exhibited higher levels of performance, work satisfaction and organizational commitment than counterparts, displaying incongruency.

Finally, Bretz & Judge (1994) illustrated empirically that individuals to whom the organizational environment appeared congruent with their organizational preferences reported a higher level of job satisfaction and had a longer tenure with their organizations than individuals experiencing less congruence of this type. Moreover, Bretz and Judge's data confirmed an indirect effect of organizational preferences—organizational environment on certain indicators of career success, such as salary and job level.

At this stage, we can conclude that: (i) Correspondence, in general, is a relationship in which the individual employee and the work organization are mutually responsive; and (ii) work adjustment, the extent to which a worker chooses to stay in his or her present organization (when faced with alternative prospects for employment), is concurrently determined by work satisfaction and satisfactoriness.

It should be noted, however, that both the individual employee and the work organization are constantly changing. Therefore, attainment of work adjustment as a particular point in time does not necessarily ensure its subsequent persistence. Consequently, adjusting to work requires that both the employee and the organization engage in a continuous and active process of mutual readjustment.

Dawis & Lofquist (1984) state that in a search for adjustment, the individual may either attempt to change the organizational environment (i.e. act on the environment) or opt for changing his or her reactions to it. In either case, however, each individual's way of interacting with the organizational environment is determined by his/her personality style. This style denotes a profile, characteristic of each individual, with respect to four distinct dimensions: (i) the degree of quickness in reacting/acting (termed *celerity*); (ii) the level of activity exhibited while reacting/acting (*pace*); (iii) the typical pattern of pace displayed while acting/reacting (*rhythm*); and (iv) the duration of the action/reaction process (*endurance*). If an individual's personality style corresponds to the personality profile required for adequate functioning in a particular organizational environment, then attainment of work adjustment becomes probable. Otherwise, either the individual or the organizational environment must change to avoid strain.

Thus, personality style constitutes an essential component of the personality factor which, along with skills, knowledge and abilities, determines Correspondence I, assuming respective job and organization requirements for these factors are satisfied.

In addition, Dawis & Lofquist (1984) assert that whenever work adjustment is disrupted, for whatever reason, affected individuals do not necessarily undertake the process of readjustment immediately. This is contingent upon a personality trait they term flexibility, meaning the degree of tolerance for discorrespondence with organizational environment before the need to launch some action in order to reduce the discorrespondence and restore work adjustment.

To put it in other words, flexibility denotes the amount of discorrespondence one is able to tolerate before being motivated to do something about it, either by acting on the environment (active adjustment) or by acting on oneself (reactive adjustment). If all attempts to regain adjustment fail, it is predicted that the individual will not remain in the frustrating organizational environment. The extent of persistence in attempting to achieve readjustment before deciding to leave is termed perseverance. This constitutes an additional personality trait conceived as an important factor for forming Correspondence I.

According to Dawis & Lofquist (1984), work adjustment *per se* is unobservable directly; rather it is both the antecedents and the outcomes that are amenable to observation and measurement. Classically, the antecedents are work satisfaction and satisfactoriness, to which we would add, following Saks (1995), organizational commitment and job involvement. The most common behavioral manifestations of the outcomes include absenteeism, voluntary turnover (or voluntary tenure), intentional organizational misbehavior and organizational citizenship behavior.

Antecedents and Outcomes of Work Adjustment

Many definitions of the concept of work satisfaction have been offered over the years (see Locke, 1976). On the whole, work satisfaction is seen as the collection of attitudes held by an individual concerning particular facets of his or her work, including working conditions, organizational policy, recognition, supervision and pay. These attitudes may be more or less favorable, depending on the discrepancy between the individual's work-related needs, desires and expectations and what is actually attainable from a specific job in a particular organizational setting. Stated briefly, work satisfaction is a function of the degree of correspondence between a worker's needs and the need-gratifying capacity of the work setting (Betz, 1969; Porter, 1963).

Reasonably well-established empirical evidence has indicated that work satisfaction with various aspects of work is negatively related to turnover. This trend tends to corroborate the connection between the level of work satisfaction and the voluntary decision to stay in an organization, as predicted by the Theory of Work Adjustment. According to Dawis & Lofquist (1984), this link is mediated by work adjustment.

Several studies have sought to elaborate this link. Hom, Caranikas-Walker, Prussia, & Griffith (1992) contend that work maladjustment is a necessary but insufficient mediating factor to account for work dissatisfaction that results in turnover. They concur with Mobley, Horner, & Hollingsworth (1978) that withdrawal cognitions (thoughts of quitting, the intention to leave the job or seeking another job) would also have to evolve as mediating precursors for turnover to occur.

Gerhart (1990) has stressed the wider contextual framework in which these mediating behaviors manifest themselves. He notes that when slumps in the economy make it hard to find alternative work, dissatisfied employees generally try to hold on to their jobs. Hulin (1991) expressed this notion in more general terms by stating that 'dissatisfaction should lead to organizational turnover only if the dissatisfied individual perceives that there are better alternatives available' (p. 446). Conversely, individuals who very much like their jobs and feel attached to their organizations may still be tempted by prospects of better career advancement elsewhere. Nevertheless, on the whole, the satisfied tend to stay, while the dissatisfied tend to leave (Blau & Boal, 1987).

In addition, workers' commitment to an organization has been found to be an important variable linked to work satisfaction (Cheloha & Farr, 1980; Hom, Katerberg, & Hulin, 1979) and to turnover (Cohern, 1993). Organizational commitment is a psychological state that both characterizes the employee's relationship with the organization and has implications for the decision to continue or discontinue membership in that organization.

Although for some time it has been fashionable for 'organizational commitment' to be treated as a unitary concept, researchers have recently provided increasing empirical evidence of the existence of a three-dimensional structure consisting of: (i) 'affective commitment'; (ii) 'continuance commitment'; and (iii) 'normative/moral commitment' (Allen & Meyer, 1990; Hackett, Bycio, & Hausdorf, 1994; Jaros, Jermier, Koehler, & Sincich, 1993).

Strong affective attachment develops when employees' experiences within an organization are consistent with their goals, values and expectations. A state of continuous commitment develops as employees recognize that they have accumulated investments or benefits that would be lost if they left. Normative/moral commitment emerges as a result of socialization experiences that emphasize the appropriateness of remaining loyal and the receipt of benefits that have created a sense of obligation to reciprocate.

Empirical findings demonstrate that employees with a strong affective commitment voluntarily stay with the organization because they identify with it and therefore *want* to stay; those with a strong continuance commitment stay on because they *need* to; and those with a strong normative/moral commitment because they feel they *ought* to do so.

Sommers (1995) has provided certain empirical evidence in support of the negative links between voluntary turnover and both affective and normative/moral commitment. Given the existing documentation of the relationship between work satisfaction and organizational commitment (Mathieu & Zajac, 1990), we may readily speculate that the relationship between work satisfaction and voluntary stay (tenure) with an organization is also partially accounted for by some of the effective components of organizational commitment.

Another variable repeatedly described as a salient determinant of voluntary turnover, though less so than organizational commitment, is job involvement (Cotton & Tuttle, 1986). Job involvement is defined as the extent to which the individual identifies psychologically with his or her job (Blau, 1985; Kanungo, 1979). This notion has also been causally linked to work satisfaction (Kanungo, 1982), which would lead us to believe that it may also be responsible in part for turnover.

The relationship of both organizational commitment and job involvement to work satisfaction should not come as a surprise. Organizational commitment draws on the belief that the organization can aid individuals in meeting some of their existence needs (Alderfer, 1969), while job involvement draws on the belief that the job has the ability to fulfil growth or psychological needs. In view of this shared frame of reference, it is only natural to assume that work satisfaction is related to both organizational commitment and job involvement. The existence needs underlying continuance commitment correspond to the extrinsic aspects of work satisfaction, while the self-actualization needs gratified by job content correspond to the intrinsic aspects of work satisfaction.

Abundant research has been conducted on the relationships between work satisfaction, absenteeism and turnover (e.g. Mitra, Jenkins, & Gupta, 1992; Mobley, 1982; Price & Mueller, 1986). For example, a meta-analysis performed by Mitra, Jenkins, & Gupta (1992), in which 33 correlations from 17 studies were combined, revealed a corrected mean correlation of 0.33 between absenteeism and turnover. Similarly, it has been demonstrated that work satisfaction affects turnover. Three additional meta-analyses (Hackett & Guion, 1985; McShane, 1985; Scott & Taylor, 1985) provide reasonable support to the employee absenteeism—work satisfaction relationship (i.e. an estimated coefficient of correlation slightly exceeding 0.20).

In his synthesis of previously published studies, Hackett (1989) uncovered a fairly substantial correlation between absenteeism and job involvement ($r = 0.36$) and a much weaker association of absenteeism with organizational commitment ($r = 0.12$). These findings led him to conclude that the intrinsically motivating aspects of the work itself (as reflected by job involvement) appear to have a stronger effect on absenteeism. We suggest this correlation be regarded with caution, since Hackett (1989) used an *overall* measure of organizational commitment, rather than investigating the possible differential patterns of the relationship between absenteeism and each of the three distinct facets of this variable, as described above, namely, affective, continuance and normative/moral commitment.

These findings clearly indicate that, beyond the singular concept of work satisfaction prescribed by the Theory of Work Adjustment, there is an entire gamut of work-related attitudes—work satisfaction, job involvement and organizational commitment—that underlie a spectrum of withdrawal behaviors, most notably, absenteeism and turnover.

So far we have dwelled upon one of the backbones of the Theory of Work Adjustment.

| Correspondence II | → work satisfaction (and additional work-related attitudes, e.g. job involvement, organizational commitment) | → work adjustment/ maladjustment | → voluntary tenure with the organization, absenteeism, or voluntary turnover |

We would now like to turn to its second conceptual component, namely:

Correspondence I   → satisfactoriness   → work   → voluntary tenure
                                           adjustment/   with the
                                           maladjustment   organization or
                                                                  voluntary/
                                                                  involuntary
                                                                  turnover

Satisfactoriness, we will recall, concerns the extent to which the organization is satisfied with the performance of the employee. The Theory of Work
Adjustment suggests that a high level of satisfactoriness is conducive to work
adjustment, the outcome of which will be voluntary tenure with the organization. Conversely, a low level of satisfactoriness engenders work maladjustment
and consequent voluntary or involuntary turnover.

Bycio, Hackett, & Alvares (1990) conducted a review of empirical findings
that indicated that a very strong relationship exists between performance and
involuntary turnover ($r = -0.51$, $r = -0.52$, in two separate studies) and between performance and voluntary turnover ($r = -0.31$, $r = -0.26$, again in two
separate studies). Additional data in Bycio, Hackett, & Alvares' (1990) investigation supports the proposition that work satisfaction and satisfactoriness
(i.e. performance) interlink with one another (mean coefficient of correlation r
$= 0.25$).

Parenthetically, Bycio, Hackett, & Alvares (1990) also supported a strong association of performance with organizational commitment (mean $r = -0.36$). Similar
findings emerged from Brett, Cron & Slocum's (1995) investigation, whose
unique contribution was to delineate a new variable, the 'extent of economic
dependency on work', which was found to moderate the relationship of both
performance—work satisfaction and performance–organizational commitment.

A different avenue of investigation was pursued by Williams & Livingstone
(1994), who revealed that productive professors were more likely to leave than
less productive professors because they could obtain sizable increases in pay
by moving on. However, untenured poorly performing professors were also
more likely to leave, this time because they realized that they would not be
granted tenure.

On the basis of these findings, the following propositions, emanating from
the Theory of Work Adjustment, seem to be tenable: (i) the probability that
individuals will be forced out of their work environment is inversely related to
satisfactoriness; and (ii) the probability that individuals will leave their work
environment inversely related to work satisfaction.

Two other possible outcomes, which appear to be located at opposite poles
of the same continuum, are organizational intentional misbehavior and organizational citizenship behavior.

Organizational intentional misbehavior is defined as any intentional action
by members of the organization which defies and violates shared organizational norms or expectations, and core societal values, mores or standards of
proper conduct (Vardi & Wiener, 1992). According to Robinson & Bennett's

(1995) typology, organizational misbehaviors consist of such elements as sabotage, lying about hours worked, verbal abuse, stealing from co-workers or the company, intentionally working slowly and wasting resources. Organizational citizenship behavior designates behavior above and beyond the call of duty, behavior essential for organizational effectiveness that goes beyond role prescriptions (Smith, Organ, & Near, 1983).

Drawing on social exchange theory (Blau, 1964; Gouldner, 1960), we can posit that when employees experience fulfillment of their work-related needs (work satisfaction) they will eventually sense a desire to reciprocate. Organ (1988) suggests that one likely avenue for employee reciprocation is organizational citizenship behavior. As indicated, this syndrome is detectable when employees engage in innovative and spontaneous activities that are discretionary, and consequently unrewarded, in the context of the organization's reward system.

Organizational intentional misbehavior, in contrast, is likely to be instigated when employees perceive their work-related needs as being strained and their values as discordant with those propounded by the organization. What this describes, in effect, is a state of intense work dissatisfaction resulting from a low level or blatant lack of Correspondence I.

Finally, ample evidence has been produced over the years of the negative effects of work maladjustment on the individual. These include psychological manifestations (e.g. burnout, depression), psychological disorders (e.g. elevated blood pressure, high level of cholesterol) and behavioral strains (e.g. excessive drinking, smoking) owing either to discorrespondence between work ability requirement and the employees' actual work-related competence (Discorrespondence I), or to the discorrespondence between work-related interests/needs and organizational/occupational commensurate rewards (Discorrespondence II) (Blau, 1981; French & Caplan, 1972; Meir & Melamed, 1986; Smith & Tziner, 1995; Tziner, 1990). Further discussion of this issue, along with a model of the process involved in linking strains with the two types of discorrespondence, can be found in Tziner & Dawis (1988). Several of this model's predictions were recently investigated and corroborated by Sutherland, Fogarty, & Pithers (1995).

In light of these findings, it seems appropriate to suggest that the Theory of Work Adjustment be amended to incorporate the antecedents and outcomes of work adjustment elaborated upon here. Figure 3.1 depicts the interrelationships of the components in such an extended theory.

HOLLAND'S CONGRUENCE THEORY (1973, 1985)

Congruence and Well-being

An alternative conceptualization of individual–work environment correspondence is offered by Holland (1973, 1985). Using the notion of congruence

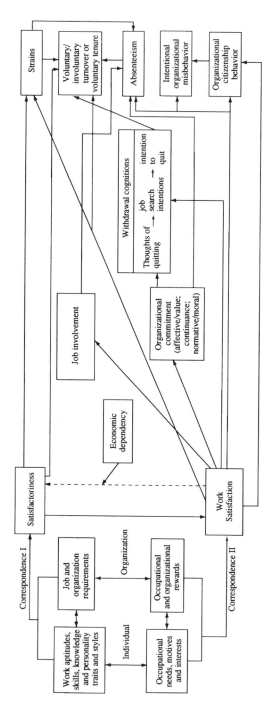

Figure 3.1   The interrelationships of the components of the extended theory of Work Adjustment

rather than correspondence, Holland claims that, in general, congruent person–environment interactions, in contrast to incongruent interactions, are conducive to well-being in the workplace, as indicated by satisfaction, stability and achievements.

Thus, according to Holland (1985), people flourish in an environment which fits their type. In his words: 'Different types require different environments. For instance, Realistic types flourish in Realistic environments because such an environment provided the opportunities and rewards a Realistic type needs' (p. 5). The fit between personality type and environment type is labeled congruence. Conceptually, it is possible to distinguish between two types of congruence, namely: (i) environmental congruence—the fit between personality type and environmental type; and (ii) occupational congruence—the fit between vocational interests and the requirement of an occupation.

It is worth noting that empirical investigations of the veracity of Holland's Congruence Theory have focused largely on satisfaction as an indicator of well-being. Thus, the following review of the findings, as well as the subsequent suggested interpretations, primarily invoke satisfaction as the indicator of well-being.

The overall question that must be addressed is: Why are congruence and work satisfaction related? The answer will have to be compatible with the variance among the established findings on the relationship between these two factors as well as with the fact that the correlations between congruence and either stability or achievements have consistently been found to be very low.

Meta-analyses by Assouline and Meir (1987) and by Tranberg, Slane, & Ekeberg (1993), reviews by Spokane (1985) and Edwards (1991) and the annotated bibliography by Holland and Gottfredson (1990) all cover studies of both environmental and occupational congruences. In the following elaboration of the relationship between congruence and satisfaction, however, a distinction is made between these two types of congruence.

Environmental Congruence

The explanation of the relationship between environmental congruence and satisfaction is based on Holland and Gottfredson (1976), Meir (1989), and Meir and Yaari (1988). In terms of the learning theory, '. . . the individual receives positive reinforcements from his/her environment for congruent behavior, and negative reinforcements for incongruent behavior. The positive reinforcements give rise to satisfaction and further congruent behavior, as well as the desire to remain in the environment. . . . Where the environment is important to the individual, such reinforcements cannot be disregarded' (Meir, 1989, pp. 226–227).

Empirically, in order to examine the level of an individual's environmental congruence, it is necessary to: (i) test the personality type of all the people in the environment; (ii) define the environmental type by finding the specific type with the highest frequency; and (iii) compare the individual's type with that of the environmental. Since the measurement of all people in a given environment is generally an unwieldy task, most studies either make do with experts' judgements as to environmental type (as the comparative basis for assigning individual congruence scores) or rely on the measurement of available respondents.

In the breakdown of correlations in Assouline and Meir's (1987) meta-analysis, it was found that the mean correlation between 'congruence with the others in one's environment' (environment congruence) and satisfaction was 0.29 (20 correlations, total n = 995, 95% confidence interval between 0.20 and 0.38). The overall mean correlation between congruence (all kinds) and satisfaction was found to be only 0.21 (53 correlations, total n = 9041, 95% confidence interval between –0.09 and 0.51). Thus, environmental congruence seems to correlate more highly with satisfaction than does occupational congruence. In light of these findings, Meir, Hadas, & Noyfeld (in press) suggest that 'a person can more easily disregard the incongruent reinforcements in his or her occupation (e.g. by compensating through avocational activity) than in his or her social environment'.

Occupational Congruence

A review of several definitions may be helpful in understanding the occupational congruence—satisfaction relationship. Within the work context, Shartle (1956) defines 'position' as a set of tasks that a single worker has to fulfill in his or her work, 'job' as the set of similar positions in a given organization, and 'occupation' as the group of similar jobs in different organizations. Thus, every worker has to perform a number of tasks with this number varying from one position to another. Lower level positions usually involve only a few tasks, in some cases only one (e.g. gathering, selecting or packing of fruit or industrial products). Generally, the higher the position, the greater the number of tasks to be performed. For example, a university rector or city mayor may have to carry out as many as 50 tasks.

We may speak of an individual's degree of satisfaction in a particular occupation as the extent to which the tasks involved make demands on the worker's time, unique skills and training. Thus, violinists will probably feel more satisfied if the greater proportion of their time and effort is devoted to playing the violin (on which, among other considerations, their reputation rests), as opposed to spending an inordinate amount of time on the administrative side of handling the orchestra.

The organizational tasks that characterize high-level jobs tend to force the individual either to develop some interest in those specific decision-making and instruction-giving aspects or to face the prospect of burnout and its inevitable negative consequences on satisfaction, stability and achievement. This burden of tasks that deflects from the optimization of professional skills goes a long way in explaining the phenomenon of top managers who are unhappy with their jobs, despite high salaries and status.

In lower level occupations, the character of the tasks is simple: the training is on-the-job, no higher education is required, the work is monotonous and repetitive, and the status and income of the worker are low. Moreover, the abilities and education of the majority of the workers on the lower level are limited, so that promotion is inhibited. However, their abilities and education are generally congruent with task requirements, so that satisfaction may well emerge and few incentives will be necessary to keep them in their jobs. Conversely, workers whose potential abilities and education exceed their task requirements and who find few outlets for self-accomplishment or skill utilization are unlikely to perceive the job as a source of satisfaction. Such people will be more prone to the benefits of extrinsic reinforcements, such as income, security and status, if they are to be retained at work.

Lack of satisfaction does not necessarily result in one's leaving the position. There might be sufficient extrinsic gratifications which justify the decision not to leave. The unsatisfied worker may also remain in a job because of lack of initiative to move to another job, lack of self-confidence, real or assumed loss of fringe benefits, instrumental commitment, lack of alternative job openings, and so on. Yet, as long as the unsatisfied worker stays put, the lack of occupational satisfaction will be reflected in his or her motivation and performance.

The basic conditions of equivalent occupations across different organizations are generally such that shifts between organizations without real change in work conditions are rare. If, however, a job in any other organization is perceived as more compatible to the workers' set of task preferences—e.g. a disliked task is less required; a favored task is more salient—a change of workplace can be expected.

For example, a full professor with tenure might move to a different university because in the new workplace less emphasis is placed on teaching undergraduates. We could thus assert that in the former university there was insufficient organizational or value congruence in teaching undergraduates.

A further illustration may be found in a study on bank tellers (Meir & Navon, 1992), in which a distinction was made between Conventional-Social and Conventional–Enterprising bank branches. Here the degree of congruence between personality type and bank type was found to be related both to the tellers' satisfaction and to their supervisors' evaluations.

The concept of 'satisfaction' is, in fact, a construct combining various aspects of satisfaction. It seems logical to suppose that these are positively interrelated within a person, as well as between people. In other words, a matrix of all positive correlations among many aspects of satisfaction can be assumed to exist. The true satisfaction score of an individual is thus the personal weighted sum of these various aspects, while the same individual's empirical satisfaction score may vary along with the salience of each aspect in particular. For example, the salience of satisfaction with the probability of being promoted is likely to change with the information that one's colleague was promoted.

Occupational (or job) satisfaction is also a more specific term which expresses a variety of feelings. It consists of a momentary good feeling, as well as a general positive estimate of the opportunities to continue to have such a good feeling without expectations of frustrations. One of the empirical measures of occupational satisfaction is the worker's evaluation of the extent of opportunities for the tasks involved in the occupation to fit his or her specific skills and task preferences, in comparison to the estimate of such opportunities in a different occupation. Similarly, job satisfaction can be assessed in part by a comparison of the extent of good feeling the worker would have in the current occupation, but in a different organization. Other measures include satisfaction with work conditions, salary, status, work values and perception of promotion possibilities.

It thus emerges that satisfaction is not constant. It varies along the time dimension because of the alterations in such varied aspects of the job as tasks or technology, perceived promotional options and burnout. This variation in satisfaction across time is true both for the general meaning of the term and for the more specific aspects of occupational satisfaction described above. Considering this degree of variation in the concept of satisfaction, we can see that it is impossible to define a single measure which could predict any specific kind of satisfaction in a correlation beyond the stability of satisfaction itself as a measure (notwithstanding the problem of error effect, as in any measuring process).

In sum, it can be said that occupational satisfaction in the workplace depends on the level of fit between the tasks an individual has to perform in his or her occupation and his or her particular skills and preferences. The level of fit is the plateau for the relation between congruence and satisfaction, and in empirical measurements this plateau is a limen which cannot be reached. This idea was behind Spokane's (1985) reference to the '0.30 magic correlational plateau' (p. 335) between congruence and satisfaction. This may well help us to understand why the mean congruence–satisfaction correlation in the meta-analysis reported by Assouline and Meir (1987) was only 0.21 and why Tranberg, Slane, & Ekeberg (1993) found the mean to be only 0.20.

For some people, occupational choice is virtually accidental (a chance meeting, a personal offer by an employer, the continuation of a temporary position), while for others this choice is the outcome of careful consideration of the options.

What advantage holds for those whose occupational choice follows a thorough survey of options and comparison of alternatives? It goes without saying that such a survey raises the probability of congruence between one's particular skills and preferred activities and the eventual occupational choice. In other words, the mean level of such measures as satisfaction, stability and achievements of those who entered their occupations through a process of reasoned occupational choice can be expected to be higher than that displayed by workers whose choice of job followed a more random or fortuitous process.

As we have noted, the mean correlations found between congruence and satisfaction are low; only about 0.20 (Assouline & Meir, 1987; Tranberg, Slane, & Ekebert, 1993). The variance between the results in the various studies seems to depend on the 'group importance' variable found by Meir, Keinan, & Segal (1986) to correlate 0.77 (rank order) with the correlation between congruence and satisfaction. Their explanation was that if the group is important to the individual, the reinforcements given by the group members for congruent or incongruent behavior produce a meaningful positive or negative impact, respectively, on the worker.

It could be argued that the correlation between congruence and satisfaction is so very low that perhaps it cannot even serve as a worthwhile goal, with or without a counsellor's help. We feel this to be an incorrect conclusion. Besides the high value which we recommend be placed on this critical objective, it is pertinent to note that even if the correlation is low, differences in satisfaction may be significant.

This important finding has been demonstrated by Meir (1995). By transforming the correlation coefficient to Binomial Effect Size Display (BESD), (Rosenthal, 1990), the superficially low 0.21 correlation found in the meta-analysis of Assouline and Meir (1987) actually showed that 'the ratio of satisfied people among those who made congruent occupational choices compared to those whose choices were incongruent was 60.4: 39.6.' (p. 343).

CONCLUSIONS

At this point the reader might well ask: To what extent are the Theory of Work Adjustment and Holland's Congruence Theory similar or different, and are they compatible?

According to the Theory of Work Adjustment (i) employee abilities, knowledge, skills and personality traits *must correspond* (Correspondence I) to work (job and organization) requirements and expectations: and (ii) employee desires (needs, interests) *must correspond* (Correspondence II) to the work (job and organization) gratifications available to fulfill these desires. These two kinds of correspondence are conceived as prerequisites for work adjustment.

The Congruence Theory deems both (i) *occupational congruence* (correspondence between employee work-related interests and work supplies available to meet them) and (ii) *environmental congruence* (correspondence of employee personality and the dominant personality type in the work milieu) as essential preconditions for attaining well-being.

It is thus obvious that *occupational congruence* concords perfectly with Correspondence II, particularly if we extend occupation to incorporate the organizational milieu wherein the work is performed. *Environmental congruence,* however, accounts only partially for the domain subsumed by Correspondence I, namely, personality traits or attributes.

Consequently, if we extend Holland's theory to encompass a variety of congruencies—for example (i) between attitudes, beliefs or values concerning modes of conduct on the one hand, and prevailing organizational norms and values in the relevant organizational milieu on the other; or (ii) between the employee's abilities, skills or knowledge on the one hand and work requirements on the other—we wind up forging a theoretical framework that is coherent with the Theory of Work Adjustment, in so far as the factors of congruence and correspondence are concerned.

It is worth noting also, that Hesketh (1995) compared a model of early career development by Feij, Whitely, Piero, & Taris (1995) with concepts deriving from the Theory of Work Adjustment in order to show that the latter offers a broader theoretical framework than the former approach, whereas the former provides ways for improving conceptualization and measurement of the Theory of Work Adjustment. Similarly, we feel that the incorporation of Holland's Theory into the Theory of Work Adjustment can make a valuable contribution to better conceptualizing and measuring the personality traits and correspondent required traits of organizational personality in the latter theory.

Additionally, as we have noted, the degree of well-being at work may be reflected in outcomes that extend beyond work satisfaction, such as absenteeism, physiological strains, voluntary tenure and organizational citizenship. Thus, the construct of well-being at work may incorporate the same indicators as the outcomes of work adjustment. In this amended form, Holland's Theory of Congruence becomes consistent with, and could in fact be integrated into, the Theory of Work Adjustment.

In conclusion, a conceptual theoretical groundwork has been laid here for a clearer understanding of the nature of work adjustment and for the means to better predict and foster this state. It remains to submit this amended Work Adjustment Theory to a thorough confirmatory empirical investigation.

Moreover, note should also be taken of the most recent findings that have examined the possible effects of non-work factors, such as life satisfaction (Judge & Waternabe, 1993), on well-being in the workplace. These should certainly be incorporated into any future investigations.

Finally, the reader will have noticed the absence herein of any discussion of the issue of correspondence (fit) operationalization. This deliberate exclusion was the result of our decision to devote this chapter to the conceptual and theoretical aspects of congruence, while integrating two dominant theories: the Theory of Work Adjustment and Holland's Congruence Theory. The issue of operationalizing congruence and the associated methodological problems is sufficiently important, and vast in scope, to merit a separate discussion, as is indeed the case in Edwards (1991) and in Hesketh & Gardner (1993). We believe that by reference to these two illuminating papers, along with the current chapter, the reader may be rewarded with a full and exhaustive treatment of both the theoretical and the practical aspects of work adjustment.

AUTHORS' NOTE

We gratefully acknowledge the SSHRC research grant (to the first author) which made it possible to prepare this chapter.

When this chapter was written, the first author was visiting with the School of Business Administration, Bar-Ilan University.

REFERENCES

Alderfer, C. P. (1969) A new theory of human needs. *Organizational Behavior and Human Performance*, **4**, 142–175.

Allen, N. J. & Meyer, J. P. (1990) The measurement and antecedents of affective continuance and normative commitment to the organization. *Journal of Occupational Psychology*, **63**, 1–18.

Assouline, M. & Meir, E. I. (1987) Meta-analysis of the relationship between congruence and well-being measures. *Journal of Vocational Behavior*, **31**, 319–332.

Betz, E. (1969) Need-reinforcer correspondence as a predictor of job satisfaction. *Personnel and Guidance Journal*, **47**, 878–883.

Blau, G. (1981) An empirical investigation of job stress, social support, service length, and job strain. *Organizational Behavior and Human Performance*, **27**, 279–302.

Blau, G. J. (1985) A multiple study investigation of the dimensionality of job involvement. *Journal of Vocational Behavior*, **27**, 19–36.

Blau, G. J. & Boal, K. B. (1987) Conceptualizing how job involvement and organizational commitment affect turnover and absenteeism. *Academy of Management Review*, **38**, 261–271.

Blau, P. (1964) *Exchange and Power in Social Life*. New York: Wiley.

Brett, J. F., Cron, W. L., & Slocum, J. W. (1995) Economic dependency on work: A moderator of the relationship between organizational commitment and performance. *Academy of Management Journal*, **38**, 261–271.

Bretz, R. D. Jr, Ash, R. A., & Dreher, G. F. (1989) Do people make the place? An examination of the attraction – selection – attrition hypothesis. *Personnel Psychology*, **42**, 561–581.

Bretz, R. D. Jr & Judge, T. A. (1994) Person–organization fit and the theory of work adjustment: Implications for satisfaction, tenure and career success. *Journal of Vocational Behavior*, **44**, 32–54.

Burke, R. J. & Dezca, E. (1982) Preferred organizational climates of type A individuals. *Journal of Vocational Behavior*, **21**, 50–59.

Bycio, P., Hackett, R. D., & Alvares, K. M. (1990) Job performance and turnover: A review and meta-analysis. *Applied Psychology: An International Review*, **39**, 47–76.

Cascio, W. F. (1991) *Managing Human Resources: Productivity, Quality of Work Life, Profits* 3rd edn. New York: McGraw-Hill.

Cheloha, R. & Farr, J. (1980) Absenteeism, job involvement, and job satisfaction in an organizational setting. *Journal of Applied Psychology*, **65**, 467–473.

Cohen, A. (1993) Organizational commitment and turnover. *Academy of Management Journal*, **36**, 1140–1157.

Cotton, J. L. & Tuttle, J. M. (1986) Employee turnover: A meta-analysis and review with implications for research. *Academy of Management Review*, 11, 55–70.

Dawis, R. V. & Lofquist, L. H. (1984) A Psychological Theory of Work Adjustment. Minneapolis: University of Minnesota Press.

Edwards, J. R. (1991) Person–job fit: A conceptual integration, literature review, and methodological critique. In C. L. Cooper and I. T. Robertson (eds), *International Review of Industrial and Organizational Psychology*, Vol. 6 (pp. 283–357). Chichester: Wiley.

Edwards, J. R. & van Harrison, R. (1993) Job demands and worker health: Three-dimensional reexamination of the relationship between person–environment fit and strain. *Journal of Applied Psychology*, 78, 628–648.

Feij, J. A., Whitely, W. T., Peiro, J. M., & Taris, T. W. (1995) The development of career enhancing strategies and content innovation: A longitudinal study of recruits. *Journal of Vocational Behavior*, 46, 231–256.

French, J. R. P. Jr & Caplan, R. D. (1972) Organizational stress and individual strain. In A. J. Marrow (ed.), *The Failure of Success* (pp. 30–66). New York: Amacon.

Friedman, M. & Rosenman, R. H. (1974) Job stress and employee behavior. *Organizational Behavior and Human Performance*, 23, 372–387.

Gerhart, B. (1990) Voluntary turnover and alternative job opportunities. *Journal of Applied Psychology*, 75, 467–476.

Gouldner, A. W. (1960) The norm of reciprocity. *American Sociological Review*, 25, 165–167.

Hackett, R. D. (1989) Work attitudes and employee absenteeism: A synthesis of the literature. *Journal of Occupational Psychology*, 62, 235–248.

Hackett, R. D., Bycio, P. & Hausdorf, P. A. (1994) Further assessments of Meyer and Allen's (1991) three-component model of organizational commitment. *Journal of Applied Psychology*, 79, 15–23.

Hackett, R. D. & Guion, R. M. (1985) A reevaluation of the absenteeism–job satisfaction relationship. *Organizational Behavior and Human Decision Processes*, 35, 165–167.

Hesketh, B. (1995) Personality and adjustment styles: A theory of work adjustment approach to career enhancing strategies. *Journal of Vocational Behavior*, 46, 274–282.

Hesketh, B. & Gardner, D. (1993) Person–environment fit models: A reconceptualization and empirical test. *Journal of Vocational Behavior*, 35, 315–442.

Holland, J. L. (1973) *Making Vocational Choices: A Theory of Careers*. Englewood Cliffs, NJ: Prentice-Hall.

Holland, J. L. (1985) *Making Vocational Choices: A Theory of Vocational Personalities and Work Environment*. Englewood Cliffs, NJ: Prentice-Hall.

Holland, J. L. & Gottfredson, G. D. (1976) Using a typology of persons and environments to explain careers: Some extensions and clarifications. *The Counseling Psychologist*, 6, 20–29.

Holland, J. L. & Gottfredson, G. D. (1990, August) *An annotated bibliography for Holland's theory of vocational personalities and work environments*. Paper presented at the annual meeting of the American Psychological Association. Boston, MA.

Hom, P. W., Caranikas-Walker, Prussia, G. E., & Griffith, R. W. (1992) A meta-analytical structural equations analysis of a model of employee turnover. *Journal of Applied Psychology*, 77, 890–909.

Hom, P. W., Katerberg, R. & Hulin, C. R. (1979) Comparative examination of three approaches to the prediction of turnover. *Journal of Applied Psychology*, 64, 280–290.

Hulin, C. (1991) Adaptation, persistence and commitment in organizations. In M. D. Dunnette and L. M. Hough (eds), *Handbook of Industrial and Organizational Psychology*, 2nd edn, Vol. 2 (pp. 445–505). Palo Alto, CA: Consulting Psychologists Press.

Jaros, S. J., Jermier, J. M., Koehler, J. W. & Sincich, T. (1993) Effects of continuance, affective and moral commitment on the withdrawal process: An evaluation of eight structural equation models. *Academy of Management Journal*, 36, 951–995.

Judge, T. A. & Watanabe, S. (1993) Another look at the job satisfaction–life satisfaction relationship. *Journal of Applied Psychology*, **78**, 939–948.

Kanungo, R. N. (1979) The concepts of alienation and involvement revisited. *Psychological Bulletin*, **86**, 119–138.

Kanungo, R. N. (1982) *Work Alienation*. New York: Praeger.

Locke, E. A. (1976) The nature and the causes of job satisfaction. In M. D. Dunnette (ed.), *Handbook of Industrial and Organization Psychology*. Chicago: Rand McNally.

Lofquist, L. H. & Dawis, R. V. (1969) *Adjustment to Work*. Minneapolis: University of Minnesota.

Mathieu, J. E. & Zajac, D. M. (1990) A review and meta-analysis of antecedents, correlates and consequences of organizational commitment. *Psychological Bulletin*, **108**, 171–194.

McShane, S. L. (1985) Job satisfaction and absenteeism: A meta-analytic reexamination. *Canadian Journal of Administrative Sciences*, **2**, 68–77.

Meir, E. I. (1989) Integrative elaboration of the congruence theory. *Journal of Vocational Behavior*, **35**, 219–230.

Meir, E. I. (1995) Elaboration of the relation between interest congruence and satisfaction. *Journal of Career Assessment*, **3**, 341–346.

Meir, E. I., Hadas, C. & Noyfeld, M. (in press) Person–environment fit in small military units. *Journal of Career Assessment*.

Meir, E. I., Keinan, & Segal Z. (1986) Group importance as a mediator between personality–environment congruence and satisfaction. *Journal of Vocational Behavior*, **28**, 60–69.

Meir, E. I. & Melamed, S. (1986) The accumulation of person–environment congruences and well-being. *Journal of Occupational Behavior*, **7**, 315–323.

Meir, E. I. & Navon, M. (1992) A longitudinal examination of congruence hypotheses. *Journal of Vocational Behavior*, **41**, 35–47.

Meir, E. I. & Yaari, Y. (1988) The relation between congruent specialty choice within occupations and satisfaction. *Journal of Vocational Behavior*, **33**, 99–112.

Mitra, A., Jenkins, D. G., & Gupta, N. (1992) A meta-analytic review of the relationship between absence and turnover. *Journal of Applied Psychology*, **77**, 879–889.

Mobley, W. H. (1982) *Employee Turnover: Causes, Consequences, and Control*. Menlo Park, CA: Addison-Wesley.

Mobley, W. H., Horner, S. O., & Hollingsworth, A. T. (1978) An evaluation of precursors of hospital employee turnover. *Journal of Applied Psychology*, **63**, 408–414.

Organ, D. W. (1988) *Organizational Citizenship Behavior*. Lexington, MA: Lexington.

Porter, L. W. (1963) Job attitudes in management: Perceived importance of needs as a function of job level. *Journal of Applied Psychology*, **47**, 144–148.

Price, J. & Mueller, G. (1986) *Absenteeism and Turnover of Hospital Employees*. Greenwich, CT: JAI Press.

Robinson, S. L. & Bennett, R. J. (1995) A typology of deviant workplace behaviors: A multidimensional scaling study. *Academy of Management Journal*, **38**, 555–572.

Rosenthal, R. (1990) How are we doing in soft psychology? *American Psychologist*, **45**, 775–776.

Saks, M. A. (1995) Longitudinal field investigation of the moderating and mediating effects of self-efficacy on the relationship between training and newcomer adjustment. *Journal of Applied Psychology*, **80**, 211–225.

Schneider, B. (1983) Interactional psychology and organizational behavior. In B. M. Staw and L.L. Cummings (eds), *Research in Organizational Behavior*, Vol. 5 (pp. 1–31). Greenwich, CT: JAI Press.

Schneider, B. (1987) E = F (P, B). The road to a radical approach to person–environment fit. *Journal of Vocational Behavior*, **31**, 353–361.

Scott, K. D. & Taylor, G. S. (1985) An examination of conflicting findings on the relationship between job satisfaction and absenteeism: A meta-analysis. *Academy of Management Journal*, **28**, 588–612.

Shartle, C. L. (1956) *Occupational Information*. New York: Prentice-Hall.

Smith, C. A., Organ, D. W., & Near, J. P. (1983) Organizational citizenship behavior: Its nature and antecedents. *Journal of Applied Psychology*, **68**, 653–663.

Smith, D. & Tziner, A. (1995) The moderating effects of affective disposition and social support on the relationship between person–environment fit and strains: An empirical investigation on nurses. Unpublished manuscript. Université de Montréal.

Sommers, M. J. (1995) Organizational commitment, turnover and absenteeism: An examination of direct and indirect effects. *Journal of Organizational Behavior*, **16**, 49–58.

Spokane, A. R. (1985) A review of research on person–environment congruence in Holland's theory of careers. *Journal of Vocational Behavior*, **26**, 306–343.

Sutherland, L. F., Fogarty, G. J. & Pithers, R. T. (1995) Congruence as a predictor of occupational stress. *Journal of Vocational Behavior*, **46**, 292–309.

Tranberg, M., Slane, S., & Ekeberg, S. E. (1993) The relation between interest congruence and satisfaction: A meta-analysis. *Journal of Vocational Behavior*, **42**, 253–264.

Turban, D. B. & Keon, T. L. (1993) Organizational attractiveness: An interactionist perspective. *Journal of Applied Psychology*, **78**, 184–193.

Tziner, A. (1990) *Organizational Staffing and Work Adjustment*. New York: Praeger.

Tziner, A., & Dawis, R. (1988) Occupational stress: A theoretical look from the perspective of work adjustment theory. *International Journal of Management*, **5**, 423–430.

Tziner, A. & Falbe, C. M. (1990) Actual and preferred climates of achievement orientation and their relationships to work attitudes and performance in two occupational strata. *Journal of Organizational Behavior*, **11**, 159–167.

Vardi, Y. & Wiener, Y. (1992) *Organizational misbehavior (OMB): A calculative-normative model*. Paper presented at the annual meeting of the Academy of Management, Las Vegas.

Williams, C. R. & Livingstone, L. P. (1994) Another look at the relationship between performance and voluntary turnover. *Academy of Management Journal*, **37**, 269–298.

Chapter 4

CONTEMPORARY RESEARCH ON ABSENCE FROM WORK: CORRELATES, CAUSES AND CONSEQUENCES

Gary Johns
Concordia University

The purpose of this chapter is to review the research literature on absence from work that has been published in the last 15 years or so. The review is meant to be fairly comprehensive in that it spans various correlates, causes, consequences, theoretical perspectives, and research methods used to study absenteeism. However, due to space limitations, it does not cover interventions used to manage attendance. This will be the subject of another paper.

The time span of 15 years is not arbitrary. Rather, it reflects the fact that it has been a good while since a more comprehensive review of this subject has been attempted. Earlier reviews include those by Porter and Steers (1973) and Muchinsky (1977). Subsequent reviews have been selective, focusing on particular theories or models of attendance (Brooke, 1986; Chadwick-Jones, Nicholson, & Brown, 1982; Mowday, Porter, & Steers, 1982; Steers & Rhodes, 1978), demographic correlates of absence (Nicholson, Brown, & Chadwick-Jones, 1977), job satisfaction and absence (Nicholson, Brown, & Chadwick-Jones, 1976), and absence management strategies (Rhodes & Steers, 1990). The reader is directed to these earlier qualitative reviews, all of which provide useful summaries of research in particular areas. In addition, since 1984, a number of meta-analyses have been conducted that provide quantitative summaries of particular correlates of absence. The conclusions of these meta-analyses will form part of the present review.

The chapter is organized around a loose series of informal 'models' that reflect various presumed correlates or causes of absence. In some cases, these models are espoused both by researchers and by lay people.

International Review of Industrial and Organizational Psychology, 1997 Volume 12
Edited by C.L. Cooper and I.T. Robertson. © 1997 John Wiley & Sons Ltd.

PROCESS AND DECISION MODELS

Process and decision models are included in the same section because both attempt to 'decompose' the causes of at least some forms of absence. Process models are more macro models that attempt to integrate a number of causal factors and thus provide some order to the extreme diversity of absence research. Decision models are more micro models that probe the cognitions underlying absence or that attempt to understand how a series of individual absences unfolds. The term *decision* does not always refer to a deliberate act but rather to a set of cognitive or temporal parameters that influence attendance patterns. Both types of models are concerned with *how* absence and attendance occur.

Process Models

Steers and Rhodes (Rhodes & Steers, 1990; Steers & Rhodes, 1984) updated their original process model of absenteeism (Steers & Rhodes, 1978). The initial model contained 24 variables grouped into eight conceptual categories: Personal characteristics, values, job situation, job satisfaction, pressures to attend, attendance motivation, ability to attend, and attendance. Brooke (1986) developed a model that contained 16 variables, although he claimed some advantages in terms of breadth of coverage.

Rhodes and Steers (1990) review five studies that provided mostly partial tests of their model. Each of these tests confirms some aspects of the model and fails to support others. The theorists conclude that 'these studies provide some support for the Steers and Rhodes model as originally proposed' (p. 52). Earlier, Fichman (1984, p. 5) came to a less positive conclusion that the 'model to date has theoretical problems and lacks strong empirical support.' Using self-reported absence data, Brooke and Price (1989) found partial support for Brooke's (1986) model. Hendrix and Spencer (1989) obtained a poor fit between Brooke's model and their data and offered a revised model.

One appreciates the sequencing of variables and the interactions suggested by the process models in comparison to some economic models that consist of one well-stocked regression equation. Nevertheless, process models struggle to represent *breadth* when it is becoming clearer that *depth* is necessary to understand absence. Expecting a complex set of linkages, generally inferred from bivariate associations, to hold up in any given sample is too much to ask. Absence is a low base rate behavior, the occurrence of which is highly constrained by contextual factors. Mid-range models that capture the essence of this point will probably fare better than broad-based process models that serve as useful teaching devices but that are incapable of being confirmed in any given sample or replicated across samples.

Decision Models

Fichman (1988) applied a Cox proportional hazard rate event history model (Cox, 1972) to the absence and attendance spells of coal miners in order to understand how these behaviors unfolded over time. The unit of analysis was an attendance spell, and the hazard rate of going absent was framed as the strength of nonwork motives. Essentially, it is the 'timing of time allocation' that is being studied with this procedure. Fichman found that the hazard rate was affected by the type (voluntary, semi-voluntary, involuntary) of prior and subsequent absence exhibited. In a later study using the same technique, Fichman (1989) found positive duration dependence, the tendency for the hazard rate of absence to increase with the duration of an attendance spell. He contrasted this with lack of support for a random model or a habit model, which would predict negative duration dependence. Harrison and Hulin (1989) also used a Cox model to study the attendance patterns of white-collar employees. These patterns revealed strong temporal effects related to day of the week, month of the year, and number of absences taken previously. Demographic variables which are usually correlated with aggregated absence did not contribute to the model, and the authors surmise that the more basic psychological variables for which they are surrogates were already reflected in the temporal patterns.

Thus far, the event history technique has not captured the imagination of other absence researchers despite its clear advantage of framing absence as a time allocation problem. The extant examples have a rather closed system quality, since the basic data simply consist of attendance patterns. What this line of work needs is some theoretically driven independent variables that are measured repeatedly over a time span that corresponds to the collection of the absence data. Both work and nonwork measures would be very attractive given Fichman's position that this is essentially a problem of motivated time allocation between these two spheres. The following study illustrates a method for accomplishing this.

In a very inventive study, Hackett, Bycio, and Guion (1989) had nurses keep a daily diary in which they rated the occurrence of various potential causes of absence and recorded how much they would have liked to be absent. This idiographic-longitudinal design allows for the examination of decision processes that are common across respondents as well as those are unique to individuals. Hard-to-justify causes were more predictive of desire to be absent than actual absence, and a number of factors predicted absenteeism among the sample as a whole (e.g. tiredness, ill health, home responsibilities, and disrupted sleep). However, the most interesting result was the power of within-person regression analysis to explain the absence behavior of individual nurses, something that was masked by group-level analysis. This finding illustrates precisely what Johns and Nicholson (1982) meant when they argued that absence has different meanings for different people.

Martocchio and Judge (1994) used an experimental design and policy capturing techniques to also examine within-person decisions. Subjects responded to 96 scenarios in which potential causes of absence were systematically manipulated and rated each in terms of likelihood of missing work. Although most reported that they would miss due to illness, there were considerable differences among respondents in the extent to which other causes were expected to provoke absence, including counterintuitive signs. The authors interpreted these results as supporting Johns and Nicholson (1982) concerning the phenomenological uniqueness of absence events. The results regarding individual differences are impressive in light of the potential for experimental demand and social desirability in such a design.

It should be noted that neither of these within-person studies examined interactions among causes. However, a good case can be made that such interactions would uniquely influence decision processes. To extend Nicholson's (1977) examples, it is the concert pianist *with* the broken finger that is likely to be absent, not the pianist or the person with a broken finger.

Finally, Martocchio and Harrison (1993) developed a decision-making theory of absence that draws on the theory of reasoned action (Ajzen & Fishbein, 1980) and the theory of planned behavior (Ajzen, 1991). Key components include attitudes toward attendance, subjective norms favoring attendance, perceived control over one's behavior, and (more recently added by Harrison) perceptions of moral obligation to attend. In general, research shows that intentions to attend (attendance motivation) mediate the relationship between actual attendance and the independent contribution of attitudes toward attendance, norms, and moral obligation, although the importance of these constructs varies sensibly across samples (Harrison, 1995; Harrison & Bell, 1995; Martocchio, 1992). This research is important because it isolates various specific theoretical levers by which attendance might be improved. In particular, research shows that perceived control over obstacles to attendance (self-efficacy) can be enhanced with self-management training (Frayne & Latham, 1987; Latham & Frayne, 1989). It is also important because of its confirmation of social influences on absence, a point to be developed below.

All in all, the decision models seem to hold more promise than the process models. However, tests of decision models have a rather descriptive quality to them. Now that we have some ideas about *how* attendance decisions are made, we need to learn more about *why* they are made. In other words, decision variables need to be positioned as mediators of theoretically or practically relevant independent variables. The other models discussed here suggest some likely candidates.

THE WITHDRAWAL MODEL

The withdrawal model has been a dominant paradigm in absence research. Under this model, absence from work is thought to represent withdrawal from aversive work circumstances. Beyond this, the exact theoretical underpinnings for this model are generally unstated, and could range from operant learning theory (Skinner, 1974) to theories of person–environment fit (Edwards, 1991) or met expectations (Porter & Steers, 1973).

Job Satisfaction

The withdrawal model has most often been examined by correlating measures of job satisfaction with absenteeism. Earlier qualitative reviews of the connection between job satisfaction and absence were not in perfect agreement. For example, Muchinsky (1977) concluded that overall satisfaction and satisfaction with work content were negatively correlated with absenteeism but that other satisfaction facets were not. Reviewing the literature and offering new data from 16 organizations, Nicholson, Brown, and Chadwick-Jones (1976) concluded that 'at best it seems that job satisfaction and absence from work are tenuously related' (p. 734). This conclusion was strongly influenced by the results from their original data, for which they claimed various methodological improvements. Still, noting cross-site differences in associations, they speculated about moderators such as norms, sanctions, and supervisory practices that might influence the absence–satisfaction connection.

Since 1984, there have been at least five meta-analyses of the relationship between job satisfaction and absence from work (Farrell & Stamm, 1988; Hackett, 1989; Hackett & Guion, 1985; McShane, 1984; Scott & Taylor, 1985). A careful examination of the three earliest of these papers reveals a number of differences in sampling, methodology (e.g. reliability corrections made), results, and conclusions drawn. Hackett (1989) provides a succinct summary of these differences, the chief of which was the inclusion of 528 correlation coefficients by Nicholson (1975) in the Hackett and Guion (1985) analysis that were not included by McShane (1984) or Scott and Taylor (1985).

Hackett (1989) reanalyzed his massive data set, with methodological refinements, with and without the Nicholson data. He corrected for unreliability in both absence and satisfaction. In the comprehensive data set, the strongest sample-size–weighted mean correlations were −0.23 between overall satisfaction and time lost and −0.21 between satisfaction with work itself and frequency. The respective figures excluding the Nicholson coefficients were −0.23 and −0.27. Correlations for other facets of satisfaction were generally much lower.

A synthesis of the existing meta-analyses suggests that the following conclusions are fairly well established regarding the connection between job satisfaction and absence:

- Overall satisfaction and satisfaction with the content of the work itself are the best predictors of absenteeism. Correcting for attenuation in both variables, the population estimate for these correlations ranges from the low to the mid 20s.

- Frequency of absence is more highly correlated with job satisfaction than is time lost.
- The potential exists for moderators of the job satisfaction–absence relationship.

Given the proliferation of zero order correlations between satisfaction and absence, there has been relatively little systematic examination of potential moderators. However, gender warrants specific scrutiny. Hackett (1989) found that satisfaction–absenteeism relationships were stronger as the proportion of women in research samples increased. As will be seen below, this corresponds to other evidence that men and women differ substantially in terms of the dynamics of absenteeism.

In concluding this discussion of the relationship between job satisfaction and absenteeism, it should be emphasized that the withdrawal model assumes that the former variable causes the latter. However, in one study (Tharenou, 1993), absenteeism was more likely to influence subsequent job satisfaction than the reverse. This finding, which will be discussed in more detail under *The Consequences of Absenteeism*, is not conducive to the withdrawal model. Thus, not all of the variance in absenteeism that is 'accounted for' by correlation with satisfaction may be indicative of withdrawal.

Organizational Commitment

If job satisfaction reflects attitudes regarding one's immediate work environment, organizational commitment reflects attachment toward the larger organization. Although satisfaction and commitment tend to be positively related, there is much evidence that they are discriminable constructs (e.g. Brooke, Russell, & Price, 1988; Mathieu & Farr, 1991). While there have been fewer studies that correlate commitment with absence, the basic withdrawal paradigm is the same as that for job satisfaction—people will be more likely to withdraw from organizations to which they lack commitment. From the other side of the coin, the Steers and Rhodes (1978) attendance model classified commitment as a pressure to attend work.

There are three extant meta-analyses that summarize the empirical evidence on this hypothesis. Mathieu and Zajac (1990) reported a mean sample-size-weighted correlation corrected for attenuation of 0.10 between commitment and attendance. This estimate was based on 24 samples that used a wide variety of absence measures. They concluded that it was unlikely that this relationship was moderated. Using seven samples, Cohen (1991) found a mean weighted and corrected correlation of −0.11 between commitment and absence. Also, he concluded that career stage, indexed by tenure, moderated this relationship. Specifically, the correlation was −0.08 for samples with a mean tenure of 3 to 8 years and −0.24 for samples with a mean tenure of 9 or more years. However, this conclusion is based on only three and two samples respectively, the latter two including only 231 subjects. Farrell and Stamm (1988) reported a mean corrected correlation of –0.12 between commitment and time lost absence in eleven samples. This figure was substantially higher, –0.23, in six samples that measured frequency of absence. In turn, the frequency estimate was moderated by occupational status, with a correlation of –0.41 for higher status samples and –0.15 for lower status samples.

Trends in these results appear to be the following: In general, the relationship between organizational commitment and absence is very low. However, when frequency of absence is the criterion, the size of the relationship approaches those found for overall and work satisfaction. The moderator analyses by Cohen and by Farrell and Stamm suggest that commitment increases in importance as a correlate of absence as people's engagement with the organizational increases via tenure or elevated position. Indeed, Cohen's (1991) thesis is that concerns with the immediate task environment (including job satisfaction) dominate early career stages and that organizational commitment becomes more important in determining work behavior in later career stages.

Given their vintage, most of the studies reviewed in the meta-analyses would have used the Organizational Commitment Questionnaire (OCQ, Mowday, Steers, & Porter, 1979) or a similar measure. This measure is generally conceded to reflect affective attachment to the organization. However, Meyer and Allen's (1991) three-component conception of commitment argues for two additional bases for attachment, normative commitment and continuance commitment. Under normative commitment, people remain attached to the organization and its goals because of ideology or felt obligation. Under continuance commitment, attachment stems from having few employment alternatives or perceiving the cost of movement as high.

Hypotheses bearing on these three forms of commitment are quite interesting in light of the general withdrawal rubric. Straightforwardly, in the spirit of the three meta-analyses reviewed earlier, affective commitment is expected to be negatively related to absenteeism. Normative commitment, due to a feeling of obligation to the organization, might be expected to stimulate attendance and, importantly, to mitigate the deleterious effects of low job satisfaction. On the other hand, continuance commitment might be expected to *stimulate* absence, especially under conditions of felt inequity (cf. Johns & Nicholson, 1982). Feeling 'locked in' might stimulate reactance (Brehm, 1966), expressed in short episodes of escape, and feeling locked in and badly treated would only exacerbate the withdrawal response.

Thus far, evidence relevant to these hypotheses is sparse. Hackett, Bycio, and Hausdorf (1994) found a negative correlation between commitment and 'culpable' absence for a sample of bus drivers using the Allen and Meyer (1990) measure. However, this relationship did not hold up when age, tenure, and general job satisfaction were controlled. In this study, normative and continuance commitment were uncorrelated with absence, while an abbreviated version of the OCQ demonstrated a consistent negative relationship. Meyer, Allen, and Smith (1993) found that affective and normative commitment to both the organization and the occupation were negatively correlated with self-reported voluntary absence in a sample of registered nurses. Continuance commitment was unrelated to absence. Mayer and Schoorman (1992) found in a sample of financial institution employees that affective but not continuance commitment was negatively related to unexcused time lost. Gellatley (1995) found that affective commitment was negatively related to absence frequency and time lost for a sample of hospital employees. Suggestively, continuance commitment due to a felt sacrifice of quitting was *positively* correlated with frequency of absence. Although this study measured perceptions of organizational fairness, it did not examine the interaction between continuance commitment and fairness to test the 'worst scenario' (locked in, badly treated) hypothesis. In another nursing sample (Somers, 1995), it was found that affective commitment was negatively related to frequency of 'annexed' absences, those tied to a weekend or holiday period. The other two forms of commitment were unrelated to annexed absences or a straight frequency measure. Somers also found that affective commitment and continuance commitment interacted to predict annexed absence. The relationship between affective commitment and absence was strongest when continuance commitment was low. This result is in line with the thesis that attitudes will be most predictive of behavior when constraints against action are low (Johns, 1991). Finally, Randall, Fedor, and Longenecker (1990) found no significant main effects or interaction between the three forms of commitment in predicting a self-reported composite of tendency to avoid being absent or late. However, the OCQ did correlate 0.16 with this measure of 'presence'.

Blau and Boal (1987) presented a theory of how organizational commitment might interact with job involvement to affect absence. It is particularly interesting in its predictions about how different types of absence might derive from various combinations of commitment and involvement. For instance, absence for individuals high on both variables is expected to be centered on medical causes, while that for those low on both variables is expected to be more calculative. For present purposes, however, the more mundane prediction is that the former individuals will exhibit the least volume of absence and the latter will exhibit the greatest. Blau (1986) confirmed this interaction between commitment and involvement for unexcused absence among nurses. However, Mathieu and Kohler (1990a) found a rather different interaction between these two attitudes with regard to absences for 'personal reasons' among bus drivers. Although they also found that absence was lowest among high involvement-high commitment drivers, absence was greatest among those with low commitment and *high* involvement.

In these two studies, the commitment measure was identical (a short form of the OCQ) and the absence measures appear very similar. This suggests the possibility that work context was important. Indeed, Mathieu and Kohler (1990a) speculate that high involvement-low commitment drivers (Blau & Boal's [1987] 'lone wolves') might have been likely to substitute regular attendance with better paid overtime, a practice seen at the transit authority. However, this is surely the calculative response that Blau and Boal predict for low-low employees, not the career enhancing motive that they attribute to lone wolves.

Very occasionally, organizational commitment has been treated as a mediator of other causes of absence. For example, Brooke's (1986) model treated commitment as a mediator of distributive justice, job satisfaction, and job involvement. Brooke and Price (1989) failed to confirm this role, although Hendrix and Spencer (1989) found mediation of satisfaction and involvement. Zaccaro and Collins (1988) measured the attendance of college fraternity members at mandatory meetings. They found that commitment to the fraternity mediated the impact of rank (i.e. holding a leadership position) and perceptions of the fraternity's interaction process on unexcused absence at required meetings. Higher rank and more favorable perceptions were associated with reduced absence via elevated commitment.

Finally, in a very interesting twist on commitment research, Ostroff (1992) found that the organizational commitment of high school teachers, aggregated at the school level, was positively related to student attendance rates. This study controlled for a number of variables (e.g. student to teacher ratio) that might have spuriously produced the association.

Thus far, although the work on commitment suggests some interesting hypotheses regarding absence, it is fair to conclude that the empirical evidence is somewhat disappointing. One can't help having the feeling that researchers need to think much more about the *context* in which various forms of commitment might influence attendance. To take one example, normative commitment might be critical for the attendance of volunteer workers whereas continuance commitment might be irrelevant. In tentative support of this idea, Harrison (995) found that moral obligation was a critical factor in the attendance motivation of volunteer workers at a homeless shelter.

Part of the context of commitment may have to do with the exact bases upon which the various forms of commitment are developed among different employees. Using a social exchange perspective, Eisenberger and colleagues (Eisenberger, Huntington, Hutchison, & Sowa, 1986; Eisenberger, Fasolo, & Davis-LaMastro, 1990) argued that absenteeism is most likely to be low when employees feel that *the organization is committed to them*. In other words, perceived organizational support will make salient a reciprocity norm that stimulates prosocial behavior in the form of attendance. Indeed, in several samples, these authors report negative correlations between perceived organizational support and absenteeism (especially frequency) that are well above those revealed in the literature for organizational commitment. This suggests that it is not commitment *per se* but the *source* of commitment that shapes attendance behavior.

Absence and Other 'Withdrawal' Behaviors

One of the most interesting aspects of the withdrawal model concerns theoretical predictions about how absenteeism might be related to other work behaviors that also could reflect withdrawal. Although lateness, absence, and turnover have been the most commonly linked variables, Hanisch and Hulin (1990) extended the argument to retirement intentions and Wise (1993) to systematic reductions in degree of labour participation, such as working part time.

Rosse and Miller (1984) and Hulin (1991) have explicated several models that have been proposed to account for possible connections among withdrawal behaviors:

- *Independent forms.* The different behaviors have different antecedents, functions, and consequences, and should thus be studied independently.
- *Compensatory forms.* The various withdrawal behaviors serve the same function such that engaging in one decreases the likelihood of using another. Holding job satisfaction constant, withdrawal behaviors should be negatively correlated.
- *Alternate forms.* The various behaviors can substitute for each other under conditions of constraint. If quitting is precluded due to economic conditions, absenteeism may increase.
- *Spillover.* Withdrawal is nonspecific avoidance such that dissatisfaction will result in an increase in all forms, which will be positively correlated.
- *Progression.* People will tend to engage in progressively more salient forms of withdrawal. For instance one might progress from daydreaming to lateness to absence to turnover to early retirement.

These models have a seductively simple appearance. However, they can be quite complicated to test. For example, Rosse and Miller (1984) observe that progression of withdrawal could reflect various causal mechanisms, including objectively worsening conditions, gradual awareness of poor fit, or experimentation with increasingly irreversible behaviors. Hulin (1991) notes that the alternate forms model predicts negative relations between withdrawal behaviors when one alternative is constrained but little relationship under other circumstances.

In order to truly test these models, the functional relationship among several types of withdrawal behaviors would have to be studied over time. In addition, antecedents, consequences, and relevant moderators would have to be examined. In practice, most of the evidence regarding these models comes from cross-sectional correlations among withdrawal behaviors and examination of the extent to which they have similar affective antecedents. Rosse and Miller (1984) provided a detailed review of the evidence on these issues, concluding that absence, lateness, and turnover do tend to be positively correlated and that they do share some common affective antecedents. By far, the clearest evidence here is that for a positive correlation between absenteeism and turn-over. Mitra, Jenkins, and Gupta (1992) reported a mean corrected correlation of 0.33 for 33 such coefficients. This result was unmoderated by type of absence measure. Since turnover does share some job satisfaction antecedents with absence (Mowday, Porter, & Steers, 1982) they concluded support for the progression form of the withdrawal model.

Mitra, Jenkins, and Gupta's (1992) data and logic do support a withdrawal thesis and do appear to rule out the independent forms model and orthodox interpretations of the compensatory and alternate forms models that specify nega-tive relationships. Interestingly, the authors found that absenteeism-turnover cor-relations were highest when national unemployment was low. It is possible that the ready availability of jobs permits withdrawal-prone absentees the opportunity to convert their tendencies into turnover. Alternatively, it is possible that this result is a spurious function of the increased base rates that have been observed for absenteeism (Markham, 1985; Markham & McKee, 1991) and turnover (Carsten & Spector, 1987) under conditions of low unemployment. If so, the results are equally conducive to the spillover and progression models.

Whatever its exact causal mechanism, demonstrating progression requires a transitive chain of events in which an increased rate of variable *a* precedes the occurrence of or an increased rate of variable *b*. There is very little such research. Rosse and Miller (1984) reviewed five studies, three of which showed some evidence of progression from lateness to absence or absence to turnover. Subsequently, several additional studies have appeared. Farrell and Peterson (1984) found that increased absenteeism preceded turnover in small samples of newly hired nurses and accountants. Evidence that this was with-drawal, *per se*, stems from a concomitant decrease in organizational commit-ment. In a sample of newly hired hospital employees, Rosse (1988) found progression *within* classes of withdrawal (lateness and absence) as well as between lateness and absence and absence and quitting. In samples of news-paper workers and nurses, Larson and Fukami (1985) found that frequency of absence was highest among those who desired to leave the organization and who perceived high ease of movement. They interpreted this as support for progression, especially since alternative forms predicts that absence would be elevated under *low* perceived ease of movement. Dalton and Mesch (1992) found that utility workers who requested and received internal job transfers exhibited about half the absence of those who wanted a transfer but had not received it (cf. Dalton & Todor, 1993). This suggests alternate forms. Wise (1993), studying nurses, found that elevated absence preceded turnover but that it reduced the odds of employees systematically reducing their labor participation by adopting part-time or casual status. This suggests that both progression (absence to turnover) and alternate forms (absence for reduced work participation) were operating. This attention to systematically reduced participation is useful in thinking about how attendance will be influenced by new forms of employment such as job sharing.

In a very interesting study, Sheridan (1985) used catastrophe theory to study the performance, absence, and turnover of nurses over time. He concluded that increased absence preceded turnover, and that this relationship was discontinuous and nonlinear. In other words, turnover was preceded by a rapid, rather than gradual, buildup of absenteeism. This study makes the important point that nonlinearity may be an important missing ingredient in models of the association among behaviors thought to reflect withdrawal.

Sheridan's (1985) primary sample consisted of recent hires. Intuitively, one might assume that progression would be most clear in such a sample due to socialization and work role transition dynamics (Nicholson & West, 1988). Indeed, he found that his cusp catastrophe model accounted for 21% of the variance in turnover in recent hires and only 14% in a replication sample with between 7 and 60 months tenure. The role of tenure was also apparent in Kanfer, Crosby, and Brandt's (1988) study of operative employees. In this research, absence did not predict turnover for people with 2 to 5 months tenure or those with over 12 months tenure. However, between 6 and 12 months, leavers exhibited more absence than stayers. In concert, these two studies suggest that if progression of withdrawal exists, it may be most demonstrable at certain earlier stages in the job cycle. Notice, however, that sheer base rate considerations may make early turnover more predictable, giving the appearance of importance to tenure (cf. Bass & Ager, 1991). Also, the results of a study by Ferris and Rowland (1987) appear to run counter to this trend. They found that organizational tenure did not moderate the relationship between absence and turnover intentions in a sample of nurses. However, tenure with supervisor did serve as a moderator. For low-tenure subjects there was a *negative* relationship between absence and intentions, while for high-tenure subjects there was a *positive* relationship.

Hulin (1991) has been a proponent of the idea that it is often unwise to study particular withdrawal behaviors (such as absenteeism) in isolation. Rather, he argues that various behavioral manifestations of withdrawal are loosely coupled attempts at adaptation to dissatisfaction that are indicative of a latent withdrawal construct. Serving the same psychological function, they can thus be aggregated to obtain a more precise (and more psychometrically tractable) fix on this construct.

Hanisch and Hulin (1990, 1991) pursued this logic in two studies that showed that self-reported absenteeism was part of a larger work withdrawal construct. All of the data in these studies were self-reported, and the absence measure was verbally anchored rather than a report of days missed (see Johns, 1994b). Also, the inclusion of 'unfavorable job behaviors' may confound deviance with withdrawal. Nevertheless, the search for a more generalized withdrawal construct may have some real theoretical merit. In passing, it must be emphasized that this construct is only relevant to that portion of absenteeism that represents job withdrawal, a presumably small proportion when one recalls the meta-analytic results for satisfaction–absence correlations. Also, by its very nature, this approach runs counter to the decomposition of absence into various components that might have different functions and different predictors (e.g. Blau, 1985; Kohler & Mathieu, 1993).

DEMOGRAPHIC MODELS

The heading of this section obviously pushes the use of the term *models* to its limit. Although correlating demographic variables with absenteeism is common, this practice has seldom been guided by some articulated theory that suggests what one should expect to find. Thus, most of the existing knowledge is incidental, fragmented, and bivariate. Nevertheless, some developments have occurred on this front during the review period.

Age and Tenure

On the surface, the likely relationships between age and tenure and absenteeism are not entirely obvious. Should young workers have better attendance because they are healthy or poorer attendance because of competing role demands? Should high tenure workers have better attendance because they enjoy the perks that come with seniority or poorer attendance because they can get away with absence? Two meta-analyses have clarified the functional relationships, although they cannot speak precisely to causes.

Correcting for unreliability in absence, Martocchio (1989) found a mean correlation between age and frequency of absence of −0.20 in 27 samples. The relationship was slightly more negative in physically demanding than undemanding jobs. However, gender was a much stronger moderator, revealing a corrected relationship of −0.27 for men and −0.03 for women. The corrected correlation between age and time lost was −0.11 in 29 samples. When samples were partitioned by gender, this figure fell to −0.07 for women. In fact, the confidence intervals for women's frequency and time lost both included zero.

Hackett (1990) also used meta-analysis to find a corrected correlation of −0.30 between age and frequency of absence in 25 samples, −0.07 between age and time lost in 37 samples, and −0.24 between age and attitudinal absence (number of absences of three days or less) in 20 samples. Controlling for tenure, these figures were −0.15, −0.01, and −0.23 respectively. Apparent relationships between *tenure* and absence were greatly reduced when age was controlled. This analysis is important, because as Hackett notes, it speaks against the idea that a negative association between age and absence is due to accrued perks or elevated satisfaction acquired with tenure. Hackett also found that age–satisfaction relationships were strongly reduced as the percentage of women in the sample increased. In 12 all-male samples, the corrected correlation between frequency and age was −0.37, while it was 0.02 in 4 all-female samples. A similar pattern existed for attitudinal absence.

In combination, these meta-analyses establish fairly firmly that younger men tend to exhibit higher levels of frequency and attitudinal absences, measures that are often thought to capture voluntariness. Women tend not to exhibit an age–absence association, and tenure is unconnected to absence when age is controlled. It should be emphasized that all of these findings were presaged in an excellent qualitative review and original analysis by Nicholson, Brown, and Chadwick-Jones (1977).

The negative relationship between age and absence frequency for men might be explained by habituation to work or elevated job satisfaction among older workers or more off-the-job distractions for younger workers. Obviously, some attention needs to be paid to mediating variables to better understand this relationship. Kohler and Mathieu (1993) found that the association between absence and a set of 'individual resource characteristics' that included age, tenure, and gender was partially mediated by a set of affective reactions to work. Unfortunately, this analysis was not fine-grained enough to speak specifically to age and absence. Older workers do tend to exhibit greater job satisfaction (Birdi, Warr, & Oswald, 1995) and organizational commitment (Mathieu & Zajac, 1990). Thus, scope exists for enhanced affect to be a mechanism for absence reduction among older workers. Finding mediators of the age–satisfaction relationship may suggest some important ways that organizations can manage absence among younger males.

In closing this section, the reader is reminded that the meta-analyses of age and absence have summarized linear relationships, although the possibility of nonlinear effects has long been recognized. The most typical expectation is that a U-shaped function might occur due to the susceptibility of older workers to illness. Although Nicholson, Brown, and Chadwick-Jones (1977) reviewed evidence and reported original data that revealed both U- and inverted U-shaped functions, little subsequent research has explored this issue.

Gender

The role that gender plays in absenteeism is extremely interesting, extremely confusing, and rather poorly researched.

Côté and Haccoun (1991) conducted a much needed meta-analysis of the relationship between gender and absenteeism. Correcting for unreliability in absenteeism, they concluded that the best population estimate of this relationship was $r = 0.24$, with women exhibiting more absence than men. This result was based on 29 data sets and did not differ much for frequency versus time lost. As noted earlier in this review, there is ample suggestion that the dynamics of absenteeism seem to differ for men and women, given the facts that age fails to predict women's absence, but that job satisfaction is more predictive of women's than men's absence.

Why are women absent more than men? The question is all the more interesting when it is recognized that women do not receive lower performance evaluations than men (Latham, Skarlicki, Irvine, & Siegel, 1993) except when they represent only a very small proportion of an employee group (Sackett, DuBois, & Noe, 1991). One often advocated theory is that the brunt of childcare responsibilities tends to fall on women and that nonwork demands thus prompt women's absence. Indeed, Goff, Mount, and Jamison (1990) found a correlation of 0.73 between gender and primary responsibility for childcare, with women assuming the major share. Kossek (1990) reviews similar evidence. A logical conclusion from this is that women should be more likely than men to exhibit elevated absence as family size increases. However, neither Zaccaro, Craig, and Quinn (1991) nor Scott and McClellan (1990) were able to demonstrate predicted interactions between gender and family size in accounting for absenteeism. In fact, the latter researchers found little evidence of gender interactions for a wide range of variables. In a study that went to some pains to measure kinship responsibility, Blegen, Mueller, and Price (1988) found it uncorrelated with one and two day absences.

Controlling for several relevant variables, Kossek (1990) determined that gender was not associated with reports of problems with childcare. However, women did have more negative attitudes about managing work and childcare arrangements. In turn, the latter variable was associated with more self-reported time taken off work due to childcare responsibilities. A mediated relationship (gender to attitudes to absence) can be inferred. It is possible that this refinement of the criterion variable is just what is needed to understand the relationship between gender and absence. However, as Johns (1994b) notes, asking about childcare responsibilities and resulting absenteeism in the same questionnaire is susceptible to problems of common method variance and self-generated validity.

A couple of studies have used household surveys to measure people's stated reasons for recent absences. Compared to using organizational records, this tactic might be assumed to increase the accuracy of reportage. Among 21 possible reasons for absence, Haccoun and Desgent (1993) discovered four gender differences. Women were more likely to report going absent due to a child's illness. Men were more likely to report going absent due to a spouse's illness, a professional appointment, or a family social function. These results are fairly similar to those of Nicholson and Payne (1987), who found three gender differences out of 12 possible reasons. Women were more likely to be absent due to both serious and minor domestic problems. Men were more likely to be absent due to personal business matters. It is worth noting that personal illness revealed no gender difference in either study.

Haccoun and Dupont (1987) used a clever design to explore gender differences in absenteeism. Specifically, they content analyzed interviews with hospital workers who had just returned from a scheduled day off or an unscheduled day off that was classified by the employer as a sickness absence. Fully 72% of the sample admitted to not being sick on the latter day. The focus of the interviews was on what activities were engaged in during the day off. Results revealed that women reported engaging in a greater range of activities on the day off, whether the day was scheduled or unscheduled. They also reported resting less than the men in either case. Instead, women appeared to be preoccupied with more purposive activities such as shopping and tending to family matters. In fact, gender and the type of day off interacted such that women were more likely to be tending to family matters on an absence day. In an echo of the household surveys, women did not report engaging in more health-related activities than men on their day off. Although this study would have been stronger as a within-subjects design, it does provide some suggestions about the role pressures that might induce greater absenteeism among women.

At least three studies have tested models that include a large number of potential causes of absenteeism separately for men and women. The general thinking is that there are complex structural differences and substantially different absence taking processes that are obscured by pooling data for both sexes. Using data from the Michigan Quality of Employment Survey, Leigh (1983) examined self-reported absence over a two-week period. He found that self-reported health status predicted absence for both men and women. However, the following variables were significantly related only to women's absence: Incidence of colds, sleep problems, smoking, overweight status, and the presence of young children in the family. VandenHeuvel and Wooden (1995) conducted a similar study using a large sample of mostly manufacturing employees from various Australian firms. Stressful life events, self-estimated health, and attitudes toward absence predicted self-reported absence for both men and women, although stressful events were more critical for women. Long commuting time and shift work were associated with absence for women but not men. The presence of dependants had little impact for either group.

A final study derived separate stress-related models for men and women using records-based absence data (Hendrix, Spenser, & Gibson, 1994). The women's model was more complex, revealing direct effects on absenteeism due to boredom, financial problems, somatic symptoms, and cold and flu episodes. Only cold and flu were directly implicated in men's absence. Both models revealed upstream effects for job stress and emotional exhaustion as mediators of job and/or family conditions.

If there is a trend in all of these results, it is subtle, suggesting that the causes of elevated absenteeism among women may be more syndromic than the result of some 'smoking pistol'. The occurrence of boredom, financial problems, commuting time, and shift work among the differentiating variables reminds us that even today it is uncommon to find gender-mixed samples that are equivalently matched on job status. Thus, some sampling bias may contribute to these differences, with women experiencing objectively less favorable job situations. However women often exhibit greater absence even when compared to men doing the same job, such as teaching (Alexanderson, Leijon, Åkerlind, Rydh, & Bjurulf, 1994; Scott & McClelland, 1990). Also, among factory employees, Johns (1978) found that women were absent more than men even when controlling for differences in job content and job satisfaction. Melamed, Ben-Avi, Luz, and Green (1995) found that women blue-collar workers were much more likely than men to exhibit sickness absence in response to objectively monotonous jobs. They suggested that women are more likely than men to use absence as a means of coping with stress. Alexanderson et al. (1994) found that women were especially likely to exhibit elevated absence when they were performing jobs numerically dominated by males (such as metal work), while there was some tendency for men to exhibit more absenteeism in women-dominated jobs (such as clerical and secretarial). One is reminded here of research which shows that token representation in work settings is associated with lower performance evaluations for women (Sackett, DuBois, & Noe, 1991).

The presence of dependants and family responsibilities figures in some studies but not others. This uneven trend, noted in earlier research, may suggest that it is not responsibilities *per se* that cause absence but how well one is equipped to deal with these responsibilities without taking a day off. In fact, Goff, Mount, and Jamison (1990) measured work–family conflict directly and found it uncorrelated with number of children under five. Thomas and Ganster (1995) found that flexible scheduling and supportive supervision increased feelings of employee control, which decreased work–family conflict and stress symptoms. Such context factors have probably confounded simple correlations between number of dependants and absenteeism.

Kossek (1990) queried respondents about their preferences for a variety of childcare options. Out of nine options, the only one that differentiated by gender was women's greater preference for job sharing and part-time work. Similarly, Scott and McClellan (1990) found that women wished to work fewer hours than men. This suggests that women may be more likely than men to need a 'safety valve' to give them time to achieve the purposive activities on a day off suggested by the Haccoun and Dupont (1987) study. Indeed, Ferris, Bergin, and Wayne (1988) found that gender interacted with ability to control anxiety to predict absence among teachers. This ability was negatively related to absence for women but not for men.

A final trend in the research reviewed above is the role of sex differences in conceptions of physical and mental health. Again, this role is subtle, because gender does not generally interact with a self-reported health status or generalized self-reports of taking days off due to illness *per se*. Nevertheless, women exhibit more generalized ill health (morbidity) than men, and they are more protective of their health in terms of physicians' visits, hospital visits, and prescription drug use (e.g. Rodin & Ickovics, 1990). As will be seen below, women seem prone to certain medical conditions which are implicated in work absence.

Given the increase in research on gender issues in organizational behavior and industrial/organizational psychology, the relative lack of attention to absenteeism is surprising. In addition, the high reliability of the gender–absence connection suggests that it is a window through which a better general understanding of absence might be achieved. One approach might be to probe the possibility that women and men share distinct absence cultures, separate normative views about the legitimacy of the behavior (Johns & Nicholson, 1982). Thomas and Thomas (1994) showed that US Navy enlisted personnel of both sexes exhibited equivalent absence from duty when pregnant women were removed from their samples. This shows that an attendance-oriented culture can erase gender differences. During roughly the same period, the expected gender difference was found for a sample of *civilian* US Navy employees (Rogers & Herting, 1993). This reflects a potential difference in absence cultures between the civilian and military contexts.

In doing research on gender and absenteeism it is wise to keep in mind the great changes that have occurred to women's employment in the past 20 years. There is every reason to believe that there might be strong cohort effects, and that research trends may change over time. For instance, the tendency for gender to moderate age and satisfaction effects may reflect career dynamics for women that are less applicable today than in the past.

THE MEDICAL MODEL

The medical model is the most paradoxical of all of the models discussed in this chapter. Previous reviews of the absence literature, focusing on the psychological and management literatures, could lead one to believe that sickness is an unlikely cause of work absence. That is, these reviews have had little to say about the possible medical causes of absence (except Brooke, 1986). It is possible that medically oriented research has been viewed as out of the scope of organizational behavior because it is thought to deal with unavoidable or involuntary behavior. On the other side of the coin, most medically oriented research has blithely ignored mainstream organizational behavior research, in the process sometimes connoting that virtually all absence is due to sickness. If the medical model is the model of choice for medically oriented researchers, it is also the most popular model people use to explain their own absence behavior to researchers (Chadwick-Jones, Nicholson, & Brown, 1982; Hackett, Bycio, & Guion, 1989; Nicholson & Payne, 1987; Xie & Johns, 1995).

None of this is to suggest that people's public or private attributions about the causes of their absence are especially accurate (Johns, 1994b). Rushmore and Youngblood (1979) found motivational correlates of records-based sickness absence. In a principal-components analysis of diary ratings and potential absence causes, Hackett, Bycio, and Guion (1989) found that tiredness, stress, and personal problems loaded on the same factor as ill health. Nicholson and Payne (1987) concluded that people underestimate their own tendency to take off work for minor medical problems. Taylor, Haynes,

Sackett, and Gibson (1981) found that work absenteeism rose dramatically among steelworkers who were diagnosed as hypertensive, a clear manifestation of the adoption of a sick role. Johnson and Ondrich (1990) found that the duration of post-injury absences from work was conditioned by economic incentives. All in all, these results suggest that much ostensible sickness absence has a strong psychological component, and that using strict medical criteria for separating voluntary from involuntary absence is probably a futile exercise.

A few words are in order about the studies cited in this section. There appears to have been a burgeoning interest in work absence among medical researchers in recent years. Traditionally, the criteria for evaluating medical treatments have been efficacy and safety. However, the medical establishment has also become interested in the economic consequences of ill health and its repair. Absenteeism is one such economic indicator. Because of the volume of research, due to space limitations, I have tried to be representative rather than exhaustive in presenting this material. Of necessity, most epidemiological research and most clinical trials use self-reported absence, and most of the research discussed here falls into these categories. Johns (1994b) reviews the psychometric properties of self-reports of absence.

Smoking and Drinking

During the review period, several studies have reaffirmed the earlier-established positive relationship between smoking and absence (Leigh, 1986; North, Syme, Feeney, Head, Shipley, & Marmot, 1993; Parkes, 1983, 1987). However, Parkes (1983) also found that frequency of absence was only elevated among 'stress smokers' who were experiencing high affective distress and unable to smoke in the hospital environment where the study was conducted. In the same vein, Manning, Osland, and Osland (1989) found elevated short-term absence among respondents who had recently ceased smoking. This was coupled with decreases in job satisfaction and self-appraised health. Taken together, the latter two studies suggest that there are some cases in which attendance gains due to improved health might be offset by absence due to stress when smoking cessation is enforced. Ault, Ekelund, Jackson, Saba, and Saurman (1991) argue that the association between smoking and absence is artifactual, and that it occurs because smokers tend to be younger, drink more alcohol, and hold lower status jobs. Given these provocative findings, I look forward to seeing studies of the impact of workplace smoking bans on absenteeism.

In common with much of the traditional research on smoking, research concerning alcohol consumption has also taken a rather mechanical approach. Thus, Marmot, North, Feeney, and Head (1993) review evidence confirming that problem drinking is associated with absenteeism. A more interesting question exists as to whether more moderate levels of consumption are associated with absence and whether abstinence holds any benefits. Among male civil servants, Marmot et al. (1993) found a U-shaped relationship between alcohol intake and short spells of absence (cf. Jenkins, 1986). Long spells increased with frequency of drinking but not alcohol consumption. Patterns were less pronounced for women, although nondrinkers exhibited higher absence rates.

Webb, Redman, Hennrikus, Kelman, Gibberd, and Sanson-Fisher (1994) present a careful review of research assessing the association between drinking and work injuries. They conclude that much of this research is flawed (e.g. no control group), and that the connection is inconclusive. Their own well-designed study found that problem drinking, but not consumption, was associated with injury-related absence. In fact, problem drinkers were almost three times as likely as non-problem drinkers to exhibit such absence. Rare for a medical study, this research also measured job satisfaction, finding that those with low levels were about twice as likely as others to exhibit absences due to injury.

Psychological Disorder

A fair amount of epidemiological research implicates psychological disorder as a cause of work absence. For example, a large-scale study of London-based civil servants found that psychological disorders (mainly neurosis) were the third most common 'medical' cause of long sickness spells among women and the fourth among men. For both sexes, such disorders were the second most prevalent cause of very long spells (Stansfeld, Feeney, Head, Canner, North, & Marmot, 1995). Jenkins (1985) had earlier reported how minor psychological disorders such as anxiety and depression accounted for the absence of British civil service executive officers. Both reports emphasize that there is good reason to believe that psychological disorders are likely to be under-reported as a cause of absence due to both poor recognition and stigma. Borgquist, Hansson, Nettlebladt, Nordström, and Lindelöw (1993) found that these 'hidden cases' not detected by general practitioners were particularly prone to absence, taking twice the sick leave of those diagnosed with psychological problems.

Using data from the Eastern Baltimore Mental Health Survey, Kouzis and Eaton (1994) found that major depression, panic disorder, and schizophrenia were causes of work absence. In a similar North Carolina survey, Broadhead, Blazer, George, and Tse (1990) also implicated major depression, although the effect was weak. Tollefson, Souetre, Thomander, and Potvin (1993) reported a positive relationship between severity of depression and work absence, and Skodol, Schwartz, Dohrenwend, Levav, and Shrout (1994) were able to implicate even minor depression as a contributor to work absence. In another large-scale study, Garrison and Eaton (1992) found that women who were secretaries were more likely to be depressed and more likely to have missed work in the previous three months than other employed women. However, they were unable to attribute the absenteeism directly to depression *per se* and suggested that both depression and absence might be part of a stress-related syndrome.

In a study conducted at First Chicago Corporation, Conti and Burton (1994) found that depression surpassed common chronic medical problems such as low back pain and heart disease in terms of average duration of absence. Depressed people were also most prone to recidivistic absence. In this study, women were more prone than men to be diagnosed with depression.

There is a strong relationship between self-reported physical illness and psychological disorder that is much less evidenced when objective physical health indicators are applied (Stansfeld, Smith, & Marmot, 1993). This suggests that self-reports of minor medical causes of absence are often camouflaging emotional distress.

In the US, the Americans with Disabilities Act of 1990 necessitates that employers provide reasonable accommodations for employees with mental health disabilities. Over the years, arbitrators have been fairly well disposed toward carefully documented cases of excessive absenteeism as grounds for dismissal. It will be interesting to see if employees begin to claim mental health problems as reasons for excessive absenteeism and ask for reasonable accommodation in terms of less demanding scheduling and so on (cf. Kaufmann, 1993).

Pain

Various lines of research have explored the connection between physical pain and absence. Migraine headaches have been particularly implicated. In the 1990 Kentucky Health Survey, 13% of household respondents reported serious headaches within the past year (Kryst & Scherl, 1994). Close to 50% of those with self-reported migraine symptoms said that they interfered with work or school attendance, while only a little more than 20% of other headache sufferers reported attendance problems. The American Migraine Study found that '50% of women [migraine sufferers] lost 3 or more days of work per year and that 31% lost 6 or more days per year. Among men, the corresponding values were 30% and 17%' (Lipton, Steward, & Von Korff, 1994, p. 218). In a large-scale study of young adults, Breslau and Davis (1993) found that 31% of migraine sufferers versus 19% of nonsufferers reported missing work in the last month.

Two points about this research deserve elaboration. First, population studies consistently show that women suffer more from migraine than men (Lipton, Steward, & Von Korff, 1994). Thus, this is one likely contributor to women's elevated absenteeism. In five of six studies summarized by Lissovoy and Lazarus (1994) women reported missing more work days due to migraine than men. Second, it is hard to separate the physical and psychological aspects of migraine. In their prospective study, Breslau and Davis (1993) found that migraine was associated with the subsequent occurrence of major depression and panic disorders, problems that are themselves implicated as causes of absenteeism.

Taylor and Burridge (1982) documented the trends in medical diagnosis for sickness absence in the British Post Office over the years, finding a marked increase in psychiatric problems and musculoskeletal difficulties such as low back pain. In relation to work attendance, low back pain has been determined to have a substantial psychological component. In a clinical study, Öhlund, Lindström, Areskoug, Eek, Peterson, and Nachemson (1994) found that self-assessments of back strength and general health were better predictors of long-term absence due to low back pain than physicians' judgments of behavioral signs. In another clinical study, Waddell, Newton, Henderson, Somerville, and Main (1993) found that there was minimal direct connection between biomedical low back pain and disability. Even controlling for biomedical severity of pain, subjective fear avoidance beliefs (beliefs that avoiding work will prevent pain) accounted for 26% of the variance in absenteeism. Depressive symptoms accounted for some additional variance.

Busch, Costa, Whitehead, and Heller (1988) found that severity of premenstrual and menstrual symptoms was related to frequency of absence, although nongynecological symptoms were much more likely to result in absence. Again, however, the role of cognitive factors is implicated. Among women with severe symptoms, attitudes toward menstruation and perceived consequences of absence are predictive of actual absence (Gruber & Wildman, 1987).

Self-efficacy regarding one's own ability to master pain may be a key mediating variable in predicting work attendance. In fact research shows that internal health locus of control is more likely than external health locus of control to be associated with reduced absence (Ivancevich, 1985; Johns, 1994c).

Since absentees often frame the reasons for their absence in medical terms, organizational behavior research would probably profit from incorporating some medical perspectives. On the other hand, the obvious psychological component to much 'sickness' absence suggests that medical approaches would profit from a more careful consideration of the work context.

THE STRESS MODEL

Spielberger and Reheiser (1994) have documented the tremendous increase in research concerning work-related stress. In the PsycLit database between 1978 and 1980, for example, there were fewer than 30 articles with the terms occupational stress, job stress, or work stress in their titles. In the period from 1990 to 1992 there were approximately 170 such articles, with steady growth during the interim. Given this trend, it is perhaps not surprising that a number of articles have appeared that attempt to link work stress with absenteeism.

From the outset, the stress literature has been mired in terminological confusion that is more sport than necessity (Kahn & Byosiere, 1992). In what follows, I use *stress* in the sense of a perception of failure to cope with job demands. Often called *strain*, this is frequently accompanied by feelings of tension and anxiety. *Stressors* are external factors thought to cause these psychological reactions.

I have intentionally separated the stress model from the medical model for the following reason. It is very common for the popular press, certain researchers, and certain institutions to impute negative medical consequences to work stress. However, this is as much social construction as it is research fact. The relationship between psychological stress and medical symptoms is complex, varied, and often far from consistent (Cohen & Williamson, 1991; Fried, Rowland, & Ferris, 1984; Kahn & Byosiere, 1992). It is certainly possible that medical symptomatology mediates the relationship between stress and some forms of absence. Alternatively, absence may be an independent reaction to stress or an alternative reaction that alleviates physiological responses. For these reasons, stress models of absence must be able to stand on their own merits rather than imputing universal (but usually untested) medical mediation.

The most common version of the stress model seems to be predicated on the following logic: Stress is bad, and elevated absence will prove it. This neoclassical twist on the withdrawal model casts absence as a dependent variable and justifies stress research to skeptical managers who may be looking for its bottom-line impact (Dwyer & Ganster, 1991). Although some research reveals little or no connection between stress or stressors and absence (e.g. Galloway, Panckhurst, Boswell, Boswell, & Green, 1984; McKee, Markham, & Scott, 1992; Rees & Cooper, 1990; Spector, Dwyer, & Jex, 1988), most of the work reviewed below does reveal a positive relationship.

A different viewpoint casts absence as an independent variable and suggests that it can be proactive and positively adaptive, at least for the individual absentee. *En extremus*, people who are absent more will exhibit *less* stress due to recuperative activities. No research has been designed to truly probe this viewpoint, although there are some hints in the results of the more conventional studies that it is worth pursuing.

In the stress literature, some of the most interesting research has concentrated on job designs that place employees at particular risk for stress and absenteeism. This work has generally been conducted under the guidance of Karasek's (1979) job demands and control model, in which high demands and low control are predicted to produce an extreme level of stress. Karasek (1990) used retrospective data to probe the reactions of white-collar workers toward job changes. He found that job reorganizations that involved increased control and that were initiated with employee participation resulted in lower self-reports of absenteeism, depression, and heart disease symptoms. In a sample of manufacturing employees, Dwyer and Ganster (1991) found that both perceived workload and 'objective' psychological demands (estimated by job analysis) interacted with perceived control to stimulate absence, generally supporting Karasek's expectations. Using all self-report data, Kristensen (1991) found that a high work pace and 'Taylorized' job design interacted to provoke the highest level of absenteeism among slaughterhouse workers. In a remarkable graphic (Figure 3), the author illustrates how absenteeism escalates with these job properties, with piecework-paid 'slaughtering of pigs, work with knife' topping the list. Finally, Melamed et al. (1995) found that both subjectively perceived monotony and objective monotony (indexed by repetition or passive underload) were positively correlated with both psychological distress and frequency of sickness absence among blue-collar workers.

This line of research is particularly relevant to the thesis that absenteeism can be used as a coping mechanism and is not simply a reaction to dissatisfaction. Constrained by a lack of control from engaging in alternative adjustment mechanisms, absenteeism becomes a viable alternative (cf. Johns, 1991). In fact, in the Dwyer and Ganster (1991) study, overall job satisfaction and satisfaction with the work itself were *positively* correlated with sick days taken. This theme is also echoed in studies of hospital workers by Arsenault and Dolan (1983) and Léonard, Van Ameringen, Dolan, and Arsenault (1987). In both studies, a composite of stressors said to be contextual or extrinsic to the job (e.g. role stressors, career ambiguity, and pay inequity) was positively correlated with absence frequency while a composite said to be content-oriented and intrinsic to the job (e.g. urgent decisions, responsibility, workload) was negatively correlated with frequency. Although a factor analysis is mentioned, the exact logic behind the intrinsic–extrinsic distinction is unclear. However, the research suggests that some kinds of potential stressors are associated with less absence. In a related vein, high psychological demands themselves were not associated with absence in the Dwyer and Ganster (1991) research. Only when coupled with low control did problems occur. In this study, the demands seem to reflect job content while degree of control is more reflective of job context. In a longitudinal study, George (1989) found that positive mood at work was negatively associated with absence. She interpreted her results as indicating that her subjects used absenteeism to control their mood states. Again, relevant to the proactivity thesis, *negative* mood was *not* correlated with absence.

A couple of studies have examined absenteeism and stress under the general rubric of person–environment fit as opposed to the 'one job absents all' thrust of the Karasek model. Using all self-reported data from nurses, Landeweerd and Boumans (1994) found that preference for work autonomy moderated the relationships between job design and absence. Nurses with little preference for autonomy tended to absent themselves from autonomous jobs, and those with a high preference tended to absent themselves from jobs in which tasks, rather than patients, were allocated. However, these interactions were not observed for 'health complaints' which addressed stress-related variables such as anxiety, depression, and irritability. In yet another study of nurses, Furnham and Walsh (1991) used measures of career congruence and career consistency to index person–environment fit (cf. Holland, 1973). Although both measures were negatively correlated with frustration, both were positively correlated with absenteeism, counter to the prediction that good fit would reduce absence. Frustration was uncorrelated with absence. The explanation for these results is unclear.

The person–environment fit approach suggests the more general question about whether certain personality characteristics moderate the relationship between stress or stressors and absence. Put another way, are certain types of people more or less likely to react to stress by absenting themselves? Arsenault and Dolan (1983) reported some tentative evidence that two types of personalities were likely to absent themselves when confronted with contextual stressors: high strivers with internal locus of control and low strivers with external local of control. They interpreted these types as engaging respectively in active versus passive avoidance.

Tang and Hammontree (1992) found that the personality trait of hardiness (Kobasa, 1979) moderated the relationship between work stress and self-reported absence among police officers. Most studies of hardiness have centered on its buffering effects in the conversion of stress into illness. Tang and Hammontree found no such effect. In addition, contrary to expectations, they found that the highest absence was exhibited by officers *high* in hardiness who were experiencing work stress. The authors' interpretation of this result is obscure. I think that it illustrates the adaptive, coping nature of absence—hardy officers might have used absence strategically in response to stress. Under my thesis, stress would be reduced after a period of absence by hardy officers. Although the study was longitudinal, this hypothesis was not tested.

Parkes (1983) found that student nurses who reported themselves to be 'stress smokers' were most likely to exhibit frequent absence in response to affective distress. Because smoking was prohibited on this job, she interpreted this interaction between smoking style and stress as indicative of the impairment of coping through smoking.

Like the Arsenault and Dolan (1983) research, other studies have reported relationships between absenteeism and variables that are commonly thought to be stressors without actually measuring stress *per se*. In other words, tests of actual mediated models (stressor → stress → absence) are rare. In a meta-analysis, Jackson and Schuler (1985) reported a mean corrected correlation of 0.47 between role ambiguity and tension or anxiety in 43 samples. Similarly, they reported corrected correlation of 0.43 between role conflict and these same variables in 23 samples. However, the corrected correlation between role ambiguity and absence was 0.13 (5 samples) and that between role conflict and absence was −0.02 (3 samples). In a subsequent well-designed study of nurses, Jamal (1984) found much higher correlations, 0.34 for ambiguity and 0.23 for conflict. Barling, MacEwen, Kelloway, and Higginbottom (1994) found that interrole conflict (i.e. work versus family) due to eldercare had direct effects on both psychological strain and self-reported partial absence (e.g. arriving late or leaving early).

Jackson and Schuler (1985) make the sensible point that one must clearly specify one's theory when making predictions about role relationships and absenteeism. For example, they note that role conflict that stems from work overload may actually discourage absence because things will only get worse if time off is taken. Similarly, they point out how inter-sender role conflict might affect the pattern rather than volume of absence or how attendance at work might relieve stress in the nonwork domain. Again, the importance of local context in the expression of the behavior is underlined.

In the work stress literature, some attention has been devoted to trying to sort out the effects of work stress from those due to nonwork factors. This is particularly relevant to absenteeism research. On one hand, stressful events off the job might be occasions for adaptive absence from work. On the other hand, attendance at work might serve as an escape from nonwork sources of stress. Tang and Hammontree (1992) found that work stress, but not general life stress, was associated with a lagged measure of absenteeism among police officers. Manning and Osland (1989) found that work stressors, life stressors, and life strain were positively correlated with several absence measures for the year preceding the stress survey but not for the year following the survey. Subjects were white-collar employees in a manufacturing concern. Among government employees, Hendrix, Spencer, and Gibson (1994) found that life stress influenced job stress and that both variables operated indirectly on absenteeism via a variety of emotional and medical mediators. Also, they concluded that there was a 'direct effect of absenteeism on job stress for females' (p. 121). At minimum, all three of these studies can be interpreted as ruling out the 'escape to work' hypothesis. Although he did not measure work stress separately, Baba (1990) found a weak positive association between life stress and absence among male professionals.

The results of the Manning and Osland and the Hendrix, Spencer, and Gibson studies raise the intriguing possibility that absence causes stress rather than *vice versa*. The most likely mechanisms by which this could occur would be a negative reaction to one's absence by the organization or increased work-load following absence. However, both of these scenarios seem highly contextual. It should be emphasized that neither of these studies was designed to determine causality. While the Manning and Osland study lacked two waves of stress data, the Hendrix, Spencer, and Gibson study used only a single wave of data for all variables.

It might be expected that absenteeism would be a particularly likely response to the extreme form of work stress known as burnout. Because of its negative qualities of depersonalization, reduced personal accomplishment, and emotional exhaustion (Maslach & Jackson, 1984), burnout would seem to prompt absence both in terms of withdrawal from aversion as well as more proactive motives. The evidence on this is mixed. Saxton, Phillips, and Blakeney (1991) found that emotional exhaustion was a key correlate of time lost among airline reservations personnel. They did not measure the other burnout dimensions. Among nurses, Firth and Britton (1989) found that emotional exhaustion, but not the other two dimensions, was positively correlated with time lost. Lawson and O'Brien (1994) determined that depersonalization was correlated with time lost in one period for developmental disabilities workers. Although the other dimensions were uncorrelated with absence, some burnout symptoms measured with activity sampling by observers were so.

Most psychological research has been concerned with chronic work stressors. However, Theorell, Leymann, Jodko, Konarski, and Norbeck (1994) report an excellent prospective longitudinal study with matched control groups of reactions to an acute stressor—'person under train' incidents among Stockholm subway drivers. Absence data were self-reported, but physiological measures were taken. Control drivers exhibited less absence than incident drivers at three weeks and from three months to one year after the incident. Drivers who were involved with seriously injured victims were absent more than those involved with mildly injured or dead victims.

Although the incorporation of a hard behavioral measure such as absenteeism has profited the stress literature, it is less certain that the study of absenteeism has been greatly illuminated by the introduction of a stress paradigm. Most of the research reviewed above framed absence as physical withdrawal. This neoclassical version of the withdrawal model evinces a certain literalmindedness that preempts some of the more interesting questions about stress and absence. One of these questions concerns the conditions under which absenteeism represents a reasonable and sensible response to stress that benefits both the employee and the organization. As noted above, some incidental evidence points to this more positive, proactive view of absence as coping. What is needed is research targeted specifically at this issue, casting absence as a variable that is reciprocally related to stress (Edwards, 1992).

The association between personality and absenteeism has not been studied very extensively. Although main effects are possible, personality's role as a moderator of the stress–absence relationship might prove to be an especially fruitful venue for study. Just what kind of people are likely to respond to stress with *absence*, as opposed to some other work behavior? And for whom is absence a reasoned and proactive behavior versus passive withdrawal?

Finally, the kind of research that I would most like to see would link absence to the social construction of stress and its variation across occupational or organizational subcultures (cf. Barley & Knight, 1992; Meyerson, 1994). This would tie stress research to the work on absence cultures covered below. A key question has to do with the conditions under which absenteeism might be institutionalized as a *legitimate* reaction to stress. Meyerson (1994) found interesting cross-site differences in the extent to which hospital social workers saw role ambiguity as enabling versus constraining or normal versus abnormal. Similarly, the sites varied in the extent to which burnout was seen as normal versus pathological or individual versus social. These differences were linked to whether a medical model or a social work model dominated each site. In this case, one would expect to see absenteeism accepted as a legitimate response to stress in hospitals where ambiguity was viewed as constraining and abnormal and an illegitimate response where it was viewed as enabling and normal.

Barley and Knight (1992) have documented and analyzed how the nursing profession has embraced work stress as a salient feature of employment. Indeed, a disproportionate number of the studies reviewed in this section has used nursing samples, as nurses seem quite open to having their stressful work legitimated as such by researchers. In Hackett, Bycio, and Guion's (1989) study of nurses' absenteeism, subjects talked quite openly about taking 'mental health days' in response to work stress, although stress was found to load on the same factor as ill health, tiredness, and personal problems. One can imagine occupational cultures, such as the military, where stress is a less acceptable reason for absence. All of this deserves research attention.

SOCIAL AND CULTURAL MODELS

Most of the other models of absence around which this chapter is organized are essentially individual-level models. That is, individual differences in demographic background, work attitudes, stress reactions, and health are purported to explain variations in attendance patterns. The limitations of this viewpoint are apparent when it is recognized that absenteeism and attendance are, respectively, the violation and fulfillment of *social* expectations that one party has for another.

One of the first descriptions of the social shaping of attendance patterns is seen in the work of Hill and Trist (1955), who showed how novice coal miners came to calibrate their attendance with that of their veteran colleagues. This early insight went largely unheeded until the limitations of individual demographic and attitudinal approaches became apparent. This resulted in a call for more social approaches to the study of absence (Chadwick-Jones, Nicholson, & Brown, 1982; Johns, 1984; Johns & Nicholson, 1982; Marcus & Smith, 1985; Nicholson & Johns, 1985). Since this mostly theoretical work was published, there has been a gradual accumulation of empirical evidence bearing on social influences on absence and attendance. In fact, if a new approach to absence can be said to have emerged during the review period, this is it. As Johns (1984) notes, this approach allows for a range of social influence from subtle social cues about acceptable attendance behavior to full-blown, highly salient absence cultures with explicit norms and elaborate monitoring and enforcement mechanisms.

In what follows, I organize the reported research in an order that reflects increasing directness and confirmability of social influence on absence and attendance. That is, the order is meant to correspond to the extent to which alternative causes are less likely and 'black boxes' are replaced by explicit social mechanisms. Nevertheless, an ideal study would exhibit all of the features of this ascending hierarchy:

1. Between-unit differences in absenteeism.
2. Normative and other social correlates of absence.
3. Cross-level and multi-level effects in which attendance patterns at a higher level are mirrored in individual behavior.

Between-Unit Differences

A large amount of research has noted, usually in passing, great variations in absence rates or patterns between distinct social units. These units span nations (Prins & de Graaf, 1986; Steers & Rhodes, 1984), industries (Meissenheimer, 1990; Wooden, 1990), occupations (Akyeampong, 1992; Meissenheimer, 1990), organizations within the same industry (Parkes, 1983), plants or geographically replicated work units within the same organization (Johns, 1987; Mathieu & Kohler, 1990b), departments within plants (Johns, 1987), and supervisory groups within departments (Johns, 1994c; Markham & McKee, 1995a, b).

Between-unit differences such as these provide a particularly visible suggestion that social mechanisms in the realm of climate or culture are at work. Although some differences are so large as to rule out certain individual-level causes (e.g. variations in health between developed nations), unmeasured individual variables (or combinations thereof) could conceivably explain these differences. Also, differences between horizontal units of analysis (e.g. plants) can be confounded by differences in vertical levels of analysis (e.g. workgroups within plants). Thus, between-unit differences in absence must be supplemented with social process information that begins to identify appropriate causal mechanisms and the level at which they operate.

Norms and Other Social Mechanisms

The social process mechanism that has received the most attention thus far is a normative mechanism. This research is especially interesting in that it is representative of 'new wave' absence research in which subjects are actually queried about their own or others' attendance behavior, a rare event in traditional research. The general question explored is whether one's perception of normative expectations is correlated with one's own attendance behavior. The methods have been varied enough to ensure that results are not overly dictated by methodological choice.

Baba and Harris (1989) found a simple rating of peer absence was a robust predictor of the respondent's own frequency and time lost in a white-collar sample. Other studies have approached this issue by having people provide verbally anchored estimates of the extent to which they felt that there were subjective norms favoring attendance. This work has used Ajzen and Fishbein's (1980) theory of reasoned action as a point of departure, predicting that such norms combine with attitudes toward absence to influence attendance via intensions. Support for the role of normative expectations in influencing intentions (and for intentions influencing absence) has been reported for financial services employees (Martocchio, 1992), homeless shelter volunteers (Harrison, 1995), students, and fitness program participants (Harrison & Bell, 1995). Furthermore, Harrison has shown that generalized and internalized moral obligations to attend supplement the other reasoned action theoretical components in explaining intentions to attend work, school, or volunteer activities, but not exercise class (Harrison, 1995; Harrison & Bell, 1995).

Other studies have bypassed the expectations aspect of norms and attempted to measure attendance norms more directly by asking people how many days or sessions their work group peers tend to miss over a particular period of time. Gellatly (1995), Harrison and Shaffer (1994), and Johns (1994a) all found that this direct normative estimate was positively correlated with the respondents' actual absence. The latter two studies also revealed that people have a consistent tendency to provide self-reports of their own absence falling significantly below this perceived norm.

Is it possible that the perceived 'norms' in these studies are simply inflated (and thus self-serving) projections of employees' own attendance records? The evidence is unclear. Johns (1994a) found a correlation of only 0.13 between individual employees' group estimates and the groups' actual absence rates. Aggregating the estimates by group boosted the correlation to 0.31. Gellatly (1995) found that the perceived norm mediated the relationship between the work groups' previous year's absence frequency rate and the individual's next year's absence frequency. The product of a model that also included demographic and attitudinal variables, these results speak against the projection thesis.

Geurts, Buunk, and Schaufeli (1994) found that feelings of disadvantageous inequity vis-à-vis one's work colleagues were associated with more tolerant personal absence standards and elevated absence frequency. In one of the two Dutch plants studied, personal standards also mediated the relationship between perceived group absence norms and absenteeism. Both group norms and personal standards were measured with a series of questions probing tolerance of absence in various circumstances. This study highlights both the role of absence norms and the use of labor withdrawal to deal with perceived inequity (Johns & Nicholson, 1982).

Gale (1993) made clever use of Jackson's (1960) methodology to construct a *group* level measure of absence norm strength that reflected both the intensity of approval of the behavior and the degree of agreement within the group. This measure partially mitigates the projection problem, and it also incorporates the connotation of legitimacy that underlies some treatments of norms. Confirming the theoretical predictions of Nicholson and Johns (1985), Gale found that absence norms regarding time lost were strongest for cohesive work groups and those in which task interdependence was high. In turn, normative tolerance for absence was positively correlated with time lost at both the individual and group levels. This relationship did not hold for frequency of absence. In a similar vein, Haccoun and Jeanrie (1995) found that *personal* tolerance for absence was correlated with self-reported time lost.

Edwards and Whitston(1993) to some extent downplay the operation of norms in their combined qualitative and quantitative study of absence in four organizations. To them, norms are 'the extent to which workers discuss both their own absence and that of others' (p. 112). They found that 29% of their sample discussed taking time off with others and 59% discussed the absence of other workers, although there was a fair degree of cross-site and within-site variation in these figures. Responses to these single-item measures were uncorrelated with actual absence, and the authors take these gross percentages as evidence that norms were unimportant. Although the authors claim to measure work group norms, most of their inferences about the operation of norms pertain to individuals, occupations, or organizations. As suggested above and illustrated below, supervisory work groups are a likely focus for normative influence.

A few other studies have examined the role of group cohesiveness with regard to absence. Spink and Carron (1992) found that both task cohesiveness and social cohesiveness were negatively correlated with absence from adult exercise classes. However, the design compared extreme groups of high and low absentees and thus might have capitalized on inflated effect sizes. Zaccaro (1991) found that task cohesion, but not social cohesion, was negatively correlated with absence from scheduled meetings by military cadets. Newsome (1993) determined that work group social cohesion was negatively associated with the absence frequency of employees in three manufacturing firms. Drago and Wooden (1992) found that a general measure of cohesiveness interacted with job satisfaction to predict self-reported absence in a cross-national data set. Cohesion was associated with low absence when satisfaction was high and high absence when satisfaction was low. These results were interpreted in normative terms. In each of these studies, cohesiveness was measured with individual-level perceptions, although Zaccaro also adjusted for group-level effects.

A couple of studies have claimed individual-level support for Nicholson and Johns's (1985) theoretical arguments about the potential importance of absence cultures. Haccoun and Jeanrie (1995) used factor analysis to derive a measure of absence culture that included items concerning employees' perception of their boss's tolerance of absence, their own tolerance of their coworkers' absence, and their own trivialization of absence. The separate scales accounted for significant variance in the self-reported time lost of hospital employees. Deery, Erwin, Iverson, and Ambrose (in press) tested a large LISREL model of absence antecedents on Australian auto workers. They found that a measure of absence culture was correlated with frequency of noncertified one and two day absences but concluded that this influence was indirect, working through job motivation. The two-item measure is said to be from Ilgen and Hollenback (1977), although I am unable to verify its location in that article.

Each of the lines of research reviewed in this section has its weak points. Tests of the theory of reasoned action are vulnerable to common method variance between subjective norms and intentions. More direct measures of absence norms are vulnerable to projection and thus to reverse causation. Little theory has been invoked to explain exactly when and how cohesiveness influences attendance or to allow for the possibility that more cohesive groups could collude to exhibit elevated absence. Studies that measure absence culture solely at the individual level of analysis are prone to ecological fallacy. Nevertheless, in concert, the reviewed research suggests that individuals are sensitive to the social connotations of absence and others' expectations about this behavior.

Cross-Level and Multi-Level Effects

A few absence studies have employed cross-level or multi-level designs (Rousseau, 1985). The former designs explore the extent to which absenteeism (or related variables) at a higher level of analysis is systematically related to individual absence. The latter designs explore the extent to which individual effects are replicated at higher levels of analysis. In both cases, positive results imply social influence in which between-unit differences in absence are supplemented with systematic social effects within and between units.

Such designs vary in their capacity to uncover social or cultural influences on absence. A 'bare-bones' cross-level design might assign group-level absence data to individuals and examine its correlation with individual-level absence. The problem with such a design is the possibility of individual differences across groups masquerading as group-level effects. Thus, it is wise to control for individual correlates of absence in such analyses, although the complexity of absence causation renders unmeasured variables a real problem. At the other extreme, a really successful cross-level design would demonstrate cross-level effects on absence *and* uncover *socially* mediated effects that reveal some conscious awareness of a group's absence culture.

Mathieu and Kohler (1990b) assigned garage-level absence data to transit operators and examined its contribution to individual absence when controlling for several demographic and affective variables. They found that garage-level time lost predicted subsequent individual time lost; no such effect was observed for frequency. These results are impressive given the relative physical isolation of bus drivers from their peers, but the study did not measure any social mechanisms that might have corresponded to possible across-garage differences in culture.

Martocchio (1994) employed a rather different form of cross-level design to study the absenteeism of clerical employees in five separate units of a Fortune 500 firm. At the individual level, he measured perceived outcomes that might encourage absence (e.g. time with friends) and deter absence (e.g. demotion) (cf. Nicholson & Johns, 1985). Then, he aggregated these responses at the work-unit level and assigned them to individuals. Controlling for demographics, work attitudes, and the individual level outcomes, he found that unit-level outcomes (interpreted as unit culture) predicted paid frequency of absence. This study contains some exploration of the context of the absence cultures that the Mathieu and Kohler (1990b) study lacked. However, although within-unit agreement justified aggregating the costs and the benefits of absence, the conceptual reasons for this agreement are not perfectly clear. This is especially the case for the benefits, which included several items that would seem to be very personal matters (e.g. time with friends and family). As Martocchio notes, this study would have benefited from the inclusion of some clear group-level constructs.

Johns (1994c) used a cross-level design in which he assigned the absence rates of utility company work groups to individual employees after removing the individual's absence data from the group's. Controlling for a number of individual-level predictors, Johns found that group level time lost accounted for variance in individual time lost; no such effect was observed for frequency. He also found that perceptions of the salience of the group's absence culture (indexed by noticing peers' absence and knowing who was absent most and least) were negatively correlated with time lost at the individual and group levels, and he also found evidence of a cross-level effect. Thus, this study replicated the Mathieu and Kohler (1990b) study while providing some supporting evidence for social mechanisms underlying the differences between groups.

George (1990) studied the absence behavior of 26 work groups in a large department store. She found that the positive affective tone of the groups (their average positive affectivity) was negatively associated with their absence frequency rate. She interpreted this as a group-level effect, an interpretation that requires both theoretical and empirical support given the fact that affectivity is generally seen to be an individual difference variable. Part of this support was provided by the partial application of within-and-between analysis (Dansereau, Alutto, & Yammarino, 1984). Yammarino and Markham (1992) have criticized this application and disputed the contention that George's data reveal group-level effects. George and James (1993) countered that the data reveal both individual and group effects, given the limits of within-and-between analysis. This exchange is instructive, if only to remind the reader that the determination of the level of analysis at which effects operate can be difficult and contentious.

In a very enlightening study, Markham and McKee (1995a) used within-and-between analysis to probe the existence of absence cultures at the work group level of garment assembly plants. They found that employee-perceived managerial standards and personal standards for absenteeism covaried with absence frequency within and between groups such as to support genuine group-level effects (but not plant effects). That is, work groups differed collectively in their views of external and internal absence standards and their absence behavior followed suit. In turn, group absence rates were also associated with supervisors' personal standards for absence. The authors state that these data provide an illustration of the operation of what Nicholson and Johns (1985) described as absence culture salience. These results are all the more interesting when it is recognized that piecerate paid cut-and-sew operations would not seem to provide the most conducive atmosphere for collective pursuits. The authors implicated the gender mix of the work groups as contributing to these cultural differences, and they also replicated their basic findings in a longitudinal follow-up (Markham & McKee, 1995b).

Taken together, these cross-level and multi-level designs provide the best quantitative evidence for social influence on absenteeism and for the existence of absence cultures. This is because they combine the illustration of between-unit differences with some indications about the content of the culture. The latter point deserves refinement with further research. Of the studies reviewed in this section, only Johns (1994c) included an explicitly social referent (monitoring *each other*'s attendance) in his design. More attention to such mechanisms will illustrate *how* variables such as costs, benefits, mood, and perceived absence standards translate into attendance patterns at the group level. Such work could also profit from comparative studies of groups that are thought on *a priori* grounds to have distinctive absence cultures. For an example, see the following section.

The two sections that follow illustrate further models of absenteeism that are mostly (*The Conflict Model*) and partly (*The Deviance Model*) social in their essence.

THE CONFLICT MODEL

Research shows that absenteeism is the focus of much conflict between employers and employees. Thus, arbitration is common in such matters as the appropriateness of attendance policies, the classification of absences as to cause, and discharge resulting from excessive absenteeism (Clay & Stephens, 1994). Beneath the tip of this legal iceberg lies a rich body of mainly qualitative research that casts absenteeism as a manifestation of unorganized conflict between management and labor. It should be emphasized that the term *unorganized* means in comparison to organized strike activity (Hyman, 1975), not necessarily *dis*organized. Thus, absence could represent both individualized and more collective manifestations of conflict with the employer.

For the absence scholar, industrial relations research guided by the conflict model is especially useful in illustrating how the labor–management interface generates and maintains distinctive patterns of absence and attendance. In many cases, apparent anomalies become understandable when the industrial relations context is taken into account. Put another way, absence cultures are best understood when the *entire* ambient social system is accounted for. Thus, Nicholson (1985) illustrates how the local community culture and emergent labor–management relations led to the remarkable practice of a bus company sending around cars to pick up absentee bus drivers in the mornings. Similarly, Adler (1993) explains how seemingly draconian attendance policies and regimented work design actually reduced apparent conflict about absence at the General Motors–Toyota joint venture auto assembly plant in California.

Turnbull and Sapsford (1992) present an interesting analysis of absenteeism over the years among British dockworkers. The essence of their findings is that mechanization and a government-mandated move from casual to permanent employment changed the meaning of absence over time and the consequent relationship between strikes and absenteeism. Over time, absence changed from the assertion of one's freedom, to a behavior tolerated by employers, to a source of entrenched conflict. In the latter two periods, the relationships between absence and strikes shifted from negative to positive. Conceptual parallels to the 'progression of withdrawal' controversy are apparent. In fact, Australian data show that increases in absence precede increases in industrial disputes (Kenyan & Dawkins, 1989).

Paul Edwards and colleagues (Edwards & Scullion, 1982, 1984; Edwards & Whitston, 1993) have studied absenteeism extensively from a conflict perspective. For them, patterns of absence and associated attitudes are one indicator of how the larger issue of managerial control gets played out in contrasting organizational settings. For example, Edwards and Scullion (1984) contrast absenteeism practices in garment factories with those in engineering factories. They conclude that the high absenteeism in the clothing plants was a more individualized response to management control. In the engineering plants, strong collective organization among the employees enabled them to control the pace and level of work in such a way that absence was less common. This even extended to informal schedules as to who would miss work when. In later research, Edwards and Whitston (1993) extended these contrasts to British Rail, a hospital, and white-collar financial work, again illustrating how attempts at management control are accommodated and resisted via attendance patterns. In this study, rich case descriptions are supplemented with quantitative responses of employees to written vignettes of absence incidents.

However, since these responses were virtually uncorrelated with demographics, work attitudes, self-reported behavior, or aggregated records-based data, the validity of the vignette responses, said to measure a construct called considerateness, is uncertain.

Two very interesting papers have used the conflict model to (re)interpret past research and practice regarding absenteeism. Nichols (1994) takes a fresh look at the much-cited Tavistock work of Hill and Trist (1953, 1955). Although this research is often described as showing absence patterns as a form of social adaptation to work, Nichols argues that the research is excessively intrapsychic (i.e. psychoanalytic), adopts a managerial perspective that blames the victim (the sick or injured absentee), and downplays absence as a symptom of conflicting interests between employees and employers. Tansey and Hyman (1992) provide a compelling description of the public relations campaign against industrial absenteeism during World War II that was spearheaded by Eddie Rickenbacker of Eastern Airlines and the Warner and Swasey company of Cleveland. They argue that this campaign reflected a nineteenth-century moral vision of the unilateral prerogatives of management, and that it ignored the true causes of absenteeism. The authors present a clever content analysis of Warner and Swasey advocacy ads appearing in *Newsweek* between 1939 and 1945, many of which stressed worker deviance, appealed to fear, and drew close connections between factory absenteeism and lost lives on the front. The excesses of unions were a common theme.

The case studies that form the bulk of the research base for the conflict model represent especially striking examples of the workings of absence cultures because they illustrate the operation of social context. However, true to their method, they suffer from limited generalizability and a severe lack of parsimony. One useful way to proceed would be to supplement the traditional methods with more quantitative, micro-level investigations of ideas suggested by the case studies. For example, some views hold that grievance filing can serve as a substitute for other expressions of conflict, such as absenteeism, while other views (such as the deviance model) would suggest that absenteeism and grievances are complementary expressions of dissidence (Klaas, Heneman, & Olson, 1991). The first view suggests a negative relationship between grievance activity and absence, while the second suggests a positive relationship. Klaas (1989) reviews research that shows that both individual grievances and grievance rates are positively related to absenteeism. Refining the argument, Klaas, Heneman, and Olson (1991) found a positive relationship between absenteeism and the filing of policy grievances and a negative relationship between absenteeism and the filing of disciplinary grievances. They reason that feelings of generalized inequity prompt both absence and policy grievances but that disciplinary grievances can forestall other forms of conflictual behavior. This kind of work is important because it speaks to both the various meanings of absence and the detailed processes that presumably underpin the conflict model.

On a final note, the conflict model may find some interesting challenges in accounting for attitudes toward absence and for attendance patterns in emerging forms of work organizations. Some studies have reported an increase in absenteeism among semi-autonomous or self-managing teams or elevated absence in comparison with traditionally managed work groups (e.g. Cordery, Mueller, & Smith, 1991). Since these responses to reduced supervision were accompanied by *improved* work attitudes, the results seem to run counter to the basic tenets of the 'absence as conflict' thesis. Indeed, Barker's (1993) qualitative study of a successful conversion to self-management in an electronics firm illustrates how attendance standards can become a major source of conflict among team members and how teams can apply indigenous sanctions that are more controlling than those of traditional management. Thus, studying absence may be one concrete vehicle for understanding emerging patterns of industrial relations.

THE DEVIANCE MODEL

The deviance model is rather broad, encompassing both stronger and weaker forms (Johns, 1994a). In the weaker form, absenteeism is viewed as deviant because of its negative consequences for organizational effectiveness and its violation of legal or psychological work contracts. In its stronger form, absenteeism is viewed as a product of negative traits that result in malingering, laziness, or disloyalty. The deviance model is partly a social model because it is concerned with attributions made by observers of the behavior and with the absentee's own awareness of these attributions.

Do observers of absenteeism tend to make negative attributions about the behavior, and do actors exhibit a parallel awareness of this negative view? Runcie (1988) defines deviance as behavior that is at odds with a norm and describes absenteeism as a 'classic example of worker deviance' (p. 134). Robinson and Bennett (1995) define deviance as the voluntary violation of important norms that threaten the functioning of an organization. They used multidimensional scaling to construct a typology of deviant workplace behavior, finding that 'calling in sick when not' was an example of what they labeled production deviance. This is deviance with minor rather than serious consequences that tends to harm the organization more than specific individuals.

Punishment is a common response to deviant behavior, and Scott and Markham (1982) have documented the strong role of discipline and punishment in organizational attendance management programs. Deviance also produces conflict between actors and observers, and research shows that dismissal or punishment for excessive absenteeism is one of the most commonly arbitrated labor disputes (Clay & Stephens, 1994; Moore, Nichol, & McHugh, 1992; Scott & Taylor, 1983). Unfortunately for the thesis being pursued here, this research on the determinants of arbitration decisions has focused totally on the discipline procedures used by organizations rather than the behavior of the absentee. Thus, arbitrators' attributions about absence *per se* remain obscure.

What is less obscure is that managers and their subordinates often differ in their norms about typical or normal absence behavior, and this undoubtedly fuels the conflict that results in arbitration. Both Johns (1994a) and Markham and McKee (1995a) found that supervisors had more stringent expectations for attendance than their subordinates. Martocchio and Judge (1995) found related differences in opinions about severity of discipline for absence, some of which were associated with the demographic similarity of the parties. Xie and Johns (1995) found good normative agreement between these parties in a sample of manufacturing employees in the People's Republic of China and explained the agreement in cultural terms.

Absentees and potential absentees seem to be aware of the negative connotations of absence and marshal selective perception to disassociate themselves from the behavior. Hackett, Bycio, and Guion (1989) determined that guilt about taking time off motivated nurses to attend even when they wished not to do so. In a review of the self-report absence literature, Johns (1994b) found a consistent tendency for people to underreport their own absence behavior. In addition, people tend to see their own attendance behavior as superior to that of their work group peers or classmates (Harrison & Shaffer, 1994; Johns, 1994a; Xie & Johns, 1995). This self-serving bias is also accompanied by a group-serving bias that attributes more absence to one's general occupation than to one's work group peers (Johns, 1994a). Xie and Johns (1995) found that this phenomenon was particularly pronounced in China. Johns (1994a, b) presents the logic that this pattern of perceptions is mainly ego-protective while considering the possibility of more cognitive mechanisms.

None of the above should be taken to imply that people are incapable of viewing the absence of others with understanding, especially when it occurs in some context that makes salient situational constraints on attendance or fair motives for absence. Edwards and Whitston (1993) illustrate this both in their qualitative data and in quantitative responses to a variety of vignettes in which employees often provided 'considerate' responses to the absence exhibited by others. Also using vignettes, Judge and Martocchio (1995) found that supervisors who made more external attributions about absence causes and who valued fairness more rendered less severe disciplinary decisions. Again using vignettes, Conlon and Stone (1992) illustrated that managers were sensitive to the volume of absence (and, to some extent, its pattern) in rendering judgements about absentees. The within-subjects designs of these studies make them potentially vulnerable to demand characteristics in which subjects exhibit excessive rationality to discriminate among absentees. Nevertheless, the larger point being made here is that the deviance model often comprises a default model when contextual information is lacking, vague, or contradictory.

Since most people get to work most of the time, excessive absenteeism represents consistent, low consensus behavior, a pattern that invites dispositional attributions (Kelley, 1972). But is there any evidence for a dispositional link to absenteeism? During the review period, the renewed interest in disposition at work (Judge, 1992) has included some research on attendance.

A dispositional facet to behavior suggests some degree of temporal consistency as a minimum condition. Indeed, past absenteeism consistently figures as one of the best predictors of current absenteeism. Farrell and Stamm's (1988) meta-analysis estimated absence history to be correlated 0.71 with current time lost (10 samples) and 0.65 with current frequency (15 samples). Going further, there is also some evidence of cross-situational consistency in the behavior. Brenner (1968) found that high school absenteeism was positively related ($r = 0.30$) to absenteeism in employment following high school. Ivancevich (1985) determined that past work absence predicted subsequent absence even among employees who were assigned to new jobs that involved substantial training and new equipment and control systems. Although these results are consistent with a dispositional thesis, they do not rule out stable off-work demands or chronic health problems as causes of absence. Also, in a cohort study, Dalton and Mesch (1992) found that employees who asked for and received job transfers exhibited lower absence rates than those who had asked for but not received a transfer. This suggests that changes of situation do affect attendance.

Further evidence for a deviant dispositional input to absence would be evidenced by the correlation of absenteeism with a constellation of other 'counterproductive' behaviors or attitudes. Chen and Spector (1992) found that self-reported absence was positively related to self-reported anger, aggression, and hostility at work. Hogan and Hogan (1989) present some factor analytic results that suggest that, as criterion variables, absences, grievances, and compensation claims load on the same factor. Normand, Salyards, and Mahoney (1990) found that US Postal Service job applicants who tested positive for illicit drug use exhibited 59% more time lost after hiring than those who tested negative. Probably the most relevant data regarding the possible dispositional substrate to absenteeism comes from the evidence on so-called integrity, honesty, or reliability tests. Although such tests are controversial (Camara & Schneider, 1994), it appears that absenteeism is part of a broad composite of counterproductive behaviors that is predictable with both overt and personality-based integrity measures (Ones, Viswesvaran, & Schmidt, 1993). In a typical study, Borofsky and Smith (1993) used the Employee Reliability Inventory as a pre-employment screening device. A pre-post comparison showed a significant reduction in unauthorized time lost following the introduction of the inventory.

The linking of attendance to the integrity construct also raises questions about its status as an example of organizational citizenship behavior. Organ (1988) asserts that reasonable attendance at work is contractual, but that excellent attendance over long periods of time goes well beyond organizational expectations. He cites such attendance as an example of the conscientiousness dimension of organizational citizenship. Mayer and Schoorman (1992) found that unexcused time lost was negatively correlated with altruism and organization-specific citizenship behaviors.

A final study located firmly in the deviance domain was conducted by Sands and Miller (1991). They examined the relationship between lunar phases and absenteeism in an insurance company. Controlling for a number of temporal variables, they found, contrary to conventional expectations, a weak *decrease* in absence when the moon was full. So much for folk wisdom.

It is my impression that managers have a tendency to overuse the deviance model as an explanation for absence. In turn, this leads them to seek out and punish individual offenders while ignoring more proactive and more culturally oriented means of managing attendance. On the other hand, researchers have probably not paid enough attention to the deviant connotations of absence. As illustrated above, these connotations strongly shape how people view their own behavior and that of their work group and occupational peers. In turn, these views stimulate politics and conflict when employees try to justify their behavior to managers (cf. Fitzgibbons, 1992). More direct study of this process would be welcome.

THE ECONOMIC MODEL

Most commonly, the economic model treats absenteeism and attendance as problems of labor supply (Chelius, 1981). People who sell their time to employers forego leisure. As wage rates increase, it is increasingly attractive to substitute work for leisure (the substitution effect). But as income increases, it is increasingly attractive to take time off for consumatory purposes (the income effect). Unconstrained, people should attend only up to the point where their internal time value (marginal rate of substitution of income for leisure) is equal to the marginal wage (Dunn & Youngblood, 1986).

This basic formulation predicts that absence will increase with the length of the workweek (due to the decreasing marginal utility of attendance), increase as nonlabor income rises, and decrease as financial penalties for absence increase (Drago & Wooden, 1992). It is ambiguous concerning the correlation between wages and absence due to the competing forces of substitution versus income, although Allen (1981a) suggests that job choice mechanisms might work in favor of substitution.

In practice, much research in this area has simply examined the relationship between wages and absenteeism. A negative relationship has often been found, suggesting the domination of substitution effects (e.g. Allen, 1981b; Barmby & Treble, 1991; Chaudhury & Ng, 1992; Drago & Wooden, 1992; Kenyon & Dawkins, 1989). Similarly, higher wages are associated with lower durations of absence from work following injury (Johnson & Ondrich, 1990). However, such effects are often weak and not always consistently observed (e.g. Leigh, 1986, 1991). Put simply, typical economic data sets lack both the process and control variables required to fish successfully in these waters. Barmby, Orme, and Treble (1991) implicate the need for data on demand side absence control mechanisms, and Drago and Wooden (1992) show that higher sick leave entitlements are associated with higher self-reported absence. More basically, however, more precise measures of the value of time are required. Using individual level data and *direct* measures of the internal value of time, Dunn and Youngblood (1986) found that employees used absence to reduce their marginal rate of substitution and achieve optimal equilibrium. Using some of the same data, Youngblood (1984) earlier illustrated that time lost increased with the value of nonwork time whereas frequency of absence was weakly influenced by work attachment, indexed by job scope and job satisfaction. Such dedicated measurement answers questions that gross economic data cannot, and Youngblood and Dunn are to be commended.

Economists have also shown an interest in the impact of unionization on absence. Allen (1984) lays out the basic question: Does unionization decrease absenteeism by improving working conditions and providing 'voice', or does it increase absenteeism by protecting absentees from sanctions? Although these precise mechanisms have not been explored, the general trend is clear: Unionized employees tend to exhibit greater absence (Allen, 1984; Chaudhury & Ng, 1992; Leigh, 1981, 1984, 1985, 1986). Wilson and Peel show that the relationship between various 'voice' and participation mechanisms and absence is in fact quite complex. However, in their sample of engineering and metal working firms, profit-sharing and share ownership plans were unambiguously associated with reduced absence rates (Peel & Wilson, 1990; Wilson & Peel, 1991).

Another prediction made by the economic model is that absenteeism should decrease when unemployment rises. Two mechanisms could underpin this prediction (Leigh, 1985). One is that employees, aware of the deviant connotations of absence, are more likely to exhibit good attendance when layoffs are possible and prospects for other employment are slim. The other is that employers use hard times to divest themselves of high-absence employees. Controlling for a number of economic variables and surrogates, Leigh (1985) found support for a negative relationship between unemployment rates and absence rates at both the industry level and the national (US) level. Kenyon and Dawkins (1989) replicated this effect with Australian national data. Markham (1985) found similar results at the national (US), regional, and organizational levels. Markham and McKee (1991) found that local unemployment was negatively correlated with plant absence rates and that attendance improvements appeared to lead unemployment rates. That is, it was as if employees anticipated tough economic times with improved attendance. These authors also found an independent effect for plant staff size—as plants declined in size, attendance figures improved.

A final prediction of the economic model, alluded to briefly above, is that absenteeism will be responsive to the economic incentives and disincentives contained in absence control plans, sick day and disability provisions, and so on. Indeed, there is substantial evidence that the provision of liberal sick days results in more absence and that policy details are strong predictors of absence (Dalton & Mesch, 1991; Dalton & Perry, 1981; Drago & Wooden, 1992; Ehrenberg, Ehrenberg, Rees, & Ehrenberg, 1991; Ng, 1989).

A few economists have presented theoretical models that extend or complement the traditional labor–leisure perspective. Gafni and Peled (1984) attempt to account for the documented increase in absenteeism that follows the diagnosis of hypertension among people previously unaware of this medical problem. They argue that the increased absence is due to an increased demand for leisure in the face of a shortened life and the decreased value of retirement savings. Given the well developed psychology of the sick role (Levine & Kozloff, 1978), this economic explanation seems implausible. Both Barmby, Sessions, and Treble (1994) and Kahana and Weiss (1992) present models that attempt to account for absenteeism given asymmetric information about employee health. The latter paper further uses game theory to compare incentives for absence in labor-managed versus traditionally managed firms.

The economic model has good potential as a vehicle for thinking about how the value of work and nonwork time influences absence and how family economic circumstances might affect attendance patterns. Unfortunately, traditional economic studies often substitute a well-filled regression equation for careful theorizing and generate data bases that are filled with single-item measures, unnecessarily dichotomized variables, and self-reported absence measures (see Johns, 1994b). More careful measurement and theorizing that integrates the economic model with other models would be welcome. Youngblood's (1984) study is a good example. Drago and Wooden (1992) illustrate how disciplinary and normative perspectives complement the traditional labor–leisure approach.

THE CONSEQUENCES OF ABSENCE

The large majority of research on absenteeism has tended to cast the behavior as a dependent variable. However, over the years, a body of work has accumulated that frames the behavior as an independent variable and then examines its consequences.

Some of the first theoretical treatment of this issue was provided by Mowday, Porter, and Steers (1982), who speculated about the positive and negative consequences of absenteeism for individuals, work groups, and organizations. Although they were able to cite almost no research on these effects, their work does highlight the possibility for conflict between these levels of analysis. That is, what might be good for one party (reduced individual stress) might be bad for another party (reduced organizational productivity).

The most systematic and thorough treatment of the possible consequences of absence is provided by Goodman and Atkin (1984) who also extended the list of stakeholders to unions, the family, and society. They outline the theoretical rationale for various consequences and provide a research agenda for several.

Does absence lower job performance? Bycio (1992) provides an indirect answer to this question with a meta-analysis of 46 studies of the relationship between individual performance and absenteeism. He determined that both supervisory performance evaluations and nonrating measures of performance quality (e.g. cash imbalances) were negatively related to various forms of absenteeism. However, credibility intervals were wide, and artifacts did not explain all the variance across studies. This finding is open to questions of both direction of causality and causal mechanism, and Bycio does a good job of working through the possibilities. Chief among these is that irritated supervisors give high absentees low evaluations. Given the finding of a connection for nonrating data and some subsidiary analyses, he concludes that there is more to this association than supervisory annoyance. Indeed, respondents to a random telephone survey reported that supervisory wrath and threats to promotion were unlikely consequences of work absence (Haccoun & Desgent, 1993), and Baba (1990) found that perceptions of such consequences were uncorrelated with absence. Bycio also explains how employee disposition (the deviance model) or progression of withdrawal (from lowered performance to absence, cf. Sheridan, 1985) could account for his results.

Tharenou (1993) provides the clearest evidence that absence can result in lower job performance at the individual level. In a longitudinal study of electrical apprentices that included two full waves of data collection, she found that prior absence was associated with subsequent lower supervisory performance ratings and course grades. In addition, she presents some evidence that suggests the ratings were not contaminated by absence. Tharenou notes that further progress in this domain will probably require the fine-grained application of event history analysis (Fichman, 1988; Harrison & Hulin, 1989) to absence and performance data. Her finding that absenteeism led to reduced course grades corresponds to Gunn's (1993) cross-sectional findings of a strong positive association between class attendance and academic performance in introductory psychology classes and the Ehrenberg et al. (1991) finding that absenteeism in school districts was associated with lower district scores on standardized tests.

All of the studies reviewed by Bycio were individual-level studies, and virtually none of them was purpose-designed to probe the fine details of the absence–performance connection. Several group-level studies have done this. Moch and Fitzgibbons (1985) found that absenteeism decreased departmental production efficiency only when it could not be anticipated or when the production process was not highly automated. Under these conditions, absenteeism resulted in the production of substantial scrap. Goodman and Leyden (1991) found that absenteeism among underground coal mining crews reduced crew familiarity, which in turn resulted in lower productivity. In related research, Goodman and Garber (1988) found that unfamiliarity due to absence resulted in increased accident rates among miners.

These group-level studies are very important because they speak to the impact of absence on productivity in terms of the context of the social system and work design. It would be interesting to see this work extended to more complex models of how automation, interdependence, and other task and technology variables condition the influence of absence. It would also be fascinating to see this line of research extended to white-collar work and to forms of 'pseudo-absence' due to business travel or telecommuting. How do such absences affect social relationships and unit performance? How does 'electronic absence' differ from conventional absence?

Clegg (1983) provided an excellent critique of causality issues in research on work 'withdrawal' and considered the possibility that absenteeism might result in subsequent job dissatisfaction, a direction of causality contrary to the conventional withdrawal model. Clegg claimed to find such evidence, and this study is frequently cited as showing reverse causality. Unfortunately, it did not include two waves of satisfaction data. Clegg controlled for prior absence when testing the job satisfaction causes absence hypothesis, but not when testing the absence causes satisfaction hypothesis. This combination of factors means that reverse causality in this study may be spurious. However, Tharenou (1993) obtained two full waves of data and did indeed conclude that increased absenteeism led to a subsequent reduction in job satisfaction, rather than the other way around. As the author herself implies, the fact that the subjects were apprentice electricians, followed from the beginning of their apprenticeship, might especially favor reverse causality. For new recruits to a rather structured work training program, early absence may trigger a downward spiral of events that precipitates negative affect.

Performance and job satisfaction are variables that are of interest to both the organization and the individual. Is there any evidence regarding the consequences of absence that is more exclusively pertinent to the individual? Earlier, it was pointed out that evidence for the stress-reductive, adjustive properties of absence is very indirect and incidental. Other than that work, the only suggestive research is that in which people explain why they are typically absent. Medical reasons tend to dominate such explanations (Hackett, Bycio, & Guion, 1989; Nicholson & Payne, 1987; Xie & Johns, 1995), suggesting physical recuperation as a common consequence. However, the reader is reminded that there are documented cross-cultural and gender differences in stated reasons for absence (Haccoun & Desgent, 1993; Xie & Johns, 1995) and gender differences in activities pursued on days taken off (Haccoun & Dupont, 1987). This suggests that the personal consequences of absence will vary substantially across individuals (cf. Johns & Nicholson, 1982, the meanings of absence).

Given Goodman and Atkin's (1984) excellent outline of needed work, research on the consequences of absence is disappointing by virtue of its low volume. Behavior is shaped by its consequences for oneself and others, and lack of awareness of these consequences sets limits on our ability to understand behavior. Perhaps the growing emphasis on increased interdependence and teamwork will provide some impetus for focusing on absence's consequences.

CONCLUSION

What do we know about the correlates, causes, and consequences of absence that we didn't know 15 years ago? Because of its less than ideal psychometric properties, absenteeism has particularly profited from the advantages of meta-analytic summary. In the domains of job satisfaction and demographics, we now have a solid base of population estimates of effect sizes, a fact that both stimulates shifts in research emphasis (from job satisfaction to commitment) and challenges researchers to explain these effects (e.g. gender and absence). In the domains of performance and turnover, wide confidence intervals in estimated correlations with absence have inspired good theoretical thinking about likely moderators.

Fifteen years ago, because few had even asked, we knew very little about how people viewed their own absence behavior or that of others. Now, we know that people have a tendency to underestimate their own absence and hold inflated views of the absence of others. Managers and employees hold different standards about how much absence is acceptable, but managers are capable of applying reasonable attributional criteria to judgments about absence. Key variables from the theory of reasoned action account for variance in intentions to be absent. Within-person decision models show that the meanings of absence vary among individuals despite some more universal causal mechanisms.

Fifteen years ago, little was known about the social and cultural dynamics of absenteeism. In my opinion, the enhancement of knowledge on this front represents the greatest advance during the review period. Meaningful cross-group differences and normative mechanisms are now well established, and it is becoming clear that supervisory groups are often critical in shaping the attendance patterns of their members. The social perspective is important because it forces the researcher to attend to a factor that seems to be critically important in matters of absence and attendance—work context. In this domain, the conflict model provides some especially good examples. As noted at several points earlier, the social perspective also holds excellent promise as a partial explanatory mechanism for phenomena covered under the other models, including how gender affects absence and how absence is or is not legitimated as a response to stress or ill health.

Fifteen years ago, with the exception of some experimental tests of interventions, the standard study of absence passed out a questionnaire in the workplace and obtained absence data from personnel records. Although this is still true, it is important to remember that the advances noted above have stemmed from a remarkable diversity of methods, including the use of observation, interviews, diaries, vignettes, self-reports, supervisory reports, telephone surveys, household visits, within-person designs, content analysis, and meta-analysis. Absence is difficult to study, and one should use what works. This diversity (uncommon in many research areas) is to be commended.

Fifteen years ago, there were very few studies of work stress and absenteeism. Now, there are many, but they do little to enhance our general understanding of absence, either because they fail to probe rigorously the possible adjustive aspects of absence or because they fail to consider when absence might be the preferred reaction to stress over other responses.

Except for the micro-level studies of time valuation, the fruits of the economic model are generally unenlightening, often replicating effects seen in firm-level studies. This is unfortunate, because the economic model seems moderately well equipped to probe some aspects of a very important issue—the impact of nonwork factors on absence. The lack of information on these factors was decried 15 years ago (Johns & Nicholson, 1982), and this is still a serious omission from the absence research agenda.

The increasing interest in absenteeism by medical researchers holds promise if absenteeism is viewed as a psychologically mediated response to medical condition and not simply as an economic indicator of the cost of sickness or the efficacy of treatment. This requires that research in the medical domain incorporate more understanding of workplace psychology and behavior.

In my opinion, progress in the past 15 years has been due to creative anarchy in theory and method. In this sense, the lack of a dominant paradigm or model has been helpful. On certain terms and conditions, some organization of this anarchy might be welcome. However, two temptations should be avoided, both of which have to do with putting quantity before quality. At one extreme, I have already alluded to the fallacy of organizing empirically with a regression equation stocked with variables from more and more models. We already have evidence that knowledge accruing from this approach is literally noncumulative (e.g. Johns, 1978) and simply trying to account for more variance is a futile task in any event (Nicholson & Martocchio, 1995). At the other extreme, organizing theoretically with a grand process model has the limitations alluded to at the beginning of the chapter.

What is needed now are probably some small theories that cross-cut two or more of the models described above. For example, one can conceive of a theory that combines differential medical susceptibility, culture, and notions of deviance to explain in part why women are often absent more than men and when they might not be. A series of such small theories would better organize our understanding of absenteeism while still respecting the wide varieties of meanings that absence holds for individuals and groups.

AUTHOR NOTE

This research was supported by grant 94ER0506 from Quebec's Fonds pour la Formation de Chercheurs et l'Aide à la Recherche and grant 410-920202 from the Social Sciences and Humanities Research Council of Canada.

REFERENCES

Adler, P. S. (1993) The 'learning bureaucracy': New United Motor Manufacturing, Inc. *Research in Organizational Behavior*, **15**, 111–194.

Ajzen, I. (1991) The theory of planned behavior. *Organizational Behavior and Human Decision Processes*, **50**, 179–211.

Ajzen, I. & Fishbein, M. (1980) *Understanding Attitudes and Predicting Social Behavior*. Englewood Cliffs, NJ: Prentice-Hall.

Akyeampong, E. B. (1992, Spring) Absences from work revisited. *Statistics Canada Perspectives*, 44–53.

Alexanderson, K., Leijon, M., Åkerlind, I., Rydh, H., & Bjurulf, P. (1994) Epidemiology of sickness absence in a Swedish county in 1985, 1986 and 1987. *Scandinavian Journal of Social Medicine*, **22**, 27–34.

Allen, N. J. & Meyer, J. P. (1990) The measurement and antecedents of affective continuance, and normative commitment to the organization. *Journal of Occupational Psychology*, **63**, 1–18.

Allen, S. G. (1981a) Compensation, safety, and absenteeism: Evidence from the paper industry. *Industrial and Labor Relations Review*, **34**, 207–218.

Allen, S. G. (1981b) An empirical model of work attendance. *Review of Economics and Statistics*, **63**, 77–87.

Allen, S. G. (1984) Trade unions, absenteeism, and exit-voice. *Industrial and Labor Relations Review*, **37**, 331–345.

Arsenault, A. & Dolan, S. (1983) The role of personality, occupation and organization in understanding the relationship between job stress, performance and absenteeism. *Journal of Occupational Psychology*, **56**, 227–240.

Ault, R. W., Ekelund, R. B. Jr, Jackson, J. D., Saba, R. S., & Saurman, D. S. (1991) Smoking and absenteeism. *Applied Economics*, **23**, 743–754.

Baba, V. V. (1990) Methodological issues in modeling absence: A comparison of least squares and tobit analyses. *Journal of Applied Psychology*, **75**, 428–432.

Baba, V. V. & Harris, M. J. (1989) Stress and absence: A cross-cultural perspective. *Research in Personnel and Human Resources Management, Suppl. 1*, 317–337.

Barker, J. R. (1993) Tightening the iron cage: Concertive control in self-managing teams. *Administrative Science Quarterly*, **38**, 408–437.

Barley, S. R. & Knight, D. B. (1992) Toward a cultural theory of stress complaints. *Research in Organizational Behavior*, **14**, 1–48.

Barling, J., MacEwen, K. E., Kelloway, K., & Higginbottom, S. F. (1994) Predictors and outcomes of elder-care-based interrole conflict. *Psychology and Aging*, **9**, 391–397.

Barmby, T. A., Orme, C. D., & Treble, J. G. (1991) Worker absenteeism: An analysis using microdata. *Economic Journal*, 101, 214–229.

Barmby, T., Sessions, J., & Treble, J. (1994) Absenteeism, efficiency wages and shirking. *Scandinavian Journal of Economics*, 96, 561–566.

Barmby, T. A. & Treble, J. G. (1991) Absenteeism in a medium-sized manufacturing plant. *Applied Economics*, 23, 161–166.

Bass, A. R. & Ager, J. (1991) Correcting point-biserial turnover correlations for comparative analysis. *Journal of Applied Psychology*, 76, 595–598.

Birdi, K., Warr, P., & Oswald, A. (1995) Age differences in three components of employee well-being. *Applied Psychology: An International Review*, 44, 345–373.

Blau, G. (1985) Relationship of extrinsic, intrinsic, and demographic predictors to various types of withdrawal behaviors. *Journal of Applied Psychology*, 70, 442–450.

Blau, G. J. (1986) Job involvement and organizational commitment as interactive predictors of tardiness and absenteeism. *Journal of Management*, 12, 577–584.

Blau, G. J. & Boal, K. B. (1987) Conceptualizing how job involvement and organizational commitment affect turnover and absenteeism. *Academy of Management Review*, 12, 288–300.

Blegen, M. A., Mueller, C. W., & Price, J. L. (1988) Measurement of kinship responsibility for organizational research. *Journal of Applied Psychology*, 73, 402–409.

Borgquist, L., Hansson, L., Nettelbladt, P., Nordström, G., & Lindelöw, G. (1993) Perceived health and high consumers of care: A study of mental health problems in a Swedish primary health care district. *Psychological Medicine*, 22, 763–770.

Borofsky, G. L. & Smith, M. (1993) Reductions in turnover, accidents, and absenteeism: The contribution of a pre-employment screening inventory. *Journal of Clinical Psychology*, 49, 109–116.

Brehm, J. W. (1966) *A Psychological Theory of Reactance*. New York: Academic Press.

Brenner, M. H. (1968) Use of high school data to predict work performance. *Journal of Applied Psychology*, 52, 29–30.

Breslau, N. & Davis, G. C. (1993) Migraine, physical health and psychiatric disorder: A prospective epidemiologic study in young adults. *Journal of Psychiatric Research*, 27, 211–221.

Broadhead, W. E., Blazer, D. G., George, L. K., & Tse, C. K. (1990) Depression, disability days, and days lost from work in a prospective epidemiologic survey. *Journal of the American Medical Association*, 264, 2524–2528.

Brooke, P. P., Russell, D. W., & Price, J. L. (1988) Discriminant validation of measures of job satisfaction, job involvement, and organizational commitment. *Journal of Applied Psychology*, 73, 139–145.

Brooke, P. P. Jr (1986) Beyond the Steers and Rhodes model of employee attendance. *Academy of Management Review*, 11, 345–361.

Brooke, P. P. Jr. & Price, J. L. (1989) The determinants of employee absenteeism: An empirical test of a causal model. *Journal of Occupational Psychology*, 62, 1–19.

Busch, C. M., Costa., P. T. J., Whitehead, W. E., & Heller, B. R. (1988) Severe perimenstrual symptoms: Prevalence and effects on absenteeism and health care seeking in a non-clinical sample. *Women & Health*, 14, 59–74.

Bycio, P. (1992) Job performance and absenteeism: A review and meta-analysis. *Human Relations*, 45, 193–220.

Camara, W. J. & Schneider, D. L. (1994) Integrity tests: Facts and unresolved issues. *American Psychologist*, 49, 112–119.

Carsten, J. M. & Spector, P. E. (1987) Unemployment, job satisfaction, and employee turnover: A meta-analytic test of the Muchinsky model. *Journal of Applied Psychology*, 72, 374–381.

Chadwick-Jones, J. K., Nicholson, N., & Brown, C. (1982) *Social Psychology of Absenteeism*. New York: Praeger.

Chaudhury, M. & Ng, I. (1992) Absenteeism predictors: Least squares, rank regression, and model selection results. *Canadian Journal of Economics*, **25**, 615–635.

Chelius, J. R. (1981) Understanding absenteeism: The potential contribution of economic theory. *Journal of Business Researh*, **9**, 409–418.

Chen, P. Y. & Spector, P. E. (1992) Relationships of work stressors with aggression, withdrawal, theft, and substance use: An exploratory study. *Journal of Occupational and Organizational Psychology*, **65**, 177–184.

Clay, J. M. & Stephens, E. C. (1994) An analysis of absenteeism arbitration cases: Factors used by arbitrators in making decisions. *International Journal of Conflict Management*, **5**, 130–142.

Clegg, C. W. (1983) Psychology of employee lateness, absence, and turnover: A methodological critique and an empirical study. *Journal of Applied Psychology*, **68**, 88–101.

Cohen, A. (1991) Career stage as a moderator of the relationships between organizational commitment and its outcomes: A meta-analysis. *Journal of Occupational Psychology*, **64**, 253–268.

Cohen, S. & Williamson, G. M. (1991) Stress and infectious disease in humans. *Psychological Bulletin*, **109**, 5–24.

Conlon, E. J. & Stone, T. H. (1992) Absence schema and managerial judgment. *Journal of Management*, **18**, 435–454.

Conti, D. J. & Burton, W. N. (1994) The economic impact of depression in a workplace. *Journal of Occupational Medicine*, **36**, 983–988.

Cordery, J. L., Mueller, W. S., & Smith, L. M. (1991) Attitudinal and behavioral effects of autonomous group working: A longitudinal field study. *Academy of Management Journal*, **34**, 464–476.

Côté, D. & Haccoun, R. R. (1991) L'absentéisme des femmes et des hommes: Une méta-analyse. *Canadian Journal of Administrative Sciences*, **8**, 130–139.

Cox, D. R. (1972) Regression models and life-tables. *Journal of the Royal Statistical Society, Series B*, **34**, 187–202.

Dalton, D. R. & Mesch, D. J. (1991) On the extent and reduction of avoidable absenteeism: An assessment of absence policy provisions. *Journal of Applied Psychology*, **76**, 810–817.

Dalton, D. R. & Mesch, D. J. (1992) The impact of employee-initiated transfer on absenteeism: A four-year cohort assessment. *Human Relations*, **45**, 291–304.

Dalton, D. R. & Perry, J. L. (1981) Absenteeism and the collective bargaining agreement: An empirical test. *Academy of Management Journal*, **24**, 425–431.

Dalton, D. R. & Todor, W. D. (1993) Turnover, transfer, and absenteeism: An interdependent perspective. *Journal of Management*, **19**, 193–219.

Dansereau, F., Alutto, J. A., & Yammarino, F. J. (1984) *Theory Testing in Organizational Behavior: The Varient Approach*. Englewood Cliffs, NJ: Prentice-Hall.

Deery, S. J., Erwin, P. J., Iverson, R. D., & Ambrose, M. L. (in press) The determinants of absenteeism: Evidence from Australian blue-collar employees. *International Journal of Human Resource Management*.

Drago, R. & Wooden, M. (1992) The determinants of labor absence: Economic factors and workgroup norms across countries. *Industrial and Labor Relations Review*, **45**, 764–778.

Dunn, L. F. & Youngblood, S. A. (1986) Absenteeism as a mechanism for approaching an optimal labor market equilibrium: An empirical study. *Review of Economics and Statistics*, **68**, 668–674.

Dwyer, D. J. & Ganster, D. C. (1991) The effects of job demands and control on employee attendance and satisfaction. *Journal of Organizational Behavior*, **12**, 595–608.

Edwards, J. R. (1991) Person–job fit: A conceptual integration, literature review, and methodological critique. *International Review of Industrial and Organizational Psychology*, **6**, 283–357.

Edwards, J. R. (1992) A cybernetic theory of stress, coping, and well-being in organizations. *Academy of Management Review*, 17, 238–274.

Edwards, P. K. & Scullion, H. (1982) *The Social Organization of Industrial Conflict: Control and Resistance in the Workplace.* Oxford: Blackwell.

Edwards, P. & Scullion, H. (1984) The social organization of industrial conflict. *Sociological Review*, 32, 547–571.

Edwards, P. & Whitston, C. (1993) *Attending to Work: The Management of Attendance and Shopfloor Order.* Oxford: Blackwell.

Ehrenberg, R. G., Ehrenberg, R. A., Rees, D. I., & Ehrenberg, E. L. (1991) School district leave policies, teacher absenteeism, and student achievement. *Journal of Human Resources*, 26, 72–105.

Eisenberger, R., Fasolo, P., & Davis-LaMastro, V. (1990) Perceived organizational support and employee diligence, commitment, and innovation. *Journal of Applied Psychology*, 75, 51–59.

Eisenberger, R., Huntington, R., Hutchison, S., & Sowa, D. (1986) Perceived organizational support. *Journal of Applied Psychology*, 71, 500–507.

Farrell, D. & Peterson, J. C. (1984) Commitment, absenteeism, and turnover of new employees: A longitudinal study. *Human Relations*, 37, 681–692.

Farrell, D. & Stamm, C. L. (1988) Meta-analysis of the correlates of employee absence. *Human Relations*, 41, 211–227.

Ferris, G. R., Bergin, T. G., & Wayne, S. J. (1988) Personal characteristics, job performance, and absenteeism of public school teachers. *Journal of Applied Social Psychology*, 18, 552–563.

Ferris, G. R. & Rowland, K. M. (1987) Tenure as a moderator of the absence–intent to leave relationship. *Human Relations*, 40, 255–266.

Fichman, M. (1984) A theoretical approach to understanding employee absence. In P. S. Goodman & R. S. Atkin (eds), *Absenteeism: New Approaches to Understanding, Measuring, and Managing Employee Absence* (pp. 1–46). San Francisco: Jossey-Bass.

Fichman, M. (1988) Motivational consequences of absence and attendance: Proportional hazard estimation of a dynamic motivation model. *Journal of Applied Psychology*, 73, 119–134.

Fichman, M. (1989) Attendance makes the heart grow fonder: A hazard rate approach to modeling attendance. *Journal of Applied Psychology*, 74, 325–335.

Firth, H. & Britton, P. (1989) 'Burnout', absence and turnover amongst British nursing staff. *Journal of Occupational Psychology*, 62, 55–59.

Fitzgibbons, D. E. (1992) A critical reexamination of employee absence: The impact of relational contracting, the negotiated order, and the employment relationship. *Research in Personnel and Human Resources Management*, 10, 73–120.

Frayne, C. A. & Latham, G. P. (1987) Application of social learning theory to employee self-management of attendance. *Journal of Applied Psychology*, 72, 387–392.

Fried, Y., Rowland, K. M., & Ferris, G. R. (1984) The physiological measurement of work stress: A critique. *Personnel Psychology*, 37, 583–615.

Furnham, A. & Walsh, J. (1991) Consequences of person–environment incongruence: Absenteeism, frustration, and stress. *Journal of Social Psychology*, 13, 187–204.

Gafni, A. & Peled, D. (1984) The effect of labelling on illness related absenteeism. *Journal of Health Economics*, 3, 173–178.

Gale, E. K. (1993) *The effect of norms and significant others' attitudes on absenteeism.* Paper presented at the annual meeting of the Society for Industrial and Organizational Psychology, San Francisco.

Galloway, D., Panckhurst, F., Bosewll, K., Boswell, C., & Green, K. (1984) Mental health, absences from work, stress and satisfaction in a sample of New Zealand primary school teachers. *Australian and New Zealand Journal of Psychiatry*, 18, 359–363.

Garrison, R. & Eaton, W. (1992) Secretaries, depression and absenteeism. *Women & Health*, **18**(4), 53–76.

Gellatly, I. R. (1995) Individual and group determinants of employee absenteeism: Test of a causal model. *Journal of Organizational Behavior*, **16**, 469–485.

George, J. M. (1989) Mood and absence. *Journal of Applied Psychology*, **74**, 317–324.

George, J. M. (1990) Personality, affect, and behavior in groups. *Journal of Applied Psychology*, **75**, 107–116.

George, J. M. & James, L. R. (1993) Personality, affect, the behavior in groups revisited: Comment on aggregation, levels of analysis, and a recent application of within and between analysis. *Journal of Applied Psychology*, **78**, 798–804.

Geurts, S. A., Buunk, B. P., & Schaufeli, W. B. (1994) Social comparisons and absenteeism: A structural modeling approach. *Journal of Applied Social Psychology*, **24**, 1871–1890.

Goff, S. J., Mount, M., K., & Jamison, R. L. (1990) Employer supported child care, work/family conflict, and absenteeism: A field study. *Personnel Psychology*, **43**, 793–809.

Goodman, P. S. & Atkin, R. S. (1984) Effects of absenteeism on individuals and organizations. In P. S. Goodman & R. S. Atkin (eds), *Absenteeism: New Approaches to Understanding, Measuring, and Managing Employee Absence* (pp. 276–321). San Francisco: Jossey-Bass.

Goodman, P. S. & Garber, S. (1988) Absenteeism and accidents in a dangerous environment: Empirical analysis of underground coal mines. *Journal of Applied Psychology*, **73**, 81–86.

Goodman, P. S. & Leyden, D. P. (1991) Familiarity and group productivity. *Journal of Applied Psychology*, **76**, 578–586.

Gruber, V. A. & Wildman, B. G. (1987) The impact of dysmehorrhea on daily activities. *Behaviour Research and Therapy*, **25**, 123–128.

Gunn, K. P. (1993) A correlation between attendance and grades in a first-year psychology class. *Canadian Psychology*, **34**, 201–202.

Haccoun, R. R. & Desgent, C. (1993) Perceived reasons and consequences of work absence: A survey of French-speaking employees in Quebec. *International Journal of Psychology*, **28**, 97–117.

Haccoun, R. R. & Dupont, S. (1987) Absence research: A critique of previous approaches and an example for a new direction. *Canadian Journal of Administrative Sciences*, **4**, 143–156.

Haccoun, R. R. & Jeanrie, C. (1995) Self reports of work absence as a function of personal attitudes towards absence, and perceptions of the organization. *Applied Psychology: An International Review*, **44**, 155–170.

Hackett, R. D. (1989) Work attitudes and employee absenteeism: A synthesis of the literature. *Journal of Occupational Psychology*, **62**, 235–248.

Hackett, R. D. (1990) Age, tenure, and employee absenteeism. *Human Relations*, **43**, 610–619.

Hackett, R. D., Bycio, P., & Guion, R. M. (1989) Absenteeism among hospital nurses: An idiographic-longitudinal analysis. *Academy of Management Journal*, **32**, 424–453.

Hackett, R. D., Bycio, P., & Hausdorf, P. A. (1994) Further assessments of Meyer and Allen's (1991) three-component model of organizational commitment. *Journal of Applied Psychology*, **79**, 15–23.

Hackett, R. D. & Guion, R. M. (1995) A reevaluation of the absenteeism–job satisfaction relationship. *Organizational Behavior and Human Decision Processes*, **35**, 340–381.

Hanisch, K. A. & Hulin, C. L. (1990) Job attitudes and organizational withdrawal: An examination of retirement and other voluntary withdrawal behaviors. *Journal of Vocational Behavior*, **37**, 60–78.

Hanisch, K. A. & Hulin, C. L. (1991) General attitudes and organizational withdrawal: An evaluation of a causal model. *Journal of Vocational Behavior*, **39**, 110–128.

Harrison, D. A. (1995) Volunteer motivation and attendance decisions: Competitive theory testing in multiple samples from a homeless shelter. *Journal of Applied Psychology*, **80**, 371–385.

Harrison, D. A. & Bell, M. P. (1995) *Social expectations and attendance decisions: Implications for absence control programs.* Paper presented at the annual meeting of the Academy of Management, Vancouver.

Harrison, D. A. & Hulin, C. L. (1989) Investigations of absenteeism: Using event history models to study the absence-taking process. *Journal of Applied Psychology*, **74**, 300–316.

Harrison, D. A. & Shaffer, M. A. (1994) Comparative examinations of self-reports and perceived absenteeism norms: Wading through Lake Wobegon. *Journal of Applied Psychology*, **79**, 240–251.

Hendrix, W. H. & Spencer, B. A. (1989) Development and test of a multivariate model of absenteeism. *Psychological Reports*, **64**, 923–938.

Hendrix, W. H., Spencer, B. A., & Gibson, G. S. (1994) Organizational and extra-organizational factors affecting stress, employee well-being, and absenteeism for males and females. *Journal of Business and Psychology*, **9**, 103–128.

Hill, J. M. M. & Trist, E. L. (1953) A consideration of industrial accidents as a means of withdrawal fro the work situation. *Human Relations*, **6**, 357–380.

Hill, J. M. M. & Trist, E. L. (1955) Changes in accidents and other absences with length of service. *Human Relations*, **8**, 121–152.

Hogan, J. & Hogan, R. (1989) How to measure employee reliability. *Journal of Applied Psychology*, **65**, 177–184.

Holland, J. L. (1973) *Making Vocational Choices: A Theory of Careers.* Englewood Cliffs, NJ: Prentice-Hall.

Hulin, C. (1991) Adaptation, persistence, and commitment in organizations. In M. D. Dunnette & L. M. Hough (eds), *Handbook of Industrial and Organizational Psychology* 2nd edn, Vol. 2 (pp. 445–505). Palo Alto, CA: Consulting Psychologists Press.

Hyman, R. (1975) *Industrial Relations: A Marxist Introduction.* London: Macmillan.

Ilgen, D. R. & Hollenback, J. H. (1977) The role of job satisfaction in absence behavior. *Organizational Behavior and Human Performance*, **19**, 148–161.

Ivancevich, J. M. (1985) Predicting absenteeism from prior absence and work attitudes. *Academy of Management Journal*, **28**, 219–228.

Jackson, J. (1960) Structural characteristics of norms In N. B. Henry (ed), *The Dynamics of Instructional Groups. Fifty-ninth Yearbook of the National Society for the Study of Education, Part II.* Chicago: University of Chicago Press.

Jackson, S. E. & Schuler, R. S. (1985) A meta-analysis and conceptual critique of research on role ambiguity and role conflict in work settings. *Organizational Behavior and Human Decision Processes*, **36**, 16–78.

Jamal, M. (1984) Job stress and job performance controversy: An empirical assessment. *Organizational Behavior and Human Performance*, **33**, 1–21.

Jenkins, R. (1985) Minor psychiatric morbidity in employed young men and women and its contribution to sickness absence. *British Journal of Industrial Medicine*, **42**, 147–154.

Jenkins, R. (1986) Sex differences in alcohol consumption and its associated morbidity in young civil servants. *British Journal of Addiction*, **81**, 525–535.

Johns, G. (1978) Attitudinal and nonattitudinal predictors of two forms of absence from work. *Organizational Behavior and Human Performance*, **22**, 431–444.

Johns, G. (1984) Unresolved issues in the study and management of abence from work. In P. S. Goodman & R. S. Atkin (eds), *Absenteeism: New Approaches to Understanding, Measuring, and Managing Employee Absence* (pp. 360–390). San Francisco: Jossey-Bass.

Johns, G. (1987, October) The great escape. *Psychology Today*, 30–33.

Johns, G. (1991) Substantive and methodological constraints on behavior and attitudes in organizational research. *Organizational Behavior and Human Decision Processes*, **49**, 80–104.

Johns, G. (1994a) Absenteeism estimates by employees and managers: Divergent perspectives and self-serving perceptions. *Journal of Applied Psychology*, **79**, 229–239.

Johns, G. (1994b) How often were you absent? A review of the use of self-reported absence data. *Journal of Applied Psychology*, **79**, 574–591.

Johns, G. (1994c) *Medical, ethical, and cultural constraints on work absence and attendance.* Presentation made at the International Congress of Applied Psychology, Madrid.

Johns, G. & Nicholson, N. (1982) The meanings of absence: New strategies for theory and research. *Research in Organizational Behavior*, **4**, 127–172.

Johnson, W. G. & Ondrich, J. (1990) The duration of post-injury absences from work. *Review of Economics and Statistics*, **72**, 578–586.

Judge, T. A. (1992) The dispositional perspective in human resources research. *Research in Personnel and Human Resources Management*, **10**, 31–72.

Judge, T. A. & Martocchio, J. J. (1995) The role of fairness orientation and supervisor attributions in absence disciplinary decisions. *Journal of Business and Psychology*, **10**, 115–137.

Kahana, N. & Weiss, A. (1992) Absenteeism: A comparison of incentives. *Journal of Comparative Economics*, **16**, 573–595.

Kahn, R. L. & Byosiere, P. (1992) Stress in organizations. In M. D. Dunnette & L. M. Hough (eds), *Handbook of Industrial and Organizational Psychology* 2nd edn, Vol. 3 (pp. 571–650). Palo Alto, CA: Consulting Psychologists Press.

Kanfer, R., Crosby, J. V., & Brandt, D. M. (1988) Investigating behavioral antecedents of turnover at three job tenure levels. *Journal of Applied Psychology*, **73**, 331–335.

Karasek, R. (1990) Lower health risk with increased job control among white collar workers. *Journal of Organizational Behavior*, **11**, 171–185.

Karasek, R. A. Jr (1979) Job demands, decision latitude, and mental strain: Implications for job redesign. *Administrative Science Quarterly*, **24**, 285–308.

Kaufmann, C. L. (1993) Reasonable accommodation to mental health disabilities at work: Legal constructs and practical applications. *Journal of Psychiatry & Law*, **21**, 153–174.

Kelley, H. H. (1972) Attribution in social interaction. E. E. Jones et al. (eds), *Attribution: Perceiving the Causes of Behavior* (pp. 1–26). Morristown, NJ: General Learning Press.

Kenyon, P. & Dawkins, P. (1989) A time series analysis of labour absence in Australia. *Review of Economics and Statistics*, **71**, 232–239.

Klass, B. S. (1989) Determinants of grievance activity and the grievance system's impact on employee behavior: An integrative perspective. *Academy of Management Review*, **14**, 445–458.

Klass, B. S., Heneman, H. G. III, & Olson, C. A. (1991) Effects of grievance activity on absenteeism. *Journal of Applied Psychology*, **76**, 818–824.

Kobasa, S. C. (1979) Stressful life events, personality, and health: An inquiry into hardiness. *Journal of Personality and Social Psychology*, **37**, 1–11.

Kohler, S. S. & Mathieu, J. E. (1993) Individual characteristics, work perceptions, and affective reactions influences on differentiated absence criteria. *Journal of Organizational Behavior*, **14**, 515–530.

Kossek, E. E. (1990) Diversity in child care assistance needs: Employee problems, preferences, and work-related outcomes. *Personnel Psychology*, **43**, 769–791.

Kouzis, A. C. & Eaton, W. W. (1994) Emotional disability days: Prevalence and predictors. *American Journal of Public Health*, **84**, 1304–1307.

Kristensen, T. S. (1991) Sickness absence and work strain among Danish slaughter-house workers: An analysis of absence from work regarded as coping behaviour. *Social Science and Medicine*, **32**, 15–27.

Kryst, S. & Scherl, E. (1994) A population-based survey of the social and personal impact of headache. *Headache*, **34**, 344–350.

Landeweerd, J. A. & Boumans, N. P. G. (1994) The effect of work dimensions and need for autonomy on nurses' work satisfaction and health. *Journal of Occupational and Organizational Psychology*, **67**, 207–217.

Larson, E. W. & Fukami, C. V. (1985) Employee absenteeism: The role of ease of movement. *Academy of Management Journal*, **28**, 464–471.

Latham, G. P. & Frayne, C. A. (1989) Self-management training for increasing job attendance: A follow-up and a replication. *Journal of Applied Psychology*, **74**, 411–416.

Latham, G. P., Skarlicki, D., Irvine, D., & Siegel, J. P. (1993) The increasing import-ance of performance appraisals to employee effectiveness in employment settings in North America. *International Review of Industrial and Organizational Psychology*, **8**, 87–132.

Lawson, D. A. & O'Brien, R. M. (1994) Behavioral and self-report measures of staff burnout in development disabilities. *Journal of Organizational Behavior Management*, **14**(2), 37–54.

Leigh, J. P. (1981) The effects of union membership on absence from work due to illness. *Journal of Labor Research*, **2**, 329–336.

Leigh, J. P. (1983) Sex differences in absenteeism. *Industrial Relations*, **22**, 349–361.

Leigh, J. P. (1984) Unionization and absenteeism. *Applied Economics*, **16**, 147–157.

Leigh, J. P. (1985) The effects of unemployment and the business cycle on absentee-ism. *Journal of Economics and Business*, **37**, 159–170.

Leigh, J. P. (1986) Correlates of absence from work due to illness. *Human Relations*, **39**, 81–100.

Leigh, J. P. (1991) Employee and job attributes as predictors of absenteeism in a national sample of workers: The importance of health and dangerous working condi-tions. *Social Science and Medicine*, **33**, 127–137.

Léonard, C., Van Ameringen, M.-R., Dolan, S. L., & Arsenault, A. (1987) Absen-téisme et assiduité au travail. Deux moyens d'adaptation au stress? *Relations Indus-trielles*, **42**, 774–789.

Levine, S. & Kozloff, M. A. (1978) The sick role: Assessment and overview. *Annual Review of Sociology*, **4**, 317–343.

Lipton, R. B., Steward, W. F., & Von Korff, M. (1994) The burden of migraine: A review of cost to society. *PharmacoEconomics*, **6**, 215–221.

Lissovoy, G. & Lazarus, S. S. (1994) The economic cost of migraine. *Neurology*, **44**(Suppl. 4), S56–S62.

Manning, M. R. & Osland, J. S. (1989) The relationship between absenteeism and stress. *Work & Stress*, **3**, 223–235.

Manning, M. R., Osland, J. S., & Osland, A. (1989) Work-related consequences of smoking cessation. *Academy of Management Journal*, **32**, 606–621.

Marcus, P. M. & Smith, C. B. (1985) Absenteeism in an organizational context. *Work and Occupations*, **12**, 251–268.

Markham, S. E. (1985) An investigation of the relationship between unemployment and absenteeism: A multi-level approach. *Academy of Management Journal*, **28**, 228–234.

Markham, S. E. & McKee, G. H. (1991) Declining organizational size and increasing unemployment rates: Predicting employee absenteeism from within- and between-plant perspectives. *Academy of Management Journal*, **34**, 952–965.

Markham, S. E. & McKee, G. H. (1995a) Group absence behavior and standards: A multilevel analysis. *Academy of Management Journal*, **38**, 1174–1190.

Markham, S. E. & McKee, G. H. (1995b) *Finding leverage points for transforming absence culture: A longitudinal investigation into the importance of work groups.* Paper presented at the annual meeting of the Academy of Management, Vancouver.

Marmot, M. G., North, F., Feeney, A., & Head, J. (1993) Alcohol consumption and sickness absence: From the Whitehall II study. *Addiction*, **88**, 369–382.

Martocchio, J. J. (1989) Age-related differences in employee absenteeism: A meta-analysis. *Psychology and Aging*, **4**, 409–414.

Martocchio, J. J. (1992) The financial cost of absence decisions. *Journal of Management*, **18**, 133–152.

Martocchio, J. J. (1994) The effects of absence culture on individual absence. *Human Relations*, **47**, 243–262.

Martocchio, J. J. & Harrison, D. A. (1993) To be there or not to be there? Questions, theories, and methods in absenteeism research. *Research in Personnel and Human Resources Management*, **11**, 259–328.

Martocchio, J. J. & Judge, T. A. (1994) A policy-capturing approach to individuals' decisions to be absent. *Organizational Behavior and Human Decision Processes*, **57**, 358–386.

Martocchio, J. J. & Judge, T. A. (1995) When we don't see eye to eye: Discrepancies between supervisors and subordinates in absence disciplinary decisions. *Journal of Management*, **21**, 251–278.

Maslach, C. & Jackson, S. E. (1984) Burnout in organizational settings. In S. Oskamp (ed), *Applied Social Psychology Annual*, Vol. 5. Beverly Hills, CA: Sage.

Mathieu, J. E. & Farr, J. L. (1991) Further evidence for the discriminant validity of measures of organizational commitment, job involvement, and job satisfaction. *Journal of Applied Psychology*, **76**, 127–133.

Mathieu, J. E. & Kohler, S. S. (1990a) A test of the interactive effects of organizational commitment and job involvement on various types of absence. *Journal of Vocational Behavior*, **36**, 33–44.

Mathieu, J. E. & Kohler, S. S. (1990b) A cross-level examination of group absence influences on individual absence. *Journal of Applied Psychology*, **75**, 217–220.

Mathieu, J. E. & Zajac, D. M. (1990) A review and meta-analysis of the antecedents, correlates, and consequences of organizational commitment. *Psychological Bulletin*, **108**, 171–194.

Mayer, R. C. & Schoorman, F. D. (1992) Predicting participation and production outcomes through a two-dimensional model of organizational commitment. *Academy of Management Journal*, **35**, 671–684.

McKee, G. H., Markham, S. E., & Scott, K. D. (1992) Job stress and employee withdrawal from work. In J. C. Quick, L. R. Murphey, & J. J. Hurrell Jr (eds), *Work and Well-being: Assessments and Interventions for Occupational Mental Health*. Washington, DC: American Psychological Association.

McShane, S. L. (1984) Job satisfaction and absenteeism: A meta-analytic re-examination. *Canadian Journal of Administrative Sciences*, **1**, 61–77.

Meisenheimer, J. R. Jr (1990, August) Employee absences in 1989: A new look at data from the CPS. *Monthly Labor Review*, 28–33.

Melamed, S., Ben-Avi, I., Luz, J., & Green, M. S. (1995) Objective and subjective work monotony: Effects of job satisfaction, psychological distress, and absenteeism in blue-collar workers. *Journal of Applied Psychology*, **80**, 29–42.

Meyer, J. P. & Allen, N. J. (1991) A three-component conceptualization of organizational commitment. *Human Resource Management Review*, **1**, 61–98.

Meyer, J. P., Allen, N. J., & Smith, C. A. (1993) Commitment to organizations and occupations: Extension and test of a three-component conceptualization. *Journal of Applied Psychology*, **78**, 538–551.

Meyerson, D. E. (1994) Interpretations of stress in institutions: The cultural production of ambiguity and burnout. *Administrative Science Quarterly*, **39**, 628–653.

Mitra, A., Jenkins, G. D., Jr, & Gupta, N. (1992) A meta-analytic review of the relationship between absence and turnover. *Journal of Applied Psychology*, 77, 879–889.

Moch, M. K. & Fitzgibbons, D. E. (1985) The relationship between absenteeism and production efficiency: An empirical assessment. *Journal of Occuaptional Psychology*, 58, 39–47.

Moore, M. L., Nichol, V. W., & McHugh, P. P. (1992) Review of no-fault absenteeism cases taken to arbitration, 1980–1989: A rights and responsibilities analysis. *Employee Responsibilities and Rights Journal*, 5, 29–48.

Mowday, R. T., Porter, L. W., & Steers, R. M. (1982) *Employee–Organization Linkages: The Psychology of Commitment, Absenteeism, and Turnover*. New York: Academic Press.

Mowday, R. T., Steers, R. M., & Porter, L. W. (1979) The measurement of organizational commitment. *Journal of Vocational Behavior*, 14, 224–247.

Muchinsky, P. M. (1977) Employee absenteeism: A review of the literature. *Journal of Vocational Behavior*, 10, 316–340.

Newsome, S. (1993) *Predicting absence without work attitudes*. Paper presented at the annual meeting of the Canadian Psychological Association, Montreal.

Ng. I. (1989) The effect of vacation and sickleave policies on absenteeism. *Canadian Journal of Administrative Sciences*, 6(4), 18–27.

Nichols, T. (1994) Industrial accidents as a means of withdrawal from the workplace according to the Tavistock Institute of Human Relations: A re-examination of a classic study. *British Journal of Sociology*, 45, 387–406.

Nicholson, N. (1975) *Industrial absence as an indicant of employee motivation and job satisfaction*. Unpublished doctoral dissertation, University of Wales, Cardiff.

Nicholson, N. (1977) Absence behaviour and attendance motivation: A conceptual synthesis. *Journal of Management Studies*, 14, 231–252.

Nicholson, N. (1985) Absence and turnover: The absentee bus crews. In C. Clegg, N. Kemp, & K. Legge (eds), *Case Studies in Organizational Behaviour* (pp. 114–121). London: Harper & Row.

Nicholson, N., Brown, C. A., & Chadwick-Jones, J. K. (1976) Absence from work and job satisfaction. *Journal of Applied Psychology*, 61, 728–737.

Nicholson, N., Brown, C. A., & Chadwick-Jones, J. K. (1977) Absence from work and personal characteristics. *Journal of Applied Psychology*, 62, 319–327.

Nicholson, N. & Johns, G. (1985) The absence culture and the psychological contract—Who's in control of absence? *Academy of Management Review*, 10, 397–407.

Nicholson, N. & Martocchio, J. J. (1995) The management of absence: What do we know? What can we do? G. R. Ferris, S. D. Rosen, & D. T. Barnum (eds), *Handbook of Human Resources Management* (pp. 567–614). Oxford: Blackwell.

Nicholson, N. & Payne, R. (1987) Absence from work: Explanations and attributions. *Applied Psychology: An International Review*, 36, 121–132.

Nicholson, N. & West, M. A. (1988) *Managerial Job Change: Men and Women in Transition*. Cambridge: Cambridge University Press.

Normand, J., Salyards, S. D., & Mahoney, J. J. (1990) An evaluation of preemployment drug testing. *Journal of Applied Psychology*, 75, 629–639.

North, F., Syme, S. L., Feeney, A., Head, J., Shipley, M., & Marmot, M. G.(1993) Explaining socioeconomic differences in sickness absence: The Whitehall II study. *British Medical Journal*, 306, 361–366.

Öhlund, C., Lindström, I., Areskoug, B., Eek, C., Peterson, L.-E., & Nachemson, A. (1994) Pain behavior in industrial subacute low back pain. Part I. Reliability: Concurrent and predictive validity of pain behavior assessments. *Pain*, 58, 201–209.

Ones, D. S., Viswesvaran, C., & Schmidt, F. L. (1993) Comprehensive meta-analysis of integrity test validities: Findings and implications for personnel selection and theories of job performance. *Journal of Applied Psychology*, 78, 679–703.

Organ, D. W. (1988) *Organizational Citizenship Behavior: The Good Soldier Syndrome.* Lexington, MA: Lexington.

Ostroff, C. (1992) The relationship between satisfaction, attitudes, and performance: An organizational level analysis. *Journal of Applied Psychology*, 77, 963–974.

Parkes, K. R. (1983) Smoking as a moderator of the relationship between affective state and absence from work. *Journal of Applied Psychology*, **68**, 698–708.

Parkes, K. R. (1987) Relative weight, smoking, and mental health as predictors of sickness and absence from work. *Journal of Applied Psychology*, 72, 275–286.

Peel, M. J. & Wilson, N. (1990) Labour absenteeism: The impact of profit sharing, voice and participation. *International Journal of Manpower*, **11**(7), 17–24.

Porter, L. W. & Steers, R. M. (1973) Organizational, work, and personal factors in employee turnover and absenteeism. *Psychological Bulletin*, 80, 151–176.

Prins, R. & de Graaf, A. (1986) Comparison of sickness absence in Belgian, German and Dutch firms. *British Journal of Industrial Medicine*, 43, 529–536.

Randall, D. M., Fedor, D. B., & Longenecker, C. O. (1990) The behavioral expression of organizational commitment. *Journal of Vocational Behavior*, 36, 210–224.

Rees, D. W. & Cooper, C. L. (1990) Occupational stress in health service employees. *Health Services Management Research*, 3, 163–172.

Rhodes, S. R. & Steers, R. M. (1990) *Managing Employee Absenteeism.* Reading, MA: Addison-Wesley.

Robinson, S. L. & Bennett, R. J. (1995) A typology of deviant workplace behaviors: A multidimensional scaling study. *Academy of Management Journal*, 38, 555–572.

Rodin, J. & Ickovics, J. R. (1990) Women's health: Review and research agenda as we approach the 21st century. *American Psychologist*, 45, 1018–1034.

Rogers, R. E. & Herting, S. R. (1993) Patterns of absenteeism among government employees. *Public Personnel Management*, 22, 215–235.

Rosse, J. G. (1988) Relations among lateness, absence, and turnover: Is there a progression of withdrawal? *Human Relations*, 41, 517–531.

Rosse, J. G. & Miller, H. E. (1984) Relationship between absenteeism and other employee behaviors. In P. S. Goodman and R. S. Atkin (eds), *Absenteeism: New Approaches to Understanding, Measuring, and Managing Absence* (pp. 194–228). San Francisco: Jossey-Bass.

Rousseau, D. M. (1985) Issues of level in organizational research: Multi-level and cross-level perspectives. *Research in Organizational Behavior*, 7, 1–37.

Runcie, J. F. (1988) 'Deviant behavior'. Achieving autonomy in a machine-paced environment. In M. O. Jones, M. D. Moore, & R. C. Snyder (eds), *Inside Organizations: Understanding the Human Dimension* (pp. 129-140). Newbury Park, CA: Sage.

Rushmore, C. H. & Youngblood, S. A. (1979) Medically-related absenteeism: Random or motivated behavior? *Journal of Occupational Medicine*, 21, 245–250.

Sackett, P. R., DuBois, C. L. Z., Noe, A. W. (1991) Tokenism in performance evaluation: The effects of work group representation on male–female and white–black differences in performance ratings. *Journal of Applied Psychology*, 76, 263–267.

Sands, J. M. & Miller, L. E. (1991) Effects of moon phase and other temporal variables on absenteeism. *Psychological Reports*, 69, 959–962.

Saxton, M. J., Phillips, J. S., & Blakeney, R. N. (1991) Antecedents and consequences of emotional exhaustion in the airline reservations service sector. *Human Relations*, 44, 583–595.

Scott, D. & Markham, S. (1982) Absenteeism control methods: A survey of practices and results. *Personnel Administrator*, 27, 73–84.

Scott, D. & Taylor, G. S. (1983) An analysis of absenteeism cases taken to arbitration: 1975–1981. *Arbitration Journal*, 38(3), 61–70.

Scott, K. D. & McClellan, E. L. (1990) Gender differences in absenteeism. *Public Personnel Management*, 19, 229–253.

Scott, K. D. & Taylor, G. S. (1985) An examination of conflicting findings on the relationship between job satisfaction and absenteeism: A meta-analysis. *Academy of Management Journal*, **28**, 599–612.

Sheridan, J. E. (1985) A catastrophe model of employee withdrawal leading to low job performance, high absenteeism, and job turnover during the first year of employment. *Academy of Management Journal*, **28**, 88–109.

Skinner, B. F. (1974) *About Behaviorism*. New York: Knopf.

Skodol, A. E., Schwartz, S., Dohrenwend, B. P., Levav, I., & Shrout, P. E. (1994) Minor depression in a cohort of young adults in Israel. *Archives of General Psychiatry*, **51**, 542–551.

Somers, M. J. (1995) Organizational commitment, turnover and absenteeism: An examination of direct and interaction effects. *Journal of Organizational Behavior*, **16**, 49–58.

Spector, P. E., Dwyer, D. J., & Jex, S. M. (1988) Relation of job stressors to affective, health, and performance outcomes: A comparison of multiple data sources. *Journal of Applied Psychology*, **73**, 11–19.

Spielberger, C. D. & Reheiser, E. C. (1994) The job stress survey: Measuring gender differences in occupational stress. *Journal of Social Behavior and Personality*, **9**, 199–218.

Spink, K. S. & Carron, A. V. (1992) Group cohesion and adherence in exercise classes. *Journal of Sport and Exercise Psychology*, **14**, 78–86.

Stansfeld, S., Feeney, A., Head, J., Canner, R., North, F., & Marmot, M. (1995) Sickness absence for psychiatric illness: The Whitehall II study. *Social Science and Medicine*, **40**, 189–197.

Stansfeld, S. A., Smith, G. D., & Marmot, M. (1993) Association between physical and psychological morbidity in the Whitehall II study. *Journal of Psychosomatic Research*, **37**, 227–238.

Steers, R. M. & Rhodes, S. R. (1978) Major influences on employee attendance: A process model. *Journal of Applied Psychology*, **63**, 391–407.

Steers, R. M. & Rhodes, S. R. (1984) Knowledge and speculation about absenteeism. In P. S. Goodman & R. S. Atkin (eds), *Absenteeism: New Approaches to Understanding, Measuring, and Managing Employee Absence* (pp. 229–275). San Francisco: Jossey-Bass.

Tang, T. L.-P. & Hammontree, M. L. (1992) The effects of hardiness, police stress, and life stress on police officers' illness and absenteeism. *Public Personnel Management*, **21**, 493–510.

Tansey, R. R. & Hyman, M. R. (1992) Public relations, advocacy ads, and the campaign against absenteeism during World War II. *Business & Professional Ethics Journal*, **11**(3 & 4), 129–164.

Taylor, D. W., Haynes, R. B., Sackett, D. L., & Gibson, E. S. (1981) Longterm follow-up of absenteeism among working men following the detection and treatment of their hypertension. *Clinical and Investigative Medicine*, **4**(3/4), 173–177.

Taylor, P. J. & Burridge, J. (1982) Trends in death, disablement, and sickness absence in the British Post Office since 1891. *British Journal of Industrial Medicine*, **39**, 1–10.

Tharenou, P. (1993) A test of reciprocal causality for absenteeism. *Journal of Organizational Behavior*, **14**, 269–290.

Theorell, T., Leymann, H., Jodko, M., Konarski, K., & Norbeck, H. E. (1994) 'Person under train' incidents from the subway driver's point of view—a prospective 1-year follow-up study: The design, and medical and psychiatric data. *Social Science and Medicine*, **38**, 471–475.

Thomas, L. T. & Ganster, D. C. (1995) Impact of family-supportive work variables on work–family conflict and strain: A control perspective. *Journal of Applied Psychology*, **80**, 6–15.

Thomas, P. J. & Thomas, M. D. (1994) Effects of sex, marital status, and parental status on absenteeism among navy enlisted personnel. *Military Psychology*, **6**, 95–108.

Tollefson, G. D., Souetre, E. J., Thomander, L., & Potvin, J. H. (1993) Comorbid anxious signs and symptoms in major depression: Impact on functional capacity and comparative treatment outcomes. *International Clinical Psychopharmacology*, **8**, 281–293.

Turnbull, P. & Sapsford, D. (1992) A sea of discontent: The tides of organised and 'unorganised' conflict on the docks. *Sociology*, **26**, 291–309.

VandenHeuvel, A. & Wooden, M. (1995) Do explanations of absenteeism differ for men and women? *Human Relations*, **48**, 1309–1330.

Waddell, G., Newton, M., Henderson, I., Somerville, D., & Main, C. J. (1993) A fear-avoidance beliefs questionnaire (FABQ) and the role of fear-avoidance beliefs in chronic low back pain and disability. *Pain*, **52**, 157–168.

Webb, G. R., Redman, S., Hennrikus, D. J., Kelman, G. R., Gibberd, R. W., & Sanson-Fisher, R. W. (1994) The relationships between high-risk and problem drinking and the occurrence of work injuries and related absences. *Journal of Studies on Alcohol*, **55**, 434–446.

Wilson, N. & Peel, M. J. (1991) The impact on absenteeism and quits of profit-sharing and other forms of employee participation. *Industrial and Labor Relations Review*, **44**, 454–468.

Wise, L. C. (1993) The erosion of nursing resources: Employee withdrawal behavior. *Research in Nursing & Health*, **16**, 67–75.

Wooden, M. (1990, December) The 'sickie': A public sector phenomenon? *Journal of Industrial Relations*, 560–576.

Xie, J. L. & Johns, G. (1995) *Perceptions of absence from work: The People's Republic of China versus Canada*. Manuscript under review.

Yammarino, F. J. & Markham, S. E. (1992) On the application of within and between analysis: Are absence and affect really group-based phenomena? *Journal of Applied Psychology*, **77**, 168–176.

Youngblood, S. A. (1984) Work, nonwork, and withdrawal. *Journal of Applied Psychology*, **69**, 106–117.

Zaccaro, S. J. (1991) Nonequivalent associations between forms of cohesiveness and group-related outcomes: Evidence for multidimensionality. *Journal of Social Psychology*, **13**, 387–399.

Zaccaro, S. J. & Collins, T. T. (1988) Excused and unexcused absenteeism in normative organizations. *Group & Organization Studies*, **13**(1), 81–99.

Zaccaro, S. J., Craig, B., & Quinn, J. (1991) Prior absenteeism, supervisory style, job satisfaction, and personal characteristics: An investigation of some mediated and moderated linkages to work absenteeism. *Organizational Behavior and Human Decision Processes*, **50**, 24–44.

Chapter 5

ORGANIZATIONAL COMMITMENT

John P. Meyer
University of Western Ontario

It has been more than 10 years since Griffin and Bateman (1986) reviewed the organizational commitment literature in Volume 1 of the *International Review of Industrial and Organizational Psychology*. In that chapter, commitment shared the spotlight with job satisfaction. Much has happened in the field since then. New approaches have been taken to the conceptualization and measurement of organizational commitment and advances have been made in the research designs and analytic techniques used to examine the development and consequences of commitment. Close to a dozen meta-analytic reviews focusing specifically on organizational commitment and its relations with other variables have been published. Finally, data are being collected in countries around the world, and interest in other forms of work-related commitment, and their interactions, is increasing.

To make the task of reviewing these developments more manageable, I will, like Griffin and Bateman, focus primarily on theory and research pertaining to organizational commitment. I will start by focusing on the results of recent meta-analytic investigations. Although the meta-analyses themselves were published within the time frame covered in this review (i.e. the 1990s), the studies included in these analyses were generally published much earlier. Consequently, the results of the meta-analyses provide a snapshot of the field as we entered the 1990s and serve to highlight the important substantive and methodological limitations that needed to be addressed. In subsequent sections of this review I will examine the progress that has been made in addressing these limitations, particularly as they pertain to the measurement of commitment and the investigation of its development and consequences. Although I will include the results of studies conducted outside North America and the UK in this discussion, I will not specifically address cross-cultural issues that arise from this research. Finally, I will conclude with some suggestions for the direction of commitment research in the future.

International Review of Industrial and Organizational Psychology, 1997 Volume 12
Edited by C.L. Cooper and I.T. Robertson. © 1997 John Wiley & Sons Ltd.

META-ANALYSES

The most comprehensive and widely cited meta-analytic review of the organizational commitment literature was that conducted by Mathieu and Zajac (1990). Mathieu and Zajac reported mean sample-weighted correlations, corrected for unreliability, between organizational commitment and 48 other work-related variables divided into three categories: antecedents (26), consequences (8), and correlates (14). I will organize my review of meta-analytic findings around these same three categories. Within each category, I will begin by summarizing the findings obtained by Mathieu and Zajac and then present the results of more recent analyses. The latter generally had a narrower focus and included more detailed assessments of moderator effects. Unless otherwise stated, all correlations reported in this section of the article are sample-weighted and corrected for attenuation due to unreliability.

Antecedents of Commitment

Among the variables Mathieu and Zajac (1990) classified as antecedents of commitment were those reflecting personal characteristics, job characteristics, group–leader relations, organizational characteristics, and role states. Of these, the strongest correlations were obtained for job characteristics, particularly job scope (enrichment), and group–leader relations (e.g. leader communication, participative leadership, task interdependence). Personal characteristics (with the exception of perceived personal competence) were generally found to have weak correlations with commitment. Sex was one of the personal characteristics found not to be related to commitment. Aven, Parker, and McEvoy (1993) confirmed this result in a more recent meta-analysis based on a larger set of studies. Few studies examined relations between commitment and organizational characteristics and those that did reported relatively weak correlations. Role states (ambiguity, conflict, overload) were not found to have meaningful links to commitment, although there was sufficient between-study variance to suggest that moderators might be operating.

Cohen and his colleagues conducted a series of meta-analyses to address more specific antecedent–commitment relations and potential moderating effects. For example, Cohen and Lowenberg (1990) reviewed the findings of studies conducted to test Becker's side-bet theory of commitment. According to Becker, commitment increases as employees make side-bets, or investments, that would be lost if they were to leave the organization. Cohen and Lowenberg found that the correlations between commitment and 11 side-bet variables (e.g. age, tenure, gender) were generally weak, and concluded that there is little evidence to support side-bet theory. They cautioned, however, that the side-bet and commitment measures used in the studies included in their analyses might not have been appropriate for testing side-bet theory (cf. Meyer & Allen, 1984).

Cohen (1992) tested for the moderating effect of occupation on the correlations between commitment and various personal and organizational antecedent variables. He found that commitment was more strongly related to personal characteristics (e.g. tenure, education, marital status, gender, motivation) for employees in blue-collar and non-professional white-collar occupations than for professionals. Correlations between commitment and organizational characteristics also varied across occupational groups, but the pattern was less consistent. For example, role ambiguity correlated more strongly with commitment among non-professionals, whereas autonomy and communication correlated more strongly with commitment among professionals. These latter findings suggest that, in general, the needs and preferences of members of these broad occupational groups differ, and that the commitment they experience varies as a function of whether these needs and preferences are satisfied at work.

In a related analysis, Cohen (1993a) examined the correlations between commitment and age and tenure within different career stages. He found that the correlation between age and commitment was stronger among younger employees (i.e. those under 30) than it was for the other age groups. In contrast, the correlation between tenure and commitment was greater among the more senior employees (i.e. those with more than nine years of experience). These findings suggest that the correlations involving age and tenure may not be linear, and might help to account for the relatively weak correlations reported by Mathieu and Zajac (1990).

Cohen and Gattiker (1994) used meta-analysis to examine the link between organizational commitment and rewards, operationalized as actual income and pay satisfaction. Across all studies, commitment was more strongly related to pay satisfaction than to actual income. These relations were moderated to some extent, however, by structural characteristics. Specifically, pay satisfaction correlated more strongly with commitment in the private versus public sector, and the correlation between actual income and commitment was greater for professional than for clerical employees.

Consequences of Commitment

Included in Mathieu and Zajac's (1990) 'consequence' category were job performance, perceived job alternatives, intention to search, intention to leave, attendance, lateness, and turnover. Not surprisingly, given the nature of the construct, the most widely investigated outcomes, and the ones with the strongest correlations with commitment (in order) were intention to search, intention to leave, and actual turnover. Correlations with the other outcome variables were disappointingly low, although there was some evidence to suggest that moderators might be operating. The only moderator variable considered by Mathieu and Zajac, however, was a methodological one. They found, in general, that relations between commitment and outcome measures were greater when an attitudinal rather than a calculative measure of commitment was used.

Randall (1990) also conducted a meta-analysis of studies examining the relations between commitment and various work outcomes. Her findings closely paralleled those of Mathieu and Zajac. In an examination of methodological moderator effects, Randall found that overall correlations tended to be slightly stronger (i) in studies using cross-sectional rather than longitudinal designs, (ii) for white-collar as opposed to blue-collar samples (a finding replicated by Cohen & Hudecek, 1993), (iii) when commitment was measured using the Organizational Commitment Questionnaire (OCQ: see Mowday, Steers, & Porter, 1979) rather than another instrument, and (iv) when objective or self-report measures of the outcome rather than supervisor ratings were used. These differences tended to be quite small, prompting Randall to conclude that the overall weak relations between commitment and behaviour cannot be explained from a methodological perspective.

Cohen (1991) examined the impact of career stage on the relation between commitment and various organizational outcomes. He found that, when age was used as the career indicator, the correlation between commitment and turnover (actual and intended) was greater among those in the early as opposed to middle or late career stages. He also found a moderating effect of career stage, defined in terms of tenure, on absenteeism and performance. In this case, the correlations were stronger for those in the late as opposed to early and middle career stages. Based on these findings, he concluded that organizations can benefit from the commitment of employees across career stages, but that the nature of the benefit (e.g. retention, performance) might differ. As for why age and tenure operated differently in moderating commitment–outcome relations, Cohen speculated that age, like turnover, has relevance not only for one's work, but for life in general. On the other hand, tenure, is a more work-specific variable, as are absenteeism and performance.

Finally, Cohen (1993b) tested for the interaction of two potential moderators of the correlation between commitment and turnover: time lapse between measures and career stage. He found evidence for such an interaction when career stage was defined in terms of age but not in terms of tenure. Although the strength of the correlation between commitment and turnover was stronger for younger employees when the interval between the measures was short, for older employees commitment predicted turnover better when the interval was longer. Cohen argued that this might be due to the fact that commitment is less stable in younger employees and, therefore, the longer the interval the more likely it is to change (along with the decision to stay or leave). In contrast, for older employees, commitment is likely to be more stable, but it might be more difficult for those with weak commitment to leave because of structural bonds, lack of alternatives, and so on. The longer the measurement interval, the more likely it is that uncommitted employees will find the means to overcome these obstacles.

Correlates of Commitment

Included in Mathieu and Zajac's (1990) category of 'correlates' of commitment were variables that, like commitment, reflect an employee's psychological reactions to work (e.g. motivation, job involvement, stress, union commitment, occupational commitment, job satisfaction). The causal connections between these variables and commitment are either unknown or the subject of debate. These variables showed some of the highest correlations with commitment of any included in the analyses. The magnitude of these correlations has raised concerns in the past about the potential for redundancy among the constructs themselves (e.g. Morrow, 1983). There is now considerable evidence, however, to suggest that construct redundancy is not a serious problem in the case of organizational commitment (e.g. Brooke, Russell, & Price, 1988; Meyer, Allen & Smith, 1993; Morrow, 1993; Mathieu & Farr, 1991; Randall & Cote, 1991; Reilly & Orsak, 1991). Nevertheless, the fact that organizational commitment is so strongly associated with these other reaction measures suggests a need to examine their connections more closely.

In a more recent meta-analysis, Wallace (1993) estimated the correlation between organizational commitment and professional commitment, a variable not included in Mathieu and Zajac's analysis. She reported a mean corrected correlation of 0.452, suggesting that commitment to an organization and a profession are not necessarily incompatible. This positive correlation does not rule out the possibility of differences in absolute levels of organizational and professional commitment, and does not preclude the possibility that conflicts might arise. Wallace also found evidence for moderator effects. Specifically, although positive in all cases, the magnitude of the correlation between professional and organizational commitment varied with degree of professionalization in an occupation and with position or rank in the employing organization. The correlations also varied depending on how professional commitment was conceptualized and measured (professional, occupational, or career commitment, or career salience). The latter finding is consistent with concerns recently expressed about the conceptualization and measurement of work commitments (see Morrow, 1993).

Summary and Implications

As noted earlier, these meta-analytic investigations serve two important purposes. First, they provide a summary of what we know about the relations between organizational commitment and other variables. The results of analyses involving antecedent variables, for example, suggest that commitment is more strongly related to characteristics of the job and work situation than to personal or structural characteristics. The analyses involving consequence variables indicate that, consistent with its historical roots (see Mowday, Porter, & Steers, 1982), commitment correlates most strongly with turnover (and related variables). Correlations with other outcome variables appear to be generally quite weak. The strongest correlations were obtained in analyses involving other 'reaction' measures. These correlations were not of sufficient magnitude, however, to suggest that organizational commitment is redundant with these other constructs (cf. Morrow, 1993).

It must be kept in mind that, although the variables included in these meta-analyses are commonly classified as antecedents, consequences, and correlates of commitment, the data used in these analyses were, for the most part, obtained in cross-sectional studies involving self-report measures. Thus, although the findings appear to reflect meaningful patterns with implications for how organizations might foster commitment in their employees and the consequences that might result, they must be interpreted with caution. At best, the results of these analyses help to place organizational commitment within a nomological network of work-related variables. The magnitudes of the correlations suggest that organizational commitment is meaningfully related to many of these variables, but the nature of the relations is as yet unclear.

A second, and arguably more important, contribution made by these meta-analyses is that they identified a number of limitations in commitment research that need to be addressed. Among the more frequently cited problems were (i) lack of clarity and consensus concerning the conceptualization and measurement of commitment, (ii) the atheoretical nature of antecedent research, including lack of attention to mediating mechanisms, (iii) the overly narrow focus of outcome research, with a general lack of attention to potential negative outcomes and to outcomes of more direct relevance to employees, (iv) the use of methods ill-suited to investigation of causal relations, and (v) the focus in both the antecedent and consequence research on main effects with a lack of systematic investigation of moderator effects. These concerns are, of course, not completely independent. In what follows, I will review recent developments in the commitment literature as they pertain to three broad issues, the conceptualization and measurement of organizational commitment, its development, and its consequences.

CONCEPTUALIZATION AND MEASUREMENT OF ORGANIZATIONAL COMMITMENT

Part of the difficulty in interpreting the results of studies (individual or meta-analytic) designed to examine the development and consequences of organizational commitment is the fact that commitment has been defined and measured in many different ways. Moreover, the definitions and measures used within a given study do not always correspond (cf. Meyer & Allen, 1984, 1991). Recent efforts to clarify the meaning of organizational commitment and to refine its measurement have taken two distinct directions. The first involved attempts to clarify the construct by illustrating that commitment can take different forms. That is, the nature of the commitment that defines the relationship between an employee and an organization can vary. The second involved making distinctions among specific entities within the organization to which employees become committed. These two approaches at classification are not incompatible. After discussing each individually, I will conclude this section with a discussion of how, in combination, the two approaches help to clarify our understanding of organizational commitment, how it develops, and its implications for individuals and organizations.

The Nature of the Commitment

Although there is a growing consensus that commitment is a multidimensional construct, various approaches have been taken to identify its dimensions. I will focus my discussion here on two of these approaches. In each case, I will describe the distinctions that have been made and, where relevant, will discuss the development and evaluation of measures. Unless it is relevant to the evaluation of measures, I will reserve discussion of research using these measures to address substantive issues (e.g. development and consequences) for subsequent sections.

Allen and Meyer (1990b, Meyer & Allen, 1991) developed a multidimensional model of commitment based on their observation that existing definitions of the construct reflected at least three distinct themes. Specifically, commitment has been viewed as an affective orientation toward the organization (e.g. Mowday, Porter, & Steers, 1982), a recognition of costs associated with leaving the organization (e.g. Becker, 1960), and a moral obligation to remain with the organization (e.g. Weiner, 1982). Common to these perspectives 'is the view that commitment is a psychological state that (a) characterizes the employee's relationship with the organization, and (b) has implications for the decision to continue membership in the organization' (Meyer & Allen, 1991, p. 67). Thus, regardless of the definition, committed employees are more likely to remain in the organization than are uncommitted employees. What differs is the nature of the psychological state being described.

Meyer and Allen (1991) argued that the psychological states reflected in these different definitions of commitment are not mutually exclusive, and that a clearer understanding of an employee's relationship with an organization can be gained by considering the strength of all three. In developing their model, therefore, they referred to these states as components, rather than types, of commitment and gave each an identifying label: affective (emotional attachment), continuance (cost-based), and normative (obligation). Finally, Meyer and Allen reasoned that the psychological states reflected in the three components of commitment would develop on the basis of quite different experiences (antecedents) and have potentially different implications for employees' behaviour (consequences), other than their tendency to remain in the organization.

Allen and Meyer (1990b) developed measures to be used in testing the three-component model. The Affective (ACS), Continuance (CCS), and Normative (NCS) Commitment Scales have been subjected to fairly extensive psychometric evaluation and have received considerable support (see Allen & Meyer, in press, for a review). For example, the three scales were found in both exploratory (Allen & Meyer, 1990b; McGee & Ford, 1987; Reilly & Orsak, 1991) and confirmatory (Dunham, Grube, & Castaneda, 1994; Hackett, Bycio, & Hausdorf, 1994; Meyer, Allen, & Gellatly, 1990; Moorman, Niehoff, & Organ, 1993; Shore & Tetrick, 1991; Somers, 1993; Vandenberghe, in press) factor analyses to measure distinguishable constructs. Moreover, studies that have examined the links between the three commitment scales and various antecedent and consequence measures (e.g. Allen & Meyer, 1990b; Bycio, Hackett, & Allen, 1995; Dunham, Grube, & Castaneda, 1994; Hackett, Bycio, & Hausdorf, 1994; Konovsky & Cropanzano, 1991; Meyer, Allen, & Smith, 1993; Randall, Fedor, & Longenecker, 1990; Shore & Wayne, 1993; Whitener & Walz, 1993) have generally found a pattern of correlations consistent with the predictions generated from the model. Finally, the three commitment constructs have been found in factor analyses to be distinguishable from related constructs including job satisfaction (Shore & Tetrick, 1991), career, job, and work values (Blau, Paul, & St. John, 1993); career commitment (Reilly & Orsak, 1991), occupational commitment (Meyer, Allen, & Smith, 1993), and perceived organizational support (Shore & Tetrick, 1991). Shore and Tetrick found that items from the ACS loaded on the same factor as items from the OCQ, which is consistent with the view that the OCQ measures primarily affective commitment (cf. Allen & Meyer, 1990b).

In spite of this supportive evidence, there have been findings that suggest the need for further refinement of the Allen and Meyer (1990b) measures. Most notably, the CCS has been found in some studies to comprise two related dimensions, one reflecting lack of alternatives, and the other high personal sacrifice (Hackett, Bycio, & Hausdorf, 1994; Meyer, Allen, & Gellatly, 1990, McGee & Ford, 1987; Sommers, 1993). The implications of this are unclear at this point. McGee and Ford found that the two subscales correlated in opposite directions with affective commitment and concluded that they measure somewhat different constructs. They advocated further development of the subscales. In contrast, others have found that the two dimensions/subscales are highly related and correlated similarly with other constructs (e.g. Hackett, Bycio, & Hausdorf, 1994; Meyer, Paunonen, Gellatly, Goffin, & Jackson, 1989). These findings, combined with evidence that the internal consistency of the full CCS is acceptable (Allen & Meyer, in press), suggest that there may be little to be gained by further development of the subscales. Nevertheless, users might be wise to evaluate the utility of using subscales on a case by case basis until this issue is resolved (Meyer, Allen, & Gellatly, 1990).

Studies have also revealed stronger than expected correlations between the ACS and NCS, suggesting that feelings of affective attachment and sense of obligation to an organization are not independent of one another (e.g. Hackett, Bycio, & Hausdorf, 1994). The two scales also tend to show similar patterns of correlation with antecedent and outcome measures; the correlations involving the ACS tend to be somewhat stronger than those involving the NCS, however (see Allen & Meyer, in press). A recent modification of the NCS did not correct these problems (Meyer, Allen, & Smith, 1993).

Finally, Vandenberg and Self (1993) found that the factor structure of the ACS and CCS was somewhat unstable during the early months of employment, and cautioned that the scales might not be appropriate for use with new employees. Meyer and Gardner (1994) conducted similar analysis, however, and found little evidence of instability. The difference in findings might be due to differences in the timing of measurement in the two studies; Vandenberg and Self obtained their measures after one day, one month and three months, whereas the measures examined by Meyer and Gardner were administered after one, six and 12 months. In light of these findings, researchers wanting to use the ACS and CCS to examine changes in commitment, and/or its correlations with other variables over time, should determine that the factor structure is indeed stable over the time frame examined.

O'Reilly and his colleagues (e.g. Caldwell, Chatman, & O'Reilly, 1990; O'Reilly & Chatman, 1986) took a somewhat different approach to categorizing the various forms of commitment. Like Meyer and Allen (1991), they argued that commitment reflects the 'psychological bond' that ties the employee to the organization, but that the nature of the bond can differ. Following from Kelman's (1958) work on attitude and behaviour change, they suggest that the psychological bond between an employee and an organization can take three distinct forms which they labelled compliance, identification, and internalization. Compliance occurs when employees adopt certain attitudes and behaviours in order to gain reward. Identification involves the acceptance of influence to maintain a satisfying relationship. Internalization occurs when the induced attitudes and behaviours are congruent with the employee's own values. O'Reilly and Chatman argued that an employee's psychological attachment to an organization can reflect varying combinations of each of these three psychological foundations.

O'Reilly and Chatman (1986) proposed that the behavioural consequences of the three forms of commitment might be quite different. To illustrate, they developed measures of compliance, identification, and internalization and examined their relations with several outcome measures (e.g. prosocial behaviour, turnover intention, and turnover). Identification and internalization were negatively related to turnover intention and turnover and positively related to prosocial behaviour. Moreover, in some analyses it was found that identification and internalization each accounted for unique variance in the outcome measures. Compliance showed the opposite pattern of relations and was also found to contribute uniquely to the prediction of turnover intention.

Although it served to sensitize researchers to the multidimensional nature of commitment, the impact of O'Reilly's classification system has been weakened somewhat by the fact that it has been difficult to distinguish identification and internalization (e.g. Caldwell, Chatman, & O'Reilly, 1990; O'Reilly, Chatman, & Caldwell, 1991; Sutton & Harrison, 1993; Vandenberg, Self, & Seo, 1994); the measures tend to correlate highly with one another and to show similar patterns of correlations with measures of other variables (for an exception, see Harris, Hirschfeld, Feild, & Mossholder, 1993). In fact, in their more recent research (Caldwell, Chatman, & O'Reilly, 1990; O'Reilly, Chatman, & Caldwell, 1991), O'Reilly and his colleagues combined the identification and internalization items to form a measure of what they called normative commitment. (Note that this construct corresponds more closely to affective commitment in Meyer and Allen's (1991) model and should not be confused with the latter's use of the term normative commitment.) Furthermore, although compliance (also referred to as instrumental commitment in more recent work) is clearly distinct from identification and internalization, one might question whether it can truly be considered commitment. For example, whereas commitment is generally assumed to reduce turnover (Mowday, Porter, & Steers, 1982), compliance has been found to correlate positively with employee turnover (O'Reilly & Chatman, 1986).

Before turning to a discussion of the focus of commitment, it should be noted that there have been several other attempts to identify and measure different forms of commitment, and to determine how these measures related to other (antecedent and consequence) variables (e.g., Jaros, Jermier, Koehler, & Sincich, 1993; Mayer & Schoorman, 1992; Penley & Gould, 1988). Space does not permit me to describe these different approaches in detail. It is important to note, however, that in some cases the same labels are used to describe quite different forms of commitment whereas, in other cases, different labels are used to describe very similar forms. Consumers of this research should, therefore, rely more on the construct definitions, or on the scale items, than on labels to determine what form of commitment is actually being measured.

The Focus of Commitment

Reichers (1985) noted that, in the organizational commitment literature, the 'organization' has typically been 'viewed as a monolithic, undifferentiated entity that elicits an identification and attachment on the part of the individual' (p. 469). She argued that, in reality, organizations comprise various 'coalitions and constituencies' (e.g. owners/managers; rank and file employees, customers/clients), each with its own goals and values that might or might not be compatible with the goals of the organization *per se*. Therefore, organizational commitment can best be understood as a collection of multiple commitments. This raises the possibility that (i) employees can have varying commitment profiles, and (ii) conflict can exist among an employee's commitments.

Reichers (1986) provided some preliminary support for this multiple-constituency perspective. More recently, Becker (1992) provided additional support by demonstrating that employees' commitments to top management, immediate supervisor, and work group contributed significantly beyond commitment to the organization to the prediction of job satisfaction, intention to quit, and prosocial organizational behaviour. Based on a reanalysis of Becker's data, however, Hunt and Morgan (1994) suggested that commitment to specific constituencies might be better viewed as exerting their influence on these outcomes through their effects on overall commitment to the organization. Nevertheless, they also noted that this mediating effect might be strongest for constituencies that are psychologically closer to the organization (e.g. top management, supervisor), and that direct effects of commitment to constituencies might be expected for outcomes that are of more direct relevance to that constituency.

In another analysis of these data, Becker and Billings (1993) used cluster analysis to identify commitment profiles (i.e. differing patterns of commitment to the various constituencies within the organization). They found four dominant profiles: '(1) the Locally Committed (employees who are attached to their supervisor and work group), (2) the Globally Committed (employees who are attached to top management and the organization), (3) the Committed (employees who are attached to both local and global foci), and (4) the Uncommitted (employees who are attached to neither local nor global foci)' (p. 177). Employees who were committed to both local and global foci had the highest level of overall job satisfaction, were least likely to intend to leave, and demonstrated the highest levels of prosocial behaviour. The locally and globally committed employees did not differ from one another in terms of general attitudes and behaviour, falling between the committed and uncommitted in all cases. Interestingly, however, when attitudes and prosocial behaviour directed at the supervisor and work group were assessed, both were found to be higher among the locally committed than among the globally committed. Again, this suggests that the benefits of assessing commitments to specific constituencies are more likely to be realized in attempts to predict constituency-relevant behaviour.

Cohen (1993c) measured commitment to the organization, occupation, union, and job in a sample of 129 white-collar employees from three organizations. He hypothesized that behaviour of relevance to a particular constituency would be best predicted by commitment to that constituency. The findings provided some support for this hypothesis. For example, the best predictor of intention to leave the organization was organizational commitment, whereas job commitment was the best predictor of job withdrawal, and union commitment was the best predictor of perceived union success. Interestingly, there was also some evidence that prediction could be enhanced by considering commitments other than that to the most relevant constituency. For example, occupational commitment contributed *positively* to the prediction of both organizational and job withdrawal intention. Job commitment contributed positively to the prediction of union activity, and occupational commitment contributed negatively to the prediction of perceived union success. The latter findings indicate that there is a potential for both compatibility and conflict among commitments.

Lawler (1992) also noted that organizations are composed of multiple subgroups. He referred to these subgroups as 'nested collectives' because each subgroup is subsumed by a larger group (e.g. work teams are part of departments, which are part of divisions, and so on). Lawler further argued that the amount of affect employees have to invest in these collectives is fixed and, therefore, the more they invest in one, the less they will have to invest in others. Finally, he proposed that employees will be most committed to the collective that is seen to afford them the greatest opportunity for self control. Typically, this is the smaller, more proximal, group (e.g. a work team). Thus, employees are more likely to develop attachments to subgroups within the organization than to the organization itself.

Although Lawler's (1992) theory has yet to receive much empirical investigation, a recent study by Yoon, Baker, and Ko (1994) is relevant. They measured commitment to the organization as well as interpersonal attachments to persons with higher or lower positions in their local work unit (vertical attachment) and to co-workers (horizontal attachments) in a large sample of employees from 62 Korean organizations. They argued that, if a subgroup approach such as that advocated by Lawler is correct, organizational commitment should correlate positively with vertical attachments and negatively with horizontal attachments. Although they found that vertical attachments correlated more strongly with organizational commitment than did horizontal attachments, the correlation with horizontal attachments was also positive. The latter finding is more consistent with a 'cohesion approach' suggesting that attachment (commitment) to subunits within the organization enhances commitment to the larger collective (i.e. the organization).

In summary, although the multiple-constituency framework has not been tested extensively, preliminary evidence indicates that there may be some value in measuring commitments to more specific foci within the organization. Existing evidence, however, does not negate the value of measuring organizational commitment at a global level. Becker (1992) found fairly strong correlations between global commitment and job satisfaction, turnover intention, and prosocial organizational behaviour. Although significant, the increment in prediction contributed by commitment to specific foci was small. It should be kept in mind, however, that when we measure commitment to the organization as a whole, we are probably measuring employees' commitment to 'top management' (Reichers, 1986), or to a combination of top management and more local subgroups (Becker & Billings, 1993; Hunt & Morgan, 1994). If our intention is to use commitment as a means of understanding or predicting behaviour of relevance to the organization as a whole (or to top management specifically), it would seem that our purpose can be well served with global measures of organizational commitment. If, on the other hand, we are interested in behaviour of relevance to more specific constituencies (e.g. the work team), better understanding and prediction might be afforded by a measure of commitment to the relevant constituency (Cohen, 1993c).

An Integration of the Multidimensional Approaches

As illustrated above, commitment can be considered multidimensional both in its form and its focus. These two approaches to developing a multidimensional framework are not incompatible. Indeed, one can envision a two-dimensional matrix with different forms of commitment listed along one axis, and the different foci along the other. The various cells within this matrix then reflect the nature of the commitment an employee has toward each individual constituency of relevance to him or her. Note that this matrix should not be used to classify employees. Rather, each employee's commitment profile should reflect varying degrees of different forms of commitment to each of the different constituencies.

At this time, it is not clear how commitments within the various cells of this two-dimensional matrix might relate to one another. According to Lawler's (1992) nested-collectives theory, there might be some dependencies, particularly among the cells reflecting affective attachments. Moreover, following Lawler's logic, if strong affective attachments to nested subgroups within the organizations are accompanied by a lower level of attachment to the organization, an interesting situation is created. In order to maintain their membership in the smaller unit, employees must remain in the larger organization, in spite of relatively low levels of affective commitment. This 'need' to remain might reflect what Allen and Meyer (1990b; Meyer & Allen, 1991) called continuance commitment. Consequently, there may be dependencies across both focus and form of commitment. Although the findings of Yoon, Baker, and Ko (1994) did not provide strong support for Lawler's theory, they too suggested a complex set of relations among commitments.

Combining the two multidimensional perspectives creates a potentially very complex model of commitment that becomes virtually impossible to test, or use, in its entirety. Nevertheless, acknowledging the complex multidimensional structure of commitment should serve to raise awareness of the fact that, in trying to understand how employees' commitment develops and relates to behaviour, we must frame our research questions more precisely than we have in the past. That is, we must specify clearly the form of commitment, and the constituency to which it is directed.

DEVELOPMENT OF COMMITMENT

There continues to be a considerable amount of research conducted to investigate the development of commitment. Although the strategy of correlating commitment with variables presumed to be its antecedents is less common today than it was during the 1970s and 80s, studies of this type are still being conducted. Typically, however, the objective of these studies has been to illustrate that different components of commitment have different antecedents (see Allen and Meyer, in press, for a review of this research as it pertains to their three-component model). In this section I will focus on three relatively recent lines of research. First, I will describe the results of studies that have used path analytic or structural equation modelling procedures to examine the 'causal' connections presumed to exist between commitment and its antecedents. Next, I will discuss theory and research pertaining to the development process (i.e. the mechanisms through which various antecedent variables exert their influence on commitment). Finally, on a more practical note, I will review the results of recent research that sheds some light on the role played by organizational human resource management (HRM) policies and practices in the development of employees' commitment.

Causal Models

Among the concerns expressed by reviewers about the earlier antecedent literature were that (i) it was largely atheoretical, and (ii) the methods used were not appropriate for establishing causal direction. More recently, there has been an increase in the use of structural equation modelling procedures to examine the development of commitment. Although they still rely on correlational data, these procedures allow more confidence in inferences about causal connections than do simple bivariate correlations. Moreover, appropriate use of these procedures requires an *a priori* theoretical rationale for the ordering of variables.

My intent here is not to provide an exhaustive review of structural equation modelling studies, but rather to provide some illustrative examples. I will first describe a series of studies designed to establish causal ordering among antecedent variables identified in earlier research. I will then summarize the results of several studies of relevance to the long-standing debate over whether job satisfaction influences organizational commitment or commitment influences job satisfaction.

Causal ordering of antecedents

Mathieu and his colleagues (Mathieu, 1988, 1991; Mathieu & Hamel, 1989) conducted a series of studies to examine the causal ordering of antecedent variables. Although, in each of these studies, self-report data were collected on a single occasion, what distinguished them from earlier antecedent studies was the use of path analysis to test theory-based causal models. In these models, variables believed to be antecedent to commitment were ordered in terms of causal priority on the basis of Lewin's (1943) field theory. According to field theory, employees' reactions to their environment (e.g. commitment to the organization) should be primarily a function of their perceptions of, and reactions to, proximal elements in their environment or life space (e.g. work experiences and satisfaction). Environmental and personal characteristics are considered to be more distal causes that are likely to exert their influence on commitment indirectly through the more proximal causes.

Mathieu (1988) tested a model of the development process in a military training context. He measured variables from each of the four broad antecedent categories identified in previous work (i.e. personal characteristics, role states, job characteristics, and work experiences), and ordered them in accord with field theory predictions. For example, personal characteristics and role states were expected to exert their influence indirectly through perceptions of, and reactions to, the training experience (i.e. training characteristics and satisfaction with training, respectively). Although the original model was found to fit the data reasonably well, Mathieu found that a revised model fitted the data better. Training characteristics continued to have the strongest direct effect on commitment, but some of the variables expected initially to have only indirect effects (e.g. achievement motivation, role strain) were found to have direct effects as well. In a similar study conducted with a larger sample, Mathieu (1991) found that general job satisfaction, when measured in place of satisfaction with training, had the strongest direct effect on commitment, and that all other variables, with the exception of achievement motivation, had only indirect effects.

Mathieu and Hamel (1989) developed a causal model to be tested in a non-military context. Data were obtained from professionals and non-professionals in two government agencies and a state university. They found that, in general, the two most proximal causes of organizational commitment were job satisfaction and mental health. Job and personal characteristics (and their interaction), as well as role strain and organizational characteristics, were all found to exert their effects indirectly through the more proximal causes. The strength of some of the indirect effects was found to differ between professionals and non-professionals, however.

Mathieu and his colleagues speculated that some of their findings might have been unique to the samples they used (i.e. military and government). Moreover, there are no doubt other important antecedent variables and mediating and moderating effects that they did not consider. Nevertheless, their findings should provide some guidance for future research.

Job satisfaction and commitment

We know from the meta-analytic findings reviewed above that commitment and satisfaction are highly related, but there has been no consensus about whether, or how, the two variables are causally connected. The findings of earlier attempts to address this issue produced mixed results. Consequently, as structural equation modelling procedures have become more sophisticated, researchers have continued to revisit this issue.

Mathieu (1991) and Lance (1991) conducted cross-sectional studies that permitted them to test for both non-recursive and recursive effects. Both found evidence for an asymmetrical reciprocal relation. That is, satisfaction and commitment were found to exert effects on each other, but the effect of satisfaction on commitment was greater than the effect of commitment on satisfaction.

Farkas and Tetrick (1989) applied structural equation modelling procedures to longitudinal data and found evidence to suggest that the causal ordering of satisfaction and commitment reverses over time, perhaps reflecting either cyclical or reciprocal effects. Vandenberg and Lance (1992) also collected longitudinal data but tested only for causal effects within-time. Their findings provided the strongest support for a commitment–causes–satisfaction model.

It appears from the results of these studies that the relation between job satisfaction and commitment might be quite complex. It is not clear at this point whether we will ever be able to determine which, if either, is causally prior. From the standpoint of understanding how organizational commitment develops, this might not be a crucial issue. It might, however, be more important in the consideration of how satisfaction and commitment relate to behaviour. I will address this issue again in the discussion of the consequences of commitment.

The Development Process

Although the results of analyses designed to evaluate the causal ordering of antecedent variables are a significant advance over previous research, they still do not address the issue of how or why these variables are related to commitment. Relatively little attention has been given to explaining or investigating the mechanisms through which the various antecedent variables exert their influence on commitment. It appears that most studies have been conducted under the assumption that commitment develops on the principle of exchange; employees commit themselves to organizations that provide them with desired outcomes. Hence, commitment is generally expected (and found) to correlate positively with desirable work characteristics and conditions, and negatively with undesirable ones. Although it might well be the case that exchange principles operate in the development of commitment, the recent recognition that commitment can take different forms makes it evident that the picture is more complicated than this.

To illustrate, consider affective, continuance, and normative commitment as described by Meyer and Allen (1991). Each represents a relatively distinct psychological state and relates somewhat differently to behaviour, yet the development of each can be explained, in part, using the principle of exchange. That is, employees who encounter positive experiences at work can develop a desire to remain and contribute (affective commitment), or a sense of moral obligation to do so (normative commitment). Moreover, if employees recognize that leaving the organization would require them to give up some of the benefits they derive from membership, they might feel a need to remain (continuance commitment). Clearly, then, there is more to the development of commitment than simple exchange.

There is little evidence in the literature of a systematic attempt to examine the development process. Nevertheless, there are several lines of research that come closer to addressing what might be considered 'mechanisms' in the development process than has been the case in the past. I will briefly discuss five such mechanisms: person–job fit, met-expectations, causal attribution, organizational justice and support, and retrospective rationalization. In most cases, the research pertaining to these mechanisms has been concerned with the development of affective commitment. In some cases, however, there might also be implications for the development of other forms of commitment as I will illustrate.

Person–job fit

It has long been argued that employees will be more satisfied with their jobs to the extent that there is a good match between what the person is looking for in a job and what the job provides (cf. Dawis, 1992; Locke, 1976). It is only recently, however, that person–job fit has been examined as a factor in the development of commitment (e.g. Meglino, Ravlin, & Adkins, 1989; Vancouver & Schmitt, 1991; O'Reilly, Chatman, & Caldwell, 1991).

Tests of the person–job fit hypothesis have typically involved computing an index of fit and correlating it with an outcome measure of interest. Consistent with this practice, Meglino, Ravlin, and Adkins (1989) computed the rank order correlations between employees' values and those of supervisors and management, O'Reilly, Chatman, and Caldwell (1991) obtained correlations between employees' culture preference ratings and measures of perceived organizational culture, and Vancouver and Schmitt (1991) calculated the sum of squared differences (reflected) between subordinate and supervisor goals. In all three studies, these fit indices were found to correlate positively with commitment.

Whether these findings can be taken as evidence to support the person–job fit hypothesis is unclear in light of recent concerns raised by Edwards and his colleagues (e.g. Edwards, 1991, 1993, 1994; Edwards & Cooper, 1990) about the meaningfulness of the fit indices used in these studies. Edwards suggested an alternative set of procedures for testing the person–job fit hypothesis, but these have yet to be applied to test the hypothesis as it pertains to the development of commitment. This is an area where further research is needed.

A related line of research has been to examine the interaction of person and job (or organization) characteristics in the prediction of commitment (e.g.

Blau, 1987; Meyer, Irving, & Allen, in press). (See Edwards and Cooper [1990] for a discussion of the difference between person–job fit and person x situation interaction.) The findings have been mixed. Whereas Blau found no evidence of a person x situation interaction in the prediction of commitment, Meyer, Irving, and Allen did. The findings reported by Meyer, Irving, and Allen, however, were not completely consistent with prediction. Although they found that experiences that contributed to employees' comfort in the organization had a stronger influence on commitment among those who placed greater value on such experiences, the opposite was found to be true for competence-related experiences. That is, the effect of competence-bolstering experiences on commitment (both affective and normative) was greater for those who initially placed less importance on such experiences. Although this somewhat counterintuitive finding was found to replicate, Meyer, Irving, and Allen could only speculate on why it occurred. Again, in light of the inconsistent and somewhat unexpected results obtained to date, this is an area where additional research is needed (cf. Mathieu & Zajac, 1990).

Met-expectations

Related to the notion that employees will be more committed to organizations when they encounter a good fit is the hypothesis that commitment will be greater when employees' experiences on the job match their pre-entry expectations (e.g. Wanous, 1980). This 'met-expectations' hypothesis has been tested in several studies and, in a recent meta-analysis, Wanous, Poland, Premack, and Davis (1992) reported a corrected average correlation of 0.39 between indices of met expectations and commitment. As was the case with person–job fit, however, there are problems associated with the procedures that have commonly been used to test the met-expectations hypothesis (see Irving & Meyer, 1994, 1995). Consequently, this correlation must be interpreted with some caution.

Irving and Meyer (1994) tested the met-expectations hypothesis using analytic procedures similar to those recommended by Edwards (1991) for tests of the person–job fit hypothesis. They found only modest support for the hypothesis. Instead, their findings suggested that commitment was greater among employees who reported positive work experiences during the early months of employment regardless of what they initially expected. Major, Kozlowski, Chao, and Gardner (1995) found that unmet expectations did have a negative impact on commitment, but that this effect was ameliorated by positive relations with managers and coworkers. Clearly, it is premature to draw firm conclusions about the role that confirmation of expectations plays in the development of commitment. There appears to be considerable agreement, however, that the first year of employment is an important time for the development of commitment (e.g. Louis, 1980; Wanous, 1980) and, therefore, more research is needed to determine how expectations and experiences combine to shape commitment during this period. Care must be taken, however, to ensure that appropriate methods are used to examine these effects.

Causal attribution

There is considerable evidence to suggest that commitment is associated with positive work experiences. The person–job fit and met-expectations hypotheses suggest the possibility that the impact of these experiences might be moderated by individual differences in needs/values and expectations. Another potential moderator is the attribution employees make for these experiences (Meyer & Allen, 1991). That is, having positive experiences at work might be more likely to contribute to the development of an affective attachment to the organization if employees view the organization as having been responsible for those experiences than if they attribute their existence to other sources (e.g. union, profession, job).

Although this attribution hypothesis has not yet been evaluated systematically, on one direct test of the hypothesis, Meyer and Allen (1995) found some evidence for a moderating effect of attribution on the relations between work experiences and their affective reactions to their organizations, jobs, and immediate supervisors. Other evidence for the role played by attributions was provided by Koys (1988, 1991) who found that the impact of desirable HRM practices on commitment was greater when employees believed that they reflected the organization's concern for the employees rather than an attempt to satisfy legal requirements. Similarly, Mellor (1992) found that employees were less committed to their union when they were led to attribute the need for organizational downsizing to the union.

Additional research is needed to determine whether, and to what extent, attribution processes are involved in the development of commitment. Evidence in support of the attribution hypothesis would help to explain inconsistencies across studies in the magnitude of correlations between specific antecedent variables and commitment. It might also help us to understand when and how various experiences are likely to influence commitment to the different constituencies within and outside organizations.

Organizational justice and support

Although it is not entirely clear whether organizational justice and support can be considered process variables *per se*, it might be argued that employees evaluate their experiences at work in terms of whether they are fair and/or they reflect a concern on the part of the organization for the well-being of the employees. If so, perceptions of justice and support could be considered more proximal causes of commitment than, say, job characteristics or organizational policies and practices. If these more distal causes exert their influence on commitment by shaping perceptions of justice and support, the latter take on the role of mediating mechanisms. At any rate, both organizational justice and support are receiving increased attention in the commitment literature, and warrant some discussion.

Like commitment, organizational justice is now generally viewed as a multidimensional construct (see Greenberg, 1990, 1993). Perhaps most relevant to the present discussion is the distinction made between the fairness of outcomes received (distributive justice) and fairness of the procedures used in determining outcomes (procedural justice). Several studies have been conducted to examine the relative strength of these two forms of justice on organizational commitment. For example, Folger and Konovsky (1989) used measures of distributive and procedural justice concerning pay raises to predict employees' pay satisfaction and organizational commitment. They found that perceptions of distributive justice accounted for more variance in pay satisfaction than did procedural justice, whereas procedural justice perceptions accounted for more variance in commitment. Similar results were reported by Sweeney and McFarlin (1993) and Konovsky and Cropanzano (1991). Together the findings support the more general position advanced by Lind and Tyler (1988) that 'procedural justice has especially strong effects on attitudes about institutions or authorities, as opposed to attitudes about specific outcomes in question' (p. 179).

These findings suggest that employees' commitment to the organization might be shaped, at least in part, by their perceptions of how fairly they are treated by the organization. Additional evidence for this claim will be provided when I discuss the impact of HRM practices on commitment below. Whether justice perceptions themselves have a direct or indirect effect on commitment is not clear. One possibility suggested in the justice literature is that, by treating employees fairly, organizations communicate their commitment to employees (e.g. Folger & Konovsky, 1989). That is, the effect of justice perceptions on commitment might be mediated by perceptions of the organization's commitment to employees.

The idea that employees become committed to organizations that demonstrate commitment to them is consistent with an exchange theory perspective. To my knowledge, however, there has been no attempt to define or measure 'organizational commitment to employees.' A construct that comes close is organizational support (Eisenberger, Huntington, Hutchison, & Sowa, 1986). Eisenberger et al. developed a 17-item instrument, the Survey of Perceived Organizational Support (SPOS), to measure employees' 'global beliefs concerning the extent to which the organization values their contributions and cares about their well-being' (p. 501). The SPOS has been found in several studies (e.g. Eisenberger, Fasolo, & Davis-LaMastro, 1990; Guzzo, Noonan, & Elron, 1994; Shore & Tetrick, 1991; Shore & Wayne, 1993; Smith & Meyer, 1996) to correlate positively with measures of affective commitment (i.e. the OCQ and ACS). There is also some evidence that the SPOS correlates positively with normative commitment (Smith & Meyer, 1996), but not with continuance commitment (Shore & Wayne, 1993; Smith & Meyer, 1996).

These findings are potentially important, and suggest that organizations wanting to foster a greater affective (or normative) commitment in their employees might do so by first providing evidence of their commitment to employees. The SPOS measures employees' perceptions of two aspects of such commitment (valuing employees' contribution and concern for their well-being). There may be other aspects of commitment to employees, however, that are not tapped by the SPOS (e.g. providing job security). This would seem to be a construct deserving of further development.

Retrospective rationalization

The mechanisms discussed to this point might best be considered examples of prospective rationality. That is, commitment develops on the basis of an assessment of what benefits are being, or will be, derived from association with the organization. Another possibility that derives largely from research in the behavioral commitment literature, is that psychological (particularly affective) commitment develops in an effort to justify previous behaviours or decisions (e.g. Kiesler, 1971; Salancik, 1977). Kiesler and Salancik identified several conditions under which a behaviour, once initiated, will tend to be repeated. These include freedom of choice, irrevocability, explicitness, publicness, and importance. Commitment to remain in an organization, therefore, should be greater when the employee feels that he/she freely chose to work for the organization, the decision cannot be undone, others know about the decision, and so on. Moreover, to be consistent with their behaviour, employees might be expected to develop a positive reaction (affective commitment) to the organization. The latter is typically explained in terms of dissonance reduction or self-justification processes (e.g. Mowday Porter, & Steers, 1982).

Retrospective rationalization processes are difficult to study and most of the evidence provided to illustrate its role in the development of organizational commitment has come from findings obtained in laboratory research (see Salancik, 1977). One exception was a study by O'Reilly and Caldwell (1981). Two more recent studies were conducted to extend the findings of O'Reilly and Caldwell. Meyer, Bobocel, and Allen (1991), like O'Reilly and Caldwell, used proxy measures of the conditions assumed to bind employees to their decision. For example, number of job offers was used as one index of volition. Of the binding variables measured (volition, irrevocability, importance), only volition was found to be positively related to commitment. Although this could be taken as evidence of retrospective rationalization, Meyer, Bobocel, and Allen argued that it might also reflect prospective rationality (i.e. those who have more choice chose better jobs). Consistent with the latter explanation, the correlation between volition and affective commitment became non-significant when perceived quality of decision was controlled. Also of interest was the finding that irrevocability (e.g. difficulty of finding another job) was not related to affective commitment as expected. Rather, it was found to correlate positively with continuance commitment (i.e. perceived cost of leaving).

Kline and Peters (1991) measured the binding variables (volition, irrevocability, publicness) directly with self-report scales administered on the first day of employment. Consistent with the retrospective rationalization hypothesis, they found that commitment correlated positively with volition and publicness and negatively with revocability (presumably the inverse of irrevocability). Of course, the positive correlation with volition could reflect quality of choice. Moreover, although revocability, as measured, was assumed to be the inverse of irrevocability, this might not have been true. For example, a negative response to the item 'I am trying out this job to see if it works out' does not necessarily imply irrevocability. It could reflect anticipated satisfaction with the job/organization. Thus, Kline and Peter's findings cannot be taken as unequivocal support for the retrospective rationalization hypothesis.

At best, the findings concerning the impact of retrospective rationality processes in the development of commitment are mixed. Past experimental evidence suggests that these processes do operate and can help to explain attitude development. There is also evidence that these effects can occur in applied settings (Staw, 1974). It is not clear, however, whether these findings have relevance for organizations wanting to foster commitment in their employees. Ethical issues aside, it might be difficult to create the conditions necessary to include retrospective rationalization processes. Failure to do so could result in organizations increasing employees' continuance rather than their affective commitment as intended (Meyer, Bobocel, & Allen, 1991).

Organizational Policies and Practices

Another line of antecedent research of relatively recent origin is the investigation of the impact of HRM policies and practices on commitment. Unlike most of the earlier antecedent research that examined employees' perceptions of their immediate work context (e.g. job characteristics, work experiences), this research focuses on the policies and practices that serve, in part, to shape those perceptions. Although HRM policies and practices are likely to be more distal antecedents of commitment, one advantage of considering them is that they are under more direct control by the organization. Again, most research to date has focused on efforts designed to foster affective commitment. This is because (i) it is only recently that multidimensional models and measures of commitment have been developed, and (ii) affective commitment has arguably the most desirable consequences for an organization.

Recruitment and selection

There has not been a great deal of research examining the impact of recruitment and selection practices on commitment, although a number of studies have provided data of relevance to this issue. For example, Premack and Wanous (1985), in their meta-analyses of effects of realistic job previews (RJP), found a positive, albeit weak, effect on commitment. As noted earlier, Wanous et al. (1992) found that met expectations, one of the intended effects of RJPs, was positively related to commitment. Although the latter finding must be interpreted with some caution because of methodological weaknesses in the studies included in the meta-analysis (see Irving & Meyer, 1994, 1995), there is at least some indication that organizational recruitment practices might contribute to the early development of commitment. More research is needed to examine this influence.

Mowday, Porter, and Steers (1982) argued that employees entering an organization might differ in their propensity to become committed. They identified three broad categories of variables that, together, determine propensity: personal characteristics (e.g. desire to establish a career in an organization, self-efficacy), pre-entry expectations, and organizational choice variables (e.g. volition, irrevocability). The propensity hypothesis has been tested in two studies (Lee, Ashford, Walsh, & Mowday, 1992; Pierce & Dunham, 1987) and both reported that propensity, measured prior to entry, predicted subsequent commitment. Lee et al. (1992) also found some evidence to suggest that propensity might influence commitment by shaping the way employees perceive their early experiences; those with a higher propensity for commitment tended to view the same objective experiences more positively than those with lower propensity.

Unfortunately, it is difficult to assess the implications of these findings because the propensity construct, as defined and operationalized, is so complex. It is not clear what components of propensity (e.g. expectation, personal characteristics) are responsible for the correlation with subsequent commitment. Until these effects can be teased apart, we will not know whether it is possible to select for propensity, or if propensity is largely shaped during the recruitment and selection processes.

Socialization and training

One way in which organizations might hope to build on employees' initial propensity for commitment is through the socialization process. Investigation of the effects of socialization practices on commitment was facilitated by Van Maanen and Schein (1979) who devised a six-dimensional classification scheme, and Jones (1986) who developed a set of measures that could be used to determine where along these dimensions an organization's socialization practices fall. These measures have now been used in several studies and the evidence clearly indicates a link between perceived socialization experiences and commitment (e.g. Allen & Meyer, 1990a; Ashforth & Saks, 1996; Baker & Feldman, 1990; Jones, 1986; Mignerey, Robin, & Gordon, 1995).

The dimension that has consistently been found to have the strongest association with commitment is *Investiture versus Divestiture* (e.g. Allen & Meyer,

1990a; Ashforth & Saks, 1996; Jones, 1986). The investiture–divestiture dimension, as measured by Jones' (1986) instrument, reflects the 'degree to which newcomers receive positive [investiture] or negative [divestiture] support after entry from experienced organizational members' (p. 265). Commitment tends to be stronger when organizations use investiture tactics.

Instilling commitment is only one of several objectives organizations attempt to achieve through socialization. A somewhat disconcerting finding reported by Jones (1986), therefore, was that the socialization practices associated with higher levels of commitment tended to be negatively associated with employees' self-reported tendency to adapt an innovative role orientation. Moreover, commitment itself was found to correlate negatively with orientation toward innovation. These findings might be of particular concern to organizations wanting to foster both a high level of commitment and a willingness to innovate in their employees. More recent research has demonstrated that commitment and innovation are not strongly related, however, and that the socialization dimensions that have the strongest influence on these two outcomes are different (Allen & Meyer, 1990a; Ashforth & Saks, 1996). Nevertheless, these findings should sensitize researchers and practitioners to the fact that socialization practices are likely to have multiple effects, and that to focus exclusively on any one might be shortsighted.

Although these findings suggest some guiding principles for the design of socialization programs, there are limitations of the research that raise questions about the generalizability of these principles. For example, tests of Van Maanen and Schein's (1979) model have been conducted largely with highly educated newcomers (e.g. MBAs) during the first year of employment (Ashforth & Saks, 1996; for an exception, see Baker & Feldman, 1990). It is unclear to what extent these findings are representative of what would be found with other less educated, or more heterogeneous, samples, or for socialization conducted during later career stages. Moreover, research to date has focused largely on the *form* of socialization without concern for the *content*. It might well be that the message conveyed to employees during socialization will be more important in determining their commitment than the structural characteristics of the practices (cf. Ashforth & Saks, 1996). Chao, O'Leary-Kelly, Wolf, Klein, and Gardner (1994) recently developed a method of classifying socialization content that might be useful in testing this hypothesis. Finally, there has been little attempt to determine how these organization-initiated socialization practices interact with employees' own information-seeking strategies (see Morrison, 1993; Ostroff & Kozlowski, 1992).

Training is often an important part of the socialization process. Although commitment is not necessarily the intended, or at least most obvious, objective of training, it can nevertheless be influenced in the process. Gaertner and Nollen (1989) found that commitment was related to employees' perceptions of organizational efforts to provide them with training, but not to their actual training experiences. They suggest that the fact that actual training experiences did not predict commitment might have been due to the fact that the measure did not reflect frequency or content of training.

Tannenbaum, Mathieu, Salas, and Cannon-Bowers (1991) assessed the commitment of recruits immediately upon arrival at a US Naval Training Command for an 8-week socialization-type training process, and again following training. They found that, overall, organizational commitment increased following training. Moreover, with pre-training commitment controlled, post-training commitment was positively related to training fulfilment (the extent to which the training fulfilled trainees' expectations and desires), satisfaction with the training experience, and training performance. Thus, it would appear that successful training experiences can contribute to the development of affective commitment. Saks (1995) obtained similar results in a study conducted with a civilian sample (accountants).

Tannenbaum et al. (1991) also found some evidence that organizational commitment might have reciprocal effects on training success. They reported a strong positive correlation between commitment and employees' motivation for training, a variable that was found to be an important predictor of training satisfaction and performance. This finding was recently replicated in a large-scale study of government supervisory and management personnel (Facteau, Dobbins, Russell, Ladd, & Kudisch, 1995). Thus, although more research is necessary, particularly in the private sector, existing evidence suggests that commitment can be affected by training experiences and can, in turn, influence employees' motivation for training.

Promotion

Policies and practices concerning the movement of employees, particularly upward movement, once they are in the organization might also be expected to have an impact on their commitment. Gaertner and Nollen (1989) found that commitment was higher among employees who had been promoted, and was also related to employees' perceptions that the company had a policy of promoting from within. Such a policy might be perceived as an example of the company's commitment to the employee as discussed earlier.

Robertson, Iles, Gratton, and Sharpley (1991) examined the impact of a management development and tiering program used by a large financial services organization to evaluate employees in early and mid-career. They found that commitment and turnover intentions were strongly influenced by the outcome of early career assessments; those who received negative feedback became less committed and more likely to consider leaving the company. Reactions to assessments conducted in mid-career (early 30s), however, were affected more by the perceived adequacy of the procedures involved than by the outcome. Thus, different strategies might be needed to maintain commitment among those given failure feedback depending on career stage.

Schwarzwald, Koslowsky, & Shalit (1992) examined the effect of promotion decisions on the commitment of a group of Israeli employees who had declared their candidacy for promotion. Those who were promoted were subsequently more committed than those who were not. Those who were not promoted also perceived greater inequity than those who were promoted and tended to be absent more frequently following the decision. Schwarzwald, Koslowsky, and Shalit suggested that equity considerations might be the mediating factor in determining the attitudinal and behavioural outcomes of failure to be promoted.

Finally, Fletcher (1991) found that the commitment of managerial candidates who went through assessment centres changed little in pre-assessment, post-assessment, and follow-up surveys. Moreover, successful and unsuccessful candidates differed little in commitment either before or after the assessment. Performance in the assessment centre did, however, affect candidates in other ways (e.g. self-esteem). In light of the findings of the studies described above, it is possible that the absence of an effect on commitment in this study was due to perceptions that the assessments were fair.

Together, these findings suggest that a policy of promotion from within can have a beneficial effect on commitment. Among those who are considered for promotion, the outcome of the decision is likely to have an effect on commitment but, for some, the perception of fairness in the decision-making process might be even more important. This suggests that companies should communicate clearly how their decisions were made and why those who did not receive the promotion were passed over.

Compensation and benefits

Although relatively little attention has been given to examining the effects of the administration of salary and benefits on commitment, one compensation-relevant practice that has received some attention is the use of Employee Stock Ownership Plans (ESOP). ESOPs are increasing in popularity for several reasons, including the belief that employees who have a stake in the company will be more committed to it (Klein, 1987). Indeed, evidence for a link between organizational commitment and ESOPs (and related systems) has now been obtained in several studies (e.g. Buchko, 1992, 1993; Florkowski & Schuster, 1992); Klein, 1987; Klein & Hall, 1988; Tucker, Nock, & Toscano, 1989; Wetzel & Gallagher, 1990). Many of these studies also addressed the issue of why ESOPs are related to commitment.

Klein (1987) identified three models that have been used to explain the link between employee ownership and commitment. According to the first of these, the Intrinsic Satisfaction Model, commitment derives directly from ownership and should therefore be proportional to the amount of stock an employee holds. The Extrinsic Satisfaction Model proposes that commitment will be proportional to the degree of financial gain the employee realizes (or has the potential to realize) as a function of holding stock in the company. Finally, according to the Instrumental Satisfaction Model, employee ownership is believed to increase commitment because it increases the actual or perceived influence that employees have in decision-making within the organization. Using data from over 2800 ESOP participants from 37 different companies, Klein found some support for both the Extrinsic and Instrumental Satisfaction models, but not for the Intrinsic Satisfaction model.

More recent studies have provided mixed support for the Instrumental Satisfaction and Extrinsic Satisfaction models, and almost no support for the Intrinsic Satisfaction model. For example, Buchko (1993) found that financial value of the ESOP was indirectly related to commitment through its influence on overall satisfaction with the plan. In contrast, perceived influence resulting from ownership was found to be directly related to both satisfaction with the plan and commitment to the organization. In a quasi-experimental study, Tucker, Nock, and Toscano (1989) found that organizational commitment increased following the introduction of an ESOP in a small clothing store, but that perceived influence did not change. Interestingly, they found that the commitment of both participants and non-participants increased following the introduction of the ESOP, and they speculated that this might have been due to a general change in the climate of the organization. Finally, in a study designed to examine the influence of profit sharing on commitment, Florkowski and Schuster (1992) found that concerns about the financial implication of the plan (i.e. performance-reward contingency; pay equity) were related to support for the plan which, in turn, was an important determinant of organizational commitment. Perceived influence was not directly related to plan support as had been anticipated, but did relate to commitment indirectly through its influence on job satisfaction.

Together these findings suggest that the introduction of an ESOP alone is not sufficient to increase affective commitment. Employees will expect to benefit either financially or in terms of their ability to influence decisions, or both. If increasing commitment is an objective, it would appear that making the plan financially meaningful, and/or increasing employees' opportunity to participate in decision-making, should be an important part of the plan. With regard to financial meaningfulness, however, it must be kept in mind that too much emphasis on this factor could actually reduce affective commitment (cf. Caldwell, Chatman, & O'Reilly, 1990; Oliver, 1990) or lead to the development of other forms of commitment. For example, an ESOP that requires that employees stay for a fixed period of time in order to receive the organization's contribution to the plan can increase the cost of leaving the organization (i.e. continuance commitment).

Even less research has been conducted to examine the impact of benefits on commitment. Nevertheless, the administration of benefits might conceivably have implications for employee commitment. Consider, for example, the potential impact of organizations' efforts to respond to the increase in the number of dual-career families by providing family-responsive benefits (e.g. flexible hours; daycare assistance). Grover and Crooker (1995) used data collected in a national survey of over 1500 US workers to examine the relation between availability of family-responsive benefits and affective organizational commitment. They found a positive correlation between the availability of such benefits and commitment, even for those who would not benefit directly. They argued that organizations that offer such benefits are perceived by employees as showing greater caring and concern (organizational support) and as being fair in their dealings with employees.

It should be noted that the correlations obtained by Grover and Crooker (1995) were not large and that there may be limits to generalizability. For example, Grover and Crooker suggested that the introduction of family-responsive benefits should be consistent with the existing culture of the organization. If employees view these benefits as having been introduced in response to external pressure or as a token gesture, they may have less impact (cf. Koys, 1988, 1991). Moreover, Grover and Crooker's explanation for their findings assumes that a norm for need-based distribution of resources exists; if the norm is for equity-based distribution, the provision of benefits that meet the needs of a select group of employees might create some resentment.

Change management

Organizations in both the public and private sectors are coming under increasing pressures to change the way they operate. Many of these changes, and the way they are implemented, can be expected to have an influence on organizational commitment. To illustrate, consider the case of organizational downsizing. It has been estimated that approximately 90% of large organizations in North America reduced their workforce in recent years (Emshoff, 1994). Unfortunately, it appears that the anticipated economic and organizational gains expected from downsizing are often not realized (Cascio, 1993). This may be due, in part, to the fact that downsizing organizations sometimes have difficulty in retaining their most valued employees (cf. Mone, 1994).

A number of recent studies have been conducted to examine how the commitment of 'survivors' is affected by downsizing. A common thread running through much of this research has been the importance of procedural justice. Survivors were likely to have higher levels of post-layoff commitment when they felt that the downsizing was unavoidable and was implemented fairly (see Konovsky & Brockner, 1993). Among the factors found to influence perceptions of justice were the level of support provided to the victims (Brockner, Grover, Reed, DeWitt, & O'Malley, 1987), the fairness of decision-making in the past (Davy, Kinicki, & Scheck, 1991), and the adequacy of the explanation provided (Brockner, DeWitt, Grover, & Reed, 1990). Other factors that contributed to commitment in addition to, or in interaction with, justice were feelings of job security (Davy, Kinicki, & Scheck, 1991), perceptions of the intrinsic quality of jobs following the layoff (Brockner, Weisenfeld, Reed, Grover, & Martin, 1993), and pre-layoff commitment (Brockner, Tyler, & Cooper-Schneider, 1992). Interestingly, those with the strongest commitment prior to the layoff were the ones most adversely affected by perceived injustice in the downsizing process.

Summary

The investigation of the development of commitment has clearly progressed beyond efforts to correlate commitment with variables presumed to be its antecedents. Structural equation modelling analyses have helped to increase our confidence in the causal ordering of variables involved in the development of commitment. Many issues remain, however, including the appropriate time lag for detecting causal effects, and whether it is better to use cross-sectional or longitudinal designs to examine reciprocal effects (cf. Farkas & Tetrick, 1989; Mathieu, 1991).

There is much to be learned yet about the processes involved in the development of commitment. What we know has been learned almost incidentally. There has been little in the way of systematic investigation of process issues. What research has been done has focused primarily on the development of affect-based commitment. We need to know more about how the various forms of commitment, and commitments to different constituencies, develop in order to understand and predict how changes in the workplace are likely to influence employees' commitment profiles.

There appears to be evidence that organizations can, intentionally or unintentionally, influence their employees' commitment through their HRM practices. Before drawing firm conclusions about the influence of any particular HRM practice, however, it is important to keep in mind that most of the research has been correlational. A correlation between an HRM practice and commitment is difficult to interpret. Organizations are likely to adapt management practices that are compatible with one another and with general organizational objectives. Consequently, when examined individually, a particular practice might be related to commitment, not because it has an impact on commitment, but because it is associated with other HRM practices, or general business strategies, that do (Huselid, 1995). It is also important to note that HRM practices were often measured using surveys administered to employees. Employees' perceptions may or may not be accurate. More attention needs to be given in future research to examining the impact of actual practices.

CONSEQUENCES

The results of the meta-analyses described earlier revealed that, with the exception of turnover-related variables, correlations between organizational commitment and outcome measures were disappointingly weak. Based on these findings, Randall (1990) concluded that 'researchers do not have a very powerful scientific foundation upon which to base claims of the importance of OC as a research topic and as an organizationally desirable attitude' (p. 375). Perhaps in an attempt to solidify that foundation, investigators have continued to examine the links between commitment and organizationally relevant outcomes. There has also been some attempt to look for links with outcomes of greater relevance to the employees themselves.

Turnover Intention and Turnover

Even though the link between organizational commitment and turnover-related variables has been relatively well established, a considerable amount of attention continues to be given to this relationship. Rather than trying to provide a comprehensive review of this research, I will focus attention on some common themes. Specifically, I will review the findings of studies undertaken to (i) examine the relations between various components of commitment and turnover-related variables, (ii) identify potential moderators of the commitment-turnover relation and (iii) assess the relative contributions of commitment and other attitude variables (e.g. job satisfaction, job involvement) to the prediction of turnover intention and turnover. I will conclude with a discussion of a somewhat contentious issue concerning the redundancy of the commitment and turnover intention constructs.

Turnover and components of commitment

Several studies have examined the correlations between turnover, or turnover intention, and two or more of Allen and Meyer's (1990b) three components of commitment. Affective commitment has consistently been found to correlate negatively with turnover intention and/or actual turnover (e.g. Carson & Bedeian, 1994; Cropanzano, James, & Konovsky, 1993; Hackett, Bycio, & Hausdorf, 1994; Jenkins, 1993; Konovsky & Cropanzano, 1991; Meyer, Allen, & Smith, 1993; Somers, 1995; Whitener & Walz, 1993). Although it has received less attention, normative commitment has also been found to correlate negatively with turnover intention and turnover (Hackett, Bycio, & Hausdorf, 1994; Meyer, Allen, & Smith, 1993; Somers, 1995). The findings have been less consistent for continuance commitment; significant negative correlations were obtained in some studies (Hackett, Bycio, & Hausdorf, 1994; Whitener & Walz, 1993) but not in others (e.g. Cropanzano, James, & Konovsky, 1993; Konovsky & Cropanzano, 1991; Somers, 1995). Somers (1995) found that, although continuance commitment did not contribute independently to the prediction of turnover intention, it did moderate the effect of affective commitment. The link between affective commitment and turnover was weaker when continuance commitment was high; presumably those with low affective commitment were less inclined to leave when the perceived cost of doing so was high.

Components of commitment identified in other multidimensional models have also been linked to commitment. Vandenberg, Self, and Seo (1994) examined the contribution of the components of commitment identified by O'Reilly and Chatman (1986), identification, internalization, and compliance, to the prediction of turnover intention and turnover, relative to the OCQ. They found internalization and compliance had only modest correlations with turnover intention and turnover (those with compliance were opposite in direction) and that, when entered into a structural equation model along with the OCQ, only the latter had a significant effect on turnover intention. The effect of the OCQ on turnover was mediated by turnover intention and job search. In a preliminary analysis, Vandenberg, Self, and Seo found that identification was not distinguishable from the OCQ and therefore did not include it in the structural equation modelling analyses.

Jaros et al. (1993) included measures of affective, continuance, and moral commitment in competitive tests of several models of the turnover process. The measures of commitment paralleled, but were not the same as, those developed by Allen and Meyer (1990b). Jaros et al. found that, in the best fitting model, affective and continuance commitment contributed significantly and independently to the prediction of withdrawal tendency, which, in turn, predicted actual turnover; moral commitment did not contribute significantly to prediction.

Ben-Bakr, Al-Shammari, Jefri, & Prasad (1994) examined the relative strength of the correlation between turnover intention and commitment in a sample of employees in various occupations and organizations in Saudi Arabia. They found a significant negative correlation for overall commitment, but when the OCQ was divided into subscales to create value commitment and continuance commitment measures (see Angle & Perry, 1981), the value commitment scale was found to correlate more strongly with turnover intention than was the continuance commitment scale. (Note, continuance commitment operationalized this way is not the same as continuance commitment as defined by Allen and Meyer, 1990b.)

Finally, Mayer and Schoorman (1992) tested a two-dimensional model of organizational commitment and its link to turnover intention and turnover. Using measures of continuance and value commitment developed by Schechter (1985), they found that both forms of commitment correlated significantly with intent to stay, and negatively with turnover. Although the correlations with intent were of roughly equal magnitude, continuance commitment correlated more strongly with actual turnover.

In sum, although affect-based forms of commitment have been found consistently to relate to turnover intention and turnover, other forms of commitment (e.g. continuance and normative commitment) also appear to play a role in the turnover process, albeit somewhat less consistently. Of particular interest is the finding that different forms of commitment may interact to influence turnover decisions (Somers, 1995). Although it has been suggested that a fuller understanding of the consequences of commitment might be gained by examining the joint influences of the different components (Meyer & Allen, 1991), there has been little systematic effort to do so. Somers' findings suggest that this may be a fruitful avenue for future investigation.

Moderator effects

Meta-analyses of the relations between commitment and turnover-related variables suggested that there might be moderator effects operating. Several studies have since attempted to identify variables that might interact with commitment to influence turnover. For example, Jenkins (1993) tested for, and found, a moderating effect of individual differences in self-monitoring on the relation between affective commitment and turnover intention. The correlation between affective commitment and turnover intention was stronger for low self-monitors than for high self-monitors.

Blau and Boal (1987) outlined a conceptual model in which they argued that organizational commitment would interact with job involvement to influence turnover. Blau and Boal (1989) conducted a partial test of the model and found, as predicted, that the interaction contributed to prediction beyond the main effects of involvement and commitment (as well as demographic variables and withdrawal cognitions). The highest turnover was found among those with low involvement and commitment, and the lowest turnover was found for those with high involvement and commitment. The interaction effect was due primarily to the fact that commitment had a stronger effect on turnover when involvement was low than involvement did when commitment was low.

Huselid and Day (1991) conducted a similar test and were able to replicate Blau and Boal's (1989) findings when they used ordinary least squares (OLS) regression analyses, but not when they used logistic regression (LR) analysis, which is more appropriate for binary dependent variables. In the latter analyses, they found neither significant main or interaction effects. At a more general level, they questioned the meaningfulness of results of much of the turnover research because of its reliance on OLS analyses.

Martin and Hafer (1995) tested Blau and Boal's (1987) interaction model using turnover intention as the criterion variable. Moreover, they tested the model separately for part-time and full-time telemarketing employees. Consistent with Blau and Boal (1989), they found evidence to support the interaction hypothesis for the combined groups, and for full-time employees only. The pattern of results obtained for part-time employees, however, was slightly different from that for full-time employees. Rather than finding the lowest turnover intentions among those with high commitment and high involvement, as was the case for the full-time employees, they found the lowest intention in the low involvement, high commitment group for part-time employees.

In sum, it appears that commitment might interact with other individual difference variables to influence turnover intention and turnover. The investigation of these interaction effects, however, has not been extensive, nor particularly systematic. Although it is important to identify other variables that influence the effect of commitment or turnover, or other outcome variables, the investigation of these moderator effects should be guided by theory and conducted with appropriate procedures.

Comparative tests of effects

There has been considerable rhetoric over the last two decades about the relative magnitude of the effects of different work attitude variables, most notably organizational commitment and job satisfaction, on employee turnover. This issue has now been addressed in a number of studies using various methodologies. In some cases, the relative magnitudes of correlations with turnover, or turnover intention, were compared. These studies have produced mixed results, with some finding stronger correlations for commitment (e.g. Ben-Bakr et al., 1994), and others for satisfaction (e.g. Rosin & Korabik, 1991). Jenkins (1993) found that the relative strength of correlations with turnover intention differed for high and low self-monitors; commitment was more strongly correlated for low self-monitors, but the reverse was true for high self-monitors.

Another approach has been to include commitment and satisfaction together as predictors in regression or structural equation modelling analyses to assess the relative strength of their independent contributions to prediction. These studies have also yielded somewhat mixed results. For example, Shore, Newton, and Thorton (1990) evaluated several models of the relations between work attitudes and behavioural intentions using cross-sectional data obtained from university employees. They found that job satisfaction and organizational commitment were both related to turnover intentions, but that commitment was a better predictor than was job satisfaction. Similarly, in a national sample of accountants, Rahim and Afza (1993) found that organizational commitment and job satisfaction both made significant independent contributions to the prediction of propensity to leave the organization, but that the contribution made by commitment was greater. Mueller, Boyer, Price, and Iverson (1994) investigated the turnover process in smaller organizations (i.e. dental offices). They found that, although commitment was negatively related to turnover intention and turnover, job satisfaction was a more important mediator of the influence of work conditions on turnover intention. Finally, Shore and Martin (1989) compared the relative contribution of commitment and satisfaction to the prediction of turnover intention for professional and clerical employees. They found that commitment was a better predictor for the latter, but satisfaction was a better predictor for the former.

Tett and Meyer (1993) examined the relative strength of the contribution of job satisfaction and organizational commitment to the prediction of turnover intention and turnover by combining meta-analyses and structural equation modelling. Specifically, they used meta-analyses to develop a matrix of correlations among four variables, organizational commitment, job satisfaction, turnover intention, and turnover. These correlations were then used to evaluate the contribution of commitment and satisfaction to prediction using structural equation modelling procedures. Their findings suggested that job satisfaction and organizational commitment contributed independently to the prediction of turnover intention, but that the effect of job satisfaction was slightly stronger. Moreover, they found that the effect of job satisfaction on turnover was mediated completely by turnover intention, but that, in addition to its indirect effect, commitment also exerted a small direct effect on turnover.

It appears from these findings that job satisfaction and organizational commitment are both implicated in the turnover process. The relative magnitude of their contributions to the prediction of turnover is still unclear however. One reason for the confusion might be that, as noted earlier, it is not clear whether, or how, satisfaction and commitment influence each other. Another reason might be that investigators have not adequately recognized the complexity of the turnover process. Lee and Mitchell (1991) outlined what they described as an 'unfolding model' of turnover that includes four somewhat different decision paths. They noted that commitment and satisfaction are only relevant to the turnover decision in a limited set of conditions identified in these decision paths.

Commitment and turnover intention: the issue of construct redundancy

It has been argued that one reason why organizational commitment might be a better predictor of turnover intention than job satisfaction and other work attitudes is that the constructs of commitment and turnover intention are redundant (at least in part). Two studies conducted recently to address this issue empirically produced mixed results. Kong, Wertheimer, Serradel, & McGhan (1994) conducted a factor analysis of OCQ items and a five-item measure of turnover intention developed by Hunt, Osborn, and Martin (1981). They found that both sets of items loaded on a single factor and, therefore, questioned whether commitment and turnover intention are different constructs. In contrast, Mueller, Wallace, and Price (1992), using confirmatory factor analysis, demonstrated that organizational commitment and turnover intention were distinguishable constructs.

The Kong et al. (1994) findings appear to be an anomaly. Although there has been only one disconfirming factor analytic study, the magnitude of the correlations reported between measures of organizational commitment and turnover intention are typically not strong enough to warrant the claim that the constructs are identical (see Tett & Meyer, 1993). Nevertheless, the question of how we should interpret the correlation between commitment and turnover intention remains. The same question applies to the comparison of correlations (e.g. job satisfaction versus organizational commitment) as discussed above.

Concern over the construct redundancy issue has perhaps been most evident in criticisms levelled at measures of commitment. It is often claimed, for example, that the OCQ includes items that assess turnover intention (e.g. Blau, 1989; Davy, Kinicki, & Scheck, 1991; Farkas & Tetrick, 1989). Are these claims legitimate? A careful reading of OCQ items reveals that there are no items that measure 'intention to leave' *per se*. At best (or worst), it can be argued that there are items that tap into 'withdrawal cognitions.' Given that commitment reflects a propensity to continue a course of action, this does not seem unreasonable.

The distinction between commitment and turnover intention can perhaps be seen more clearly by considering the different forms that commitment itself can take. According to Meyer and Allen (1991), commitment has been described as a *desire*, a *need*, or an *obligation* to continue a course of action. None of these is synonymous with *intention* to continue. Rather, each can contribute to such an intention. Moreover, the absence of a desire, a need, or an obligation to remain does not imply an intention to leave. For example, an employee with a low desire to remain may nevertheless have a strong intention to remain because of a strong need or sense of obligation.

In sum, then, the correlation between commitment and turnover intention should best be considered a reflection of the association between a psychological state and a behavioural intention, and as suggesting that one might be used to predict the other. It does not reflect construct redundancy. Moreover, it should be kept in mind that the (presumed) problem does not exist when commitment is evaluated as a predictor of turnover which is, after all, what we are ultimately interested in predicting.

Absenteeism and Tardiness

Little has changed in the investigation of the relation between commitment and absenteeism other than the fact that studies are now being conducted to determine whether the strength and/or direction varies across different forms of commitment. For example, several investigators have examined the relation between absenteeism and two or more of Allen and Meyer's (1990b) three components of commitment. Gellatly (1995) correlated affective and continuance commitment measures obtained from nurses and food service workers in a chronic care hospital with indices of their absence frequency and total days absent over a 12-month period following the survey. Affective commitment correlated significantly in the negative direction with both indices; continuance commitment did not correlate significantly with either index. When included in a structural equation model with other individual- and group-level variables, affective commitment was still found to contribute significantly to the prediction of absence frequency.

Hackett, Bycio, and Hausdorf (1994) correlated affective, continuance, and normative commitment scores obtained from a sample of bus drivers with indices of culpable and non-culpable absence. The only significant correlation they found was between affective commitment and culpable absence. This correlation was not significant when age, tenure, and job satisfaction were controlled.

Somers (1995) examined the relations between absence (total and annexed) and affective, continuance, and normative commitment in a sample of nurses. He found that only affective commitment predicted absence, albeit modestly, and then only annexed absence. As was the case with turnover intention noted above, however, Somers also found a significant interaction effect of affective and continuance commitment. The link between affective commitment and absence was greater for those who were low in continuance commitment. The highest rate of absence was found among those with both low affective and continuance commitment. These employees may have been using absence as an escape, or as an opportunity to find alternative employment.

These findings suggest that, as was the case with turnover, affect-based measures of commitment show the strongest and most consistent relation to voluntary absence. There may, of course, be factors that moderate this relation, as was suggested by the meta-analyses reviewed earlier. Indeed, Mathieu and Kohler (1990) found some evidence for a moderating effect of job involvement. There is also some evidence that other forms of commitment may have an effect on commitment, but the findings are less consistent. This could reflect the operation of moderators. Alternatively, the lack of consistency across studies might simply reflect chance fluctuation around a relatively low true correlation. There have, as yet, been too few studies using non-affect-based measures of commitment to determine which of these two possibilities is most likely. Based on the findings of Somers (1995), it might be useful to look for interaction effects among the components of commitment in future research.

Turning to tardiness, recent research has generally confirmed that, even when significant, the correlation between commitment and lateness behaviour tends to be relatively weak (e.g. Blau, 1995). Blau (1994) argued that one explanation for this weak relation might be the inadequate conceptualization of the tardiness construct. He identified and measured three different forms of lateness behaviour: increasing chronic, stable periodic, and unavoidable. He found that affective commitment was most strongly related to chronic lateness, accounting for 17% of the variance in a sample of hospital employees and 14% of the variance in bank employees.

There have been too few studies to draw firm conclusions about the link between commitment and lateness behaviour. Future research should consider the distinctions in tardiness behaviour made by Blau (1994). One potential avenue for research would be to examine whether the different forms of lateness behaviour relate differently to different forms of commitment.

Another might be to determine whether lateness is better predicted by commitment to some organizational constituencies than others.

In-role Job Performance

The meta-analytic findings concerning the relation between organizational commitment and in-role job performance paralleled those obtained in earlier meta-analyses involving job satisfaction (e.g. Iaffaldano & Muchinsky, 1985); the corrected mean correlation is positive but relatively weak. This is not surprising given that there are many factors contributing to employees' performance, some of which might be unrelated to commitment or satisfaction (e.g. ability, resources). Consistent with these meta-analytic findings, significant correlations have been found between commitment and performance in some recent studies (e.g. Cropanzano, Jamer, & Konovsky, 1993; Johnston & Snizek, 1991; Saks, 1995) but not in others (e.g. Ganster & Dwyer, 1995; Schweiger & DeNisi, 1991).

Again, there are at least two explanations for the inconsistent findings. First, the inconsistency might simply reflect chance fluctuations around a weak true correlation. Alternatively, there might be meaningful moderators operating. For example, Brett, Cron, and Slocum (1995) found a moderating effect of financial requirements on the relation between organizational commitment and sales performance in two organizations. The link between commitment and performance was stronger when financial requirements were low. Because pay was based on performance, a high financial need would provide a powerful incentive for performance, and reduce the impact that commitment might have.

One way in which recent research has extended the meta-analytic findings is the demonstration that the strength, and even the direction, of the correlation can vary depending on the form of commitment being considered. For example, Meyer et al. (1989) found that the affective commitment of managers in a food service company was positively related to their district managers' ratings of performance and promotability, whereas their continuance commitment was negatively related to these ratings. A similar finding was reported by Cropanzano, James, and Konovsky (1993) with employees in a pathology laboratory.

Hackett, Bycio, and Hausdorf (1994) correlated measures of affective, continuance, and normative commitment with four indices of performance (commendations, complaints, accidents, in-service rating checklist) in a sample of bus drivers. When age, tenure, and satisfaction were controlled, the only significant correlations that remained were those between affective commitment and accident rate (negative), and between continuance commitment and the receipt of commendations (negative).

Angle and Lawson (1994) examined the relations between two forms of commitment, affective and continuance, and supervisor rating of performance among employees in a Fortune 500 manufacturing organization. They found that neither affective nor continuance commitment was related to the global measure of performance. When they examined correlations with facet measures of performance, however, they found that affective commitment was positively related to ratings of dependability and initiative, but not to organization/accomplishment or judgment. Continuance commitment was not significantly related to any of the facet measures. Angle and Lawson argued, therefore, that the link between commitment and performance might depend not only on the nature of the commitment measure, but also on the type of performance being measured. For example, affective commitment might be more strongly related to measures of performance that reflect motivation rather than ability. Consistent with the latter suggestion, in a sample of life insurance agents in Singapore, Leong, Randall, and Cote (1994) found that commitment influenced job performance through its effects on levels of exertion (working harder), and well-directed effort (working smarter).

Most studies of the commitment–performance relation have been conducted at the individual level of analysis. Ostroff (1992) examined the link using an organization-level analysis. The commitment of over 13,808 teachers in 298 schools was measured and averages were computed within school. These school averages were then related to various indices of school performance (e.g. student achievement and satisfaction). Ostroff found that commitment was related to most indices of performance in the predicted direction. Although there are problems with comparison, she noted that the magnitude of the correlations obtained in this study tended to be somewhat stronger than those obtained in studies using an individual level of analysis. One possible explanation for this finding is that commitment contributes to employees' tendency to engage in unique, and perhaps idiosyncratic, forms of behaviour that are not captured in measures of individual performance, but are nevertheless reflected in the performance of the overall unit to which they are directed.

Extra-role Performance and Organizational Citizenship

Unlike in-role performance that is highly regulated and has various non-motivational determinants, extra-role performance (Katz, 1964) and organizational citizenship behaviour (Organ, 1988) are, by definition, discretionary. Consequently, there is reason to suspect that employees' commitment to an organization would have a stronger and more consistent link to behaviour that falls outside the defined role than to in-role performance. Such has been found to be the case with job satisfaction (see Organ, 1988).

A number of studies have examined the link between commitment and various indices of extra-role performance and citizenship, and most have reported significant correlations (e.g. Aryee & Heng, 1990; Munene, 1995; Wittig-Berman & Lang, 1990). One exception was a study by Williams and

Anderson (1991) using O'Reilly and Chatman's (1986) measures of identification and internalization. In a recent meta-analytic investigation of the correlates of citizenship behaviour, Organ and Ryan (1995) found a corrected mean correlation of 0.316 with organizational commitment. This correlation is larger than that typically found in meta-analyses of the relation between commitment and in-role performance.

Like the investigation of other outcome measures, a recent development has been to consider relations between extra-role behaviour and different forms of commitment. For example, Meyer, Allen, and Smith (1993) found positive correlations between nurses' affective commitment and their self-reports of helping others and effective use of time; normative commitment was also found to be positively related to the use of time measure. Continuance commitment was not related to either measure. Meyer, Allen, and Smith also asked nurses to indicate how they believed they would to react to dissatisfying conditions at work. They found that affective and normative commitment were positively related to the tendency to seek change (voice) or accept the condition (loyalty), and negatively related to the tendency to passively withdraw (neglect). Continuance commitment was unrelated to voice and loyalty, but positively related to neglect.

In a structural equation modelling analysis of data obtained from employees in a national cable television company, Moorman, Neihoff, and Organ (1993) found evidence for a relation between affective commitment and citizenship behaviour (supervisor ratings), but this relation disappeared when perceptions of procedural justice were controlled. Positive zero-order correlations were obtained between affective commitment and measures of several components of OCB. Some positive correlations, albeit weaker, were also obtained for continuance commitment.

Shore and Wayne (1993) found that affective commitment correlated positively with several components (altruism, compliance, and favours) of organizational citizenship behaviour, as rated by supervisors of employees in a large multinational firm; continuance commitment correlated negatively with two components (altruism and compliance). When affective commitment and perceived organizational support were entered together in regression analyses to predict citizenship, affective commitment did not make a significant unique contribution, whereas perceived support did. When continuance commitment and perceived support were entered together, both made significant contributions, and the effect of continuance commitment continued to be negative.

Morrison (1994) took a somewhat different perspective to the study of citizenship behaviour. She argued, and found, that employees differ in what they personally define as in-role and extra-role (citizenship) behaviour. She also found that affective and normative commitment were related to perceived job breadth. That is, those with stronger affective and normative commitment were more likely to view what have traditionally been considered citizenship behaviours as components of their job. Relations with affective commitment were generally stronger and more consistent (across behaviour categories) than those involving normative commitment.

In another slightly different twist to examining the relation between commitment and citizenship behaviour, Shore, Barksdale, and Shore (1995) asked managers to estimate the affective and continuance commitment of their employees. They found that citizenship behaviour predicted perceived affective commitment, whereas side-bets (a composite of education, age, job tenure, and organization tenure) predicted perceived continuance commitment. Supervisor ratings of employees' affective commitment were positively related to their own judgments of managerial potential and promotability, and to their employees' ratings of leader reward behaviour. Supervisor ratings of continuance commitment were negatively related to judgments of potential and promotability as well as to the extent they fulfil employees' requests. Interestingly, citizenship was a better predictor of manager-rated affective commitment than was performance, perhaps because the discretionary nature of citizenship behaviour made it more informative.

Because citizenship behaviour is discretionary, it can be directed at different targets. Therefore, in addition to considering how citizenship behaviour might relate differently to different forms of commitment, it is also important to consider whether, and how, it relates to commitment to different constituencies within, or outside, the organization. Some evidence that prosocial organizational behaviour relates differently to commitment to different constituencies within the organization was provided by Becker and Billings (1993) in a study described earlier. In another study along these lines, Gregersen (1993) examined the relations between supervisor ratings of extra-role behaviour and a global measure of organizational commitment as well as several facet measures (i.e. commitment to supervisor, top management, co-workers and customers). He also tested for moderating effects of tenure. Gregersen found that extra-role behaviour was not related to any form of commitment for those who were in the company for less than two years, but that it was positively related to global commitment for those with two to eight years in the company, and to commitment to immediate supervisor for those with a tenure of two to eight, and more than eight, years. Extra-role behaviour was negatively related to commitment to top management for the more senior employees.

In sum, these findings suggest that commitment to the organization might exert its strongest effects on citizenship and extra-role behaviours. The effects, however, might be quite complex. Additional research is needed to determine what forms of behaviour are related to what forms of commitment, to what constituencies, and under what conditions.

Employee Health and Well-being

The overwhelming majority of studies examining the consequences of commitment have focused on outcomes of relevance to the employing organization. It is only recently that outcomes of immediate and more direct relevance to the employees themselves have been investigated. For example, Romzek (1989) examined the correlations between commitment and various indices of non-work and career satisfaction in a sample of public-service employees. She found that commitment to the organization correlated positively with these measures. Although her data cannot be taken as evidence that commitment to an organization will actually contribute to employees' life and career satisfaction, she pointed out that the findings contradict the claim made by some that committing oneself to an organization necessitates a sacrifice in these other areas (cf. Cohen & Kirchmeyer, 1995).

Begley and Czajka (1993) measured the commitment of hospital employees before and after a major divisional consolidation. They found that commitment served to buffer the impact of stress on a measure of displeasure (a combination of job dissatisfaction, intent to quit, and irritation). Job displeasure was positively associated with stress only when commitment was low.

Ostroff and Kozlowski (1992) surveyed recent university graduates within the first few months of their starting career-oriented employment in a broad range of organizations, and again five months later. They found a significant negative correlation between commitment and self-reported psychological and physical stress, and a significant positive correlation with adjustment to the work situation, at both times. Wittig-Berman and Lang (1990) correlated the commitment of employed MBA students with self- and other-reports of symptoms of stress and with self-reports of alienation. They found that commitment was negatively related to both stress and alienation.

Summary

The findings of research conducted since the publication of the meta-analytic reviews described earlier continue to demonstrate relatively modest correlations between commitment and the outcome variables it has been assumed to influence. On a more positive note, however, it is clear that affective commitment has modest correlations with a number of different behaviours. Thus, organizations might expect to reap small benefits in several different ways by having affectively committed employees. The strongest correlations tended to be found with behaviours over which employees have the greatest control (e.g. turnover, citizenship). The influence of discretion is nicely illustrated by Somer's (1995) finding that the correlation between affective commitment and turnover intention was stronger among employees with lower continuance commitment. Presumably those with higher levels of continuance commitment felt they had less freedom to leave.

If our primary objective is to predict specific behaviours, Randall (1990) was correct in suggesting that we could do a better job using reasoned action models (e.g. Ajzen & Fishbein, 1980). These models have been found to yield quite accurate prediction. Nevertheless, they have been characterized by Roznowski and Hulin (1992) as *idiot savants* in recognition of the fact that they do one thing, but only one thing, very well. Employers are arguably more interested in knowing that their employees will take the organization's interests into consideration across situations than they are in predicting any one type of behaviour. Morrison's (1994) finding that more committed employees define their jobs more broadly (i.e. citizenship behaviours are viewed as in-role) illustrates the value of commitment in this regard. Similarly, Ostroff's (1992) finding that the correlation between commitment and performance is greater when both are measured at a group level suggests that committed employees can contribute to organizational effectiveness in ways that are not necessarily reflected in measures of an individual's performance.

The findings also illustrate the importance of distinguishing among different forms of commitment, and among commitments to different constituencies, in the investigation of commitment–behaviour relations. Moreover, they suggest that commitment might interact with other personal and situational characteristics to influence behaviour, but it is not clear at this point what the most important moderators might be.

Research continues to focus primarily on the positive consequences of commitment in spite of reminders that there may be negative consequences as well (e.g. Randall, 1987). There have been only a few studies that examined the relation between commitment and behaviour that, arguably, might have negative implications for the organization or employee. For example, Somers and Casal (1994) found some evidence for an inverted-U shaped relation between affective commitment and whistle-blowing behaviour. Grover (1993) found that committed employees were less likely than uncommitted employees to indicate that they would mis-report their behaviour to authorities, although both committed and uncommitted employees said they would be more likely to mis-report if they felt there was a conflict between their organizational and professional roles. Finally, Wahn (1993) found a positive correlation between continuance commitment and self-reports of unethical conduct. There is clearly a need for more research examining the potential 'down side' of commitment.

Finally, a word of caution is in order. Most of the research reviewed in this section was correlational. Therefore, although it is tempting to conclude that (affective) commitment has the desirable consequences discussed above, we cannot rule out other interpretations of the findings. It is possible, for example, that commitment is a consequence rather than a cause of an 'outcome' variable. For example, Brown, Cron, and Leigh (1993) provided data to suggest that employees' sales performance exerted an influence on their work attitudes, including commitment, by enhancing their feelings of success. Another possibility is that commitment and the outcome variables of interest are related only because they have a common cause. For example, Schweiger and DeNisi (1991) reported a significant negative correlation between commitment and stress. It would be tempting to conclude that commitment reduces stress but, in this case, it is more likely that both stress and commitment were influenced by reactions to an ongoing merger.

CONCLUSIONS

There has been considerable change in the organizational commitment literature since Griffin and Bateman conducted their review in 1986. Although they noted at that time that commitment might take different forms, there has been a much more systematic attempt to examine the multidimensional nature of organizational commitment, both in form and focus, in the last 10 years. There have also been advances made in the methods used to study the development and consequences of commitment. In particular, researchers have moved away from a reliance on bivariate correlations and are taking advantage of developments in structural equation modelling techniques to investigate causal connections on both the antecedent and consequence sides. These procedures still rely on patterns of covariance to infer causality, however, and must be interpreted with caution. A few attempts have been made to use quasi-experimental procedures to examine the influence of organizational practices (e.g. merger, promotion) on commitment. We need more of this kind of research in the future.

Throughout this review I have suggested areas where additional research is needed to build on current developments. Among the most important of these, I think, is the study of process. Much of the research directed at understanding how commitment develops has rested on untested assumptions about underlying mechanisms. The need to examine process has been highlighted by the recognition that commitment can take different forms and that each develops in different ways. For example, without understanding process, we are less well equipped to predict which, if any, form of commitment is likely to be affected by changes in conditions at work. For example, will the introduction of an attractive benefit program contribute to employees' affective attachment to the company, make them feel obligated to reciprocate, or increase their perception of the economic costs of leaving? Preliminary evidence suggests that the answer depends on how the practice is perceived, but we need to know much more about how these perceptions are shaped and get translated into commitment.

Additional research is also needed to clarify further the distinctions that have been made among forms of commitment. Even in the more well-developed multidimensional models, there is disagreement about the number of dimensions and how they are related. There is also a need for additional research to determine how employees become committed to different constituencies within organizations, and how these commitments interact to shape behaviour. Finally, there is a need for more systematic investigation of (i) moderators of relations with antecedent and outcome variables, (ii) potential negative consequences of commitment, and consequences of greater relevance to employees, and (iii) the impact of specific organizational policies and practices on employees' commitment.

It goes without saying that, in addressing these substantive issues, care must be taken to ensure that appropriate methods are being used. New developments in analytic procedures have contributed to the advances in commitment research noted above. In light of these methodological developments, however, it might be necessary to go back and re-examine findings that we have perhaps taken for granted. The impact of person–job fit and met-expectations are examples. In the same vein, we must be sensitive to developments in the conceptualization and measurement of constructs included in our models of commitment. Absenteeism and tardiness are good examples here.

Another important issue that needs to be addressed involves both substantive and methodological considerations. The models of commitment discussed here have, for the most part, been developed and tested in Western countries. There is a need for more systematic research to determine whether these models apply elsewhere. Although studies have been conducted in non-Western countries, without systematic cross-cultural research, it is impossible to know whether any discrepancies in the findings reflect true cultural differences in constructs and/or the way they relate to one another, or are due to problems with the way the constructs are measured, including difficulties with translation.

Finally, a major challenge ahead will be to determine how the changes being experienced by organizations throughout the world (e.g. downsizing, mergers and acquisitions, re-engineering, globalization) affect the role played by organizational commitment. Two quite discrepant scenarios can be envisioned. On the one hand, it is possible that as organizations become more streamlined, and the need for flexibility and adaptability increases, having a committed workforce will become less important, and perhaps even a liability. On the other hand, as organizations become leaner, they rely more heavily on those who remain to fulfil their mission. These employees are also likely to be given much more responsibility for managing their own behaviour. As I noted earlier, it is under conditions where employees have greater discretion that global attitudes, including organizational commitment, are likely to exert their strongest effects.

Even if employee commitment to the organization itself becomes less of an issue in the future, it is unlikely that concerns over commitment in general will disappear. In the process of studying organizational commitment we have learned much about what commitment is, how it develops, and how it influences behaviour, that should generalize to other work-related (e.g. career, occupation, union) commitments. As we expand the study of commitment to these other contexts, we should not ignore what has been learned in the study of commitment to the organization.

ACKNOWLEDGEMENTS

Preparation of this chapter was supported by a grant from the Social Sciences and Humanities Research Council of Canada. I am grateful to Meridith Black and Julie McCarthy for their assistance in the literature search and preparation of the manuscript.

REFERENCES

Ajzen, I. & Fishbein, M. (1980) *Understanding Attitudes and Predicting Social Behavior*. Englewood Cliffs, NJ: Prentice-Hall.

Allen, N. J. & Meyer, J. P. (1990a) Organizational socialization tactics: A longitudinal analysis of links to newcomers' commitment and role orientation. *Academy of Management Journal*, **33**, 847–858.

Allen, N. J. & Meyer, J. P. (1990b) The measurement and antecedents of affective, continuance, and normative commitment to the organization. *Journal of Occupational Psychology*, **63**, 1–18.

Allen, N. J. & Meyer, J. P. (in press) Affective, continuance, and normative commitment to the organization: An examination of construct validity. *Journal of Vocational Behavior*.

Angle, H. L. & Lawson, M. B. (1994) Organizational commitment and employees' performance ratings: Both type of commitment and type of performance count. *Psychological Reports*, 1539–1551.

Angle, H. L. & Perry, J. L. (1981) An empirical assessment of organizational commitment and organizational effectiveness. *Administrative Science Quarterly*, **27**, 1–14.

Aryee, S. & Heng, L. J. (1990) A note on the applicability of an organizational commitment model. *Work and Occupations*, **17**, 229–239.

Ashforth, B. E. & Saks, A. M. (1996) Socialization tactics: Longitudinal effects on newcomer adjustment. *Academy of Management Journal*, **39**, 149–178.

Aven, F. F., Parker, B., & McEvoy, G. M. (1993) Gender and attitudinal commitment to organizations: A meta-analysis Special Issue: Loyalty in a multi-commitment world, *Journal of Business Research*, **26**, 63–73.

Baker III, H. E. & Feldman, D. C. (1990) Strategies of organizational socialization and their impact on newcomer adjustment. *Journal of Managerial Issues*, **2**, 198–212.

Becker, H. S. (1960) Notes on the concept of commitment. *American Journal of Sociology*, **66**, 32–42.

Becker, T. E. (1992) Foci and bases of commitment: Are they distinctions worth making? *Academy of Management Journal*, **35**, 232–244.

Becker, T. E. & Billings, R. S. (1993) Profiles of Commitment: An Empirical Test. *Journal of Organizational Behavior*, **14**, 177–190.

Begley, T. M. & Czajka, J. M. (1993) Panel analysis of the moderating effects of commitment on job satisfaction, intent to quit, and health following organizational change. *Journal of Applied Psychology*, **78**, 552–556.

Ben-Bakr, K. A., Al-Shammari, I. S., Jefri, O. A., & Prasad, J. N. (1994) Organizational commitment, satisfaction, and turnover in Saudi organizations: A predictive study. *Journal of Socio-Economics*, **23**, 449–456.

Blau, G. J. (1987) Using a person–environment fit model to predict job involvement and organizational commitment. *Journal of Vocational Behavior*, **30**, 240–257.

Blau, G. (1989) Testing the generalizability of a career commitment measure and its impact on employee turnover. *Journal of Vocational Behavior*, **35**, 88–103.

Blau, G. (1994) Developing and testing a taxonomy of lateness behavior. *Journal of Applied Psychology*, 79, 959–970.

Blau, G. (1995) Influence of group lateness on individual lateness: A cross-level examination. *Academy of Management Journal*, 38, 1483–1496.

Blau, G. & Boal, K. (1987) Conceptualizing how job involvement and organizational commitment affect turnover and absenteeism. *Academy of Management Review*, 12, 288–300.

Blau, G. & Boal, K. (1989) Using job involvement and organizational commitment interactively to predict turnover. *Journal of Management*, 15, 115–127.

Blau, G., Paul, A., & St. John, N. (1993) On developing a general index of work commitment. *Journal of Vocational Behavior*, 42, 298–314.

Brett, J. E., Cron, W. L., & Slocum, J. W. (1995) Economic dependency on work: A moderator of the relationship between organizational commitment and performance. *Academy of Management Journal*, 38, 261–271.

Brockner, J., DeWitt, R., Grover, S. L., & Reed, T. (1990) When it is especially important to explain why: Factors affecting the relationship between managers' explanations of a layoff and survivors' reaction to the layoff. *Journal of Experimental Social Psychology*, 26, 389–407.

Brockner, J., Grover, S., Reed, T., DeWitt, R., & O'Malley, M. (1987) Survivors' reactions to layoffs: We get by with a little help from our friends. *Administrative Science Quarterly*, 32, 526–542.

Brockner, J. B., Tyler, T. R., & Cooper-Schneider, R. (1992) The influence of prior commitment to an institution on reactions to perceived unfairness: The higher they are, the harder they fall. *Administrative Science Quarterly*, 37, 241–261.

Brockner, J., Weisenfeld, B. M., Reed, T., Grover, S., & Martin, C. (1993) Interactive effect of job content and content on the reactions of layoff survivors. *Journal of Personality and Social Psychology*, 64, 187–197.

Brooke, P. P., Russell, D. W., & Price, J. L. (1988) Discriminant validation of measures of job satisfaction, job involvement, and organizational commitment. *Journal of Applied Psychology*, 73, 139–145.

Brown, S. P., Cron, W. L., & Leigh, T. W. (1993) Do feelings of success mediate sales performance–work attitude relationships? *Journal of the Academy of Marketing Science*, 21, 91–100.

Buchko, A. A. (1992) Employee ownership, attitudes, and turnover: An empirical assessment. *Human Relations*, 45, 711–733.

Buchko, A. A. (1993) The effects of employee ownership on employee attitudes: An integrated causal model and path analysis. *Journal of Management Studies*, 30, 633–657.

Bycio, P., Hackett, R. D., & Allen J. S. (1995) Further assessments of Bass's (1985) conceptualization of transactional and transformational leadership. *Journal of Applied Psychology*, 80, 468–478.

Caldwell, D. F., Chatman, J. A. & O'Reilly, C. A. (1990) Building organizational commitment: A multi-firm study. *Journal of Occupational Psychology*, 63, 245–261.

Carson, K. D. & Bedeian, A. G. (1994) Career commitment: Construction of a measure and examination of its psychometric properties. *Journal of Vocational Behavior*, 44, 237–262.

Cascio, W. F. (1993) Downsizing: What do we know? What have we learned? *Academy of Management Executive*, 7, 95–104.

Chao, G. T., O'Leary-Kelly, A. M., Wolf, S., Klein, H. J., & Gardner, P. D. (1994) Organizational socialization: Its content and consequences. *Journal of Applied Psychology*, 79, 730–743.

Cohen, A. (1991) Career stage as a moderator of the relationships between organizational commitment and its outcomes: A meta-analysis. *Journal of Occupational Psychology*, 64, 253–268.

Cohen, A. (1992) Antecedents of organizational commitment across occupational groups: A meta-analysis. *Journal of Organizational Behavior*, **13**, 539–558.

Cohen, A (1993a) Age and tenure in relation to organizational commitment: A meta-analysis. *Basic and Applied Social Psychology*, **14**, 143–159.

Cohen, A. (1993b) On the discriminant validity of the Meyer and Allen (1984) measure of organizational commitment: How does it fit with the work commitment construct? In N. S. Bruning (ed.), *Proceedings of the Annual Meeting of the Administrative Science Association of Canada: Organizational Behaviour*, **14**, 82–91.

Cohen, A. (1993c) Work commitment in relation to withdrawal intentions and union effectiveness. *Journal of Business Research*, **26**, 75–90.

Cohen, A. & Gattiker, U. E. (1994) Rewards and organizational commitment across structural characteristics: A meta-analysis. *Journal of Business and Psychology*, **9**, 137–157.

Cohen, A., & Hudecek, N. (1993) Organizational commitment–turnover relationship across occupational groups: A meta-analysis. *Group and Organization Management*, **18**, 188–213.

Cohen, A. & Kirchmeyer, C. (1995) A multidimensional approach to the relation between organizational commitment and nonwork participation. *Journal of Vocational Behavior*, **46**, 189–202.

Cohen, A. & Lowenberg, G. (1990) A re-examination of the side-bet theory as applied to organizational commitment: A meta-analysis. *Human Relations*, **43**, 1015-1050.

Cropanzano, R., James, K., & Konovsky, M. A. (1993) Dispositional affectivity as a predictor of work attitude and job performance. *Journal of Organizational Behavior*, **14**, 595–606.

Davy, J. A., Kinicki, A. J., & Scheck, C. L. (1991) Developing and testing a model of survivor responses to layoffs. *Journal of Vocational Behavior*, **38**, 302–317.

Dawis, R. V. (1992) Person–environment fit and job satisfaction. In C. J. Cranny, P., C. Smith, and E. F. Stone (eds), *Job Satisfaction*, New York: Lexington Books.

Dunham, R.B., Grube, J. A., & Castaneda, M. B. (1994) Organizational commitment: The utility of an integrative definition. *Journal of Applied Psychology*, **79**, 370–380.

Edwards, J. R. (1991) Person–job fit: A conceptual integration, literature review, and methodological critique. In C. L. Cooper, and I. T. Robertson (eds), *International Review of Industrial and Organizational Psychology*, Vol. 6. New York: Wiley.

Edwards, J. R. (1993) Problems with the use of profile similarity indices in the study of congruence in organizational research. *Personnel Psychology*, **46**, 641–665.

Edwards, J. R. (1994) The study of congruence in organizational behavior research: Critique and a proposed alternative. *Journal of Organizational Behavior and Human Decision Processes*, **58**, 51–100.

Edwards, J. R. & Cooper, C. L. (1990) The person–environment fit approach to stress: Recurring problems and some suggested solutions. *Journal of Organizational Behavior*, **11**, 293–307.

Eisenberger, R., Fasolo, P., & Davis-LaMastro, V. (1990) Perceived organizational support and employee diligence, commitment, and innovatin. *Journal of Applied Psychology*, **75**, 51–59.

Eisenberger, R., Huntington, R., Hutchison, S., & Sowa, D. (1986) Perceived organizational support. *Journal of Applied Psychology*, **71**, 500–507.

Emshoff, J. R. (1994) How to increase employee loyalty while you downsize. *Business Horizons*, **37**, 49–57.

Facteau, J. D., Dobbins, G. H., Russell, J. E. A., Ladd, R. T., & Kudisch, J. D. (1995) The influence of general perceptions of the training environment on pretraining motivation and perceived training transfer. *Journal of Management*, **21**, 1–25.

Farkas, A. J. & Tetrick, L. E. (1989) A three-wave longitudinal analysis on the causal ordering of satisfaction and commitment on turnover decision. *Journal of Applied Psychology*, **74**, 855–868.

Fletcher, C. (1991) Candidates' reactions to assessment centres and their outcomes: A longitudinal study. *Journal of Occupational Psychology*, **64**, 117–127.

Florkowski, G. W. & Schuster, M. H. (1992) Support for profit sharing and organizational commitment: A path analysis. *Human Relations*, **45**, 507–523.

Folger, R. & Konovsky, M. A. (1989) Effects of procedural and distributive justice on reactions to pay raise decisions. *Academy of Management Journal*, **32**, 115–130.

Gaertner, K. N. & Nollen, S. D. (1989) Career experiences, perceptions of employment practices, and psychological commitment to the organization. *Human Relations*, **42**, 975–991.

Ganster, D. C. & Dwyer, D. J. (1995) The effects of under staffing on individual and group performance in professional and trade occupations. *Journal of Management*, **21**, 175–190.

Gellatly, I. R. (1995) Individual and group determinants of employee absenteeism: Test of a causal model. *Journal of Organizational Behavior*, **16**, 469–485.

Greenberg, J. (1990) Organizational justice: Yesterday, today and tomorrow. *Journal of Management*, **16**, 399–432.

Greenberg, J. (1993) Stealing in the name of justice: Informational and interpersonal moderators of theft reactions to underpayment inequity. *Organizational Behavior and Human Decision Processes*, **54**, 81–103.

Gregersen, H. B. (1993) Multiple commitments at work and extrarole behavior during three stages of organizational tenure. *Journal of Business Research*, **26**, 31–47.

Griffin, R. W. & Bateman, T. S. (1986) Job satisfaction and organizational commitment. In C. L. Cooper and I. Robertson (eds), *International Review of Industrial and Organizational Psychology*, Vol. 2. New York: Wiley.

Grover, S. L. (1993) Why professionals lie: The impact of professional role conflict on reporting accuracy. *Organizational Behavior and Human Decision Processes*, **55**, 251–272.

Grover, S. L. & Crooker, K. J. (1995) Who appreciates family-responsive human resource policies: The impact of family-friendly policies on the organizational attachment of parents and non-parents. *Personnel Psychology*, **48**, 271–288.

Guzzo, R. A., Noonan, K. A., & Elron, E. (1994) Expatriate managers and the psychological contract. *Journal of Applied Psychology*, **79**, 617–626.

Hackett, R. D., Bycio, P., & Hausdorf, P. A. (1994) Further assessments of Meyer and Allen's (1991) three-component model of organizational commitment. *Journal of Applied Psychology*, **79**, 15–23.

Harris, S. G., Hirschfeld, R. R., Feild, H. S. & Mossholder, K. W. (1993) Psychological attachment: Relationships with job characteristics, attitudes, and preferences for newcomer development. *Group and Organization Management*, **18**, 459–481.

Hunt, J. G., Osborn, R. N., & Martin, H. J. (1981) A multiple influence model of leadership. *Technical Report No. 520, US Army Research Institute for Behavioral and Social Sciences*, Alexandria, VA.

Hunt, S. D. & Morgan, R. M. (1994) Organizational commitment: One of many commitments or key mediating construct? *Academy of Management Journal*, **37**, 1568–1587.

Huselid, M. A. (1995) The impact of human resource management practices on turnover, productivity, and corporate financial performance. *Academy of Management Journal*, **38**, 635–672.

Huselid, M. A. & Day, N. E. (1991) Organizational commitment, job involvement, and turnover: A substantive and methodological analysis. *Journal of Applied Psychology*, **76**, 380–391.

Iaffaldano, M. T. & Muchinsky, P. M. (1985) Job satisfaction and performance: A meta-analysis. *Psychological Bulletin*, **97**, 251–273.

Irving, G. P. & Meyer, J. P. (1994) Reexamination of the met-expectations hypothesis: A longitudinal analysis. *Journal of Applied Psychology*, **79**, 937–949.

Irving, G. P. & Meyer, J. P. (1995) On using direct measures of met expectations: A methodological note. *Journal of Management*, 21, 1159–1175.

Jaros, S. J., Jermier, J. M. Koehler, J. W., & Sincich, T. (1993) Effects of continuance, affective, and moral commitment on the withdrawal process: An evaluation of eight structural equation models. *Academy of Management Journal*, 36, 951–995.

Jenkins, J. M. (1993) Self-monitoring and turnover: The impact of personality on intent to leave. *Journal of Organizational Behavior*, 14, 83–91.

Johnston III, G. P. & Snizek, W. (1991) Combining head and heart in complex organizations: A test of Etzioni's dual compliance structure hypothesis. *Human Relations*, 44, 1255–1272.

Jones, G. R. (1986) Socialization tactics, self-efficacy, and newcomers' adjustments to organizations. *Academy of Management Journal*, 29, 262–279.

Katz, D. (1964) The motivational basis of organizational behavior. *Behavioral Science*, 9, 131–146.

Kelman, H. C. (1958) Compliance, identification, and internalization: Three processes of attitude change. *Journal of Conflict Resolution*, 2, 51–60.

Kiesler, C. A (1971) *The Psychology of Commitment: Experiments Linking Behavior to Belief*. New York: Academic Press.

Klein, K. J. (1987) Employee stock ownership and employee attitudes: A test of three models. *Journal of Applied Psychology*, 72, 319–332.

Klein, K. J. & Hall, R. J. (1988) Correlates of employee satisfaction with stock ownership: Who likes an ESOP most? *Journal of Applied Psychology*, 73, 630–638.

Kline, C. J. & Peters, L. H. (1991) Behavioral commitment and tenure of new employees: A replication and extension. *Academy of Management Journal*, 34, 194–204.

Kong, S. X., Wertheimer, J. S., Serradell, J., & McGhan, W. F. (1994) Psychometric evaluation of measures of organizational commitment and intention to quit among pharmaceutical scientists. *Pharmaceutical Research*, 11, 171–180.

Konovsky, M. A. & Brockner, J. (1993) Managing victim and survivor layoff reactions: A procedural justice perspective. In R. Cropanzano (ed.), *Justice in the Workplace*. Hillsdale, NJ: Erlbaum.

Konovsky, M. A. & Cropanzano, R. (1991) Perceived fairness of employee drug testing as a predictor of employee attitudes and job performance. *Journal of Applied Psychology*, 76, 698–707.

Koys, D. J. (1988) Human resource management and a culture of respect: Effects on employee's organizational commitment. *Employee Responsibilities and Rights Journal*, 1, 57–68.

Koys, D. J. (1991) Fairness, legal compliance, and organizational commitment. *Employee Responsibilities and Rights Journal*, 4, 283–291.

Lance, C. E. (1991) Evaluation of a structural model relating job satisfaction, organizational commitment and precursors to voluntary turnover. *Multivariate Behavioral Research*, 26, 137–162.

Lawler, E. J. (1992) Affective attachment to nested groups: A choice process theory. *American Sociological Review*, 57, 327–339.

Lee, T. W., Ashford, S. J., Walsh, J. P., & Mowday, R. T. (1992) Commitment propensity, organizational commitment, and voluntary turnover: A longitudinal study of organizational entry processes. *Journal of Management*, 18, 15–32.

Lee, T. W. & Mitchell, T. R. (1991) The unfolding effects of organization commitment and anticipated job satisfaction on voluntary employee turnover. *Motivation and Emotion*, 15, 99–121.

Leong, S. M. Randall, D. M., & Cote, J. A. (1994) Exploring the organizational commitment-performance linkage in marketing: A study of life insurance salespeople. *Journal of Business Research*, 29, 57–63.

Lewin, K. (1943) Defining the 'field at a given time'. *Psychological Review*, 50, 292–310.

Lind, E. A. & Tyler, T. R. (1988) *The Social Psychology of Procedural Justice.* New York: Plenum Press.

Locke, E. A. (1976) The nature and consequences of job satisfaction. In M. D. Dunnette (ed.), *Handbook of Industrial and Organizational Psychology*, Chicago: Rand McNally.

Louis, M. R. (1980) Surprise and sense-making: What newcomers experience in entering unfamiliar organizational settings. *Administrative Science Quarterly*, 25, 226–251.

Major, D. A., Kozlowski, S. W. J., Chao, G. T., & Gardner, P. D. (1995) A longitudinal investigation of newcomer experiences, early socialization outcomes, and the moderating effects of role development factors. *Journal of Applied Psychology*, 80, 418–431.

Martin, T. N. & Hafer, J. C. (1995) The multiplicative interaction effects of job involvement and organizational commitment on the turnover intentions of full and part-time employees. *Journal of Vocational Behavior*, 46, 310–331.

Mathieu, J. E. (1988) A causal model of organizational commitment in a military training environment. *Journal of Vocational Behavior*, 34, 321–335.

Mathieu, J. E. (1991) A cross-level nonrecursive model of the antecedents of organizational commitment and satisfaction. *Journal of Applied Psychology*, 76, 607–618.

Mathieu, J. E. & Farr, J. L. (1991) Further evidence for the discriminant validity of measures of organizational commitment, job involvement, and job satisfaction. *Journal of Applied Psychology*, 76, 127–133.

Mathieu, J. E. & Hamel, K. (1989) A causal model of the antecedents of organizational commitment among professionals and nonprofessionals. *Journal of Vocational Behavior*, 34, 299–317.

Mathieu, J. E. & Kohler, S. S. (1990) A test of the interactive effects of organizational commitment and job involvement on various types of absence. *Journal of Vocational Behavior*, 36, 33–44.

Mathieu, J. E. & Zajac, D. M. (1990) A review and meta-analysis of the antecedents, correlates, and consequences of organizational commitment. *Psychological Bulletin*, 108, 171–194.

Mayer, R. C. & Schoorman, F. D. (1992) Predicting participation and production outcomes through a two-dimensional model of organizational commitment. *Academy of Management Journal*, 35, 671–684.

McGee, G. W. & Ford, R. C. (1987) Two (or more?) dimensions of organizational commitment: Reexamination of the Affective and Continuance Commitment Scales. *Journal of Applied Psychology*, 72, 638–642.

Meglino, B. M., Ravlin, E. C., & Adkins, C. L. (1989) A work values approach to corporate culture: A field test of the value congruence process and its relationship to individual outcomes. *Journal of Applied Psychology*, 74, 424–432.

Mellor, S. (1992) The influence of layoff severity on postlayoff union commitment among survivors: The moderating effect of the perceived legitimacy of a layoff account. *Personnel Psychology*, 45, 579–600.

Meyer, J. P. & Allen, N. J. (1984) Testing the 'side-bet theory' of organizational commitment: Some methodological considerations. *Journal of Applied Psychology*, 69, 372–378.

Meyer, J. P. & Allen, N. J. (1991) A three-component conceptualization of organizational commitment. *Human Resource Management Review*, 1, 61–89.

Meyer, J. P. & Allen, N. J. (1995, May) *Work characteristic and work attitude relations: Moderating effect of attributions.* Paper presented at the annual meeting of the Society of Industrial and Organizational Psychology, Orlando, Florida.

Meyer, J. P., Allen, N. J., & Gellatly, I. R. (1990) Affective and continuance commitment to the organization: Evaluation of measures and analysis of concurrent and time-lagged relations. *Journal of Applied Psychology*, 75, 710–720.

Meyer, J. P., Allen, N. J., & Smith, C. A. (1993) Commitment to organizations and occupations: Extension and test of a three-component conceptualization. *Journal of Applied Psychology*, **78**, 538–551.

Meyer, J. P., Bobocel, D. R., & Allen, N. J. (1991) Development of organizational commitment during the first year of employment: A longitudinal study of pre- and post-entry influences. *Journal of Management*, **17**, 717–733.

Meyer, J. P. & Gardner, R. C. (1994, March) *Assessment of change in organizational commitment during the first year of employment: An application of confirmatory factor analysis*. Paper presented at the Academy of Management, Research Methods Division, Conference on Causal Modelling, West Lafayette, Indiana.

Meyer, J. P., Irving, G. P. & Allen, N. J. (in press) Examination of the combined effects of work values and early work experiences on organizational commitment. *Journal of Organizational Behavior*.

Meyer, J. P., Paunonen, S. V., Gellatly, I. H., Goffin, R. D., & Jackson, D. N. (1989) Organizational commitment and job performance: It's the nature of the commitment that counts. *Journal of Applied Psychology*, **74**, 152–156.

Mignerey, J. T., Rubin, R. B., & Gordon, W. I. (1995) Organizational entry: An investigation of newcomer communication behavior and uncertainty. *Communication Research*, **22**, 54–85.

Mone, M. A. (1994) Relationships between self-concepts, aspirations, emotional responses, and intent to leave a downsizing organization. *Human Resource Management*, **33**, 281–298.

Moorman, R. H., Niehoff, B. P., & Organ, D. W. (1993) Treating employees fairly and organizational citizenship behavior: Sorting the effects of job satisfaction, organizational commitment, and procedural justice. *Employee Responsibilities and Rights Journal*, **6**, 209–225.

Morrison, E. W. (1993) Longitudinal study of the effects of information seeking on newcomer socialization. *Journal of Applied Psychology*, **78**, 173–183.

Morrison, E. W. (1994) Role definitions and organizational citizenship behavior: The importance of the employee's perspective. *Academy of Management Journal*, **37**, 1543–1567.

Morrow, P. C. (1983) Concept redundancy in organizational research: The case of work commitment. *Academy of Management Review*, **8**, 486–500.

Morrow, P. C. (1993) *The Theory and Measurement of Work Commitment*. Greenwich, CT: JAI Press.

Mowday, R. T., Porter, L. W., & Steers, R. M. (1982) *Employee–Organization Linkages: The Psychology of Commitment, Absenteeism, and Turnover*. New York: Academic Press.

Mowday, R. T., Steers, R. M. & Porter, L. W. (1979) The measurement of organizational commitment. *Journal of Vocational Behavior*, **14**, 224–247.

Mueller, C. W., Boyer, E. M., Price, J. L., & Iverson, R. D. (1994) Employee attachment and noncoercive conditions of work: The case of dental hygienists. *Work and Occupations*, **21**, 179–212.

Mueller, C. W., Wallace, J. E., & Price, J. L. (1992) Employee commitment: Resolving some issues. *Work and Occupations*, **19**, 211–236.

Munene, J. C. (1995) 'Not on seat': An investigation of some correlates of organizational citizenship behavior in Nigeria. *Applied Psychology: An International Review*, **44**, 111–222.

Oliver, N. (1990) Work rewards, work values, and organizational commitment in an employee-owned firm: Evidence from the UK. *Human Relations*, **43**, 513–526.

O'Reilly, C. A. & Caldwell, D. F. (1981) The commitment and job tenure of new employees: Some evidence of postdecisional justification. *Administrative Science Quarterly*, **26**, 597–616.

O'Reilly, C. A. & Chatman, J. (1986) Organizational commitment and psychological attachment: The effects of compliance, identification, and internalization on prosocial behavior. *Journal of Applied Psychology*, 71, 492–499.

O'Reilly, C. A., Chatman, J., & Caldwell, D. F. (1991) People and organizational culture: A profile comparison approach to assessing person–organization fit. *Academy of Management Journal*, 34, 487–516.

Organ, D. W. (1988) *Organizational Citizenship Behavior: The Good Soldier Syndrome.* Lexington, MA: Lexington Books.

Organ, D. W. & Ryan, K. (1995) A meta-analytic review of attitudinal and dispositional predictors of organizational citizenship behavior. *Personnel Psychology*, 48, 775–802.

Ostrof, C. (1992) The relationship between satisfaction, attitudes, and performance: An organizational level analysis. *Journal of Applied Psychology*, 77, 963–974.

Ostroff, C. & Kozlowski, S. W. J. (1992) Organizational socialization as a learning process: The role of information acquisition. *Personnel Psychology*, 45, 849–874.

Penley, L. E. & Gould, S. (1988) Etzioni's model of organizational involvement: A perspective for understanding commitment to organizations. *Journal of Organizational Behavior*, 9, 43–59.

Pierce, J. L. & Dunham, R. B. (1987) Organizational commitment: Pre-employment propensity and initial work experiences. *Journal of Management*, 13, 163–178.

Premack, S. L. & Wanous, J. P. (1985) A meta-analysis of realistic job preview experiments. *Journal of Applied Psychology*, 70, 706–719.

Rahim, M. A. & Afza, M. (1993) Leader power, commitment, saisfaction, compliance, and propensity to leave a job among US accountants. *Journal of Social Psychology*, 133, 611–625.

Randall, D. M. (1987) Commitment and the organization: The organization man revisited. *Academy of Management Review*, 12, 460–471.

Randall, D. M. (1990) The consequences of organizational commitment: Methodological investigation. *Journal of Organizational Behavior*, 11, 361–378.

Randall, D. M. & Cote, J. A. (1991) Interrelationships of work commitment constructs. *Work and Occupations*, 18, 194–211.

Randall, D. M., Fedor, D. B. & Longenecker, C. O. (1990) The behavioral expression of organizational commitment. *Journal of Vocational Behavior*, 36, 210–224.

Reichers, A. E. (1985) A review and reconceptualization of organizational commitment. *Academy of Management Review*, 10, 465–476.

Reichers, A. E. (1986) Conflict and organizational commitments', *Journal of Applied Psychology*, 71, 508–514.

Reilly, N. P. & Orsak, C. L. (1991) A career stage analysis of career and organizational commitment in nursing. *Journal of Vocational Behavior*, 39, 311–330.

Robertson, I. T., Iles, P. A., Gratton, L., & Sharpley, D. (1991) The impact of personnel selection and assessment methods on candidates. *Human Relations*, 44, 963–982.

Romzek, B. S. (1989) Personal consequences of employee commitment. *Academy of Management Journal*, 32, 649–661.

Rosin, H. M. & Korabik, K. (1991) Workplace variables, affective responses, and intention to leave among women managers. *Journal of Occupational Psychology*, 64, 317–330.

Roznowski, M. & Hulin, C. (1992) The scientific merit of valid measures of general constructs with special reference to job satisfaction and job withdrawal. In C. J. Cranny, P. C. Smith, and E. F. Stone (eds), *Job Satisfaction*. New York: Lexington Books.

Saks, A. M. (1995) Longitudinal field investigation of the moderating and mediating effects of self-efficacy on the relationship between training and newcomer adjustment. *Journal of Applied Psychology*, 80, 211–225.

Salancik, G. R. (1977) Commitment and the control of organizational behavior. In B. M. Staw and G. R. Salancik, (eds), *New Directions in Organizational Behavior.* Chicago: St. Clair Press.

Schechter, D. S. (1985) *Value and continuance commitment: A field test of a dual conceptualization of organizational commitment.* Unpublished Master's thesis, University of Maryland, College Park.

Schwarzwald, J., Koslowsky, M., & Shalit, B. (1992) A field study of employees' attitudes and behaviors after promotion decisions. *Journal of Applied Psychology,* 77, 511–514.

Schweiger, D. M. & DeNisi, A. S. (1991) Communication with employees following a merger: A longitudinal field experiment. *Academy of Management Journal,* 34, 110–135.

Shore, L. M., Barksdale, K., & Shore, T. H. (1995) Managerial perceptions of employee commitment to the organization. *Academy of Management Journal,* 38, 1593–1615.

Shore, L. M. & Martin, H. J. (1989) Job satisfaction and organizational commitment in relation to work performance and turnover intentions. *Human Relations,* 42, 625–638.

Shore, L. M., Newton, L. A., & Thorton III, G. C. (1990) Job and organizational attitudes in relation to employee behavioral intentions. *Journal of Organizational Behavior,* 11, 57–67.

Shore, L. M. & Tetrick, L. E. (1991) A construct validity study of the Survey of Perceived Organizational Support. *Journal of Appled Psychology,* 76, 637–643.

Shore, L. M. & Wayne, S. J. (1993) Commitment and employee behavior: Comparison of affective and continuance commitment with perceived organizational support. *Journal of Applied Psychology,* 78, 774–780.

Smith, C. A. & Meyer, J. P. (1996, April) *HRM practices and organizational commitment: Test of a mediation model.* Paper presented at the annual meeting of the Society for Industrial and Organizational Psychology, San Diego, CA.

Somers, M. J. (1993) A test of the relationship between affective and continuance commitment using non-recursive models. *Journal of Occupational and Organizational Psychology,* 66, 185–192.

Somers, M. J. (1995) Organizational commitment, turnover and absenteeism: An examination of direct and interaction effects. *Journal of Organizational Behavior,* 16, 49–58.

Somers, M. J. & Casal, J. C. (1994) Organizational commitment and whistle-blowing. *Group and Organization Management,* 19, 270–284.

Staw, B. M. (1974) Attitudinal and behavioral consequences of changing a major organizational reward: A natural field experiment. *Journal of Personality and Social Psychology,* 6, 742–751.

Sutton, C. D. & Harrison, A. W. (1993) Validity assessment of compliance, identification, and internalization as dimensions of organizational commitment. *Educational and Psychological Measurement,* 53, 217–223.

Sweeney, P. D. & McFarlin, D. B. (1993) Workers' evaluations of the 'ends' and the 'means': An examination of four models of distributive and procedural justice. *Organizational Behavior and Human Decision Processes,* 55, 23–40.

Tannenbaum, S. I., Mathieu, J. E., Salas, E., & Cannon-Bowers, J. A. (1991) Meeting trainees' expectations: The influence of training fulfilment on the development of commitment, self-efficacy, and motivation. *Journal of Applied Psychology,* 76, 759–769.

Tett, R. P. & Meyer, J. P. (1993) Job satisfaction, organizational commitment, turnover intention and turnover: Path analyses based on meta-analytic findings. *Personnel Psychology,* 46, 259–293.

Tucker, J., Nock, S. L., & Toscano, D. J. (1989) Employee ownership and perceptions at work. *Work and Occupations*, **16**, 26–42.

Vancouver, J. B. & Schmitt, N. W. (1991) An exploratory examination of person–organization fit: Organizational goal congruence. *Personnel Psychology*, **44**, 333–352.

Vandenberg, R. J. & Lance, C. E. (1992) Examining the causal order of job satisfaction and organizational commitment. *Journal of Management*, **18**, 153–167.

Vandenberg, R. J. & Self, R. M. (1993) Assessing newcomers' changing commitments to the organization during the first 6 months of work. *Journal of Applied Psychology*, **78**, 557–568.

Vandenberg, R. J., Self, R. M., & Seo, J. H. (1994) A critical examination of the internalization, identification, and compliance commitment measures. *Journal of Management*, **20**, 123–140.

Vandenberghe, C. (1996) Assessing organizational commitment in a Belgian context: Evidence for the three-dimensional model. *Applied Psychology: An International Review*, **45**, 371–386.

Van Maanen, J. & Schein, E. H. (1979) Toward a theory of organizational socialization. *Research in Organizational Behavior*, **1**, 209–264.

Wahn, J. (1993) Organizational dependence and the likelihood of complying with organization pressures to behave unethically. *Journal of Business Ethics*, **12**, 245–251.

Wallace, J. E. (1993) Professional and organizational commitment: Compatible or incompatible? *Journal of Vocational Behavior*, **42**, 333–349.

Wanous, J. P. (1980) *Organizational Entry*. Reading, MA: Addison-Wesley.

Wanous, J. P., Poland, T. D., Premack, S. L., & Davis, S. K. (1992) The effects of met expectations on newcomer attitudes and behaviors: A review and meta-analysis. *Journal of Applied Psychology*, **77**, 288–297.

Weiner, Y. (1982) Commitment in organizations: A normative view. *Academy of Management Review*, **7**, 418–428.

Wetzel, K. W. & Gallagher, D. G. (1990) A comparative analysis of organizational commitment among workers in the cooperative and private sectors. *Economic and Industrial Democracy*, **11**, 93–109.

Whitener, E. M. & Walz, P. M. (1993) Exchange theory determinants of affective and continuance commitment and turnover. *Journal of Vocational Behavior*, **42**, 265–281.

Williams, L. J. & Anderson, S. E. (1991) Job satisfaction and organizational commitment as predictors of organizational citizenship and in-role behaviors. *Journal of Management*, **17**, 601–617.

Wittig-Berman, U. & Lang, D. (1990) Organizational commitment and its outcomes: Differing effects of value commitment and continuance commitment on stress reactions, alienation and organization-serving behaviors. *Work and Stress*, **4**, 167–177.

Yoon, J., Baker, M. R., & Ko, J. W. (1994) Interpersonal attachment and organizational commitment: Subgroup hypothesis revisited', *Human Relations*, **47**, 329–351.

Chapter 6

THE EXPLANATION OF CONSUMER BEHAVIOUR: FROM SOCIAL COGNITION TO ENVIRONMENTAL CONTROL

Gordon Foxall
University of Birmingham

I/O AND CONSUMER PSYCHOLOGY

Consumer behaviour once fell within the purview of I/O psychology, though this amounted to little more than industrial psychology texts' incorporating a sketch of consumer behaviour and market research as a concluding chapter. Now that I/O psychology is primarily orientated towards behaviour internal to the firm or other organisation, even this link with consumer research has become tenuous. Yet the behaviour of organisations is incomprehensible without reference to their publics and that of business firms cannot be fully understood in the absence of knowledge about the principal context in which they operate: the consumers with whom they effect transactions. The analysis of intra-firm relations might profitably begin with reference to their markets; for, assuming that firms are responsive, their behaviour must be understood as contingent upon that of their customers. Despite the potential for collaboration between I/O psychology and consumer psychology, however, and the commonalities of their theoretical and methodological backgrounds (Jacoby, 1983), little cross-disciplinary work has been undertaken which links intra-organisational behaviour to its external referents or, for that matter, consumption to the realm of production (du Gay, 1995). If I/O psychologists have tended to concentrate on intra-organisational behaviour, consumer psychologists have generally developed theories, perspectives and empirical knowledge that has treated consumer behaviour as devoid of contact with marketing and other relevant organisations.

Consumer psychology is a burgeoning field (Kassarjian, 1982; Bettman, 1986; Cohen & Chakravarti, 1990; Tybout & Artz, 1994) which prospers,

International Review of Industrial and Organizational Psychology, 1997 Volume 12
Edited by C.L. Cooper and I.T. Robertson. © 1997 John Wiley & Sons Ltd.

nevertheless, within severe intellectual limitations. It has become divorced from noncognitive explanations and from consideration of the context within which purchase and consumption occur. Moreover, despite the recent emergence of hermeneutical and postmodern perspectives in consumer research (Brown, 1995; Featherstone, 1991; Hirschman & Holbrook, 1992; Holbrook, 1995; Sherry, 1991, 1995; Shields, 1992), the prevailing normal science component of consumer research remains staunchly cognitivist. Consumer research has no coherent theoretical framework to classify the situations in which consumer behaviour occurs, nor to account systematically for patterns of consumer behaviour in various contexts (Foxall & Hackett, 1992, 1994; Hackett & Foxall, 1994, 1995; Hackett, Foxall, & Van Raaij, 1993; Timmermans, 1993). Such a framework must incorporate both the spatial and temporal components of the consumer situation as well as its social and regulatory influences and its outcomes.

The restrictive influence of scientific paradigms needs no elaboration (Kuhn, 1962). It is in the nature of paradigms to preclude multiple explanations, to pre-empt alternative theories, and this is precisely what the assumption that cognitive structures determine behaviour achieves for the dominant field of social cognition. As a leading proponent answers his own question with cool authority: 'Is social cognition sovereign? Of course it is' (Ostrom, 1994, p. xi). Cognitivism constituted the normal science component of psychology itself for over three decades. And, since applied psychology embodies the paradigmatic preoccupations of its parent, models of consumer behaviour have been inescapably cognitive in orientation (e.g. Nicosia, 1966; Howard & Sheth, 1969). But there is danger in such inevitability, for paradigms other than that which provides the normal science component of the discipline may be overlooked despite their potential to illumine its subject matter by engendering debate and synthesis, novel problems, hypotheses and methods.

This chapter argues that only by incorporating research orientations and findings from noncognitive psychology, can consumer researchers account for the situational influences on consumer choice. A complete view can never result from a single paradigm and scientific progress relies on contrast and comparative evaluation (Feyerabend, 1975; Laudan, 1984). The chapter therefore examines an alternative perspective on consumer behaviour derived from a critical reading of operant theory (Foxall, 1990). The review is concerned initially with the recent literature on the central outcomes of social cognition: attitudes and behaviour and the consistency required of them by social cognitive models of consumer behaviour. The cognitive modelling of consumer choice, especially at the level of the brand, depends for its validity and credibility upon there being sufficient correspondence between pre-behavioural measures such as attitudes and intentions and behaviour itself for the latter to be predictable from the former. The main difficulty with cognitive consumer research has been the inability of the models in question to predict consumer choice. Perhaps the most sophisticated attempt to do so, the

Howard–Sheth model (Howard & Sheth, 1969; Howard, 1977, 1983, 1989), derived from the choice models of the Carnegie–Mellon School, has been extensively tested. But only under the most gruelling conditions of situational consistency can the required correlational correspondence between measures of intention and measures of behaviour be demonstrated, and the results of attitude–intentions–behaviour research are as consistent with a behaviourist model of choice as with a cognitive (Foxall, 1983, 1987, 1996a, 1997).

The review is also concerned, therefore, with the recent literature of behaviour analysis especialy as it relates to verbal responding and private events. The alternative paradigm from which this literature is derived is compatible with a great deal of evidence and thought on the prediction of behaviour gained through cognitive reasoning and method, but it avoids the problem of having to demonstrate consistency across situations. This literature suggests an alternative approach to understanding consumer choice in its social and marketing context. That alternative approach, which has been developed over the last fifteen years (Foxall, 1996a), begins with an analysis of consumer behaviour that relates it to its environmental determinants. The neo-Skinnerian perspective thus created is particularly apposite given the need to understand both consumer and business behaviour in contingent relationship with one another. It is argued that a model of consumer choice based on a behaviour analytic framework can account for the phenomena of consumer choice as well as the more familiar cognitive models.

SOCIAL COGNITION OF CONSUMER BEHAVIOUR

The Socal Cognitive Consumer

Consumer behaviour embodies all the activities of buyers, ex-buyers and potential buyers from prepurchase to postpurchase, consumption to discontinuance. It extends from the awareness of a want, through the search and evaluation of possible means of satisfying it, and the act of purchase itself, to the evaluation of the purchased item in use, which directly impacts upon the probability of repurchase (Alba, Hutchinson, & Lynch, 1991). The models of consumer behaviour that emerged in the 1960s, on which the central paradigm for academic consumer research still relies almost exclusively, are a distinctive meld of cognitive and social psychologies (Andreasen, 1965; Nicosia 1966; Engel, Kollat, & Blackwell, 1968; Howard & Sheth, 1969). Fundamental components of this paradigm are the goal-oriented reception, encoding, representation and processing of information; equally important is the way this cognitive procedure is linked to behaviour in the sequence of belief-, attitude-, and intention-formation. The initial emphasis was upon high involvement processing but, by successive elaborations, several of the models have accommodated low involvement processing (Engel, Blackwell, &

Miniard, 1995; Howard, 1989) which may influence capacity for recall without requiring prior evaluation (Hawkins & Hoch, 1992). The style of consumer decision making also impacts the cognitive framework within which consumer behaviour develops (Bagozzi & Foxall, 1996; Bates & Mitchell, 1995; Bettman, Johnson, & Payne, 1991; Foxall, 1993c, 1994d,e; Foxall & Bhate, 1993a,b,c). The theoretical underpinnings of consumer psychology thus anticipated the social cognition movement of the 1980s and 1990s (Fiske, 1993; Ostrom, Prior, & Simpson, 1981; Wyer & Srull, 1986, 1989, 1994a,b), including the possibility that implicit cognitive events influence social behaviour (Greenwald & Banaji, 1995; Janiszewski, 1988; Schwartz & Reisberg, 1991). Prior to this development, cognitive psychology was little concerned with attitudinal and intentional outputs of information processing, while social psychology largely avoided cognitive concerns. In anteceding the advent of social cognition, consumer researchers made theoretical and methodological advances, notably in the area of attitudinal–intentional–behavioural consistency, which are contributions to social psychology as well as to consumer research. The fields of social cognition and consumer psychology are now inextricably intertwined: social cognition theories furnish the dominant paradigm for consumer psychology, while numerous academic consumer researchers have reputations in both fields (e.g. Bagozzi, 1992; Folkes & Kiesler, 1991; Kardes, 1994; Petty, Unnava & Strathman, 1991; Petty, Priester, & Wegener, 1994; Van Raaij, 1991).

Attitude-consistent Behaviour

Attitude is a mediating variable corresponding to mental processes or states which account for the consistency of an individual's favourable–unfavourable and cross-situational responses towards an object. An attitude is 'a psychological tendency that is expressed by evaluating a particular entity with some degree of favor or disfavor' (Eagly & Chaiken, 1993, p. 1; cf. Olson & Zanna, 1993; Tesser & Shaffer, 1990). 'Psychological tendency' denotes an intrapersonal state, and 'evaluative' encompasses all varieties of evaluation responding: overt or covert, and—an espousal of the traditional tricomponential view of attitude structure and function—cognitive, affective or behavioural. Attitudes develop out of evaluative responding of one of these three kinds, are mentally represented in memory, and are activated in the presence of the object to which they refer with the effect of shaping further behaviour towards it (Eagly & Chaiken, 1993). But it is not the behaviour involved in the formation of attitudes which has received the lion's share of attention from attitude researchers and theorists; rather, that to which attitudes are understood to lead. Since the pioneering conceptualisation and measurement in the third and fourth decades of this century (Bogardus, 1925; Likert, 1932), attitude has been portrayed as an organocentric predisposition to behave consistently towards the object to which it refers wherever it is encountered. The verbal statements by which attitudes are recorded in response to questionnaires have been assumed to express accurately the underlying 'real' or 'true' attitude held in mind and thus predict and explain its nonverbal manifestations. Foundational definitions of attitude therefore emphasised its motivating capacity: in Allport's (1935, p. 810) words, an attitude is 'a mental and neural state of readiness, organized through experience, exerting a directive or dynamic influence upon the individual's response to all objects and situations with which it is related'. The tacit assumption was then, as it generally is now, that to know an individual's attitude was equivalent to being able to predict his or her actions (Fazio & Zanna, 1981, p. 162). The attitude–behaviour relationship came to be most contingent in those definitions which claimed that only if consistent behaviour followed from measures of cognition, affect or conation, could an attitude be held to exist (Doob, 1947; Fazio, 1986: 205; cf. Pieters, 1988; Pieters & Van Raaij, 1988; Van Raaij, 1988).

Attitude psychology thereafter has a familiar history: while its most optimistic phase culminated in the mid-1960s, its most successful era extends from the mid-1970s to the present. The objectives of attitude study naturally embrace far more than the prediction of behaviour but, within social psychology and consumer research, and especially in the analysis of social cognition in which both fields have a current interest (Wyer & Srull, 1994a,b), the external validity of attitude measures continues to maintain a central position. Marketing models of consumer choice require the demonstrability of attitude-consistent behaviour (Foxall, 1983; cf. Castleberry, Barnard, Barwise, Ehrenberg, & Dall'Olmo Riley, 1994). The evidence of attitudinal-behavioural consistency that has accrued during the last twenty years or so can be fully comprehended and interpreted only through a short detour into the period of pessimism that intervened between those of optimism and success. The original objective of attitude psychology to predict behaviour towards an object from measures of a person's attitude towards that object, became problematical as a result of Wicker's (1969) review of 42 mainly experimental studies of behaviour with respect to various attitude objects. Wicker lambasted the notion that attitudes and behaviour were empirically consistent on the grounds that correlations were typically small, even if statistically significant. His conclusion was that 'taken as a whole, these studies suggest that it is considerably more likely that attitudes will be unrelated or only slightly related to overt behaviours than that attitudes will be closely related to actions' (Wicker, 1969, p.65). Not only were the correlations between attitudes and behaviour low—few exceeded 0.3 and the average was about 0.15—even the direction of causality between the variables was in doubt (as it remains: Bagozzi, in press). Fishbein summed up the position: '. . . what little evidence there is to support any relationship between attitudes and behavior comes from studies showing that a person tends to bring his attitude into line with his behavior rather than from studies demonstrating that behavior is a function of attitude' (Fishbein, 1972).

The empirical evidence for attitudinal-behavioural consistency led to pessimistic conclusions: published studies indicated at best only very weak relationships between attitude towards an object and behaviours performed with respect to it; attitude change was not an inevitable precursor of behavioural change; and attitudes might be nothing more than postbehavioural epiphenomena. But the disappointment was quickly to lead to innovations in methodology and conceptualisation that have since revolutionised the field (Upmeyer, 1989). Two broad courses of research have been pursued since the beginning of the 1970s in the attempt to come to terms with the critical conclusions of Wicker and others. The approach associated predominantly with Fazio and Zanna (e.g. 1978a,b, 1981) retains the original problem of demonstrating a relationship of consistency between global attitude towards an object and behaviour enacted towards that object. That associated predominantly with Fishbein and Ajzen (e.g. 1975; Ajzen, 1988; Ajzen & Fishbein, 1980) and, by extension, with Bagozzi and Warshaw (1990) has adopted a narrower route to the conceptualisation and measurement of attitudes and behaviours, and has concentrated on identifying and implementing the methodological developments necessary if the latter are to be accurately predicted from the former. Fazio's (1990) *ex post* categorisation of these approaches suggests that they are complementary (cf. Olson & Zanna, 1993). The 'global' approach has dealt with attitude elicitation that is apparently spontaneous, reliant on little if any mental processing and leading directly to action. The information processing associated with it is reminiscent of, though not identical with, the peripheral route to persuasion of the elaboration likelihood model (Petty & Cacioppo, 1984a,b) which continues to inspire empirical work in consumer research (e.g. Davies & Wright, 1994; MacKenzie & Hoffman, 1992; MacKenzie & Spreng, 1992; Miniard, Sirdeshmukh, & Innis, 1992; Schumann, Petty, & Clemons, 1990), and of the heuristic processing proposed by Chaiken (1989). For a complementary account, see Holbrook, O'Shaughnessy, and Bell (1990). The 'reasoned' approach has concentrated on the mental processing involved in deliberating on the consequences of undertaking an action before forming an intention to do so. It assumes a level of information processing more reminiscent of the central route to persuasion (Petty & Cacioppo, 1986a,b) and of systematic processing (Bohner, Moskowitz, & Chaiken, 1995).

Spontaneous Processing

Fazio (1986; Fazio & Zanna, 1981) focuses on the original general-to-specific problem of correlating global attitude measures with specific behaviour criteria. While some attitude–behaviour correlations are low using this approach, some are high and an important goal of this research programme has been to understand *under what circumstances* attitudes correlate with behaviour. It is the nonattitudinal variables, which people fail to take into account when they form and report attitudes towards targets, that confound attitude–behaviour consistency. Therefore, these investigators have argued that nonattitudinal factors be taken into consideration in the prediction of behaviour from attitudes to objects. The variations in correlations between attitudes and behaviours depend on the variability in nonattitudinal factors from situation to situation, which is considerable. That is, nonattitudinal factors *moderate* the relationship of attitude towards an object and behaviour towards that object (Eagly & Chaiken, 1993).

Attitudes as object-evaluation associations

Fazio (1986, p.214) defines an attitude as involving 'categorization of an object along an evaluative dimension': specifically, an attitude is an association between a given object and a given evaluation (Fazio, 1989, p. 155; Fazio, Chen, McDonel, & Sherman, 1982). This corresponds to the affective element of the tricomponential portrayal of attitude. The simple idea that an attitude is an association suggests that the strength of attitudes—and hence their capacity to influence behaviour—will vary, just as the strength of any relationship which is the result of associative learning will vary (Fazio, 1989, p.155). Fazio's model of the attitude–behaviour process thus attempts to answer the question '*When* is attitude related to behaviour?' rather than the more pervasive *why?* It assumes that social behaviour is substantially determined by the way in which the individual perceives the immediate situation in which the attitude object is presented as well as the way in which he or she perceives the object itself. Because situations are generally ambiguous, the individual's definition of any particular situation depends on how he or she interprets it. Hence, behaviour is guided by perceptions of the attitude object but also by perceptions of the situation in which it occurs, and that setting is said to determine the event. For instance, behaviour towards a particular person (attitude object) depends on the individual's perception of him or her: but the style of that behaviour will differ depending on whether the attitude object is encountered in his or her home, or a store, or at a party, or in church. 'It is this definition of the event—perceptions that involve both the attitude object and the situation in which the object is encountered—that the model postulates to act as the primary determinant of an individual's behavior' (Fazio, 1986, p.208).

When attitudes guide behaviour

The extent to which an attitude guides behaviour depends on the manner of its formation. Attitudes formed from *direct* experience with the attitude object are expected to differ from those stemming from *indirect* experience (e.g. word of mouth, advertising) in terms of their capacity to predict behaviour. Especially when they have to articulate an attitude, for example to a researcher or to fill out a questionnaire, people draw on past experiences which are described in the light of present circumstances; moreover, even enquiries about intentions can influence behaviour (Morwitz, Johnson, & Schmittlein, 1993). There is corroborative evidence that the attitudes of people who have had direct experience with an attitude object (target) correlate moderately with subsequent attitude-relevant behaviours; attitudes where such experience is lacking correlate only weakly. Attitude–behaviour consistency is higher when the preceding sequence has been behaviour-to-attitude-to-behaviour, rather than when it has been simply attitude-to-behaviour.

Whether an attitude guides behaviour depends also on the accessibility of the attitude from memory (Berger, 1992; Kardes, 1988; cf. Bargh, 1994). Attitudes formed behaviourally lead to a stronger object-evaluation bond than those formed indirectly and are as a result more easily accessed from memory. This is consistent with Bem's (1972) view that the difficulty people encounter in assessing their attitudes (their evaluations of an object) is overcome by engaging in behaviour with the object or by observing their own behaviour with it. Information gained through behaviour or behavioural observation is more trustworthy than that presented by another person or medium (Stayman & Kardes, 1992).

Dealing with direct experience

A feasible deduction from Fazio's demonstration of the significance of direct experience with the attitude object is that the consequences of relevant past behaviour are responsible wholly or in part for the probability of current responding in the presence of the attitude object. Current behaviour could then be explained as having come under the stimulus control of the attitude object, such control having been established through the reinforcement resulting from previous experience with the stimulus. In other words, the entire episode might be depicted as operant conditioning and investigation might be directed towards identifying the consequences of behaviour that accounted for its future probability. However, the explanation that has predominated is cognitive: attitudes formed through direct experience are held to be more accessible from memory than those formed indirectly. And accessibility, measured as verbal response latency (i.e. the speed with which the attitude is activated or recalled in the presence of the attitude object) is hypothesised to be directly proportional to behaviour change (Fazio & Zanna, 1981; Fazio, Powell, & Williams, 1989; Fazio et al., 1982). The strength of an attitude, its capacity to influence behaviour in the presence of the attitude object, increases with such structural attitude qualities as clarity, confidence, stability and certainty (Bargh, Chaiken, Govender, & Pratto, 1992; Doll & Ajzen, 1992; Downing, Judd, & Brauer, 1992). An attitude's strength is also increased through its repeated verbal expression (Fazio et al., 1982), though repeated expression is also related to attitude polarisation (Downing, Judd, & Brauer,

1992; Smith, Haugtvedt, & Petty, 1994). Accessible attitudes are, moreover, activated automatically in the presence of the attitude stimulus—without conscious and volitional cognitive processing (Eagly & Chaiken, 1993, p.197; see also Bargh et al., 1992; Blascovich, Ernst, Tomaka, Kelsey, Salomon, & Fazio, 1993; Fazio, 1994; Haugtvedt & Petty, 1992; Myers-Levy, 1991; Tesser, Martin, & Mendolia, 1994). Not all of the evidence supports this: there are contra-indications that *all* attitudes are automatically activated in the presence of the attitude object, regardless of their accessibility (Bargh et al., 1992). Prior knowledge about the attitude object also increases attitudinal-behavioural consistency presumably because such knowledge is attained through direct experience (Eagly & Chaiken, 1993, pp.200–201; cf. Tripp, Jensen, & Carlson, 1994). As will be documented, there is empirical evidence that such verbal repetition increases the chance that the evaluative behaviour described as an attitude will become a self-instruction that guides further responding.

Deliberative Processing

Compatibility

Many familiar conclusions of attitude researchers in the era since Wicker's (1969) review and (1971) call for the abandonment of the attitude concept derive from the application of Fishbein's (1967) intentions model which gave rise to the theory of reasoned action (Fishbein & Ajzen, 1975) and the theory of planned behaviour (Ajzen, 1985). The emphasis is largely on the methodological refinements required in order to increase the accuracy of prediction (Bagozzi & Warshaw, 1990, 1992). This group of attitude theories revolves around the belief that the degrees of specificity with which attitudinal and behavioural measures are each defined must be identical if high correlations are to be found between them. Global attitude measures are therefore consistent with multiple-act measures of behaviour towards the attitude object. It follows that the prediction of single acts is only likely to result from equally narrow measures of attitude, those that correspond exactly in level of specificity to the act to be predicted; those, moreover, that are framed as measures of the respondent's attitude towards performing that act in closely designated circumstances (Fishbein & Ajzen, 1975). This is not the initial intellectual problem posed by attitude research (Cohen, 1964), but its pragmatic departure from the constructions inherent in that problem has produced a reformation in the technology of behavioural prediction (Ajzen & Fishbein, 1980). Nor is the requirement of situational compatibility confined to measuring attitude towards a specific target behaviour rather than attitude towards an object: Ajzen and Fishbein's (1977) analysis of numerous studies of attitudinal-behavioural consistency revealed that high correlations are probable only when the measures of attitude and behaviour coincide with reference to the precise *action* to be performed, the *target* towards which the action is to be directed, the *context* in which the action would occur, and its *timing*. A further important recognition was that measures of the cognitive precursors of attitude will be highly predictive only when there is maximal temporal contiguity of the behavioural and antecedent measures (Ajzen & Fishbein, 1980). The greater the temporal gap between attitude or intention and the behaviour to which they refer, and hence the extent of situational intervention that potentially separates them, the lower will be their correlative consistency. Though this remains a significant problem in all of the theories reviewed below, it is not necessarily a handicap to prediction. Even a temporal gap of some fifteen years does not impede prediction in some cases, though the correlations may be positively influenced by the use of self-report measures of behaviour (Randall & Wolff, 1994). Certainly, there appears abundant empirical evidence that the intention which *immediately* precedes behaviour is highly predictive (Ericsson & Simon, 1993) and that is all that the models now considered explicitly claim.

The theory of reasoned action

The theory of reasoned action (TRA), which represents a culmination of Fishbein's and Ajzen's work on the prediction of attitude-consistent behaviours, incorporates both these observations and several other innovations (Fishbein & Ajzen, 1975). The theory predicts not behaviours themselves but intentions to engage in them provided, first, that reasons can be adduced for doing so, and, second, that there is no hindrance to the respondent's doing so. It thus refers to reasoned behaviour that is under the individual's volitional control. Such behaviour, despite the authors' caution in delineating the predictive scope of their model, is assumed to approximate intentions towards its performance. Intentions are, in their turn, determined by two belief-based cognitions. The first, attitude towards performing the target behaviour, is measured as the respondent's belief that a particular action will have a given outcome or consequence, weighted by his or her evaluation of that outcome. Only *salient* behavioural beliefs enter into the calculation of behavioural attitude. The second cognitive variable that determines intention is the respondent's subjective norm, his or her perceptions of the evaluations that important social referents ('significant others') would hold towards the respondent's performing the target action, weighted by his or her motivation to comply with them. Subjective norm is an attempt to capture the nonattitudinal influences on intention and, by implication, behaviour. By permitting this consideration of perceived social pressure to enter the calculation of behavioural intentions, the theory takes account of some at least of the situational interventions that may reduce the consistency of the attitude–behaviour sequence. There is empirical evidence that people actually distinguish behavioural and normative beliefs (Trafimow & Fishbein, 1995).

The initial problem of attitude research has thus been modified further by the assumptions that the relationship between attitude and behaviour is mediated by the behavioural intention that is the immediate precursor of the targeted action, and that behavioural intention is determined by both attitudinal and nonattitudinal factors (Sparks, Hedderley, & Shepherd, 1991). But this approach has proved successful in as much as the prediction of behaviour, albeit under the specialised circumstances to which the theory applies, has been achieved. A meta-analysis of studies employing the TRA (Sheppard, Hartwick, & Warshaw, 1988) found an average correlation of behavioural intention with behaviour of 0.53, while a more recent meta-analysis (Van den Putte, 1993) reports an average of 0.62. Hence, the achievement of the TRA is that if its variables are measured under conditions maximally conducive to high correlations, which refer to conditions of close contextual correspondence, high correlations are usually obtained by the TRA. The theory found a pivotal place in consumer research, academic (*Journal of Consumer Research,* 1994) and commercial (East, 1990, 1997; Foxall, 1983, 1984). The fascination continues (e.g. Ball, Lamb, & Brodie, 1992; Berger, 1992; Berger, Ratchford, & Haines, 1994; Haugtvedt & Wegener, 1994; Haugtvedt, Schumann, Schneier, & Warren, 1994; Mick, 1992; Percy & Rossiter, 1992; Nataraajan, 1993; Yi, 1990).

But there are criticisms, too (Bagozzi, 1984, 1985, 1988). Sheppard, Hartwick, and Warshaw (1988) point out that the TRA deals with the prediction of behaviours rather than the outcomes of behaviours: it is concerned for instance to predict the likelihood of one's studying for an examination, not that of one's passing it. The amount of studying one does is largely under personal volitional control but whether one's hard studying is accompanied by success in the examination depends on factors that lie beyond that control: the cooperation of others in the household or library might not be forthcoming, the books one most needs may not be available, one may not have invested sufficient time and effort in attaining study skills, and so on (Liska, 1984). Even if one is fully motivated and puts total effort into the task, circumstances may impede one's performance and achievement of the goal (Ramsey, Lord, Wallace, & Pugh, 1994; Sheppard, Hartwick, & Warshaw, 1988). The TRA cannot predict goal achievement because that outcome relies upon situational factors which make the attainment of a goal uncertain. The TRA also concentrates on the prediction of single, specified behaviours which are not in competition with other behaviours. It thus avoids situations of choice within the class of intended behaviours or consequences (Dabholkar, 1994). The attributes taken into consideration in expectancy-value models such as the TRA correspond to attributes of the product class: to the extent that brands within that class are perceptively identical, brand choice may be unpredictable (Ehrenberg, 1972). Most consumers are neither entirely brand nor store loyal and have more than one brand/outlet in mind when shopping for a particular product. The availability of choice, leading to the possible selection of one item or behaviour from alternatives, is a situational constraint. Given the multi-brand purchasing behaviours of consumers (Ehrenberg & Uncles, 1995), and their multi-store purchasing patterns (Keng & Ehrenberg, 1984), it is doubtful whether such specific behaviours can be predicted by models of this sort.

Most significantly, the TRA has been criticised for not considering the full gamut of nonattitudinal personal and situational factors likely to influence the strength of the attitude–behaviour relationship or enhance the prediction of behaviour (Brown & Stayman, 1992; Olson & Zanna, 1993). The authors of the TRA are adamant that behaviour is determined by behavioural intention and that all contributing influences are subsumed by the two elements that determine it: attitude towards performing the target act and subjective norm with reference to performing that act (Ajzen & Fishbein, 1980; Fishbein & Ajzen, 1975). Yet this principle of sufficiency has been proved inaccurate by empirical work that has incorporated additional factors to increase the predictability of intentions and/or behaviour (Bagozzi & Van Loo, 1991). Factors not comprehended by the theory which have been found to improve the predictability of behaviour include (Eagly & Chaiken, 1993; cf. Shepherd & Towler, 1992; Shepherd, Sparks, Bellier, & Raats, 1991/2; Towler & Shepherd 1991/2): personal norm (Beck & Ajzen, 1991; Boyd & Wandersman, 1991; Manstead & Parker, 1995; Parker, Manstead, & Stradling, 1995; Richardson, Shepherd, & Elliman, 1993); self-identity (Granberg & Holmberg, 1990; Sparks & Shepherd, 1992; Sparks, Shepherd, & Frewer, 1995); self-schemas (Bagozzi & Kimmel, 1996); size and content of consideration set (Pieters & Verplanken, 1995); availability of relevant skills, resources and cooperation (Liska, 1984; Fishbein & Stasson, 1990); action control (Bagozzi & Kimmel, 1996); past behaviour/habit (Bagozzi, 1981; Bagozzi & Kimmel, 1995; Bagozzi & Warshaw, 1990, 1992; Bentler & Speckart, 1979, 1981; East, 1992, 1993; Fredericks & Dossett, 1983; Towler & Shepherd, 1991/2); amount of reasoning during intention formation (Pieters & Verplanken, 1995); perceived control/confidence (Giles & Cairns, 1995; Marsh & Matheson, 1983; Pieters & Verplanken, 1995; Sparks, Hedderley, & Shepherd, 1992; Sparks, Shepherd, & Frewer, 1995; Terry & O'Leary, 1995); attitude functions (Maio & Olson, 1994); and affect (Bagozzi, 1994; Bagozzi & Moore, 1994; Bagozzi, Baumgartner, & Pieters, 1966).

Behaviour requiring resources, skills and cooperation in order to be enacted is problematical. Consumer behaviour usually requires all three, yet restricting the TRA to behaviour that is volitional means it requires only motivation on the part of the individual. Studies that have supported the model have dealt with only simple behaviours that require little if anything by way of resources and skills. Fishbein and Ajzen argue that such considerations have an effect on intention and thus were taken care of in their model. Also Fishbein and Ajzen stressed that the intention that mattered for purposes of prediction was that obtaining immediately before the opportunity to engage in the behaviour arose. Understanding what occurs between intention and behaviour has become a big part of predicting actions (Eagly & Chaiken, 1993).

The theory of planned behaviour (TPB)

The TPB (Ajzen, 1985) incorporates just one of these additional variables. *Perceived behavioural control* is posited—along with attitude towards the act and subjective norm—to determine behavioural intentions. (East, 1997, points out that researchers such as Marsh and Matheson, 1983, who included a measure of confidence in the TRA were anticipating the development of the TPB.) Further, when perceived and actual behavioural control coincide or are closely approximate, perceived behavioural control is expected to exert a direct determinative influence on behaviour. Thus, in contrast to the TRA, this theory applies if volitional control is limited. Moreover, the extent to which perceived behavioural control adds significantly to the prediction of intentions is apparent from Ajzen's (1991) analysis of the results of several studies employing his theory which shows that the average multiple correlation was 0.71. A comparison of the theories of reasoned action and planned behaviour by Madden, Ellen, and Ajzen (1992) involved a spectrum of ten behaviours from those rated comparatively difficult to control (e.g. shopping) to those rated comparatively easy (e.g. renting a video); the inclusion of perceived behavioural control in addition to the reasoned action variables resulted in a significant increase in explained behavioural variance. As predicted by TPB, perceived behavioural control was more important in the case of the behaviours rated as low in controllability. Manstead and Parker (1995, p.72) conclude that the TPB has improved on the predictive performance of the TRA and extended the range of behaviours to which it can be applied.

The wide range of applications to which the TPB has been put leads East (1997) to the view that it has now substantially superseded the TRA. These applications include: addictions (Godin, Valois, LePage, & Desharnais, 1992; Morojele & Stephenson, 1992); blood and organ donation (Giles & Cairns, 1995; Borgida, Conner, & Manteufel, 1992); excessive drinking (Schlegel, Davernas, & Zanna, 1992); control of infant sugar intake (Beale & Manstead, 1991); contraceptive use and sexual behaviour (Boldero, Moore, & Rosenthal, 1992; Chan & Fishbein, 1993; Dewit & Teunis, 1994; Kashima, Gallois, & McCamish, 1993; Morrison, Gillmore, & Baker, 1995; White, Terry, & Hogg, 1994; Richard, 1994; Richard, van der Pligt, & de Vries, 1995); job seeking (van Ryn & Vinokur, 1990); physical exercise (Ajzen & Driver, 1992; Courneya, 1995; Godin, Valois, & LePage, 1993; Harrison & Liska, 1994; Kimiecik, 1992; Norman & Smith, 1995); health care (Anderson, Campbell, & Shepherd, 1995; DeVellis, Blalock, & Sandler, 1990; McCaul, Sandgren, O'Neill, & Hinsz, 1993); food acceptance and choice (Dennison & Shepherd, 1995; Raats, Shepherd, & Sparks, 1995; Sparks & Shepherd, 1992); collective action (Kelly & Breinlinger, 1995); recycling (Boldero, 1995; Taylor & Todd,

1995); internet use (Klobas, 1995); risky driving (Parker, Manstead, & Stradling, 1995; Parker, Reason, Manstead, & Stradling, in press; Parker, Manstead, Stradling, Reason, & Baxter, 1992); avoidance of accidents (Richard, Dedobbeleer, Champagne, & Potvin, 1994; Rutter, Quine, & Chesham, 1995); entrepreneurial behaviour (Desroches & Chebat, 1995); gift purchasing (Netemeyer, Andrews, & Durvasula, 1993; Sahni, 1994); share applications (East, 1993); complaining (East, 1996); voting (Watters, 1989); intention to play with video games (Doll & Ajzen, 1992; Netemeyer & Burton, 1990); class attendance and scholarly accomplishment (Ajzen & Madden, 1986); leisure behaviour (Ajzen & Driver, 1991, 1992); 'green' consumerism (Sparks & Shepherd, 1992; Sparks, Shepherd, & Frewer, 1995).

The TPB is, nevertheless problematical on several grounds of conceptualisation and method. Like the TRA, it assumes temporal contiguity between intention and behaviour so that precise situational correspondence is still essential to accurate prediction (Netemeyer, Burton, & Johnston, 1991). The operationalisation of the theory is beset by the problem of measuring perceived behavioural control—directly as opposed to recording control beliefs—(Manstead & Parker, 1995). Moreover, as Eagly and Chaiken (1993, p.189) point out, the assumption of a causal link between perceived control and intention presumes people decide to engage in a behaviour because they feel they can achieve it. This raises problems in the case of antisocial or negatively self-evaluated behaviours such as risky driving (Manstead & Parker, 1995). Another, technical, problem is that the theory introduces only one new variable when we have seen that other factors—habit, perceived moral obligation, self-identity—may also predict behaviour over and above the terms of the TRA. The theory is based on the principle of sufficiency—though the variables involved have been expanded by one from the TRA: there is continuing evidence that factors such as self-identity and moral judgement add predictive power over and above the measures formally incorporated into the TPB (see, for instance, Raats, Shepherd, & Sparks, 1995; Sparks & Shepherd, 1995; Sparks, Shepherd, & Frewer, 1995). Manstead and Parker (1995) argue strongly that personal norms and the affective evaluation of behaviour may account for variance in behavioural intentions beyond that accounted for by the TPB (cf. Allen, Machleit, & Kleine, 1992).

Prior behaviour, in particular, is an independent determinant of intention and behaviour and several of the extra-TRA variables, including perceived behavioural control, are presumably related to prior behaviour (e.g. Morojele & Stephenson, 1992; see also East, 1997; Foxall, 1996, 1997; cf. Thompson, Haziris, & Alekos, 1994; Thompson, Thompson, & Hill, 1995). East (1997) argues that 'experience elaborates the belief basis of planned behaviour constructs'. As the consumer progresses from novice to experienced buyer, his or her behaviour is influenced more by attitudes towards the behaviour and perceived behavioural control and less by subjective norm (East, 1992). The consumer who lacks specific and detailed knowledge of, say, a product falls back on simple notions or heuristics: social pressures to act in a particular manner will be more easily known or guessed than the benefits and costs of executing a novel behaviour (East, 1997). This is paralleled by the finding that extrinsic cues such as product price and appearance are used in decision making by consumers with little or no direct experience of consuming the item (Rao & Monroe, 1988); moreover, the less consumers are familiar with a product the more they tend to infer its quality from its price and to have lower price limits suggesting that they have little idea of the product qualities worth paying for (Rao & Sieben, 1992). East (1997) interprets this to mean that 'experience seems to result in detailed product knowledge that is used to change the way in which consumer judgements are made'. The progression is from a necessary reliance on subjective norms to the chance to use behaviour-specific attitudes which have been developed in the course of behaving. Consistent with this, novice computer buyers rely disproportionately on subjective norms, while it seems likely that experienced computer users would hardly base their decisions on social pressures rather than behavioural attitudes and perceived control (East, 1992). There is further empirical confirmation in the case of television viewing intentions that subjective norm is the stronger influence among novices (who lack experience and knowledge of the service, breakfast-time broadcasting) as compared with experienced viewers whose intentions are more predictable from behavioural attitudes (East, 1992). Also, nonusers of mineral water tend to be far more strongly influenced by subjective norm than are users (Knox & de Chernatony, 1994). Past behaviour correlates more highly with behavioural attitude and perceived behavioural control than with subjective norm for other consumer behaviours including applying for shares in a privatised utility, redress seeking, theatre-going, complaining in a restaurant, taking out a pension scheme, and playing the National Lottery (East, 1997). East's data also indicate that the inclusion of a measure of past behaviour in a regression equation predicting intention from the TPB variables reduces the beta weights to a greater degree for behavioural attitude and perceived behavioural control than for subjective norm. Subjective norm, after all, is unlikely to be affected by or to increase in salience as a result of experience. One approach to the problems remaining in the TPB has been to investigate how people formulate plans and translate intentions into behaviour, something the theory fails to address (Eagly & Chaiken, 1993). It is, however, a theme confronted by the theories of self-regulation and, especially, the theory of trying.

The theories of self-regulation and trying

An attempt to uncover the factors responsible for the translation of intentions into behaviour was made by Bagozzi (1986, 1992, 1993; Bagozzi, Baumgartner, & Yi, 1992a,b) in the theory of self-regulation. The novel thinking behind this approach is that attitude provides only a measure of the extent to which an individual is affectively involved with a behaviour: his or her motivation to act in the specified way depends on their desire to engage in the behaviour. It can be hypothesised, therefore, that desires would show a stronger effect on intentions than would attitudes, that attitude affects would ideally disappear, and that if desires contain explanatory content over and above that provided by subjective norm and past behaviour, they will predict intentions even though these additional variables are included in the measure of antecedents to intention (Bagozzi & Kimmel, 1995). Bagozzi and Warshaw (1990) argue that goal attainment is determined by trying, that is cognitive and behavioural activities that mediate the expression of an intention to achieve a goal and its actual achievement. Trying thus incorporates the effectual tasks on which the attainment of a goal depends (Eagly & Chaiken, 1993, p.190). This essentially behaviour-based approach takes into consideration the planning people engage in to achieve remote goals.

The theory of trying aims to explain the link between intention and behaviour by investigating the striving people undertake in order to perform a behaviour or attain a goal (Bagozzi & Kimmel, 1995, p.5). It assumes that when individuals *try* to achieve such a goal they discern it as potentially burdensome to the extent that it has only a probability of success; that is, they are concerned about the likely outcome in view of the expenditure of effort that performing the behaviour will entail. They will specifically be concerned with the possibilities of two final consequences—succeeding, having tried, and failing despite trying—and they will certainly incur the intermediate consequences inherent in the process of striving itself. This approach differs from the TRA and TPB in three respects. First, those theories measure attitude as an overall and unidimensional construct, averaging the effects of separate component attitudes and thereby masking their individual effect on intention which may differ from situation to situation. The three component attitudes, confirmed in a study of respondents' trying to lose weight (Bagozzi & Warshaw, 1990) are towards (i) success, (ii) failure, and (iii) the process of striving. Second, the theory of trying posits a novel idea of the manner in which attitudes operate in influencing intentions: attitudes towards success and failure will result in intentions to engage in a particular behaviour to the degree that expectations of success are high and expectations of failure are low. Bagozzi and Warshaw (1990) found evidence for the interaction of attitude towards success and expectations of success, and of a significant main effect of attitude towards the process; they found mixed support for the interaction of attitudes towards failure and expectations of failure. Third, the theory of trying explicitly includes the effect of past behaviour on current trying. Despite Ajzen's (1987, p.41) denial of the usefulness of including past behaviour in causal theories of human action, numerous studies indicate the importance of this variable. Bentler and Speckart (1979) compared the TRA with (i) an alternative model that incorporated, in addition to the usual TRA variables, a direct causal path from attitude to behaviour not mediated by intention and (ii) a further model that added past behaviour, which was assumed to affect behaviour both directly and via intention. This final model provided the best fit with the data: direct paths from attitude to behaviour and from past behaviour to behaviour were supported. Attitude and past behaviour explained variability not explained by intentions, though drug consumption, the focal behaviour investigated, is not necessarily volitional (Eagly & Chaiken, 1993).

Other studies show that measures of past behaviour improve predictions of behaviour over those provided by attitudes/subjective norm/intention alone: for example giving up smoking (Marsh & Matheson, 1983; Sutton, Marsh, & Matheson, 1987); studying and exercise (Bentler & Speckart, 1981); students' class attendance (Ajzen & Madden, 1986; Fredericks & Dossett, 1983); voting (Echabe, Rovira, & Garate, 1988); seat belt use (Budd, North, & Spencer, 1984; Mittal, 1988; Sutton & Hallett, 1989; Wittenbraker, Gibbs, & Kahle, 1983); blood donation (Bagozzi, 1981; Charng, Piliavin, & Callero, 1988); and in consumer behaviour (East, 1992, 1993, 1996). It is apparent from these studies that past behaviour influences current behaviour without being mediated by intentions, and that past behaviour may influence intentions without being mediated by attitude or subjective norm. Bagozzi and Warshaw (1990) measured past behaviour in two ways: frequency and recency, both of which were expected to impact the target act under investigation; of the two, only the frequency of past behaviour was expected to impact intention to perform the act. They reported that both the frequency and recency of past trying had a direct influence on subsequent trying; moreover, frequency also influenced intentions to try to lose weight.

Bagozzi and Kimmel (1995) compared the four theories considered thus far in a study of two activities thought to have low perceived behavioural control: exercising and dieting. In the case of the TRA, intentions entirely predicted exercising and dieting responses but, while intentions for both were predicted by attitudes, subjective norms predicted intentions for neither. Their test of the TPB revealed that exercising was predicted by perceived behavioural control but not by intentions; however, intentions but not perceived behavioural control predicted dieting. Results for the prediction of intentions were also mixed: perceived behavioural control predicted this variable in the case of exercising but did not achieve this in the case of dieting. The direct influence of perceived behavioural control is thus substantiated for exercising; but neither the hypothesised direct nor the indirect effect of perceived control on dieting was confirmed. Attitudes again predicted intentions for both actions but subjective norms failed to do so in either instance. As proposed by the theory of self-regulation, desires strongly influenced intentions for both behaviours; intention to exercise was impacted by attitude but not intention to diet; moreover, subjective norm again failed to predict intention in either case. But behaviour related significantly to intention for both exercising and dieting. When past behaviour measures were used to augment the theory of self-regulation, both frequency and recency significantly impacted behaviour but the effect of intention on behaviour became nonsignificant. The findings provide mixed evidence for the theory of trying. While intention predicted dieting but not exercising, frequency and recency each had a significant impact on both behaviours. A significant interaction between attitude towards success and expectation of success was found only in the case of exercising; frequency and subjective norms also had a significant effect for this behaviour but neither attitudes towards the process nor the interaction of attitude towards failure and expectations thereof fulfilled the hypothesised relationships. Intentions for dieting were functions of frequency, subjective norms, and attitudes towards the process of striving, but neither of the hypothesised interactions was confirmed.

Madden and Sprott (1995) partially confirm Bagozzi and Kimmel's results. They compared the TRA, TPB and the theory of trying in two contexts: renting a video cassette, representing high volitional control, and obtaining a good night's sleep, representing low volitional control. The TPB's predictions of intention exceeded those of the TRA, but were no more predictive of behaviour once intentions had been taken into account. For the theory of trying, Madden and Sprott failed to confirm Bagozzi and Warshaw's (1990) finding that frequency and recency significantly affected trying. Intentions to try may subsume these effects for such familiar behaviours: indeed, past behaviour in the form of recency of trying impacted significantly on intention in both cases. Past behaviour improved the predictions of behaviour generated by the TRA and TPB in the case of sleeping but not video rental. Past trying frequency improved predictions of intention for both behaviours over those produced by the TRA and TPB, a confirmation of the results reported by Bagozzi and Kimmel (1995). A test of the TRA and an augmented version containing measures of the frequency and recency of past behaviour as covariates (Bagozzi & Warshaw, 1992) also indicates the importance of past behaviour as an explanatory variable. The investigation demonstrates the capacity of the TRA to predict some behaviours under some circumstances when it is not augmented by measures of past behaviour. For losing weight, the theory performed as expected: behaviour was predicted by intentions, and intentions were predicted by attitude and subjective norm. Neither attitudes nor subjective norm predicted behaviour, that is the effect of each on behaviour was fully mediated by intention. However, initiating a conversation with an attractive stranger was not predicted by intentions; attitude predicted intention but subjective norm had no impact upon it; and behaviour was directly influenced by attitude. These results on the whole are not consistent with the TRA (Bagozzi & Warshaw, 1992, p.628). When the past behaviour was added to the analysis, neither of the behaviours investigated could be attributed to processes of reasoning or volition (Bagozzi & Warshaw, 1992, p.630). For neither behaviour was there an influence from intentions to behaviour; nor did attitude have a direct effect on either behaviour. The TRA thus fails to explain behaviour once the effects of frequency and recency of are controlled for. Intentions to lose weight or initiate a conversation were unstable after the partialling-out of frequency and recency effects, indicating that neither behaviour can be attributed to volitional control. 'Significantly, strong recency effects are found for trying to lose weight . . . and initiating a conversation . . . No other determinants of behaviour are found . . .' (ibid.) Bagozzi and Warshaw (1992, p.631) conclude that because of the failure of attitude, subjective norm and intention to act as antecedents of behaviour doubt is case on their role in the explanation of human action. In a reversal of the explanatory sequence presumed by the TRA, their results indicate that intentions and attitudes arise out of behaviour.

Dealing with prior behaviour

Despite the implications of these findings with respect to past behaviour, authors of deliberative processing models generally seek the rationale for the relation between past and current behaviours in cognitive theory. Hence, Bagozzi and Warshaw (1992, p.605) propose that frequency effects on intentions operate when attitudes fail: either because the information needed to form a belief and/or evaluation is absent or because it is unclear. Inability to access or comprehend one's attitude will similarly increase the salience of frequency effects for intention formation. Frequency might exert a direct effect on behaviour when the individual has formed no plan of action, even though his or her attitude and intention are in place, or when choice involves a multitude of similar options, or when there is no time pressure to act. But, in addition, 'frequency effects might reflect desires or cognitive urges' (ibid.; Bagozzi, 1991). Frequency effects on behaviour are also likely when 'cognitions and evaluations are primitive or undergoing change' or because the behaviour in question is 'mindless or scripted, such as biting one's fingernails' (ibid.; Abelson, 1981; Langer, 1989b). Further, an inability to activate intentions, caused by absence of control, situational interventions, or 'internal impediments' may stand in the way of a conscious intention activating behaviour (Bagozzi & Yi, 1989; Bagozzi, Yi, & Baumgartner, 1990; cf. Warshaw, Sheppard, & Hartwick, 1990). Frequency of past behaviour can also substitute for actual control (Ajzen & Madden, 1986; Beale & Manstead, 1991). Recency acts upon intentions by increasing availability and anchoring/adjustment biases into reports thereof (Tversky & Kahneman, 1974). Recent behaviour exerts a disproportionate influence on the perceived likelihood of an event; and on the anchor value used to estimate subjective probability of an event; both influence one's intention to perform it. When intentions do not automatically lead to behaviour, recency of behaving may act to 'capture any residual automatic reactions that are triggered by conditioned releasers or stimulated directly by learned dispositions to respond' (Bagozzi & Warshaw,

1992, p.606). Finally, situational factors may just block an intended behaviour and recency effects may operate by suggesting alternative paths to the goal. In summary, past behaviour will predict current when cognitive determinants are absent or ineffective or goal attainment is blocked; and when behaviour is either mindless or scripted or incapable of fulfilment even though it is attitude-driven or intentional. The analysis also carries the implication that routine (mindless/scripted/low involvement) behaviour is to be accounted for by behavioural variables whilst novel (high involvement) behaviour is to be accounted for by cognitive variables. As the following section on the behaviour analysis of choice and decision making indicates, however, there is no reason to accept this. Either behavioural explanation can cover both or the behavioural and cognitive approaches to explanation should be seen as complementary rather than supplementary: cognitive accounts for proximal causation, behavioural for distal.

Syntheses of Attitude–Behaviour Relationships

Several attempts have been made to produce syntheses of the evidence on spontaneous and deliberative attitude–behaviour relationships and the cognitive processes inferred to underlie them: though see Eagly and Chaiken (1993, p.204) who argue that these approaches cannot properly be considered alternatives. Several of these attempts enquire *when* each method of processing is relevant and raise the possibility that they may work in tandem.

MODE: motivation and opportunity as determinants

Fazio (1990) points to two ways in which attitudes guide behaviour—spontaneously and through deliberation—and argues that one or other of these processing modes will be activated according to the circumstances of *m*otivation and *o*pportunity present. Deliberative processing is probable when the expected costliness of the prospective behaviour induces rational evaluation of the merits and demerits of assuming a given course of action. At this time, motivation to avoid the expense of making and acting upon a poor judgement overrides the spontaneous mechanism whereby attitudes might be activated from memory without cognitive effort. If an opportunity to do so is available, the individual can be expected to engage in extensive prebehavioural mental deliberation. Where the motivation to avoid heavy costs misjudgement is low and/or an opportunity to deliberate is not forthcoming, attitudinal influences on behaviour will occur via spontaneous processing. The extent to which attitude influences behaviour in these circumstances reflects the strength of evaluative association that has been built with respect to the attitude object through direct experience or by means of verbal rehearsal of the attitude. Provided that this association is sufficiently strong, the individual's definition of the event will be wholly or predominantly attitude-determined.

When the attitude association is weak, however, this definition of the event will be based mainly on nonattitudinal factors: behaviour towards the attitude object will then depend predominantly on the salient features of the attitude object itself and the situation (Fazio, 1990, pp.93–94).

HSM: the heuristic-systematic model

A broadly similar spectrum underlies Chaiken's (1980) heuristic-systematic model (HSM) which arrays processing strategies on the basis of the amount of cognitive effort they involve. The extremes of the processing continuum she proposes are *systematic* processing which is potentially effortful, requiring the evaluation of multiple interpretations of the situation before a definitive impression is formulated, and *heuristic* processing which requires minimal information handling, relying on established rules to make sense of the current situation. Assuming that individuals minimise effortful activity, systematic processing is likely only when the person is highly motivated and has the cognitive capacity and resources to engage in it. Individuals are also assumed to balance effort minimisation with the confidence they feel in their social perceptions. When heuristics based on experience can be substituted for systematic processing, they will be activated by elements of the current situation that signify their relevance (Bohner, Moskowitz, & Chaiken, 1995). But decision making may result from the simultaneous activation of both processes, reflecting both 'content-related thinking' (systematic) and 'cue-related evaluations' (heuristic) (van Knippenberg, Lossie, & Wilke, 1994). Recent reviews of the empirical work prompted by the HSM can be found in Eagly and Chaiken (1993); in addition, Bohner, Moskowitz, and Chaiken (1995) present the most recent version of the model and review research which has applied the model in the spheres of mood, persuasion and minority influence.

Eagly–Chaiken composite model

Eagly and Chaiken (1993) present an integrative model of the attitude–behaviour relationship which incorporates both the attitudes towards objects ('targets') implicated in spontaneous processing and the attitudes towards behaviours implicated in deliberative processing. Each kind of attitude is operational at a different stage in a dynamic sequence leading to behaviour. Attitude towards a behaviour is determined by *habit* (successive instances of an action that occur automatically or at least in the absence of self-instruction); *attitude towards the target*; and the three sets of outcomes: *utilitarian*, rewards and penalties expected to follow from the performance of the behaviour, *normative*, the endorsement or denunciation expected of significant others towards the action, plus the self-administered rewards like pride and punishments like guilt resulting from internal moral rules; and, when these self-administered consequences relate to the self-concept, *self-identity*. Attitude towards behaviour impacts in turn upon intention which impacts upon behaviour. Intention is also partly determined by normative and self-identity outcomes; and behaviour, by habit and attitude towards behaviour (Eagly & Chaiken, 1993, pp.209–211). This is corroborated by the functional approach to attitude theory and research taken by Shavitt (1989) who proposes that an object may evoke one or more of three functions: *utilitarian* (coffee, for instance) which arises from the reinforcing and punishing outcomes of using the item; *social identity* (e.g. a wedding ring) that communicates social status, identity and prestige; and *ego-defensive/self-esteem* (e.g. one's appearance). Shavitt has shown that many objects evoke a single attitude function and that promotional appeals based on the appropriate function for each product are more persuasive than appeals based on different criteria.

COMMENTARY: THE IMPORT OF PRIOR BEHAVIOUR

The Precedence of Cognitive Explanation

Prior behaviour as an explanatory variable

So much in the preceding account points to the determinative role of prior behaviour that this variable apparently has the potential to modify the paradigm for attitude research, shifting the emphasis from intra-personal sources of explanation towards a behaviour-based perspective. More than being just an additional influence that increases attitudinal/intentional-behavioural consistency or accounts for inconsistency, prior behaviour has a determinative influence on behaviour inasmuch as its inclusion in models has direct implciations for the predictive and explicative power of cognitive variables and may even render them redundant. As will be shown, its influence on 'intentions' can be interpreted in a behaviour analytic account as an influence on verbal behaviour which acts as an instruction to further responding. The pressure of the evidence is for the incorporation of prior behaviour more fully into explanations of behaviour. However, although prior behaviour is finding a place at the level of measurement, the implications of the empirical findings for this factor impinge little on the epistemology of attitude researchers and theorists. By and large, they have opted for a cognitive framework to embrace the influence of prior behaviour on current responding. The nonattitudinal variables considered by Eagly and Chaiken to moderate attitude towards an object and behaviour towards that object include 'vested interest' (which is surely an aspect of learning history); and personality, including moral reasoning level, and having a *doer* self-image (both of which can be conceptualised as arising in the individual's learning history). But these authors do not consider these further, let alone as denotive of a history of reinforcement and punishment, because they do not fit into a unified theoretical framework. Rather they press on with their assumption that 'attitude–behavior correspondence is affected by the nature of the attitude and by the implications that that attitude is perceived to have for the behaviour that is assessed' (Eagly & Chaiken, 1993, p.194). One might be forgiven for detecting that the social cognitive paradigm has been allowed to select the approach to explanation. Some authors speak of learning history as determinative (Eiser, 1987; Eiser & van der Pligt, 1988, p.41) but still find their ultimate explanation in cognitivism.

Cognitive rationale of prior behaviour

Some reviewers have been willing to accommodate behavioural as well as cognitive precursors of attitude as factors that increase attitudinal-behavioural consistency. Eagly and Chaiken (1993, p.202) sum up their extensive review of the factors involved in generating such consistency: 'Attitudes that are based on *more* input are likely to relate more strongly to attitude-relevant behaviors, whether this input is behavioral or cognitive. Thus, research on behavioral experience has shown that increased behavioral input increases attitude–behavior correspondence, and research on prior knowledge has suggested that increased cognitive input has the same impact. Unfortunately, research on affective experience is lacking, but increased input from this source may similarly increase attitude–behavior correspondence.' Yet this approach, though it tries to incorporate both behavioural and cognitive influences evenhandedly, is limited in two ways by its implicit acceptance of a cognitive reference structure.

First, there is an overwhelming inclination towards explaining attitudinal-behavioural consistency in cognitive terms. The general thrust of the evidence gained subsequently to Wicker's (1969) review and the disappointment and consternation it has generated tended towards the importance of including noncognitive factors in the prediction of behaviour. But current attitude theory does not reflect this sufficiently. Extra-attitudinal cognitive factors were, of course, always implicated in the quest for greater consistency, but seminal contributions have emphasized situational and behavioural influences (Foxall, 1983, 1984, 1996; Seibold, 1980). The implication of the tight situational compatibility required of measures of target behaviour and measures of its antecedent cognitive predictors (Ajzen & Fishbein, 1977) is that situational factors are highly significant for the correlational consistency of attitudes/ intentions and behaviour. Only when the situational influences governing both the prebehavioural and the behavioural variables are functionally equivalent are high correlations found. That the intertemporal period between prebehavioural and behavioural measures must be minimal if high correlations are to be found corroborates this view by pointing to the undesirability of unexpected situational demands reducing the predictive value of measured intentions (Foxall, 1983, 1984, 1996). Fishbein and Ajzen's (1980) claim that situational factors that intervene between intention and behaviour can be ignored for purposes of prediction since the changes will likely cancel one another out and thus not influence the predictive accuracy of the intention also requires comment. While the problem of prediction has been overcome—albeit only to the extent that, for the individual, the predictive intention is that which immediately precedes the opportunity to behave in accordance with it—that of explanation remains. For there can be no claim to have explained behaviour in terms of its antecedent reasons if situational interventions can play so large a part in the determination of behaviour (Sarver, 1983). This is no deterrent to Fishbein and Ajzen whose insistence on attributing behaviour to intentions—and in turn to attitudes and subjective norms—reveals a deliberate predilection to *interpret* behaviour by reference to underlying causative mental dispositions. The practical importance of predictive methods closely following theoretical expectations is clear from the marketing of new consumer products in which process about 80% of innovations fail at the point of market acceptance even when their launch has been preceded by sophisticated market research based on the measurement of prospective consumers' attitudes and intentions. Only behaviour with the product, including product tests and test marketing, predicts trial and repeat purchase with any acceptable degree of accuracy (Foxall, 1984). But the point here is that context and situation deserve a more central place in the explanation of behaviour which is denied them by the partiality inherent in acceptance of the preeminence of the cognitive paradigm. Yet the reasons why past and current behaviour are consistent are discussed by attitude theorists in predominantly cognitive terms: the possibility that the consistency is due to environmental influences does not appear to enter their research agenda. Moreover, the tripartite comprehension of attitude prevails as the paradigm for further investigation and explication.

Second, although Eagly and Chaiken mention in passing a behaviouristic approach, their apparent understanding of the possibilities thereof seems severely limited. They accept, for instance, that including measures of past behaviour is reasonable from a behaviourist standpoint which holds that 'behaviour is influenced by habit, or more generally, by various types of conditioned releasers or learned predispositions to respond that are not readily encompassed by the concepts of attitude and intention' (Eagly & Chaiken, 1993, p.179). But this avoids the fact that the explanatory power of past behaviour is frequently sufficient to make cognitive variables superfluous; that a behaviour analytic theory may be capable of explaining or interpreting the evidence on attitudinal-behavioural consistency in full; and that in any case the reason for including a behaviourist perspective is to identify the consequences that past behaviour has produced to account for the consistency of that prior responding and thus to use those consequences to predict future behaviour.

Prior behaviour as habit

Another tendency is to refer to repetitious behaviour as habit. Triandis (1977, 1980) defined habit as 'situation-specific sequences that are or have become automatic, so that they occur without self-instruction' (Triandis, 1980, p.204). In similar vein, Eagly and Chaiken (1993, p.180) comment that 'the concept of habit implies that a behaviour has become so routinised through repetition that a person has ceased to make any conscious decision to act yet still behaves in the accustomed way'. Another way of putting this is that habitual behaviour is that maintained by direct contact with the contingencies of reinforcement rather than instructed through verbal behaviour. The alternative paradigm to which this description belongs suggests a means by which the import of prior behaviour may be more fully understood. However, this is not the usual emphasis in attitude theory and research. Ronis, Yates and Kirscht (1989, p.218) refer to a habit as an action that has been carried out with such frequency that it has become automatic; its performance is devoid of conscious thinking. A great deal of consumer behaviour is apparently of this kind: Ehrenberg and Uncles (1995). How is such behaviour to be explained? Unfortunately, it is often 'explained' in terms that are frankly tautological. Hence Ronis, Yates, and Kirscht (1989, p.217) argue that 'the continued repetition of behaviours is often determined by habits rather than by attitudes or beliefs'. But this is meaningless given their definition of habit: a habit, as they understand it and as the word is used in everyday discourse, *is* the repeated behaviour. Such behaviour must be accounted for—unless we think it is uncaused—by reference to other factors; in an operant account, for instance, it would be ascribed to the contingenies of reinforcement. These authors attribute the causative habits to repeated behaviour (p.219), an assignation that completes the tautology of their argument. Eagly and Chaiken similarly refer to habits as 'nonattitudinal determinants of behaviour' and as one of several 'psychological tendencies that regulate behavior' (Eagly & Chaiken, 1993, pp.216, 671).

Ronis, Yates, and Kirscht (1989, pp.216–218) uncontroversially point out that the explanation of habit requires that attention be given to two component processes: *initiation*, that in which the behaviour comes about, requiring decision making; and *persistence* which implies automaticity, lack of conscious direction. They associate attitudes with initiation, but not persistence. A decision, almost by definition, involves conscious thought and reflection on one or more alternatives to the chosen behaviour. They also point out that initiation (novel behaviour) is predictable from attitudes, while persistence is not; that prior behaviour is also a strong predictor of novelty; and that habit predicts future behaviour more effectively than intentions (Ronis, Yates, & Kirscht, 1989, p.221). In other words, attitudes correlate with habitual behaviour under some circumstances, not others. In a behaviour analysis, there is evidence that nonverbal behaviour is consistent with rules in the long term only if the contingencies bear out the rules. Moreover, note that the behaviour analytic demonstration is that behaviourist explanation can account for both decision and habit: it is not the case that behaviour analysis is confined to habit while decision is accounted for as social cognitivism.

Taking Account of Preceding Behaviour

The factor that emerges again and again as predictive of current behaviour, *preceding* behaviour, has two components. The first is the set of similar responses performed by the individual in the past, what attitude theorists and researchers including Fishbein, Ajzen, Bagozzi and Warshaw have referred to as past behaviour or prior behaviour. This stream of similar responses cannot be considered in the absence of the consequences it has produced and their implications for the probability that similar behaviour of the same kind will be emitted again. In the terminology of behaviour analysis, and on the assumption that they are similarly reinforced, these responses belong to the same operant class and their future rate of emission depends upon the learning history of the individual. The second sense in which preceding behaviour may be understood is that of the verbal behaviour which instructs the current responding of an individual. This verbal behaviour might consist of instructions or rules articulated by someone else or of the self-instructions generated by the individual for him/herself. These verbal discriminative stimuli are the antecedent source of the rule-governed behaviour of humans: such behaviour is distinguished form the contingency-shaped behaviour of nonhumans and, on occasion, humans. The broader category of verbal behaviour, which includes both the rule-provision of the speaker and the rule-compliance of the listener, allows radical behaviourism to investigate and interpret the phenomena of thinking, reasoning, problem-solving and deciding that have traditionally fallen within the purview of cognitive psychology (Skinner, 1974; Ribes, 1991, 1992). The paradigm which offers understanding of the role of instructed behaviour and underpins the argument made here is behaviour analysis.

BEHAVIOUR ANALYSIS OF CONSUMER CHOICE

Science and Interpretation

The radical behaviourist paradigm explains behaviour by reference to the contingent relationships of a response and the consequences it produces in the presence of an antecedent stimulus (Skinner, 1969; cf. Malott, 1986). The 'three-term contingency' represented in this statement comprises the central explanatory device of the paradigm: $S^D - R - S^{R/A}$ where S^D is a discriminative (antecedent, setting) stimulus, R is a response, and $S^{R/A}$ is a positive or aversive (consequent) stimulus (Skinner, 1953, p.110; see also Hineline, 1992; Iversen, 1992; Morris & Midgley, 1990; Morris, Todd, Midgley, Schneider, & Johnson, 1990). On the assumption that behaviour is a function of its consequences, causal reference to theoretical entities such as attitudes and intentions is redundant (Skinner, 1971, p.18). The antecedent stimulus is never an initiating cause of behaviour (Skinner, 1988a) but signals the availability of reinforcement contingent upon the emission of the appropriate response. When learning has occurred, behaviour may come under the proximal control of the antecedent (discriminative) stimulus in the absence of the reinforcing consequence; however, such stimulus control is lost if the pertinent reinforcer is not occasionally available as a contingent consequence of responding. The variables of which behaviour is ultimately a function are the consequences such behaviour has produced in the learning history of the individual (Delprato & Midgley, 1992; cf. Morris, 1991).

Radical behaviourism is often identified with laboratory experimentation and with the application of a scientific method derived from Machian positivism to the relatively simple operant behaviour of nonhumans (Todd & Morris, 1992; cf. Phillips, 1992). The results it gains there are further assumed to be uncritically extrapolated to the human sphere, leading to prescriptions for social control and cultural engineering unsupported by either direct empirical evidence or a coherent theory of human behaviour. This view overlooks two considerations: first the large proportion of operant research which nowadays involves human participants, especially in the context of verbal behaviour; second the role of interpretation in operant accounts of complex behaviour. Research on verbal behaviour is reviewed below but the subject of radical behaviourist interpretation requires elaboration at this point. Interpretation is necessary wherever the elements of the three-term contingency, though possibly observable, are not amenable to public confirmation and when they cannot engender the degree of prediction and or control that can be secured in the laboratory. Thus interpretation is indispensable when the precise consequent and antecedent stimuli that control complex behaviour are not consensually obvious (e.g. what attributes of the product class are sufficient for reinforcement of purchasing to take place? What are the exact discriminative stimuli under the control of which eating chocolate occurs?) Interpretation is also required to account for phenomena that are observable by only one individual—private events such as *my* thoughts and feelings. I can only infer that the behaviour of another personl is controlled by similar stimuli that are private to him or her (Mackenzie, 1988; Skinner, 1988b). Interpretation is equally inescapable when self-rules are elusive to the observer (and perhaps to the actor). Sometimes only an interpretation that infers such rules from overt behaviour can fill in the gaps. By presenting an understanding of consumer choice as influenced by environmental considerations, a behaviour analysis has the potential to augment consumer research which currently lacks a theory of situational control of consumer choice. However, mention of this paradigm in marketing and consumer research (e.g. Berry & Kunkel, 1970; Nord & Peter, 1980; Rothschild & Gaidis, 1981; cf. Foxall, 1987) presumes that its explanatory system can be extrapolated unadorned from experimental research with nonhumans to complex human interactions such as purchase and consumption. A behaviour analytic account of human behaviour must take full measure of the situational and speciational peculiarities of the context in which that behaviour takes place. Such an exposition must be conversant with the experimental analysis of human behaviour and the ramifications of radical behaviourist interpretation (Foxall, 1995a). Both require that particular attention be accorded the human capacity for verbal control of behaviour.

Verbal Behaviour

Verbal behaviour of the speaker

While the operant behaviour of nonhumans is shaped entirely by direct contact with the environment (Lowe, 1989), that of humans frequently comes under an additional source of control. That control is verbal, as when the actions of a young boy are modified as a result of the instructions given him by his mother irrespective of his direct experience of the contingencies to which her instructions refer. The analysis of rule-governed, as contrasted with contingency-shaped, behaviour is a longstanding theme in operant psychology, as is that of verbal behaviour in general (Skinner, 1945, 1957, 1969). Skinner (1957) defined verbal behaviour as behaviour that is reinforced through the mediation of other persons: it impinges upon the social, rather than the physical environment (Moore, 1994). As a behavioural phenomenon, verbal behaviour is defined functionally, not logically, and the style of its analysis does not differ from that of any other operant behaviour (Moore, 1994, p.289; Skinner, 1957). Consonant with the metatheoretical stance of radical behaviourism (Skinner, 1945), such functional analysis diverges fundamentally from the formalism preferred by most linguists, including the formal standpoint from which Chomsky (1959) launched his critical review of Skinner's *Verbal Behavior* (MacCorquodale, 1969, 1979; Richelle, 1993, pp.120–128). Some strands of the recent upsurge in research on verbal responding arise too from criticism of Skinner, including his concentration on the verbal behaviour of the speaker rather than the listener (Hayes & Hayes, 1989; cf. Skinner, 1989), his failure to consider reference and postulation (L.J. Hayes, 1991, 1994; Parrott, 1986), and the 'unwarranted dominance' of Skinner's book in its acceptance as the sole behaviour theoretic approach to verbal responding and its consequent overshadowing of other theoretical approaches including relational frame analysis (S. C. Hayes, 1994; Hayes & Hayes, 1992a).

Instructed behaviour

When a listener's behaviour results from the verbal activity of a speaker, it is said to be instructed or rule-governed. The rule may act as a verbal discriminative stimulus which takes the place of the contingencies themselves (cf. S. C. Hayes, 1989; Horne & Lowe, 1993, 1996). The provision of rules is especially pertinent in changing behaviour the consequences of which are delayed, improbable or small (Malott, 1989). If it is effective over time, such control requires a degree of consistency between the instructions and the contingencies they describe. But instructed behaviour has noteworthy properties of its own arising from its insensitivity to changes in the consequences of responding (Catania, Matthews, & Shimoff, 1990; Catania, Shimoff, & Matthews, 1989). Instructed behaviour is always subject to two sets of contingencies (indeed, this may be its definitive characteristic; S. C. Hayes, 1989): the social consequences that maintain the rule-following, and the natural contingencies that eventually take over if the instruction is effective (e.g. Baum, 1994). If the instructed behaviour is to be effectively learned, the consequences of rule-compliance must be more powerful than the natural consequences that would follow trial-and-success behaviour in the absence of the instruction. Since these natural contingencies are often remote, delayed and weak, learning from them alone (i.e. in the absence of instructions) would be slow or dangerous—as in the case of learning to drive a car—or possibly never-acting. This may be partly why instructed behaviour is often insensitive to changes in the natural contingencies. Shaped behaviour does not show this insensitivity: the acquisition of a practical skill such as glassblowing must, in many of its aspects, be directly shaped by hands-on experience that confers positive consequences as learning takes place.

The functional categorization of rule-following presents difficulties, though that suggested by Zettle and Hayes (1982), paralleling Skinner's (1957) definitions of the functional units of speaker behaviour, has prompted both empirical and theoretical investigations (S. C. Hayes, 1989; Hayes & Hayes, 1989; Chase & Danforth, 1991; Malott, 1989). Skinner posited two such units in particular, manding and tacting. The *mand* denotes the consequences contingent upon following the instructions of the speaker or of imitating his or her example. Much advertising consists of mands—'Buy three and get one free!' 'Don't forget the fruit gums, mum'—which indicate contingencies that are under the control of the speaker. *Tacts* present the listener with a part of the environment which he or she thus contacts and, depending on learning history, behaves towards. A trade mark or logo may be followed by making a purchase or entering a store. Zettle and Hayes suggest units of analysis for the listener's responding that match these phases of the speaker's behaviour. Corresponding to manding is *pliance* which is rule-governed behaviour controlled by consequences that the speaker (or his/her agent) regulates (or claims to regulate). The rule, known as a *ply*, refers, therefore, to the social consequences of compliance or noncompliance: 'Keeping my breath fresh will get me more dates'. Corresponding to *tacting* is *tracking* which is instructed behaviour which, according to the rule, is under the control of the nonsocial environment. A *track* specifies the arrangement of contingencies within that physical or temporal context: 'If I turn left at the next intersection, I'll come to Sainsbury's'. 'If I arrive by five, the shop will still be open'. A third functional unit of listener behaviour has no corresponding unit for the speaker: the *augmental* (Zettle & Hayes, 1982) is a highly motivating rule that states emphatically how a particular behaviour will be reinforced or will avoid punishment. 'Just one more packet top and I can claim my watch!' The reason for the difficulty of defining plying and tracking exclusively is that a single rule often embodies elements of both (Poppen, 1989): sometimes both elements of such a rule require the same behaviour to be performed (in which case the rule is a *congruent*); sometimes there is conflict (when the rule is known as a *contrant*).

Private events

A substantial proportion of recent work in the theoretical and experimental analysis of behaviour has focused on verbal behaviour, providing a noncognitive account of such phenomena as thinking, reasoning and decision making (Catania, 1992b; S. C. Hayes, 1989; Hayes & Chase, 1991; Hayes & Hayes, 1992b; Hayes, Hayes, Sato, & Ono, 1994; Skinner, 1945, 1969). Indeed, the essential point of divergence of radical from methodological behaviourism lies in the former's embracing private events as a part of its subject matter (Moore, 1994; Baum, 1994). These private events are not treated as unobservables though thoughts and feelings are observed by only one person. Radical behaviourists *infer* however that other people have private events which act as verbal discriminative stimuli for their behaviour (Mackenzie, 1988). But this is a far cry still from the treatment of unobservables by social cognitivists: to the radical behaviourist such 'mental way stations' (Skinner, 1963) are no more than explanatory fictions that bring inquiry to a premature end by diverting attention from the ultimate causes of behaviour which lie in the environment. Some behaviour analysts have cast private events as possible proximal causes of behaviour (e.g. Malott & Garcia, 1991), though others have argued against this (e.g. Hayes, Brownstein, Haas, & Greenway, 1986) partly on the grounds that only entities which can be manipulated in an experimental analysis of behaviour should be admitted. For nonbehaviourists, however, the assumption that private events are proximal causes of behaviour blurs the distinction between behaviourist and cognitive modes of explanation (Overskeid, 1995).

Consistency of verbal and nonverbal behaviours

Words and events are linked by a web of contingencies arranged by the verbal community (Catania, 1992a, p.250). The relationship between what a person says and what he or she does is central to the establishment and maintenance of social life. This, the heart of the attitude–behaviour problem, is reformulated in a behavioural analysis into how and when verbal rules come to guide behaviour. These rules may originate in one of two ways: the behaviour may be instructed by others or it may be self-instructed as the individual describes the apparent contingencies to him or herself. So an individual's behaviour may be changed either by instruction or by shaping what he or she says about it; in the latter case, 'one's own verbal behaviour may thus become effective as an instructional stimulus' (Catania, 1992a, p.251). Of the two, shaped verbal behaviour has a greater effect on the individual's propensity to act than either direct shaping through modification of the contingencies or instruction (Catania, Matthews, & Shimoff, 1990, p.217), that is encouraging a person to formulate his or her own rules by altering the contingencies that govern their verbal behaviour is the most effective persuasive strategy (though the danger of false rules, leading to superstitious behaviour, is ever-present: Ono, 1994). The resulting behaviour is then sensitive to the natural contingencies only to the extent that changes in those contingencies result in changes in the corresponding verbal behaviour (Catania, Matthews, & Shimoff, 1990, p.217). The corollary is that only changes in the contingencies that are mediated by verbal behaviour, self-instructing, will change behaviour. None of this implies that behaviour formed through instruction does not come into contact with the contingencies. The natural contingencies remain the ultimate causes of behaviour and, therefore, rule-governed behaviour will at some point become contingency-shaped. Perhaps it is from the contingencies that we can ultimately predict behaviour most successfully, as well as explain it. Hence the contingency category analysis of consumer behaviour must include reference to both rules that are the proximal causes of behaviour and the natural contingencies in which their distal causes reside.

Guerin (1994a,b) argues that attitudes and intentions can be behaviouristically interpreted. Hence attitudes constitute 'a generalized affective response to stimuli and contexts': the things that individuals report they like, favour or prefer are those which have relatively strong reinforcing effects (1994a, p.236). Beliefs, consisting predominantly of intraverbals and tacts, do not control either attitudes or overt behaviour, any more than attitudes control behaviour. Attitudes are simply a commentary on one's behaviour which one makes to oneself (ibid.), though we should wish to add that they are an *evaluative* commentary (Lalljee, Brown, & Ginsburg, 1984). But attitudes are not comments on elusive beliefs or latent behavioural processes: rather, the elements on which they provide a commentary are the individual's overt (public) and covert (private) behaviours. This goes beyond the simpler behaviouristic stratagem of using the term attitude to describe the consistency of behaviour: while this is sometimes a useful approach (Foxall, 1983, 1996), it fails to acknowledge the evaluative nature of verbal behaviour and its capacity to direct other verbal and nonverbal behaviours: that is to provide a truly behaviouristic counterpart to the attitude concept of social cognition. The distinction is that between attitudes as verbal behaviour that is contingency-shaped (under the direct control of the environment)—as in saying that 'This book is enjoyable' because I have been reading it and have found it so—and attitudes under social control—as in saying the same thing about a book I have not read but about which my mentor has expressed a favourable view. The result of an operant analysis of such verbal behaviour is a functional view of attitudes. Functioning as tacts, attitudes may be simply reports on the environment, replies to questions, social rituals or self-regulating verbal behaviours that involve self-reinforcements (Guerin, 1994a, pp.237–238). Expressed to others, attitudes may also function as mands.

The so-called 'problem' of attitudinal-behavioural consistency disappears on this view: both attitudinal and nonattitudinal acts are operant behaviours in their own right, each maintained by its own context of contingencies. Consistency cannot be expected unless the contingencies happen to be functionally equivalent, perhaps as a result of a verbal community arranging the contingencies so as to produce consistency. For Guerin (1994a), the interesting problem for behaviourists is isolating the effect of attitudes on the person who hears them spoken; since the verbal control of behaviour falls far short of perfection, the surprising thing is that any degree of consistency at all is observable, especially in view of the large repertoires of behaviour that people have and the reinforcement available for inconsistency (lying, for instance: Sato & Sugiyama, 1994). The compatibility required for the predictive success of the TRA and other models that stress deliberative processing thus demands the verbal detailing of specific contingencies rather than the provision of generalised statements about possible outcomes. Such statements of attitude and intention act as verbal instructions to guide behaviour. Actual responding is predictable from them in circumstances where the individual has control over the contingencies of the situation, where he or she is familiar with behaving in that context and the consequences that have previously followed it. The evaluative beliefs elicited by questionnaires based on such theories actually record what the respondent takes to be the contingencies entailed in acting in a particular way (belief strength) and the likelihood of reinforcement/punishment resulting from the performance of the behaviour in question (evaluation). The summation of these evaluative beliefs entails the combination of the positive and negative aspects of the contingencies, which Guerin (1994a, p.244) likens to 'a multiple contingency Matching Law for verbally governed behavior'. Both the beliefs and their evaluations have their origins in the individual respondent's learning history. Subjective norm similarly records the contingencies laid down by the respondent's verbal community, reflecting social pressure (Guerin, 1992). But learning history is significant here and is overlooked by cognitivists only because it is not immediately obvious, leading to the ontological inference that the causes of behaviour must lie within the individual. Guerin (1994a, p. 245) sums up: 'The TRA brings together the major variables also dealt with by behaviour analysis: verbally governed behavior, verbal tacts about contingencies and reports of their value, combining the multiple contingencies involved to get an overall prediction, and the verbal community contingencies . . .'.

Behavioural Interpretation of Consumer Decision Making

The behavioural perspective model

To construct an operant interpretation of consumer behaviour, it is necessary to redefine the elements of the three-term contingency in three respects (Foxall, 1990). First, the nature of the setting variables and the influence they exert must be clarified in view of the complexity of the environments in which human economic behaviour takes place. Second, the nature of reinforcement must be refined in the context of human behaviour which, even in the operant laboratory, is multiply motivated. Third, the nature and influence of verbal behaviour, which regulates behaviour only in humans, must be considered. The behavioural perspective model (BPM) proposes that consumer behaviour is situated at the intersection of the behaviour setting in which it occurs (the spatial perspective) and the learning history of the consumer (the temporal perspective) (Foxall, 1990). The resulting construct of the *consumer situation* has been used to interpret observed patterns of consumer behaviour including purchase and consumption, saving and domestic asset management, the adoption and diffusion of innovations and 'green' consumption (Foxall, 1993a, 1994a,b,c, 1995c). The interpretation proceeds essentially in terms of the three-term contingency, albeit critically appraised and represented in line with the provisions outlined above (Figure 6.1). The consumer behaviour setting consists of the current discriminative stimuli that signal reinforcement and punishment contingent upon the emission of a purchase or consumption response. The discriminative stimuli that compose the setting may be physical (e.g. point-of-sale advertising, the product array, a store logo), social (principally the physical presence of co-shoppers, other diners in a restaurant, the waiter, the salesperson), temporal (the hours of opening of a store, the duration of a special offer, Christmas) or regulatory (self- and other-rules that specify contingencies). Rule-governed behaviour is actually a social phenomenon but deserves separate treatment (Guerin, 1994a; Hyten & Burns, 1986). The consequences of responding in the setting which have played a role in shaping the individual's learning history and which are now signalled as behaviourally contingent by these setting elements, have three functions. Aversive consequences that are suffered punish the behaviour that produced them, that is, make it less probable in future. Any behaviour that avoids or escapes aversive consequences is (negatively) reinforced, that is, made more probable in similar circumstances in the future. Positive consequences of a behaviour also strengthen or reinforce it, that is, increase its probability of recurrence (Foxall, 1992a). Such positive reinforcement may occur in two ways.

Hedonic reinforcement refers to the acceptance of positive benefits of purchasing, owning or consuming economic products and services (goods); these benefits are utilitarian, conferring material satisfactions, the utility of

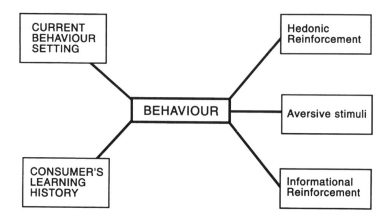

Figure 6.1   Summary of the behavioural perspective model

orthodox microeconomic theory. Hedonic reinforcers are frequently referred to as incentives both in general discourse and in applied behaviour analysis. *Informational* reinforcement is performance feedback, an indication of how well the consumer is doing. It may confer social status and/or self-satisfaction, or it may simply constitute a reference point denoting progress to date. Informational reinforcement is associated with verbal behaviour because the meaning of the behaviour is always mediated by a person, usually someone other than the actor but perhaps by him/herself. There is empirical evidence that hedonic and informational reinforcement have separate influences in behaviour in both human operant experiments conducted under laboratory conditions (Wearden, 1988), in token economy studies, and in the field of experiments of applied behaviour analysis directed towards the reduction of environmentally deleterious consumption (Foxall, 1995, 1996).

The extent to which consumer behaviour can be attributed to control by environmental contingencies varies with the closedness of the setting in which it takes place. The animal laboratory, from which principles of operant behaviourism were derived, presents a particularly closed setting, one in which the elements of the three-term contingency can be objectively identified and behaviour therefore traced unambiguously to its environmental effects. The further behaviour settings stray from this degree of closedness, the harder it is for the operant psychologist to ascribe activities within them unreservedly to operant conditioning. Even in the animal laboratory, there exists scope for alternative interpretations: in terms, for instance, of classical conditioning or cognitive decision making. The human operant laboratory, for example, presents a less closed context, one from which escape is relatively easy; while nonhumans face no option but being in the setting, human participants on occasion remove themselves from the experimental situation. The settings in which human consumer behaviour takes place are more open still: though a continuum of such settings is evident, from the relatively closed confines of a large group awareness training session to the relatively open variety store. Closed and open settings may also be distinguished in terms of the verbal behaviour that characterises each. In closed settings, the other-instructions and contingencies are precise: in order to get a passport, a consumer must obey the rules to the letter. In open settings, the consumer has more control over his or her behaviour through self-instructions, and specific other-rules are less likely to be determinative. There may be several other-rule configurations to 'choose' from; further, there is the possibility of behaviour being directly controlled by the contingencies: as one spots new products, devises new ways of finding presents, and so on. Even if the view is taken that most consumer behaviour is rule-governed, open settings allow self-rules to a far greater extent than closed. Moreover, human behaviour that is entirely contingency-shaped is rare. Self-rules, devised and followed by the same individual, are particularly effective instructions, which may be more isolated from the contingencies than other-rules (Catania, Matthews, & Shimoff, 1990, p.227). Employing dichotomous variables to represent the causative elements of the model, actual consumer situations can be categorised among eight contingency configurations, depending on whether the consumer behaviour setting is relatively closed or relatively open, whether hedonic reinforcement is relatively high or low, and whether informational reinforcement is relatively high or low. Moreover, depending on the strength of the sources of reinforcement, four operant classes of consumer behaviour can be defined: accomplishment (where both are high), pleasure (where hedonic reinforcement is high but information is low), accumulation (where informational reinforcement is high but hedonic is low), and maintenance (where both are low) (Foxall, 1993b). The consumer situations and behaviours assigned to each of these eight contingency categories are defined functionally rather than morphologically and topographically identical behaviours may be assigned at different times to different operant classes and contingency categories depending on the interpretation of the combination of contingencies maintaining them. The labels employed in Figure 6.2 are, therefore, ultimatey arbitrary, though they have proved useful in the interpretation of consumer behaviour (Foxall, 1994a).

	BEHAVIOR SETTING SCOPE		
	Closed ← → Open		
ACCOMPLISHMENT	CONTINGENCY CATEGORY 2 FULFILLMENT	CONTINGENCY CATEGORY 1 STATUS GOODS	HIGH HEDONIC HIGH INFORMATIONAL
PLEASURE	CONTINGENCY CATEGORY 4 INESCAPABLE ENTERTAINMENT	CONTINGENCY CATEGORY 3 POPULAR ENTERTAINMENT	HIGH HEDONIC LOW INFORMATIONAL
ACCUMULATION	CONTINGENCY CATEGORY 6 TOKEN-BASED BUYING	CONTINGENCY CATEGORY 5 SAVING AND COLLECTING	LOW HEDONIC HIGH INFORMATIONAL
MAINTENANCE	CONTINGENCY CATEGORY 8 MANDATORY CONSUMPTION	CONTINGENCY CATEGORY 7 ROUTINE PURCHASING	LOW HEDONIC LOW INFORMATIONAL

Figure 6.2   Contingency category matrix

Learning history

The importance of learning history is amply demonstrated by the repeated finding that prior behaviour is an important determinant of current responding. It is not sufficient to attribute the influence of prior behaviour simply to 'habit', which is to redescribe it rather than explain it. The continuance of behaviour is to be accounted for by the consequences it produces and whether or not a stream of behaviour is continued into the near future depends on the stimulus control which influences it and the maintenance of the pattern of reinforcement that is its distal cause. The deliberative processing models such as the TRA are centrally concerned with the self-reported consequences of behaving in a given way, which constitutes a personal summary of the respondent's learning history. The elicitation of subjective norm beliefs and evaluations is also indicative of a history of rule-compliance. The spontaneous processing models emphasise direct experience with the attitude object, which both constitutes a learning history in itself and serves to establish the attitude object as a discriminative stimulus for further responding. The rehearsal of attitude statements, especially if they have their origin in other-instructions, constitutes prior *verbal* behaviour which also exerts an environmental influence on the probability of current responding. The potency of a learning history is manifested within a particular behaviour setting: prior learning establishes what will act as a discriminative stimulus in that setting by embodying the consequences, reinforcing and punishing, of earlier behaviour in the presence of the relevant setting elements. The functional approach to attitude theory and research taken by Shavitt (1989) corroborates the BPM by indicating several functions of behavioural consequence in controlling verbal and nonverbal current responding (usually via preceding verbal behaviour/ instructional control). The bases of the attitude functions she proposes appear closely related to the nature of the reinforcement associated with these products—hedonic (utilitarian) and informational (social identity). The distinction between hedonic and informational reinforcement is consonant with that between the utilitarian and soical identity functions of attitudes (Shavitt, 1989). Shavitt argues that the function of a person's attitude towards an air conditioner is principally utilitarian 'because one's attitude toward it should be based largely on rewards (e.g. comfort) and punishments (e.g. high energy bills) intrinsically associated with it . . . [O]ne's attitude toward an air conditioner should guide behaviors that maintain the rewards and avoid the punishments associated with this object (e.g. using the air conditioner on a hot day, turning it off at times to conserve energy)' (p.324). However, an individual's attitude towards a wedding ring performs contrasting functions: 'one's attitude toward it should be based largely on what it symbolizes. Furthermore, wedding rings are worn (in public) primarily to communicate information to others about the wearer, and one's attitude toward wedding rings and what they symbolize should guide this behavior' (ibid.).

The components of Eagly and Chaiken (1993) composite model are also supportive of the BPM: all of the determinants of attitude towards behaviour— habit, attitudes towards the target, utilitarian, normative and self-identity outcomes—are indicative of learning history. Habits form only if the behaviour of which they are composed is sequentially reinforced; attitudes towards target develop only through experience; and, although conceptualised as expectations of what will result from behaving in a specified way, the outcomes can result only from environmental history, either in the form of contingency-shaping or through instruction. Moreover, utilitarian outcomes closely resemble the hedonic reinforcement of the BPM, while normative (including self-identity) outcomes are akin to informational reinforcement. The BPM links past behaviour, behaviour setting elements, and outcomes by arguing that learning history primes elements of the setting to act as discriminative stimuli for hedonic and informational reinforcement/punishment contingent upon the performance of specific responses. Like Eagly and Chaiken's model, the BPM is untested but it provides an alternative, noncognitive synthesis of empirical results gained in both attitude research and operant investigations of instructed behaviour.

Consumer decision making as behaviour

How do the mechanisms for decision making and persuasion proposed by Fazio's MODE model (1990), the Elaboration Likelihood Model (Petty &

Cacioppo, 1984a) and the Heuristic-Systematic Model (Chaiken, 1980) relate to consumer decision making in behavioural perspective? In the BPM interpretation 'motivation' is supplied by the individual's learning history or lack thereof. It is this which determines the likelihood that the outcome of a particular action will be relatively costly or rewarding and which leads to more or less prebehavioural reviewing of the contingencies, that is, the probability of particular positive and aversive outcomes emerging from each of the behaviours available. This review is not mental processing: it is behaviour, verbal behaviour which is often private. Where deliberation takes place it consists of a review of rules, self-rules generated on the basis of direct learning experience of the contingencies, and other-rules provided by those whose instructions have proved accurate and reinforcing if followed in the past and/or who themselves have relevant experience of the consequences which can be publicly ascertained. Self-rules correspond to the attitude towards the act of the Fishbein–Ajzen formula: how else would one identify learning history through self-report than by asking an individual what he or she believed would be the outcome of acting in a given way in specific circumstances and weighting this by his or her appraisal of those consequences? Questions that elicit attitude towards the act may be equally understood as indicating a history of reinforcement. The rules revealed in this manner ('Eating fresh greens every day will result in a clear complexion') are akin to the tracks identified by Zettle and Hayes (1982): they specify how to get to a particular goal point. By this time, behaviour is 'scripted' (Langer, 1989a,b), following not from conscious intentions or plans but under the control of self-rules and/or immediate stimuli. Other-rules correspond to the subjective norm of the Fishbein–Ajzen model: acting as plys, they specify the social consequences of compliance or non-compliance with a specified course of action. Evidence for the progression from other-rules, via deliberation, experience and self-observation, to action based on self-rules is provided by research on the TPB by East (1992, 1997) which was reviewed above. (A comparative review of the cognitive and behaviourist approaches to problem solving is found in Reese, 1994; cf. Chase & Bjamadottir, 1992; Reese, 1992a,b; Ito, 1994.)

The probability of a particular response depends also upon the non-regularity components of the consumer behaviour setting, the physical, social and temporal discriminative stimuli given meaning in any particular setting by the individual's learning history. Where they have figured in the past as controlling antecedents, they will now act to signal the kinds of consequences that are contingent on each possible response. They will thus play an integral role in prebehavioural deliberation, each setting the occasion for behaviour with predictable results in the form of positive and aversive consequences. When the history of the individual is such that known consequences have followed regularly and unimpeded from specific acts, the discriminative stimuli in the current setting will provide signals that quickly result in the performance of the requisite behaviour; when the individual has little appropriate learning history, or the history is ambiguous with respect to the kinds of reinforcer or punisher likely to result from behaviour, the magnitude of these consequences and their probability, greater deliberation including the formulation, weighing and use of rules will be normal.

The self- and other-instructions activated to a greater or lesser extent in either deliberative or spontaneous processing, plus the power of current discriminative stimuli—conferred in a history of reinforcement and punishment—determine the probability of a specific response. The immediate prebehavioural verbal self-instruction or prediction the individual is capable of making (on the question of introspection entering into rule-formulation, see Moore, 1994; on that of self-editing in rule-formulation, see Hyten and Chase, 1991; cf. Vaughan, 1991)—equivalent to what deliberation theorists call his or her behavioural intention—is another kind of rule, an augmental, the proximal motivating factor leading to the consummation of a particular act.

Behaviour formed through direct experience is contingency-shaped: its persistence is due to continued reinforcement and its emission is likely to come under the stimulus control of the physical, social and temporal elements of the behaviour setting. Such behaviour may be described as 'spontaneous' or 'automatic'—finger tapping, for instance—when it is entirely under the control of these historical and current contingencies (Catania, 1992a). However, it is unlikely that a great deal of human behaviour is formed and maintained entirely through the direct action of the environmental contingencies. Humans are rule-formulating animals and routine/habitual behaviour is likely to be guided by self-rules, formed through experience and observation, and taking the form largely of tracks. Private tracking probably controls a great deal of repetitive consumer behaviour such as weekly or monthly supermarket shopping. Although such behaviour as brand choice shows 100% loyalty in only a small minority of the users of a product class, most consumers' mutli-brand purchasing is confined to a small repertoire of tried and tested brands in each class (Ehrenberg & Uncles, 1995). Brand choice within this repertoire may look haphazard but it is far from random. It differs from finger tapping in that it is highly functional and economically/consumption rational, and most consumers have no difficulty in describing the rules employed in finding and selecting brands of fast-moving consumer goods, as protocol analysis readily shows (O'Shaughnessy, 1987). Self-rules in the form of tracks are undoubtedly analogous to global attitudes towards the object—in this case a known subset of substitutable brands within a product class—which are easily/automatically elicited by the discriminative stimuli in the purchase setting. Formed through repeated purchasing, observation and imitation, including a long period of consumer socialisation, they are readily available to guide immediate, familiar purchasing in the presence of such antecedent controlling stimuli as the label on a can, a familiar brand name or a logo. This resembles the spontaneous processing in the presence of a known attitude object identified by Fazio as prerequisite to unpremeditated, automatic, routine processing.

Behaviour instructed by the rules provided by others is formed through indirect experience: TV advertisements, neighbours' recommendations, parents' approbation and so on. Such rules are most likely to be effective when the listener's relevant learning history is minimal or nonexistent and/or when the behaviour setting in which he or she is acting is closed (the latter a function of how much control the speaker has over the setting). Other-instructions are far more likely to be productive in situations unfamiliar to the listener, when a novel course of action is commended—perhaps buying a radically innovative product or moving house or just trying a new make of computer disc. Such behaviours usually require some degree of deliberation since no self-rules exist to 'spontaneously' guide action. Depending on the consumer's history of rule-compliance, he or she will be more or less disposed to follow the other-instructions without demur: a friend whose advice has proved worthwhile may be able to offer recommendations that are immediately taken up and acted upon, providing the new sphere of consumption is not too far removed from that previously instructed. But a stranger appearing in a TV commercial may not be able to rely on audience members' having so motivating a reinforcement history with respect to following other-rules. Other-rules of these kinds take the form of plys: in the absence of direct experience on the part of the listener, and especially if the rules come from a remote/unfamiliar/impersonal source, they are more likely to lead to deliberation than immediate action. The consequent review of the contingencies is not mental but behavioural (Skinner, 1974), a series of private events in which the ultimate causes of behaviour are scrutinised. Verbal rules towards specific courses of action (like attitudes towards target behaviours in the cognitive theories) may result from this process. The consumer who initially had no self-rules for the proposed course of action (because he or she had little or no direct experience thereof, little or no relevant learning history) eventually may form such rules, translating the plys provided by others into the private tracks necessary to guide particular behaviour in a clearly defined situation (corresponding to that defined in terms of target, action, timing and context by the multi-attribute modellers).

To reach a decision, determining to adopt one action among several, is to form a behavioural intention in the deliberative models; in the BPM, it appears to involve a third kind of rule, an augmental, which motivates the individual to behave in a specific manner. Augmentals of this kind result from deliberation and are succeeded by positive motivation, perhaps the outcome of a cost-benefit analysis that indicates that the reinforcing consequences of the proposed act are likely to exceed the aversive, a review of the contingencies that suggests one action will generate greater net benefits than any other. If the action is performed and reinforced, the plys provided as other-rules gradually become track-based self-rules and, ultimately, the contingencies themselves exert a greater share of control than instructions: the behaviour becomes routinised and apparently habitual. Much behaviour is of course a mixture of contingency-shaped and rule-governed, subject to adjustment as new contingencies arise and as new instructions from others and oneself emerge to be evaluated and otherwise deliberated upon. Guerin (1994a, p.192) distinguishes two kinds of decision making which have the capacity to bring together the findings of social cognitive research and those of behaviour analysis. 'Intuitive decision making', he writes, 'refers to behaving in accordance with the multiple environmental contingencies acting at that time [while] non-intuitive means that decision behavior has become verbally governed in some way and verbal rules are controlling the decision behaviour through pliance or tracking.' The preceding analysis goes beyond this, however, eschewing the simple dichotomy it implies. The theory expounded above casts behaviour where there is little direct learning history as guided by other-rules (plys), and that where there is a well-established learning history as guided by prior contingency shaping and the discriminative stimuli of the current behaviour setting including self-rules (tracks). Between the two is a period of contingency shaping through which the self-rules that come to guide behaviour apparently spontaneously are formulated. At this stage, the nonverbal contingencies that guide current behaviour are notoriously difficult to distinguish from the self-rules that may do so (Hackenberg & Joker, 1994; Hayes et al., 1986). The choice of explanation is methodologically based: some behaviour analysts refuse to admit variables represented by private events that are not amenable to an experimental analysis to their subject matter (e.g. S. C. Hayes, 1986); others are willing to interpret observed behaviour in terms of nonpublicly available entities of this kind (e.g. Catania, 1992a; Horne & Lowe, 1993).

Hence, the debate about the direction of causation between attitudes and behaviour is redundant: a consumer who has simply seen an advertisement for a brand will have an attitude in the sense of being able to express some verbal evaluations, prehaps only in the form of echoics (Skinner, 1957) though he or she may be capable of some minimal verbal evaluation of the brand. But such an attitude is less likely to act as a self-instruction to guide behaviour than that which is formed through experience with the brand.

CONCLUSION

Impressive as the social cognitive account of consumer behaviour is, its contents can be construed equally plausibly but with wholly different consequences by behaviour analysis. This is not simply a case of redescribing cognitive events in behaviouristic terminology: the findings of research into verbal behaviour parallel those on social cognition in providing an empirical basis for an explanation of cognitive events and processes which stresses their environmental origin and the contextual causation of all behaviour, verbal and nonverbal. The social cognition research programme actually points towards a more behaviour-based understanding of consumer choice through the emerging emphasis on prior behaviour as an explanatory and predictive variable for current behaviour. Studies of attitudinal-behavioural relationships have in fact identified the importance of two central ingredients of the behaviour analytic approach. These are the preceding verbal instructions that guide current behaviour, and contingency-shaped prior behaviour as a major predictor of current and future responding. But the prevailing social cognition paradigm has (naturally, within its own confines) interpreted these influences as reducible to cognitive phenomena. Contemporaneously with the social cognitive research on attitudes and behaviour over the last decade or so, a separate research programme has investigated instructed behaviour within an operant psychological framework of conceptualisation and analysis. What is surprising perhaps is that the empirical results and theoretical conclusions of the two paradigms are largely compatible, though the implications of the behaviour analytical approach present distinct alternatives paradigmatically, practically and as a signpost to future research. They support the view that behaviour may be construed as a function of environmental rather than intra-personal variables; they suggest that the response to consumer behaviour in the marketing organisation operates quite differently from its description in the marketing literature; and they require a research programme founded on a dissimilar ontological and methodological basis to that which currently predominates.

Far from being a paradigm that has been superseded and supplanted by the cognitive revolution, behaviourism is a flourishing area of intellectual activity in both its neo-Skinnerian and post-Skinnerian accentuations (e.g. Alessi, 1992; Fallon, 1992; Hayes, Hayes, Reese, & Sarbin, 1993; Kimble, 1994; Lee, 1988, 1992; Morris, 1993a,b; Rachlin, 1992, 1995; Staddon, 1993; Thompson, 1994). But Skinner's (1967, pp.109–110) expectation that it will provide the clearest model of human behaviour exaggerates. Nevertheless, the incorporation of a behaviour analytic account of consumer choice in the repertoire of available paradigms has three important implications for consumer research. First, it allows the development of an empirically based explanation of the situational influences on consumer behaviour, an aspect of consumer research that is currently underdeveloped. Second, it encourages the interaction of alternative paradigms on which the scientific progress of consumer research depends. Third, it stimulates an explanation of organisational response to consumer behaviour which stresses the role of environmental variables in marketing management. The BPM is, moreover, receiving empirical support (Foxall, 1996b).

While operant consumer research provides ontological diversity, however, it does not resolve all the epistemological problems of cognitive explanation. The encouragement of ontological diversity nonetheless represents an advance for a subdiscipline which has sought so little to emancipate itself from the strictures of social cognition. Further diversity is now necessary. The development of a general operant theory of the firm requires the input of I/O as well as consumer and marketing psychology. While consumer psychologists are capable of extending the operant analysis of purchase and consumption, and other behavioural scientists in marketing can enlarge upon the account of organisational response given here, there is also a need for an intra-firm analysis of managerial behaviour directed towards the market place which tests the capacity of operant theory to provide an explanation of what Leibenstein (1979) referred to as the micro-micro level of analysis. Current applications of operant psychology to industrial behaviour are far too instrumental to accomplish this explicatory task. The creation of an operant theory of the firm which interprets the behaviour of managers generally, marketing managers particularly, and the consumers who make up the key component of the firm's environment deserves priority.

ACKNOWLEDGEMENTS

I am grateful to Professor Richard Bagozzi (University of Michigan), Dr Robert East (Kingston University), Professor John O'Shaughnessy (University of Cambridge), Dr Richard Shepherd (Food Research Institute). The usual disclaimer applies.

REFERENCES

Abelson, R. P. (1981) Psychological status of the script concept. *American Psychologist*, **36**, 715–729.

Ajzen, I. (1985) From intentions to actions: A theory of planned behavior. In J. Kuhl & J. Beckman (eds), *Action Control: From Cognition to Behavior* (pp.11–39). Berlin: Springer-Verlag.

Ajzen, I. (1987) Attitudes, traits, and actions: Dispositional prediction of behavior in personality and social psychology. *Advances in Experimental Social Psychology*, **20**, 1–63. Berkovitz, L. (ed.), Academic Press, San Diego.

Ajzen, I. (1988) *Attitudes, Personality and Behavior*. Milton Keynes: Open University Press.

Ajzen, I. (1991) The theory of planned behavior. *Organizational Behavior and Human Decision Processes*, **50**, 179–211.

Ajzen, I. & Driver, B. E. (1991) Predictions of leisure participation from behavioral, normative, and control beliefs. *Leisure Sciences*, **13**, 185–204.

Ajzen, I. & Driver, B. E. (1992) Application of the theory of planned behavior to leisure choice. *Journal of Leisure Research*, **24**, 207–224.

Ajzen, I. & Fishbein, M. (1977) Attitude–behavior relations: A theoretical analysis and review of empirical research. *Psychological Bulletin*, **84**, 888–918.

Ajzen, I. & Fishbein, M. (1980) *Understanding Attitudes and Predicting Social Behavior*. Englewood Cliffs, NJ: Prentice-Hall.

Ajzen, I. & Madden, T. J. (1986) Prediction of goal-directed behavior: Attitudes, intentions, and perceived behavioral control. *Journal of Experimental Social Psychology*, **22**, 453–474.

Alba, J. W., Hutchinson, J. W., & Lynch, J. G. (1991) Memory and decision making. In T. S. Robertson & H. H. Kassarjian (eds), *Handbook of Consumer Behavior* (pp. 1–49) Englewood Cliffs, NJ: Prentice-Hall.

Alessi, G. (1992) Models of proximate and ultimate causation in psychology. *American Psychologist*, 47, 1359–1370.

Allen, C. T., Machleit, K. A., & Kleine, S. S. (1992) A comparison of attitudes and emotions as predictors of behavior at diverse levels of behavioral experience. *Journal of Consumer Research*, 18, 493–504.

Allport, G. W. (1935) Attitudes. In C. Murchison (ed.), *Handbook of Social Psychology* (pp. 798–844) Worcester, MA: Clark University Press.

Anderson, A. S., Campbell, D. M., & Shepherd, R. (1995) The influence of dietary advice on nutrient intake during pregnancy. *British Journal of Nutrition*, 73, 163–177.

Andreasen, A. (1965) Attitudes and customer behavior: A decision model. In L. E. Preston (ed.), *New Research in Marketing*. Berkeley, CA: University of California Press.

Bagozzi, R. P. (1981) Attitudes, intentions, and behavior: A test of some key hypotheses. *Journal of Personality and Social Psychology*, 41, 607–627.

Bagozzi, R. P. (1984) Expectancy–value attitude models: An analysis of critical measurement issues. *International Journal of Research in Marketing*, 1, 295–310.

Bagozzi, R. P. (1985) Expectancy–value attitude models: An analysis of critical theoretical issues. *International Journal of Research in Marketing*, 2, 43–60.

Bagozzi, R. P. (1986) Attitude formation under the theory of reasoned action and a purposeful behaviour reformulation. *British Journal of Social Psychology*, 25, 95–107.

Bagozzi, R. P. (1988) The rebirth of attitude research in marketing. *Journal of the Market Research Society*, 30, 163–195.

Bagozzi, R. P. (1991) Enactment processes in the theory of reasoned action. Unpublished manuscript. University of Michigan.

Bagozzi, R. P. (1992) The self-regulation of attitudes, intentions, and behavior. *Social Psychology Quarterly*, 55, 178–204.

Bagozzi, R. P. (1993) On the neglect of volition in consumer research: A critique and proposal. *Psychology and Marketing*, 10, 215–237.

Bagozzi, R. P. (1994) Effects of arousal on organization of positive and negative affect and cognitions: Application to attitude theory. *Structural Equation Modeling*, 1, 222–252.

Bagozzi, R. P. (in press) The role of arousal in the creation and control of the halo effect in attitude models. *Psychology and Marketing*.

Bagozzi, R. P., Baumgartner, H., & Pieters, R. (1996) Goal-directed emotions. Unpublished paper. University of Michigan.

Bagozzi, R. P., Baumgartner, H., & Yi, Y. (1992a) Appraisal processes in the enactment of intentions to use coupons. *Psychology and Marketing*, 9, 469–486.

Bagozzi, R. P., Baumgartner, H., & Yi, Y. (1992b) State versus action orientation and the theory of reasoned action: An application to coupon usaged, *Journal of Consumer Research*, 18, 505–518.

Bagozzi, R. P. & Foxall, G. R. (1996) Construct validation of a measure of adaptive-innovative cognitive styles in consumption. *International Journal of Research in Marketing*, 13, 201–213.

Bagozzi, R. P. & Kimmel, S. K. (1995) A comparison of leading theories for the prediction of goal-directed behaviours. *British Journal of Social Psychology*, 34, 472–461.

Bagozzi, R. P. & Kimmel, S. K. (1996) The role of self-schemas and action control in the regulation of goal-directed behaviors: making attitude theory more social. Unpublished paper. University of Michigan.

Bagozzi, R. P. & Moore, D. J. (1994) Public service advertisements: emotion and empathy guide prosocial behavior. *Journal of Marketing*, 58, 56–70.

Bagozzi, R. P. & Van Loo, M. F. (1991) Motivational and reasoned processes in the theory of consumer choice. In R. Frantz, H. Singh, & J. Gerber (eds), *Handbook of*

Behavioral Economics, Vol. 2B: *Behavioral Decision Making* (pp. 401–437). Greenwich, CT: JAI.

Bagozzi, R. P. & Warshaw, P. R. (1990) Trying to consume. *Journal of Consumer Research*, 17, 127–140.

Bagozzi, R. P. & Warshaw, P. R. (1992) An examination of the etiology of the attitude–behavior relation for goal-directed behaviors. *Multivariate Behavioral Research*, 27, 601–634.

Bagozzi, R. P. & Yi, Y. (1989) The degree of intention formation as a moderator of the attitude–behavioral relationship. *Social Psychology Quarterly*, 52, 266–279.

Bagozzi, R. P., Yi, Y. & Baumgartner, H. (1990) The level of effort required for behavior as a moderator of the attitude–behavior relation. *Eropean Journal of Social Psychology*, 20, 45–59.

Ball, D., Lamb, C., & Brodie, R. V. (1992) Segmentation and market structure when both consumer and situational characteristics are explanatory. *Psychology and Marketing*, 9, 395–408.

Bargh, J. A. (1994) The four horsemen of automaticity: Awareness, intention, efficiency, and control in social cognition. In R. S. Wyer & T. K. Srull (eds), *Handbook of Social Cognition. Vol. 1: Basic Processes*. Second edition (pp. 1–40). Hillsdale, NJ: Erlbaum.

Bargh, J. A., Chaiken, S. Govender, R. & Pratto, F. (1992) The generality of the automatic attitude activation effect. *Journal of Personality and Social Psychology*, 62, 893–912.

Bates, L. & Mitchell, V.-W. (1995) Consumer decision-making typologies: A review of the literature and suggestions for further research'. Unpublished paper. Manchester School of Management.

Baum, W. M. (1994) *Understanding Behaviorism: Science, Behavior and Culture*. New York: Harper Collins.

Beale, D. A. & Manstead, A. S. R. (1991) Predicting mothers' intentions to limit frequency of infants' sugar intake: Testing the theory of planned behavior. *Journal of Applied Social Psychology*, 21, 409–431.

Beck, L. & Ajzen, I. (1991) Predicting dishonest actions using the theory of planned behavior. *Journal of Research in Personality*, 25, 285–301.

Bem, D. (1972) Self-perception theory. In L. Berkovitz (ed.), *Advances in Experimental Social Psychology*, Vol. 6 (pp. 1–62). San Diego, CA: Academic Press.

Bentler, P. M. & Speckart, G. (1979) Models of attitude–behavior relations. *Psychological Review*, 86, 452–464.

Bentler, P. M. & Speckart, G. (1981) Attitudes 'cause' behaviors: A structural equation analysis. *Journal of Personality and Social Psychology*, 40, 226–238.

Berger, I. E. (1992) The nature of attitude accessibility and attitude confidence: A triangulated experiment. *Journal of Consumer Psychology*, 1, 103–124.

Berger, I. E., Ratchford, B. T., & Haines, G. T. (1994) Subjective product knowledge as a mediator of the relationship between attitudes and purchase intentions for a durable product. *Journal of Economic Psychology*, 15, 301–314.

Berry, L. L. & Kunkel, J. H. (1970) In pursuit of consumer theory. *Decision Sciences*, 1, 25–39.

Bettman, J. R. (1986) Consumer psychology. *Annual Review of Psychology*, 37, 257–289.

Bettman, J. R., Johnson, E. J., & Payne, J. W. (1991) Consumer decision making. In T. S. Robertson & H. H. Kassarjian (eds), *Handbook of Consumer Behavior* (pp. 50–84) Englewood Cliffs, NJ: Prentice-Hall.

Blascovich, J., Ernst, J. M., Tomaka, J., Kelsey, R. M., Salomon, K. L., & Fazio, R. H. (1993) Attitude accessibility as a moderator of automatic reactivity during decision making. *Journal of Personality and Social Psychology*, 64, 165–176.

Bogardus, E. S. (1925) Measuring social distances. *Journal of Applied Sociology*, **9**, 299–308.

Bohner, G., Moskowitz, G. B., & Chaiken, S. (1995) The interplay of heuristic and systematic processing of social information. In W. Stroebe & M. Hewstone (eds), *European Review of Social Psychology*, Vol. 6 (pp. 33–68). Chichester: Wiley.

Boldero, J. (1995) The prediction of household recycling of newspapers—the role of attitudes, intentions and situational factors. *Journal of Applied Social Psychology*, **25**, 440–462.

Boldero, J., Moore, S., & Rosenthal, D. (1992) Intentions, context and safe sex. *Journal of Applied Social Psychology*, **22**, 1374–1396.

Borgida, E., Conner, C., & Manteufel, L. (1992) Understanding living kidney donation: A behavioural decision making perspective. In S. Spacapan & S. Oskamp (eds), *Helping and Being Helped: Naturalistic Studies* (pp. 183–212). Newbury Park, CA: Sage.

Boyd, B. & Wandersman, A. (1991) Predicting undergraduate condom use with the Fishbein and Ajzen and the Triandis attitude–behavior models: Implications for public health interventions. *Journal of Applied Social Psychology*, **21**, 1810–1830.

Brown, S. (1995) *Postmodern Marketing*. London: Routledge.

Brown, S. P. & Stayman, D. M. (1992) Antecedents and consequences of attitude toward the ad: A meta-analysis. *Journal of Consumer Research*, **19**, 34–51.

Budd, R. J., North, D., & Spencer, C. (1984) Understanding seat-belt use: A test of Bentler and Speckart's extension of the 'theory of reasoned action'. *European Journal of Social Psychology*, **14**, 69–78.

Castleberry, S. B., Barnard, N. R., Barwise, T. P., Ehrenberg, A. S. C., & Dall'Olmo Riley, F. (1994) Individual attitude variations over time. *Journal of Marketing Management*, **10**, 153–162.

Catania, A. C. (1992a) *Learning*. Third edition. Englewood Cliffs, NJ: Prentice-Hall.

Catania, A. C. (1992b) B. F. Skinner, organism. *American Psychologist*, **47**, 1521–1530.

Catania, A. C., Matthews, B. A., & Shimoff, E. H. (1990) Properties of rule-governed behaviour and their implications. In D. E. Blackman & H. Lejeune (eds), *Behaviour Analysis in Theory and Practice: Contributions and Controversies* (pp. 215–230). London: Erlbaum.

Catania, A. C., Shimoff, E., & Matthews, B. A. (1989) An experimental analysis of rule-governed behavior. In S. C. Hayes (ed.), *Rule-Governed Behavior: Cognition, Contingencies, and Instructional Control* (pp.119–150). New York: Plenum.

Chaiken, S. (1980) Heuristic versus systematic information processing and the use of source versus message cues in persuasion. *Journal of Personality and Social Psychology*, **39**, 752–766.

Chan, D. K. S. & Fishbein, M. (1993) Determinants of college women's intentions to tell their partners to use condoms. *Journal of Applied Social Psychology*, **23**, 1455–1470.

Charng, H., Piliavin, J. A., & Callero, P. L. (1988) Role identity and reasoned action in the prediction of repeated behavior. *Social Psychology Quarterly*, **51**, 133–151.

Chase, P. N. & Bjamadottir, G. S. (1992) Instructing variability: Some features of a problem-solving repertoire. In S. C. Hayes & L. J. Hayes (eds), *Understanding Verbal Relations* (pp. 181–196). Reno, NV: Context Press.

Chase, P. N. & Danforth, J. S. (1991) The roles of rules in concept formation. In L. J. Hayes & P. N. Chase (eds), *Dialogues on Verbal Behavior* (pp. 205–225). Reno, NV: Context Press.

Chomsky, N. (1959) Review of B. F. Skinner's *Verbal Behavior*. *Lanuage*, **35**, 26–58.

Coase, R. H. (1988) *The Firm, the Market, and the Law*. Chicago: University of Chicago Press.

Cohen, A. (1964) *Attitude Change and Social Influence*. New York: Basic Books.

Cohen, J. B. & Chakravarti, D. (1990) Consumer psychology. *Annual Review of Psychology*, 41, 243–288.

Courneya, K. S. (1995) Understanding readiness for regular physical activity in older individuals: An application of the theory of planned behavior. *Health Psychology*, 14, 80–87.

Dabholkar, P. A. (1994) Incorporating choice into an attitudinal framework: Analyzing models of mental comparison processes. *Journal of Consumer Research*, 21, 100–118.

Davies, M. A. P. & Wright, L. T. (1994) The importance of labelling examined in food marketing. *European Journal of Marketing*, 28(2), 57–67.

Delprato, Dennis, J. & Bryan, D. Midgley (1992) Some fundamentals of B. F. Skinner's behaviorism. *American Psychologist*, 47, 1507–1520.

Dennison, C. M. & Shepherd, R. (1995) Adolescent food choice: An application of the theory of planned behaviour. *Journal of Human Nutrition and Dietetics*, 8, 9–23.

Desroches, J. J. Y. & Chebat, J. C. (1995) Why Quebec businesses go public: Attitudes and the decision making process. *Revue Canadienne des Sciences de l'Administration*, 12, 27–37.

DeVellis, B. M., Blalock, S. J., & Sandler, R. S. (1990) Predicting participation in cancer screening: The role of perceived behavioural control. *Journal of Applied Social Psychology*, 20, 639–660.

Dewit, J. B. F. & Teunis, G. J. P. (1994) Behavioral risk reduction strategies to prevent HIV-infection among homosexual men. *Aids Education and Prevention*, 6, 493–505.

Doll, J. & Ajzen, I. (1992) Accessibility and stability of predictors in the theory of planned behavior. *Journal of Personality and Social Psychology*, 63, 754–765.

Doob, L. W. (1947) The behavior of attitudes. *Psychological Review*, 54, 135–156.

Downing, J. W., Judd, C. M., & Brauer, M. (1992) Effects of repeated expressions on attitude extremity. *Journal of Personality and Social Psychology*, 62, 17–29.

Eagly, A. H. & Chaiken, S. (1993) *The Psychology of Attitudes*. Fort Worth, TX: Harcourt Brace Jovanovich.

East, R. (1990) *Changing Consumer Behaviour*. London: Cassell.

East, R. (1992) The effect of experience on the decision making of expert and novice buyers. *Journal of Marketing Management*, 8, 167–176.

East, R. (1993) Investment decisions and the theory of planned behaviour. *Journal of Economic Psychology*, 14, 337–375.

East, R. (1996) Redress seeking as planned behavior. *Journal of Consumer Satisfaction, Dissatisfaction and Complaining Behavior*, 9, 27–34.

East, R. (1997) *Consumer Behaviour: Advances and Applications in Marketing*. London: Prentice-Hall.

Echabe, A. E., Rovira, D. P., & Garate, J. F. V. (1988) Testing Ajzen and Fishbein's attitude model: The prediction of voting. *European Journal of Social Psychology*, 18, 181–189.

Ehrenberg, A. S. C. (1972) *Repeat Buying*. Amsterdam: North Holland. Second edition, 1988, London: Griffin.

Ehrenberg, A. S. C. & Uncles, M. D. Dirichlet-type Markets: A Review. Unpublished manuscript. South Bank Business School, London.

Eiser, J. R. (1987) *The Expression of Attitude*. New York: Springer-Verlag.

Eiser, J. R. & van der Pligt, J. (1988) *Attitudes and Decisions*. London: Routledge.

Engel, J. F., Blackwell, R. D., & Miniard, P. W. (1995) *Consumer Behavior*. Eighth edition. Fort Worth, TX: Dryden.

Engel, J. F., Kollat, D. T., & Blackwell, R. D. (1968) *Consumer Behavior*. New York: Holt, Rinehart & Winston.

Ericsson, K. A. & Simon, H. A. (1993) *Protocol Analysis: Verbal Reports as Data*. Cambridge, MA: MIT Press.

Fallon, D. (1992) An existential look at B. F. Skinner. *American Psychologist*, **47**, 1441–1453.

Fazio, R. H. (1986) How do attitudes guide behavior? In R. M. Sorrentino & E. T. Higgins (eds), *Handbook of Motivation and Cognition: Foundations of Social Behavior* (pp. 204–243). Chichester: Wiley.

Fazio, R. H. (1989) On the power and functionality of attitudes: The role of attitude accessibility. In A. R. Pratkanis, A. J. Breckler, & A. G. Greenwald (eds), *Attitude Structure and Function* (pp. 153–180). Hillsdale, NJ: Erlbaum.

Fazio, R. H. (1990) Multiple processes by which attitudes guide behavior: The MODE model as an integrative framework. In M. P. Zanna (ed.), *Advances in Experimental Social Psychology*, Vol. 23 (pp. 75–109). San Diego, CA: Academic Press.

Fazio, R. H. (1994) Attitudes as object-evaluation associations: Determinants, consequences, and correlates of attitude accessibility. In R. E. Petty & J. A. Krosnick (eds), *Attitude Strength: Antecedents and Consequences*, Hillsdale, NJ: Erlbaum.

Fazio, R. H. & Zanna, M. P. (1987a) Attitudinal qualities relating to the strength of the attitude–behavior relationship. *Journal of Experimental Social Psychology*, **14**, 398–408.

Fazio, R. H., Chen, J., McDonel, E. C., & Sherman, S. J. (1982) Attitude accessibility, attitude–behavior consistency, and the strength of the object-evaluation association. *Journal of Experimental Social Psychology*, **18**, 339–357.

Fazio, R. H., Powell, M. C., & Williams, C. J. (1989) The role of attitude accessibility in the attitude-to-behavior process. *Journal of Consumer Research*, **16**, 280–288.

Fazio, R. H. & Zanna, M. P. (1987b) On the predictive validity of attitudes: The roles of direct experience and confidence. *Journal of Personality*, **46**, 228–243.

Fazio, R. H. & Zanna, M. P. (1981) Direct experience and attitude-behavior consistency. *Advances in Experimental Social Psychology*, **14**, 161–202.

Featherstone, M. (1991) *Consumer Culture and Postmodernism*. London: Sage.

Feyerabend, P. (1970) Consolations for the specialist. In I. Lakatos & A. Musgrave (eds), *Criticism and the Growth of Knowledge*. Cambridge: Cambridge University Press.

Feyerabend, P. (1975) *Against Method*. London: NLB.

Fishbein, M. (1967) (ed.) *Readings in Attitude Theory and Measurement*. New York: Wiley.

Fishbein, M. (1972) The search for attitudinal-behavioral consistency. In J. S. Cohen (ed.), *Behavioral Science Foundations of Consumer Behavior*. New York: Free Press.

Fishbein, M. & Ajzen, I. (1975) *Belief, Attitude, Intention and Behavior*. Reading, MA: Addison-Wesley.

Fishbein, M. & Stasson, M. (1990) The role of desires, self-predictions, and perceived control in the prediction of training session attendance. *Journal of Applied Social Psychology*, **20**, 173–198.

Fiske, S. T. (1993) Social cognition and social perception. *Annual Review of Psychology*, **44**, 155–194.

Folkes, V. S. & Kiesler, T. (1991) Social cognition: Consumers' inferences about the self and others. In T. S. Robertson & H. H. Kassarjian (eds), *Handbook of Consumer Behaviour* (pp. 281–315). Englewood Cliffs, NJ: Prentice-Hall.

Foxall, G. R. (1983) *Consumer Choice*, London: Macmillan; New York: St. Martin's Press.

Foxall, G. R. (1984) Consumers' intentions and behaviour. *Journal of the Market Research Society*, **26**, 231–241.

Foxall, G. R. (1987) Radical behaviourism and consumer research: Theoretcial promise and empirical problems. *International Journal of Research in Marketing*, **4**, 111–129.

Foxall, G. R. (1990) *Consumer Psychology in Behavioural Perspective*. London and New York: Routledge.

Foxall, G. R. (1992a) The consumer situation: An integrative model for research in marketing. *Journal of Marketing Management*, **8**, 392–404.

Foxall, G. R. (1992b) The Behavioral Perspective Model of purchase and consumption: From consumer theory to marketing management. *Journal of the Academy of Marketing Science*, **20**, 189–198.

Foxall, G. R. (1993a) Consumer behaviour as an evolutionary process. *European Journal of Marketing*, **27**(8), 46–57.

Foxall, G. R. (1993b) Situated consumer behavior: A behavioral interpretation of purchase and consumption. In J. A. Costa & R. W. Belk (eds), *Research in Consumer Behavior*, Vol. 6 (pp. 113–152), Greenwich, CT: JAI.

Foxall, G. R. (1993c) Variety seeking and cognitive style. *British Food Journal*, **95**(7), 32–36.

Foxall, G. R. (1994a) Behavior analysis and consumer psychology. *Journal of Economic Psychology*, **15**, 5–91.

Foxall, G. R. (1994b) Consumer choice as an evolutionary process: An operant interpretation of adopter behavior. *Advances in Consumer Research*, **21**, 312–317.

Foxall, G. R. (1994c) Environment-impacting consumer behaviour: A framework for social marketing and demarketing. In M. J. Baker (ed.), *Perspectives on Marketing Management*, Vol. 4 (pp.27–53), Chichester: Wiley.

Foxall, G. R. (1994d) Consumer initiators: Adaptors and innovators. *British Journal of Management*, **5**, S3–S12.

Foxall, G. R. (1994e) Consumer decision-making. In M. J. Baker (ed.), *The Marketing Book*, (pp.193–215). London: Butterworth-Heinemann.

Foxall, G. R. (1995a) Science and interpretation in consumer research: A radical behaviourist perspective. *European Journal of Marketing*, **29**(9), 3–99.

Foxall, G. R. (1995b) The psychological basis of marketing. In M. J. Baker (ed.), *The Companion Encyclopedia of Marketing*. London and New York: Routledge.

Foxall, G. R. (1995c) Environment-impacting consumer behavior: An operant analysis. *Advances in Consumer Research*, **22**, 262–268.

Foxall, G. R. (1995d) Cognitive styles of consumer initiators. *Technovation*, **15**, 269–288.

Foxall, G. R. (1996a) *Consumers in Context: The BPM Research Program*. London and New York: Routledge.

Foxall, G. R. (1996b) Consensual availability and predictive validity of the BPM interpretation of consumer behaviour'. Working Paper in Consumer Research #96/03. Research Centre for Consumer Behaviour, University of Birmingham.

Foxall, G. R. (1997) *Consumer Choice and Marketing Response*. London: Macmillan; New York: St. Martin's Press.

Foxall, G. R. & Bhate, S. (1993a) Cognitive style and personal involvement as explicators of consumers' innovative purchasing of 'healthy' food brands. *European Journal of Marketing*, **27**(2), 6–17.

Foxall, G. R. & Bhate, S. (1993b) Cognitive style and use-innovativeness for applications software in home computing: Implications for new product strategy. *Technovation*, **13**, 311–323.

Foxall, G. R. & Bhate, S. (1993c) Cognitive styles, personal involvement and innovative purchasing of 'healthy' food brands. *Journal of Economic Psychology*, **11**, 33–56.

Foxall, G. R. & Hackett, P. (1992) Consumers' perceptions of micro-retail location: Wayfinding and cognitive mapping in planned and organic shopping environments. *International Review of Retail, Distributive and Consumer Research*, **2**, 309–327.

Foxall, G. R. & Hackett, P. (1994) Consumer satisfaction with Birmingham's International Convention Centre. *Service Industries Journal*, **14**, 369–380.

Fredericks, A. J. & Dossett, D. L. (1983) Attitude–behavior relations: A comparison of the Fishbein–Ajzen and Bentler–Speckart models. *Journal of Personality and Social Psychology*, **45**, 501–512.

du Gay, P. (1995) *Consumption and Identity at Work*. London: Sage.

Giles, M. & Cairns, E. (1995) Blood donation and Ajzen's theory of planned behaviour: An examination of perceived behavioural control. *British Journal of Social Psychology*, **34**, 173–188.

Godin, G., Valois, P. & LePage, L. (1993) The pattern of influence of perceived behavioral control upon exercising behavior—an application of Ajzen's theory of planned behavior. *Journal of Behavioral Medicine*, **16**, 81–102.

Godin, G., Valois, P., LePage, L., & Desharnais, M. (1992) Predictors of smoking behaviour: An applicaion of Ajzen's theory of planned behaviour. *British Journal of Addiction*, **87**, 1335–1343.

Granberg, D. & Holmberg, S. (1990) The intention–behavior relationship among US and Swedish voters. *Social Psychology Quarterly*, **53**, 44–54.

Greenwald, A. G. & Banaji, M. R. (1995) Implicit social cognition: Attitudes, self-esteem, and stereotypes. *Psychological Review*, **102**, 4–27.

Guerin, B. (1992) Behavior analysis and the social construction of knowledge. *American Psychologist*, **47**, 1423–1432.

Guerin, B. (1994a) *Analyzing Social Behavior: Behavior Analysis and the Social Sciences*. Reno, NV: Context Press.

Guerin, B. (1994b) Attitudes and beliefs as verbal behavior. *The Behavior Analyst*, **17**.

Hackenberg, T. D. & Joker, V. R. (1994) Instructional versus schedule control of humans' choices in situations of diminishing returns. *Journal of the Experimental Analysis of Behavior*, **62**, 367–383.

Hackett, P. & Foxall, G. R. (1994) A factor analytic study of consumers' location specific values: A traditional high street and a modern shopping mall. *Journal of Marketing Management*, **10**, 163–178.

Hackett, P. & Foxall, G. R. (1995) The structure of consumers' place evaluations. *Environment and Behavior*, **27**, 354–379.

Hackett, P., Foxall, G. R., & Van Raaij, W. F. (1993) Consumers in retail environments. In T. Garling & R. G. Golledge (eds) *Behavior and Environment: Psychological and Geographical Approaches* (pp.378–399). Amsterdam: Elsevier.

Harrison, D. A. & Liska, L. Z. (1994) Promoting regular exercise in organizational fitness programs: Health related differences in motivational building-blocks. *Personnel Psychology*, **47**, 47–71.

Haugtvedt, C. P. & Petty, R. E. (1992) Personality and persuasion: Need for cognition moderates the persistence and resistance of attitudes. *Journal of Personality and Social Psychology*, **62**, 308–319.

Haugtvedt, C. P., Schumann, D. W., Schneier, W. L., & Warren, W. L. (1994) Advertising repetition and variation strategies: Implications for understanding attitude strength. *Journal of Consumer Research*, **21**, 176–189.

Haugtvedt, C. P. & Wegener, D. T. (1994) Message order effects in persuasion: An attitude strength perspective. *Journal of Consumer Research*, **21**, 205–218.

Hawkins, S. A. & Hoch, S. J. (1992) Low-involvement learning: Memory without evaluation. *Journal of Consumer Research*, **19**, 212–225.

Hayes, L. J. (1991) Substitution and reference. In L. J. Hayes & P. N. Chase (eds) *Dialogues on Verbal Behavior* (pp.3–18). Reno, NV: Context Press.

Hayes, L. J. (1994) Thinking. In S. C. Hayes, L. J. Hayes, M. Sato, & K. Ono (eds), *Behavior Analysis of Language and Cognition* (pp.149–164). Reno, NV: Context Press.

Hayes, L. J. & Chase, P. N. (1991) (eds) *Dialogues on Verbal Behavior*. Reno, NV: Context Press.

Hayes, S. C. (1986) The case of the silent dog—verbal reports and the analysis of rules. *Journal of the Experimental Analysis of Behavior*, **45**, 351–363.

Hayes, S. C. (1989) (ed.), *Rule-Governed Behavior: Cognition, Contingencies, and Instructional Control*. New York: Plenum.

Hayes, S. C. (1994) Relational frame theory: A functional approach to verbal events. In S. C. Hayes, L. J. Hayes, M. Sato & K. Ono (eds) *Behavior Analysis of Language and Cognition* (pp.9–30). Reno, NV: Context Press.

Hayes, S. C., Brownstein, A. J., Haas, J. R., & Greenway, D. E. (1986) Instructions, multiple schedules, and extinction: Distinguishing rule-governed from schedule-controlled behavior. *Journal of the Experimental Analysis of Behavior*, **46**, 137–147.

Hayes, S. C. & Hayes, L. J. (1989) The verbal action of the listener as a basis for rule-governance. In S. C. Hayes (ed.), *Rule-Governed Behavior: Cognition, Contingencies, and Instructional Control* (pp.153–190). New York: Plenum.

Hayes, S. C. & Hayes, L. J. (1992a) Verbal relations and the evolution of behavior analysis. *American Psychologist*, **47**, 1383–1395.

Hayes, S. C. & Hayes, L. J. (1992b) (eds), *Understanding Verbal Relations*. Reno, NV: Context Press.

Hayes, S. C. & Hayes, L. J., Reese, H. W., & Sarbin, T. R. (1993), *Varieties of Scientific Contextualism*. Reno, NV: Context Press.

Hayes, S. C., Hayes, L. J., Sato, M., & Ono, K. (1994) (eds), *Behavior Analysis of Language and Cognition*. Reno, NV: Context Press.

Hineline, P. (1992) A self-interpretive behaviour analysis. *American Psychologist*, **47**, 1274–1286.

Hirschman, E. C. & Holbrook, M. B. (1992) *Postmodern Consumer Research: The Study of Consumption as Text*. Newbury Park, CA: Sage.

Holbrook, M. M. (1995) *Consumer Research: Introspective Essays on the Study of Consumption*. Newbury Park, CA: Sage.

Holbrook, M. B., O'Shaughnessy, J. & Bell, S. (1990) Actions and reactions in the consumption experience: The complementary roles of reasons and emotions in consumer behavior. In E. C. Hirschman (ed.), *Research in Consumer Behavior*, Vol. 4 (pp.131–163). Greenwick, CT: JAI.

Horne, P. J. & Lowe, C. F. (1993) Determinants of human performance on concurrent schedules. *Journal of the Experimental Analysis of Behavior*, **59**, 29–60.

Horne, P. J. & Lowe, C. F. (1996) On the origins of naming and other symbolic behavior. *Journal of the Experimental Analysis of Behavior*, **65**, 185–242.

Howard, J. A. (1977) *Consumer Behavior: Application of Theory*. New York: McGraw-Hill.

Howard, J. A. (1983) Marketing theory of the firm. *Journal of Marketing*, **47**, 90–100.

Howard, J. A. (1989) *Consumer Behavior in Marketing Strategy*. Englewood Cliffs, NJ: Prentice-Hall.

Howard, J. A. & Sheth, J. N. (1969) *The Theory of Buyer Behavior*. New York: Wiley.

Hyten, C. M. & Burns, R. (1986) Social relations and social behavior. In H. W. Reese & L. J. Parrott (eds), *Behavior Science: Philosophical, Methodological, and Empirical Advances* (pp.163–183). Hillsdale, NJ: Erlbaum.

Hyten, C. M. & Chase, P. N. (1991) An analysis of self-editing: Method and preliminary findings. In L. J. Hayes and P. N. Chase (eds), *Dialogues on Verbal Behavior* (pp.67–81). Reno, NV: Context Press.

Ito, Y. (1994) Models and problem solving: Effects and use of the 'views of probability'. In S. C. Hayes, L. J. Hayes, M. Sato, & K. Ono (eds), *Behavior Analysis of Language and Cognition* (pp.259–280). Reno, NV: Context Press.

Iversen, I. H. (1992) Skinner's early research: From Reflexology to operant conditioning. *American Psychologist*, **47**, 1318–1328.

Jacoby, J. (1983) Consumer and industrial psychology: Prospects for theory corroboration and mutual contribution. In M. D. Dunnette (ed.), *Handbook of Industrial and Organizational Psychology* (pp.1031–1061). New York: Wiley.

Janiszewski, C. (1988) Preconscious processing effects: The independence of attitude formation and conscious thought. *Journal of Consumer Research*, **15**, 199–209.

Journal of Consumer Research (1994). Summaries and Index Volumes 1–20. June 1974 through March 1994. *Journal of Consumer Research*, **21**, Supplement, 1–117.

Kardes, F. R. (1988) Spontaneous inference processes in advertising: The effects of conclusion omission and involvement on persuasion. *Journal of Consumer Research*, **15**, 225–233.

Kardes, F. R. (1994) Consumer judgment and decision process. In R. S. Wyer & T. K. Srull (1994) (eds), *Handbook on Social Cognition. Vol. 2: Application*. Second edition. Hillsdale, NJ: Erlbaum.

Kashima, Y., Gallois, C., & McCamish, M. (1993) The theory of reasoned action and cooperative behaviour: It takes two to use a condom. *British Journal of Social Psychology*, **32**, 227–239.

Kassarjian, H. H. (1982) Consumer psychology. *Annual Review of Psychology*, **33**, 619–649.

Kelly, C. & Breinlinger, S. (1995) Attitudes, intentions and behavior: A study of women's participation in collective action. *Journal of Applied Social Psychology*, **25**, 1430–1445.

Keng, K. A. & Ehrenberg, A. S. C. (1984) Patterns of store choice. *Journal of Marketing Research*, **21**, 399–409.

Kimble, G. A. (1994) A new formula for behaviorism. *Psychological Review*, **101**, 254–258.

Kimiecik, J. (1992) Predicting vigorous activity of corporate employees: Comparing the theories of reasoned action and planned behavior. *Journal of Sport and Exercise Psychology*, **14**, 192–206.

Klobas, J. E. (1995) Beyond information quality: Fitness for purpose and electronic information resource us. *Journal of Information Science*, **21**, 95–114.

Knox, S. & de Chernatony, L. (1994) Attitude, personal norms and intentions. In M. Jenkins & S. Knox (eds), *Advances in Consumer Marketing* (pp.85–98). London: Kogan Page.

Kuhn, T. S. (1962) *The Structure of Scientific Revolutions*. Chicago, IL: Chicago University Press (Second Edition 1970).

Lalljee, M., Brown, L. B., & Ginsburg, G. P. (1984) Attitudes: Disposition, behaviour or evaluation? *British Journal of Social Psychology*, **23**, 233–244.

Langer, E. J. (1989a) *Mindfulness*. Reading, MA: Addison-Wesley.

Langer, E. J. (1989b) Minding matters: The consequences of mindlessness-mindfulness. In L. Berkowitz (ed.), *Advances in Experimental Social Psychology*, Vol. 22 (pp.137–173). San Diego, CA: Academic Press.

Laudan, L. (1984) *Science and Values: The Aims of Science and their Role in Scientific Debate*. Berkeley, CA: University of California Press.

Lee, V. L. (1988) *Beyond Behaviorism*, London: Erlbaum.

Lee, V. L. (1992) Transdermal interpretation of the subject matter of behavior analysis. *American Psychologist*, **47**, 1337–1343.

Leibenstein, H. (1979) A branch of economics is missing: Micro-micro theory. *Journal of Economic Literature*, **17**, 477–502.

Likert, R. (1932) A technique for the measurement of attitudes. *Archives of Psychology*, **140**, 5–53.

Liska, A. E. (1984) A critical examination of the causal structure of the Fishbein/Ajzen attitude–behavior model. *Social Psychology Quarterly*, **47**, 621–674.

Lowe, C. F. (1989) *From Conditioning to Consciousness: The Cultural Origins of Mind*. Bangor: University College of North Wales.

Mackenzie, B. (1988) The challenge to Skinner's theory of behavior. In A. C. Catania & S. Harnad (eds), *The Selection of Behavior. The Operant Behaviorism of B. F. Skinner: Comments and Consequences* (pp.111–113). New York: Cambridge University Press.

Mackenzie, S. B. & Hoffman, D. L. (1992) How does motivation moderate the impact of central and peripheral processing on brand attitudes and intentions? *Journal of Consumer Research*, **18**, 519–529.

Mackenzie, S. B. & Spreng, R. A. (1992) How does motivation moderate the impact of central and peripheral processing on brand attitudes and intentions? *Journal of Consumer Research*, **18**, 519–529.

MacCorquodale, K. (1969) B. F. Skinner's *Verbal Behavior*: A retrospective appreciation. *Journal of the Experimental Analysis of Behavior*, **12**, 831–841.

MacCorquodale, K. (1970) On Chomsky's review of Skinner's *Verbal Behavior*. *Journal of the Experimental Analysis of Behavior*, **13**, 85–99.

Madden, T. J., Ellen, P. S., & Ajzen, I. (1992) A comparison of the theory of planned behavior and the theory of reasoned action. *Personality and Social Psychology Bulletin*, **18**, 3–9.

Madden, T. J. & Sprott (1995) A comparison of theoretical extensions to the theory of reasoned action. *Proceedings of the Society of Consumer Psychology* (pp.1–9), 1995 Annual Convention, La Jolla, CA.

Maier, N. R. F. (1965) *Psychology in Industry*. Boston, MA: Houghton Mifflin.

Maio, G. R. & Olson, J. M. (1994) Value–attitude–behaviour relations: The moderating role of attitude functions. *British Journal of Social Psychology*, **33**, 301–312.

Malott, R. (1986) Self-management, rule-governed behavior and everyday life. In H. W. Reese & L. J. Parrott (eds), *Behavior Science: Philosophical, Methodological, and Empirical Advances* (pp.207–228). Hillsdale, NJ: Erlbaum.

Malott, R. W. (1989) The achievement of evasive goals: Control by rules describing contingencies that are not direct acting. In S. C. Hayes (ed.), *Rule-Governed Behavior: Cognition, Contingencies, and Instructional Control* (pp.269–324). New York: Plenum.

Malott, R. W. & Garcia, M. E. (1991) Role of private events in rule-governed behavior. In L. J. Hayes & P. N. Chase (eds), *Dialogues on Verbal Behavior* (pp.237–254). Reno, NV: Context Press.

Manstead, A. S. R. & Parker, D. (1995) Evaluating and extending the theory of planned behaviour. In W. Stroebe & M. Hewstone (eds), *European Review of Social Psychology*, Vol. 6 (pp.69–95). Chichester: Wiley.

Marsh, A. & Matheson, J. (1983) *Smoking Attitudes and Behaviour*. London: HMSO.

McCaul, K. D., Sandgren, A. K., O'Neill, H. K., & Hinsz, V. B. (1993) The value of the theory of planned behavior, perceived control and self-efficacy expectations for predicting health-protective behaviors. *Basic and Applied Social Psychology*, **14**, 231–252.

Mick, D. G. (1992) Levels of subjective comprehension in advertising processing and their relations to ad perceptions, attitudes, and memory. *Journal of Consumer Research*, **18**, 411–424.

Miniard, P. W., Sirdeshmukh, D., & Innis, D. E. (1992) Peripheral persuasion and brand choice. *Journal of Consumer Research*, **19**, 226–239.

Mittal, B. (1988) Achieving higher seat belt usage: The role of habit in bridging the attitude–behavior gap. *Journal of Applied Social Psychology*, **18**, 993–1016.

Moore, J. (1994) On introspection and verbal reports. In S. C. Hayes, L. J. Hayes, M. Sato, & K. Ono (eds), *Behavior Analysis of Language and Cognition* (pp.281–299). Reno, NV: Context Press.

Morojele, N. K. & Stephenson, G. M. (1992) The Minnesota model in the treatment of addiction: A social psychological assessment of changes in beliefs and attributions. *Journal of Community and Applied Social Psychology*, **2**, 254–41.

Morris, E. K. (1991) The contextualism that is behaviour analysis: An alternative to cognitive psychology. In A. Still & A. Costall (eds), *Against Cognitivism: Alternative Foundations for Cognitive Psychology* (pp.123–149). Hemel Hempstead: Harvester Wheatsheaf.

Morris, E. K. (1993a) Behavior analysis and mechanism: One is not the other. *The Behavior Analyst*, **16**, 25–43.

Morris, E. K. (1993b) Mechanism and contextualism in behavior analysis: Just some observations. *The Behavior Analyst*, **16**, 255–268.

Morris, E. K. & Midgley, B. D. (1990) Some historical and conceptual foundations of ecobehavioral analysis. In S. R. Schroeder (ed.), *Ecobehavioral Analysis and Development Disabilities* (pp.1–32). New York: Springer-Verlag.

Morris, E. K., Todd, J. T., Midgley, B. D., Schneider, S. M., & Johnson, L. M. (1990) The history of behavior analysis: some historiography and a bibliography. *The Behavior Analyst*, **13**, 131–158.

Morrison, D. M., Gillmore, M. R., & Baker, S. A. (1995) Determinants of condom use among high-risk heterosexual adults: A test of the theory of reasoned action. *Journal of Applied Social Psychology*, **25**, 651–676.

Morwitz, V. G., Johnson, E., & Schmittlein, D. (1993) Does measuring intent change behavior? *Journal of Consumer Research*, **20**, 46–61.

Myers-Levy, J. (1991) Elaborating on elaboration: The distinction between relational and item-specific elaboration. *Journal of Consumer Research* **18**, 358–367.

Nataraajan, R. (1993) Prediction of choice in a technically complex, essentially intangible, highly experiential and rapidly evolving consumer product. *Psychology and Marketing*, **10**, 367–379.

Netemeyer, R. G., Andrews, J. C., & Durvasala, S. (1993) A comparison of three behavioral intentions models: The case of Valentine's Day gift-giving. *Advances in Consumer Research*, **20**, 135–141.

Netemeyer, R. G. & Burton, S. (1990) Examining the relationships between voting behavior, intention, perceived behavioral control, and expectations. *Journal of Applied Social Psychology*, **20**, 661–680.

Netemeyer, R. G., Burton, S., & Johnston, M. (1991) A comparison of two models for the prediction of volitional and goal-directed behaviors: A confirmatory analysis approach. *Social Psychology Quarterly*, **54**, 87–100.

Nicosia, F. M. (1966) *Consumer Decision Processes.* Englewood Cliffs, NJ: Prentice-Hall.

Nord, W. R. & Peter, J. P. (1980) A behavior modification perspective on marketing. *Journal of Marketing*, **44**, 36–47.

Norman, P. & Smith, L. (1995) The theory of planned behavior and exercise: An investigation into the role of prior behavior, behavioral intentions, and attitude variability. *European Journal of Social Psychology*, **25**, 403–415.

Olson, J. M. & Zanna, M. P. (1993) Attitudes and attitude change. *Annual Review of Psychology*, **44**, 117–154.

Ono, K. (1994) Verbal control of superstitious behavior: Superstitions as false rules. In S. C. Hayes, L. J. Hayes, M. Sato, & K. Ono (eds), *Behavior Analysis of Language and Cognition* (pp.181–196). Reno, NV: Context Press.

O'Shaughnessy, J. (1987) *Why People Buy.* New York: Oxford University Press.

Ostrom, T. M. (1994) Foreword. In R. S. Wyer & T. K. Srull (eds), *Handbook of Social Cognition. Vol. 1: Basic Processes* (pp.vii–xii). Hillsdale, NJ: Erlbaum.

Ostrom, T. M., Prior, J. B., & Simpson, D. D. (1981) The organization of social information. In E. T. Higgins, C. P. Herman, & M. P. Zanna (eds), *Social Cognition: The Ontario Symposium* (pp.3–38). Hillsdale, NJ: Erlbaum.

Overskeid, G. (1995) Cognitive or behaviourist—who can tell the difference? The case of implicit and explicit knowledge. *British Journal of Psychology*, **46**, 312–319.

Parker, D., Manstead, S. R., & Stradling, S. G. (1995) Extending the theory of planned behaviour: The role of the personal norm. *British Journal of Social Psychology*, **34**, 127–138.

Parker, D., Manstead, A. S. R., Stradling, S. G., Reason, J. T., & Baxter, J. S. (1992) Intentions to commit driving violations: An application of the theory of planned behavior. *Journal of Applied Psychology*, **77**, 94–101.

Parker, D., Reason, J. T., Manstead, A. S. R., & Stradling, S. G. (in press) Driving errors, driving violations, and accident involvement. *Ergonomics.*

Parrott, L. J. (1986) The role of postulation in the analysis of inapparent events. In H. W. Reese & L. J. Parrott (eds), *Behavior Science: Philosophical, Methodological, and Empirical Advances* (pp.35–60). Hillsdale, NJ: Erlbaum.

Percy, L. & Rossiter, J. R. (1992) A model of brand awareness and brand attitude advertising strategies. *Psychology and Marketing,* **9,** 262–274.

Petty, R. E. & Cacioppo, J. T. (1984a) The effects of involvement on responses to argument quantity and quality: Central and peripheral routes to persuasion. *Journal of Personality and Social Psychology,* **46,** 69–81.

Petty, R. E. & Cacioppo, J. T. (1984b) Source factors and the elaboration likelihood model of persuasion. *Advances in Consumer Research,* **11,** 668–672.

Petty, R. E. & Cacioppo, J. T. (1986a) *Communication and Persuasion: Central and Peripheral Routes to Attitude Change.* New York: Springer-Verlag.

Petty, R. E. & Cacioppo, J. T. (1986b) The elaboration likelihood model of persuasion. In L. Berkowitz (ed.), *Advances in Experimental Social Psychology,* **19,** 123–205.

Petty, R. E., Priester, J. R. & Wegener, D. T. (1994) Cognitive processes in attitude change. In R. S. Wyer & T. K. Srull (1994) (eds) *Handbook of Social Cognition. Vol. 2: Application.* Second edition. Hillsdale, NJ: Erlbaum.

Petty, R. E., Unnava, R., & Strathman, A. J. (1991) Theories of attitude change. In T. S. Robertson & H. H. Kassarjian (eds), *Handbook of Consumer Behavior* (pp.241–280). Englewood Cliffs, NJ: Prentice-Hall.

Phillips, D. C. (1992) *The Social Scientist's Bestiary: A Guide to Fabled Threats to, and Defences of, Naturalistic Social Science.* Oxford: Pergamon.

Pieters, R. G. M. (1988) Attitude–behavior relationships. In W. F. Van Raaij, G. M. Van Veldhoven, & K.-E. Warneryd (eds), *Handbook of Economic Psychology* (pp.144–204). Dordrecht: Kluwer.

Pieters, R. G. M. & Van Raaij, W. F. (1988) The role of affect in economic behavior. In W. F. Van Raaij, G. M. Van Veldhoven, & K.-E. Warneryd (eds), *Handbook of Economic Psychology* (pp.108–142). Dordrecht: Kluwer.

Pieters, R. G. M. & Verplanken, B. (1995) Intention–behaviour consistency: Effects of consideration set size, involvement and need for cognition. *European Journal of Social Psychology,* **25,** 531–543.

Poppen, R. L. (1989) Some clinical implications of rule-governed behavior. In S. C. Hayes (ed.), *Rule-governed Behavior* (pp.325–357). New York: Plenum.

Raats, M. N., Shepherd, R., & Sparks, P. (1995) Including moral dimensions of choice within the structure of the theory of planned behavior. *Journal of Applied Social Psychology,* **25,** 484–494.

Rachlin, H. (1992) Teleological behaivorism. *American Psychologist,* **47,** 1371–1382.

Rachlin, H. (1995) *Behavior and Mind: The Roots of Modern Psychology.* New York: Oxford University Press.

Ramsey, S. L., Lord, C. G., Wallace, D. S., & Pugh, M. A. (1994) The role of subtypes in attitudes towards superordinate social categories. *British Journal of Social Psychology,* **33,** 387–403.

Randall, D. M. & Wolff, J. A. (1994) The time interval in the intention–behaviour relationship. *British Journal of Social Psychology,* **33,** 405–418.

Rao, A. R. & Monroe, K. B. (1988) The moderating effect of prior knowledge on cue utilization in product evaluations. *Journal of Consumer Research,* **15,** 253–263.

Rao, A. R. & Sieben, W. A. (1992) The effects of prior knowledge on price acceptability and the type of information examined. *Journal of Consumer Research,* **19,** 256–270.

Reese, H. W. (1992a) Rules as nonverbal entities. In S. C. Hayes & L. J. Hayes (eds), *Understanding Verbal Relations* (pp.121–134). Reno, NV: Context Press.

Reese, H. W. (1992b) Problem solving by algorithms and heuristics. In S. C. Hayes & L. J. Hayes (eds), *Understanding Verbal Relations* (pp.153–180). Reno, NV: Context Press.

Reese, H. W. (1994) Cognitive and behavioral approaches to problem-solving. In S. C. Hayes, L. J. Hayes, M. Sato & K. Ono (eds), *Behavior Analysis of Language and Cognition* (pp.197–258). Reno, NV: Context Press.

Ribes, E. (1991) Language as contingency-substitution behavior. In L. J. Hayes & P. N. Chase (eds), *Dialogues on Verbal Behavior* (pp.47–58). Reno, NV: Context Press.

Ribes, E. (1992) An analysis of thinking. In S. C. Hayes & L. J. Hayes (eds), *Understanding Verbal Relations* (pp.209–224). Reno, NV: Context Press.

Richard, L., Dedobbeleer, N., Champagne, F., & Potvin, L. (1994) Predicting child restraint device use: A comparison of two models. *Journal of Applied Social Psychology*, 24, 1837–1847.

Richard, R. (1994) Regret is what you get: the impact of anticipated feelings and emotions on human behaviour. Unpublished doctoral dissertation. University of Amsterdam.

Richard, R., van der Pligt, J., & de Vries, N. (1995) Anticipated affective reactions and prevention of AIDS. *British Journal of Social Psychology*, 34, 9–21.

Richardson, N. J., Shepherd, R., & Elliman, N. A. (1993) Current attitudes and future influences on meat consumption in the UK. *Appetite*, 21, 41–51.

Richelle, M. N. (1993) *B. F. Skinner: A Reappraisal*. London: Erlbaum.

Ronis, D. L., Yates, J. F., & Kirscht, J. P. (1989) Attitudes, decisions and habits as determinants of repeated behavior. In A. R. Pratkanis, S. J. Breckler, & A. G. Greenwald (eds), *Attitude Structure and Function* (pp. 213–240). Hillsdale, NJ: Erlbaum.

Rothschild, M. L. & Gaidis, W. C. (1981) Behavioral learning theory: Its relevance to marketing and promotions. *Journal of Marketing*, 45. 70–78.

Rutter, D. R., Quine, L., & Chesham, D. J. (1995) Predicting safe riding behavior and accidents: Demography, beliefs, and behavior in motorcycling safety. *Psychology and Health*, 10, 369–386.

Sahni, A. (1994) Incorporating perceptions of financial control in purchase prediction: An empirical examination of the theory of planned behavior. *Advances in Consumer Research*, 21, 442–448.

Sarver, V. T. (1983) Ajzen and Fishbein's 'theory of reasoned action': A critical assessment. *Journal for the Theory of Social Behaviour*, 13, 155–163.

Sato, M. & Sugiyama, N. (1994) Lying. In S. C. Hayes, L. J. Hayes, M. Sato, & K. Ono (eds), *Behavior Analysis of Language and Cognition* (pp.165–180). Reno, NV: Context Press.

Schlegel, R. P., Davernas, J. R., & Zanna, M. P. (1992) Problem drinking: A problem for the theory of reasoned action. *Journal of Applied Social Psychology*, 22, 358–385.

Schumann, D. W., Petty, R. E., & Clemons, D. S. (1990) Predicting the effectiveness of different strategies of advertising variation: A test of the repetition-variation hypotheses. *Journal of Consumer Research*, 17, 192–202.

Schwartz, B. & Reisberg, D. (1991) *Learning and Memory*. New York: Norton.

Seibold, D. (1980) Attitude–verbal report–behavior relationships as causal processes: Formulation, test, and communication implications. In D. P. Cushman & R. D. McPhee (eds), *Message–Attitude–Behavior Relationship* (pp.195–244). New York: Academic Press.

Shavitt, S. (1989) Operationalizing functional theories of attitude. In A. R. Pratkanis, S. J. Breckler, & A. G. Greenwald (eds), *Attitude Structure and Function* (pp.311–337). Hillsdale, NJ: Erlbaum.

Shepherd, R., Sparks, P., Bellier, S., & Raats, M. M. (1991/2) Attitudes and choice of flavoured milks: Extension of Fishbein and Ajzen's theory of reasoned action. *Food Quality and Preferences*, 3, 157–164.

Shepherd, R. & Towler, G. (1992) Nutrition knowledge, attitudes and fat intake: Application of the theory of reasoned action. *Journal of Human Nutrition and Dietetics*, 5, 387–397.

Sheppard, B. H., Hartwick, J., & Warshaw, P. R. (1988) The theory of reasoned action: A meta-analysis of past research with recommendations for modifications and future research. *Journal of Consumer Research*, **15**, 325–343.

Sherry, J. F. (1991) Postmodern alternatives: The interpretive turn in consumer research. In T. S. Robertson & H. H. Kassarjian (eds), *Handbook of Consumer Behavior* (pp.548–591). Englewood Cliffs, NJ: Prentice-Hall.

Sherry, J. F. (1995) (ed.), *Contemporary Marketing and Consumer Behavior: An Anthropological Sourcebook*. Newbury Park, CA: Sage.

Shields, R. (1992) (ed.), *Lifestyle Shopping: The Subject of Consumption*. London: Routledge.

Skinner, B. F. (1938) *The Behavior of Organisms*. New York: Century.

Skinner, B. F. (1945) The operational analysis of psychological terms. *Psychological Review*, **52**, 270–277, 291–294.

Skinner, B. F. (1950) Are theories of learning necessary? *Psychological Review*, **57**, 193–216.

Skinner, B. F. (1953) *Science and Human Behavior*. New York: Macmillan.

Skinner, B. F. (1957) *Verbal Behavior*. New York: Century.

Skinner, B. F. (1963) Behaviorism at fifty. *Science*, **140**, 951–958.

Skinner, B. F. (1967) B. F. Skinner. In E. G. Boring & G. Lindzey (eds), *A History of Psychology in Autobiography*, Vol. V. New York: Appleton, Century, Crofts.

Skinner, B. F. (1969) *Contingencies of Reinforcement: A Theoretical Analysis*. Englewood Cliffs, NJ: Prentice-Hall.

Skinner, B. F. (1971) *Beyond Freedom and Dignity*. New York: Knopf.

Skinner, B. F. (1974) *About Behaviorism*. New York: Knopf.

Skinner, B. F. (1988a) Reply to Schnaitter. In A. C. Catania & S. Harnad (eds), *The Selection of Behavior. The Operant Behaviorism of B. F. Skinner: Comments and Consequences* (p.354). New York: Cambridge University Press.

Skinner, B. F. (1988b) Reply to Mackenzie. In A. C. Catania & S. Harnad (eds), *The Selection of Behavior. The Operant Behaviorism of B. F. Skinner: Comments and Consequences* (pp.113–114). New York: Cambridge University Press.

Skinner, B. F. (1989) The behavior of the listener. In S. C. Hayes (ed.), *Rule-governed Behavior: Cognition, Contingencies, and Instructional Control* (pp.85–96). New York: Plenum.

Skinner, B. F. (1990) Can psychology be a science of mind? *American Psychologist*, **45**, 1206–1210.

Smith, S. M., Haugtvedt, C. P., & Petty, R. E. (1994) Need for cognition and the effects of repeated expression on attitude accessibility and extremity. *Advances in Consumer Research*, **21**, 234–237.

Sparks, P., Hedderley, D., & Shepherd, R. (1991) Expectancy-value models of attitudes: A note on the relationship between theory and methodology. *European Journal of Social Psychology*, **21**, 261–271.

Sparks, P., Hedderley, D., & Shepherd, R. (1992) An investigation into the relationship between perceived control, attitude variability and the consumption of two common foods. *European Journal of Social Psychology*, **22**, 55–71.

Sparks, P. & Shepherd, R. (1992) Self-identity and the theory of planned behavior: Assessing the role of identification with 'green consumerism'. *Social Psychology Quarterly*, **55**, 388–399.

Sparks, P., Shepherd, R., & Frewer, L. J. (1995) Assessing and structuring attitudes toward the use of gene technology in food production: The role of perceived ethical obligation. *Basic and Applied Social Psychology*, **16**, 267–285.

Staddon, J. E. R. (1993) *Behaviorism*. London: Duckworth.

Stayman, D. M. & Kardes, F. R. (1992) Spontaneous inference processes in advertising: Effects of need for cognition and self-monitoring on inference generation and utilization. *Journal of Consumer Psychology*, **1**, 125–142.

Sutton, S. A. & Hallett, R. (1989) Understanding seat belt intentions and behavior: A decision making approach. *Journal of Applied Social Psychology*, **19**, 1310–1325.

Sutton, S. A., Marsh, A., & Matheson, J. (1987) Explaining smokers' decisions to stop. Test of an expectancy-value model. *Social Behaviour*, **2**, 35–50.

Taylor, S. & Todd, P. (1995) An integrated model of waste management behavior: A test of household recycling and composting intentions. *Environment and Behavior*, **27**, 603–630.

Terry, D. J., & O'Leary, J. E. (1995) The theory of planned behaviour: The effects of perceived behavioural control and self-efficacy. *British Journal of Social Psychology*, **34**, 199–220.

Tesser, A., Martin, L. L., & Mendolia, M. (1994) The role of thought in changing attitude strength. In R. E. Petty & J. A. Krosnick (eds), *Attitude Strength: Antecedents and Consequences*. Hillsdale, NJ: Erlbaum.

Tesser, A. & Shaffer, D. (1990) Attitudes and attitude change. *Annual Review of Psychology*, **41**, 479–524.

Thompson, K. E., Haziris, N. & Alekos, P. J. (1994) Attitudes and food choice behaviour. *British Food Journal*, **96**(11), 9–13.

Thompson, K. E., Thompson, N. J., & Hill, R. W. (1995) The role of attitude, normative and control beliefs in drink choice behaviour. Unpublished paper. Cranfield University.

Thompson, R. F. (1994) Behaviorism and neuroscience. *Psychological Review*, **101**, 259–265.

Timmermans, H. (1993) Retail environments and spatial shopping behavior. In T. Garling & R. G. Gollege (eds), *Behavior and Environment: Psychological and Geographical Approaches* (pp.342–377). Amsterdam: Elsevier.

Todd, J. T. & Morris, E. K. (1992) Case histories in the great power of steady misrepresentation. *American Psychologist*, **47**, 1441–1453.

Towler, G. & Shepherd, R. (1991/92) Modification of Fishbein and Ajzen's theory of reasoned action to predict chip consumption. *Food Quality and Preference*, **3**, 37–45.

Towler, G. & Shepherd, R. (1992) Application of Fishbein and Ajzen's expectancy-value model of understanding fat intake. *Appetite*, **18**, 15–27.

Trafimow, D. & Fishbein, M. (1995) Do people really distinguish between behavioural and normative beliefs? *British Journal of Social Psychology*, **34**, 257–266.

Triandis, H. C. (1977) *Interpersonal Behavior*. Monterey, CA: Brooks/Cole.

Triandis, H. (1980) Values, attitudes and interpersonal behavior. In H. E. Howe & M. M. Page (eds), *Nebraska Symposium on Motivation 1979*, Vol. 27 (pp.195–259). Lincoln: University of Nebraska Press.

Tripp, C., Jensen, T. D., & Carlson, L. (1994) The effects of multiple product endorsements by celebrities on consumers' attitudes and intentions. *Journal of Consumer Research*, **20**, 535–547.

Tversky, A. & Kahneman, D. (1974) Judgment under uncertainty: Heuristics and biases. *Science*, **185**, 1124–1131.

Tybout, A. M. & Artz, N. (1994) Consumer Psychology. *Annual Review of Psychology*, **45**, 131–169.

Upmeyer, A. (1989) (ed.), *Attitudes and Behavioral Decisions*. New York: Springer-Verlag.

Van den Putte, B. (1993) On the theory of reasoned action. Unpublished doctoral dissertation. University of Amsterdam.

van Knippenberg, D., Lossie, N., & Wilke, H. (1994) In-group prototypicality and persuasion: Determinants of heuristic and systematic message processing. *British Journal of Social Psychology*, **33**, 289–300.

Van Raaij, W. F. (1988) Information processing and decision making. Cognitive aspects of economic behavior. In W. F. Van Raaij, G. M. Van Veldhoven, & K.-E.

Warneryd (1998) (eds), *Handbook of Economic Psychology* (pp.74–106). Dordrecht: Kluwer.

Van Raaij, W. F. (1991) The formation and use of expectations in consumer decision making. In T. S. Robertson & H. H. Kassarjian (eds), *Handbook of Consumer Behaviour* (pp.401–418). Englewood Cliffs, NJ: Prentice-Hall.

van Ryn, M. & Vinokur, A. D. (1990) The role of experimentally manipulated self-efficacy in determining job search behavior among the unemployed. Unpublished manuscript. University of Michigan.

Vaughan, M. E. (1991) Toward a methodology for studying verbal behavior. In L. J. Hayes & P. N. Chase (eds), *Dialogues on Verbal Behavior* (pp.82–84). Reno, NV: Context Press.

Warshaw, P. R., Sheppard, B. H., & Hartwick, J. (1990) The intention and self-prediction of goals and behaviors. In R. P. Bagozzi (ed.) *Advances in Marketing Communications Research*. Greenwich, CT: JAI.

Watters, A. E. (1989) Reasoned/intuitive action: an individual difference moderator of the attitude–behavior relationship in the 1988 US presidential election. Unpublished thesis. University of Michigan.

Wearden, J. (1988) Some neglected problems in the analysis of human operant behaviour. In G. C. L. Davey & C. Cullen (eds), *Human Operant Conditioning and Behaviour Modification*. Chichester: Wiley.

White, K. M., Terry, D. J., & Hogg, M. A. (1994) Safer sex behavior: The role of attitudes, norms and control factors. *Journal of Applied Social Psychology*, **24**, 2164–2192.

Wicker, A. W. (1969) Attitude versus actions: The relationship of verbal and overt behavioural responses to attitude objects. *Social Issues*, **25**, 41–78.

Wicker, A. W. (1971) An examination of the 'other variables' explanation of attitude–behavior inconsistency. *Journal of Personality and Social Psychology*, **19**, 18–30.

Wittenbraker, J., Gibbs, B. L., & Khale, L. R. (1983) Seat belt attitudes, habits, and behaviors: An adaptive amendment to the Fishbein model. *Journal of Applied Social Psychology*, **13**, 406–421.

Wyer, R. S. & Srull, T. K. (1986) Human cognition in its social context. *Psychological Review*, **93**, 322–359.

Wyer, R. S. & Srull, T. K. (1989) *Memory and Cognition in its Social Context*. Hillsdale, NJ: Erlbaum.

Wyer, R. S. & Srull, T. K. (1994a) (eds), *Handbook of Social Cognition. Vol. 1: Basic Processes*. Second edition. Hillsdale, NJ: Erlbaum.

Wyer, R. S. & Srull, T. K. (1994b) (eds), *Handbook of Social Cognition. Vol. 2: Application*. Second edition. Hillsdale, NJ: Erlbaum.

Yi, Y. (1990) The indirect effects of advertisements designed to change product attribute beliefs. *Psychology and Marketing*, **7**, 47–63.

Zettle, R. D. & Hayes, S. C. (1982) Rule-governed behavior: A potential framework for cognitive-behavioral therapy. In P. C. Kendall (ed.), *Advances in Cognitive-behavioral Research and Therapy* (pp.73–117). New York: Academic Press.

Chapter 7

DRUG AND ALCOHOL PROGRAMS IN THE WORKPLACE: A REVIEW OF RECENT LITERATURE

Michael M. Harris
University of Missouri
and
Michael L. Trusty
Anheuser–Busch Companies

INTRODUCTION

Although workplace drug and alcohol programs have become quite common in the USA, Industrial/Organizational (I/O) psychologists have played a relatively minor role in this area. The purpose of this chapter is to acquaint and update I/O psychologists on issues and problems in this area. The present chapter focuses on research published towards the end of 1991 through 1995. Readers interested in a review covering an earlier period of time should examine Harris and Heft (1992).

The chapter is divided into three major sections. First, research on workplace drug testing programs will be discussed. Second, literature on Employee Assistance Programs (EAPs) will be summarized. Following each of these sections, suggestions for future research will be provided. Finally, we conclude with a review of research on drug and alcohol programs in parts of the world besides North America, and offer a brief overview of legal issues affecting workplace drug and alcohol programs.

We turn now to workplace drug testing. Following a brief introduction to this topic, we review research on different types of drug tests, and summarize findings regarding the relationship between drug use and job outcomes. We then proceed to describe literature on applicant/employee reactions to drug screening programs. We conclude with a discussion of criticisms of drug tests, and offer suggestions for needed research on this topic.

International Review of Industrial and Organizational Psychology, 1997 Volume 12
Edited by C.L. Cooper and I.T. Robertson. © 1997 John Wiley & Sons Ltd.

WORKPLACE DRUG TESTING

Introduction

Harris and Heft (1992) found that a large number of companies in the US used drug testing, and that researchers had considered several different types of tests, the validity and cost-effectiveness of drug screening, and applicant/employee reactions to these tests. A review of recent literature indicates that despite some controversies regarding such tests (e.g. see below), drug testing has not waned. Murphy and Thornton (1992), for example, surveyed 324 companies that recruited students from Colorado State University (of which 57% responded) and found that 41% tested candidates and/or employees for drug use. Interestingly, nearly a third of the companies with a drug testing program did random testing; almost 70% reported that a positive test result was confirmed by a second test. Murphy and Thornton reported results on a number of other interesting issues, such as the policies followed if an employee fails the test, test administration and program management, and general policies regarding drug screening. Readers interested in establishing drug testing programs and policies will find this paper of value in understanding what other organizations are doing.

Types of Tests

Harris and Heft (1992) categorized drug tests into three types: physiological, paper-and-pencil, and impairment-based measures. They noted that the first category was by far the most popular, and included procedures such as urinalysis, blood, and hair tests, as well as other less well-known measures (e.g. saliva tests). Use of paper-and-pencil measures appeared to be far less common; impairment tests, which generally relied on hand–eye coordination tasks, were recommended by some drug testing critics, but relatively little seemed to be known about them. Following Harris and Heft, we begin with a review of the physiological tests, followed by discussion of paper-and-pencil measures and impairment tests.

Physiological

Harris and Heft (1992, 1993) observed that urinalysis was, despite some problems, the most popular procedure for drug screening. Simmering and Ones (1994) reviewed numerous other physiological screening procedures, including hair analysis, plasma or blood analysis, fingernail tests and saliva analysis. Each procedure had advantages and disadvantages. Perhaps because urinalysis testing is the most popular, and many of the initial problems with this technique (e.g. poor reliability) have been reduced (Harris & Heft, 1993), no new research on urinalysis was located. However, a number of studies and reports on hair testing were found. These are summarized next.

Hair testing

Hair testing has a number of potential advantages over urinalysis. One major advantage is that the collection of the specimen is much less invasive than urinalysis. Hair also requires no special storage, while urine samples do. Hair samples last considerably longer than do urine samples. Finally, hair samples can determine use of drugs several months prior to the test and can indicate the amount and patterns of drugs used (Mieczkowski, 1992; Simmering & Ones, 1994). On the other hand, hair tests do have some shortcomings. Hair tests will not indicate very recent drug use (e.g. within five to seven days). When head hair is not available, axillary and pubic hair must be used, which may absorb drug traces differently. Third, questions have been raised as to whether passive exposure can affect the hair test, the impact of various approaches to try to 'beat' the test (e.g. washing of one's hair), and whether different types of hair (e.g. fine versus coarse) will affect the analysis (Mieczkowski, 1992). Major groups, such as the National Institute for Drug Abuse, have concluded that insufficient evidence exists to date for hair testing to be accepted as an appropriate method for drug screening (Normand, Lempert, & O'Brien, 1994). The chief concern raised by these groups is that there are no generally accepted analytic procedures or standards for hair tests.

Although we found no studies in the workplace setting, some studies conducted in the penal system have compared hair tests to urinalysis. For example, Feucht, Stephens, and Walker (1994) found that hair analysis identified many more cocaine users (50) than did urinalysis (8), as did Mieczkowski and Newell (1993). However, equal numbers of marijuana users were identified by both procedures. The authors concluded that hair analysis may be more effective in identifying cocaine users than marijuana users. Because there was no way to determine actual drug use in these populations, an alternative explanation is that the hair test leads to more false positives than the urinalysis test.

In sum, despite increased interest in the hair test, it remains to be seen whether this procedure really is an improvement over urinalysis. Anecdotally, we know of at least one large organization that is using hair tests. Whether such tests become as commonly used as the urinalysis test remains to be seen.

Paper-and-pencil tests

Harris and Heft (1992) summarized a few papers addressing paper-and-pencil tests of alcohol and drug use. They concluded that 'results across studies are inconsistent, few validity studies have been published or even reported' (p.247) and many issues remained as to their use in the workplace. An examination of recent literature showed this state of affairs has changed little. Schmidt, Viswesvaran, and Ones (1993) reported a meta-analysis of the validity of integrity tests for predicting drug and alcohol use. Based on 50 studies (N = 25 594), they found corrected validities to range between 0.23 to 0.48 depending on the nature of the sample (e.g. employee versus student) and the specific criterion (i.e. alcohol versus illegal drug). In all cases, the lower 90% credibility value was greater than zero. They concluded that the operational validity is probably 0.30, and that the tests were of value in reducing substance abuse among employees. The studies used for the meta-analysis, however, suffered from at least two shortcomings. First, all of the studies were based on concurrent validation strategies, although predictive studies are more relevant (Schmidt, Viswesvaran, & Ones, 1993). Second, almost all of the studies used self-admissions as criteria. Studies using external criteria may reveal different results (Sackett & Harris, 1984).

Marcoulides, Mills, and Unterbrink (1993) examined the Drug Avoidance Scale (DAS), a paper-and-pencil test, and its relationship with a urinalysis test, for 246 job applicants for a security service company. Marcoulides, Mills and Unterbrink indicated that there was a strong relationship between the DAS and the urinalysis test, but did not provide an effect size.

In sum, despite some interest in paper-and-pencil measures of drug and alcohol use, there appears to be very little new here. Issues such as faking would need to be carefully considered with such measures. It seems likely that at least for the time being, companies will continue to rely on measures other than self-reported attitudes towards drugs or self-reported use.

Impairment-based tests

Harris and Heft (1992) noted that some critics of drug testing advocated an impairment-based test, which would seem to provide the most direct assessment of performance problems. However, like Harris and Heft, we were unable to locate any scientific studies examining such a test. Comer (1993) described a number of potential advantages of one impairment-based test, which required employees to use a joy stick to maintain a cursor in the center of a video screen (readers may note that this seems quite similar to certain video games!). The advantages of this device included minimum testing time (about one minute), reasonable costs (about $100–$200 per employee per year), immediate results, and sensitivity to a wide variety of work impairments (Comer, 1993). Problems with the technique clearly remain, however. The general manager of a transportation company that used this impairment-based test found that the difficulty of the test varied from day to day, which would probably cause frequent false positives and false negatives. The general manager even reported that he passed the test after he had, in his opinion, become too intoxicated to drive a vehicle (Comer, 1994). Hence, anecdotal evidence indicates that impairment-based tests also have shortcomings.

Is Drug Use Related to Job Outcomes?

Although there have been numerous studies addressing the relationship between drug use and job outcomes, the literature is inconsistent. One reason for the inconsistency is that a number of different criteria have been examined, and as described below, the relationships appear to differ from criterion to criterion. Second, some studies have controlled for various factors (e.g. age) in assessing the relationship between drug use and job outcomes, while others have not. Third, even if a statistical relationship is located between drug use and job outcomes, the *size* of the relationship may be small (Harris & Heft, 1993). What follows next is an overview of research on drug use with different criteria, including absenteeism/turnover, accidents, other job behavior, and wages.

Drug use and absenteeism/turnover

A number of studies, including McDaniel (1988), Kandel and Yamaguchi (1987), and Zwerling, Ryan, and Orav (1990), have examined the relationship between drug use and turnover. Although these studies have used a variety of different measures of drug use (e.g. self-report, urinalysis), they consistently report significant relationships with turnover (Normand, Lempert, & O'Brien, 1994). However, examination of the magnitude of this relationship indicates that it is relatively small; for example, McDaniel reported a correlation of 0.08 between self-reported drug use and turnover. Harris and Heft (1993) estimated a correlation of 0.04 between urinalysis tests and involuntary turnover in Normand, Salyards, and Mahoney's (1990) study.

Accidents

While many people assume that drug and alcohol use is a frequent cause of workplace accidents, research shows mixed findings regarding the relationship between drug use and accidents. For example, in similar studies of US Postal workers, Normand, Salyards, and Mahoney (1990) did not find a relationship between drug use and accidents, while Zwerling, Ryan, and Orav (1990) reported a significant relationship between them. Normand, Lempert, and O'Brien (1994) provided a comprehensive review of this literature, and reported mixed results as to the relationship between drug use and accidents. They offered several reasons for this. For example, workplace accidents are relatively rare; as discussed below, the number of employees working while intoxicated is reasonably small, though it probably differs from industry to industry. Moreover, workers who are impaired may simply miss work or avoid performing dangerous tasks. Yet another possibility is that the emphasis on drug and alcohol prevention and testing and extensive publicity to various workplace accidents (e.g. the *Exxon Valdez* oil tanker incident in 1989) has greatly reduced the number of workers who are intoxicated on the job. Finally, Normand, Lempert, and O'Brien (1994) suggested that alcohol and drug use was related to accident rate in the transportation industry; however there was less evidence of this relationship in other industries. Thus, while there is some evidence for a relationship between drug and alcohol use and accidents, the magnitude appears to be smaller than people have assumed.

Other job behavior

Some recent research has examined the relationship between drug use and employees' job attitudes. Lehman and Simpson (1992) found that self-reported drug use was significantly related to a variety of self-reported behavior on the job, including antagonistic work behavior (e.g. arguing with coworkers), even after controlling for factors such as job satisfaction and pay level. However, all of the data were based on self-reports.

Wages

While drug and alcohol use has been found either to be significantly related or not at all related to higher turnover and other problems at the workplace, some research has found greater drug use to be related to higher wages earned by employees. Gill and Michaels (1992) found that after controlling for self-selection effects as well as various demographic factors, users of illegal drugs on average earned higher wages than non-users. Further, users of 'hard' drugs were more likely to be employed than workers who did not use such drugs. Register and Williams (1992) found that when on-the-job and long-term marijuana use was controlled for, general marijuana use was related to higher wages. However, both on-the-job and long-term marijuana use were associated with lower wages. Register and Williams interpreted their results as suggesting that 'after-hours use [of marijuana] might actually increase the worker's productivity on the following day if such use tends to reduce stress and anxiety' (p. 445).

In sum, different studies have come to different conclusions about the relationship between drug use and job outcomes. Harris and Heft (1993) raised a number of questions about this relationship relative to other tests. They pointed out that if the purpose of the drug test is for preemployment screening, there may be other methods (e.g. cognitive ability tests) that are just as valid, if not more valid. They also asked whether drug testing would provide *incremental* validity over other tests; for example, if an organization already uses a cognitive ability test, the drug test may provide little or no additional validity. In defense of the use of drug testing, however, Harris and Heft (1993) pointed to certain advantages of this approach over other traditional tests, such as greater acceptability to unions and less concern over adverse impact problems. Third, they questioned whether there is a linear relationship between drug use and job outcomes. That is, they suggested that low drug use may not negatively affect performance, such as suggested by Register and Williams (1992). In response to this criticism, Harris and Heft (1993) cited a study by Blank and Fenton (1989) that supported a linear relationship such that even low levels of drug use were associated with higher rates of turnover compared with non-drug users.

Why is Drug Use Associated with Workplace Problems?

Assuming that drug use is in fact associated with workplace problems, such as turnover, accidents, and other behavior, some have asked *why* this relationship exists. Harris and Heft (1992) offered two possible explanations. One, use of drugs may create physiological and behavioral changes. Secnd, drug use and job behavior may be related because they are both caused by a third variable, such as a propensity for deviant behavior. Or, both explanations may be right (Normand, Lempert, & O'Brien, 1994, p.132). One recent study addressed these possibilities. Holcom and Lehman (1995) obtained self-reports of substance use, job performance, and general deviance (e.g. attitudes toward risk-taking and non-conformity). Although substance use was highly correlated with job performance, a structural equations model revealed that substance use was not related to job performance once general deviance was taken into account. This study, then, supports the second explanation for a link between drug use and job behavior, namely, that they have a spurious relationship.

Applicant/Employee Reactions

Harris and Heft (1993) reviewed a number of studies addressing applicant and employee reactions to drug testing programs, and highlighted conflicting results. Specifically, Crant and Bateman (1990) found that applicants were less favorably predisposed to an organization with a drug testing program; Rosse and Ringer (1991) found that the presence of such a program had little or no effect on subjects. Harris and Heft offered two methodological reasons to explain the differences. Harris and Heft also reviewed literature suggesting that the nature of the job affects perceptions of the drug screening, and concluded that perceived danger of the job, particularly to the public, was a major determinant of its acceptability. Finally, Harris and Heft noted two studies that had been done in an actual setting. One of these studies compared the importance of procedural justice issues to perceptions of outcome fairness, and found that the former was more critical. A second study, which involved college students' drug testing, revealed that despite many concerns on the part of participants, they felt that the program offered some advantages (e.g. existence of the drug test provided a socially acceptable reason for not using drugs). Harris and Heft (1993) offered several suggestions for future research, including application of research on recruitment, continued investigation of the specific components that affect employee perceptions, and greater use of field rather than laboratory studies.

Recent research on employee and applicant reactions to drug testing has produced some interesting results. First, Mastrangelo (1995) examined undergraduate students' reactions to companies with and without preemployment and random drug screening. Contrary to earlier studies, he found that subjects generally *preferred* an organization that had random drug screening. He also reported a significant interaction with attitudes towards drug testing, such that subjects who favored drug testing were far more favorable towards a company that did such screening. Subjects who were extremely opposed to drug testing were more favorable towards companies that did not have such programs. Kravitz, Stinson, and Chavez (1994) compared college students' ratings of the overall appropriateness and invasiveness of a variety of employment procedures, including interviews, references, personality tests, and cognitive ability tests. They found that averaged across different target jobs (e.g. production worker, manager), a drug test was seen as only slightly less appropriate than a job skills test and accomplishment record, and more appropriate than many other devices including references, cognitive ability tests, and personality measures. In terms of invasiveness, a drug test was about average compared to other procedures: it was viewed as more invasive than references or a cognitive ability test, but less invasive than an honesty test, personality measure, or criminal record check.

Based on these results, it would appear that the use of drug testing has become more acceptable to employees and job applicants. Indeed, contrary to earlier studies, the results from Kravitz, Stinson, and Chavez (1994) suggested that the drug test appears to be at least as well regarded as tools commonly recommended by I/O psychologists, such as personality and cognitive ability tests. Whether this indicates that people have come to see the advantages of drug testing, have become resigned to such procedures, or some traditional tests are held in much lower regard than I/O psychologists realize, is unclear. In support of the first explanation, Verespej (1992) reported a significant decrease in the number of respondents (who were predominantly professional employees and middle- and top-level managers) who regarded drug testing as an invasion of privacy in 1991 compared to a survey done in 1987. Specifically, while 30% viewed drug testing as an invasion of privacy in 1987, fewer than 20% perceived drug testing as an invasion of privacy in 1991. Respondents provided a number of reasons for their support of such screening, including concern over safety, negative impact of drug use on quality and productivity, and perceived financial costs of drug use to the company.

Several recent studies were found that addressed Harris and Heft's (1993) call for further research on the effects of drug testing program features. Crant and Bateman (1993) manipulated the consequence of the testing program (i.e. rehabilitation or termination) and the type of testing (for cause or random). They found that neither factor affected college students' attitudes toward, intention to apply, or willingness to accept a job offer. Raciot and Williams (1993) examined the effect of presence or absence of prior warning of test, testing program consequence (i.e. rehabilitation versus termination), and relevance of safty to the job (i.e. job could lead to serious accidents versus job unlikely to lead to harm) in an experimental design using college students. Raciot and Williams found significant effects of the latter two factors on such variables as the perceived invasiveness and fairness of the testing program; warning did not have a significant effect. Kravitz and Brock (in press) conducted a series of laboratory studies with college students that tested five independent variables: consequences of the testing program (i.e. termination versus rehabilitation), relevance of safety to the job, false positive rate, false negative rate, and the ability of the test to distinguish between current drug impairment and previous drug use. Kravitz and Brock found at least some evidence to support the effect of all five factors on attitudes toward the testing program. Another variable considered by Kravitz and Brock was belief in a just world; as hypothesized, subjects who believed in a just world were more likely to support a drug testing program.

While all of the above studies were performed in a laboratory setting with college students responding to descriptions of hypothetical organizations, Tepper and Braun (1995) examined actual employee reactions to their organizations' random drug testing program. Because the drug testing was required by Federal law, and the respondents worked in jobs where safety issues were of concern, one might expect that reactions would be relatively positive. Mean responses to the three variables which formed the criterion (all of which addressed perceived invasiveness; e.g. 'The drug testing policy in my company is an invasion of privacy'), were roughly neutral. A hierarchical regression analysis indicated that four predictors accounted for 35% of the variance in the criterion: number of times tested (the more often tested, the more negative the reactions), managerial status (managers had more positive attitudes), perceived accuracy (the more accurate the test was perceived to be, the more positive attitudes were), and perceived severity (the more severe the consequences of being drug positive, the more negative the attitudes).

Although the above studies suggest a great deal of congruence between laboratory and field research, Tepper (1994) demonstrated that employees may respond quite differently to a drug screening program, depending on whether or not they have been subjected to the test. In a series of three independent studies, Tepper found that while safety and drug test consequences interacted together to affect perceptions of the program in a laboratory study, a completely different effect was found with employees responding to an actual drug screen. A third study revealed that the dimensions considered by the respondents differ, depending on whether or not they had actually been tested. While employees who had not been tested were most concerned about *distributive* justice aspects, employees who had been tested were more concerned about *procedural* justice aspects.

Drug Testing: An Ongoing Debate

Despite the popularity of workplace drug testing, debate among academics regarding the use of such screening tools has appeared. The arguments against drug testing, and responses to them, are reviewed next.

Drug tests are not valid predictors

Critics of drug testing have argued that evidence for the validity of drug tests is minimal at best (Comer, 1994; Crow & Hartman, 1992; MacDonald, Wells & Fry, 1993). Although the studies reviewed above indicated at least some relationship does exist, the magnitude appears small. In response to this criticism, one might respond that although the relationship is small, there are studies indicating that drug tests are at least somewhat predictive of some job outcomes, including accidents. If we do find that drug tests are predictive of an outcome such as accidents, wouldn't it be unfair to *not* use them? At the same time, as discussed below, several reasons for use of drug testing besides prediction, such as deterrence, have been suggested. Thus, it is possible that drug tests serve some important purposes besides prediction, even though empirical research has not yet been conducted on these issues.

Drug tests are not cost-effective

Even assuming that drug tests are valid predictors of various job outcomes, they may not be cost-effective (Hartman & Crow, 1993; MacDonald, Wells, & Fry, 1993). As summarized by Harris and Heft (1993), the cost-effectiveness or utility of drug testing is a source of much disagreement. Part of the reason for the disagreement is that the two major studies which estimated the cost-effectiveness of drug testing (Normand, Salyards, & Mahoney, 1990 and Zwerling, Ryan, & Orav, 1992) used quite different formulas. Based on their formula, Zwerling, Ryan, and Orav even argued that drug testing was not really cost-effective in Normand, Salyards, and Mahoney's (1990) study. Hartman and Crow (1993) pointed to additional problems with utility analyses, and argued that utility analysis may not provide accurate estimates.

A proponent of drug testing might counter that while utility analysis may not be completely accurate, it is a widely accepted procedure for determining cost-effectiveness (Boudreau, 1991). Moreover, Normand, Salyards, and Mahoney (1990) used standard formulas that have been carefully developed and tested elsewhere (e.g. Cascio, 1987). While certain gains may be slightly overestimated, Normand, Salyards, and Mahoney probably underestimated other gains. From a different perspective, Cavanaugh and Prasad (1994) offered a variety of reasons, besides increased productivity and fewer accidents, as to why companies use drug and alcohol testing. Among the reasons offered are the need to reinforce rationality, uphold moral authority, retain an image of control, and signal corporate responsibility and concern for societal problems. Of course, some might argue that these purposes themselves are misguided or wrong. However, it has been suggested that a preemployment drug testing program may serve as a deterrent, as job candidates who use drugs decide to withdraw from the selection process or simply never apply for the job (Harris & Heft, 1993). Similarly, a random or 'for cause' drug testing program may serve as a deterrent to drug use and serve as a signal to employees that safety is important. Such effects may be difficult to study, but could represent an important organizational benefit.

Drug use is not a prevalent problem

Some have argued that the prevalency of substance use in the workplace is much lower than people think (Crow & Hartman, 1992). The implication is that low prevalence reduces the need for drug testing. This is certainly the case from a predictive viewpoint. Relatedly, some criticize drug testing on the grounds that it ignores other forms of substance abuse, particularly alcohol consumption, that are far more problematic (Comer, 1994).

Normand, Lempert, and O'Brien (1994) provided an excellent summary of research examining the prevalence of substance abuse, including unpublished surveys. Results from a major study, the National Household Survey (conducted in 1990), indicated that for full-time employed workers 18 and older, 7% had used an illicit drug during the past month, while 6.8% indicated heavy alcohol consumption. Workers in some industries reported higher rates of drug and alcohol consumption than others. For example, full-time male workers between the ages of 18 and 34 in the construction industry were the most likely group to take illegal drugs in the past month (20%) and to engage in heavy alcohol use (26%). Professionals were least likely to use illegal drugs (only 9% reported usage); the least likely workers to engage in heavy drinking were in the repair services (9%). Based on these findings, as well as results from other sources, Normand, Lempert, and O'Brien suggested that overall 'approximately 7 percent of workers reported having used an illicit drug and approximately 6 percent reported having drunk heavily in the last month' (p.99). Do these results suggest that drug use is too rare to make a testing program cost effective? Not necessarily. Utility analysis indicates that the cost-effectiveness of a test depends on several factors, only one of which is the base rate (Boudreau, 1991). These data also suggest that certain industries may find greater benefits from a drug testing program than others. It is also interesting that heavy drinking rates were quite comparable to rates of illegal drug use. The assumption, then, that alcohol use is much more of a problem than illicit subtance use may be incorrect.

Drug testing is unfair to applicants and employees

While there are various laws that restrict or even ban the use of drug testing in certain cases, some industries require drug testing (Harris & Heft, 1992).

Several researchers have argued, however, that drug testing is unfair to applicants and employees. There are a number of different points to this objection. First, some argue that applicants and employees should not be required to disclose information about or be subjected to tests for matters not relevant to the company (Comer, 1994). Since drug use after work hours may not have an effect on on-the-job behavior (and even if it does, so do many other activities, such as staying up late at night), this argument suggests that drug testing (other than perhaps 'for cause' reasons) would be unfair, much as asking about a person's age, race, or religion would be deemed irrelevant and unfair. A proponent of drug testing might respond that this issue gets at where one draws the limit between privacy and the company's right to know. While age, race, and religion are personal matters, the fact that one might have committed a crime at some point, for example, is something the company has a right to know. Similarly, illicit drug use, which is a crime in the USA, is something the organization has the right to know about because it may affect work.

Second, some argue that the drug validity evidence that does exist is merely due to a spurious relationship between race, job outcomes, and drug test (Comer, 1994; Horgan, 1990). In response to this claim, Harris and Heft (1993) pointed to research indicating that race neither moderates (e.g. McDaniel, 1988) nor mediates (e.g. Normand, Salyards, & Mahoney, 1990; Zwerling, Ryan, & Orav, 1990) the relationship between drug test and job outcomes. Moreover, critics have not offered empirical data to support the notion of a spurious relationship.

A third point critics raise is that drug testing is disliked by applicants and employees (Comer, 1994). In response to this argument, as reviewed above, recent research indicates that many respondents actually prefer organizations that do drug testing. In addition, research summarized above indicates that employees may feel either positively or negatively about a drug screening program, depending on how it is designed and implemented.

In sum, we agree that drug testing is a debatable issue. Our hope is that the debate serves as an impetus for further empirical research in the area, and as a stimulus for more careful thinking about the advantages and disadvantages of drug testing.

Workplace Drug Testing: Suggestions for Future Research

Based on our review, we have several suggestions for future research on workplace drug testing programs. One area of research that requires further investigation concerns the relationship between drug use and job outcomes. Although this same recommendation was offered by Harris and Heft (1992), more work is still needed on this issue, using a variety of different criteria. It will also be important to continue to examine different demographic, attitudinal, and situational factors that may mediate or moderate this relationship.

Although a relatively large data base has been gathered for some criteria (e.g. accidents), there is a noticeable lack of research for other criteria (e.g. general job performance).

A second important area for research is to compare different tests in terms of reliability, validity, and cost-effectiveness. Far too little is known about how procedures such as urinalysis, hair tests, and paper-and-pencil measures compare along these dimensions. It is possible that the best test to use will depend on the particular purpose. For example, a hair test may be most useful for random tests, while urinalysis might be most appropriate for preemployment screening. Perhaps most importantly, research is needed to examine all possible effects of a drug testing program. For example, do such programs really have a deterrence effect? Do certain types of programs have a negative effect on employee attitudes and behavior (e.g. turnover)?

Third, more research is needed to examine *why* drug use is related to job outcomes. While two possibilities were described here, research on wage advantages of drug users suggests that the linkage may be much more complex. For example, it is possible that while drug use has detrimental effects on certain types of performance (e.g. eye–hand coordination), its relaxant effect faciliates other types of performance.

Fourth, more studies are needed, particularly in actual settings, to understand applicant and employee reactions to drug testing programs. Research on applicant reactions to various tests (e.g., Macan, Avedon, Paese, & Smith, 1994; Smither, Reilly, Millsap, Pearlman, & Stoffey, 1993) has suggested a variety of factors, such as perceived face validity, that affect perceptions. Research comparing different types of drug screening programs (e.g. preemployment testing, random testing, 'for cause' testing) might find that different factors affect perceptions of the tests. Further, research by Tepper (1994) points to the need to separately examine employees who have been tested and those who have not been tested.

Finally, practically all of the published research has examined applicant or employee reactions to *urinalysis tests*. While some researchers have assumed that employees and applicants will react more favorably to alternative tests (e.g. the hair test; an impairment test), there is no empirical research to support those assertions. Field studies regarding this issue are sorely needed.

EMPLOYEE ASSISTANCE PROGRAMS

Harris and Heft (1992) divided research on EAPs into four basic areas: supervisor reactions to EAPs, employee reactions to EAPs, EAP adoption/implementation, and evaluation of EAPs. We first discuss some descriptive information regarding EAPs, followed by a review of recent literature in each of these four areas.

EAPs: Descriptive Information

As reported by Harris and Heft (1992), EAPs have become popular in industry, business, and government in the last few decades; there is no evidence to suggest any change in this state of affairs. According to Blum and Roman (1992), almost half of full-time employees in the USA who are not self-employed have access to an employer-provided EAP. Despite their popularity, research indicates that they are not frequently used. Harley (1991) found that on average, supervisors referred only one subordinate out of 100 over a six year period. Burke (1994) found that fewer than 6% of one company's employees had used the EAP, presumably at any point during their employment with the organization. Park (1992) reported that out of a total employee population of just under 2000, only 621 employees had initiated contact with the EAP staff over the last six years. Assuming the number of employees remained the same over the six years, this represents a usage rate of about 5%, which meshes with the estimate by Blum and Roman (1992). Given that most EAP programs address issues besides drug and alcohol use, such as depression, the percentage of workers using them seems quite low.

In the largest data base of employees using an EAP (Blum & Roman, 1992; 6400 employees who used an EAP from 84 work facilities), there was a nearly even mix of men (45%) and women (55%), most of whom were white (70%) or black (22%). Over half (52%) were married. Employees represented all levels of education, job level, and income. In terms of referral source, employees using the EAP reported a number of agents that were influential in their decision to seek help. The most commonly cited influential agents (in terms of the number of employees reporting) were: self (29%), supervisor (31%), coworker who used the EAP (25%) and coworker who had not used the EAP (25%). The employee's spouse was rated as influential by 19% of the respondents. Interestingly, the company records indicated the following sources for referral agent: self (44%), informal supervisor (16%), formal supervisor (11%), and peer (14%).

Finally, EAP staff diagnosed most clients as having two or more problems. Somewhat surprisingly, the most commonly diagnosed problem was psychological/emotional issues (44% of the clients were diagnosed as such), followed by marital problems (28%) and other family problems (31%). Relatively few clients were diagnosed with either an alcohol or drug problem (16% were diagnosed with an alcohol problem, 3% with a cocaine problem, and 4% with 'other' drug problems). Drug and alcohol use, then, appears to be much less of a factor in EAP use than one would imagine (though a portion of clients came to the EAP because of drug or alcohol use of a family member). One implication is that EAPs are used far more often for problems other than alcohol and drugs. Whether employees are going to other help sources for treatment of alcohol and drug problems, or whether they tend to ignore these problems and avoid seeking help, is unclear.

Supervisor Reactions to EAPs

Harris and Heft (1992) identified a number of studies addressing the role of the supervisor in EAP referrals. Much of this literature was based on a model developed by Gerstein and his colleagues (e.g. Gerstein, 1990), which adapted a bystander intervention theory from social psychology to explain the conditions under which supervisors would be willing to refer a subordinate.

In the last few years, Gerstein and his colleagues continued to examine the role of the supervisor in EAP referrals. Gerstein, Lynn, and Brown (1991) examined the effect of two factors: severity of the employee's problem and type of setting (e.g. school, hospital, or manufacturing business) on subjects' willingness to refer hypothetical employees. Although setting did not affect willingness to refer, the more severe the employee's problem was, the more willing subjects were to refer. Gerstein, Lynn, and Brown (1991) interpreted both results in accord with their theoretical model. Gerstein, Wheeler, and Gaber (1994) found that while a training program on handling troubled employees was not significantly related to number of employees actually referred by the supervisor, span of control was related. That is, in accord with their hypothesis, Gerstein, Wheeler, and Gaber (1994) found that supervisors with a smaller span of control tended to have referred more employees. Gerstein, Moore, Duffey, and Dainas (1993) examined the relationship between the sex of the referring supervisor and the sex of the employee. They found that while there was no main effect of either variable on EAP referrals, the interaction was statistically significant. Thus, female supervisors were more likely to refer women than men to the EAP. However, male supervisors were equally likely to refer men and women. Again, Gerstein et al. (1993) interpreted this result in light of their theoretical model, which suggests that individuals are more likely to help others they feel similar to.

Harley (1991) examined some factors that might precipitate supervisors' referral of an employee to the EAP. He found that job performance and the occurrence of a dramatic event at work involving the subordinate (e.g. arriving at work intoxicated) were significant predictors of supervisors' referral to the EAP. Based on these results, Harley concluded that contrary to EAP philosophy, supervisors use the EAP referral as a last resort, rather than as an early attempt to improve subordinate behavior.

Employee Reactions to EAPs

Harris and Heft (1992) suggested that despite the importance of employee perceptions and attitudes in the decision to use an EAP, there was a dearth of research on this important topic. The little literature that did exist suggested several variables that were important in an employee's decision, such as familiarity with the EAP, confidentiality, and opportunity to attend during work hours.

A number of recent articles were located that addressed employee reactions to an EAP. Two major dependent variables were examined in this line of research: satisfaction with the EAP and willingness to go to the EAP. With regard to the former variable, Burke (1994) found that employees who used the EAP were generally satisfied, with the average response ranging from 3.6 to 4.1 on a 1–5 scale (1 = very dissatisfied; 5 = very satisfied). Park (1992) found that 93% of the employees were either satisfied or very satisfied with the EAP and 91% would ask for additional help from the EAP.

A larger number of studies examined employes' willingness to use an EAP. In perhaps the most sophisticated study of this variable, Milne, Blum, and Roman (1994) tested a structural equation model using five predictors of propensity to use the EAP: confidentiality/trust, familiarity with the EAP, perceived support of top management for the EAP, perceived support of one's supervisor for the EAP, and accessibility of the EAP. Not only did confidentiality/trust have a direct effect on propensity to use the EAP, but it also served as a mediator for all four other predictors. Milne, Blum, and Roman concluded that 'confidence in the EAP is a highly significant contributor to propensity to use the program' (p.140).

Hall, Vacc, and Kissling (1991) examined a plethora of predictors of willingness to use an EAP, including demogrpahic factors (e.g. sex), social support network, attitudes towards the EAP (e.g. perceived efficacy of the EAP), and perceptions of alternative help sources. Although all factors were statistically significant, attitudes towards the EAP comprised the best predictors. Several predicted interactions were also significant.

May (1992) addressed the impact of different referral sources on expectations of the EAP using a laboratory study, in which some subjects were told to imagine that their supervisor had referred them, while the other subjects were told to assume they had self-referred. There was, however, no significant effect of referral source. May offered several possible explanations for the lack of differences, including the artificial nature of the study.

Several studies have examined demographic predictors of employees who use the EAP. Sullivan and Poverny (1992) examined the EAP of a large university located in southern California. They found that in proportion to their numbers, staff tended to utilize the EAP more frequently than faculty. Younger employees tended to use the EAP more frequently than older employees, and professional/supervisory staff were more likely to use the EAP than non-exempt staff. Sullivan and Poverny suggested that some of these patterns may have been due to different health plans, since faculty tended to have a health insurance programs that offered other options (e.g. psychological counseling). Although Gerstein et al. (1993) found that neither employee race nor sex were related to actual EAP use, Gerstein, Wheeler, and Gaber (1994) reported a significant relationship between organizational level and actual EAP use wherein mid-level staff were more likely to use the EAP than were higher-level or lower-level employees.

Evaluation of EAPs

Despite their prevalence, past reviews have noted there is a dearth of rigorous evaluation of EAPs (Harris & Heft, 1992). One of the most widely publicized evaluations was conducted at McDonnell–Douglas. In that study, employees who used the EAP were compared with employees who had received treatment for problems from other sources. The former group was found to have lower absenteeism, fewer terminations, and lower medical costs as compared to the latter group (Author, 1993). Interestingly, the difference between the two groups emerged over several years, rather than immediately. Nevertheless, questions have been raised regarding the methodology used in this study (Normand, Lempert, & O'Brien, 1994). For example, there was no evidence whether these two groups were comparable on variables such as age, sex, and income.

No recent studies were located that provided rigorous evaluations of EAPs. However, several papers were found that examined aspects related to EAP effectiveness. Yu, Chen, Harshman, & McCarthy (1991) compared three groups of employees who sought treatment for substance abuse. Group 1 (N = 73) consisted of employees whose treatment costs exceeded $300 the first year of the study and had no additional treatment in the next two years; Group 2 (N = 18) consisted of employees whose treatment costs were $300 or more over the three years covered in the study; Group 3 (N = 32) consisted of employees who failed to follow through with their treatment or whose treatment costs were less than $300 (e.g. they were unable to obtain much treatment due to scheduling problems). Examination of medical costs for each of the three groups indicated that Group 1 experienced an average decline of 48% in medical expenses, while medical expenses increased for employees in Groups 2 (93%) and 3 (116%). A key implication is that substance abuse treatment may, in the long run, be quite cost-effective. On the other hand, the increase in medical expenses of participants in Group 2 suggests that substance abuse treatment is no automatic panacea. Yu et al. offered several reasons as to why employees in Group 2 showed dramatic increases in medical costs, such as greater reliance on medical treatment and non-random sampling procedures.

Walsh, Hingson, Merrigan et al. (1991) examined alternative treatment programs following entry into the EAP. Subjects (N = 227) were randomly assigned into one of three treatments: (i) inpatient hospitalization; (ii) joining an Alcoholics Anonymous (AA) group; or (iii) opportunity to use a program of their choice. A variety of dependent variables were measured over a two-year period, including need for additional treatment, length of sobriety, and job outcomes (e.g. number of terminations). The results showed significant differences between the three groups on a number of measures, including need for additional treatment and length of sobriety. In most cases, Group 1 employees showed significantly fewer problems (e.g. intoxication) than the other two groups. The AA group and the choice group were generally not significantly different from one another. Interestingly, however, because of the cost of hospitalization, the expenses associated with the treatment (including initial treatment) for Group 1 and Group 2 were virtually identical. There were no significant differences on any of the job outcomes. Finally, at the end of the study, amount of alcohol consumed, number of people classified as alcoholic, and number of job problems experienced declined greatly for all three groups. Thus, these results suggested that use of an EAP over a two-year period may dramatically reduce substance abuse problems. Nevertheless, without a control group receiving no treatment, it is difficult to draw rigorous conclusions about the efficacy of an EAP program versus no EAP program.

Foote and Erfurt (1991) compared a strategy wherein some employees using the EAP received a follow-up contact with a counsellor, while other employees received the regular treatment (i.e. no follow-up contact). They found limited support for a difference between these two groups—the major exception was that employees in the follow-up group had significantly lower treatment costs. No information was provided as to whether the additional costs of follow-up contact outweighed the benefits.

By way of summary, Harris and Heft (1992) predicted that 'rigorous evaluation studies [of EAPs] . . . will be slow in coming, if indeed they appear at all' (p.258). Several years later, this prediction appears to have been accurate. On a positive note, however, Harris and Heft urged that additional research be conducted on specific aspects of EAPs; the literature summarized above indicates that there has been some progress in that direction. More informed choices can be now made as to which features (e.g. what sources should be used by the EAP) to incorporate in an EAP.

EAP Adoption/Implementation

Harris and Heft noted several studies examining adoption and implementation of EAPs. Only one new study was located in this area. Bennett, Blum, and Roman (1994) found that controlling for various other variables, companies in low unemployment areas and low turnover rates were most likely to have adopted an EAP. Bennett, Blum, and Roman offered two different explanations for their finding. One, businesses experiencing high turnover might feel that investing in employees who have a high likelihood of leaving is not cost-effective. Second, organizations that have an EAP might foster greater employee commitment, thereby reducing their turnover rate. Obviously, these explanations have very different theoretical and practical implications.

Employee Assistance Programs: Suggestions for Future Research

While research on EAPs has certainly increased in the last few years, and some theoretical models have been developed in this area, a great deal of work remains. One issue that clearly stands out is the need for further work on the referral process. Particularly in light of the small number of employees who make use of an EAP, the need to better understand the dynamics of how employees decide to go remains critical.

As reviewed above, Gerstein and his colleagues have developed a model to understand supervisors' willingness to refer an employee; however, no comprehensive, well-developed model has been developed that addresses the self-referral process and what leads employees to actually go to an EAP. Towards that end, we suggest application of image theory (Beach, 1990) to understand this process. Although a detailed description of image theory and how it might apply to EAP use is beyond the scope of this paper, a brief overview is warranted. Image theory assumes that people use three basic structures of knowledges, or images, in making decisions. One image incorporates one's values (e.g. morals, ethics, or more generally, principles). These values form the core standards for making decisions. The next image, referred to as trajectory, constitutes one's short- and long-term goals or desired outcomes. An example from the work context may be promotion to area manager. The third image, the strategic image, involves plans and methods for attaining these goals. Image theory assumes that people must somehow process constant information and deal with continuous decision. In order to do this, people adopt a very simple method of information processing, referred to as screening. Screening is based on simple heuristics, in which decisions are rejected if they do not meet certain basic criteria. Only if these basic criteria are met will the individual consider the information or decisions in greater detail. Lee and Mitchell (1994) have addressed the notion of 'shocks', or events that force the individual to make much more careful judgments and decisions.

In the present context, an employee with a drinking or drug problem may have certain values or principles that relate to substance use (e.g. 'a little alcohol never hurt anyone'), which in turn lead him or her to reject the need to go to the EAP. It may be that only a shock (e.g. a strong warning from his or her supervisor about poor job performance) will force the employee to consider the need for an EAP more carefully, and thus lead him or her to go to the EAP.

Application of image theory offers some potentially interesting areas for research. First, given that image theory assumes two basic types of decision making processes, depending on the point in process, the factors considered in choosing to use or not use the EAP may differ as a function of the issues facing the employee. Second, image theory would lead one to consider different approaches in addressing employee problems. For example, for certain employees, some types of shocks (e.g. a supervisory reprimand versus a coworker confrontation) may be more helpful than others, depending on their value image. In short, image theory is a relatively new approach to understanding how people make decisions. Although its application to the workplace is even more recent, it has been used to understand turnover (Lee & Mitchell, 1994) and job search and choice (Stevens & Beach, 1994).

Related to all this work is the importance of different sources that appear to serve as encouragement to utilize the EAP. As Blum and Roman (1992) indicated, coworkers appear to play a greater role than heretofore has been recognized.

In terms of EAP effectiveness, given that their presence appears to be so well entrenched in industry, business and government today, we suspect that there is only limited interest among practitioners in demonstrating their utility. However, there is likely to be greater interest in how to best design EAPs, and how to broaden their appeal to employees. It is therefore in these latter two areas that more research is likely to appear. In this regard, we reviewed some research that addressed the effectiveness of different aspects of an EAP. Much more work is needed here.

With regard to why employees choose to use the EAP, most of the research has addressed employees in general, and whether or not they are willing to go. Perhaps it would be more beneficial to study why employees who could have gone to an EAP chose to go to other help sources. Research by Sullivan and Poverny (1992) provides some possible directions for research on this issue; follow-up work is clearly needed.

Finally, in terms of EAP adoption, there is very little research. Anecdotal and testimonial evidence comes from organizations that have adopted EAPs; a study examining organizations that decide not to use an EAP would be quite valuable. For example, are these organizations simply not convinced that an EAP would be cost-effective? Or, do these organizations have a view that employees with a problem should seek help on their own?

WORKPLACE DRUG AND ALCOHOL PROGRAMS AND PRACTICES OUTSIDE NORTH AMERICA

Although the vast majority of research on workplace drug and alcohol programs was conducted in North America, there has been some writing and research on this issue in other countries as well. We located literature on three countries: New Zealand, Sweden, and Germany. A summary of this literature follows next.

New Zealand

Inkson (n.d.) conducted a survey of alcohol programs and practices in companies with 100 or more employees ($N = 305$) located in New Zealand. They found that respondents perceived alcohol to be a relatively unimportant problem, with 53% indicating that alcohol abuse is a 'minor' problem, and almost 20% indicating that alcohol abuse was not a concern. Only 2% felt that alcohol abuse was a major concern. Nevertheless, over half of the respondents agreed that there may be hidden problems created by alcohol in their organization. Almost half (47%) of the respondents indicated that their company did not have a policy for dealing with alcohol problems, while 30% stated that the policy existed but not in written form. Slightly more than 20% had a written policy. In terms of actions that would be taken with an employee having an alcohol problem, few respondents indicated that a rehabilitation program or formal assistance program (e.g. EAP) would be provided. Inkson also queried respondents as to how actual situations involving an alcohol problem had been dealt with. Contrary to the previous statements, disciplinary action was indicated in about one-third of the cases, whereas some type of counseling treatment was mentioned in well over half of the situations.

Pringle (in press) surveyed senior managers from 60 medium and large private-sector companies in New Zealand. These businesses were from a mix of industries, including manufacturing, construction, transportation, and financial services. A large percentage of respondents (87%) indicated that they used alcohol as part of their work activities; whether the alcohol was consumed at the work site, at home, or other locations (e.g. restaurants) was not clear. However, managers of 5 out of 6 companies reported that alcohol was kept on their premises (typically in a senior manager's office or boardroom). Most of the respondents had some contact with a problem drinker at work. The most common action cited for dealing with a problem drinker at work was talk or referral for counseling (28%), termination or warning (25%), or no action if his or her work was acceptable (22%).

In terms of company policies and practices, Pringle (in press) reported that only 25% of the companies had a formal, written policy on alcohol, which is very close to the number reported by Inkson (n.d.). None of these companies had an EAP. Alcohol was reported to have a variety of important uses in the workplace. Specifically, respondents viewed alcohol as a necessary aspect of client interaction (e.g. for entertainment), as a reward to employees (e.g. for celebrating a successful sale), and as a gift to important individuals. As observed by Pringle, alcohol 'is part and parcel of business life' (p.15).

Unlike the USA, then, there appears to be far less emphasis on substance abuse issues in the New Zealand workplace. Moreover, the little attnetion that has been paid focuses on alchol abuse, and not illegal substances. Finally, cultural norms appear to be less disparaging of alcohol use than perhaps is the case in the USA.

Sweden

Karlsson (1990) reviewed drug and alcohol programs in Sweden. In terms of the prevalence of drug and alcohol usage, Karlsson reported that 10% of males and 1–2% of females were estimated to be alcohol abusers in the general population. Less information was available as to the percentage of drug users in the general population. Research examining the prevalence of drug and alcohol problems in the workforce was quite sparse, especially compared to research in the USA, but one study had indicated that 4% of men and 1% of women abused drugs.

With regard to drug and alcohol programs, Karlsson observed that Swedish work laws provide for a myriad of rules regarding the treatment of employees with drug and alcohol problems. For instance, the Work Environment Act affects how the company addresses substance abuse problems; other laws make it difficult for workers to be terminated. Together, these laws have led many companies to adopt alcohol and drug programs. Based on an analysis of seven companies (ranging from manufacturing firms to a state-owned nuclear power plant) with such programs, Karlsson found a number of interesting findings. First, very few employees had made use of the services (less than 1% of the workforce). The supervisors and managers were perceived as a major problem that had to be overcome. None of the companies had conducted a formal evaluation of the program; yet the program was widely believed to be very effective, based on the number of employees who had returned or been able to remain on the job. Finally, four of the seven companies had an alcohol and drug testing program. Only one of them, however, conducted this testing at the preemployment stage; the other three tested 'for cause'. The most commonly used approaches were urinalysis and a breath test. Interestingly, one company, a paper mill, had recently begun testing because two employees were found to be drug-users.

Thus, as in the USA, alcohol and perhaps drug problems are viewed as important workplace problems. EAPs seem quite widespread in Sweden. Some of the issues identified by Karlsson (e.g. low usage rate) are similar to concerns in the USA. Drug testing does not appear to be as prevalent in Sweden as it is in the USA.

Germany

While many companies appear to have adopted alcohol and drug programs and policies in Germany, research on them is scarce (Fuchs & Rummel, 1993). It is estimated that 5% of employees are alcoholics, while another 10% are at risk for becoming alcohol abusers in Germany. Fuchs and Rummel surveyed 377 managers of a company with an alcohol and drug program three years after its inception. They found that most respondents understood that alcohol problems were not due to a lack of the person's willpower, and agreed that alcohol use in the workplace was not permitted. At the same time, about half of the managers indicated that use of alcohol may be necessary when interacting with customers. Fuchs and Rummel asserted that this attitude contradicts the need to refrain from alcohol at the workplace. In terms of other issues related to the alcohol prevention program, Fuchs and Rummel reported relatively positive findings regarding such things as respondents' willingness to refer, attitudes towards the program, and so forth. Given increased attention to drug and alcohol problems, further research is likely to be of interest to German companies.

LEGAL ISSUES IN DRUG AND ALCOHOL PROGRAMS

Alcohol and drug programs in the workplace have resulted in a variety of lawsuits. Segal (1994) provides a well-written practical guide to legal issues surrounding drug and alcohol testing. Among the issues he raises are common law invasion of privacy restrictions, the role of the union in approving a drug testing program, need for reasonable suspicion testing, and civil rights laws (e.g. Americans with Disabilities Act; Civil Rights Act of 1964). Segal describes how use of a drug test based on suspected addiction to support a termination may be cause for legal action by the employee. Harris and Heft (1993) reviewed other laws, such as state regulations, that affect drug and alcohol testing.

Parliman and Edwards (1992) reviewed employer liability issues in connection with an EAP. They described two types of lawsuits that workers have filed in this regard. The first type of lawsuit involves a claim that the company's action involved a violation of right to privacy. For example, in one lawsuit, the company allegedly met with the psychologist who had treated an employee at the EAP, and asked him about the employee's problems. Despite the fact that the employee had not authorized the psychologist to share their conversation, he proceeded to share information about her personal problems with company representatives. After the company terminated the employee, she sued for invasion of privacy and subsequently won. The second type of lawsuit involves charges of infliction of severe emotional distress. In a court case involving this legal concept, an employee who was suffering from depression as well as an alcohol problem met with an EAP counselor for help. During the meeting, which the employee's supervisor also attended, the employee was told that he must go for inpatient alcohol treatment or be fired. Moreover, the employee had to inform the company of his decision by the end of the day. When the employee asked for an extension of the deadline, he was told that a postponement of the deadline would result in his dismissal. At that point, he was told he was fired; the next day, the company reversed its decision, but the employee proceeded to sue. Ultimately, a jury gave him $30 000 in compensatory pay and $100 000 in punitive damages. Clearly, companies that have an EAP must be careful to ensure they do not violate pertinent laws.

CONCLUSION

We have reviewed recent literature on drug and alcohol programs in the workplace. This area remains an important one for organizations, and companies will continue to devote resources to such programs. We suggested a number of issues for future research. While I/O psychologists have so far been involved in a few limited questions regarding workplace drug and alcohol programs, we believe they have an important role to play in terms of research, practice, and public policy recommendations.

ACKNOWLEDGEMENT

The authors would like to thank Leslie Greising for typing the references and reviewing the chapter.

REFERENCES

Author (1993) How McDonnell Douglas cost-justified its EAP. *Personnel Journal*, 72, 48.

Beach, L. R. (1990) *Image Theory: Decision Making in Personal and Organizational Contexts*. Chichester: Wiley.

Bennett, N., Blum, T. C., & Roman, P. M. (1994) Presence of drug screening and employee assistance programs: Exclusive and inclusive human resource management practices. *Journal of Organizational Behavior*, 15, 549–560.

Blank, D. L. & Fenton, J. W. (1989) Early employment testing for marijuana: Demographic and employee retention patterns. In S. W. Gust and J. M. Walsh (eds), *Drugs in the Workplace: Research and Evaluation Data* (pp.139–150), Rockville, MD: National Institute on Drug Abuse.

Blum, T. C. & Roman, P. M. (1992) A description of clients using employee assistance programs. *Alcohol Health and Research World*, 16(2), 120–128.

Boudreau, J. (1991) Utility analysis for decisions in human resource management. In M. Dunnette and L. Hough (eds), *Handbook of Industrial and Organizational Psychology* (pp.621–745). Palo Alto, CA: Consulting Psychologists Press.

Burke, R. J. (1994) Utilization of employees' assistance program in a public accounting firm: Some preliminary data. *Psychological Reports*, 75, 264–266.

Cascio, W. F. (1987) *Costing Human Resources: The Financial Impact of Behavior in Organizations*, Second edition. Boston: Kent.

Cavanaugh, J. M. & Prasad, P. (1994) Drug testing as symbolic managerial action: In response to 'A case against workplace drug testing'. *Organization Science*, 5(2), 267–271.

Comer, D. R. (1993) Workplace drug testing reconsidered. *Journal of Managerial Issues*, 5(4), 517–531.

Comer, D. R. (1994) A case against workplace drug testing. *Organization Science*, 5(2), 259–271.

Crant, J. M. & Bateman, T. S. (1990) An experimental test of the impact of drug-testing programs on potential job applicants' attitudes and intentions. *Journal of Applied Psychology*, 75, 127–131.

Crant, J. M. & Bateman, T. S. (1993) Potential job applicant reactions to employee drug testing: The effect of program characteristics and individual differences. *Journal of Business and Psychology*, 7(3), 279–290.

Crow, S. M. & Hartman, S. J. (1992) Drugs in the workplace: Overstating the problems and the cures. *Journal of Drug Issues*, 22(4), 923–937.

Feucht, T. E. Stephens, R. C., & Walker, M. L. (1994) Drug use among juvenile arrestees: A comparison of self-report, urinalysis and hair assay. *Journal of Drug Issues*, 24(1), 99–116.

Foote, A. & Erfurt, J. C. (1991) Effects of EAP follow-up on prevention of relapse among substance abuse clients. *Journal of Studies on Alcohol*, 52, 241–248.

Fuchs, R. & Rummel, M. (1993) Chemical dependency at work and organisational development: A management training programme aimed at the superiors of an institute for financial services. In J. Bellabarba, R. Fuchs, L. Rainer, & M. Rummel (Chairs), *Chemical Dependency at Work Employees Assistance Programmes (Substance*

Abuse): Our work in the Context of Company Internal Health Promotion Programmes. Symposium presented at the Sixth European Congress on Work and Organizational Psychology in Alicante, Spain.

Gerstein, L. H. (1990) The bystander-equity model of supervisory helping behavior: Past and future research on the prevention of employee problems. In P. M. Roman (ed.) *Alcohol Problem Intervention in the Workplace.* New York: Quorum Books.

Gerstein, L., Lynn, D., & Brown, P. (1991) Type of setting, employee substance abuse, and hypothetical supervisors' EAP referrals. *Journal of Drug Issues,* 21(4), 817–824.

Gerstein, L., Moore, D. T., Duffey, K., & Dainas, C. (1993) The effects of biological sex and ethnicity on EAP utilization and referrals. *Consulting Psychology Journal,* 45(4), 23–27.

Gerstein, L., Wheeler, J. L., & Gaber, T. G. (1994) The relation of the supervisory training and span of control to EAP referrals. *Consulting Psychology Journal,* 46, 19–22.

Gill, A. M. & Michaels, R. J. (1992) Does drug use lower wages? *Industrial and Labor Relations Review,* 45, 419–434.

Hall, L., Vacc, N. A., & Kissling, G. (1991) Likelihood to use employee assistance programs: The effects of sociodemographic, social-psychological, sociocultural, organizational, and community factors. *Journal of Employment Counseling,* 28, 63–73.

Harley, D. A. (1991) Impaired job performance and worksite trigger incidents: Factors influencing supervisory EAP referrals. *Employee Assistance Quarterly,* 6(3), 51–70.

Harris, M. M. & Heft, L. L. (1992) Alcohol and drug use in the workplace: Issues, controversies, and directions for future research. *Journal of Management,* 18, 239–266.

Harris, M. M. & Heft, L. L. (1993). 'Preemployment urinalysis drug testing: A critical review of psychometric and legal issues and effects on applicants', *Human Resource Management Review,* 3(4), 271–291.

Hartman, S. J. & Crow, S. M. (1993) Drugs in the workplace: Setting Harris straight. *Journal of Drug Issues,* 23(4), 733–738.

Holcum, M. L. & Lehman, W. E. K. (1995, May) A Structural Model of Negative Job Performance: Assessing the Causal Roles of Deviance and Substance Use. Paper presented at the annual meeting of the Society for Industrial Organizational Psychology, Orlando, Florida.

Horgan, J. (1990) Test negative: A look at the 'evidence' justifying illicit-drug tests. *Scientific American,* 262 (March), 18–19.

Inkson, J. H. K. (n.d.) Employers' Attitudes to Alcohol Abuse Among Employes: A Preliminary Study, Unpublished manuscript.

Kandel, D. B. & Yamaguchi, K. (1987) Job mobility and drug use: An event history analysis. *American Journal of Sociology,* 92, 836–878.

Karlsson, C. (1990) *Programmes on Alcohol and Drugs at Swedish Workplaces.* ALNA Council of Sweden.

Kravitz, D. A. & Brock, P. (in press) Evaluations of drug testing programs. *Employee Responsibilities and Rights Journal.*

Kravitz, D. A., Stinson, V., & Chavez, T. L. (1994, April) Perceived Fairness of Tests Used in Making Selection and Promotion Decisions. Paper presented at the Annual Meeting of the Society for Industrial Organizational Psychology, Nashville, Tennessee.

Lee, T. W. & Mitchell, T. R. (1994) An alternative approach: The unfolding model of voluntary employee turnover. *Academy of Management Review,* 19(1), 51–89.

Lehman, W. E. K. & Simpson, D. D. (1992) Employee substance abuse and on-the-job behaviors. *Journal of Applied Psychology,* 77, 309–321.

MacDonald, S., Wells, S., & Fry, R. (1993) The limitations of drug screening in the workplace. *International Labour Review,* 132(1), 95–113.

Macan, T. H., Avedon, M. J., Paese, M., & Smith, D. E. (1994) The effects of applicants' reactions to cognitive ability tests and an assessment center. *Personnel Psychology*, 47(4), 715–738.

Marcoulides, G. A., Mills, R. B., & Unterbrink, H. (1993) Improving pre-employment screening: Drug testing in the workplace. *Journal of Managerial Issues*, 5(2), 290–300.

Mastrangelo, P. (1995) Do college students still prefer companies without employ-ment drug testing? Paper presented at the tenth annual conference of the Society for Industrial and Organizational Psychology, Orlando, FL.

May, K. M. (1992) Referrals to employee assistance programs: A pilot analogue study of expectations about counseling. *Journal of Mental Health Counseling*, 14(2), 208–224.

McDaniel, M. (1988) Does pre-employment drug predict on-the-job suitability? *Personnel Psychology*, 41, 717–729.

Mieczkowski, T. (1992) New approaches in drug testing: A review of hair analysis. *Annals of the American Academy of Political and Social Science*, 521, 132–150.

Mieczkowski, T. & Newel, R. (1993) Comparing hair and urine assays for cocaine and marijuana. *Federal Probation*, 57(2), 59–67.

Milne, S. H., Blum, T. C., & Roman, P. M. (1994) Factors influencing employees' propensity to use an employee asisstance program. *Personnel Psychology*, 47, 123–145.

Murphy, K. R. & Thornton, G. C. (1992) Characteristics of employee drug testing policies. *Journal of Business and Psychology*, 6(3), 295–309.

Normand, J., Lempert, R. O., & O'Brien, C. P. (1994) *Under the Influence? Drugs and the American Work Force*. Washington DC: National Academy Press.

Normand, J., Salyards, S., & Mahoney, J. (1990) An evaluation of pre-employment drug testing. *Journal of Applied Psychology*, 75, 629–639.

Park, D. A. (1992) Client satisfaction evaluation: University employee assistance pro-gram. *Employee Assistance Quarterly*, 8(2), 15–34.

Parliman, G. C. & Edwards, E. L. (1992) Employee assistance programs: An em-ployer's guide to emerging liability issues. *Employee Relations Law Journal*, 17(4), 593–601.

Pringle, J. K. (in press) Managers' alcohol use: Roles and symbolic functions. *Journal of Business and Psychology*, 9(4).

Raciot, B. M. & Williams, K. J. (1993) Perceived invasiveness and fairness of drug-testing procedures for current employees. *Journal of Applied Social Psychology*, 23, 1879–1891.

Register, C. A. & Williams, D. R. (1992) Labor market effects of marijuana and cocaine use among young men. *Industrial and Labor Relations Review*, 45, 435–448.

Rosse, J. G. & Ringer, R. C. (1991, April) Applicant Reactions to Paper-and-Pencil Forms of Drug Testing. Paper presented at the annual meeting of the Society for Industrial and Organizational Psychology, St. Louis, Missouri.

Sackett, P. R. & Harris, M. M. (1984) Honesty testing for personnel selection: A review and critique. *Personnel Psychology*, 37, 221–245.

Schmidt, F. L., Viswevaran, V., & Ones, D. S. (1993, August) Validity of Integrity Tests for Predicting Drug and Alcohol Abuse. Paper presented at the American Psychological Association Convention, Toronto, Canada.

Segal, J. A. (1994) Urine or you're out. *HR Magazine*, 39, 30–38.

Simmering, M. J. & Ones, D. S. (1994, July) Pre-employment Drug Testing Methods in the United States. Paper presented at the 23rd International Congress of Applied Psychology, Madrid, Spain.

Smither, J. W., Reilly, R. R., Millsap, R. E., Perlman, K., & Stoffey, R. W. (1993) Applicant reactions to selection procedures. *Personnel Psychology*, 46, 49–76.

Stevens, C. K. & Beach, L. R. (1994) Application of Image Theory to Job Search and Choice Processes: New Directions for Theory and Research. Unpublished paper.

Sullivan, R. & Poverny, L. (1992) Differential patterns of EAP service utilization among university faculty and staff. *Employee Assistance Quarterly*, **8**(1), 1–12.

Tepper, B. J. (1994) Investigation of general and program-specific attitudes toward corporate drug-testing policies. *Journal of Applied Psychology*, **79**, 392–401.

Tepper, B. J. & Braun, C. K. (1995) Does the experience of organizational justice mitigate the invasion of privacy engendered by random drug testing? An empirical investigation. *Basic and Applied Social Psychology*, **16**(1&2), 211–225.

Verespej, M. A. (1992) Drug users—not testing—anger workers. *Industry Week*, **241**(4), 33-34.

Walsh, D. C., Hingson, R. W., Merrigan, D. M., Levenson, S. M., Cupples, L. A., Heeren, T., Coffman, G. A., Becker, C. A., Barker, T. A., Hamilton, S. K., McGuire, T. C., & Kelly, C. A. (1991) A randomized trial of treatment options for alcohol-abusing workers. *New England Journal of Medicine*, **325**(11), 775–782.

Yu, J., Chen, P. J., Harshman, E. J., & McCarthy, E. G. (1991) An analysis of substance abuse patterns, medical expenses and effectiveness of treatment in the workplace. *Employee Benefits Journal*, **18**, 26–30.

Zwerling, C. Ryan, J., & Orav, E. J. (1990) The efficacy of preemployment drug screening for marijuana and cocaine in predicting employment outcome. *Journal of the American Medical Association*, **264**, 2639–2643.

Zwerling, C., Ryan, J., & Orav, E. J. (1992) Costs and benefits of preemployment drug screening. *Journal of the American Medical Association*, **26**, 91–93.

Chapter 8

PROGRESS IN ORGANIZATIONAL JUSTICE: TUNNELING THROUGH THE MAZE

Russell Cropanzano
Colorado State University
and
Jerald Greenberg
Ohio State University

One of the topics of greatest interest to scientists in the fields of industrial-organizational psychology, human resources management, and organizational behavior in recent years has been *organizational justice*—people's perceptions of fairness in organizations. Whether we're talking about the fairness of large-scale organizational policies, such as pay systems, or individual practices at the local level, such as determining priorities for vacation scheduling in an office, questions of fairness on the job are ubiquitous. As both scentists and practitioners have become sensitive to the importance of such matters, the literature on organizational justice has proliferated. Witness, for example, the large number of books (e.g. Cropanzano, 1993; Folger & Cropanzano, in press; Greenberg, 1996a; Sheppard, Lewicki, & Minton, 1993; Steensma & Vermunt, 1991; Tyler, 1990; Vermunt & Steensma, 1991), and conceptual articles (e.g. Brockner & Weisenfeld, 1996; Folger, 1994; Greenberg, 1990a, 1993c; Lind, 1995; Lind & Earley, 1992; Tyler & Dawes, 1993; Tyler & Lind, 1992; Tyler & Smith, in press) that have appeared in recent years. Further evidence of the topic's current appeal is reflected by the fact that organizational justice consistently has been among the most popular topics of papers submitted for consideration on the program of the Organizational Behavior Division of the Academy of Management during the years 1993–1995. From our perspective, attention to matters of organizational justice appears to show no sign of abating in the foreseeable future.

With the recent growth in contributions to the organizational justice literature, the need has arisen to gain perspective on the field—to assess where it has been and where it is going. Insofar as previous reviews of the literature

International Review of Industrial and Organizational Psychology, 1997 Volume 12
Edited by C.L. Cooper and I.T. Robertson. © 1997 John Wiley & Sons Ltd.

have covered earlier periods, in the present review we will concentrate on work appearing between 1990 and 1995—a span during which considerable growth may have left observers of the organizational justice literature feeling somewhat uncertain as to its major issues and directions. We attempt to remedy this situation in the present chapter. Specifically, we intend to shed light on recent progress in the field of organizational justice by 'tunneling through the maze' of ideas it has generated—highlighting major conceptual and applied advances, and putting them in perspective. In doing so, we hope to help readers see light at the end of the tunnel that may encourage them to enter, and that will guide them in their journey toward understanding organizational justice.

JUSTICE: ITS FUNDAMENTAL NATURE IN ORGANIZATIONS

Before starting this journey, it is important to specify our orientation. In keeping with social science tradition, our treatment of justice is completely *descriptive* in orientation—focusing on people's perceptions of what constitutes fairness, and their reactions to unfair situations. This is in contrast to the large body of work in moral philosophy (e.g. for a review, see Cohen & Greenberg, 1982) which is inherently *prescriptive*, specifying what should be done to achieve justice (for more on this distinction, see Greenberg & Bies, 1992). As such, when organizational scientists talk about justice, they generally are referring to individual perceptions, one's evaluations as to the appropriateness of a given outcome or process. Thus, as the term is used here, justice is subjective—as perceived by a person.

Questions about justice arise whenever decisions are made about the allocation of resources. For example, in organizations the manner in which profits are disbursed among investors or pay is distributed to employees may animate justice concerns. Indeed, the very fact that people work in order to receive economic gains (e.g. pay) and social benefits (e.g. status) suggests that organizations are settings in which matters of justice are likely to be salient (Greenberg & Tyler, 1987). Given the centrality of these outcomes for work life, it should come as no surprise that fairness is something that individuals use to define their relationships to their employers. It is with this idea in mind, that Greenberg (1987a) coined the term 'organizational justice' to refer to theories of social and interpersonal fairness that may be applied to understanding behavior in organizations. In this connection it is important to note that concerns about fairness are not unique to organizations and that much of our understanding of justice is based on other settings and disciplines (for reviews, see Bierhoff, Cohen & Greenberg, 1986; Cohen, 1986; Greenberg & Cohen, 1982a; Tyler & Smith, in press). However, as we will illustrate in this chapter, organizations have proven to be a rich venue for studying matters of fairness. Indeed, we have learned a great deal about organizations by studying justice and a great deal about justice by examining it within organizations.

In general, the study of organizational justice has focused on two major issues: employees' responses to the things they receive—that is, *outcomes*—and the means by which they obtain these outcomes—that is, *procedures*. It is almost tautological to claim that all allocation decisions are about outcomes. In fact, work settings may be characterized by the outcomes stemming from them. For example, performance appraisal results in some rating or ranking, a promotion decision culminates in a new job, a pay review results in a raise, a selection interview results in a hiring decision, and so on. Of course, outcomes also can be negative as well as positive. For example, decisions are also made about how to punish a poor performer, and whom to terminate during cutbacks. Allocations result in a certain configuration or pattern whereby some individuals get more and others get less. Individuals' evaluations of these outcomes are referred to as judgments of *distributive justice* (Leventhal, 1976a).

Although concerns about distributive justice are critical in organizations, and were the first form of justice to capture the attention of organizational scientists (see Greenberg, 1987a), they comprise only part of the story where organizational justice is concerned. Outcomes do not simply appear; they result from a specific set of processes or procedures. For example, people may raise questions about *how* their performance ratings, promotion decisions, pay raises, or selection decisions were determined. Were these based on procedures that are themselves fair? As we will detail in this chapter, people's perceptions of the fairness of the procedures used to determine allocations— referred to as *procedural justice*—are of considerable importance in organizations. Indeed, there are many benefits that result from perceived fair procedures, and problems that result from perceived unfair procedures.

Insofar as the concept of procedural justice was introduced into the study of organizations during a period in which interest in distributive justice was waning (Folger & Greenberg, 1985; Greenberg & Folger, 1983) it quickly became the center of attention among justice researchers (Greenberg & Tyler, 1987). Not surprisingly, contemporary empirical work has emphasized procedural justice. The balance of material in the present chapter reflects this trend: Although we review recent investigations of both types of fairness, procedural justice receives somewhat more attention. This skew reflects only the prevailing balance of attention in the literature, and not our judgment about their relative importance. Indeed, we have advocated the importance of both distributive and procedural justice in our own work (e.g. Folger & Cropanzano, in press; Greenberg, 1996a).

In the first half of this chapter we will review the latest advances in both distributive justice and procedural justice. We will discuss the basic concepts and review recent evidence examining these concepts within work organizations. Following a historical perspective, we will first examine distributive justice and then move to procedural justice. In the third section we will discuss recent evidence concerning the manner in which these two types of justice operate jointly to predict work outcomes. Then, in the second half of the chapter we will review organizational justice research focusing on applications. Specifically, we will describe evidence demonstrating the role of justice in various organizational practices and phenomena, such as strategic planning, staffing, drug testing, conflict-resolution, layoffs, organizational citizenship behavior, and employee theft. Throughout this chapter we will not only critically analyze the present state of knowledge, but also make recommendations for new directions that deserve to be taken in the future.

DISTRIBUTIVE JUSTICE

The concept of distributive justice can be traced back to Aristotle's *Nichomachean Ethics*: 'that which is manifested in distributions of honour or money or the things that fall to be divided among those who have a share in the constitution' (Ross, 1925, Book V, p. 1130). However, it was Homans (1961) whose conceptualization provided the modern roots of attention to distributive justice. According to Homans' 'rule of distributive justice', it is expected among parties to a social exchange relationship: (i) that the reward of each will be proportional to the costs of each, and (ii) that net rewards, or profits, will be proportional to their investments. Extending this concept to the context of organizations, Adams (1965) proposed his theory of inequity, according to which people are motivated to avoid the tension that results from states in which the ratio of one's own outcomes (i.e. rewards) compared to one's inputs (i.e. contributions) is unequal to the corresponding ratio of a comparison other. Complete historical overviews of these concepts are beyond the scope of the present work; for more information the reader is invited to consult Cohen and Greenberg (1982), Greenberg (1982), Törnblom (1990) and Tyler and Smith (in press). Following the lead of these earlier works, a distinction may be made between studies of how people judge and respond to unfair distributions (i.e. research focusing on recipients' behavior) and people's decisions about the allocation norms that should be followed (i.e. research focusing on allocators' behavior). Several studies within each category have been conducted in recent years.

Reactions to Allocation Outcomes

The study of distributive justice in organizations today focuses primarily on people's perceptions of the fairness of the outcomes (benefits or punishments) they receive—that is, their evaluations of the end state of the allocation process. In keeping with traditional equity theory research (for a review, see Greenberg, 1982), contemporary studies have found that people tend to be less satisfied with outcomes they perceive to be unfair than those they perceive to be fair. Such perceptions have been shown to result in poor performance (e.g. Cowherd & Levine, 1992; Pfeffer & Langton, 1993) and high rates of withdrawal behavior, such as turnover and absenteeism (e.g. Hulin, 1991;

Schwarzald, Koslowsky, & Shalit, 1992). In view of these costly consequences of perceived distributive injustice, and following from earlier conceptualizations (e.g. Leventhal, Karuza, & Fry, 1980), recent work has focused on understanding the processes by which individuals form judgments of distributive fairness.

This process is more complex than one may expect on an intuitive basis. It is not simply the case that people's perceptions of fairness are determined exclusively by self-fulfiling motives—that is, the more one gets, the more satisfied one is (although this motive is potent, to be sure; Greenberg, 1983, 1987b). One's absolute level of resources, in and of itself, is only one determinant of fairness (Summers & Hendrix, 1991; Sweeney, McFarlin, & Inderrieden, 1990). Rather, individuals base their evaluations of distributive justice not only one what they receive, but as suggested by Homans (1961) and Adams (1965), what they receive *relative* to some standard or referent. Although the comparative nature of distributive standards is rooted in theory, confusion has long existed in the literature as to the choice of comparison standards (Austin, 1977).

This is especially true in organizations, where comparison standards are often social in nature. For example, people may evaluate the fairness of their own pay by comparing it to the pay believed to be received by someone else. There are also other referent standards that may be used. For example, people may compare the adequacy of the rewards they receive to their expectations, needs, or general societal norms. This practice is quite plausible insofar as the value of many organizational outcomes cannot be classified objectively. Consequently, these evaluations can be based solely on social comparisons. Consider, for example, an outcome such as pay. The fairness of a specific level of pay may be difficult to evaluate in the absence of information about job title, the pay of similar others, one's pay history, and the like. Only by reference to such standards can pay outcomes be judged as 'adequate' or 'inadequate'. These issues are discussed in greater detail by Kulik and Ambrose (1992), and also have been the subject of recent research.

Illustrating the dynamics of referent standards, Sweeney, McFarlin, and Inderrieden (1990) measured pay satisfaction, actual salary, and various sorts of referents (including both social comparisons and personal expectations) in three large-scale survey studies. They found that although salary level was related to satisfaction, the various referents contributed substantial variance beyond objective information about the amount of one's income. Apparently, satisfaction with outcomes is determined not only by the magnitude of the outcomes received, but also by how these outcomes compare to referent standards.

The results of such comparisons have been found to affect important organizational outcomes. Consider, for example, Schwarzwald, Koslowsky, and Shalit's (1992) field study of work attitudes and absenteeism among individuals being considered for promotion. After failing to earn new positions, individuals had increases in absenteeism, and experienced lower feelings of commitment and higher feelings of inequity. The researchers reasoned that the promoted coworkers acted as referents. That is, individuals who were not initially disadvantaged now felt inequitably underpaid relative to those who had earned a promotion. Such inequities can have adverse effects on job performance. For example, Cowherd and Levine (1992) found that workers produced higher quality products when there was only a small pay differential between themselves and managers compared to when this differential was large. To the extent that large differences may have been perceived to be undeserved in view of relative work contributions, it follows from equity theory that people would withold their inputs, thereby accounting for the results. This finding is consistent with several classic tests of equity theory reporting that inequitably underpaid individuals produce low quality goods (for a review, see Greenberg, 1982).

A limitation of these studies—indeed, of most distributive justice research— is that the investigators measured people's referents and fairness perceptions at only a single point in time. This is problematic insofar as people's choices of referents may be dynamic and adjust to changing conditions. This possibility was demonstrated in a longitudinal study by Stepina and Perrewe (1991). These researchers first measured employees' comparative referents with regard to four job facets: compensation, security, job complexity, and supervision. Then, two years later these measures were readministered to the same participants. With regard to the security, job complexity, and supervision facets, referent choice was stable among those who perceived themselves to be advantaged relative to their referents. In contrast, those who believed themselves to be relatively disadvantaged were more likely to select a new (and lower) referent, thereby producing greater felt equity. However, for the compensation facet, consistent standards were used throughout the two-year period. People were less likely to alter their compensation referents and maintained the same points of comparison for the duration of the study. This stability existed even among employees who felt they were disadvantaged. Insofar as these findings illustrate the dynamic nature of referent comparisons—at least with respect to some dimensions—care needs to be exercised in interpreting people's reactions to inequity.

We close this section by pointing to some unfinished business: drawing a distinction between outcomes that are *unfavorable*, and those that are *unfair* from a distributive justice perspective. An unfavorable outcome is one that is not as advantageous as it could be, whereas an unfair outcome is one that is lower than it should be compared to some referent. Indeed, receiving a low allocation of a desired resource may be considered quite fair to the extent that one's limited contributions so merit. Although this distinction is conceptually explicit, some researchers have been more careful about separating these two constructs than others (for discussions of this problem, see Flinder & Hauenstein, 1994; Lind & Tyler, 1988; Lowe & Vodanovich, 1995). To take but two examples, both Cropanzano and Folger (1991) and Brockner and Wiesenfeld (in press) use the two terms interchangeably. This practice creates considerable conceptual confusion insofar as it can become unclear whether certain predictions or findings apply to outcomes that are inequitable, or simply unfavorable. Accordingly, we encourage future researchers to be more careful about distinguishing between these two terms.

Reward Allocation Behavior

Thus far, we have discussed distributive justice only from the perspective of the person who receives the allocation. If that allocation is believed to be inappropriate relative to some standard, then the recipient is likely to experience distributive injustice. However, following the work of Leventhal (1976a), we also can consider distributive justice from the perspective of the individual making the allocation. Indeed, several recent studies (e.g. Kabanoff, 1991; Skitka & Tetlock, 1992) have examined the rules by which decision makers distribute resources.

Perhaps the easiest way to describe decision rules is to start with the case that is presumed to be philosophically 'pure'—that is, a situation in which self-interest is eliminated, a condition of impartiality. To achieve this hypothetical state, the philosopher John Rawls (1971) proposed a thought experiment referred to as the 'original position'. Imagine that a group of people have assembled to plan a future society. They possess a rudimentary understanding of human nature, interpersonal relationships, and so on. However, they know absolutely nothing about the future economy, technology, or challenges that their new civilization will face. The planners even lack knowledge about themselves and the other people with whom they will be sharing their new society. No one knows what their own social position, abilities, and even preferences will be. In other words, everyone in the planning group is working from behind a 'veil of ignorance'. It is impossible to be self-serving when one does not even know one's own interests! Under these conditions, Rawls (1971) believed that individuals would decide to divide benefits in a way that made the worst-off person as well-off as possible. In other words, things would probably be allocated based on a rule of equality, or perhaps even need (cf. Deutsch, 1975).

The conditions necessary to test Rawls' (1971) supposition can never exist in the real world. No one can actually set-up a new society behind a veil of ignorance. However, the 'original position' can be approximated in the laboratory. In two imaginative experiments, Lissowski, Tyszka, and Okrasa (1991) had Polish undergraduates perform an experimental task. Before beginning, the students had to agree on a payment rule; some individuals could be paid more generously than others. After (or if) the group had reached a decision, individuals were assigned to their payment condition by lot. The bulk of these groups were able to reach consensus regarding a payment rule. However, they did not behave as suggested by Rawls (1971). Instead, subjects selected a distribution principle that maximized the average income (not the minimum income, as Rawls suggested), while simultaneously maintaining a so-called 'floor constraint'. That is, individuals also retained a minimum income for the worst-off member of their 'society'. Similar results were obtained by Frohlich, Oppenheimer, and Eavy (1987a,b) using samples of American and Canadian subjects. Although this situation is artificial in the extreme, the findings underscore a key point: When allocators do not know what outcomes will benefit themselves, they take steps to ensure their own well-being, and that of all concerned.

The implications of this fact come into focus when we consider that people generally make allocation decisions with some specific purpose in mind—typically either normative (e.g. being fair) or instrumental (e.g. stimulating performance or maintaining harmony) in nature (Greenberg & Cohen, 1982b; Skitka & Tetlock, 1992). For example, Kabanoff (1991), James (1993), and Martin and Harder (1994) all maintain that people in North American organizations are likely to distribute economic resources based upon a rule of equity. That is, rewards are assigned on the basis of merit: Those who contribute the most, earn the most. Kabanoff (1991) argues that equity distributions are used to spur productivity (for additional evidence see also James, 1993). The basic idea is simple (and consistent with expectancy theory; Vroom, 1964): To the extent that better performers receive higher rewards, people desiring these rewards will strive to attain high levels of performance (cf. Deutsch, 1975, 1985).

However, the matter appears to be more complicated than decision makers may realize. Although research does suggest that equitable rewards can boost positive work behaviors, such as work performance (Greenberg, 1990a; Sheppard, Lewicki, & Minton, 1993), this is by no means a foregone conclusion. The problem managers face is in ensuring that individuals on the low end of the pay scale will perceive their pay as equitable. Those who receive the allocations may not have the same perceptions as those who make them. If they do not, then it seems possible that an attempt to create equity from the organization's perspective could create unfair resource dispersion from the perspective of disadvantaged employees. To the extent that this occurs, the performance-boosting benefits of 'equity' (as defined by the persons assigning the outcomes) will simply not result. In fact, performance may even decline (cf. Greenberg & Cohen, 1982).

Evidence bearing on this point is provided in a noteworthy study by Pfeffer and Davis-Blake (1992) examining 'wage dispersion' (i.e. variability in salary) among university and college administrators. When wage dispersion was high, turnover was lower among individuals with high salaries and higher among individuals with low salaries. In a follow-up study among university and college faculty, Pfeffer and Langton (1993) found that as salary dispersion increased, research productivity dropped and faculty became less collaborative.

Harder (1992) reached similar conclusions in a study of professional athletes. To the extent that the colleges and universities were attempting to achieve pay equity (and it seems unlikely that they would be doing otherwise), their efforts would appear to have failed. Not only did performance fail to improve, but in some cases it declined. This is not to say that equity is unimportant. In fact, Greenberg (1990a), Kulik and Ambrose (1992), Sheppard, Lewicki, & Minton (1993), and Cropanzano and Randall (1993) all review evidence demonstrating that equity can indeed lead to positive work behaviors. However, the equitable feelings that produce these benefits are based on the perceptions of the recipient, and these may *not* coincide with those of the decision maker.

Our discussion thus far has focused on only one organizational reward—pay. Although money is a critically important reward in organizations (Miceli, 1993; Miceli & Lane, 1991), it is not the only reward that is distributed. Indeed, in their classic resource exchange theory, Foa and Foa (1974) have described a variety of valued resources that may be allocated following different normative standards than those which may be used for distributing money. In keeping with this tradition, the allocation of neo-economic outcomes has been studied in two in-basket experiments conducted by Martin and Harder (1994). Participants in these studies were managers who were asked to divide hypothetical rewards between recipients. Some of the rewards were financial (e.g. profits) and others were socioemotional (e.g. friendliness). The researchers found that different types of rewards were allocated following different standards. Specifically, whereas socioemotional rewards were most frequently divided equally, financial rewards were most frequently divided in accordance with people's relative contributions (i.e. equitably). These findings suggest that although it may be considered distributively fair to distinguish between recipients with respect to financial rewards, considered to be deserved by virtue of meritorious contributions, socioemotional rewards are not considered suitable for distinction in this manner. Rather, socioemotional rewards deserve to be provided equally to all, regardless of their performance-relevant contributions. This is in keeping with research showing that allocators are reluctant to distinguish between recipients with whom they have friendly relations (for a review and conceptual model, see Greenberg & Cohen, 1982b).

Another variable shown to influence the making of reward-allocation decisions is national culture (for a review, see Gergen, Morse, & Gergen, 1980). As Greenberg (1982) concluded a decade-and-a-half ago after reviewing cross-cultural differences in the use of justice norms, 'cultural norms of various nations appear to make the equity norm more or less prevalent' (p.424). Among the most reliable cultural differences found has been the tendency for people from collectivistic societies, such as the Chinese, to prefer equal allocations insofar as these promote group harmony, and for people from individualistic societies, such as Americans, to prefer equitable allocations insofar as allocations proportional to contributions promote productivity (Miles & Greenberg, 1993). Although such findings are consistent with Hofstede's (1980)

conceptualization of culture, an emphasis on cultural differences diverts attention from the more immediate situational demands of a social setting. Recogniz-
ing this possibility, James (1993) and Triandis (1994) have raised the possibility
that different cultures may value different transactional goals, and that these
may be met by following different allocation practices.

Testing this notion, Bond, Leung, and Schwartz (1992, Study 1) had undergraduates from Israel and Hong Kong allocate rewards among members of
a work group and indicate why they had made their allocation decisions.
Interestingly, they found that the preferred distributions were largely based on
subjects' expectancies that their decisions would produce positive consequences. In other words, the decision was not based on what was valued by
their culture, but instead, on the outcomes one could expect to obtain: Subjects followed either equity or equality, depending on their beliefs about the
consequences of doing so. Cultural differences by themselves did a limited job
of predicting allocation behavior.

Chen (1995) has suggested that this may be the case because cultural
differences are subject to change over time, and that multiple cultural forces
may make preferences for allocation norms uncertain. Moreover, cultural
differences in sensitivity to various goals are dynamic in nature. For example,
there have been recent shifts in goal priorities within both American and
Chinese companies: American organizations have become more humanistic,
and less likely to be driven purely by profit, whereas Chinese organizations
(following reforms initiated in 1978) have become more profit-driven, and less
driven by interest in achieving harmony. As a result of these changes, Chen
(1995) predicted that employees of contemporary American organizations
would prefer equal allocations of material rewards whereas their Chinese
counterparts would prefer equitable allocations. Chen had large numbers of
American and Chinese employees of various companies, and at various levels,
complete an in-basket exercise that allowed them to express preferences for
various reward-allocation practices. It was found that allocation preferences
were in keeping with the cultural shifts Chen described: Americans were more
likely to make equal allocations of rewards, whereas the Chinese were more
likely to make equitable allocations of rewards. Although these findings are
completely opposite to those long noted, they illustrate the same dynamic in
operation: People make reward allocation decisions that are consistent with
the goals that are salient at the time, and these may well be reliably differentiated by culture. In fact, it is precisely because of this reversal that our confidence in the validity of this phenomenon is enhanced.

PROCEDURAL JUSTICE

In the mid-1970s several theorists (e.g. Deutsch, 1975, Leventhal, 1976b;
Thibaut & Walker, 1975) first called our attention to the idea that justice

demands paying attention not only to the 'ends' of social exchange, but also to the 'means' whereby those ends are attained. As noted earlier, this idea has been referred to as *procedural justice*—the perceived fairness of the procedures used to determine outcomes. Thibaut and Walker's (1975) research comparing various legal systems led to the conclusion that procedures perceived to be fair are ones that give people a voice in the procedures affecting them. Around this same time, Leventhal (1976b, 1980; Leventhal, Karuza, & Fry, 1980) proposed that fair processes involve more than just voice. He argued that procedures may be considered fair to the extent that they adhere to six criteria—they are: applied consistently, free from bias, accurate, correctable, representative of all concerns, and based on prevailing ethical standards. A few years later, Greenberg and his associates (e.g. Folger & Greenberg, 1985; Greenberg, 1987a; Greenberg & Folger, 1983; Greenberg & Tyler, 1987) articulated how the concept of procedural justice may be applied to the study of organizations. The subsequent work in this area has been considerable (for reviews, see Greenberg, 1990a, 1996; Sheppard, Lewicki, & Minton, 1993; Tyler & Smith, in press), and has seen a great deal of conceptual and practical development during the period covered by this review.

Perhaps the major reason for the popularity of the study of procedural justice in organizations is that fair procedures have been associated with a wide variety of desirable outcomes. For example, substantial evidence has demonstrated that procedurally fair treatment makes individuals more accepting of smoking bans (Greenberg, 1994a), pay systems (Miceli, 1993; Miceli & Lane, 1991), parental leave policies (Grover, 1991), and disciplinary actions (Ball, Treviño, & Sims, 1994). In fact, justice concerns appear to feature prominently in virtually all human resource interventions (for reviews see Folger & Cropanzano, in press; Greenberg, 1996a; Tyler & Smith, in press). Generally, people are more accepting of decisions that result from fair procedures than those that result from unfair procedures.

Furthermore, people who accept organizational decisions tend to cooperate with authority figures (Lind, 1995; Tyler & Dawes, 1993; Tyler & Lind, 1992). This occurs even among people who are harmed or inconvenienced by their organizations in some way—the very individuals whose favor may be difficult to court. For example, Tyler and Degoey (1995) found that the more strongly individuals believed that officials went about making water-rationing decisions on a fair basis, the more likely they were to cooperate with those decisions. Similarly, Greenberg (1994a) found that smokers more strongly accepted a smoking ban when they believed it was imposed by their company following fair procedures than when following unfair procedures. In another context, Schaubroeck, May, and Brown (1994) found that salaried employees reacted less negatively to a pay freeze when that freeze was implemented in a procedurally fair fashion than when it was implemented in an unfair fashion. Similarly, Greenberg (1990b) found that people were less likely to steal in response to pay cuts when these appeared to be the result of fair procedures than when they stemmed from unfair procedures. Taken together, these findings illustrate that the effectiveness of organizational procedures may be enhanced by incorporating process attributes that are perceived to be fair.

However, the matter is more involved than this. Employees use their experience with fair or unfair allocation procedures as information that reflects on the organization as a whole. As such, procedural fairness may be used as the basis by which people establish larger relationships with their employers, enhancing their loyalty toward the organization and their willingness to exert effort on its behalf (Tyler & Lind, 1992). In this regard, research has shown that compared to those who believe that their organizations' decision-making processes are unfair, those who perceive them to be fair exhibit higher levels of organizational commitment (Tyler, 1991), greater trust in management (Konovsky & Pugh, 1994), lower turnover intentions (Dailey & Kirk, 1992), a lower likelihood of litigation (Bies & Tyler, 1993), more generous citizenship behaviors (Konovsky & Pugh, 1994; Organ & Moorman, 1993), and to some extent, higher job performance (although the evidence for this connection is tentative, see Gilliland, 1994; Konovsky & Cropanzano, 1991; Lee, 1995).

Clearly, procedural justice has wide-ranging beneficial effects on organizational functioning. In this light, we will examine the components of procedural justice in more detail. When people make fairness evaluations they appear to be sensitive to two distinct 'focal determinants' (Greenberg, 1993b): *structural determinants*—those dealing with the environmental context within which interaction occurs—and *social determinants*—those dealing with the treatment of individuals. We will now turn our attention to each of these. Following this discussion, we will address the issue of *why* procedural justice produces the beneficial effects described above.

Structural Aspects of Procedural Justice

From a structural perspective a procedure may be considered procedurally fair to the extent that it is based on explicit formal organizational policies that people expect to lead to fair distributions (Greenberg, 1993b). The central issue investigated in this regard has to do with identifying the specific determinants of procedural fairness. Both Thibaut and Walker's (1975) findings about the importance of voice and Leventhal's (1976b, 1980; Leventhal, Karuza, & Fry, 1980) list of six criteria have proven useful in this regard, although these guidelines are highly abstract and general in nature.

In the past few years, however, several theorists have built upon these conceptualizations by proposing various structural determinants of procedural justice that are expected to operate in specific organizational settings. For example:

● Building on the empirical work of Greenberg (1986a), Folger, Konovsky, and Cropanzano (1992) proposed that three factors contribute to the perceived fairness of performance evaluations: adequate notice, fair hearing, and judgment based on evidence—each of which has been supported in empirical research (Taylor, Tracy, Renard, Harrison, & Carroll, 1995).

- In the context of strategic planning, Kim and Mauborgne (1991, 1993) identified such process attributes as bilateral communication, ability to refute, consistency, and the presence of a social account as determinants of fairness.
- In the domain of workplace drug screening, Konovsky and Cropanzano (1993), reviewed research suggesting that fair drug screening procedures are ones that are accurate, allow for corrections to be made, provide opportunities for voice, and that are administered with advance notice. With the exception of this last criterion, these other variables are all completely predictable from procedural justice theories.
- Gilliland (1993) identified nine procedural rules expected to enhance the fairness of personnel selection decisions: job relatedness, the opportunity to perform, reconsideration opportunity, consistency, feedback, selection information, honesty, two-way communication, and the propriety of questions. Although these are closely linked to procedural justice theories, Gilliland (1993) also identified two additional rules that may contribute to the perceived fairness of selection decisions, but which have not been previously identified by justice theorists: ease of faking answers, and the invasiveness of questions.

For the most part, these contributions have identified determinants of fairness consistent with Leventhal's (1976b, 1980) rules and the use of voice identified by Thibaut and Walker (1975). In keeping with earlier studies (Greenberg, 1986; Sheppard & Lewicki, 1987), it would appear that these general determinants of fairness *do* apply in organizations although they may take different forms in different contexts. Moreover, it is also possible that some unique determinants of fairness manifest themselves in different organizational settings.

The notion that procedural fairness may be context-sensitive is not meant to imply that completely idiosyncratic criteria are used in different settings—that is, justice is not totally context-specific. Rather, it appears that many of the same general procedural guidelines are brought to all organizational environments although their relative weights and specific forms are shaped by the demands of the context in which they operate. In other words, general determinants of fairness may come to life by being altered to fit their settings. It is with this idea in mind that Greenberg (1996a) has recommended carefully tailoring measures of procedural justice to the specific settings in which they are being assessed: 'What makes a set of questions appropriate in one context may not make them equally appropriate in another. Questions about justice should be carefully matched to the context of interest . . .' (p.402). To the extent that research measures tapping justice perceptions are context-sensitive, our confidence in interpreting them may be enhanced.

Social Aspects of Procedural Justice

Following largely from the work of Bies and his associates (e.g. Folger & Bies, 1989; Greenberg, Bies, & Eskew, 1991; Tyler & Bies, 1990), interest in the structural aspects of procedural justice has been supplemented by the social aspects of procedural justice. The basic idea is that people are concerned with the quality of the interpersonal treatment they receive at the hands of decision-makers—what many researchers have referred to as *interactional justice* (Bies & Moag, 1986). In tracing the history of this concept, Greenberg (1993b) noted that interactional justice was originally treated as a separate construct, a third type of justice (e.g. Bies, 1987). Although subsequent research demonstrated the importance of interpersonal determinants of fairness, the concept became increasingly difficult to distinguish from structural procedural justice. For one thing, both the formal procedures and the interpersonal interactions jointly comprise the process that leads to an allocation decision. Additionally, inter-actional and structural procedural justice had similar consequences and corre-lates (e.g. Clemmer, 1993). Indeed, some studies found them to be highly related to one another (e.g. Konovsky & Cropanzano, 1991; Koper, Van Knippenberg, Bouhuijs, Vermunt, & Wilke, 1993). For these reasons, most current researchers now treat interactional justice as a social aspect of pro-cedural fairness as opposed to separate forms of justice (e.g. Tyler & Bies, 1990; Tyler & Lind, 1992), and we will follow suit.

Following the lead of Greenberg (1993b) and Tyler and Bies (1990) we also will distinguish between two aspects of interpersonal treatment. The first is *social sensitivity*—the extent to which people believe that they have been treated with dignity and respect. The second is *informational justification*—the extent to which people believe they have adequate information about the procedures affecting them. Below we discuss each.

Social sensitivity: The role of dignity and respect

Although it is commonsensical to claim that people like being treated in an interpersonally sensitive manner, it represents a conceptual extension to claim that such treatment contributes to perceptions of fairness. Indeed, several researchers have found that treating people with dignity and respect enhances their perceptions of fairness and their acceptance of the outcomes associated with the discussion. For example, in their study of grievance resolution pro-cedures used by coal miners, Shapiro and Brett (1993) found that fair deci-sions were believed to be made by adjudicating parties who demonstrated high degrees of knowledge, impartiality, and a willingness to consider the grievants' perspectives and feelings. Similarly, in a field experiment Greenberg (1994a) had company officials explain a pending company-wide smoking ban to workers in a manner that demonstrated either high or low levels of sensitivity to the nature of the disruption they were likely to face. As expected, he found that employees were more accepting of the ban, believing it to be fairer, when higher levels of sensitivity were shown.

Interestingly, it is not only perceptions of fairness that are enhanced by socially sensitive treatment, but a general reluctance to retaliate against harmdoers in response to unfair outcomes. For example, Greenberg (1994b) studied theft reactions following from underpayment. Although all underpaid people stole, those who were treated in a direspectful manner stole objects that were of no value to themselves, but that were of value to their employers. In other words, disrespectful treatment, adding insult to the injury of unfair treatment, encouraged people to retaliate against their employers—seeking to harm them in exchange for harming themselves, even if so doing did nothing more than even the score between them symbolically.

It is important to note that the importance of social sensitivity as a determinant of justice is not limited to Americans. Leung, Chiu, and Au (1993) conducted a study in Hong Kong in which they examined observers' responses to hypothetical industrial actions such as strikes and sit-ins. Respondents were found to be more sympathetic to industrial actions when management had treated workers with a lack of consideration and respect. This research provides a useful cross-cultural addition to the burgeoning literature on the social determinants of fairness. More such cross-cultural work of this type is needed (cf. Lind & Earley, 1992), not only to determine the generalizability of existing phenomena, but also to determine the extent to which normative differences with respect to politeness and social sensitivity qualify existing conclusions.

Informational justification: The role of social accounts

In addition to fairness defined in terms of courteous treatment, research also supports the idea that fairness demands having access to information regarding the reasons underlying how outcomes are determined. For example, Daly and Geyer (1994) surveyed employees' reactions to a major facilities relocation. They found that individuals responded more positively when the move was adequately explained than when no such explanation was given. In a follow-up study, these same researchers found that adequate explanations were effective in maintaining workers' feelings of organizational commitment during periods of organizational decline (Daly & Geyer, 1995). The benefits of informational justifications for undesirable outcomes have been exhibited consistently in several additional empirical studies conducted in a wide variety of settings (e.g. Brockner, DeWitt, Grover, & Reed, 1990; Greenberg, 1993a, 1994a; Konovsky & Folger, 1991a; Schaubroeck, May & Brown, 1994). All of these studies demonstrate that providing people with information that justifies the need for negative outcomes enhances the extent to which they come to accept those outcomes as fair.

Recent studies have examined various characteristics of informtion that contribute to its perceived adequacy in mitigating reactions to undesirable outcomes. For example, in a laboratory study Shapiro (1991) assessed the perceived adequacy of three different types of causal accounts: an external attribution to an uncontrollable event, an internal attribution to an altruistic motive, and an internal attribution to a selfish motive. She found that the most effective excuses were external in nature, events over which actors had no control. By contrast, explanations that led to the belief that the actor was selfish were considered least adequate. In fact, explanations that are not particularly convincing might not only be inadequate when it comes to cultivating positive impressions, but may backfire, leading to negative impressions (Greenberg, 1996b).

It is not only the adequacy of information that contributes to its effectiveness in mitigating reactions to unfair situations, but also the medium by which that information is conveyed. In this connection, Shapiro, Butner, and Barry (1994, Study 2) compared the perceived adequacy of accounts presented in face-to-face verbal interaction and in written notes. They found that the added richness of face-to-face verbal interaction enhanced perceptions of the adequacy of messages compared to the same messages presented in written form. These findings are in keeping with earlier studies suggesting that communciations media differ with respect to the degree of information they convey, and that richer media are considered preferable for communicating socially sensitive information (Lengel & Daft, 1988). In an era in which working people frequently interact by using such impersonal means as computers, fax machines, and satellite transmissions, Shapiro, Batner, and Barry's (1994, Study 2) findings are worthy of further consideration.

Not only might information presented via one medium be more effective than the same information presented via another medium, but also, the same explanation may be more effective in some situations than in others. Brockner et al. (1990) examined this possibility using a sample of layoff survivors. Although survivors responded negatively when their coworkers lost their jobs, justifications attenuated these negative reactions. These mitigating accounts were most effective under two conditions: when the workers were uncertain about the way that their employer was allocating organizational resources, and when the layoff was especially important to the survivors. According to Brockner et al. (1990), uncertainty and importance created a high need for information, and social accounts are useful in this regard. On the other hand, when uncertainty was low and the layoffs were unimportant, survivors' need for information was lower, and the accounts given had less impact.

Why Do Procedures Matter?

As we have noted, research suggests that matters of justice involve more than just economic gain; they also involve the manner in which people are treated. The question of why this occurs has been the topic of considerable recent research. In general, two approaches have been suggested, both of which have received empirical support—the *instrumental model* and the *relational model*. We now will review the evidence for each.

The instrumental model

The instrumental, or self-interest, model of procedural justice accepts the traditional notion that economic incentives promote fairness. It simply claims that individuals may take a long-term focus when evaluating their economic gains. As a result, people may become tolerant of short-term economic losses so long as they expect that advantageous outcomes will be forthcoming in the future. Procedural justice is highly valued insofar as it suggests the existence of a system that will yield the greatest benefits in the long run. Thus, short-term failures can be overlooked when there is some promise of future gain (for reviews, see Greenberg, 1990a, Shapiro, 1993; Tyler, 1990).

There is a good deal of evidence suggesting that individuals value procedural justice, in part, for instrumental reasons. Perhaps the most compelling evidence for the instrumental model is that people evaluate processes more favorably when they lead to positive outcomes than when they lead to negative outcomes. This effect has been observed repeatedly (e.g. Ambrose, Harland, & Kulik, 1991; Conlon, 1993; Conlon & Fasolo, 1990; Conlon & Ross, 1993; Flinder & Hauenstein, 1994; Krzystofiak, Lillis, & Newman, 1995; Lind, Kanfer, & Earley, 1990; Lind, Kulik, Ambrose, & de Vera Park, 1993; Lowe & Vodanovich, 1995), although sometimes the effect sizes are small (e.g. Tyler, 1989, 1991) and exceptions occur (e.g. Giacobbe-Miller, 1995; Tyler, 1994).

If the instrumental model identified the only cause of procedural justice, then one would expect that process fairness would be entirely determined by short-term and long-term economic concerns. On the other hand, to the extent that noninstrumental considerations matter, then process characteristics should enhance perceptions of procedural justice even when no direct economic benefits are expected. To test this possibility, researchers have examined the impact of process characteristics (such as voice or advance notice) under conditions in which advantageous outcomes are precluded. For example, in a laboratory experiment conducted by Lind, Kanfer, and Earley, (1990) undergraduate subjects were assigned performance goals, the successful attainment of which would lead to a desired reward. Some subjects were given an effective voice in determining their goal. For others, their voice had no effect on the outcome. Finally, in a control group subjects had no voice whatsoever. The lowest levels of perceived fairness were reported by subjects in the control group, for whom no voice was allowed. The highest levels of perceived fairness were found when voice was permitted and capable of influencing the goal. In this condition, voice is presumed to have both an instrumental effect—increasing the opportunity to meet the goal—and a noninstrumental effect—enhancing the belief that one's input is welcomed.

Most relevant to our point is that even when individuals could not influence their outcomes, they still reported greater fairness when they had voice than when they didn't have voice.

Parallel findings were obtained by Cropanzano and Randall (1995). These researchers were interested in investigating the effects of advance notice on perceptions of procedural justice. Subjects were assigned to work on an anagram-solving task. High performance on this task would yield a bonus unit of experimental credit. Some individuals were disadvantaged due to a change in the scoring procedure. When the change was announced in advance, perceptions of procedural fairness were relatively high. However, when the change was announced after the task was conducted, perceptions of procedural fairness were much lower. Thus, although the outcomes were identical in both conditions, the manner in which the change was announced had an effect on the perceived fairness of those outcomes. The noninstrumental, purely procedural variable, advance notice, raised procedural justice perceptions despite the fact that procedures had no impact on outcomes—that is, they had no instrumental effects.

Evidence of this phenomenon is not limited exclusively to the lab. Conlon (1993) examined defendants' procedural justice judgments after appealing parking violations. He found that both instrumental considerations (the value of the fine) and noninstrumental considerations (voice in the legal procedure) affected perceptions of process fairness, although the effects of the instrumental factors were substantially larger. Slightly different results were obtained in a field study by Shapiro and Brett (1993). These researchers assessed the reactions of coal miners to various grievance procedures. Like Conlon (1993), Shapiro and Brett (1993) found evidence for both instrumental and noninstrumental determinants of procedural justice. However, in this study the noninstrumental concerns explained the preponderance of variance.

Taken together, these investigations suggest that although instrumental concerns are important, people also formulate procedural justice judgments based on other considerations. However, none of the work reviewed thus far directly measured these 'other concerns'. Although these concerns appear to be important, without such direct measurement they cannot be explicitly identified. Fortunately, research has begun to address this issue by suggesting a complementary model of procedural justice.

The relational model

The relational model (formally called the group-value model) has been proposed as a supplement to the instrumental model (for reviews see Lind, 1995; Lind & Tyler, 1988; Tyler, 1990; Tyler & Dawes, 1993; Tyler & Lind, 1992). Proponents of the relational model agree that people join groups as a means of obtaining valuable economic resources. In this sense, the relational and instrumental models are consistent. However, the relational model maintains that groups offer more than material rewards. Group affiliation is also a means of achieving social status and self-esteem, and these considerations are every bit as potent as the economic incentives emphasized by the instrumental approach. Even within the most individualistic cultures people need to be valued by some group or groups (Lind & Earley, 1992), in as much as this is an important means by which people acquire a sense of personal worth (Tyler & Lind, 1992). For this reason, people tend to be keenly aware of their positions within groups and the groups' potential for providing them with these valuable social rewards.

Tyler (1989, 1990) has argued that people have three *relational concerns*, and that these stem from people's desires for dignity and worth—neutrality, trust, and standing. *Neutrality* is something that a decision-maker expresses to an individual. If neutrality exists, then the decision-maker is free from tendentiousness and bias. He or she uses facts and not opinions and attempts to make choices that create a level playing field for all. Neutrality implies openness and honesty, and the absence of any hidden agendas. *Trust* refers to the degree to which people believe that the decision-maker intends to act in a fair manner. Employees generally wish to count on the trustworthiness of authority figures. *Standing* is something that an individual possesses, but that is conveyed by the decision-maker. When a person's standing is high, his or her status has been affirmed, such as by implementing procedures with politeness and care.

Evidence for the relational model generally has been supportive: Procedural fairness perceptions are enhanced when these three relational concerns have been fulfilled (for reviews, see Lind & Tyler, 1992; Tyler, 1990). For example, there is good support for the relational model in the context of citizens' interactions with civil authorities (Tyler, 1989, 1994). However, only now is the evidence beginning to accumulate in organizational settings. In two field studies, Lind et al. (1993) examined the manner in which individuals reacted to court-ordered arbitration in response to a lawsuit. They found that when relational concerns were met, the litigants had greater perceptions of procedural justice. These feelings, in turn, led them to accept the arbitrated settlement. Although these findings support the relational model, it is important to note that they do not contradict the instrumental approach. In fact, Lind et al. (1993) present evidence suggesting that outcome favorability may impact procedural justice judgments as well as the acceptance of outcomes themselves. Analogous results were obtained by Giacobbe-Miller (1995) in a study of labor–management disputes.

Brockner, Tyler, and Cooper-Schneider (1992) examined the relational model from a different perspective. They argued that if individuals are guided by relational concerns, then those who are most committed to their institutions will be the most upset by violations of procedural justice. This would suggest an interaction between commitment and procedural justice such that procedural justice is more strongly related to various outcomes when commitment is high. When commitment is low, however, the effects of procedural justice should be weaker. Supportive results were obtained in two field studies, one dealing with layoff survivors (Brockner, Tyler, & Cooper-Schneider, 1992, Study 1), and the other examining citizen interactions with legal authorities (Brockner, Tyler, & Cooper-Schneider, 1992, Study 2).

In conclusion, evidence supports both the instrumental and relational models of procedural justice. Both perspectives provide important insight into the underlying reasons why procedural justice has been shown to be so important in organizations.

THE RELATIONSHIP BETWEEN PROCEDURAL AND DISTRIBUTIVE JUSTICE

Thus far, our discussion of organizational justice has focused on the unique impact of distributive justice and procedural justice. However, from the time that the concept of procedural justice was first introduced to the social sciences, theorists have acknowledged that it may be related to distributive justice (Leventhal, 1976a, 1980; Thibaut & Walker, 1975), although the nature of this relationship was not systematically studied. Recently, however, theorists have focused on two possibilities that we will review here—that distributive justice and procedural justice operate independently, as main effects, and that they operate jointly, as interacting effects.

The Two-Factor Model: Different Effects of Different Types of Justice

In a review article, Greenberg (1990a) distinguished between the different consequences that procedural and distributive justice appeared to have: Procedural justice was linked to system satisfaction whereas distributive justice was linked to outcome satisfaction. To a great extent, this distinction continues to hold today. Evidence suggests that distributive justice primarily influences one's satisfaction with the outcome in question or the results of some decision (Brockner & Wiesenfeld, in press). For example, the belief that one's pay is not suitable compensation for one's achievements results in perceptions of inequity that, in turn, produce low pay satisfaction (Harder, 1992; McFarlin & Sweeney, 1992; Sweeney & McFarlin, 1993; Sweeney, McFarlin, & Inderrieden, 1990; Summers & Hendrix, 1991). By contrast, procedural justice primarily influences attitudes and behaviors that are relevant to the larger organization. Procedures, in other words, are central determinants of one's trust in management and loyalty to the institution or system that rendered the decision in question (Krystofiak, Lillis, & Newman, 1995; Lind, 1995; Tyler & Degoey, 1995). Continuing with pay as an example, evidence suggests that when pay decisions are made using fair procedures, people are likely to remain committed to their organizations—even when the decisions are unfavorable (Cooper, Dyck, & Frohlich, 1992; McFarlin & Sweeney, 1992; Schaubroeck, May, & Brown, 1994; Sweeney & McFarlin, 1993). Sweeney and McFarlin (1993) have dubbed these different effects the *two-factor model*: Although procedures and outcomes are both important determinants of justice, they affect different factors.

Despite considerable evidence supporting the two-factor model (for reviews, see Lind & Earley, 1992; Tyler, 1990; Tyler & Lind, 1992), the evidence is not unequivocal. Lowe and Vodanovich (1995), for example, suggested that the relationship of distributive justice and procedural justice to organizationally relevant criteria may vary over time. They propose that perceptions of organizational outcomes are most strongly influenced by distributive injustices immediately after the injustices occur. As time elapses, however, this effect dissipates. Employees then adapt a longer-term perspective and alter their impressions of organizations so that these are more firmly based upon procedures. If this reasoning is correct, then support for the two-factor model should only appear as time has passed following defining-episodes of distributive injustice.

Lowe and Vodanovich (1995) tested these ideas using a sample of university employees who had undergone a restructuring of their job classifications, an event that triggered feelings of distributive injustice in many employees. Their survey, administered two months after the restructuring occurred (while respondents apparently were still feeling the sting), found that feelings of organizational commitment were more strongly linked to the unfavorability of the outcome than they were to the procedures whereby these outcomes were determined. Unfortunately, insofar as the investigators failed to administer a follow-up survey to assess the extent to which procedures became more important with the passage of time, their hypotheses were not completely tested. However, their idea warrants future research. Based on our earlier conclusions regarding the mitigating influences of explanations, these may be expected to be likely moderators of the time-sensitive effects Lowe and Vodanovich (1995) proposed. After all, as time passes it is likely that people will receive information that qualifies their interpretation of earlier events.

The Interaction Model:
Conjoint Effects of Distributive and Procedural Justice

According to the two-factor model, procedures and outcomes predict different types of reactions, and therefore it speaks only to main effects. Additional research, however, suggests that procedural justice and distributive justice interact (for reviews, see Brockner & Wiesenfeld, 1996; Cropanzano & Folger, 1991). Following Brockner and Wiesenfeld (1966), this interaction can be described from the perspective of either the procedures or the

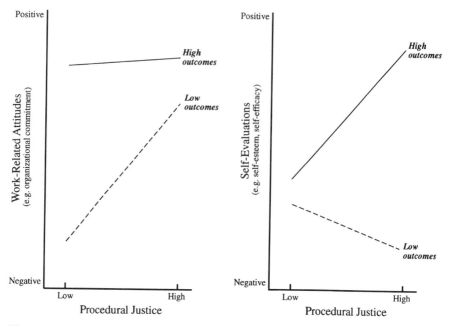

Figure 8.1   General form of procedure-by-outcome interactions for work-related attitudes (left panel) and self-evaluations (right panel)

outcomes (see left panel of Figure 8.1). One might say that procedural justice is more strongly related to work attitudes when outcomes are low than when they are high. Conversely, one also might say that outcomes are more strongly related to work attitudes when procedures are unfair than when they are fair. Brockner and Wiesenfeld (1996) examined the evidence documenting the existence of this interaction and offered several possible explanations for it.

Work-related attitudes

Notably, Brockner and Wiesenfeld (1996) suggested that the procedure-by-outcome interaction has been generally associated with organizationally relevant outcomes. For example, in research, conducted by Brockner et al. (1990) and by Daly and Geyer (1994) the procedure-by-outcome interaction significantly predicted organizational commitment. However, less research has linked the procedure-by-outcome interaction to criteria that could clearly be considered personal, such as pay satisfaction. The work of McFarlin and Sweeney (1992) is an exception. These researchers found that the procedure-by-outcome interaction was significant for commitment, but not for pay satisfaction. Clearly, more research is needed before definite conclusions can be drawn about the nature of the procedure-by-outcome interaction. At this point, however, the available evidence suggests that the procedure-by-outcome interaction behaves the same as the procedural main effect described in conjunction with the two-factor model—that is, the interaction is more clearly related to attitudes toward the system or institution than attitudes toward one's job.

It is important to note that the interaction effect has not been consistently obtained. Researchers either have not tested for it (cf. Brockner and Wiesenfeld, in press), or have found it to be nonsignificant in their research (Cropanzano & Konovsky, 1995; Lowe & Vodanovich, 1995). Nonsignificant interactions are particularly likely to occur in studies (e.g. Lowe & Vodanovich, 1995) in which sample sizes are too low to have adequate statistical power to detect interactions (cf. Stone, 1988). Interaction effects also might not be found in the case of certain dependent variables which may be sensitive only to the main effects of outcome. For example, in the context of workplace drug screening, Cropanzano and Konovsky (1995) found that some process characteristics (e.g. voice, advance notice) interacted with outcome negativity as expected whereas another (i.e. the presence or absence of a grievance system) did not. Such findings suggest that it may be misleading to ignore the possibility that all determinants of fair procedures do not have the same effects. As noted in our earlier discussion of context-sensitive variables, some determinants of procedural justice may have different effects than others.

Brockner and Siegel (1995) have offered a novel interpretation of the interaction effect. They claim that it is not procedures themselves that interact with outcomes, but that outcome favorability moderates the effect of trust: The relevant interaction is between trust and outcomes; procedures are not directly involved. Brockner and Siegel (1995) hypothesize that procedural justice is still important, but indirectly, insofar as it serves as the primary determinant of trust. Nevertheless, it is trust that takes part in the actual interaction. To date, the evidence for this idea is limited, but promising. For example, in a retrospective study Siegel, Brockner, and Tyler (1995) asked workers to recall problems they had with their supervisors. Consistent with Brockner and Siegel's (1995) reasoning, outcome favorability interacted with both procedures and trust to predict employees' acceptance of the supervisors' decisions. However, the trust-by-outcome interaction accounted for considerably more variance. Moreover, when both interactions were simultaneously used to predict decision acceptance, only the trust-by-outcome interaction remained significant; the procedure-by-outcome interaction was not. Although it is premature to draw firm conclusions about the role of trust in determining the acceptance of outcomes, it does appear to be an important factor.

Self-evaluations

Thus far, we have seen that procedures and outcomes may interact to foster different reactions to different aspects of the work environment. Insightful as this work has been, none of it has examined self-relevant cognitions. However, in light of literature demonstrating the importance of self-esteem (e.g. Brockner, 1988) and self-efficacy (e.g. Gist & Mitchell, 1992) in organizations, attention deserves to be paid to what fair or unfair treatment leads people to think about themselves.

Several recent studies have examined how procedures and outcomes work together to influence self-esteem and perceptions of self-efficacy. For the most part, these studies find a different interaction pattern than the one previously described (see right panel of Figure 8.1). For example, in two laboratory experiments Koper et al. (1993), gave university students bogus feedback about their performance on a test of basic abilities. When the students were given positive feedback and the test was believed to have been graded fairly (i.e. carefully and accurately), state self-esteem was relatively high. However, when the students were given negative feedback, the fairness of the test-grading procedure had little impact on their self-esteem. These studies suggest that procedures and outcomes interact to predict self-relevant cognitions such that outcome favorability exerts a stronger effect on state self-esteem when fair procedures are used compared to when unfair procedures are used. In a related field study, Gilliland (1994) examined the impact of procedures and outcomes on self-efficacy. He found that when people were not hired (an unfavorable outcome) using a test that was job-related (a fair procedure), their self-efficacy perceptions were low. However, unfair tests had less effect on self-efficacy than did fair tests. Gilliland's (1994) findings are generally consistent with the self-esteem research reviewed previously. As summarized in Figure 8.1, the interactions obtained by both Koper et al. (1993) and Gilliland (1994), measuring self-relevant perceptions, were different from those found in the earlier cited studies measuring organizational attitudes.

Why might this interaction occur? Tyler and Degoey (1995) consider the question from the perspective of the relational model: When a process is fair, individuals see themselves as valued; when a process is unfair, they see themselves as less valued. For this reason, people should evaluate themselves more positively when procedures are fair, and less positively when procedures are unfair. This explanation implies that it is the fairness of the presentation, and not the favorability of the feedback, that determines self-esteem. One might posit from Tyler and Degoey (1995), therefore, that people's self-esteem will be raised even when feedback is negative, so long as a fair process is maintained. This hypothesis, however, has not received support. In fact, procedural fairness does not exhibit a positive relationship to self-evaluations in the case of negative feedback. Rather, evidence suggests that people receiving negative feedback evaluate themselves less positively when that feedback is considered procedurally fair than when it is considered procedurally unfair (Gilliland, 1994; Koper et al., 1993). In other words, people receiving negative feedback may feel better about themselves when the process used to assess their performance is considered to be unfair than when it is considered to be fair. Tyler and Degoey's (1995) reasoning cannot account for these findings.

Thus, we need a model that explains why people react favorably to feedback that is procedurally fair and positive, while also reacting unfavorably to feedback that is procedurally fair and negative. We can resolve this issue by considering the dimension along which the feedback is diagnostic. For Tyler and Degoey (1995) the principal dimension in question is the individual's relationship with the group. They maintain that procedures, more than outcomes, provide information about this relationship. However, performance feedback supplies information about other things as well. In particular, feedback also can suggest things about a person's skills and abilities. In the studies by Koper et al. (1993) and Gilliland (1994), subjects received some type of evaluative feedback, such as their basic abilities or their abilities to do their jobs. A fair process might lead individuals to more fully accept their feedback as valid. Thus, when the procedures are believed to be fair, the negative feedback resulting from these procedures will have greater diagnostic value. However, when a procedure is unfair, the value of the feedback resulting from it is circumspect, and may be readily dismissed. To state the matter more succinctly, information has greater force when it is based on fair procedures compared to unfair procedures. For this reason, fairly given positive feedback leads people to evaluate themselves more favorably, whereas fairly given negative feedback leads people to evaluate themselves less favorably. This analysis suggests that allocation procedures may trigger more than just the concern for personal dignity. They also may provide information about how people should evaluate their own abilities and skills.

JUSTICE RESEARCH IN ORGANIZATIONAL SETTINGS: TOWARD PRACTICAL APPLICATIONS

Greenberg (1990a, 1993c, 1996a) has argued that the major value of studying organizational justice phenomena lies in the insight it provides with respect to understanding and managing various aspects of organizational behavior. Specifically, he claims that general, context-neutral studies of fairness are less informative than those examining fairness issues arising in specific organizational settings (Greenberg, 1996a). There are three reasons for this. First, studying the perceived fairness of organizational phenomena is a valuable way of learning about those phenomena themselves. Second, unique aspects of justice are likely to arise in specific organizational contexts. And finally, studying justice concepts in various organizational settings provides a good opportunity to assess their generalizability. Greenberg's point is that studying justice in organizations not only sheds light on matters of justice, but also on organizations themselves. For this reason, he advocates applying justice concepts to a broad set of organizational phenomena.

When the study of organizational justice first emerged, Greenberg identified several aspects of organizational settings that stood to benefit from being analyzed through the lens of organizational justice (e.g. Greenberg, 1987a). Indeed, he conducted justice-directed *post hoc* analyses of such phenomena as performance evaluations (Greenberg, 1986b,c), comparable worth (Greenberg & McCarty, 1990) and various human resources management practices (Greenberg & Folger, 1983; Folger & Greenberg, 1985). Today, researchers have not only accepted, but embraced the premise that 'justice matters' in organizations, and they have conducted many investigations focusing on the role of justice in organizations. Indeed, the past few years have seen many significant applications of justice concepts to organizational issues. In view of the voluminous nature of this literature, we will review only the highlights of this work (for a more complete presentation, see Folger & Cropanzano, in press).

Strategic Planning

Earlier, we noted that among the benefits derived from using fair procedures is that they enhance employees' acceptance of institutional authorities. This is likely to be especially important in the context of strategic planning, in which it is vital to organizational success that employees endorse their firms' strategic plans (Miller & Cardinal, 1994). Recent research suggests that one important determinant of the acceptance of strategic plans is the extent to which employees believe that the plans were formulated and implemented in a procedurally fair manner. In general, research has shown that organizational changes that are believed to be based on fair procedures are better accepted than those believed to be based on unfair procedures (Novelli, Kirkman, & Shapiro, 1995).

This phenomenon is demonstrated clearly in a survey of subsidiary managers from multinational coporations conducted by Kim and Mauborgne (1991). These researchers were interested in determining the extent to which managers believed that their companies' headquarters used procedurally fair decision techniques during the planning process. They found, as expected, that perceptions of procedural justice were positively associated with feelings of organizational commitment, trust in the head office, social harmony, and satisfaction with the outcomes of the planning process. Moreover, the procedural justice effects were greater than the impact of outcome fairness. The same researchers later replicated and extended these findings in a longitudinal study. Kim and Mauborgne (1993) found that procedural justice was associated positively with perceptions of commitment, trust, and outcome satisfaction. They also found that these feelings, in turn, led managers to be supportive of the strategic plan.

A complementary approach was taken by Korsgaard, Schweiger, and Sapienza (1995). These researchers were interested in the strategic planning process used by members of intact management teams. They presented a hypothetical business case to team members who were participating in an executive training program. Consistent with the field research of Kim and Mauborgne (1991, 1993), Korsgaard and her colleagues found that perceptions of procedural fairness were affected significantly by two independent variables: allowing team members to influence the decision, and consideration of their viewpoints. These feelings of procedural justice, in turn, led to higher levels of trust, decision commitment, and group attachment. In sum, research has shown that fair procedures enhance employees' acceptance of their organizations' strategic plans.

Organizational Staffing

Historically, when industrial/organizational psychologists have discussed 'selection fairness' they were referring to various psychometric properties of assessment instruments, such as concerns of differential validity, adverse impact, and so forth. This literature continues to be important (Arvey & Sackett, 1993). However, more recent work has begun to examine the test-takers' perceptions of fairness (Arvey, 1992), especially distributive and procedural justice (for reviews, see Gilliland, 1993; Schuler, 1993a; Singer, 1993). Generally speaking, this work suggests that staffing procedures perceived as being unfair have pernicious consequences.

Gilliland (1993) maintains that selection tests incite concerns about all three aspects of procedural justice—structural characteristics (what Gilliland calls 'formal characteristics'), explanations and interpersonal treatment. This work is important insofar as some selection methodologies are less likely to engender fairness perceptions than others (Gilliland, 1994; Singer, 1992). Perceived injustice, in turn, gives rise to a host of negative outcomes, such as poor work attitudes and lower job performance (Gilliland, 1994). For example, Gilliland (1994) found that workers who believed that they were selected by unfair means had poorer work attitudes and lower job performance than those who believed they were selected by fair means. Similarly, several studies by Singer (1992, 1993) found that individuals who believed that staffing procedures were unfair were less likely to accept a job than those who believed them to be fair. (It should be noted, however, that this effect may be stronger when job opportunities are considered sequentially than when they are examined in pairs; Bazerman, Schroth, Shah, et al., 1994, Study 2.)

Fortunately, these consequences can be avoided by incorporating procedural justice into selection systems. In fact, research conducted over the past few years can serve as explicit guides as to how this may be accomplished. With this in mind, we will consider the fairness of several of the most widely used staffing procedures (see also reviews by Folger and Cropanzano, in press; Gilliland, 1993).

Interviews

Employment interviews, especially the unstructured variety, are used very widely (Harris, Dworking, & Park, 1990). Studies have found that applicants view them as fair (Harland & Biasotto, 1993; Kravitz, Stinson, & Chavez, in press; Smither, Reilly, Millsap, et al., 1993), although these results can vary depending on the content of the interview (Rynes & Connerley, 1993). Job applicants even expect to participate in unstructured interviews—in fact, they consider selection procedures unfair when interviews are not used (Singer, 1992, 1993). Although these findings paint an encouraging picture of the benefits of unstructured interviews, it remains problematic that unstructured interviews yield lower validity coefficients than their structured counterparts (Latham & Finnegan, 1993). At the same time, however, applicants perceive unstructured interviews to be more fair than structured interviews (Latham & Finnegan, 1993; Schuler, 1993b). This probably stems from the fact that unstructured interviews provide greater opportunities for candidates to express themselves, thereby providing voice—a well-established criterion of procedural justice (Thibaut & Walker, 1975). In so far as there are justice-enhancing benefits associated with unstructured interviews, and validity-enhancing benefits associated with structured interviews, it would appear wise to consider using both types of interviews in the selection process.

Assessment centers and work simulations

Both Gilliland (1993) and Singer (1993) suggest that perceptions of fairness are enhanced when a selection instrument is ostensibly job-related or 'transparent' (Schuler, 1993a)—that is, when it has 'face validity' (Mosier, 1947). Various work simulations and assessment centers have this quality (Finkle, 1976). Applicants can readily reocgnize the tests' relevance for the job and, therefore, should view these tools favorably. In fact, considerable research suggests that this is the case. For example, in surveys conducted by Rynes and Connerley (1993), and Kravitz, Stinson, and Chavez (in press), it was found that work simulations and job-sample tests consistently were among the most favored selection devices. Studies of assessment centers yield similar results (Davis, 1993; Macan, Avedon, Paese, & Smith, 1994). These findings are encouraging insofar as work simulations and assessment centers yield substantial validity coefficients (Thornton & Cleveland, 1990). Thus, work simulations appear to constitute a selection instrument that is both useful and fair.

Biographical inventories

If face-valid assessment tools are perceived to be fair it follows that those with questionable face validity, and inherent opportunities for violations of privacy, would be considered unfair. This appears to be the case in studies of biographical inventories. Indeed, Smither et al. (1993) found that biographical inventories were believed to be less fair than other selection techniques.

Similarly, Kluger and Rothstein (1993) found that applicants generally held negative opinions of organizations that used biographical inventories. Likewise, Stoffey, Millsap, Smither, and Reilly (1991) found that the use of biodata lowered applicants' job-pursuit intentions. These findings, considered along with the fact that the US government has long restricted the kinds of questions that can be asked on an application blank (Lowell & DeLoach, 1984), raise serious questions about the costs that may be incurred by the continued use of biographical inventories as selection tools.

Personality tests

The issue of perceived job-relevance of test procedures and invasions of privacy manifests itself as well in the context of personality tests. Research has shown that personality tests are sometimes valid predictors of job performance (Guion, 1991), although this depends greatly on the personality trait measured and on the characteristics of the particular job (Tett, Jackson, & Rothstein, 1991). Generally, however, applicants do not like personality inventories. In fact, many people react negatively to them (Ambrose & Rosse, 1993; Harland & Biasotto, 1993; Kavitz, Stinson, & Chavez, in press; Rosse, Miller, & Stecher, 1994; Rynes & Connerley, 1993) and form negative opinions of the organizations using them (Smither et al., 1993). For example, in a large-scale survey of employees, Westin (1978) found that 44% of the respondents wanted personality testing banned. Not surprisingly, applicants selected by use of personality inventories are less likely to accept job offers than individuals selected by other means (Rosse, Ringer, & Miller, in press). In view of this negative picture, it should come as no surprise to find that managers are reluctant to use personality tests (Harris, Dworkin, & Park, 1990).

Despite these concerns, there may be something that can be done to enhance the acceptance of personality tests. Many personality instruments were originally designed for diagnosing personality disorders in clinical populations (for a review, see Guion, 1965). As a result, some of the questions may come across as invasive and offensive when used in nonclinical settings. If so, then it may be possible to revise offending items or to select only those items that are relevant to occupational settings. Doing so may enhance the perceived fairness of personality screening. Some evidence suggests that this will indeed occur. For example, Jones (1991) discovered that test-takers responded far more favorably when only work-related personality items were used in selection tests than when these were supplemented by unrelated items. The suggestion to limit the focus of personality tests is in keeping with the trend toward using narrow, situationally explicit, personality variables in personnel testing (Guion, 1991). Of course, to the extent that items from established personality inventories are revised or omitted, it is essential to revalidate them to ensure that their predictive power has not been attenuated.

Reference checks

Reference checks are in widespread use (Harris, Dworkin, & Park, 1990) despite the fact that they do not have particularly high levels of statistical validity (except, perhaps in certain limited conditions; Knouse, 1989). Regardless, applicants do consider reference checks to be fair. A study by Rynes and Connerley (1993), for example, found that applicants preferred reference checks to other selection techniques. Additionally, in a study in which people were asked to assess their reactions to various selection devices Kravitz, Stinson, and Chavez (in press) found that reference letters were judged quite favorably.

Cognitive abilities tests

Cognitive abilities, or so-called 'intelligence', tests are useful tools for predicting job performance (Wigdor & Sackett, 1993). However, several studies suggest that job applicants often reject them. Kluger and Rothstein (1993, Study 1) gave subjects negative feedback regarding their performance on one of four selection tests. Responses were especially negative among people who scored low on a test of cognitive ability. In a follow-up study the researchers found that the actual and perceived difficulty of the intelligence tests may have lowered test-takers' perceptions of control and distracted them (Kluger & Rothstein, 1993, Study 2). Similar results also were obtained by Macan et al. (1994).

This is not to say that people's feelings about intelligence tests are completely negative. For example, Rosse, Miller, and Stecher (1994) found that the inclusion of a cognitive ability test in a battery with a personality test actually improved people's reactions to the personality test. In addition, of the 16 selection instruments evaluated by participants in the study by Kravitz and his associates (in press), cognitive abilities tests were ranked seventh— approximately in the middle of their list. Test-takers' reactions also may depend less on the type of test and more on the particular test items. In support of this contention, Rynes and Connerley (1993) found that intelligence tests were evaluated more favorably when they included job-related items than when they did not. Likewise, Smither et al. (1993) discovered that cognitive ability tests with concrete items were perceived more positively than those containing abstract items.

To conclude this section, many recent studies have demonstrated that certain characteristics can be incorporated into selection procedures to enhance their perceived fairness. Moreover, perceived fair procedures lead to a variety of beneficial personal and organizational outcomes. Clearly, research and theory on organizational justice holds a great deal of promise when it comes to identifying ways of enhancing people's reactions to selection instruments.

Workplace Drug Screening

Although drug testing can be a valid predictor of work behavior, surveys have shown that people's reactions to this practice are highly variable (for a review, see Konovsky & Cropanzano, 1993). Many individuals perceive drug screening favorably whereas others do not (Labig, 1992; Murphy, Thornton, & Prue, 1991; Murphy, Thornton, & Reynolds, 1990). Nonetheless, studies have documented at least some concerns regarding drug-testing fairness (e.g. Harris, Dworking, & Park, 1990), although some other staffing methods are considered even less fair (Kravitz, Stinson, & Chavez, in press; Rosse, Ringer, & Miller, in press; Rynes & Connerley, 1993).

These findings are of more than academic interest. Notably, Konovsky and Cropanzano (1991) found that those employees who believed that a workplace drug screening program was procedurally unfair also had lower organizational commitment, lower job satisfaction, higher turnover intentions, and lower assessments of their work performance by their supervisors. Generally consistent results also were obtained in a role-playing study conducted by Crant and Bateman (1990). To the extent that unfair drug screening procedures may interfere with an organization's effectiveness, it is important for managers to recognize the characteristics of fair and unfair practices, and to promote the use of fair practices.

There are several possible reasons why diverse evaluations of drug testing are found. One possibility is that there are individual differences in people's attitudes toward drug testing. Research by Crant and Bateman (1993) and by Rosse, Miller, and Ringer (in press) suggests that people who use illegal drugs tend to have more negative opinions of drug testing programs than those who do not. This is in keeping with the self-interest bias in procedural justice perceptions to which we alluded earlier (cf. Grover, 1991).

However, as we have already discussed, self-interest appears to be only one determinant of procedural fairness judgments. Evaluations of drug screening also may vary because drug screening programs themselves are highly diverse. Any particular drug test may or may not have associated with it a variety of procedural safeguards (Konovsky & Cropanzano, 1993). Furthermore, even if these safeguards do exist, they may not be evident to the test-taker (suggesting that it is important for people who are behaving fairly to publicize their efforts; Greenberg, 1990c). For example, Tepper and Braun (1995) found that employees felt favorable toward drug testing procedures to the extent that they believed these procedures yielded accurate results (i.e. Leventhal's, 1980, 'accuracy' rule was followed), and that leniency was shown to those who tested positively.

In another recent study, Cropanzano and Konovsky (1995) determined that drug screening was considered fair to the extent that the procedure used contained elements of voice, advance notice, justifications, a grievance system, and when testing was conducted 'for cause'. (As mentioned earlier, all five of these process attributes except presence/absence of a grievance system interacted with outcome negativity.) Taken together, research suggests that drug testing can indeed give rise to perceptions of injustice. However, to the extent that the system is designed in a manner that incorporates appropriate procedural safeguards, these concerns may be assuaged.

Organizational Image Management

Earlier, we discussed the use of social accounts as a means of legitimizing the behavior of individuals. Extending this line of thinking, we also can see that it is not only individuals who need to have their behavior justified as fair, but organizations as well (Gatewood, Gowan, & Lautenschlager, 1993). In fact, recent research suggests that organizations go through similar processes of image-maintenance—especially following actions that might be seen as unfair (cf. Greenberg, 1990c). Although attention to this topic is fairly recent, some interesting findings already have emerged.

In a qualitative study Dutton and Dukerich (1991) examined the manner in which the New York and New Jersey Port Authority responded to the large number of homeless people congregating in their transportation facilities. Port Authority officials were concerned that these individuals constituted an obstacle for effective service delivery. As such, they took a variety of measures, many of which were subsequently criticized by the media. Among other things, Dutton and Dukerich (1991) were interested in how the Port Authority responded to these critiques.

Initially, officials denied engaging in some of the more controversial behaviors. However, as public outcry grew, the Port Authority's image further eroded in the public eye. As a result, the organization shifted its reactions from denial to a series of 'legitimizing actions' such as making a capital investment in new facilities for the homeless, and forming a task force on the problem. One might say that the Port Authority partially acquiesced to its critics and began to address their concerns. Presumably, had denial been more effective as an impression-management technique, these other institutional changes would not have been initiated.

Another perspective on organizational accounts is provided by the work of Elsbach and Sutton (1992) in their study of two social-activist groups: The AIDS Coalition to Unleash Power (ACT-UP) and Earth First! ACT-UP and Earth First! members engage in many activities that are widely accepted as legitimate. Indeed, most people wish to assist AIDS sufferers and to protect the environment, or at least, believe that it is reasonable to do so. Nevertheless, in the course of pursuing these goals, members of these organizations sometimes engaged in actions that were perceived as illegitimate (e.g. the disruption of a religious service by ACT-UP members, and an injurious tree-spiking incident committed by members of Earth First!). The investigators were interested in how these two organizations could maintain a positive public image in the face of these questionable actions.

Elsbach and Sutton (1992) found evidence that these organizations actually anticipated the need to provide social accounts, and built provisions for doing so into their structures. This was done in two ways. First, ACT-UP and Earth First! engaged in 'institutional conformity'. That is, their visible structures and actions were consistent with the values and norms of the larger society. Few people, for example, would object to a group that provides assistance to AIDS victims or that educates people about ecology. (As such, these activities are much like the legitimizing actions observed by Dutton and Dukerich, 1991.) Second, the organizations adopted a highly de-centralized structure. The roles of different chapters or spokespersons were separated from the rest of the organization. For example, Earth First! members went so far as to create an *ad hoc* group that engaged in tree-spiking. These two structural adaptations came in handy after an illegitimate event occurred.

Following controversial events ACT-UP and Earth First! were able to rely on their structures for help. For one, they could point to many legitimate activities in which they participated. This had a chilling effect on criticism insofar as any broad attacks on the organization would also constitute attacks on these favorable activities. Second, they were able to dissociate the organization from those individuals who performed the illegitimate activity. For example, ACT-UP has local chapters that operate in a relatively autonomous fashion. The overall organization simply attributed the attack on the church to the over-zealous New York chapter, thereby protecting its image by distancing itself from those illegitimate actions. Indeed, Elsbach and Sutton (1992) provide evidence that these accounts were effective at putting an end to the public censure.

In a more recent investigation on this topic, Elsbach (1994) studied the manner in which the California cattle industry responded to various allegations of wrongdoing. Her focus here was less on structure and more on the nature of the social accounts themselves. In particular, Elsbach (1994, Study 1) found that the accounts used by the maligned cattle industry took two broad forms. There were *denials*, whereby industry spokespeople maintained that nothing bad had occurred. There also were *acknowledgements*—concessions that something bad had happened, accompanied by explanations as to why the problem was not really so severe or why it was not the fault of most ranchers. (The analogous behavior on the part of individuals has been referred to as *justifications* by Tedeschi & Reiss, 1981, and *techniques of neutralization* by Sykes & Matza, 1957.)

Each of these two forms of accounts could have one of two different types of contents. One content referred to *characteristics of the institution*, such as the legitimate goals pursued by ranchers. Another content referred to *characteristics of the technology*, such as the efficiency of modern ranching techniques. Combining form and context, Elsbach (1994, Study 2) identified four prototypical accounts:

- denial based on institutional reasons (e.g. there is no safety problem due to federal monitoring);

- denial based on technical reasons (e.g. cattle are handled compassionately because that's what is profitable);
- acknowledgement, but explained by institutional reasons (e.g. grazing in a state park reduces fire hazards); and
- acknowledgement, but explained by technical reasons (e.g. enforcing a ban on growth hormones would not be economically viable).

All four of these prototypical acounts received at least some use. However, Elsbach (1994, Studies 2 and 3) found that acknowledgements did a better job than denials at maintaining the industry's image. Additionally, accounts based on institutional characteristics were more effective than those based on technical characteristics. As one might expect, the form and the content of the account also worked together. The most effective explanation of all was an acknowledgement that something negative had occurred, but that explained the event in terms of an institutional characteristic of the industry.

Although research on social accounts at the level of the organization is still in its infancy, the work conducted thus far has considerable promise. Such research represents an innovative application of organizational justice, as it moves from the level of the individual to the level of the firm as a whole. This leads us to wonder whether justice findings in other domains would generalize as readily across levels of analysis. Clearly, this represents a promising avenue for future inquiry.

Informal Conflict Resolution

Managers frequently are required to intervene in disputes between subordinates (for reviews see Dworkin, 1994; Karambayya & Brett, 1994; Wall & Callister, 1995). When they do, they are said to be acting as 'informal' third-parties, as compared to the 'formal' interventions by judges and arbitrators (Kolb, 1986). Although there are many important considerations involved in making third-party interventions effective (Elangovan, 1995), maintaining justice is one of the most important. Indeed, research has shown that managers who behave fairly resolve conflict more effectively than those who do not (Cropanzano, Aguinis, Schminke, & Denham, 1996; Karambayya, Brett, & Lytle, 1992; Kozan & Ilter, 1994). The role of justice in informal conflict resolution has a long history (for an overview, see Folger & Cropanzano, in press), although our discussion will focus only on recent contributions to this literature.

How much participation do managers allow?

As we have already discussed, giving people voice in the procedures affecting them is likely to enhance their perceptions of the fairness of those procedures and the resulting outcomes. This generalization holds true in the domain of conflict resolution as well. For example, in a field study conducted in a school Rasinski (1992, Study 1) found that a large percentage of teachers preferred to resolve conflicts between students in a participative fashion rather than in a nonparticipative fashion. Likewise, in a role-playing study, Cropanzano et al. (1996) discovered that simulated disputants in the US, the Dominican Republic, and Argentina preferred that their supervisors intervened in a way that preserved their voice in the matter. Cropanzano et al.'s (1996) respondents also believed that participative procedures were more fair and more likely to alleviate future tensions than nonparticipative procedures. Finally, in a laboratory experiment Schoorman and Champagne (1994) gave simulated supervisors negative information about their subordinates. Although this information harmed the supervisor–subordinate relationship, they found that if the two individuals openly discussed the problem, their relationship improved. This finding suggests that participation could act to strengthen the interpersonal ties between workers and managers. In view of such evidence it should come as no surprise to find that practitioners widely recommend using participative interventions for most types of conflicts (e.g. Weeks, 1992).

Research has shown that the beneficial effects of participative conflict resolution practices are not limited to American samples. For example, in a study of Turkish workers Kozan and Ilter (1994) found that managers typically used a participative process in their conflict resolution efforts. Specifically, Turkish supervisors were most likely to mediate (i.e. let the two disputants speak freely, but reserve control over the decision to themselves) and facilitate (lower tension levels, but let the subordinates work through the problem). In addition, when the supervisors used these voice-oriented strategies, subordinates reported more favorable outcomes than when they did not use such tactics. Despite this, it is most common for American managers to intervene in an autocratic fashion (see Dworkin, 1994; Folger & Cropanzano, in press), although this can vary substantially depending upon the nature of the dispute (Shapiro & Rosen, 1994). In general, American managers tend to control both the discussion of the problem as well as the choice of a settlement.

Several studies shed light on the underlying reasons for this autocratic preference. For example, Sheppard, Blumenfeld-Jones, Minton, and Hyder (1994) interviewed managers concerning the manner in which they had settled recent disputes. In keeping with previous research, they found that autocratic approaches were preferred. Part of the reason for this had to do with managerial goals. When supervisors were concerned with the need for a fast, high-quality decision, they relied on an autocratic strategy. However, when quality and speed were of less concern, supervisors were more participative. In addition, Sheppard et al. (1994) also found that the major reason why American managers use autocratic tactics had to do with the way they frame conflicts. That is, they think of their conflict-resolution obligations as decisions that have to be made, much as their other managerial tasks. Consequently, they make these decisions in much the same autocratic fashion.

Another reason why American supervisors tend to make conflict-resolution decisions autocratically is that they may not know any better. In an interesting experiment, Karambayya, Brett, and Lytle (1992) had inexperienced MBA students and actual managers role-play a simulated organizational dispute. The subjects either were or were not granted formal power. It was found that if subjects lacked formal power, they did not intervene in an autocratic fashion, and were more participative. This was true of both MBA students and actual managers. However, among those individuals who were granted formal power, significant differences emerged. The inexperienced MBA students utilized autocratic tactics, whereas the more experienced managers used more participative strategies. Finally, regardless of the condition, the simulated disputants reported that the outcomes were fairer and more effective when they were given voice in the procedures than when voice was not allowed. These findings support the notion that supervisors learn from experience, initially using less effective, autocratic approaches and gradually learning to use more participative procedures. These findings lend cause for optimism about the potential effectivness of efforts at training managers to enhance their dispute-resolution skills (Kolb, 1985).

Timing of third-party interventions

Closely related to the issue of participation in dispute resolution is the matter of timing. People in conflict with each other often prefer to resolve their disagreements by themselves (cf. Bergmann & Volkema, 1994; Rasinski, 1992). This enables both parties to control both the process and the outcome, and avoids relinquishing control to intervening authority figures. However, when a supervisor intervenes prematurely, control is stripped from the disputants. To the extent that disputants believe they did not have sufficient time to resolve their differences on their own, they are likely to believe that they were treated unfairly and to feel dissatisfied with those managers who stepped-in too quickly. These ideas were directly tested by Conlon and Fasolo (1990), who examined disputants' reactions to a simulated conflict. As expected, a hasty intervention by informal third parties lowered the disputants' perceptions of procedural fairness.

Third-party partisanship

When managers intervene in conflicts they typically are not dispassionate observers. They often have vested interests—sometimes, legitimate ones—in the way conflicts are settled. From the perspective of the disputant, however, these interests may introduce unacceptable bias into the decision-making process. In other words, supervisors may be unable to provide the neutrality that Tyler and Lind (1992) maintain is important to procedural justice. As an obvious example, when the adjudicating third party is affiliated with one of the disputants, justice is compromised. For example, several studies have found that when third parties benefited from the outcomes of the settlements they made, disputants were prone to question the fairness of the process (Welton & Pruitt, 1987; Wittmer, Carnevale, & Walker, 1991).

As obvious as these findings may be, third-party affiliations also can have some unusual effects. In one experiment, subjects either did or did not observe a third party chatting in a friendly fashion with the opposing disputant (Lind & Lissak, 1985). This friendly discourse was perceived to be improper insofar as it might bias the outcome of the decision. The effects of this type of impropriety depended upon the outcome that the third party assigned. When the outcome was unfavorable, subjects responded very negatively, attributing the result to biased decision-making. However, when the outcome was favorable, subjects responded quite positively. The cordial relations between the third paty and their opponent served to lower the subjects' expectations of receiving beneficial outcomes. When these negative expectations were not met, disputants were very pleased. (This is akin to the augmentation effect in impression management demonstrated recently by Greenberg, 1996b.)

These ideas were further tested by Conlon and Ross (1993). In two laboratory experiments they found that when a third party was partisan, the non-affiliated disputant lowered his or her expectations. This made settlements easier to achieve. In addition, favorable outcomes were evaluated positively in as much as these were substantially greater than imagined coming from a partisan decision-maker. Conlon and Ross's findings (1993) suggest that partisanship is not necessarily harmful. To a large extent, it depends on the circumstances and the nature of the settlement. However, to the extent that it can be avoided and neutrality can be demonstrated, the tactic of manipulating expectations via displays of partisanship can be avoided in the first place.

Layoffs

As organizations have downsized and restructured their operations in recent years, layoffs have become a troubling fact of organizational life for millions of Americans (Richman, 1993), and experts predict that the hardships they endure will continue in the future (Cascio, 1995). Research in organizational justice appears to provide some valuable insights into ways of mitigating the negative impact of job loss on both victims of layoffs (those who lost their jobs) and survivors (those who remain on the job after others have been laid off) (for reviews, see Brockner, 1994; Brockner & Greenberg, 1990; Konovsky & Brockner, 1993).

Layoff victims

Several studies have examined the impact of various determinants of fairness on the reactions of layoff victims. For example, Konovsky and Folger (1991a) surveyed people who had been laid off from a variety of different industries. They found that formal procedures predicted victims' willingness to speak positively about their companies and to eschew government regulation of layoffs. Interestingly, however, neither social accounts nor benefits level (an index of outcome favorability) were associated with these outcomes.

However, in a more recent study, Greenberg, Lind, Scott, and Welchans (1995) found that the fairness of the social treatment people received as their layoffs were announced had a great effect not only on their perceptions of fairness, but also on their interest in seeking legal damages against their former employers. Their interviews of a large number of laid-off people indicated that 40% considered initiating a lawsuit or an EEOC complaint. Some 23% actually talked to a lawyer or EEOC official, and 7% actually filed a suit or a complaint. Logistic regression analyses found that the strongest predictor of the willingness to consider legal action, or to actually take action, was respondents' perceptions that they were treated without dignity or in a disrespectful fashion at the time of their dismissal. In fact, whereas only 16% of those treated well thought about suing, 66% of those treated poorly thought about suing. Additional evidence suggests that victims' reactions to layoffs depended on the degree of harm the layoff caused them: the perceived fairness of the layoff procedures predicted the reactions of victims who felt harmed by the layoffs better than it did the reactions of those who were less adversely affected. These findings replicate an identical reaction identified by Brockner et al. (1994, Study 1).

Layoff survivors

Considerable research also has examined the reactions of layoff survivors. As one might imagine, survivors do not respond positively to watching their coworkers lose their jobs, often arousing 'survivor guilt'. As we described earlier, Brockner et al. (1990) found that when a justification was provided for others' layoffs, survivors responded more positively than when an explanation was lacking. However, this occurred only under conditions in which survivors had a high need for information—that is, when individuals were uncertain about the process used to determine the layoffs and when these negative outcomes were important to them. Although social accounts are important, this is only the case when these accounts are believed to be true. Mellor (1992) examined survivors' commitment to their union following layoffs. The company blamed the job terminations on the union. Survivors who believed this account expressed low commitment to their union when the layoff was severe. However, when the account was not believed or when the layoffs were less severe, commitment to the union was higher.

Brockner et al. (1994, Studies 2 and 3) also examined survivors' reactions to layoffs as a function of procedural justice, operationalized as advance notice of a forthcoming layoff, and outcomes, the level of layoff benefits provided.

They found the expected interaction: Procedures were stronger determinants of employees' responses to layoffs when benefits were unfavorable compared to when they were favorable. These findings need to be considered in light of those obtained by Brockner et al. (1990). In each case, an aspect of procedural justice (be it a social account or advance notice) was an important predictor of reactions, but only when the outcome was severely negative (i.e. when the endangered job was important or the level of benefits was low). These findings provide strong support for the interaction model of justice described earlier. They also send a clear message to organizations who are forced to layoff employees: To minimize negative reactions among survivors, conduct layoffs fairly (such as by fully explaining its need and by giving advance notice), and clearly elucidate that these practices were followed. Reaping the benefits of carrying out fair procedures frequently requires calling others' attention to them (Greenberg, 1990c).

Organizational Citizenship Behaviors

To the extent that people are strongly committed to organizations they believe have treated them fairly, it follows that they would be willing to contribute to its well-being, even if this involves going above and beyond the call of duty. This is the idea behind organizational citizenship behaviors (OCBs)—those helpful and supportive actions by employees that are not part of their formal job description. Examples include showing courtesy to others, being conscientious about work, being a 'good sport' about doing extra work, and generally protecting the organization's property. Insofar as people may have only limited control over some of their work outcomes, and may be reluctant to lower them in response to underpayment, work output may not be the most sensitive indicant of feelings of injustice (Greenberg, 1982). However, given that OCBs are discretionary, and people are free to engage in them or to forgo them if they wish, these behaviors may be highly reactive to fair and unfair treatment (Greenberg, 1993d). Not surprisingly, considerable attention has been paid to understanding the relationship between justice and OCBs (for a review, see Organ & Moorman, 1993).

As Organ (1990) and Reed and Kelly (1993) discuss, OCBs are based on employees' notions of social exchange. When an organization treats individuals fairly, they are likely to reciprocate by exerting extra effort on the firm's behalf (cf. Organ & Konovsky, 1989). Empirical evidence suggests that justice, especially procedural justice, is related to OCB (e.g. Ball, Treviño, & Sims, 1994; Konovsky & Folger, 1991b). Some OCB studies have demonstrated this effect, although they have been nonspecific as to the type of justice involved. For example, Deluga (1994) found that a general measure of fairness was associated with several aspects of OCB. Likewise, Konovsky and Organ (in press) found that a composite variable that they called justice/ satisfaction predicted various OCB dimensions.

One of the earliest studies to examine different types of justice was conducted in a Taiwanese government ministry. Farh, Podsakoff, and Organ (1990) found that procedural justice was related to the altruism dimension of OCB. However, for the compliance dimension, procedural justice did not account for a significant amount of the variance above and beyond the effect of job scope. Extending the work of Farh, Podsakoff, and Organ (1990) in an American sample, Moorman (1991) assessed five dimensions of OCB: altruism, courtesy, sportsmanship, conscientiousness, and civic virtue. Neither distributive justice nor formal procedural justice predicted any of these dimensions. However, interactional justice predicted all but civic virtue. Similarly, Lee (1995) also found that the social aspects of justice predicted all of these dimensions except civic virtue, but that formal procedures were related to OCB. Finally, Niehoff and Moorman (1993) obtained a mixed pattern. Formal procedures predicted courtesy, sportsmanship, and conscientiousness, although interactional justice was associated with only sportsmanship. Further muddying the waters, Konovsky, Elliott, and Pugh (1995) found that procedural justice was the better predictor of OCB in an American sample, whereas distributive justice was the better predictor of OCB in a Mexican sample.

The best summary that can be given at this time is that procedural justice is a better predictor of OCB than distributive justice (for Americans, at least). However, it remains unclear which particular components of procedural justice, structural or social, best predict which particular forms of OCB. The picture is further complicated by the possibility that procedural justice may be an indirect predictor of OCB. This possibility has been suggested by Konovsky, Elliott, and Pugh (1995), who found that procedural justice was correlated with trust in their survey of hospital workers. Trust, in turn, was associated with OCB. These findings call our attention to the possibility that procedural justice is only correlated with OCB by way of its influence on trust. This possibility is in keeping with the role of trust as a mediator of procedural justice identified by Brockner and Siegel (in press; Siegel, Brockner, & Tyler, 1995).

Employee Theft

Our discussion of the link between justice and prosocial acts of organizaitonal citizenship may be juxtaposed with an emerging literature on justice and the antisocial act of employee theft (Greenberg, 1997). From the perspective of distributive justice, stealing company property may be understood as an attempt to re-establish equity between the parties involved in a social exchange relationship (for a review, see Greenberg & Scott, 1996). Specifically, in terms of equity theory (Adams, 1965), employees who believe they are receiving insufficient outcomes (e.g. pay) in exchange for their work contributions may effectively raise these outcomes by stealing, thereby redressing their perceived inequities with their employers.

Greenberg has empirically demonstrated this phenomenon in a series of studies. In the first, a quasi-experiment conducted in an organization, Greenberg (1990b) compared the theft rates within three manufacturing plants belonging to the same company. In two of these factories (comprising the experimental groups), all employees encountered a pay-cut of 15% over a 10-week period as the company's response to a financial crisis. A third plant, with demographically similar employees, in which there were no pay cuts, served as the control group. Insofar as employees in the first two plants received lower pay than they had in the past, they were considered to have suffered underpayment inequity. To assess theft, standard measures of shrinkage were taken by agents unaware of the study. Consistent with equity theory, Greenberg (1990b) found that theft rates were significantly higher within the plants in which employees' pay was cut than in the control group. These differences are particularly dramatic when one considers that theft rates were consistently low in all three plants both before the pay cut, and also after regular rates of pay were reinstated.

Going beyond this straightforward test of equity theory, this investigation also considered the social determinants of justice by examining the manner in which the pay cut was explained to the workers in the two experimental groups. Employees at one plant, selected at random, were given an elaborate and caring explanation of the need for pay to be cut (the adequate explanation condition). By contrast, workers in the other experimental plant were given limited information about the need for the pay cut, accompanied by only superficial expressions of remorse (the inadequate explanation condition). The differences between these two plants was striking: Over twice as much theft occurred in the plant whose employees received the inadequate explanation compared to the plant whose employees received the adequate explanation.

These dramatic findings are limited by the confounding of two key variables—the amount of information presented about the reason for the pay cut, and the amount of sensitivity shown regarding the impact of the pay cut. To eliminate this confounding, Greenberg (1993a) independently manipulated these variables in a follow-up experiment conducted in a laboratory setting. Undergraduates were hired to perform a clerical task in exchange for $5 per hour, a rate shown in pretesting to be perceived as fair. After performing the task, a random half of the participants (the underpaid group) were told that they would be paid only $3. The other half of the participants (the equitably paid group) were told they would be paid the $5 promised.

As he announced the pay rate, Greenberg systematically manipulated the quality of the information used as the basis for establishing the pay rate, giving an explanation that was either extremely thorough and based on ostensibly verified facts (the high valid information condition) or one that was extremely incomplete and based on questionable facts (the low valid information condition). He also manipulated, via his remarks, the amount of remorse and concern shown for having caused the underpayment, demonstrating either great amounts (the high social sensitivity condition) or very limited amounts (the low social sensitivity condition). After treating the subjects in these manners, the experiment left subjects alone in a room with an ostensibly unknown sum of money and invited them to take the amount they were supposed to take (i.e. $3 in the underpayment group and $5 in the equitable payment group). However, because the experimenter knew the exact amount of money left on the desk, he was able to determine precisely how much was taken. Amounts of in excess of the stated wages were considered theft.

Consistent with equity theory, subjects who were equitably paid did not steal, whereas those who were underpaid did steal. In particular, the amount they stole was dependent upon the way they were treated. Subjects receiving high amounts of information stole less than those receiving low amounts. Likewise, those treated with high levels of social sensitivity stole less than those receiving low levels. Furthermore, these effects combined in an additive fashion: Those receiving high amounts of both variables stole the least, whereas those receiving low amounts of both stole the most.

These findings suggest not only that pay inequity induces theft, but also that the amount of theft in which the people engage depends on the nature of the interpersonal treatment they receive: Positive treatment (i.e., thorough information presented in a socially sensitive manner) at the hands of an authority figure lowers theft. People are interested in evening the score with those who have treated them inequitably, and use theft as a device for doing so—particularly when the source of the inequity shows little concern and remorse. When Greenberg's (1993a) subjects stole the money they may have been attempting to make up for the underpayment they received at the hands of the investigator, or they may have been attempting to retaliate against the investigator by taking too much money. Indeed, both restitution and retaliation are possible responses to theft-induced inequities. Because taking more money than one is supposed to simultaneously advantages oneself and disadvantages the authority figure, it is impossible to distinguish between the restitution and retaliation motives for theft. Acknowledging this limitation, Greenberg (1994b) replicated and extended this study in a manner that made it possible to deduce subjects' underlying motives for stealing.

The task subjects performed consisted of counting small round objects and packaging them into rolls so they could be easily counted. In one condition the objects were 25¢ coins (quarters). In another condition, they were similarly sized objects—lithium batteries said to be valuable experimental prototypes. Subjects performed the task alone in rooms in which buckets of either quarters or batteries were put in front of them. Some subjects encountered an underpayment inequity as they completed the task: they were told that they would only be paid $3 for the half-hour's work instead of the $6.00 they were initially promised. After this announcement was made, the experimenter left the room, but not before giving subjects three $1 bills. Subjects then completed a questionnaire while in the presence of the coins or batteries they were count-ing. As in the Greenberg (1993a) study, the explanation for this surprising negative turn of events was either thoroughly explained or not thoroughly explained, and in a manner that demonstrated either a high or low level of dignity and personal concern. Because the number of batteries or coins in the bucket was known in advance (although subjects were led to believe other-wise), it was possible to determine if they had stolen anything. It was reasoned that any theft of the batteries could be interpreted as an act of retaliation insofar as it only would harm the company but be of no value to the subjects themselves. However, theft of the quarters would mutually harm the company while benefiting themselves (making the motive at least retaliation, but also possibly restitution). Thus, in this study, the items stolen were taken as cues to the underlying motives for the theft.

When the subjects were working with quarters, the results replicated those of Greenberg (1993a). That is, both information and sensitivity independently affected theft: When both were high theft was lowest; when both were low, theft was highest; and when one factor was high and the other low, theft was intermediate. However, when subjects were working with allegedly valuable lithium batteries the only variable that affected theft was the amount of respect and dignity shown while explaining the inequity. When the level of dignity displayed was high, theft was low or nonexistent. However, when it was low, the level of theft rose considerably. By contrast, the amount of information presented about the reasons for the unexpectedly low pay had no effects on the stealing of batteries; the level of theft observed in this condition was quite low. These results suggest that the combined effects of treating people ineq-uitably while failing to treat them with dignity and respect led them to retaliate against the source of their harm, the authority figure.

The sociologist Kemper (1996) has referred to this type of retaliative behavior as *reciprocal deviance*—the deviance that results when an authority figure defaults on his or her obligations to an individual. In fact the acts of 'striking back' observed here in response to an inequity, are conceptually consistent with the inequitable conditions Kemper (1966) identified as inviting reciprocal deviance. However, it is interesting to note that it was not just the inequity that triggered theft, but the inequity augmented by a lack of personal sensitivity. This com-bination appears to have added insult to injury, triggering an interest in retalia-tion. This is not to say that the retaliation response is purely without benefit for the harmdoer. Although acts of reciprocal deviance may fail to redress an ineq-uity financially, they may do so symbolically. That is, if one cannot directly benefit oneself, then at least one can derive satisfaction from knowing that one has harmed another who has harmed oneself.

Taken together, the Greenberg studies (1990b, 1993a, 1994b) suggest that it is not only the magnitude of the inequity that determines theft, but also the *way* that inequity is presented—that is, the treatment of employees. Further illustrat-ing this point, Greenberg (1994c) administered a questionnaire to workers assessing their perceptions of various aspects of unfairness in their workplace. The respondents were approached as they recorded their 'punch out' times on a piece of paper while the investigator surreptitiously noted the actual times they stopped in front of the clock. (A sign informed the workers that the time clock was being repaired, and directed them to record their names and 'punch out' times on a form provided for that purpose. A large digital clock was placed where the time clock was usually found.) By comparing the actual 'punch out' times with those recorded, a measure of time theft was created—the reporting of more time than actually worked. Although the actual amount of time theft was rather low, variance in this measure was significantly accounted for by responses to several questionnaire items. Two variables best predicted time theft: the amount of compassion shown by supervisors, and the degree of respect employers show for employees. By contrast, general measures of pay fairness were weaker predictors of theft. Again, these findings suggest that theft is associated with unfair treatment of an interpersonal nature. Uncaring, inconsiderate supervision is a key determinant of employee theft.

In summary, it appears that employee theft is more than simply an attempt to restore a mathematical balance between outcomes and inputs. Such inequities appear to be necessary for theft to occur, but may not always be sufficient. What needs to be added to the formula for predicting employee theft is improper social treatment—variously called social insensitivity, lack of dignity, rudeness, disrespect, or lack of compassion. Thus, whereas insufficient outcomes may stimulate awareness of inequitable states, it requires social insensitivity to this condition to trigger the theft response.

CONCLUSION

Our review of the recent literature on organizational justice has distinguished between various types of justice and has examined the relationships between them. We saw that fairness is an important determinant of a variety of important work outcomes, such as commitment, turnover intentions, and organizational citizenship behaviors. Especially consequential is the manner in which organizational justice theories have been applied to a host of managerial practices, including selection, theft-prevention, and conflict-resolution. When fairness is incorporated into these practices, beneficial outcomes accrue to both individuals and the organizations employing them.

If nothing else, our analysis demonstrates that justice is a common theme that cuts across all aspects of work life, providing coherence and unity to an array of organizational practices that otherwise might appear unconnected. This is not to say that fairness is the only, or even the most important consideration in organizational practice. Our point is more modest—but only slightly so: Justice can be a consideration in virtually everything that an organization does because it is through its policies and procedures that a company defines its relationship to each employee. In other words, fairness partially determines how an organization and its members treat one another. It provides a framework within which individuals and institutions interact. This relationship, when characterized by fairness and mutual respect, is a healthy source of morale and productive behavior (Rosen, 1991). We believe that it is implicit recognition of this important point that has stimulated so much attention to matters of organizational justice in recent years. In a field lacking any established research paradigm or unifying theory, and only limited conceptual agreement, the maze of research on organizational justice has grown increasingly complex. Hopefully, by tunneling through this maze, our guided tour of the literature has convinced readers that the journey is worthwhile.

AUTHOR NOTE

Preparation of this chapter was provided in part by National Science Foundation grant number SBR-9224169 awarded to Jerald Greenberg.

REFERENCES

Adams, J. S. (1965) Inequity in social exchange. In L. Berkowitz (ed.), *Advances in Experimental Social Psychology*, Vol. 2 (pp. 267–299). New York: Adcademic Press.

Ambrose, M. L., Harland, L. K., & Kulik, C. T. (1991) Influence of social comparisons on perceptions of organizational fairness. *Journal of Applied Psychology*, **76**, 239–246.

Ambrose, M. L. & Rosse, J. G. (1993) Relational justice and personality testing: Sometimes nice guys do finish last. Unpublished manuscript. University of Colorado, Boulder, CO.

Arvey, R. D. (1992) Fairness and ethical considerations in employee selection. In D. M. Saunders (ed.), *New Approaches in Employee Selection*, Vol. 1 (pp. 1–19). Greenwich, CT: JAI Press.

Arvey, R. D. & Sackett, P. R. (1993) Fairness in selection: Current developments and perspectives. In N. Schmitt & W. Borman (eds), *Personnel Selection* (pp. 171–202). San Francisco: Jossey-Bass.

Austin, W. (1977) Equity theory and social comparison processes. In J. M. Suls & R. M. Miller (eds), *Social Comparison Processes* (pp. 279–306). Washington, DC: Hemisphere.

Ball, G. A., Treviño, L. K., & Sims, H. P., Jr (1994) Just and unjust punishment: Influences on subordinate performance and citizenship. *Academy of Management Journal*, **37**, 299–322.

Bazerman, M. H., Schroth, H. A., Shah, P. P., Diekmann, K. A., & Tenbrunsel, A. E. (1994) The inconsistent role of comparison others and procedural justice in reactions to hypothetical job descriptions: Implications for job acceptance decisions. *Organizational Behavior and Human Decision Processes*, **60**, 326–352.

Bergmann, T. J. & Volkema, R. J. (1994) Issues, behavioral responses and consequences in interpersonal conflicts. *Journal of Organizational Behavior*, **15**, 467–471.

Bierhoff, H. W., Cohen, R. L., & Greenberg, J. (1986) *Justice in Social Relations*. New York: Plenum.

Bies, R. J. (1987) The predicament of injustice: The management of moral outrage. In L. L. Cummings & B. M. Staw (eds), *Research in Organizational Behavior,* Vol. 9 (pp. 289–319). Greenwich, CT: JAI Press.

Bies, R. J. & Moag, J. S. (1986) Interactional justice: Communication criteria of fairness. In R. J. Lewicki, B. H. Sheppard, & M. Bazerman (eds), *Research on Negotiation in Organizations,* Vol. 1 (pp. 43–55). Greenwich, CT: JAI Press.

Bies, R. J. & Tyler, T. R. (1993) The 'litigation mentality' in organizations: A test of alternative psychological explanations. *Organizational Science,* 4, 352–366.

Bond, M. H., Leung, K., & Schwartz, S. (1992) Explaining choices in procedural and distributive justice across cultures. *International Journal of Psychology,* 27, 211–225.

Brockner, J. (1988) *Self-esteem at Work: Reserach, Theory, and Practice.* Lexington, MA: Lexington Press.

Brockner, J. (1994) Perceived fairness and survivors' reactions to layoffs, or how downsizing organizations can do well by doing good. *Social Justice Research,* 7, 345–363.

Brockner, J., DeWitt, R. L., Grover, S., & Reed, T. (1990) When it is especially important to explain why: Factors affecting the relationship between managers' explanations of a layoff and survivors' reactions to the layoff. *Journal of Experimental Social Psychology,* 26, 389–407.

Brockner, J. & Greenberg, J. (1990) The impact of layoffs on survivors: An organizational justice perspective. In J. S. Carroll (eds), *Applied Social Psychology and Organizational Settings* (pp. 45–75). Hillsdale, NJ: Erlbaum.

Brockner, J., Konovsky, M., Cooper-Schneider, R., Folger, R., Martin, C., & Bies, R. J. (1994) Interactive effects of procedural justice and outcome negativity on victims and survivors of job loss. *Academy of Management Journal,* 37, 397–409.

Brockner, J. & Siegel, P. (1995) Understanding the interaction between procedural and distributive justice. In R. M. Kramer & T. R. Tyler (eds), *Trust in Organizations.* Newbury Park, CA: Sage.

Brockner, J., Tyler, T. R., & Cooper-Schneider, R. (1992) The influence of prior commitment to an institution on reactions to perceived unfairness: The higher they are, the harder they fall. *Administrative Science Quarterly,* 37, 241–261.

Brockner, J. & Wiesenfeld, B. M (1996) An integrative framework for explaining reactions to decisions: The interactive effects of outcomes and procedures. *Psychological Bulletin,* 120, 189–208.

Cascio, W. F. (1995) Whither industrial and organizational psychology in a changing world of work? *American Psychologist,* 50, 928–939.

Chen, C. C. (1995) New trends in rewards allocation preferences: A Sino-US comparison. *Academy of Management Journal,* 38, 408–428.

Clemmer, E. C. (1993) An investigation into the relationship of fairness and customer satisfaction with services. In R. Cropanzano (ed.), *Justice in the Workplace: Approaching Fairness in Human Resource Management* (pp. 193–207). Hillsdale, NJ: Erlbaum.

Cohen, R. L. (1986) *Justice: Views from the Social Sciences.* New York: Plenum.

Cohen, R. L. & Greenberg, J. (1982) The justice concept in social psychology. In J. Greenberg & R. L. Cohen (eds), *Equity and Justice in Social Behavior* (pp. 1–41). New York: Academic Press.

Conlon, D. E. (1993) Some tests of the self-interest and group-value models of procedural justice: Evidence from an organizational appeal procedure. *Academy of Management Journal,* 36, 1109–1124.

Conlon, D. E. & Fasolo, P. M. (1990) Influence of speed of third-party intervention and outcome on negotiator and constituent fairness judgments. *Academy of Management Journal,* 33, 833–846.

Conlon, D. E. & Ross, W. H. (1993) The effects of partisan third parties on negotiator behavior and outcome perception. *Journal of Applied Psychology,* 78, 280–290.

Cooper, C. L., Dyck, B., & Frohlich, N. (1992) Improving the effectiveness of gain-sharing: The role of fairness and participation. *Administrative Science Quarterly*, 37, 471–490.

Cowherd, D. M. & Levine, D. I. (1992) Product quality and pay equity between lower-level employees and top management: An investigation of distributive justice theory. *Administrative Science Quarterly*, 37, 302–320.

Crant, J. M. & Bateman, T. S. (1990) An experimental test of the impact of drug-testing programs on potential job applicants' attitudes and intentions. *Journal of Applied Psychology*, 75, 127–131.

Crant, J. M. & Bateman, T. S. (1993) Potential job applicant reactions to employee drug testing: The effects of program characteristics and individual differences. *Journal of Business and Psychology*, 7, 279–290.

Cropanzano, R. (ed.) (1993) *Justice in the Workplace: Approaching Fairness in Human Resource Management*. Hillsdale, NJ: Erlbaum.

Cropanzano, R., Aguinis, H., Schminke, M., & Denham, D. L. (August 1996) Disputant reactions to managerial conflict intervention strategies: A comparison among Argentina, the Dominican Republic, Mexico and the United States. In J. G. Rosse (chair), *Justice and Fairness in Organizations*. Symposium conducted at the 1996 meeting of the Academy of Management. Cincinnati, OH.

Cropanzano, R. & Folger, R. (1991) Procedural justice and worker motivation. In R. M. Steers & L. W. Porter (eds), *Motivation and Work Behavior*. Fifth edition (pp. 131–143). New York: McGraw-Hill.

Cropanzano, R. & Konovsky, M. A. (1995) Resolving the justice dilemma by improving the outcomes: The case of employee drug screening. *Journal of Business and Psychology*, 10, 221–243.

Cropanzano, R. & Randall, M. L. (1993). Injustice and work behavior: A historical review. In R. Cropanzano (ed.), *Justice in the Workplace: Approaching Fairness in Human Resource Management* (pp. 1–20). Hillsdale, NJ: Erlbaum.

Cropanzano, R. & Randall, M. L. (1995) Advance notice as a means of reducing relative deprivation. *Social Justice Research*, 8, 217–238.

Dailey, R. C. & Kirk, D. J. (1992) Distributive and procedural justice as antecedents of job dissatisfaction and intent to turnover. *Human Relations*, 45, 305–317.

Daly, J. P. & Geyer, P. D. (1994) The role of fairness in implementing large-scale change: Employee evaluations of process and outcome in seven facility relocations. *Journal of Organizational Behavior*, 15, 623–638.

Daly, J. P. & Geyer, P. D. (1995) Procedural fairness and organizational commitment under conditions of growth and decline. *Social Justice Research*, 8, 137–151.

Davis, R. (1993) When applicants rate the examinations: Feedback from 2000 people. In B. Nevo & R. S. Jäger (eds), *Educational and Psychological Testing: The Test Taker's Outlook* (pp. 221–237). Toronto, Canada: Hogrefe & Huber.

Deluga, R. J. (1994) Supervisor trust building, leader-member exchange and organizational citizenship behaviour. *Journal of Occupational and Organizational Psychology*, 67, 315–326.

Deutsch, M. (1975) Equity, equality, and need: What determines which value will be used as the basis for distributive justice? *Journal of Social Issues*, 31(3), 137–149.

Deutsch, M. (1985) *Distributive Justice: A Social-Psychological Perspective*. New Haven, CT: Yale University Press.

Dutton, J. E. & Dukerich, J. M. (1991) Keeping an eye on the mirror: Image and identity in organizational adaptation. *Academy of Management Journal*, 34, 517–554.

Dworkin, J. B. (1994) Managerial third party dispute resolution: An overview and introduction to the special issue. *Employee Responsibilities and Rights Journal*, 7, 1–8.

Elangovan, A. R. (1995) Managerial third-party dispute intervention: A perspective model of strategy selection. *Academy of Management Review*, 20, 800–830.

Elsbach, K. D. (1994) Managing organizational legitimacy in the California cattle industry: The construction and effectiveness of verbal accounts. *Administrative Science Quarterly*, **39**, 57–88.

Elsbach, K. D. & Sutton, R. I. (1992) Acquiring organizational legitimacy through illegitimate actions: A marriage of institutional and impression management theories. *Academy of Management Journal*, **35**, 699–738.

Farh, J., Podsakoff, P. M., & Organ, D. W. (1990) Accounting for organizational citizenship behavior: Leader fairness and task scope versus satisfaction. *Journal of Management*, **16**. 705–721.

Finkle, R. B. (1976) Managerial assessment centers. In M. D. Dunnette (ed.), *Handbook of Industrial and Organizational Psychology*. Second edition (pp. 861–888). Chicago: Rand McNally.

Flinder, S. W. & Hauenstein, M. A. N. (1994) Antecedents of distributive and procedural justice perceptions. Unpublished manuscript, Virginia Polytechnic Institution and State University, Blacksburg, VA.

Foa, U. G. & Foa, E. B. (1974) *Social Structures of the Mind*. Springfield, IL: Charles C. Thomas.

Folger, R. (1994) Workplace justice and employee worth. *Social Justice Research*, **7**, 225–241.

Folger, R. & Bies, R. J. (1989) Managerial responsibilities and procedural justice. *Employee Responsibilities and Rights Journal*, **2**, 79–90.

Folger, R. & Cropanzano, R. (in press) *Organizational Justice and Human Resource Management*. Thousand Oaks, CA: Sage.

Folger, R. & Greenberg, J. (1985) Procedural justice: An interpretative analysis of personnel systems. In K. Rowland & G. Ferris (eds), *Research in Personnel and Human Resources Management*, Vol. 3 (pp. 141–183). Greenwich, CT: JAI Press.

Folger, R., Konovsky, M. A., & Cropanzano, R. (1992) A due process metaphor for performance appraisal. In B. M. Staw & L. L. Cummings (eds), *Research in Organizational Behavior*, Vol. 14 (pp. 129–177). Greenwich, CT: JAI Press.

Frohlich, N., Oppenheimer, J. A., & Eavy, C. L. (1987a) Laboratory results on Rawls's distributive justice. *British Journal of Political Science*, **17**, 1–21.

Frohlich, N., Oppenheimer, J. A., & Eavy, C. L. (1987b) Choice of principles of distributive justice in experimental groups. *American Journal of Political Science*, **45**, 606–636.

Gatewood, R. D., Gowan, M., & Lautenschlager, G. J. (1993) Corporate image, recruitment image, and initial job choice decisions. *Academy of Management Journal*, **36**, 414–427.

Gergen, K. J., Morse, S. J., & Gergen, M. M. (1980) Behavior exchange in cross-cultural perspective. In H. C. Triandis & R. W. Brislin (eds), *Handbook of Cross-cultural Psychology: Social Psychology*, Vol. 5 (pp. 121–153). Boston: Allyn & Bacon.

Giacobbe-Miller, J. (1995) A test of the group-values and control models of procedural justice from competing perspectives of labor and management. *Personnel Psychology*, **48**, 115–142.

Gilliland, S. W. (1993) The perceived fairness of selection systems: An organizational justice perspective. *Academy of Management Review*, **18**, 694–734.

Gilliland, S. W. (1994) Effects of procedural and distributive justice on reactions to a selection system. *Journal of Applied Psychology*, **79**, 691–701.

Gist, M. E. & Mitchell, T. R. (1992) Self-efficacy: A theoretical analysis of its determinants and malleability. *Academy of Management Journal*, **17**, 183–211.

Greenberg, J. (1982) Approaching equity and avoiding inequity in groups and organizations. In J. Greenberg & R. L. Cohen (eds), *Equity and Justice in Social Behavior* (pp. 389–435). New York: Academic Press.

Greenberg, J. (1983) Overcoming egocentric bias in perceived fairness through self-awareness. *Social Psychology Quarterly*, **46**, 152–156.

Greenberg, J. (1986a) Determinants of perceived fairness of performance evaluations. *Journal of Applied Psychology*, **71**, 340–342.

Greenberg, J. (1986b) The distributive justice of organizational performance evaluations. In H. W. Bierhoff, R. L. Cohen & J. Greenberg (eds), *Justice in Social Relations* (pp. 337–351). New York: Plenum.

Greenberg, J. (1986c) Organizational performance appraisal procedures: What makes them fair? In R. J. Lewicki, B. H. Sheppard, & M. H. Bazerman (eds), *Research on Negotiation in Organizations* Vol. 1 (pp. 25–41). Greenwich, CT: JAI Press.

Greenberg, J. (1987a) A taxonomy of organizational justice theories. *Academy of Management Review*, **12**, 9–22.

Greenberg, J. (1987b) Reactions to procedural injustice in payment distributions: Do the means justify the ends? *Journal of Applied Psychology*, **72**, 55–61.

Greenberg, J. (1990a) Organizational justice: Yesterday, today, and tomorow. *Journal of Management*, **16**, 399–432.

Greenberg, J. (1990b) Employee theft as a reaction to underpayment inequity: The hidden cost of pay cuts. *Journal of Applied Psychology*, **75**, 561–568.

Greenberg, J. (1990c) Looking fair vs being fair: Managing impressions of organizational justice. In B. M. Staw & L. L. Cummings (eds), *Research in Organizational Behavior*, Vol. 12 (pp. 111–157). Greenwich, CT: JAI Press.

Greenberg, J. (1993a) Stealing in the name of justice: Informational and interpersonal moderators of theft reactions to underpayment inequity. *Organizational Behavior and Human Decision Processes*, **54**, 81–103.

Greenberg, J. (1993b) The social side of fairness: Interpersonal and informational classes of organizational justice. In R. Cropanzano (ed.), *Justice in the Workplace: Approaching Fairness in Human Resource Management* (pp. 79–103). Hillsdale, NJ: Erlbaum.

Greenberg, J. (1993c) The intellectual adolescence of organizational justice: You've come a long way, maybe. *Social Justice Research*, **6**, 135–147.

Greenberg, J. (1993d) Justice and organizational citizenship: A commentary on the state of the science. *Employee Responsibilities and Rights Journal*, **6**, 227–237.

Greenberg, J. (1994a) Using socially fair treatment to promote acceptance of a work site smoking ban. *Journal of Applied Psychology*, **79**, 288–297.

Greenberg, J. (1994b) Restitution and retaliation as motives for inequity-induced pilferage. Unpublished manuscript, Ohio State University.

Greenberg, J. (1994c) Interpersonal determinants of time theft in the workplace. Unpublished manuscript, Ohio State University.

Greenberg, J. (1996a) *The Quest for Justice on the Job: Essays and Experiments*. Thousand Oaks, CA: Sage.

Greenberg, J. (1996b) 'Forgive me, I'm new': Three experimental demonstrations of the effects of attempts to excuse poor performance. *Organizational Behavior and Human Decision Processes*, **66**, 165–178.

Greenberg, J. (1997) The STEAL Motive: Managing the social determinants of employee theft. In R. Giacalone & J. Greenberg (eds), *Antisocial Behavior in the Workplace* (pp. 85–108). Thousand Oaks, CA: Sage.

Greenberg, J. & Bies, R. J. (1992) Establishing the role of empirical studies of organizational justice in philosophical inquiries into business ethics. *Journal of Business Ethics*, **11**, 433–444.

Greenberg, J., Bies, R. J., & Eskew, D. E. (1991) Establishing fairness in the eye of the beholder: Managing impressions of organizational justice. In R. Giacalone & P. Rosenfeld (eds), *Applied Impression Management: How Image Making Affects Managerial Decisions* (pp. 111–132). Newbury Park, CA: Sage.

Greenberg, J. & Cohen, R. L. (1982a) *Equity and Justice in Social Behavior*. New York: Academic Press.

Greenberg, J. & Cohen, R. L. (1982b) Why justice? Normative and instrumental interpretations. In J. Greenberg & R. L. Cohen (eds), *Equity and Justice in Social Behavior* (pp. 437–469). New York: Academic Press.

Greenberg, J. & Folger, R. (1983) Procedural justice, participation, and the fair process effect in groups and organizations. In P. B. Paulus (ed.), *Basic Group Processes* (pp. 235–256). New York: Springer-Verlag.

Greenberg, J., Lind, E. A., Scott, K. S., & Welchans, T. D. (1995) [Wrongful termination litigation in response to perceived injustice among layoff victims.] Unpublished raw data.

Greenberg, J. & McCarty, C. (1990) Comparable worth: A matter of justice. In G. R. Ferris & K. M. Rowland (eds), *Research in Personnel and Human Resources Management*, Vol. 8 (pp. 265–301). Greenwich, CT: JAI Press.

Greenberg, J. & Scott, K. S. (1996) Why do employees bite the hands that feed them? Employee theft as a social exchange process. In B. M. Staw & L. L. Cummings (eds), *Research in Organizational Behavior* (pp. 111–166). Greenwich, CT: JAI Press.

Greenberg, J. & Tyler, T. R. (1987) Why procedural justice in organizations? *Social Justice Research*, **1**, 127–142.

Grover, S. L. (1991) Predicting the perceived fairness of parental leave policies. *Journal of Applied Psychology*, **76**, 247–255.

Guion, R. M. (1965) *Personnel Testing*. New York: McGraw-Hill.

Guion, R. M. (1991) Personnel assessment, selection, and placement. In M. D. Dunnette & L. M. Hough (eds), *Handbook of Industrial and Organizational Psychology*. Second edition, Vol. 2 (pp. 327–398). Palo Alto, CA: Consulting Psychologists Press.

Harder, J. W. (1992) Play for pay: Effects of inequity in pay-for-performance context. *Administrative Science Quarterly*, **37**, 321–335.

Harland, L. K. & Biasotto, M. M. (1993, August) An evaluation of the procedural fairness of personality tests. Paper presented at the annual meeting of the Academy of Management, Atlanta, GA.

Harris, M. M., Dworkin, J. B., & Park, J. (1990) Preemployment screening procedures: How human resource managers perceive them. *Journal of Business and Psychology*, **4**, 279–292.

Hofstede, G. (1980) *Culture's Consequences*. London: Sage.

Homans, G. C. (1986) *Social Behavior: Its Elementary Forms*. New York: Harcourt, Brace, & World.

Hulin, C. L. (1991) Adaptation, persistence, and commitment in organizations. In M. D. Dunnette & L. M. Hough (eds), *Handbook of Industrial and Organizational Psychology*. Second edition, Vol. 2 (pp. 445–506). Palo Alto, CA: Consulting Psychologists Press.

James, K. (1993) The social context of organizational justice: Cultural, intergroup, and structural effects on justice behaviors and perceptions. In R. Cropanzano (ed.), *Justice in the Workplace: Approaching Fairness in Human Resource Management* (pp. 21–50). Hillsdale, NJ: Erlbaum.

Jones, J. W. (1991) Assessing privacy invasiveness of psychological test items: Job relevant versus clinical masures of integrity. *Journal of Business and Psychology*, **5**, 531–535.

Kabanoff, B. (1991) Equity, equality, power, and conflict. *Academy of Management Review*, **16**, 416–441.

Karambayya, R. & Brett, J. M. (1994) Managerial third parties: Intervention strategies, process, and consequences. In J. Folger & T. Jones (eds), *New Directions in Mediation: Communication Research and Perspectives* (pp. 175–192). Thousand Oaks, CA: Sage.

Karambayya, R., Brett, J. M., & Lytle, A. (1992) Effects of formal authority and experience on third-party roles, outcomes, and perceptions of fairness. *Academy of Management Journal*, **35**, 426–438.

Kemper, T. D. (1966) Representative roles and the legitimization of deviance. *Social Problems*, **13**, 288–298.

Kim, W. C. & Mauborgne, R. A. (1991) Implementing global strategies: The role of procedural justice. *Strategic Management Journal*, **12**, 125–143.

Kim, W. C. & Mauborgne, R. A. (1993) Procedural justice, attitudes, and subsidiary top management compliance with multinationals' corporate strategic decsions. *Academy of Management Journal*, **36**, 502–526.

Kluger, A. N. & Rothstein, H. R. (1993) The influence of selection test type on applicant reactions to employment testing. *Journal of Business and Psychology*, **8**, 3–25.

Knouse, S. P. (1989) Impression management and letters of recommendation. In R. A. Giacalone & R. Rosenfeld (eds), *Impression Management in the Organization* (pp. 283–296). Hillsdale, NJ: Erlbaum.

Kolb, D. M. (1985) To be a mediator: Expressive tactics in mediation. *Journal of Social Issues*, **41**, 1–25.

Kolb, D. M. (1986) Who are organizational third parties and what do they do? In R. J. Lewicki, B. H. Sheppard, & M. H. Bazerman (eds), *Research on Negotiation in Organizations* (pp. 207–228). Greenwich, CT: JAI Press.

Konovsky, M. A. & Brockner, J. (1993) Managing victim and survivor layoff reactions: A procedural justice perspective. In R. Cropanzano (ed.), *Justice in the Workplace: Approaching Fairness in Human Resource Management* (pp. 133–153). Hillsdale, NJ: Erlbaum.

Konovsky, M. A. & Cropanzano, R. (1991) The perceived fairness of employee drug testing as a predictor of employee attitudes and job performance. *Journal of Applied Psychology*, **76**, 698–707.

Konovsky, M. A. & Cropanzano, R. (1993) Justice considerations in employee drug testing. In R. Cropanzano (ed.), *Justice in the Workplace: Approaching Fairness in Human Resource Management* (pp. 171–192). Hillsdale, NJ: Erlbaum.

Konovsky, M. A., Elliott, J., & Pugh, S. D. (1995, August) The dispositional and contextual predictors of citizenship behavior in Mexico. Paper presented at the annual meeting of the Academy of Management, Vancouver, BC, Canada.

Konovsky, M. A. & Folger, R. (1991a) The effects of procedures, social accounts, and benefits level on victims' layoff reactions. *Journal of Applied Social Psychology*, **21**, 630–650.

Konovsky, M. A. & Folger, R. (1991b, August) The effects of procedural and distributive justice on organizational citizenship behavior. Paper presented at the annual meeting of the Academy of Management, Miami Beach, FL.

Konovsky, M. A. & Organ, D. W. (in press) Dispositional and contextual determinants of organizational citizenship behaviors. *Journal of Organizational Behavior*.

Konovsky, M. A. & Pugh, S. D. (1994) Citizenship behavior and social exchange. *Academy of Management Journal*, **37**, 656–669.

Koper, G., Van Knippenberg, D., Bouhuijs, F., Vermunt, R., & Wilke, H. (1993) Procedural fairness and self-esteem. *European Journal of Social Psychology*, **23**, 313–325.

Korsgaard, M. A., Schweiger, D. M., & Sapienza, H. J. (1995) Building commitment, attachment, and trust in strategic decision-making teams: The role of procedural justice. *Academy of Management Journal*, **38**, 60–84.

Kozan, M. K., & Ilter, S. S. (1994) Third party roles played by Turkish managers in subordinates' conflicts. *Journal of Organizational Behavior*, **15**, 453–466.

Kravitz, D. A., Stinson, V., & Chavez, T. L. (in press) Evaluations of tests used for making selection and promotion decisions. *International Journal of Selection and Assessment*.

Krzystofiak, F. J., Lillis, M., & Newman, J. M. (1995, August) Justice along the scarcity continuum. Paper presented at the annual meeting of the Academy of Management. Vancouver, BC, Canada.

Kulik, C. T. & Ambrose, M. L. (1992) Personal and situational determinants of referent choice. *Academy of Management Review*, **17**, 212–237.

Labig, C. E. Jr (1992) Supervisory and nonsupervisory employee attitude about drug testing. *Employee Responsibilities and Rights Journal*, **5**, 131–141.

Latham, G. P. & Finnegan, B. J. (1993) Perceived practicality of unstructured, patterned, and situational interviews. In H. Schuler, J. L. Farr, & M. Smith (eds), *Personnel Selection and Assessment: Individual and Organizational Perspectives* (pp. 41–55). Hillsdale, NJ: Erlbaum.

Lee, C. (1995) Prosocial organizational behaviors: The roles of workplace justice, achievement striving, and pay satisfaction. *Journal of Business and Psychology*, **10**, 197–206.

Lengel, R. H. & Daft, R. L. (1988) The selection of communication media as an executive skill. *Academy of Management Executive*, **2**, 225–232.

Leung, K., Chiu, W.-H., & Au, Y.-F. (1993) Sympathy and support for industrial actions: A justice analysis. *Journal of Applied Psychology*, **78**, 781–787.

Leventhal, G. S. (1976a) The distribution of rewards and resources in groups and organizations. In L. Berkowitz & E. Walster (eds), *Advances in Experimental Social Psychology*, Vol. 9 (pp. 91–131). New York: Academic Press.

Leventhal, G. S. (1976b) Fairness in social relationships. In J. W. Thibaut, J. T. Spence, & R. C. Carson (eds), *Contemporary Topics in Social Psychology* (pp. 211–240). Morristown, NJ: General Learning Press.

Leventhal, G. S. (1980) What should be done with equity theory? In K. J. Gergen, M. S. Greenberg, & R. H. Willis (eds), *Social Exchanges: Advances in Theory and Research* (pp. 27–55). New York: Plenum.

Leventhal, G. S., Karuza, J., & Fry, W. R. (1980) Beyond fairness: A theory of allocation preferences. In G. Milkula (ed.), *Justice and Social Interaction* (pp. 167–218). New York: Springer-Verlag.

Lind, E. A. (1995) Justice and authority relations in organizations. In R. Cropanzano & M. K. Kacmar (eds), *Organizational Politics, Justice, and Support: Managing the Social Climate of the Workplace* (pp. 83–96). Westport, CT: Quorum Books.

Lind, E. A. & Earley, P. C. (1992) Procedural justice and culture. *International Journal of Psychology*, **27**, 227–242.

Lind, E. A., Kanfer, R., & Earley, P. C. (1990) Voice, control, and procedural justice: Instrumental and noninstrumental concerns in fairness judgments. *Journal of Personality and Social Psychology*, **59**, 952–959.

Lind, E. A., Kulik, C. A., Ambrose, M., & de Vera Park, M. V. (1993) Individual and corporate dispute resolution: Using procedural fairness as a decision heuristic. *Administrative Science Quarterly*, **38**, 224–251.

Lind, E. A. & Lissak, R. I. (1985) Apparent impropriety and procedural fairness judgments. *Journal of Experimental Social Psychology*, **21**, 19–29.

Lind, E. A. & Tyler, T. R. (1988) *The Social Psychology of Procedural Justice*. New York: Plenum.

Lissowski, G., Tyszka, T., & Okrasa, W. (1991) Principles of distributive justice: Experiments in Poland and America. *Journal of Conflict Resolution*, **35**, 98–119.

Lowe, R. H. & Vodanovich, S. H. (1995) A field study of distributive and procedural justice as predictors of satisfaction and organizational commitment. *Journal of Business and Psychology*, **10**. 99–114.

Lowell, R. S. & DeLoach, J. A. (1984) Equal employment opportunity: Are you overlooking the application form? In R. S. Schuler & S. A. Youngblood (eds), *Reading in Personnel and Human Resource Management*. Second edition (pp. 115–120). St Paul, MN: West.

Macan, T. H., Avedon, M. J., Paese, M., & Smith, D. E. (1994) The effects of applicants' reactions to cognitive ability tests and an assessment center. *Personnel Psychology*, **47** 715–738.

Martin, J. & Harder, J. W. (1994) Bread and roses: Justice and the distribution of financial and socioemotional rewards in organizations. *Social Justice Research*, 7, 241–264.

McFarlin, D. B. & Sweeney, P. D. (1992) Distributive and procedural justice as predictors of satisfaction with personal and organizational outcomes. *Academy of Management Journal*, 35, 626–637.

Mellor, S. (1992) The influence of layoff severity on postlayoff union commitment among survivors: The moderating effect of the perceived legitimacy of a layoff account. *Personnel Psychology*, 45, 579–600.

Miceli, M. P. (1993) Justice and pay system satisfaction. In R. Cropanzano (ed.), *Justice in the Workplace: Approaching Fairness in Human Resource Management* (pp. 257–283). Hillsdale, NJ: Erlbaum.

Miceli, M. P. & Lane, M. C. (1991) Antecedents of pay satisfaction: A review and extension. In K. M. Rowland & G. R. Ferris (eds), *Research in Personnel and Human Resources Management*, Vol. 9 (pp. 235–309). Greenwich, CT: JAI Press.

Miles, J.A. & Greenberg, J. (1993) Cross-national differences in preferences for distributive justice norms: The challenge of establishing fair resource allocations in the European Community. In J. B. Shaw, P. S., Kirkbride, & K. M Rowlands (eds), *Research in Personnel and Human Resources Management* (Suppl. 3, pp. 133–156). Greenwich, CT: JAI Press.

Miller, C. C. & Cardinal, L. B. (1994) Strategic planning and firm performance: A synthesis of more than two decades of research. *Academy of Management Journal*, 37, 1649–1665.

Moorman, R. H. (1991) Relationship between organizational justice and organizational citizenship behaviors: Do fairness perceptions influence employee citizenship? *Journal of Applied Psychology*, 76, 845–855.

Mosier, C. I. (1947) A critical examination of the concept of face validity. *Educational and Psychological Measurement*, 7, 5–12.

Murphy, K. R., Thornton, G. C., III., & Prue, K. (1991) Influence of job characteristics on the acceptability of employee drug testing. *Journal of Applied Psychology*, 76, 447–453.

Murphy, K. R., Thornton, G. C., III., & Reynolds, D. H. (1990) College students' attitudes toward employee drug testing programs. *Personnel Psychology*, 43, 615–631.

Niehoff, B. P. & Moorman, R. H. (1993) Justice as a mediator of the relationship between methods of monitoring and organizational citizenship behavior. *Academy of Management Journal*, 36, 527–556.

Novelli, L., Jr, Kirkman, B. L., & Shapiro, D. L. (1995) Effective implementation of organizational change: An organizational justice perspective. In C. L. Cooper & D. M. Rousseau (eds), *Trends in Organizational Behavior*, Vol. 2 (pp. 15–36). Chichester, UK: Wiley.

Organ, D. W. (1990) The motivational basis of organizational citizenship behavior. In B. M. Staw & L. L. Cummings (eds), *Research in Organizational Behavior*, Vol. 12 (pp. 43–72). Greenwich, CT: JAI Press.

Organ, D. W. & Konovsky, M. A. (1989) Cognitive versus affective determinants of organizational citizenship behavior. *Journal of Applied Psychology*, 74, 157–164.

Organ, D. W. & Moorman, R. H. (1993) Fairness and organizational citizenship behavior: What are the connections? *Social Justice Research*, 6, 5–18.

Pfeffer, J. & Davis-Blake, A. (1992) Salary dispersion, location in the salary distribution, and turnover among college administrators. *Industrial and Labor Relations Review*, 45, 753–763.

Pfeffer, J. & Langton, N. (1993) The effects of wage dispersion on satisfaction, productivity, and working collaboratively: Evidence from college and university faculty. *Administrative Science Quarterly*, 38, 382–407.

Rasinski, K. A. (1992) Preference for decision control in organizational decision making. *Social Justice Research*, **5**, 343–357.

Rawls, J. (1971) *A Theory of Justice*. Cambridge, MA: Harvard University Press.

Reed, T. F. & Kelly, D. (1993) An exchange theory of organizational citizenship. In G. R. Ferris (ed.), *Research in Personnel and Human Resources Management*, Vol. 11 (pp. 41–82). Greenwich, CT: JAI Press.

Richman, L. S. (1993, September 20) When will the layoffs end? *Fortune*, pp. 54–56.

Rosen, R. H. (1991) *The Healthy Company*. New York: Jeremy P. Archer/Perigree.

Ross, W. D. (ed.) (1925) *The Oxford Translation of Aristotle. Vol. IX: The Nicomachean Ethics*. London: Oxford University Press.

Rosse, J. G., Miller, J. L., & Ringer, R. C. (in press) The deterrent value of drug and integrity testing. *Journal of Business and Psychology*.

Rosse, J. G., Miller, J. L., & Stecher, M. D. (1994) A field study of job applicants' reactions to personality and cognitive ability testing. *Journal of Applied Psychology*, **79**, 987–992.

Rosse, J. G., Ringer, R. C., & Miller, J. L. (in press) Personality and drug testing: An exploration of perceived fairness of alternatives to urinalysis. *Journal of Business and Psychology*.

Rynes, S. L. & Connerley, M. L. (1993) Applicant reactions to alternative selection procedures. *Journal of Business and Psychology*, **7**, 261–277.

Schaubroeck, J., May, D. R., & Brown, F. W. (1994) Procedural justice explanations and employee reactions to economic hardship: A field experiment. *Journal of Applied Psychology*, **79**, 455–460.

Schoorman, F. D. & Champagne, M. V. (1994) Managers as informal third parties: The impact of supervisor–subordinate relationships on interventions. *Employee Responsibilities and Rights Journal*, **7**, 73–84.

Schuler, H. (1993a) Social validity of selection situations: A concept and some empirical results. In H. Schuler, J. L. Farr, & M. Smith (eds), *Personnel Selection and Assessment: Individual and Organizational Perspectives* (pp. 11–26). Hillsdale, NJ: Erlbaum.

Schuler, H. (1993b) Is there a dilemma between validity and acceptance in the employment interview? In B. Nevo & R. S. Jäger (eds), *Educational and Psychological Testing: The Test Taker's Outlook* (pp. 239–250). Toronto, Canada: Hogrefe & Huber.

Schwarzwald, J., Koslowsky, M. & Shalit, B. (1992) A field study of employees' attitudes and behaviors after promotion decisions. *Journal of Applied Psychology*, **77**, 511–514.

Shapiro, D. L. (1991) The effects of explanations on negative reactions to deceit. *Administrative Science Quarterly*, **36**, 614–630.

Shapiro, D. L. (1993) Reconciling theoretical differences among procedural justice researchers by re-evaluating what it means to have one's view 'considered': Implications for third-party managers. In R. Cropanzano (ed.), *Justice in the Workplace: Approaching Fairness in Human Resource Management* (pp. 51–78). Hillsdale, NJ: Erlbaum.

Shapiro, D. L. & Brett, J. M. (1993) Comparing three processes underlying judgments of procedural justice: A field study of mediation and arbitration. *Journal of Personality and Social Psychology*, **65**, 1167–1177.

Shapiro, D. L., Buttner, E. H., & Barry, B. (1994) Explanations for rejection decisions: What factors enhance their perceived adequacy and moderate their enhancement of justice perceptions? *Organizational Behavior and Human Decision Processes*, **58**, 346–368.

Shapiro, D. L. & Rosen, B. (1994) An investigation of managerial interventions in employee disputes. *Employee Responsibilities and Rights Journal*, **7**, 37–51.

Sheppard, B. H., Blumenfeld-Jones, K., Minton, W. J., & Hyder, E. (1994) Informal conflict intervention: Advice and dissent. *Employee Responsibilities and Rights Journal*, 7, 53–72.

Sheppard, B. H. & Lewicki, R. J. (1987) Toward general principles of managerial fairness. *Social Justice Research*, 1, 161–176.

Sheppard, B. H., Lewicki, R. J., & Minton, J. W. (1993) *Organizational Justice: The Search for Fairness in the Workplace*. Lexington, MA: Lexington Press.

Siegel, P., Brockner, J., & Tyler, T. (August, 1995) Revisiting the relationship between procedural and distributive justice: The role of trust. Paper presented at the Annual Meeting of the Academy of Management. Vancouver, BC, Canada.

Singer, M. S. (1992) Procedural justice in managerial selection: Identification of fairness determinants and associations of fairness perceptions. *Social Justice Research*, 5, 49–70.

Singer, M. S. (1993) *Fairness in Personnel Selection*. Aldershot, New Zealand: Avebury.

Skitka, L. J. & Tetlock, P. E. (1992) Allocating scarce resources: A contingency model of distributive justice. *Journal of Experimental Social Psychology*, 28, 491–522.

Smither, J. W., Reilly, R. R., Millsap, R. E., Pearlman, K., & Stoffey, R. W. (1993) Applicants' reactions to selection procedures. *Personnel Psychology*, 46, 49–75.

Steensma, H. & Vermunt, R. (1991) *Social Justice in Human Relations. Vol. 2: Societal and Psychological Consequences of Justice and Injustice*. New York: Plenum.

Stepina, L. P. & Perrewe, P. L. (1991) The stability of comparative referent choice and feelings of inequity: A longitudinal field study. *Journal of Organizational Behavior*, 12, 185–200.

Stoffey, R. W., Millsap, R. E., Smither, J. W., & Reilly, R. R. (1991, April) The influence of selection procedures on attitudes about the organization and job pursuit intentions. In R. R. Reilly (Chair), *Perceived validity of selection procedures: Implications for organizations*. Symposium presented at the annual meeting of the Society for Industrial and Organizational Psychology, Saint Louis, MO.

Stone, E. F. (1988) Moderator variables in research: A review and analysis of conceptual and methodological issues. In K. R. Rowland & G. R. Ferris (eds), *Research in Personnel and Human Resources Management* Vol. 6 (pp. 191–230). Greenwich, CT: JAI.

Summers, T. P. & Hendrix, W. H. (1991) Modeling the role of pay equity perceptions: A field study. *Journal of Occupational Psychology*, 64, 145–157.

Sweeney, P. D. & McFarlin, D. B. (1993) Workers' evaluations of the 'ends' and the 'means': An examination of four models of distributive and procedural justice. *Organizational Behavior and Human Decision Processes*, 55, 23–40.

Sweeney, P. D., McFarlin, D. B., & Inderrieden, E. J. (1990) Using relative deprivation theory to explain satisfaction with income and pay level: A multistudy examination. *Academy of Management Journal*, 33, 423–436.

Sykes, G. & Matza, D. (1957) Techniques of neutralization: A theory of delinquency. *American Journal of Sociology*, 22, 664–670.

Taylor, M. S., Tracy, K. B., Renard, M. K., Harrison, J. K., & Carroll, S. J. (1995) Due process in performance appraisal: A quasi-experiment in procedural justice. *Administrative Science Quarterly*, 40, 495–523.

Tedeschi, J. T. & Reiss, M. (1981) Verbal strategies in impression management. In C. Antaki (ed.), *The Psychology of Ordinary Explanations of Social Behaviour* (pp. 271–309). London: Academic Press.

Tepper, B. J. & Braun, C. K. (1995) Does the experience of organizational justice mitigate the invasion of privacy engendered by random drug testing? An empirical investigation. *Basic and Applied Social Psychology*, 16, 211–225.

Tett, R. P., Jackson, D. N., & Rothstein, M. (1991) Personality measures as predictors of job performance: A meta-analysis. *Personnel Psychology*, 44, 703–742.

Thibaut, J. & Walker, L. (1975) *Procedural Justice: A Psychological Analysis*. Hillsdale, NJ: Erlbaum.
Thornton, G. C., III & Cleveland, J. C. (1990) Developing managerial talent through simulation. *American Psychologist*, **45**, 190–199.
Törnblom, K. Y. (1990) The social psychology of distributive justice. In K. Scherer (ed.), *The Nature and Administration of Justice: Interdisciplinary Approaches* (pp. 45–70). Cambridge, UK: Cambridge University Press.
Treviño, L. K. & Ball, G. A. (1992) The social implications of punishing unethical behavior: Observers' cognitive and affective reactions. *Journal of Management*, **18**, 751–768.
Triandis, H. C. (1994) *Culture and Social Behavior*. New York: McGraw-Hill.
Tyler, T. R. (1989) The psychology of procedural justice: A test of the group-value model. *Journal of Personality and Social Psychology*, **57**, 830–838.
Tyler, T. R. (1990) *Why People Obey the Law: Procedural Justice, Legitimacy, and Compliance*. New Haven, CT: Yale University Press.
Tyler, T. R. (1991) Using procedures to justify outcomes: Testing the viability of a procedural justice strategy for managing conflict and allocating resources in work organizations. *Basic and Applied Social Psychology*, **12**, 259–279.
Tyler, T. R. (1994) Psychological models of the justice motive: Antecedents of distributive and procedural justice. *Journal of Personality and Social Psychology*, **67**, 850–863.
Tyler, T. R. & Bies, R. J. (1990) Beyond formal procedures: The interpersonal context of procedural justice. In J. S. Carroll (ed.), *Applied Social Psychology and Organizational Settings* (pp. 77–98). Hillsdale, NJ: Erlbaum.
Tyler, T. R. & Dawes, R. M. (1993) Fairness in groups: Comparing self-interest and social identity perspectives. In B. A. Mellers & J. Baron (eds), *Psychological Perspectives on Justice: Theory and Applications* (pp. 87–108). New York: Cambridge University Press.
Tyler, T. R. & Degoey, P. (1995) Collective restraint in social dilemmas: Procedural justice and social identification effects on support for authorities. *Journal of Personality and Social Psychology*, **69**, 482–497.
Tyler, T. R. & Lind, E. A. (1992) A relational model of authority in groups. In M. P. Zanna (ed.), *Advances in Experimental Social Psychology*, Vol. 25 (pp. 115–191). San Diego, CA: Academic Press.
Tyler, T. R. & Smith, H. J. (in press) Social justice and social movements. In D. Gilbert, S. T. Fiske, & G. Lindzey (eds), *Handbook of Social Psychology*. Fourth edition. New York: McGraw-Hill.
Vermunt, R. & Steensma, H. (1991) *Social Justice in Human Relations, Vol. 1: Societal and Psychological Origins of Justice*. New York: Plenum.
Vroom, V. (1964) *Work and Motivation*. New York: Wiley.
Wall, J. A. & Callister, R. R. (1995) Conflict and its management. *Journal of Management*, **21**, 515–558.
Weeks, D. (1992) *The Eight Essential Steps to Conflict Resolution: Preserving Relationships at Work, at Home, and in the Community*. New York: Putnam.
Welton, G. L. & Pruitt, D. G. (1987) The mediation process: The effect of mediator bias and disputant power. *Personality and Social Psychology Bulletin*, **13**, 123–133.
Westin, A. F. (1978) Privacy and personnel records: A look at employee attitudes. *Civil Liberties Review*, **4**(5), 28–34.
Wigdor, A. K. & Sackett, P. R. (1993) Employment testing and public policy: The case of the General Aptitude Test Battery. In H. Schuler, J. L. Farr, & M. Smith (eds), *Personnel Selection and Assessment: Individual and Organizational Perspectives* (pp. 183–204). Hillsdale, NJ: Erlbaum.
Wittmer, J. M., Carnevale, P. J., & Walker, M. E. (1991) General alignment and oversupport in biased mediation. *Journal of Conflict Resolution*, **35**, 594–610.

Chapter 9

GENETIC INFLUENCE ON MENTAL ABILITIES, PERSONALITY, VOCATIONAL INTERESTS AND WORK ATTITUDES

Thomas J. Bouchard, Jr
University of Minnesota

It is unusual but not unprecedented for researchers in Industrial/ Organizational psychology to think of their discipline in broad biological and evolutionary terms (Arvey & Bouchard, 1994; Bernhard & Glantz, 1992). The focus of most practitioners is appropriately on proximal mechanisms and practical matters. Nevertheless, at times it is instructive to view one's discipline from a larger and somewhat novel perspective. There are two quite different ways in which one can approach the topic of genetic influence on psychological traits; they correspond very closely to the classic distinction made by Cronbach (1957) years ago between the two disciplines of scientific psychology, namely the study of main effects (experimental) and the study of natural variation (individual differences). In the biological realm evolutionary psychologists correspond to the experimentalists. They believe that the important phenomena are fixed adaptations on which human beings do not differ. This view is well expressed by the dominant theoreticians in this domain, Leda Cosmides and John Tooby. They wrote, 'it follows that humans, and other complex, long-lived, outbreeding organisms, must be very nearly uniform in those genes that underlie our complex adaptations' (Tooby & Cosmides, 1992, p. 79). This view does not, however, stand undisputed (Bouchard, Lykken, Tellegen, & McGue, in press; Wilson, 1994). Behavior geneticists have a natural kinship with individual difference psychology as both classes of investigators are interested in the etiology of variation in psychological characteristics (Plomin, DeFries, & McClearn, 1990; Willerman, 1979). As with most dichotomies there is considerable truth in both positions. This chapter will focus only on genetic sources of variance underlying work-related traits and not the human universals of evolutionary psychology. It is,

International Review of Industrial and Organizational Psychology, 1997 Volume 12
Edited by C.L. Cooper and I.T. Robertson. © 1997 John Wiley & Sons Ltd.

however, our opinion that behavior genetics and evolutionary psychology are natural allies (Bouchard et al., in press; Crawford & Anderson, 1989; Segal, 1993; Wilson, 1994). Both approaches take as their starting point the assumption that the only viable explanation of life on this planet and its fantastic diversity is Darwin's theory of evolution by natural selection.[1] The theory of evolution via natural selection remains controversial even among some intellectuals (Degler, 1991). In my view the best contemporary broad scale treatment of the topic is Dennett's book, *Darwin's Dangerous Idea*. Dennett (1995) concludes that the idea of evolution via natural selection is so powerful that it should be considered a universal solvent 'capable of cutting right to the heart of everything in sight . . . At every stage in the tumultuous controversies that have accompanied the evolution of Darwin's dangerous idea, there has been a defiance born of fear: "You'll never explain this!" and the challenge has been taken up: "Watch me!" And in spite of—indeed, partly because of—the huge emotional investments the opponents have made in winning their sides of the argument, the picture has become clearer and clearer' (p.521). Cziko (1995) has extended Darwin's idea of selection theory even further and many of his ideas will be of interest to I/O psychologists.

The most important reason for introducing behavior genetic ideas to I/O psychologists is a practical one, namely to aid in constructing valid explanatory models of work-related phenomena. As I hope to show, the evidence for genetic influence on most psychological traits is now sufficiently persuasive that it is no longer acceptable to assume that the preponderance of the reliable variance in any psychological trait is environmental in origin. Social scientists have always been fully aware of the fallacy of interpreting correlations as indicators of causation. Nevertheless, correlations between some kinds of variables such as life stress events, which we will demonstrate are influenced by genetic factors, have been incorporated into theoretical models as environmental causes of a variety of outcomes with nary a thought given to the possibility that the interpretation might be erroneous and the direction of causation reversed. As I/Q psychologists extend their theoretical models and incorporate additional nonwork variables (family variables, home situations, etc.), a move that is to be applauded, the possibility of misattribution of direction of causation becomes even more serious.

A BRIEF INTRODUCTION TO QUANTITATIVE GENETICS

In order to understand the logic of behavior genetic studies it is necessary to have some comprehension of quantitative genetic methods. It is a simple matter to introduce quantitative genetic theory to I/O psychologists because similar theoretical reasoning underlies much of their work. The easiest way to introduce these genetic 'models' is via reliability theory. A common interpretation of the Hoyt parallel form reliability is via true and error score theory.

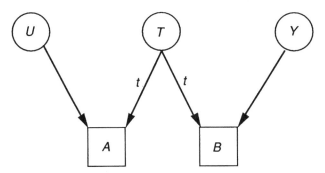

Figure 9.1 Path diagram showing the path model that underlies the interpretation of the Hoyt parallel form reliability coefficient

The correlation between parallel forms of a test is interpreted as reflecting the variance in test A and test B as caused by the influence of the true score (a latent construct). This idea is shown in the path diagram in Figure 9.1. This correlation is computed via analysis of variance, and a correlation computed in this fashion is called an intraclass correlation (Hayes, 1973, p.535).

According to convention the boxes represent variables, the circles represent latent constructs, the directional arrows represent causal influences (if the arrow pointed in the other direction this would imply that the test could be a cause of the true score, an implausible situation). In this diagram, T is the influence of a true score (in substantive terms the true score might be a trait of some sort, that is, the hypothetical construct intelligence), U and Y are sources of error variance and A and B represent test scores. The lower case 't' is a path coefficient, and it represents the degree of influence of T on each test. Following the rules of path analysis, the correlation between test A and B is the cross-product of the path coefficients linking the two tests. Thus $r_{AB} = t^2$. and $t = \sqrt{r_{AB}}$. The important fact to note here is that the correlation between the two tests is a direct measure of the true score variance. *The correlation is not squared* (Bouchard, Lykken, McGue, Segal, & Tellegen, 1990b; Jensen, 1971). For a concise introduction to path models see Loehlin (1992b).

Consider the situation where, instead of administering two tests to each individual we administer the same test to a sample of monozygotic twins who have been reared apart (MZA twins). On the assumption that the twins have been reared in uncorrelated trait relevant environments, the only reason they should show any similarity is because of common genetic influences. The model in Figure 9.1 applies. Instead of T being the causal influence, it is now G (Genetic influence). The paths represent the influence of heredity (h) and $r_{MZA} = h_b^2$; h_b^2 is the traditional symbol for broad heritability (all genetic influences). The correlation between MZA twins for any given trait provides a direct estimate of the broad heritability. For the same reason the Hoyt reliability is not squared neither is the MZA correlation (Bouchard et al., 1990b).

The correlation for dizygotic twins reared apart (DZA) is treated in the same manner. Under the assumption of a simple additive genetic model, the DZA correlation estimates half the genetic variance. This is because we know from genetic theory that on average DZ twins share half their segregating genes by descent. If there are nonadditive genetic factors at work they are entirely shared by MZ twins and hardly shared at all by DZ twins. Thus DZA and DZT (dizygotic twins reared together) correlations less than half the MZA and MZT (monozygotic twins reared together) correlations are suggestive of nonadditive genetic factors (Li, 1987; Lykken, McGue, Tellegen, & Bouchard, 1992). Broad heritability includes these non-additive genetic factors and narrow heritability (h_n^2) does not. Narrow heritability includes only additive factors that can be passed directly from parents to offspring.

To represent the correlation between MZT twins in the form of a path model we add an additional latent causal factor to account for their similarity, namely common environmental influence (C) with a path labeled (c). The equation has the following form $r_{MZT} = h^2 + c^2$. Analogously the correlation for dizygotic twins reared together (DZT) is $r_{DZT} = 0.5h^2 + c^2$. The ordinary twin method, which makes use only of twins reared together, estimates genetic influence with the following formula, $h^2 = 2(r_{MZT} - r_{DZT})$. This method assumes a simple additive model and identical common family environmental influences for both types of twins. Modern twin studies make use of much more sophisticated model fitting procedures which can incorporate a very large number of different kinships simultaneously (Neale & Cardon, 1992).

GENETIC INFLUENCE ON IQ

The idea that the IQ is a fundamental variable of great importance in the shaping of modern industrialized societies, primarily through its partitioning of individuals by occupation, is an old one that has been recently put forward again in *The Bell Curve*, by Herrnstein and Murray (1994). The public controversy generated by that book suggests that the validity, utility and fairness of IQ tests are issues that remain to be settled in the public mind. Similar, but more circumscribed debates, continue to be carried on in scientific journals (Barrett, 1994; Barrett & Depinet, 1991; McClelland, 1993, 1994; Schmidt & Hunter, 1993; Snow, 1995; Sternberg & Wagner, 1993). Even a cursory look at this literature will reveal that this controversy is driven to a considerable degree by the claim that IQ is heavily influenced by genetic factors. Informative follow-up works dealing with *The Bell Curve* controversy are Hunt (1995), Jacoby and Glauberman (1995), Neisser, Boodoo, Bouchard, Boykin, Brody, Ceci et al. (1996), Sternberg and Grigorenko (1996). A useful and readable up-to-date summary of the broader IQ controversy can be found in Seligman (1992) and Gardner, Kornhaber, and Wake (1996). A more technical treatment can be found in Brody (1992). It is not possible at present to locate genes that directly influence IQ except at the lower tail, in which case numerous developmental processes are interfered with, and the depression of IQ is one of numerous consequences (Bouchard, 1993b; Flint, Wilkie, Buckle, Winter, Holland, & McDermid, 1995; Martin, 1993; McKusick, 1992; Thapar, Gottesman, Owen, O'Donovan, & McGuffin, 1994). Molecular genetic techniques are evolving rapidly and while quantitative trait loci (QTLs or polygenes) for IQ are expected to be identified in the near future (Cardon, 1995; Plomin, 1995; Plomin, McClearn, Smith, Skuder, Vigneti, Chorney et al., 1995; Plomin, Owen, & McGuffin, 1994; Skuder, Plomin, McClearn, Smith, Vignetti, Chorney et al., 1995), it appears that the first gene known to influence a normal human quantitative psychological trait is one that influences personality (Benjamin, Li, Patterson, Greenberg, Murphy, & Hamer, 1996; Cloninger, Adolfsson, & Svrakic, 1996; Ebstein, Novick, Umansky, Priel, Osher, Blaine et al., 1996), specifically novelty-seeking. For the foreseeable future, however, we will have to rely upon fallible observational methods, experiments of nature (twins) and experiments of society (adoption) and converging lines of evidence to demonstrate genetic influence on IQ and other psychological traits. Generating evidence in support of the idea that there is genetic influence on psychological traits is essentially a problem in construct validity (Bouchard, 1993b; Bouchard, in press, a).

The Influence of Age on the Heritability of IQ

In the recent past there was a great deal of heterogeneity in heritability estimates of IQ. This heterogeneity was often explained away by asserting that heritability is a population statistic and could be expected to vary from study to study. Two factors have led to a marked change in this perception. First, the advent of meta-analysis has led to the conclusion that much of the variation in the kinship correlations that underlie heritability estimates is simply due to artifacts (Caruso, 1983), a conclusion clearly predicted as a consequence of the application of meta-analysis to other domains (Hunter & Schmidt, 1990). Second, it has now become clear that the heritability of IQ increases with age rather than decreases as most psychologists would predict. The evidence comes from two quite different lines of evidence, studies of ordinary twins and studies of unrelated individuals reared together. When the results of the ordinary twin studies found in the literature (Bouchard & McGue, 1981) are organized by age we find that after about age 20 MZT correlatons rise and DZT correlations drop (McGue, Bouchard, Iacono, & Lykken, 1993). The consequence is that the magnitude of the influence of common environment decreases and the magnitude of the influence of herdity increases. Similar effects can be shown in contemporary twin studies (Finkel, Pedersen, McGue, & McClearn, 1995; McGue et al., 1993), except that in very old age there may be a drop in genetic influence. The decline in common environmental influence with age is also demonstrated with unrelated individuals reared together (URT). The only reason such individuals should be alike (aside from placement effects, a bias in favor of an environmental hypothesis) is common environmental influences.[2] The weighted average correlation for individuals assessed in childhood is 0.29 ($N = 1882$) (Bouchard & McGue, 1981). When assessed in adolescence/adulthood the weighted average correlation (based on five samples) is 0.04 ($N = 398$) (Loehlin, Horn, & Willerman, in press; Scarr & Weinberg, 1978; Scarr, Weinberg, & Waldman, 1993; Teasdale & Owen, 1984). Only one study has assessed URTs both in childhood and adulthood; that study did find a decline in common environmental influence (Loehlin, Horn, & Willerman, in press). Contrary to popular belief, therefore, the heritability of the IQ of adults is higher than that of children.

The Magnitude of Genetic Influence on IQ

Modern studies of adult MZT and DZT twins suggest that the broad heritability of IQ is in the range 0.50 to 0.80 (Finkel et al., 1995; McGue et al., 1993; Plomin, Pedersen, Lichtenstein, & McClearn, 1994; Sundet, Tambs, Magnus, & Berg, 1988; Tambs, Sundet, & Magnus, 1984). Studies of adult MZA twins confirm this conclusion (Bouchard, Lykken, McGue, Segal, & Tellegen, 1990a; Bouchard, in press; Plomin et al., 1994; Saudino, Plomin, Pedersen, & McClearn, 1994). This conclusion is reinforced by two additional studies that did not use twins. The Texas adoption studies report a narrow heritability of 0.78 (for true scores in the population) based on a comprehensive analysis of fourteen kinships of mostly adults (children average 17 years of age) (Loehlin, Horn, & Willerman, in press). A Danish adoption study utilizing four groups of sibling pairs (full-siblings reared apart, maternal half-siblings reared apart, paternal half-siblings reared apart and unrelated reared together) drew IQ test scores from the draft board records (males tested between the ages of 18 and 26) and derived a heritability of 0.96 based on model fitting of the data (Teasdale & Owen, 1984). Three lines of evidence, twins reared apart, twins reared together and adoption studies all converge on the conclusion that the heritability of adult IQ is in the 0.50 to 0.80 range. All these studies have been carried out in Western societies and all fail to adequately sample the real extremes of poverty and wealth so the limitations of the observed values should be kept in mind.

GENETIC INFLUENCE ON SPECIAL MENTAL ABILITIES

Special mental abilities show a somewhat lower heritability than does IQ. Nichols (1978) provided the first meta-analysis of the twin-reared-together literature on this topic. Bouchard, Segal and Lykken (1990) later updated this review. These analyses suggest that with the exception of memory, for which heritability is perhaps a little lower (Thapar, Petrill, & Thompson, 1994), estimates of the heritability of most special mental abilities are in the range 0.4 to 0.6. Tambs, Sundet, and Magnus (1988) report similar results for some special abilities (technical comprehension and arithmetic skills) based on a military sample of 18–19-year-old twins who were in the compulsory Norwegian military service. Most of the behavior genetic research on mental abilities, like the research on IQ, has been carried out on young people. The MZA studies reported by Bouchard, Segal, and Lykken (1990) and Pedersen, Plomin, Nesselroade, and McClearn (1992), however, confirm that these estimates are probably reasonable for older adults as well. There is now also evidence that both variability and stability in cognitive abilities later in life are largely genetic in origin (Plomin et al., 1994).

One can address this question in a somewhat different manner, by asking the question: 'Are special mental abilities heritable after the general factor has been removed?' The answer is yes, there is something genetic beyond g and it is not insubstantial for most special mental abilities. The evidence for this conclusion comes from studies of ordinary twins (Tambs et al., 1988) adoptees (Brooks, Fulker, & DeFries, 1990; Cardon, Fulker, DeFries, & Plomin, 1992; Loehlin, Horn, & Willerman, 1994), and twins reared apart (Pedersen, Plomin, & McClearn, 1994).

INFORMATION PROCESSING SKILLS

The cognitive revolution of the 70s and 80s led to a great deal of research aimed at describing the component process underlying IQ measures (Carpenter, Just, & Shell, 1990; Kyllonen & Christal, 1990; Snow & Swanson, 1992). Jensen (1992) has argued that, 'the nature of g must be understood in terms of information processing rather than in terms of the specific knowledge and skills that are seen in the content of conventional mental tests' (p.271). Other investigators in the field have doubts about the theoretical promise of this approach (Lohman, 1994). There are many different information processing conceptualizations of cognitive processes, and it is not clear which one behavior geneticists should focus on. Surprisingly, this approach has not led to the construction of useful instruments to replace IQ tests; as Snow has noted, 'Such descriptions, however, remain today at a theoretical level. No G measures now in use display distinctions derived from this work' (Snow, 1995, p.18). Nevertheless, it is likely that some information processing measures will contribute to our understanding of g and contribute to the prediction of job performance through g while other measures will contribute to our understanding of job performance independent of g (Chaiken, 1994), and perhaps independently of special mental abilities. Consequently the degree of genetic influence on such measures is of some interest. McGue and Bouchard (1989) reported a wide range of heritabilities (based on MZA and DZA twins) for numerous information processing measures. Three factors derived from the various measures yielded heritabilities of 0.54 (Basic Information Processing Speed), 0.27 (Acquisition Speed), and 0.58 (Spatial Speed) showing that highly reliable composite information processing measures do show substantial genetic influence. Petrill, Thompson, and Detterman (1995) have shown similar effects using a variety of different measures administered to MZT and DZT twins of school age. There certainly is a relationship between some information processing measures and IQ. Vernon and Weese (1993) have demonstrated this in university students, and Petrill, Thompson, and Detterman (1995) have shown it in elementary school children. Studies with adults, however, show that cognitive speed cannot account for all individual differences in IQ (Bors & Forkin, 1995). Baker, Vernon, & Ho (1991) have shown this relationship is sometimes entirely mediated by genetic factors. Other times the relationship is more complex (Petrill, Thompson, & Detterman, 1995). The findings in this domain are still in a rudimentary state of development, and no general conclusion can be drawn with confidence.

PERSONALITY

The literature on genetic influence on personality traits is very large and could not be comprehensively reviewed in the space available (Bouchard, in press, b). There is compelling evidence that prediction of job performance can be accomplished as effectively with broad personality constructs as with narrow constructs (Ones, in press); consequently it will not be too misleading if we focus only on the Big Five, however see Hough (1992). One of the Big Five, Conscientiousness, has been shown by Barrick and Mount (1991) in a major meta-analysis, to have consistent relations with job performance across multiple measures and across all occupational groups. Loehlin (1992a) carried out the equivalent of a meta-analysis of all the kinship correlations available in the psychological literature through about 1990 and fitted genetic models to them. Recently I reorganized the data from the previous meta-analysis by Nichols (1978) along the lines of the Big Five scheme and compared those findings with comparable measures in the Minnesota Study of Twins Reared Apart (MISTRA) as well as Loehlin's analysis (Bouchard, 1994). The results are shown in Figure 9.2.

All three analyses clearly demonstrate that these higher order personality traits are strongly influenced by genetic factors with heritabilities of about 0.40. They also show very modest common environmental influence. The specific values for the MISTRA data can be found in Bouchard and Pedersen (in press) where discrepancies between the MISTRA findings and those of the Swedish Adoption Twin Study of Aging (SATSA) are discussed—SATSA finds lower heritabilities than MISTRA. A detailed discussion of the criticisms

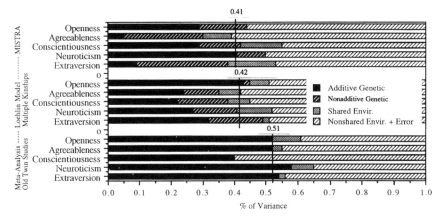

Figure 9.2   Percentage of variance accounted for in the 'Big Five' personality traits by various genetic and environmental influences for three data sets. The solid lines indicate the mean Falconer heritability for the older twin data and the mean broad heritability from model fitting for the other data sets

of behavior genetic findings in the personality domain can be found in Hoffman (1991). A critique of the Hoffman article can be found in Bouchard (1993a).

VOCATIONAL INTERESTS

The importance of the domain of vocational interest measurement for applied work has been well established since the early work of E. K. Strong (Campbell, 1968). In spite of very early work on genetic influences on interests (Carter, 1932) it is still widely believed that variance in interests is largely influenced by environmental factors. In a recent theoretical treatment of vocational interests in the *Psychological Bulletin* Gati (1991) claimed that: 'Although there is evidence for the contribution of genetic factors to interests, these factors account for less than 5% of the interest variance' (p.312). This view is in serious error. Nichols (1978) provided an excellent meta-analysis of the twin literature up to the date of his review. He organized the data under six major interests, Practical, Science, Business, Clerical, Helping and Artistic, the respective Falconer heritabilities were 0.26, 0.50, 0.30, 0.36, 0.36, and 0.36. As with other behavior genetic domains most of the subjects in these studies were very young people. Moloney, Bouchard and Segal (1991) reported heritabilities for the Strong Campbell Interests Inventory (SCII) (Hansen & Campbell, 1985) and the Jackson Vocational Interest Survey (JVIS) (Jackson, 1977) derived from adult MZA and DZA twins. The heritabilities for the SCII Holland General Occupational Themes (which are quite comparable to the six interest areas reported by Nichols) were Realistic 0.28, Investigative 0.42, Enterprising 0.44, Conventional 0.23, Social 0.40 and Artistic 0.35. Ten factors were derived from a factor analysis of the SCII and the JVIS and the heritabilities of the six factors that matched the Holland General Occupational Themes listed above were 0.41, 0.66, 0.50, 0.38, 0.52 and 0.50. These later data show the sizable increase in heritability that occurs as improvement in measurement characteristics occurs. This latter point has also been made by a large study of twins reared together (Lykken, Bouchard, McGue, & Tellegen, 1993). In this study a large sample of vocational intererst, recreational interest, and talent items was administered to 924 pairs of adult twins reared together; 39 factors and 11 superfactors were derived from the data. The mean heritability of the factors was 0.48 and of the superfactors 0.53. When the MISTRA MZA twins were scored on these factors and superfactors the correlations (heritability estimates in their own right) were 0.41 and 0.48. These are all lower bound estimates as the item pool used in this study was developed for research purposes. The range of scale reliabilities was very large; the correlation between the MZT twin similarities on all 50 factors and the 3-year retest stability of the factors was 0.86. If the item pool were subject to refinement (drop the least reliable items, refine ambiguous items, etc.) the heritabilities of the final scales undoubtedly go up somewhat.

Finally, a comprehensive analysis of data gathered on eight kinships (MZT, DZT, MZA, DZA, adopted parent × offspring, adoptive siblings, biological parent × offspring, and biological siblings) in five studies (Grotevant, 1979; Grotevant & Cooper, 1985; Grotevant, Scarr, & Weinberg, 1977; Loehlin & Nichols, 1976; Moloney, Bouchard, & Segal, 1991) was carried out on the common scales scoreable from the various forms of the Strong inventory used in these studies (Betsworth, Bouchard, Cooper, Grotevant, Hansen, Scarr et al., 1993). The median heritability of all scales was 0.36, as was the median heritability of Holland General Occupational Themes. In this study all the measures were shorter and therefore less reliable than the original full-length scales. Consequently, the study underestimates the heritabilities that would be obtained on scales scored from the standard instrument.

It seems clear that the heritability of well-measured vocational interests is in the range 0.40 to 0.50, about eight to nine times stronger than suggested by Gati.

JOB SATISFACTION

Arvey, Bouchard, Segal and Abrahams (1989) reported the first study of genetic influence on job satisfaction. That study made use of data from 34 pairs of MZA twins who completed the Minnesota Job Satisfaction Questionnaire (MSQ). The authors had predicted on intuitive grounds that intrinsic satisfaction would be higher than extrinsic satisfaction. The intraclass correlations (broad heritabilities) were 0.32 for intrinsic satisfaction, 0.11 for extrinsic satisfaction and 0.31 for general satisfaction. A correlation of 0.31 was significant in this sample, but the difference between the intrinsic and extrinsic satisfaction correlations was not significant. A single item measure of job satisfaction yielded an intraclass correlation of 0.16 (n.s.). This report elicited a spirited critique (Cropanzano & James, 1990) and a detailed reply (Bouchard, Arvey, Keller, & Segal, 1992). Arvey, McCall, Bouchard, Taubman and Cavanaugh (1994) carried out two studies of MZT and DZT twins to test the robustness of these preliminary findings. The first study, of 95 MZT and 80 DZT twins, made use of the MSQ. Model fitting yielded heritability estimates of 0.23 for intrinsic satisfaction, 0.00 for extrinsic satisfaction and 0.16 for general satisfaction. The second study was based on data (1236 MZT and 1165 DZT twins from the National Academy of Sciences and National Research Council (NAS-NRC) twin sample) previously gathered by Behrman, Hrubec, Taubman and Wales (1980). These twins completed a single item (4 point scale) measure of General Job Satisfaction as well as rating 16 characteristics associated with work (to be discussed below). The heritability of this measure of general job satisfaction was 0.27, quite a bit larger than the 0.16 found with the single item measure in the original study and close to the figure 0.31 found for the general satisfaction measure based on multiple items. It is worth noting that in both of the replication studies the DZT correlations were very low, suggesting that job satisfaction may contain considerable nonadditive variance.

WORK ATTITUDES AND VALUES

Tesser (1993) has recently noted that the idea that social attitudes might be influenced by genetic factors is foreign to social scientists. He quotes (McGuire (1985) as follows: 'Attitude theorists typically abhor hypothesizing genetic influence' (p.253).[3] Indeed the most recent *Annual Review of Psychology* chapter on the topic reported no references to genetic influence on attitudes (Tesser & Schaffer, 1990). The picture has, however, changed somewhat, and Tesser (1993) has attempted to integrate findings from behavior genetics into attitude research. He cites all the relevant literature that I am aware of except for Eaves and Eysenck (1974). Here I will focus only on studies directly relevant to work.

Keller, Arvey, Bouchard, Segal, and Dawis (1992) administered the Minnesota Importance Questionnaire (MIQ) to 23 MZA and 20 DZA twins. The MIQ measures 20 work values at the scale level and 6 higher order values at the factor level. The heritability of the higher values was Achievement 0.56, Comfort 0.32, Status 0.43, Altruism 0.18, Safety 0.42, and Autonomy 0.34. A second study by Arvey et al. (1994) (sample described above) largely replicated the findings of this modest initial study. The participants responded to

16 characteristics associated with work and were asked 'As best you can remember, what factors influenced your decision to enter the occupational field you are in at the present time?' Sample items were: personal or political contacts, pay offered including fringes, chance for interesting work, chance to help others, job security, and family business. The last item serves as a check on the method as it represents a potentially strong common environmental influence and would be expected to show little genetic influence. In fact the best fitting model for this measure was a common environmental influence of 0.67. Unique environmental influences and error account for the remaining variance. The average heritability for the remaining 15 values was 0.35, a large figure for single dichotomous items. There is little doubt that better measurement would yield higher heritabilities. The first principal component of these values accounted for only 14% of the total variance. It, however, yielded a heritability of 0.43.

In a related vein SATSA has reported on the heritability, based on the four group design, of orgnaizational climate measured with the Work Environment Scale (WES). The WES has 9 scales; four of them yielded significant heritabilities (supervisor support 0.20, Autonomy, 0.26, Work pressure 0.25, Clarity 0.23. A specially created annoyance scale yielded a heritability of 0.27, and the general factor yielded a heritability of 0.30. These findings are similar to those involving measures of parental environmental influences (Hur & Bouchard, 1995).

Education and Occupational Status

Using the NAS-NRC sample Behrman, Hrubec, Taubman and Wales (1980) estimate that 88% of the variance in educational achievement, 35% of the variance in occupational status and 45% of the variance in mature earning are due to genetic factors. Tambs, Sundet, Magnus and Berg (1989), using twins from a Norwegian military sample, report heritabilities of 0.43 and 0.51 for occupational status and educational level respectively, although the results vary for groups born in different years. Both the Behrman et al. study and the Norwegian studies dealt only with males. There are important gender effects in this domain. Scarr and Weinberg (1994), using an adoption sample, have shown that with regard to educational and occupational attainment 'biological sons are more influenced by their family backgrounds than daughters, regardless of genetic relatedness' and that 'young women's achievements are not as predictable from their own earlier achievements as are those of their brothers' (p.301). Studies from Sweden also yield heritabilities of about 0.40 for occupational status (Lichtenstein, Pedersen, & McClearn, 1992).

The point of this section is not to provide a precise estimate of genetic influence on educational level or occupational status, but rather to again caution the reader regarding the ambiguity underlying commonly observed correlations based on data gathered from biological families.

LIFE EVENTS AND OCCUPATIONAL STRESS

A recent finding in behavior genetics, that life events have a genetic basis, challenges a core belief of many psychologists. The typical view in psychology is that life events or life changes are important environmental 'causal' influences on mental and physical health (Holmes & Rahe, 1967; Paykel, 1971; Rabkin & Struening, 1976). For a dissenting view see Hudgens (1974). While a number of authors recognized that life stress events are sometimes initiated by the individual, it was still assumed that the mediation was via personality traits, etc. that were themselves largely under environmental influence.

A paper from SATSA provided the first demonstration that life events were to some extent under genetic influence and that controllable life events showed the most extensive genetic influence (Plomin, Lichtenstein, Pedersen, McClearn, & Nesselroade, 1990). The same four group design used to study personality was applied to responses to a 25-item self-report life events questionnaire. The most recent analysis of that data is shown in Table 9.1.

Table 9.1 Twin intraclass correlations and heritabilities for four older adult twin groups for ratings of life events

Life events scale	Twin type				Model-fitting heritability
	MZA (45–49)	DZA (107–125)	MZT (90–98)	DZT (112–127)	
Total score	0.43	0.07	0.24	0.19	0.31*
Events to self	0.27	0.21	0.27	0.10	0.30*
Events to others	0.22	0.06	0.11	0.15	0.18*

* $p < 0.05$
Source: Data from Plomin (1994a) p. 91.

Table 9.1 is from a recent book by Plomin (1994a). The original report of the above study (Plomin et al., 1990) classified events somewhat differently, namely according to desirability and controllability. Not surprisingly controllable events had a much higher heritability than uncontrollable events (0.43 vs 0.18). Comparable results have been reported for controllable ($h^2 = 0.53$) and uncontrollable ($h^2 = 0.23$) events in MISTRA (Moster, 1991). The Moster study also reported results for the standard Holmes and Rahe (Holmes & Rahe, 1967) scale ($h^2 = 0.42$), the Paykel (Paykel, 1971) scale ($h^2 = 0.41$) and total life events ($h^2 = 0.50$). Consequently we know that standard instruments in this domain yield significantly heritable scores. The MISTRA findings, however, are based on modest sample sizes and only on data from MZA and DZA twins. It is of considerable interest that even what are classified as uncontrollable events yield heritabilities of about 0.20. Kendler, Neale, Kessler, Heath, and Eaves (1993) carried out a twin study of life events using a

Table 9.2 Genetic and environmental parameters for personal life events/difficulties

Category of life events	Additive genetic variance	Common environmental variance	Unique environmental variance plus error
Interpersonal difficulties	0.18	0.21	0.61
Robbed/assaulted	0.33	—	0.67
Financial problems	0.39	—	0.61
Illness/injury	0.21	—	0.79
Marriage problems	0.14	—	0.86
Work difficulties	—	0.29	0.71
Total	0.26	0.18	0.57

Source: Kendler et al. (1993)

very large sample of ordinary twins from the Virginia Twin Registry. They divided their self-report items into two classes, network events which had primary impact on the individuals in the respondents social network (father had an accident) and personal events which had their primary impact on the respondent. As expected all of the network events yield a significant common environmental influence and do not have any genetic loading. The personal events and their genetic and environmental loading are given in Table 9.2. The Total Score reflects both classes of events.

Every class of personal events except for work difficulties yielded a genetic effect. Moster (1991) included a group of occupational items in her study and consistent with the Kendler et al. study the genetic parameter was essentially zero. These findings have profound consequences for the interpretation of findings in the domain of life stress research as they reverse the direction of causation for many of the findings.

The study of occupational stress has a long history in I/O psychology (Cooper & Payne, 1988). It is a specialized facet of the more generic field discussed above. Studies in this domain have regularly measured stress using some sort of inventory or questionnaire, related scores to physical and mental health and implicitly ascribed causal status to occupational stress (Cooper & Kirkcaldy, 1994). The very preliminary findings related to work difficulties reported in the above studies lend support to the assumption that work difficulties are environmentally mediated. It should be kept in mind however that the measures used in these studies are quite limited in their scope and no behavior genetic studies have been carried out with a specific focus on occupational stress. Based on work in the life events domain reviewed above and other studies dealing with health but not discussed here (Lichtenstein, Harris, Pedersen, & McClearn, 1992; Lichtenstein, Harris, Pedersen, & McClearn, 1993; Lichtenstein & Pedersen, 1995; Lichtenstein, Pedersen, Plomin, De-Faire, & McClearn, 1989; Pedersen, Lichtenstein, Plomin, DeFaire,

McClearn, & Matthews, 1989) there is a reasonable likelihood that occupational stress measures would be shown to be partially influenced by genetic factors. A particularly interesting study of twin members of a very specialized occupation—military personnel—showed that the heritability of combat exposure was 0.47 and the heritability of received combat decoration was 0.54 (True, Rice, Eisen, Goldberg, Lyons, & Nowak, 1993). In neither instance was the common family environmental influence significantly different from zero. The same group has demonstrated a genetic liability to post traumatic stress syndrome (True et al., 1993).

While they would appear to have less relevance to the I/O context it is worth noting that measures of social support (Biegel, Farkas, Abell, Goodin, & Friedman, 1989) which are widely interpreted as reflecting environmental measures also reflect genetic variance (Bergeman, Plomin, Pedersen, McClearn, & Nesselroade, 1990; Kessler, Kendler, Heath, Neale, & Eaves, 1992).

Behavior genetic studies of life stress, combat exposure, and social support can be considered a subset of genetic studies in behavioral medicine (Turner, Cardon, & Hewitt, 1995), a newly emerging field of direct relevance to many I/O psychologists.

A THEORETICAL PERSPECTIVE

Except for its utilization of genetic theory and a highly generalized affiliation with the theory of evolution the field of behavior genetics does not have a theoretical frame of reference of its own. Most behavior genetic studies of ordinary individual differences represent no more than the application of behavior genetic methods to a convenient set of psychological traits. A number of attempts at theory building have, however, been launched and they illustrate how difficult it will be to incorporate the empirical findings of this discipline into mainstream psychology. Scarr, for example, has formulated a developmental theory of how people make their own environments (Scarr & McCartney, 1983). When she presented the most recent version of the theory as her presidential address to the Society for Research in Child Development (Scarr, 1992) it ignited a storm of protest (Baumrind, 1993; Jackson, 1993). Scarr has replied to the specific criticism (Scarr, 1993) and highlighted in detail how contemporary socialization theory fails to account for the facts when it is pitted against the findings of behavior genetics. Other relevant papers dealing with the same ideas are (Bouchard et al., in press; Plomin, 1994b; Scarr, in press, a,b). These papers constitute an informative set of readings for I/O psychologists as I/O psychology faces many of the same issues regarding how to incorporate the findings of behavior genetics. For many individuals, particularly those in higher level positions and the professions, the world of work is a 'created environment' and Scarr's ideas have considerable relevance. I doubt, however, that their application to the world of work will engender nearly as much controversy as it has in developmental psychology as I/O psychologists have a history of being well ahead of other parts of psychology in the assimilation of novel and powerful new methodologies.

AUTHOR NOTES

Preparation of this chapter was supported by grants to the Minnesota Study of Twins Reared Apart, from the Pioneer Fund and the David H. Koch Charitable Trust. I would like to thank my colleague Margaret Keyes for numerous suggestions that greatly improved the manuscript. The errors that remain are mine.

1. While Darwin spoke of 'his theory' as an integrated whole, modern scholarship shows that it is actually six theories. Mayr (1991) lists five, evolution as such, common descent, multiplication of species, gradualism and natural selection. Mayr virtually ignores what is actually a sixth theory that itself was ignored for almost a hundred years: namely the theory of sexual selection (Darwin, 1871). Sexual selection has now been largely incorporated into the Neo-Darwinian paradigm (Cronin, 1991; Ridley, 1993).
2. This model is also identical to the one shown in Figure 9.1 with (T) being replaced by common environmental influence (CE). Again the correlation is not squared.
3. McGuire, however, did not dismiss the possibility out of hand and cited the relevant sociobiological literature.

REFERENCES

Arvey, R. D. & Bouchard, T. J., Jr. (1994) Genetics, twins, and organizational behavior. In B. A. Staw & L. L. Cummings (eds), *Research in Organizational Behavior* (pp.47–82). New York: JAI Press.

Arvey R. D., Bouchard, T. J., Jr, Segal, N. L., & Abraham, L. M. (1989) Job satisfaction: Environmental and genetic components. *Journal of Applied Psychology*, 74, 187–192.

Arvey, R. D., McCall, B., Bouchard, T. J., Jr, Taubman, P., & Cavanaugh (1994) Genetic influence on job satisfaction and work values. *Personality and Individual Differences*, 17 21–33.

Baker, L. A., Vernon, P. A., & Ho, H. Z. (1991) The genetic correlation between intelligence and speed of information processing. *Behavior Genetics*, 21, 351–367.

Barrett, G. V. (1994) Empirical data say it all. *American Psychologist*, 49, 69–71.

Barrett, G. V. & Depinet, R. L. (1991) A reconsideration of testing for competence rather than for intelligence. *American Psychologist*, 46(10), 1012—1024.

Barrick, M. R. & Mount, M. K. (1991) The Big Five personality dimensions and job performance: A meta-analysis. *Personnel Psychology*, 44, 1–26.

Baumrind, D. (1993) The average expectable environment is not good enough: A response to Scarr. *Child Development*, 64, 1299–1317.

Behrman, J. R., Hrubec, Z., Taubman, P., & Wales, T. J. (1980) *Socioeconomic Success: A Study of the Effects of Genetic Endowments, Family Environment, and Schooling*. New York: North-Holland.

Benjamin, J., Li, L., Patterson, C., Greenberg, B., Murphy, D. L., & Hamer, D. H. (1996) Population and familial association between the D4 dopamine receptor gene and measures of novelty seeking. *Nature Genetics*, **12**, 81–84.

Bergeman, C. S., Plomin, R., Pedersen, N. L., McClearn, G. E., & Nesselroade, J. R. (1990) Genetic and environmental influences on social support: The Swedish Adoption/Twin Study of Aging. *Journal of Gerontology: Psychological Sciences*, **45**, 101–106.

Bernhard, G. & Glantz, K. (1992) *Staying Human in the Organization: Our Biological Heritage and the Workplace*. New York: Praeger.

Betsworth, D. G., Bouchard, T. J., Jr, Cooper, C. R., Grotevant, H. D., Hansen, J. C., Scarr, S., & Weinberg, R. A. (1993) Genetic and environmental influences on vocational interests assessed using adoptive and biological families and twins reared apart and together. *Journal of Vocational Behavior*, **44**, 263–278.

Biegel, D. E., Farkas, K. J., Abell, N., Goodin, J., & Friedman, B. (eds) (1989) *Social Support Networks: A Biography, 1983–1987*. New York: Greenwood Press.

Bors, D. A. & Forkin, B. (1995) Age, speed of information processing, recall, and fluid intelligence. *Intelligence*, **20**, 229–248.

Bouchard, T. J., Jr (1993a) Genetic and environmental influences on adult personality: Evaluating the evidence. In I. Deary & J. Hettema (eds), *Basic Issues in Personality*. Dordrecht: Kluwer.

Bouchard, T. J., Jr (1993b) The genetic architecture of human intelligence. In P. A. Vernon (eds), *Biological Approaches to the Study of Human Intelligence* (pp. 33–93). Norwood, NJ: Ablex.

Bouchard, T. J., Jr (1994) Genes, environment and personality. *Science*, **264**, 1700–1701.

Bouchard, T. J., Jr (in press, a). Behavior genetic studies of intelligence, yesterday and today: The long journey from plausibility to proof. *Journal of Biosocial Science*.

Bouchard, T. J., Jr (in press, b). The genetics of personality. In K. Blum & E. P. Noble (eds), *Handbook of Psychoeurogenetics*. Boca Raton, FL: CRC Press.

Bouchard, T. J., Jr, Arvey, R. D., Keller, L. M., & Segal, N. L. (1992) Genetic influences on Job Satisfaction: A reply to Cropanzano and James. *Journal of Applied Psychology*, **77**, 89–93.

Bouchard, T. J., Jr, Lykken, D. T., McGue, M., Segal, N. L., & Tellegen, A. (1990a) Sources of human psychological differences: The Minnesota study of twins reared apart. *Science*, **250**, 223–228.

Bouchard, T. J., Jr, Lykken, D. T., McGue, M., Segal, N. L., & Tellegen, A. (1990b) When kin correlations are not squared. *Science*, **250**, 1498.

Bouchard, T. J., Jr, Lykken, D. T., Tellegen, A. T., & McGue, M. (in press) Genes, drives, environment and experience: EPD theory—Revised. In C. P. Benbow & D. Lubinski (eds), *Psychometrics and Social Issues Concerning Intellectual Talent*. Baltimore, MD: Johns Hopkins University Press.

Bouchard, T. J., Jr & McGue, M. (1981) Familial studies of intelligence: A review. *Science*, **212**, 1055–1059.

Bouchard, T. J., Jr, & Pedersen, N. (in preparation) Twins reared apart: Nature's double experiment. In E. L. Grigorenko & S. Scarr (eds), *On the Way to Individuality: Current Methodological Issues in Behavioral Genetics*.

Bouchard, T. J., Jr, Segal, N. L., & Lykken, D. T. (1990) Genetic and environmental influences on special mental abilities in a sample of twins reared apart. *Acta Geneticae Medicae et Gemellologiae*, **39**, 193–206.

Bouchard, T. J. Jr (in press) IQ similarity in twins reared apart: Findings and response to critics. In R. J. Sternberg & E. L. Grigorenko (eds), *Intelligence: Heredity and Environment*. New York: Cambridge University Press.

Brody, N. (1992) *Intelligence. Second edition*. San Diego: Academic Press.

Brooks, A., Fulker, D. W., & DeFries, J. C. (1990) Reading performance and general cognitive ability: A multivariate genetic analysis of twin data. *Personality and Individual Differences*, **11**, 141–146.

Campbell, D. P. (1968) The Strong Vocational Interest Blank: 1927–1967. In P. McReynolds (ed.), *Advances in Psychological Assessment* (pp.105–130). Palo Alto, CA: Science and Behavior Books.

Cardon, L. R. (1995) Quantitative trait loci: Mapping genes for complex traits. In J. R. Turner, L. R. Cardon, & J. K. Hewitt (eds), *Behavior Genetic Approaches in Behavioral Medicine* (pp.237–250). New York: Plenum.

Cardon, L. R., Fulker, D. W., DeFries, J. C., & Plomin, R. (1992) Multivariate genetic analysis of specific cognitive abilities in the Colorado Adoption project at age 7. *Intelligence*, **16**, 383–400.

Carpenter, P. A., Just, M. A., & Shell, P. (1990) What one intelligence test measures: A theoretical account of the processing in the Raven Progressive Matrices Test. *Psychological Review*, **97**, 404–431.

Carter, H. D. (1932) Twin similarities in occupational interests. *Journal of Educational Psychology*, **23**, 641–655.

Caruso, D. R. (1983) Sample differences in genetics and intelligence data: Sibling and parent–offspring studies. *Behavior Genetics*, **13**, 453–458.

Chaiken, S. R. (1994) The inspection time not studied: Processing speed ability unrelated to psychometric intelligence. *Intelligence*, **19**, 295–316.

Cloninger, C. R., Adolfsson, R., & Svrakic, N. M. (1996) Mapping genes for human personality. *Nature Genetics*, **12**, 3–4.

Cooper, C. L. & Kirkcaldy, B. D. (1994) A model of job stress and physical health: The role of individual differences. *Personality and Individual Differences*, **16**, 653–657.

Cooper, C. L. & Payne, R. (1988) *Causes, Coping and Consequences of Stress at Work*. Chichester: Wiley.

Crawford, C. B. & Anderson, J. L. (1989) Sociobiology: An environmental discipline? *American Psychologist*, **44**, 1449–1459.

Cronbach, L. J. (1957) The two disciplines of scientific psychology. *American Psychologist*, **12**, 671–684.

Cronin, H. (1991) *The Ant and the Peacock: Altruism and Sexual Selection from Darwin to Today*. Cambridge: Cambridge University Press.

Cropanzano, R. & James, K. (1990) Some methodological considerations for the behavior genetic analysis of work attitudes. *Journal of Applied Psychology*, **75**, 433–439.

Cziko, G. (1995) *Without Miracles: Universal Selection Theory and the Second Darwinian Revolution*. Cambridge, MA: MIT Press.

Darwin, C. (1871) *The Descent of Man, and Selection in Relation to Sex*. London: John Murray.

Degler, C. N. (1991) *In Search of Human Nature: The Decline and Revival of Darwinism in American Social Thought*. Oxford: Oxford University Press.

Dennett, D. C. (1995) *Darwin's Dangerous Idea: Evolution and the Meaning of Life*. New York: Simon & Schuster.

Eaves, L. J. & Eysenck, H. J. (1974) Genetics and the development of social attitudes. *Nature*, **249**, 288–289.

Ebstein, R. P., Novick, O., Umansky, R., Priel, B., Osher, Y., Blaine, D., Bennett, E. R., Nemanov, L., Katz, M., & Belmaker, R. H. (1996) Dopamine D4 receptor (D4DR) exon III polymorphism associated with the human personality trait of novelty seeking. *Nature Genetics*, **12**, 78–80.

Finkel, D., Pedersen, N. L., McGue, M., & McClearn, G. E. (1995) Heritability of cognitive abilities in adult twins: Comparison of Minnesota and Swedish data. *Behavior Genetics*, **25**, 421–431.

Flint, J., Wilkie, A. O. M., Buckle, V. J., Winter, R. M., Holland, A. J., & McDermid, H. E. (1995) The detection of subtelomeric chromosomal rearrangements in idiopathic mental retardation. *Nature Genetics*, **9**, 132–140.

Gardner, H., Kornhaber, M. L., & Wake, W. K. (1996) *Intelligence: Multiple Perspectives*. New York: Harcourt Brace.

Gati, I. (1991) The structure of vocational interests. *Psychological Bulletin*, **109**, 309–324.

Grotevant, H. D. (1979) Interest development in adolescents from adoptive and biological families. *Child Development*, **50**, 854–860.

Grotevant, H. D. & Cooper, C. R. (1985) Patterns of interaction in family relationships and the development of identity exploration in adolescence. *Child Development*, **56**, 415–428.

Grotevant, H. D., Scarr, S., & Weinberg, R. A. (1977) Patterns of interest similarity in adoptive and biological families. *Journal of Personality and Social Psychology*, **35**, 667–676.

Hansen, J. C. & Campbell, D. P. (1985) *Manual for the SVIB-SCII*. Fourth edition. Stanford, CA: Stanford University Press.

Hayes, W. L. (1973) *Statistics for the Social Sciences*. Second edition. New York: Holt, Rinehart & Winston.

Herrnstein, R. J. & Murray, C. (1994) *The Bell Curve: Intelligence and Class Structure in American Life*. New York: Free Press.

Hoffman, L. W. (1991) The influence of the family environment on personality: Evidence for sibling differences. *Psychological Bulletin*, **110**, 187–203.

Holmes, T. H. & Rahe, R. M. (1967) The social readjustment rating scale. *Journal of Psychosomatic Medicine*, **11**, 213–218.

Hough, L. (1992) The 'Big Five' personality variables—Construct confusion: Description versus prediction. *Human Performance*, **5**, 139–155.

Hudgens, R. W. (1974) Personal catastrophe and depression: A consideration of the subject with respect to medically ill adolescents, and a requiem for retrospective life-event studies. In B. S. Dohrenwend & B. P. Dohrenwend (eds), *Stressful Life Events: Their Nature and Effects* (pp.119–134). New York: Wiley.

Hunt, E. (1995) The role of intelligence in modern society. *American Scientist*, **83**, 356–368.

Hunter, J. E. & Schmidt, F. L. (1990) *Methods of Meta-analysis: Correcting Error and Bias in Research Findings*. Newbury Park, CA: Sage.

Hur, Y.-M. & Bouchard, T. J. J. (1995) Genetic influence on perceptions of childhood family environment: A reared apart twins study. *Child Development*, **66**, 330–345.

Jackson, D. J. (1977) *Jackson Vocational Interest Survey Manual*. Port Huron, MI: Research Psychologists Press.

Jackson, J. F. (1993) Human behavioral genetics, Scarr's theory, and her views on interventions: A critical review and commentary on their implications for African-American children. *Child Development*, **64**, 1318–1332.

Jacoby, R. & Glauberman, N. (ed.) (1995) *The Bell Curve Debate: History, Documents, Opinions*. New York: Random House.

Jensen, A. R. (1971) Note on why genetic correlations are not squared. *Psychological Bulletin*, **75**, 223–224.

Jensen, A. R. (1992) Understanding g in terms of information processing. *Educational Psychology Review*, **4**, 271–308.

Keller, L. M., Arvey, R. D., Bouchard, T. J., Jr, Segal, N. L., & Dawis, R. V. (1992) Work values: Genetic and environmental influences. *Journal of Applied Psychology*, **77**, 79–88.

Kendler, K. S., Neale, M., Kessler, R., Heath, A., & Eaves, L. (1993) A twin study of recent life events and difficulties. *Archives of General Psychiatry*, **50**, 789–796.

Kessler, R. C., Kendler, K. S., Heath, A., Neale, M. C., & Eaves, L. J. (1992) Social support, depressed mood, and adjustment to stress: A genetic epidemiological investigation. *Journal of Personality and Social Psychology*, **62**, 257–272.

Kyllonen, P. C. & Christal, R. E. (1990) Reasoning ability is (little more than) working memory capacity?! *Intelligence*, **14**, 389–433.

Li, C. C. (1987) A genetic model for emergenesis. *American Journal of Human Genetics*, **41**, 517–523.

Lichtenstein, P., Harris, J. R., Pedersen, N. L., & McClearn, G. E. (1992) Socioeconomic status and physical health, how are they related? An empirical study based on twins reared apart and twins reared together. *Social Science and Medicine*, **36**, 441–450.

Lichtenstein, P., Harris, J. R., Pedersen, N. L., & McClearn, G. E. (1993) Socioeconomic status and physical health, how are they related? An empirical study based on twins reared apart and twins reared together. *Social Science and Medicine*, **36**, 441–450.

Lichtenstein, P. & Pedersen, N. L. (1995) Social relationships, stressful life events, and self-reported physical health: Genetic and environmental influences. *Psychology and Health*, **10**, 295–319.

Lichtenstein, P., Pedersen, N. L., & McClearn, G. E. (1992) The origins of individual differences in occupational status and educational level. *Acta Sociologica*, **35**, 13–31.

Lichtenstein, P., Pedersen, N. L., Plomin, R., DeFaire, U., & McClearn, G. E. (1989) Type A behavior pattern, related personality traits and self-reported coronary heart disease. *Personality and Individual Differences*, **10**, 419–426.

Loehlin, J. C. (1992a) *Genes and Environment in Personality Development*. Newbury Park, CA: Sage.

Loehlin, J. C. (1992b) *Latent Variable Models: An Introduction to Factor Analysis, Path, and Structural Analysis*. Second edition, Hillsdale, NJ: Erlbaum.

Loehlin, J. C., Horn, J.M., & Willerman, L. (1994) Differential inheritance of mental abilities in the Texas adoption project. *Intelligence*, **19**, 325–336.

Loehlin, J. C., Horn, J. M., & Willerman, L. (in press) Heredity, environment and IQ in the Texas adoption study. In R. J. Sternberg & E. L. Grigorenko (eds), *Heredity, Environment and Intelligence*. New York: Cambridge University Press.

Loehlin, J. C. & Nichols, R. C. (1976) *Heredity, Environment, & Personality: A Study of 850 Sets of Twins*. Austin: University of Texas Press.

Lohman, D. F. (1994) Component scores as residual variation (or why the intercept correlates best). *Intelligence*, **19**, 1–12.

Lykken, D. T., Bouchard, T. J., Jr, McGue, M., & Tellegen, A. (1993) Heritabilty of interests: A twin study. *Journal of Applied Psychology*, **78**, 649–661.

Lykken, D. T., McGue, M., Tellegen, A., & Bouchard, T. J., Jr (1992) Emergenesis: Genetic traits that may not run in families. *American Psychologist*, **47**, 1565–1577.

Martin, J. B. (1993) Molecular genetics of neurological diseases. *Science*, **262**, 674–676.

Mayr, E. (1991) *One Long Argument: Charles Darwin and the Genesis of Modern Evolutionary Thought*. Cambridge, MA: Harvard University Press.

McClelland, D. C. (1993) Intelligence is not the best predictor of job performance. *Current Directions in Psychological Science*, **2**, 5–6.

McClelland, D. C. (1994) The knowledge–testing–educational complex strikes back. *American Psychologist*, **49**, 66–69.

McGue, M., & Bouchard, T. J., Jr (1989) Genetic and environmental determinants of information processing and special mental abilities: A twin analysis. In R. J. Sternberg (eds), *Advances in the Psychology of Human Intelligence* (pp.7–44). Hillsdale, NJ: Erlbaum.

McGue, M., Bouchard, T. J., Jr, Iacono, W. G., & Lykken, D. T. (1993) Behavior genetics of cognitive ability: A life-span perspective. In R. Plomin & G. E. McClearn (eds), *Nature, Nurture and Psychology,* (pp.59–76). Washington, DC: American Psychological Association.

McGuire, W. J. (1985) Attitudes and attitude change. In G. Lindzey & E. Aronson (eds), *Handbook of Social Psychology* (pp.233–346). New York: Random House.

McKusick, V. A. (1992) *Mendelian Inheritance in Man: Catalogs of Autosomal Dominant, Autosomal Recessive, and X-linked Phenotypes.* Baltimore, MD: Johns Hopkins University Press.

Moloney, D. P., Bouchard, T. J., Jr, & Segal, N. L. (1991) A genetic and environmental analysis of the vocational interests of monozygotic and dizygotic twins reared apart. *Journal of Vocational Behavior,* **39,** 76–109.

Moster, M. (1991) Stressful life events: Genetic and environmental components and their relationship to affective symptomatology. PhD Dissertation, University of Minnesota.

Neale, M. C. & Cardon, L. R. (eds) (1992) *Methodology for Genetic Studies of Twins and Families.* Dordrecht: Kluwer.

Neisser, U., Boodoo, G., Bouchard, T. J., Jr, Boykin, A. W., Brody, N., Ceci, S. J., Halpern, D. F., Loehlin, J. C., Perloff, R., Sternberg, R. J., & Urbina, S. (1996) Intelligence: Knowns and Unknowns. *American Psychologist,* **51,** 77–101.

Nichols, R. C. (1978) Twin studies of ability, personality and interests. *Homo,* **29,** 158–173.

Ones, D. S. (in press) Bandwidth–fidelity dilemma in personality measurement for personnel selection. *Journal of Organizational Behavior.*

Paykel, E. S.(1971) Scaling of life events. *Archives of General Psychiatry,* **25,** 340–347.

Pedersen, N. L. Lichtenstein, P., Plomin, R., DeFaire, U., McClearn, G. E., & Matthews, K. A. (1989) Genetic and environmental influences for Type A-like measures and related traits: A study of twins reared apart and twins reared together. *Psychosomatic Medicine,* **51,** 428–440.

Pedersen, N. L., Plomin, R., & McClearn, G. E. (1994) Is there G beyond *g*? (Is there genetic influence on specific cognitive abilities independent of genetic influence on general cognitive ability?). *Intelligence,* **18,** 133–143.

Pedersen, N. L., Plomin, R., Nesselroade, J. R., & McClearn, G. E. (1992) A quantitative genetic analysis of cognitive abilities during the second half of the life span. *Psychological Science,* **3,** 346–353.

Petrill, S. A., Thompson, L. A., & Detterman, D. K. (1995) The genetic and environmental variance underlying elementary cognitive tasks. *Behavior Genetics,* **25,** 199–210.

Plomin, R. (ed.) (1994a) *Genetics and Experience: The Interplay Between Nature and Nurture.* Thousand Oaks, CA: Sage.

Plomin, R. (1994b) The nature of nurture: The environment beyond the family. In R. Plomin (ed.), *Genetics and Experience: The Interplay Between Nature and Nurture* (pp. 82–101). Thousand Oaks: Sage.

Plomin, R. (1995) Molecular genetics and psychology. *Current Directions in Psychological Science,* **4,** 114–117.

Plomin, R., DeFries, J. C., & McClearn, G. E. (1990) *Behavioral Genetics: A Primer.* Third edition. New York: W. H. Freeman.

Plomin, R., Lichtenstein, P., Pedersen, N. L., McClearn, G. E., & Nesselroade, J. R. (1990) Genetic influences on life events during the last half of the life span. *Psychology and Aging,* **5,** 25–30.

Plomin, R., McClearn, G. E., Smith, D. L., Skuder, P., Vigneti, S. Chorney, M. J., Chorney, K., Kasarda, S., Thompson., L. A., Detterman, D. K., Petrill, S. A., Daniels, J., Owen, M. J., & McGuffin, P. (1995) Allelic associations between 100 DNA markers and high versus low IQ. *Intelligence,* **21,** 31–48.

Plomin, R., Owen, M. J., & McGuffin, P. (1994) The genetic basis of complex human behavior. *Science,* **264,** 1733–1739.

Plomin, R., Pedersen, N. L., Lichtenstein, P., & McClearn, G. E. (1994). Variability and stability in cognitive abilities are largely genetic later in life. *Behavior Genetics*, **24**, 207–215.

Rabkin, J. C. & Struening, E. L. (1976) Life events, stress and illness. *Science*, **194**, 1013–1020.

Ridley, M. (1993) *The Red Queen: Sex and the Evolution of Human Nature*. New York: Penguin Books.

Saudino, K. J., Plomin, R., Pedersen, N. L., & McClearn, G. E. (1994) The etiology of high and low cognitive ability during the second half of the life span. *Intelligence*, **19**, 359–371.

Scarr, S. (1992) Developmental theories for the 1990s: Development and individual differences. *Child Development*, **63**, 1–19.

Scarr, S. (1993) Biological and cultural diversity: The legacy of Darwin for development. *Child Development*, **64**, 1333–1353.

Scarr, S. (in press, a) Behavior genetic and socialization theories of intelligence: Truce and reconciliation. In R. J. Sternberg & E. L. Grigorenko (eds), *Intelligence: Heredity and Environment*. New York: Cambridge University Press.

Scarr, S. (in press, b) How people make their own environments: Implications for parents and policy makers. *Psychology, Public Policy, and Law*.

Scarr, S. & McCartney, K. (1983) How people make their own environments: A theory of genotype→environment effects. *Child Development*, **54** (424–435).

Scarr, S. & Weinberg, R. A. (1978) The influence of family background on intellectual attainment. *American Sociological Review*, **43**, 674–692.

Scarr, S. & Weinberg, R. A. (1994) Educational and occupational achievements of brothers and sisters in adoptive and biologically related families. *Behavior Genetics*, **24**, 301–325.

Scarr, S., Weinberg, R. A., & Waldman, I. D. (1993) IQ correlations in transracial adoptive families. *Intelligence*, **17**, 541–555.

Schmidt, F. L. & Hunter, J. E. (1993) Tacit knowledge, practical intelligence, general mental ability, and job knowledge. *Current Directions in Psychological Science*, **2**, 8–9.

Segal, N. L. (1993) Twin sibling and adoption methods: Tests of evolutionary hypotheses. *American Psychologist*, **48**, 943–956.

Seligman, D. (1992) *A Question of Intelligence*. Secaucus, NJ: Birch Lane Press.

Skuder, P., Plomin, R., McClearn, G. E., Smith, D. L., Vignetti, S., Chorney, M. J., Chorney, K., Kasarda, S., Thompson, L. A., Detterman, D. K., Petrill, S. A., Daniels, J., Owen, M. J., & McGuffin, P. (1995) A polymorphism in mitochondrial DNA associated with IQ? *Intelligence*, **21**, 1–12.

Snow, R. E. (1995) Validity of IQ as a measure of cognitive ability. In *Workshop on IQ Testing and Educational Decision Making*. San Diego, CA.

Snow, R. E. & Swanson, J. (1992) Instructional psychology: Aptitude, adaptation, and assessment. *Annual Review of Psychology*, **43**, 583–626.

Sternberg, R. J. & Grigorenko, E. L. (1996) *Intelligence: Heredity and Environment*. New York: Cambridge University Press.

Sternberg, R. J. & Wagner, R. K. (1993) The *g*-ocentric view of intelligence and job performance is wrong. *Current Directions in Psychological Science*, **2**, 1–5.

Sundet, J. M., Tambs, K., Magnus, P., & Berg, K. (1988) On the question of secular trends in the heritabilty of intelligence test scores: A study of Norwegian twins. *Intelligence*, **12**, 47–59.

Tambs, K., Sundet, J. M., & Magnus, P. (1984) Heritability analysis of the WAIS subtests: A study of twins, *Intelligence*, **8**, 283–293.

Tambs, K., Sundet, J. M., & Magnus, P. (1988) Genetic and environmental effects on the covariance structure of the Norwegian army ability tests: A study of twins. *Personality and Individual Differences*, **9**, 791–799.

Tambs, K., Sundet, J. M., Magnus, P., & Berg, K. (1989) Genetic and environmental contributions to the covariance between occupational status, educational attainment, and IQ: A study of twins. *Behavior Genetics*, **19**, 209–222.

Teasdale, T. W. & Owen, D. R. (1984) Heritability and family environment in intelligence and educational level—a sibling study. *Nature*, **309**, 620–622.

Tesser, A. (1993) The importance of heritability in psychological research: The case of attitudes. Psychological Review, 100, 129–142.

Tesser, A. & Schaffer, D. (1990) Attitudes and attitude change. *Annual Review of Psychology*, **41**, 479–523.

Thapar, A., Gottesman, I. I., Owen, M. J., O'Donovan, M. C., & McGuffin, P. (1994) The genetics of mental retardation. *British Journal of Psychiatry*, **164**, 747–758.

Thapar, A., Petrill, S. A., & Thompson, L. A. (1994) The heritability of memory in the Western Reserve twin project. *Behavior Genetics*, **24**, 155–160.

Tooby, J. & Cosmides, L. (1992) The psychological foundations of culture. In J. H. Barkow, L. Cosmides, & J. Tooby (eds), *The Adapted Mind: Evolutionary Psychology and the Generation of Culture* (pp.19–36). Oxford: Oxford University Press.

True, W. R., Rice, J., Eisen, S. A., Goldberg, J., Lyons, M. J., & Nowak, J. (1993) A twin study of genetic and environmental contributions to liability for post traumatic stress symptoms. *Archives of General Psychiatry*, **50**, 257–264.

Turner, J. R., Cardon, L. R., & Hewitt, J. K. (eds) (1995) *Behavior Genetic Approaches in Behavioral Medicine*. New York: Plenum.

Vernon, P. A. & Weese, S. E. (1993) Predicting intelligence with multiple speed of information-processing tests. *Personality and Individual Differences*, **14**, 413–419.

Willerman, L. (1979) *The Psychology of Individual and Group Differences*. San Francisco: Freeman.

Wilson, D. S. (1994) Adaptive genetic variation and human evolutionary psychology. *Ethology and Sociobiology*, **15**, 219–235.

INDEX

Index compiled by Caroline Sheard

International Review of Industrial and Organizational Psychology

CONTENTS OF PREVIOUS VOLUMES

VOLUME 9—1994

VOLUME 8—1993

Innovation in Organizations, Anderson and King; **Management Development,** Baldwin and Padgett; **The Increasing Importance of Performance Appraisals to Employee Effectiveness in Organizational Settings in North America,** Latham, Skarlicki, Irvine and Siegel; **Measurement Issues in Industrial and Organizational Psychology,** Hesketh; **Medical and Physiological Aspects of Job Interventions,** Theorell; **Goal Orientation and Action Control Theory,** Farr, Hofmann and Ringenbach; **Corporate Culture,** Furnham and Gunter; **Organizational Downsizing: Strategies, Interventions, and Research Implications,** Kozlowski, Chao, Smith and Hedlund; **Group Processes in Organizations,** Argote and McGrath.

VOLUME 7—1992

Work Motivation, Kanfer; **Selection Methods,** Smith and George; **Research Design in Industrial and Organizational Psychology,** Schaubroeck and Kuehn; **A Consideration of the Validity and Meaning of Self-Report Measures of Job Conditions,** Spector; **Emotions in Work and Achievement,** Pekrun and Frese; **The Psychology of Industrial Relations,** Hartley; **Women in Management,** Burke and McKeen; **Use of Background Data in Organizational Decisions,** Stokes and Reddy; **Job Transfer,** Brett, Stroh and Reilly; **Shopfloor Work Organization and Advanced Manufacturing Technology,** Wall and Davids.

VOLUME 6—1991

Recent Developments in Industrial and Organizational Psychology in People's Republic of China, Wang; **Mediated Communications and New Organizational Forms,** Andriessen; **Performance Measurement,** Ilgen and Schneider; **Ergonomics,** Megaw; **Ageing and Work,** Davies, Matthews and Wong; **Methodological Issues in Personnel Selection Research,** Schuler and Guldin;

Mental Health Counseling in Industry, Swanson and Murphy; Person–Job Fit, Edwards; Job Satisfaction, Arvey, Carter and Buerkley.

VOLUME 5—1990

Laboratory vs. Field Research in Industrial and Organizational Psychology, Dipboye; Managerial Delegation, Hackman and Dunphy; Cross-cultural Issues in Organizational Psychology, Bhagat, Kedia, Crawford and Kaplan; Decision Making in Organizations, Koopman and Pool; Ethics in the Workplace, Freeman; Feedback Systems in Organizations, Algera; Linking Environmental and Industrial/Organizational Psychology, Ornstein; Cognitive Illusions and Personnel Management Decisions, Brodt; Vocational Guidance, Taylor and Giannantonio.

VOLUME 4—1989

Selection Interviewing, Keenan; Burnout in Work Organizations, Shirom; Cognitive Processes in Industrial and Organizational Psychology, Lord and Maher; Cognitive Style and Complexity, Streufert and Nogami; Coaching and Practice Effects in Personnel Selection, Sackett, Burris and Ryan; Retirement, Talaga and Beehr; Quality Circles, Van Fleet and Griffin; Control in the Workplace, Ganster and Fusilier; Job Analysis, Spector, Brannick and Coovert; Japanese Management, Smith and Misumi; Causal Modelling in Organizational Research, James and James.

VOLUME 3—1988

The Significance of Race and Ethnicity for Understanding Organizational Behavior, Alderfer and Thomas; Training and Development in Work Organizations, Goldstein and Gessner; Leadership Theory and Research, Fiedler and House; Theory Building in Industrial and Organizational Psychology, Webster and Starbuck; The Construction of Climate in Organizational Research, Rousseau; Approaches to Managerial Selection, Robertson and Iles; Psychological Measurement, Murphy; Careers, Driver; Health Promotion at Work, Matteson and Ivancevich; Recent Developments in the Study of Personality and Organizational Behavior, Adler and Weiss.

VOLUME 2—1987

Organization Theory, Bedeian; Behavioural Approaches to Organizations, Luthans and Martinko; Job and Work Design, Wall and Martin; Human Interfaces with Advanced Manufacturing Systems, Wilson and Rutherford; Human–Computer Interaction in the Office, Frese; Occupational Stress and Health, Mackay and Cooper; Industrial Accidents, Sheehy and Chapman; Interpersonal Conflicts in Organizations, Greenhalgh; Work and Family, Burke and Greenglass; Applications of Meta-analysis, Hunter and Rothstein Hirsh.

VOLUME 1—1986

Related titles of interest from Wiley...

Creating Tomorrow's Organizations
A Handbook for Future Research in Organizational Behavior
Edited by **Cary L. Cooper** and **Susan Jackson**

In this Handbook, leading scholars in OB provide their ideas about new types of research within five broad topic domains: OB in a multinational or global environment; OB reaching beyond traditional boundaries; New forms and new processes for organizing; Future careers; New methods and constructs in future OB research.

0-471-97239-8   **628pp**   **1997**   **Hardback**

Handbook of Work and Health Psychology
Edited by **Marc J. Schabracq, Cary L. Cooper** and
Jacques A.M. Winnubst

Covers the concepts and problems which define the field, the diagnosis of individual stress and psychosocial work hazards, interventions and methods for a wide range of specific problems, and, finally, preventive programmes for health promotion and counseling at work.

0-471-95789-5   600pp   1996   Hardback

Handbook of Work Group Psychology
Edited by **Michael A. West**

Provides a comprehensive, critical and up-to-date overview of all the key areas in the context of organizational and work groups.

0-471-95790-9   500pp   1996   Hardback

Trends in Organizational Behavior
Edited by **Cary L. Cooper** and **Denise Rousseau**

This annual series provides a quick and up-to-date account of latest research. New and more innovative OB research towards issues reflecting the increasing interdependence in organizations (between persons, across groups and between work and home life) are highlighted.

0-471-97203-7   150pp   1997   Volume 4   Paperback
0-471-96585-5   192pp   1996   Volume 3   Paperback
0-471-95692-9   152pp   1995   Volume 2   Paperback
0-471-94344-4   158pp   1994   Volume 1   Paperback